The Structure and Reform of Direct Taxation

THE INSTITUTE FOR FISCAL STUDIES

The Structure and Reform of Direct Taxation

Report of a Committee chaired by
Professor J. E. Meade

London
GEORGE ALLEN & UNWIN
Boston   Sydney

First published in 1978
Second impression 1978

ISBN 0 04 336064 5 Hardback
ISBN 0 04 336065 3 Paperback

George Allen & Unwin (Publishers) Ltd
40 Museum Street London WC1A 1LU

The Institute for Fiscal Studies
62 Chandos Place London WC2N 4HG

British Library Cataloguing in Publication Data

The structure and reform of direct taxation.
1. Taxation – Great Britain
I. Meade, James Edward   II. Institute
for Fiscal Studies
336.2'94   HJ2619   77-30594

ISBN 0–04–336064–5

Printed in Great Britain in 10 on 11 point Times by
William Clowes & Sons Limited,
London Beccles and Colchester.

Contents

Appendixes

Foreword

The Institute for Fiscal Studies set up the Committee chaired by Professor Meade with a brief to take a fundamental look at the UK tax structure. For too long, we felt, tax reforms have been approached *ad hoc*, without regard to their effects on the evolution of the tax structure as a whole. As a result many parts of our system seem to lack a rational base. Conflicting objectives are pursued at random; and even particular objectives are pursued in contradictory ways.

We therefore wanted the Committee to look at the system as a whole and asked them to produce a statement of the objectives of taxation (including an assessment of any conflicts between different objectives); to comment on the present system in the light of these objectives; and to make recommendations for reform. At the same time we hoped that the Committee would adopt a practical approach: to aim at those reforms which would be able to command the widest possible support in the hope that political argument might in future be concerned with the rates of tax rather than the structure; and also to bear in mind the need to avoid radical upheavals in the system. Major reforms are clearly more easily digestible if they can be assimilated gradually over a longer period.

We recognised that what we asked of the Committee was in many ways an impossible task, especially since we originally envisaged that the Committee should report after twelve months. The reason for setting such a short time-table was that we felt that the Committee could either make a general judgement on the system, which it might be able to formulate within a year; or else would have to look at the system in detail, rather on the lines of the Royal Commission on the Taxation of Incomes and Profits of 1955, in which case many years of study would be involved.

In the event, the Committee could not complete its task within twelve months. It decided to restrict the scope of its study to a look at direct taxation only. However it also felt that general recommendations about the tax structure would be of limited value, or would carry little conviction, without an examination of some of the detailed administrative problems which such recommendations might raise (or solve). Even so, the Report was completed within two years, by the end of June 1977 – a remarkable achievement.

The views expressed in this study are the views of the Committee themselves and not those of the IFS. The IFS itself has no views: its purpose is to promote worthwhile studies rather than to champion causes. However we wish to congratulate the Committee on the immense amount of work it has accomplished in such a relatively short time and on the quality of its Report.

The members of the Committee were all leading experts with many professional commitments in addition to their work for the Committee. The production of a Report with such a wealth of ideas and of discussion of the practical issues was possible only because of the great amount of time and thought which they were ready to devote to the Committee's work. We hope and believe that this Report will be a rich quarry for tax reformers and a valuable reference point for students of taxation for decades to come.

The composition of the Committee was designed to combine the experience of academics with that of practitioners in different fields and also to embrace different political viewpoints. The Committee was originally composed of Professor A. B. Atkinson (economist), J. F. Avery Jones (solicitor), D. J. Ironside (accountant), Professor C. T. Sandford (economist), Professor G. Whittington (accountant), J. R. M. Willis (ex-Deputy Chairman of the Inland Revenue) and S. H. Wright (merchant banker, ex-Treasury). Four research secretaries were appointed to assist them, namely, J. S. Flemming, J. A. Kay, M. A. King (all economists) and M. G. Macdonald (lawyer and accountant).

Professor Meade himself started work at the beginning of July 1975, and the Committee started officially in October 1975. In the course of time the Committee underwent several changes. (i) In January 1976 Miss Carole Pleming was appointed as a general research assistant. (ii) Donald Ironside was appointed Deputy Chairman and took over most of the organisational work of the Committee. (iii) Stanley Wright, who was to have started full membership in January 1976 because of his previous commitment to the Layfield Committee on Local Government Finance, served on the Committee for only a short while (during which he made a most useful contribution) and then found that his other commitments prevented him from playing a full part. He accordingly resigned in April 1976. (iv) In practice it became impossible to distinguish between the role of research secretaries and Committee members. It was therefore decided in 1976 that the four research secretaries should become full members of the Committee. (v) L. R. Bell (accountant), who had commented widely on some of the early work of the Committee, was invited to become a member of it in September 1976. (vi) Professor Atkinson found that on his appointment to the Chair of Political Economy at University College, London as from October 1976, he could not continue and he therefore resigned. The final membership of the Committee is listed at the end of this Foreword.

Lastly, we would like to express our sincere thanks to the Trusts and Foundations and other bodies who financed the Committee's work. The study would not have been possible without the generous help of the Association of Certified Accountants, the Esmée Fairbairn Charitable Trust, the Gatsby Trust, the Leverhulme Trust, the Wolfson Foundation and two other Trusts which wish to remain anonymous.

DICK TAVERNE
Director
The Institute for Fiscal Studies

Final Membership of the Committee

Professor J. E. Meade, CB, FBA *(Chairman)*	Emeritus Professor of Political Economy, University of Cambridge
D. J. Ironside (Deputy Chairman)	Partner, Thomson McLintock & Co., Chartered Accountants; Visiting Fellow, University of Bath
J. F. Avery Jones	Partner, Speechly Bircham, London, Solicitors; Joint Editor, *British Tax Review*
L. R. Bell	Retired partner, Thomson McLintock & Co., Chartered Accountants
J. S. Flemming	Fellow in Economics, Nuffield College, Oxford; Managing Editor, *Economic Journal*
J. A. Kay	Fellow in Economics, St John's College, Oxford
M. A. King	Fellow, St John's College, Cambridge and University Lecturer in Economics (from October 1977 Esmée Fairbairn Professor of Investment, University of Birmingham)
M. G. Macdonald	Lecturer in Tax Law and Policy and Accounting Theory (now Senior Lecturer in Accounting), University of Kent
Professor C. T. Sandford	Professor of Political Economy, University of Bath
Professor G. Whittington	Professor of Accounting and Finance, University of Bristol
J. R. M. Willis, CB, CMG	Retired Deputy Chairman, Board of Inland Revenue, Visiting Professor, University of Bath

Preface by the Chairman

The Director of the Institute for Fiscal Studies in his Foreword to our Report has explained the origins, purpose, and composition of our Committee. Our Report is very much a joint effort with many important contributions from different members of the Committee. Indeed one of the most significant and encouraging aspects of our work has been the outcome of the dialogue between analytical economists and experienced practitioners in tax administration, law and accountancy. At first these two groups could barely understand each other's languages; but by the end of our two years' work they were engaging in fruitful co-operative searches for solutions of difficult problems.

This could not have happened had it not been for the atmosphere in which the Committee worked. A Chairman could not possibly have had a better qualified or a more co-operative group of colleagues. They were all recognised authorities on their subject. But in addition they were persons who, although they approached the subject with different and sometimes strongly held views and from different professional approaches, always preferred reasoned agreement to disagreement.

It would be invidious for me to single out particular members, with one exception. The Committee, as all the members would agree, owes a special debt of gratitude to Donald Ironside, who as Deputy Chairman played so important a role in organising our proceedings, chairing our meetings and planning our programmes of work. Without his inspiring but unsparing energy our deliberations would never have reached a conclusion.

Our Report is a joint effort, but I take this opportunity of expressing a personal view. Our economy has become too stagnant; restoration of standards of living and many desirable increases in economic welfare depend upon higher productivity. At the same time a modern humane society demands that effective action should be taken to prevent poverty and to remove unacceptable inequalities of opportunity, wealth and privilege. There may be some degree of inevitable conflict between these two objectives of 'efficiency' and 'equality'. But the clash can be minimised by an appropriate choice of social, political and economic policies and institutions; and the structure of the tax system is one important element in the outcome.

An appropriate structure for this purpose would be the combination of (i) a 'new Beveridge' development of social welfare to remove the poverty trap and to set an effective and satisfactory floor to standards of living and (ii) arrangements for the taxation of wealth, in particular of inherited wealth, which would effectively encourage a wider dispersion in the ownership of property with (iii) a basic reform of direct taxation which levied a charge on what people took out of the economic system in high levels of consumption rather than on what they put into the system through their savings and enterprise.

This last ingredient is of the utmost importance. By shifting the tax base in this way all forms of enterprise – big or small, privately owned, state owned or labour-managed – would be able to plough back their own profits or to borrow the savings of others free of tax for all forms of economic development. But at the same time wealthy persons who were maintaining a high standard of living by dissaving from their capital wealth would be more heavily taxed than at present.

A possible political reaction to this would, I suppose, be for the 'left' to reject it because it gave an opportunity for private capitalist enterprise (as well as for state enterprise and labour-managed enterprise) to invest more and to expand employment opportunities, and for the 'right' to reject it because it would hit the rich who were living on inherited property. My hope is that the opposite would happen – that the 'left' would welcome the egalitarian overtones and the 'right' the opening up of opportunities and incentives for all forms of enterprise. Indeed, if we are to find a reasonable base of political consensus for our mixed economy, I can see no better fiscal contribution to this end than a tax structure of this kind.

This is not to suggest that there should be one gigantic upheaval to replace our present system overnight with an 'ideal' new system. The important point is to achieve broad agreement on the shape of the tax structure which should be the final goal towards which step-by-step changes over the coming years should lead us. In the final Chapter of our Report we have attempted both to summarise in more detail the ingredients of a tax structure of the kind outlined above and also to consider by what processes of gradual change one might move towards it.

We have gone out of our way in our Report to discover and to display to the reader all the difficulties and snags that exist in the implementation of such a set of tax reforms. It would be irresponsible to do otherwise. But I hope that we shall not thereby give a false impression. There are difficulties, snags, and blemishes in all tax systems (not least in our own existing tax system, or lack of system, which, if presented for the first time as a blueprint for action, would undoubtedly be dismissed as impracticable); and I doubt very much whether the difficulties are worse with the package of tax reforms which I have just outlined than with any other reasonable tax package. The reader will not, I hope, be misled by our having devoted much space in our Report to a full and careful analysis of all the difficulties connected with our proposals.

There is one tiresome and annoying blemish in our Report which it is, alas, now too late to remove before publication. We have worked out all our analyses of the present tax structure and all our examples of reforms on the basis of the rates of tax and scale of personal tax allowances which the Chancellor of the Exchequer declared in his April budget to be his ultimate intention for 1977/78. But in mid-July changes have been announced; in particular the basic rate of tax is to be 34 per cent and not 33 per cent as previously envisaged and personal tax allowances are to be raised to £845 instead of £805 for the single individual and to £1,295 instead of £1,225 for the married man.[1] Our Report is now submitted to the publishers in its final form; and it would be impossible without inordinate delay to rework all our examples. Our conclusions would not be changed in any essential way by such reworkings; but it will, I fear, be a tiresome annoyance to some of our readers that what we treat in the examples in our report as the scale of taxation operating in 1977/78 is in fact not strictly accurate.

In the course of our work we have been helped by many persons, who have prepared papers for us, have commented on drafts of parts of our report, and have discussed problems with us. We have had visits from, and discussions about an expenditure tax with, Professor Lord Kaldor author of the classic work of 1955 on *The Expenditure Tax*, Professor Bradford who was working in the US Treasury on *Blueprints for Basic Tax Reform* in which an expenditure tax is discussed as one of the possible basic tax reforms for the United States, and Professor Lodin, author of 'Progressiv utgiftsskatt – ett alternativ?', which is an account of an expenditure tax devised by him for the Swedish Royal Commission on Taxation. Dr N. Barr of the London School of Economics and Dr Gordon Hughes of Christ's College, Cambridge, have prepared papers for us and discussed them with us. We have received comments on drafts of parts of our Report from among others Mr R. T. Esam, Mr E. C. Meade, Professor R. R. Nield, and Professor W. B. Reddaway. Professor A. B. Atkinson and Mr Stanley Wright after they had ceased to be members of our Committee continued to help us with comments on some draft Chapters of our Report. Mrs Dowley of Nuffield College, Oxford, has done some important statistical work for us.

We have had comments from and discussions with officials of the Treasury and the Inland Revenue, who gave us much help at times when they were busy on other and more pressing matters. We have had the advantage of a discussion with members of the IFS at a seminar arranged for that purpose.

We are extremely grateful for all this help. But it is, of course, to be understood that none of the persons who have helped us in these ways is responsible for any views which are expressed in our Report.

We received continual help and encouragement in our work from Dick Taverne, Director of the IFS; and we would like to thank Thelma Liesner and other members of the staff of the IFS, and also Pauline Wright of Thomson McLintock and Co., for their help in arrangements for our meetings and conferences and in the preparation of our Report. In particular we would express our gratitude to our assistant Miss Carole Pleming whose service to us throughout our work has been invaluable.

J. E. MEADE
22 *July* 1977

[1] Subsequently in October 1977 the Chancellor announced among other changes that the personal tax allowances for 1977/78 were to be increased further to £945 for the single individual and £1,455 for the married man. In Sections 1 and 2 of Appendix 5.1 we have noted the result of these changes.

Glossary of Acronyms

(References are to those places in the text where the meaning of the term is described.)

ACT   advance corporation tax (Chapter 4, p. 59).

AGAWAT age–gap–annual–wealth–accessions tax (Chapter 15, p. 333).

AT   accessions tax (Chapter 15, p. 319).

AWT   annual wealth tax (Chapter 16, p. 350).

CGT   capital gains tax (Chapter 6, p. 56).

CIT   comprehensive income tax (Chapter 7, p. 127).

CT   corporation tax (Chapter 6, p. 58).

CTT   capital transfer tax (Chapter 15, p. 319).

DTR   double taxation relief (Chapter 20, p. 412).

ET   expenditure tax (Chapter 8, p. 150).

GIET   gifts inclusive expenditure tax (Chapter 9, p. 183).

IT   income tax.

ITVAT   income tax form of value-added tax (Appendix 8.3).

LAWAT linear–annual–wealth–accessions tax (Chapter 15, p. 330).

LET   local expenditure tax (Chapter 11, p. 218).

LIT   local income tax (Chapter 11, p. 218).

PAWAT progressive–annual–wealth–accessions tax (Chapter 15, p. 320).

R a corporate tax base including only all transactions in real goods and services (Chapter 12, p. 230).

$R+F$ a corporate tax base including all transactions in real goods and services and financial services, but excluding financial transactions with shareholders (Chapter 12, p. 233).

S a corporate tax base including only all financial transactions with shareholders (Chapter 12, p. 233).

TTET   two-tier expenditure tax (Chapter 8, p. 160).

UET   universal expenditure tax (Chapter 8, p. 160).

VAT   value-added tax (Chapter 10, p. 208).

Glossary of Technical Terms

(References are to those places in the text where the terms are more fully defined or described.)

advance corporation tax: corporation tax paid by a company when paying a dividend (Chapter 4, p. 59).

annual value: the monetary equivalent of the annual yield of an asset that provides its benefits in a non-monetary form (Chapter 4, p. 54; Chapter 11, p. 217).

bracket indexation: the adjustment of the money steps in a progressive rate schedule by some general price index (Chapter 6, p. 100).

capital allowances: allowances given under tax law for the depreciation of assets used in business (Chapter 4, pp. 50–53; Appendix 4.1, section 2).

capital–income adjustment: the money adjustment made to the opening stock of wealth before measuring the change in real wealth for a period (Chapter 6, p. 101).

conditional benefit/social dividend: a benefit or social dividend payable only to those meeting certain conditions (Chapter 13, p. 274).

domicile: the place where, particularly under UK law, an individual is regarded as having his permanent home (Appendix 21.1).

double taxation relief: relief given to a taxpayer in one country in respect of tax paid in another country (Chapter 20, p. 412).

economic or true depreciation: the actual year-by-year fall in value of an asset over its working (cash-generating) life (Chapter 7, p. 143).

expenditure–tax adjustment: the adjustment that must be made to a taxpayer's income in order to compute his expenditure for a period (Chapter 8, p. 151).

franked: the term describing income, expenditure or wealth which is treated as having paid tax (Chapter 15, p. 321).

imputation: the administrative arrangement whereby tax paid by a company is treated in whole or part as having been paid by a shareholder (Chapter 4, pp. 58–59).

ordinarily resident: a status under the UK tax law dependent on habitual residence in that country (Appendix 21.1).

registered asset: an asset the acquisition or disposal of which is included in the expenditure–tax adjustment (Chapter 9, p. 175).

resident: the treatment of an individual for tax purposes as if he lives in a particular country (Appendix 21.1).

social dividend: a cash benefit payable by the state to individuals (Chapter 13, p. 271).

tax credit: an amount of tax that is credited as having been paid in respect of an item of income, expenditure or wealth (Chapter 4, pp. 58–59).

tax-exclusive rate: a rate of tax to be applied to a tax base exclusive of the tax itself (Note on the Distinction between a Tax-inclusive and a Tax-exclusive Basis for Rates of Taxation, pp. 28–29).

tax-inclusive rate: a rate of tax to be applied to a tax base inclusive of the tax itself (Note on the Distinction between a Tax-inclusive and a Tax-exclusive Basis for Rates of Taxation, pp. 28–29).

unconditional benefit/social dividend: a benefit or social dividend payable as of right to all individuals without qualification requirements (Chapter 13, p. 274).

unregistered asset: an asset the acquisition or disposal of which is not included in the expenditure-tax adjustment (Chapter 9, p. 175).

PART ONE INTRODUCTION

In this Part we explain the scope and purpose of our inquiry and consider in general terms what are some of the main characteristics of a good structure for a system of direct taxes.

1 Scope and Purpose of the Study

We were set up as a Committee to make a study of the structure of the UK tax system as a whole. There is a widespread view, the justification for which we illustrate in Part Two of this Report, that, as a result of many successive independent changes and *ad hoc* modifications first of this tax and then of that tax, the whole system now contains a number of anomalous complications and inconsistencies, which have been much intensified by current rates of inflation. In present inflationary conditions and with the high rates of tax necessary to finance the present high levels of public expenditure, these anomalies can have very grave and important effects on the economy. Accordingly it was thought fit to set up a Committee to undertake a radical review of the tax structure as a whole.

But the very fact that over recent years there have been so many changes in the tax system suggests that an essential need is to put a stop to this bewildering process of altering each element in the tax structure as soon as the taxpayer gets used to it and arranges his affairs appropriately. Uncertainty and lack of confidence in the stability of present arrangements are serious impediments to the national effort to improve our economic performance.

These two points of view are not very easily reconciled. As so often in this wicked world, one cannot have one's cake and eat it; but one can compromise, and eat half and keep half. Accordingly we have tried to respond to this difficult situation in the following way. In Part Three of our Report we have embarked on a root-and-branch radical analysis of the tax structure based on first principles, a process which, for good or bad, we were set up to carry out. In discussing the possible radical restructurings of the tax system we have paid close attention to the transitional problems involved; and in the final Part Four of our Report we have placed emphasis on the fact that we cannot jump by one revolutionary movement from the existing tax structure to a completely new one. Accordingly in that Part we have paid great attention to the sort of gradual modifications which would lead one nearer to, rather than further away from, the desired new structure. The root-and-branch analysis can be regarded as defining the ultimate goal against which the desirability of any step-by-step changes can be judged.

In this Report we have restricted our attention to the structure and operation of the main direct taxes, such as the income tax, the capital gains tax, the corporation tax, the capital transfer tax, and the proposed Wealth Tax. As part of this corpus of direct taxes, we have included for certain purposes the present structure of social security contributions and benefits, which for many purposes must be regarded as negative direct taxes, and also the value-added tax, which in many respects is similar to a general direct tax on consumption expenditure. Given the time and the resources available to us, we have tried to make a thorough going examination of this part of the tax structure rather than to make a more superficial examination which would cover a wider range of taxes.

We would justify this limitation of the scope of our inquiry on the grounds that the main anomalous complications and inconsistencies in the present UK tax structure are the result either of special inappropriate provisions in one or other of these direct taxes or, above all, of the way in which the provisions of these taxes interlink and react on each other. This latter topic has played a central role in our inquiry. For example, as we demonstrate in Part Two of our Report it is the combined effect of the provisions of the income tax, the capital gains tax, and the corporation tax which gives rise to some of the most marked and, one imagines, wholly unplanned distortions in the capital market; and it is the combined effect of the unrelated provisions of the income tax and of the arrangements for social security which give rise to what are also, one imagines, wholly unplanned disincentives in the labour market. The examination of structural effects of this kind and the suggestion of alternative structural tax arrangements which would avoid these distorting effects have constituted a large part of the substance of our work.

This fact that a large part of our work consists in a search for ways of getting rid of these unplanned distortions may leave the reader with a wrong impression of the underlying object of our analysis. We search continually for tax arrangements which will be as neutral as possible in their effects in the market in influencing the taxpayer's decisions and choices. The purpose of this search is to find a structure which will introduce as few *unplanned* distortions as possible. In other words it is our view that one should as far as possible start from the firm basis of a general interlocking structure of direct taxes which is as neutral as possible in its effects on market decisions. This does not, of course, rule out the introduction of a limited number of *ad hoc* modifications which are specifically *planned* to influence market decisions in one way or another.[1]

Thus the fact that we have not in this Report considered specific taxes or charges to discourage polluting activities, or special subsidies to employment in specially depressed regions, or specially heavy excise duties on particular commodities like alcoholic drinks and tobacco, should not be taken to imply that we disapprove of them because they are not 'neutral' in their effects.

There are other very important aspects of the present UK tax system which we have not attempted in this Report to examine. We have not considered tax problems of devolution nor the problems of local taxation except in so far as they impinge directly upon the operation of the main national direct taxes. We have not examined the special problems of the taxation of oil revenues or of land and development values. We have not investigated the

[1] Modifications of the main tax structure which lead to a loss of revenue are as important as increases in public expenditure in putting a strain on the rest of the tax structure. For this reason we would welcome the institution of an annual statement of such tax remissions or 'tax expenditures' in order that losses of revenue may be subjected to the same scrutiny as increases in public expenditure.

tax problems involved in short term demand management for the macroeconomic control of economic activity. We have no intention of denying the great importance of these topics. We can only repeat that in the time available to us we could not cover everything, that we consider the basic interlocking relationships of the main direct taxes to have proved to be a most important subject for analysis, and that it is against the background of such a preliminary study that further work on these other topics might well be organised.

We have conducted our inquiry primarily from the national point of view. In doing so we have, of course, taken into account the main international problems which would arise from the tax changes which we discuss. We have explained these problems at considerable length in Chapters 20 and 21 where we have described a number of possible ways of dealing with them. But the main focus of our inquiry has been on the domestic effects of different tax arrangements, and it is on the study of these effects that we have concentrated the time and resources at our disposal. As a result, the analysis and proposals in Chapters 20 and 21 should be regarded as rather more tentative than those in the rest of our Report.

In any reforms which we have analysed for the main direct taxes we have made every effort to take note of, and to present to the reader a full account of, the administrative and similar difficulties which the changes would involve. We have taken such administrative problems very seriously. But we have been less worried about the fact that some of the new tax arrangements which we discuss are unfamiliar and may for that reason not be immediately politically possible. History suggests that what is not 'politically possible' can change quite radically and quite rapidly over the years; and nothing can become politically possible unless it is first proposed and discussed by some body of persons.

But there is one political aspect of our proposals which we have had very much in mind. As we have argued, stability in the tax structure is a necessary condition for business and for individual taxpayers to plan their affairs with confidence for the future. But one cannot hope to achieve any stability in the tax structure unless one can find a combination of taxes which commands a fairly wide political consensus among the main parties and is treated by each of them as a structure which each could live with if and when each came to form a government. This does not, of course, mean that there must be 100 per cent political agreement on all tax matters. Limited alterations of the tax system or changes in rates (provided that they are not on such a scale as in effect to alter the basic tax structure) must provide opportunity for the expression of different political philosophies, which put different emphases on different social and economic objectives. But one must attempt to find a broad stable framework within which all governments will be able to operate.

We have attempted to consider tax structures which might meet this criterion. Thus the combination of a progressive expenditure tax, of a reform of social security, and of a progressive tax on inherited wealth is one such combination which we discuss. A progressive expenditure tax is a tax which by exempting savings and investment from tax gives a maximum opportunity for economic growth and development in a mixed economy, but which simultaneously levies a heavy charge on those who live at a high standard of consumption whether it is based on a high income or on the dissipation of capital wealth, while a reform of social security could put a floor to poverty, and a progressive tax on inherited wealth could encourage a wider dispersion of the ownership of property. This is only one example of possible candidates which we discuss for tax systems; but for all of them we have in mind the crucial need to consider combinations which could command a wide political appeal.

It is very possible that quite extensive changes in the existing tax system must be made if a structure is to be found which might command a fairly wide political consensus. We may well have to face extensive change in order to find a stable and lasting resting place; and this is a main reason why we do not regard our radical approach to reform of the present tax system as being inimical to the ultimate objective of avoiding continuous tax changes.

Whatever form the ultimate tax structure may take, the rates of taxation will depend not only upon the nature of that tax structure but also upon the level of government expenditure. In making our assessment of the relative merits of different tax systems, we have taken into account the extent to which each provides a wider or narrower tax base and therefore implies a lower or higher average rate of tax. But we have not considered it to be part of our task to pass any judgements on the levels of public expenditures, except for those parts of the social security system which we must inevitably treat as negative taxes. But the ultimate level of tax rates will depend basically on the levels of public expenditures; and different treatments of the payoff between high tax rates and high levels of public expenditure constitute one of the ways in which differences in political philosophies will show themselves within any given tax structure.

Another way in which differences of political emphasis will show themselves within the framework of any given tax structure is in the degree of progressiveness of the rate structure. Different governments will put different emphases on the relative importance of economic incentives and of a more equal distribution of standards of living as social objectives, and such differences of emphasis will affect their views on the best pattern for progressive tax schedules. Later in this Report (Chapter 14) we say something on the principles underlying this choice; but we make no far reaching proposals on what in our view constitutes the best pattern. Indeed it is doubtful whether we could have reached agreement on such a question even if we had tried to do so.

Thus we do not profess to say much about the general level of tax rates or on the degree of progression in the relevant tax schedules within any given tax structure. But we do claim to have said some interesting things, and possibly a few useful things, about the choice of the tax structure itself and about possible step-by-step processes of moving towards the chosen system.

2 The Characteristics of a Good Tax Structure

We have explained in Chapter 1 the limitations of our inquiry. Thus, except as they impinge directly on our main inquiry, we are not concerned with such matters as the total level of public expenditure and the consequent need for tax revenue, the distribution of taxing powers between different authorities, possible methods of linking the levying of taxes with the expenditure of the revenue, and the political problems of the accountability of taxing and spending authorities to the public.

As we interpret the phrase 'the structure of direct taxes in the United Kingdom' we are seeking answers to questions of the following kind: Do the various direct taxes make a coherent whole, or do they overlap and impinge on each other in an inconsistent and undesirable manner? Are there any ways in which, for example, the tax bases of the particular direct taxes and the rules relating one such tax to another could be modified so as to make the whole structure simpler, more effective and fairer in its operation?

In order to answer such questions one must have in mind what one would regard as the desirable characteristics of a tax structure. We consider the most important of these under the following six headings:

1 Incentives and economic efficiency
2 Distributional effects
3 International aspects
4 Simplicity and costs of administration and compliance
5 Flexibility and stability
6 Transitional problems.

1 INCENTIVES AND ECONOMIC EFFICIENCY

There are many channels through which a tax system may affect economic efficiency. It can have important effects on incentives and opportunities to work, to save, to invest in capital developments, to take risks and innovate, to use resources efficiently and to allocate them to uses which best serve the needs of society.

To a large extent these efficiency effects depend upon the total level of taxation. If the need for tax revenue to finance a large public sector is high, some tax rates will inevitably be high with inevitable effects upon some economic opportunities and incentives. We have not regarded it as part of our task to consider what is the proper balance between the public and private sectors of the economy and what, in consequence, is the proper target for total tax revenue. But there are different ways of raising a given tax revenue with differing effects upon economic opportunities and incentives; and this aspect of the matter we do regard as being at the heart of our inquiry.

The economist distinguishes between the *'income effect'* and the *'substitution effect'* of a tax burden. Thus heavier taxes on income will reduce the taxpayer's spendable income, and this consideration alone would probably make it desirable for him to work harder to restore in part his post-tax income (the 'income effect'); but at the same time a higher marginal tax rate will reduce the net spendable income which he can get from an extra hour's work, and this reduction in the extra goods which he can earn from an hour's work will tend to make him prefer leisure to work (the 'substitution effect').

'Income effects' are not a symptom of economic inefficiency and waste; they are merely the result of the most effective way of meeting the inevitable cost of given tax burdens. But 'substitution effects' are an indication of economic inefficiencies and wastes, even if they do no more than offset the influence of the 'income effects'. They may take many forms. The doctor may emigrate to substitute higher foreign earnings for lower earnings at home, and some part of the differential may be due to differences in rates of tax. The wage earner may reduce his hours of work in order to substitute untaxed domestic leisure or do-it-yourself activity at home for taxed work. The housewife may substitute untaxed domestic work for taxed earnings outside the home. A business executive may refuse promotion and thus substitute his present occupation for the alternative more productive job, because the low post-tax increase in his earnings in the higher paid job would not compensate for the cost of movement to that job or for the additional strain or risk of possible failure in the higher paid and more responsible post which he is being offered. An active businessman may substitute an easy life for the energy and worry needed to improve the efficient use of his resources, because the post-tax increase in his profit makes the payoff unattractive. A saver may substitute present consumption for future consumption by himself or his heirs, because of the tax on the yield from his savings. And so on.

Suppose that Mr Smith by working an extra hour a week could add £100 a year to the value of the output of the concern in which he is employed; but suppose that because of income tax he would keep only £60 out of any additional £100 paid to him in wages. If, while he continued to pay the same total amount in tax, Mr Smith would prefer to do an extra hour's work for an extra £100 a year but in fact prefers the leisure because he is offered only an additional £60 net of tax, then the tax has caused an economic inefficiency. If he had done the extra hour's work and had received the full £100, Mr Smith would have been better off; and no one need have been worse off, because Mr Smith would have been taking out of the community's real product no more than he added to it by his own extra labour.

Or suppose that Mr Brown by saving an extra £100 this year would have reduced the demands on real resources this year by an amount which, if invested in real capital equipment, would have added to the annual community's product a net annual output worth £10 a year; but suppose that because of income tax Mr Brown could keep only £6 a year out of any £10 a year in dividends or interest that an expanding business could offer him on his savings. If Mr Brown would prefer £10 a year to spend in future years to having £100 to spend on consumption this year, but would prefer £100 to spend this year to having only £6 a year to spend in future years, then the tax will have been the cause of an economic inefficiency. If Mr Brown had through his savings released the £100 of resources for productive investment and had been paid the full £10 a year return on it, he would have been better off; and no one else need have been worse off, because Mr Brown would in the future years have been taking out of the national product only as much as the investment of his own savings had added to it.

Taxation may cause other kinds of distortion. Thus it may lead to the substitution of one form of business organisation for another. For example, differences in the tax treatment of unincorporated businesses and of incorporated businesses may lead to the choice of a form of business organisation which is not the most appropriate and efficient for the particular purpose in hand. Or taxation may lead to the substitution of a less profitable but steady business for a more profitable but fluctuating business, because with a progressive tax system the tax burden on a given average income is higher if the income fluctuates than if it is steady.

The importance to be attached to each of these possible forms of inefficiency depends upon the extent of each relevant substitution effect. Obtaining and interpreting the relevant information is difficult, and in fact little is known about the importance of these substitution effects.[1] But in principle it is a question of fact whether in any particular sector of economic activity these substitution effects are large or small. Would fewer doctors emigrate if their total tax burden were not reduced by doing so? If the decision had no effect on their present or future tax burdens, would people save much more than at present if they could obtain the pre-tax instead of the post-tax rate of return on any additional savings? Do manual workers with a given real income in fact significantly reduce their hours of work if the marginal post-tax rate for overtime is reduced? Avoidance of economic inefficiencies would involve avoidance of high marginal rates of tax where these substitution sensitivities were great.

One corollary of this need to keep marginal tax rates down is a general presumption in favour of tax systems which provide a broad basis for revenue-raising purposes. To raise a given revenue by means of low rates of tax spread over a large tax base may be assumed to cause less marked 'substitution' distortions than to raise the same revenue by concentrating high rates of tax on a few activities, unless special circumstances suggest that those particular activities show exceptionally low substitution sensitivities. For this reason it is of great importance to resist erosion of the tax

---

[1] In Appendix 2.1 we give a brief account of the existing studies which have been made of the effects of taxation on the amount of work done. The results of these studies are rather inconclusive, partly because it is difficult to distinguish between the income effects and the substitution effects of taxation. The case in which there appears to be the most marked disincentive effects of high rates of tax is in discouraging married women to seek paid work.

base through a multiplication of exemptions and reliefs; and it may point to reliance on a tax system which comprises a number of different taxes rather than to reliance on only one or two taxes in order to keep down the marginal rates of tax on any one line of activity.

If all markets for goods and services were competitive and perfect, these direct 'substitution effects' of the taxes themselves would be our only concern in considering the efficiency effects of a tax system; and in all the examples so far given in this chapter we have been tacitly assuming this to be the case. But the fact that not all markets for goods and services are perfect and competitive introduces other considerations in assessing these efficiency effects.

In general, competitive market forces will tend to attract the allocation of resources into those activities which best satisfy the desires of the buyers of the goods and services concerned and for which, therefore, consumers are ready to offer a high price relatively to the cost of resources used in their production. But there are in the real world a number of impediments to this process. Lack of information about market conditions may lead to wasteful inertia. Or the existence of economies of large scale production may mean that small changes are unattractive so that highly organised large structural changes are necessary to improve efficiency. Or monopolistic restrictions by large productive concerns or by groups of workers may impede change. Wealthy people may be able to invest their capital at higher rates of yield and to borrow at lower rates of interest than poorer persons who have less credit and less access to capital markets; and such imperfections on the capital market will cause the ability to borrow and to lend at rates which correspond more or less nearly to the true social returns on capital to differ from case to case.

Another example may be provided by the fact that fully effective economic activity, particularly in the modern world, depends upon bringing together the specialised skills and resources of different persons. This is a function of effective markets. Mr A has the bright idea, Mr B lends the money, Mr C runs the business, Mr D does the manual work, and so on. Markets for risk capital, management executives, manual labour, patents, etc. may bring these together into a single effective business enterprise. But they may fail to do so. The man with the bright idea may not be able to persuade the man with the risk capital that it is a good idea. He may therefore have to start by himself, providing not only the bright idea but his own very limited capital and his own labour and enterprise in running the business, which can then begin to grow only by the saving and the ploughing back into his business of his own profits. The reduction by tax of the amount of such profits available for ploughing back will in such a case have an effect upon the concern which is not simply a matter of the correct 'income effects' or the undesirable 'substitution effects' of the choice between present and future consumption of resources. The holding back by tax of one of the elements of success (namely the amount of profits which can be ploughed back) may limit the extent to which the other elements of success such as innovation, enterprise and effort can be used to good effect, simply because in the absence of perfect markets for these separate factors all these elements must be combined in the same individual package.

Another form of market imperfection is where there are certain social costs (or benefits) involved in an economic activity which for one reason or another escape the calculus of private costs (or gains). An example of such social costs are the wear and tear of the highway, the policing and control of traffic, the noise, the congestion and the danger to life and limb that can be involved in extensive road traffic.

In a number of these cases the best form of corrective action lies in measures other than fiscal incentives – e.g. through retraining, state enterprise, wage or price regulation, social control of monopolies, special financial institutions to correct imperfections in the capital market, and so on. But there may in some cases be an appropriate place for fiscal incentives designed directly to counteract the effects of market imperfections.

One possible case is the use of fiscal incentives to promote regional development where unassisted individual developments would be unattractive to private enterprise, although simultaneous all-round development would turn the whole into an efficient and profitable region.

Another case is the imposition of special taxes on motor vehicles and petrol to take the place of those social costs of motoring which are not otherwise met by the private motorist. Where there are social costs which are not included in private market costs, these social costs may be represented by taxation or similar levies in order to improve the society's allocation of resources between their various uses.

The implications of market imperfections are, however, in fact much more far-reaching than is suggested by the above examples, all of which are concerned with tax arrangements which operate *directly* in causing or in counteracting a particular market imperfection. But tax arrangements may have far-reaching *indirect* effects in stimulating or restricting other economic activities which are themselves the subject of some form of market imperfection. The nature of these indirect effects is described in more detail in Appendix 2.2. One simple example must serve here to illustrate the point. Suppose that Mr Smith is induced by the income tax to substitute leisure for earned income, thus being the subject of a direct inefficiency of the kind described on p. 8 above. But suppose further that as a result he can no longer afford to purchase some luxury good the production of which causes some form of environmental pollution. Then there results some indirect offsetting increase in economic efficiency through the reduction of the polluting activity. As made clear in Appendix 2.2, it is not possible to take into account all the indirect effects of given tax arrangements on economic efficiency. The question arises how far one should go in trying to devise a tax system which takes account of such indirect effects. We return to this question at the end of Chapter 3 (pp. 43–44).

2 DISTRIBUTIONAL EFFECTS

Any system of taxes is bound to have distributional effects even if it is only a
matter of deciding who should bear the burden of the tax revenue needed to
finance some particular level of budgetary expenditure. In some cases it is
possible and appropriate to tax those particular members of society who will
benefit from the particular budgetary expenditure. For example, social
security has been regarded at least partly in this light, with the implication
that the insured should pay contributions which are related to the benefits
which they may expect to derive from the scheme. But in many cases, such
as national defence, it is difficult or impossible to attribute different amounts
of the benefits of the public expenditure to particular individuals or groups
of individuals. Moreover, in modern society the distributional aspects of a
fiscal system are often more pervasive and more purposive than the simple
determination of who should bear the burden of an otherwise given level of
government expenditure; progressive taxation combined with social security
benefits and other elements of social expenditure (e.g. on education or
health) are often expressly designed to improve the relative position of the
poorer members of society.

In addition to the effect of a tax system on redistribution between rich and
poor (the effects on *'vertical'* redistribution), the equity of a tax system must
also be judged by the extent to which it treats fairly and equally those members
of society who are equally rich or poor (the *'horizontal'* equity criterion).

The following points are clear:

1 A good tax system should be horizontally equitable, i.e. should treat
   like with like.
2 A modern tax system must be so constructed as to be capable of use for
   vertical redistribution between rich and poor.
3 There will almost inevitably be some clash between the criteria of economic efficiency (which require low *marginal* tax rates) and of vertical
   redistribution (which will require high *average* rates of tax on the rich);
   but a good tax system is one which minimises this clash and promotes a
   given redistribution with a minimum loss of efficiency.
4 The final choice of redistributional aims for a tax system involves basic
   value judgements about the nature of a good society, which are matters
   for political decision and are not the direct concern of the Committee;
   but a good tax structure is one which is sufficiently flexible to allow scope
   in a democratic society for different political choices (e.g. by variations
   in rates of tax).

Moreover, in considering the distributional effects of a fiscal system,
account must be taken of certain elements of public expenditure. This is
most obvious in the case of direct social transfer payments (sickness and
unemployment benefits, old age pensions, child benefits, family income
supplement, supplementary benefit, and so on). Indeed, the very fact that
some schemes (discussed in Chapter 13) for the reform of this part of the

UK fiscal and welfare arrangements are called '*negative income tax*' schemes makes the point unambiguously. But other forms of public expenditure (such as the cost of rent and rate rebates or allowances, the subsidisation of the price of essential foodstuffs, the provision of free health and education) may be expressly designed in part or whole to influence distribution.

So much for general principles. Unfortunately, in considering the tax side of the budget equation neither 'horizontal equity' nor 'vertical redistribution' are in fact straightforward simple objectives, and in judging any particular tax structure it is necessary to consider in more detail how these ideas should be interpreted.

In the case of 'horizontal equity' it is often a matter of passing judgement on the effects of a change in a tax structure rather than on the nature of the tax structure itself. In this respect there is an element of truth in the adage that 'an old tax is a good tax'. If there were no existing special tax on the profits of corporate as contrasted with unincorporated business, it could be argued that a proposal to introduce such a tax with its consequential effects on share values was not horizontally equitable on the grounds that it was inequitable to tax one man who received a certain income from profits and to exempt from tax another man who received the same income from profits simply because the one arose from corporate business and the other from an unincorporated concern. But the situation is different if the tax has already been introduced and has been in operation for many years without any expectation of its removal. Businessmen will have made their choices between the corporate or unincorporated form for their concerns, and investors will have put their funds into various forms of property, on a comparison of expected post-tax rates of return. To remove the special tax on corporate profits would then give an unexpected advantage to the holders of ordinary shares in corporate enterprises, these shareholders being a quite different set of persons (indeed possibly a totally different generation of persons) from those who owned the shares and were therefore hurt when the tax was first introduced. Everyone in the present generation will have made the same free choice between corporate and unincorporated concerns in the knowledge that the tax existed and on the assumption that it would continue. Its abolition would now favour one man more than another, though both have the same post-tax incomes.

Another example of this problem is the taxation of the imputed annual value of owner-occupied houses. The removal of the Schedule A tax on such imputed income raised problems of horizontal equity as between those persons who had chosen to put their property into stock exchange securities and to rent a dwelling with the taxed proceeds and those persons of equal wealth who had chosen to put their property directly into an owner-occupied house, the income from which was then relieved of tax with the consequential effect of increasing the value of the house. But when many years have passed and the majority of owner occupiers are persons who have made the choice between the one form of investment or the other on the basis that the one form is taxed and the other is not, a problem of horizontal equity would arise with any unexpected reimposition of the tax.

From the point of view of horizontal equity there is thus some truth in the view that an old tax is a good tax. But this aspect of the matter is not, of course, an over-riding one. Indeed, a Committee which is set up to consider possible improvements in a tax structure can hardly take as a working rule that whatever exists, simply because it exists, necessarily constitutes the best of all possible worlds. But the fact that changes in tax raise questions of horizontal equity does mean that any proposals for tax changes which have significant effects of this kind must take this aspect of the matter into account. Where necessary, it is possible to propose *ad hoc* temporary measures which will offset any unfairness or else to propose that the change be introduced only gradually so that people can adjust by small degrees to the new situation. Indeed, this in itself is an argument in favour of open discussion of the merits of a tax change, well in advance of the change itself, since it is the sudden unexpected nature of a tax change which raises in its most acute form the question of horizontal inequity.

Both horizontal equity and the vertical distribution of tax burdens are in fact difficult notions to make at all precise. No doubt, if Mr Smith and Mr Brown have the same 'taxable capacity', they should bear the same tax burden, and if Mr Smith's taxable capacity is greater than Mr Brown's, Mr Smith should bear the greater tax burden. But on examination 'taxable capacity' always turns out to be very difficult to define and to be a matter on which opinions will differ rather widely.

Horizontal equity implies that people who are equally well off should bear equal tax burdens. Vertical redistribution involves redistribution from those who are better off to those who are worse off. Thus any distributional principles involve some measurement of how well off a taxpayer is. But it is not always easy to determine what are the relevant aspects of welfare for tax purposes. One or two examples of this difficulty must suffice.

(1) Is it similarity of opportunity or similarity of outcome which is relevant? Messrs Smith and Jones both start with the same opportunities. Smith goes in for a risky career as a professional musician while Jones chooses a safe job as a civil servant. They both choose with their eyes open, taking into account the risks involved. If Smith succeeds he will be much better off than Jones; if he fails he will be much worse off. If there is a highly progressive tax system, Smith will be heavily taxed if he succeeds and he may be somewhat subsidised if he is totally impoverished. This is to judge horizontal equity on the basis of outcome rather than opportunity, a result which is presumably inevitable if a tax system is simultaneously devised to promote vertical redistribution.

(2) Should differences in needs or tastes be considered in comparing taxable capacities?

There are some differences in needs which may well be considered relevant in the assessment of taxable capacity. An obvious case is the need for a larger income to provide a given standard of living for those persons who, because of incapacity of one kind or another, have greater needs for help and attention. But how should such needs be assessed? Should the deaf as well as the blind receive special tax treatment?

As for differences in tastes, presumably no one would support the view that Brown should be taxed more lightly than Robinson because Brown enjoyed expensive hobbies and pleasures, whereas Robinson was equally content with a simple life. But some differences in tastes may not be wholly irrelevant.

A complex and perplexing combination of differing tastes and needs is to be observed in the contrast between single adults and married couples with families. Some persons enjoy the life of a bachelor or spinster and remain single; other persons enjoy marriage and spend their income on the production of children – an expensive hobby if ever there was one! But the children themselves once produced have needs. However, the needs of an infant are not the same as those of an adult, and a group living together has not the same needs as the sum of the needs of the same persons living separately. Horizontal equity and taxable capacity raise the familiar but difficult problem of comparison of the taxable capacity of persons in different family conditions. Should family expenditure on children be regarded simply as a way in which the parents choose to enjoy the expenditure of their income, or as a measure of the increased needs of the family, or as partly one and partly the other?

(3)   This leads to the closely connected question of the nature of the tax units which it is fair to employ for comparisons of taxable capacity. Is it the individual, the nuclear family, the extended family, the household or some other form of community? Suppose Granny has no income at all but lives with her wealthy son and daughter-in-law. Is Granny wealthy for tax purposes, or should she receive supplementary benefit? If a rich man marries a poor woman, is the man still rich and the woman still poor, or does it average out for tax purposes? What if a rich man lives with a poor woman without the legal bond of marriage?

(4)   Even when it has been decided whose welfare it is that is to be considered (e.g. the individual's or the family's), there remains the basic question what type of redistribution of welfare among tax units it is wished to promote. A frequent answer is 'less inequality'. But there is no simple single measurement of the degree of equality or inequality in any distribution. There is a very large number of types of change in a distributional pattern, and the relative importance which is attached to these different possibilities raises basic value judgements about the nature of the good society. One attitude is to be concerned primarily, even solely, with raising the standards of the poorest members of society. On this view little or no importance will be attached to the degree of inequality or equality between those in the middle and top ranges who are well above the minimum level. Others will regard it as offensive that there should be very large concentrations of riches at the top, and would regard it as a matter of importance to reduce inequalities between the rich and the poor even if this involved no improvement in the standard of living of the poor. Indeed some persons might put such an emphasis on the moral merits of an egalitarian society without distinctions of riches and poverty that they would advocate carrying the taxation of the rich to a point at which the effect on incentives might so reduce the national

income that there was even some net reduction in material standards of living throughout the population.

We have not in this chapter considered what actual distributional effects will be caused by different types of tax structure.[2] But we have attempted to consider at some length the different questions which may be raised in judging the merits of different distributional objectives for a good tax structure. Nearly all these questions involve value judgements, which constitute a basic task for political decisions. The Committee does not regard it as part of its function to make such political decisions. On the other hand, it is quite impossible for us to disregard these issues. To carry out our discussion of the choices open between various tax systems it would be quite impossible to leave every single distributional option open and unresolved. What we have tried to do can be summarised under two headings:

1   We have tried to be open, frank, and unbiased in explaining the distributional issues of the tax structures examined.
2   In reaching any decisions which involve value judgements we have tried to confine ourselves to value judgements which, in our opinion, would command a wide measure of political agreement.

3   INTERNATIONAL ASPECTS

Throughout the world the main structure of taxation is a concern of national governments. But the national economies which these governments influence by their tax policies are in large measure open economies with very extensive and important economic and financial relations with each other. In particular the experience of the 1930s taught Western industrialised countries the dangers of embarking upon autarkic restrictions on international transactions to the impoverishment of each other. As a consequence, since World War II they have built up a system of international economic and financial relations which is based upon relatively free movements of goods, capital and people between them, a system which for a quarter of a century was accompanied by a most remarkable economic development and prosperity. The trouble with the United Kingdom since World War II was until recently, not so much the absence of sustained prosperity and growth, but rather that UK growth lagged behind the exceptionally high rates achieved by the country's neighbours and competitors.

This system is now subject to a new challenge in the unprecedented experience of simultaneous international recession and inflation. The code of good behaviour in international economic and financial relationships is under review, with the object of re-establishing and maintaining a system of reasonably free transactions between the countries concerned in order to avoid mutually destructive restrictions.

---

[2] For an account of some of the difficulties involved in assessing the actual direct and indirect distributional effects of different taxes, see Appendix 2.2.

The Committee has accordingly conducted its survey of the UK tax structure on the assumption that the international order will continue to be relatively free and liberal. This itself sets certain constraints on the UK fiscal system. To some extent these constraints arise not so much from the form of the national tax structure, but rather as a result of the level and the distribution of total national tax burdens. The more intimate and free are the international economic and financial relationships, the more important it becomes for the national governments concerned not to get too far out of step in their general fiscal systems. Any large scale movement of capital and of persons of exceptional ability and enterprise to countries with low tax burdens on the rich and successful, combined with any large scale congregation of persons of small ability and of unenterprising and slack temperaments in countries with markedly egalitarian fiscal systems, would be a recipe for economic disaster. Experience suggests that there can be quite marked differences in national tax burdens without these resulting in extensive movements of capital and of persons to the low tax centres; but the fact remains that some loss will occur and that this loss will be the greater, the more freely persons and capital learn to move and the greater are the differences of tax burdens.

But the incentive for inefficient international movements of capital and persons may be due not only to the general level and distribution of national tax burdens but also to differences in the structure and form of national taxes – a possibility which is more directly the concern of the Committee. Two examples of this sort of consideration must suffice:

1 There may be little difference in the total tax burdens in a number of countries on a relatively rich man over the total course of his life. But if one of these countries assesses the tax liability on the taxpayer's consumption, while the other countries assess it on the taxpayer's income, the taxpayer may choose to reside in the consumption tax country during his working life when his income is high but his consumption is restrained because he is saving for his retirement, and to emigrate to one of the income tax countries when he retires and his income is low but his consumption remains relatively high.

2 A second example may be given by differences in the structure of corporation tax in different countries. The total burden may be the same in two countries. However, one country may allow 100 per cent initial capital allowances to be deducted for tax purposes from company profits, but disallow the deduction of interest payments on the company's indebtedness; whereas another country in the assessment of taxable profits may disallow the deduction of 100 per cent initial capital allowances, but allow the deduction of interest payments. Such a situation would give a tax incentive for equity capital to move into the former country and for loan capital to move to the latter.

So far we have discussed these international issues solely in terms of the general implications of a relatively open and liberal international system.

But international constraints on a national tax structure may arise in more precise forms from specific international treaty or other obligations. Such obligations in the case of the United Kingdom can be enumerated under three headings:

1   There are the general obligations undertaken as a member of international organisations of broad scope, such as the International Monetary Fund and the General Agreement on Tariffs and Trade.
2   There are the more specific obligations and programmes for tax harmonisation of the European Economic Community.
3   There are a number of bilateral double taxation agreements with many other countries containing specific rules for the treatment in the one country of the taxes levied in the other.

In considering various possible tax structures the Committee has had to bear in mind the existence of such specific obligations.

For a country like the United Kingdom an extremely important criterion for a good tax structure is the ease with which it can be fitted into the existing system of international economic and financial relationships and obligations. Given the tax structures of other countries, would a given tax structure in the United Kingdom be likely to lead to serious distortions in the movements of goods, capital and persons? How difficult would it be to modify it in such a way as to avoid any such distortions? Is the tax structure so modified compatible with existing international obligations? If not, what prospect is there of obtaining some appropriate change in those obligations?

4   SIMPLICITY AND COSTS OF ADMINISTRATION AND COMPLIANCE

In addition to being efficient and just and compatible with the country's international position, a good tax system should also be coherent, simple and straightforward.

In a democratic society one of the most important aspects of a tax system is that the taxing authorities should be accountable to the electorate at large. This can be so only if the tax system is such that the man and woman in the street can comprehend clearly what is the nature of the taxpayer's liability. Tax burdens which are disguised by inflationary movements of prices, or by complexities in the devising or the administration of the tax, or by uncertainties in its application cannot properly meet this criterion of simplicity. There are many aspects to this quality.

In the first place, it should be clear to the taxpayer what is and what is not taxable. Different taxes score differently on this head. In the case of an income tax there are well-known difficulties in defining precisely what is an income, what is a capital gain and what is a simple capital receipt. In the case of a tax on consumption there would be the, perhaps somewhat easier, problem of defining precisely what items of expenditure were to be defined as items of current expenditure.

Closely allied to this question of the clear definition of what is to be taxed is the question of certainty as to the amount of tax which should be paid on each taxable object. On this head also different taxes score differently. Problems of valuation are particularly important in this connection. For example, a wealth tax which involves continuous valuation of all capital assets, the greater part of which are not being continuously bought and sold in a well organised market, will involve much less certainty of tax burden than a tax which is levied upon acquisition or disposal of capital assets, the majority of which will be subject to market dealings or to valuation for the purpose of carrying out the terms of a will at the time of change of ownership.

Moreover, precision of definition of the tax base and of the consequential tax liability is not the only element in ease of understanding. The taxpayer should, as far as possible, be able not only to see clearly what is to be taxed, but also to understand the purpose which it is intended to serve by choosing the particular form of tax. The principle on which the tax base is chosen should itself be simple and easy to perceive.

The difference between a uniform and universal tax on value added and a proportionate income tax with 100 per cent initial capital allowances (discussed below, pp. 154–155), will provide a good example of the distinction between two different meanings of 'ease of understanding'. Both taxes may be equally simple and straightforward in the sense that the taxpayer would know clearly what was and what was not taxable. But while (as we shall argue) both taxes would in fact operate effectively as a tax on consumption, the taxpayer might realise that this was so in the case of a VAT but fail to see that this was so in the case of the income tax with 100 per cent initial capital allowances.

A tax system cannot be simple and easy to understand unless it makes a coherent whole. This aspect of a good tax system lies at the heart of the matter for the Committee, since it is the main purpose of the Committee to examine the tax structure as a whole and to judge whether the different parts are consistent with each other. In a federal society a very important aspect of coherence is the question whether the taxing powers of the different and independent layers of government are consistent with each other or whether they clash badly from the point of view of their effects on incentives or on a fair distribution of burdens. In the United Kingdom the acute federal problem does not as yet arise. But, as was made clear in the last section, the same problem arises in a diluted form in the question whether the domestic system of taxes fits in coherently with the tax regimes in other countries. Internally a similar question arises. Do the taxing powers of local (and, if they were to exist, devolved and regional) authorities fit in consistently with the structure of central government taxation?

A tax system must be acceptable to the public, and simplicity of the system is necessary for acceptability. Moreover, a tax system based on one or two simple clear-cut principles will make unjustifiable concessions to special interests more obvious and therefore easier to resist.

Another aspect of the simplicity of a tax system is to be found in the ease of its administration. Ease of understanding by the taxpayer and simplicity of administration may often be combined, but they are by no means always to be found together. The old purchase tax levied on consumption goods at the wholesale stage was to all intents and purposes a tax on consumption; but a tax on retail sales of goods, levied directly as payment was made for them over the counter by the final consumer for personal consumption, would have been easier than the purchase tax for the consumer to recognise as a tax on consumption. It would, however, have constituted a more difficult task for the tax authorities to administer, to control and to enforce.

In the case of ease of administration a distinction must be drawn between complexity of administration and costs of administration. Normally complexity leads to costs; but although these two things may often go together it is not necessarily always the case. A good example of such a distinction may be provided from certain proposals for a negative income tax, which we shall discuss at a later stage. A system which involved every adult citizen in drawing a weekly social dividend from the post office would in many administrative respects be straightforward and uncomplicated; but the mere size of the operation might involve a considerable expense in providing an administrative staff on the required scale.

The costs of application of a given system of taxation must be judged not only by their official administrative costs but also by the costs which the private taxpayers must incur in order to cope with their tax liabilities. There is evidence[3] that such private compliance costs are often heavy and in many cases much heavier than the official administrative costs themselves. Such costs of compliance may be reduced by ensuring that the tax system is simple, straightforward and precise – qualities which are desirable in themselves in order to make the tax system easy to understand; for the more straightforward are the taxpayer's obligations, the less time and trouble need be spent on the preparation of tax returns and appeals. Moreover, there is less scope for the expenditure of time and resources on the search for complicated ways to reduce legal liabilities to tax. But even in the case of a straightforward precise tax the private costs of compliance may be considerable when, as in the case of the deduction of tax on wages at the source by the employer through a pay-as-you-earn (PAYE) scheme, a private body or person is used to collect the tax revenue.

The total social cost of tax collection must include private compliance costs and official administrative costs. In some cases (e.g. PAYE) the cheapest method of collecting a tax may well be to make use of private individuals or businesses as agents for the collection of tax. Moreover, it is arguable that the imposition of some of the costs of tax gathering on private persons and companies may itself lead to a desirable insistence on simplicity for tax arrangements in the interests of reduction of collection costs, and that to leave to competing firms the task of tax collection may induce a healthy search for the most efficient methods of carrying out the operation.

On the other hand, other things being equal, there are at least three reasons for tipping the balance away from compliance costs on to official administrative costs where it is reasonably possible to make a choice of administrative arrangements which have this effect.

[3] See Appendix 22.1.

1   Administrative costs are themselves met from taxation which can itself
     be determined with reference to fairness of tax burden, whereas com-
     pliance costs fall on the private taxpayer and can be markedly regressive
     in their incidence.
2   Compliance costs are likely to be much resented by taxpayers, particularly
     where much time and trouble must be spent by small taxpayers only to
     show a very low or indeed a nil liability to tax.
3   Administrative costs are easier of ascertainment and more open to
     public scrutiny than are compliance costs.

5   FLEXIBILITY AND STABILITY

A good tax structure must be flexible for two rather distinct purposes, the
first being primarily economic and the second primarily political.

In the former category there must be recognition of the need to be able to
adjust total tax burdens reasonably rapidly and frequently in the interests of
demand management. One of the tools of control in the hands of Western
governments is to plan total taxation in part as a means for the stimulation
or restriction of the total demand for goods and services by the private
sector of the economy. Fashions change in the relative emphasis placed on
monetary policy and on fiscal policy for this purpose; but unless and until
there is general political agreement that fiscal policy should not be used for
this purpose, one criterion for an acceptable tax structure is that it should
contain important elements which can be varied flexibly for this purpose.

But in a democratic community flexibility in a tax system is needed for a
more basically political reason. Different political parties represent in part
different political, social and economic philosophies. In a healthy democratic
society there must be broad political consensus – or at least willingness to
compromise – over certain basic matters; but there must at the same time
be the possibility of changes of emphasis in economic policy as one government succeeds another. Such changes of emphasis will show themselves in
the trade-off which is preferred among the various objectives of a good tax
system: How much adverse effect on incentives will one government accept
in order to obtain a given decrease in inequalities of standards of living? How
complicated is one government prepared to make the tax rules in order to
achieve a given measure of horizontal equity in taxation? How far is one
government ready to control international movements of goods, capital or
persons in order to achieve a given domestic objective? And so on.

But at the same time there is a clear need for a certain stability in taxation
in order that persons may be in a position to make reasonably far-sighted
plans. Fundamental uncertainty breeds lack of confidence and is a serious
impediment to production and prosperity.

Obviously there is some clash between the requirement of flexibility and
the requirement of stability. Infinite flexibility and changeless stability are
not natural bedfellows. Excessive fluctuations in rates of tax will themselves
lead to uncertainties and lack of confidence in future plans. But above all a

prerequisite for the necessary degree of stability is the avoidance of frequent upheavals in the whole tax structure – the avoidance, that is to say, of a state of affairs in which each new government repeals a whole set of taxes which have been introduced by its predecessor and introduces a whole set of new taxes, only to see these repealed on the subsequent return of its rivals to office.

The Committee therefore has to place great importance on the question whether it is possible to find a structure of taxes which (given a reasonable degree of political give and take) might be acceptable to all political parties because it could be sufficiently flexible in its rate structure and detailed operation to enable different emphases to be put on different tax objectives from time to time. Whether such a question can be answered in the affirmative depends upon whether a sufficient degree of basic political consensus can be achieved. The Committee assumes that for any such political consensus there must be a combination of at least two essential ingredients:

1 The tax system must leave room in a mixed economy for the operation of effective incentives for private enterprise.
2 The tax system must at the same time give scope for effective modification of the distribution of income and property, which would otherwise result from the unmodified operation of the free enterprise sector of the economy.

6 TRANSITIONAL PROBLEMS

What is sauce for the goose is also sauce for the gander. The Committee would perhaps be open to legitimate criticism if, having preached the need for the different political parties to recognise the virtues of stability in a tax structure, it proceeded to recommend a totally new and improved tax structure, the introduction of which would involve a gigantic upheaval. Any inconsistency may be more apparent than real, since it may in fact be necessary to alter the tax structure in order to find one on the subsequent stability of which the main political parties could agree.

Nevertheless the avoidance of further upheaval is a major objective. An important criterion in judging a new tax proposal is therefore not merely the quality of the system itself when it is in operation, but also the ease or difficulty with which the transition from the old to the new structure can be made.

Whether a tax change should be made thus depends not only upon the desirable characteristics which that tax would have once it was in full operation, but also upon the difficulties of transition, including the need for the taxpayer to learn to understand the new system. Once more there is this element of truth in the statement that an old tax is a good tax. The question must be asked whether special measures can be devised without excessive cost or unfairness to meet adequately otherwise unacceptable transitional effects. Alternatively, could the tax be introduced by gradual stages in such a way as adequately to ease transitional hardships?

To devise relatively easy means of transition is in all cases an important objective. In addition, in recent years there have been such rapid and frequent changes in the tax structure that there may well be a case for the postponement of some further changes, however desirable they may be for the longer run. In such a case the wise course may be to have the new structure in mind as an agreed ultimate objective in order to be able to make sure that any smaller changes which may be made from time to time lead towards, rather than away from, the final goal.

The length of time that would be necessary fully to introduce some of the radical restructurings of the system of direct taxes which we discuss in this Report must not be underestimated. Time would be needed for further study, for the evolution of the necessary degree of political consensus, for the gradual introduction of small changes which would make subsequent larger changes easier, and for the step-by-step introduction of those larger changes themselves. The whole process would be a matter of a decade or more; but an essential first step is to obtain some idea of the basic features of a generally acceptable final goal.

CONCLUSIONS

The choice of tax structure must take into account many factors: the effects on economic incentives; its fairness as between persons of similar taxable capacity; its effects upon distribution between rich and poor; whether it is compatible with desirable international economic relations; and its simplicity, ease of understanding, and absence of excessive administrative costs. The transition from one tax structure to another inevitably takes time and involves costs which must be set against any gains expected from the new structure. Where these various characteristics conflict, it is an essential function of the political process to determine how much weight to give to each of them.

Appendix 2.1   The Effects of Taxation on Labour Supply

The purpose of this appendix is to outline the general conclusions of empirical studies on the effects of taxation on labour supply. For a comprehensive survey the reader should see Godfrey (1975),[1] Stern (1976)[2] and Hollister (1976).[3]

Survey studies have sought to establish directly from those working whether income taxation affects their labour supply. Individually the surveys suffer from limitations – of methodology, sample size or coverage – but the general conclusions are impressively similar, i.e. that the net effects of income tax on work effort are minor. (For the welfare effects see Chapter 2, pp. 8–9.) One American study[4] noted that those with marginal tax rates in the middle of the rate schedule quoted disincentives more than others. Few of the UK studies have been concerned with high earning taxpayers, but two which were[5, 6] contained some indication that more disincentives were experienced by those with the highest marginal tax rates. As the latest survey studies relate to the late 1960s or the beginning of the 1970s it is possible that the disincentive effects may now be more pronounced than these surveys suggest, since marginal implicit and explicit tax rates have risen since those years at most income levels.

Econometric studies showing differences in hours worked according to different wage rates are based on the application of economic theories of labour supply to collected statistical data. The theory specifies certain factors considered to be likely determinants of the number of hours worked, and data on these factors is collected and then analysed using appropriate statistical techniques to isolate which factors do in fact determine the hours worked. Specified factors will include the wage rate, but clearly other factors will be present in real-world labour-supply decisions: unearned income including social benefits, family type, work status and method of payment to name but a few. The extent to which the results of econometric studies can be considered to be of general application will depend on how far these numerous factors have been incorporated in the original economic theory and how representative are the data used.

The econometric studies to date have largely referred to the United States, have covered the lower income groups and thus tended to ignore progressive rates, and have been based on data up to 1967. What generally emerges is that the effect on married women of a change in wage rate is very different from that on male earners, an increase in the wage rate having a large and positive effect on the hours of paid work supplied by the married women. One study also suggests that the effect of an increase in the husband's wage rate has a large and negative effect on the wife's supply, a finding which if valid might be significant in the context of higher income groups and tax units.

Finally there have been income maintenance experiments carried out in the United States from 1968 to 1973. The studies compared the behaviour of randomly selected groups of families who were given varying levels of transfer payments and faced different implicit marginal tax rates, and a control group who received no such benefit nor faced similar tax rates.

Evidence of the effects on labour supply was only one of several results given by the experiment. It tended to confirm the nature of the response suggested by the econometric studies: male earners are affected only a little while married women are more responsive, this response being primarily at the participation level.

REFERENCES

1 L. Godfrey, *Theoretical and Empirical Aspects of the Effects of Taxation on Labour Supply* (Paris: OECD, 1975).
2 N. Stern, 'Taxation and labour supply' in *Taxation and Incentives* (London: IFS, 1976).
3 R. Hollister, 'Incentive and disincentive effects of taxation on lower income groups: the American experience' in *Taxation and Incentives* (London: IFS, 1976).
4 R. Barlow, H. E. Brazer, and J. N. Morgan, *Economic Behaviour of the Affluent* (Washington: Brookings Institution, 1966).
5 G. F. Break, 'Effects of taxation on incentives', *British Tax Review* (June 1957).
6 D. B. Fields and W. T. Stanbury, 'Incentives, disincentives and the income tax: further empirical evidence', *Public Finance,* no. 3 (1970).

Appendix 2.2   The Theory of the Efficiency and Distributional Effects of Taxation

Economic inefficiencies exist when there are divergences between values and costs. If the value to consumers of an additional loaf of bread is high relatively to its cost while the value of an additional shirt is low relatively to its cost, economic efficiency will be increased if resources of a given cost are shifted from producing low valued shirts to high valued loaves.

Any changes which decrease the quantities of things which are highly valued relatively to their costs at the expense of things which are lowly valued relatively to their costs will increase economic inefficiencies, and vice versa.

There are at least three types of factor which may cause divergences between social values and social costs:

1   There are social costs which fail to enter into market prices, such as pollution or congestion caused by certain activities. In these cases values will be lower than social costs and economic efficiency will be increased if resources are moved from such activities into activities whose social costs are not greater than their values.
2   Monopolies and other forms of market imperfection may restrict supplies and thus through scarcity maintain the value to consumers of the restricted goods above their social costs.
3   Finally, taxes themselves will cause a divergence between values and costs. For example, an indirect tax on a commodity will mean that the value of the good to the buyer (which includes the tax) is greater than the cost of real resources to the supplier (which excludes the tax).

If a taxpayer were liable to pay a poll tax of the same given sum however he chose to behave, and if there were no divergences between costs and values, the tax would have no direct effect on efficiency. The taxpayer would be made poorer and for this reason might buy less meat and more potatoes (the income effect of the tax); but that would simply be the most efficient way for him to use the restricted resources at his disposal. However, if the tax were not a fixed poll tax but a tax on one product, say potatoes, and if because of the higher price of potatoes the taxpayer bought less of them and more of other foods than he would have done under the poll tax, there would be an inefficiency (the substitution effect of the tax). The tax would have caused a divergence between the value to the consumer of potatoes and their cost of production, and the quantity produced and sold would be inefficiently low as a result.

An income tax or a general expenditure tax taxes all of the taxpayer's activities except his leisure activities. A fixed poll tax might well induce a taxpayer to work more in order to make up for some part of his loss of spendable income; he would not, now that he was poorer, be able to 'afford' so much leisure (the income effect). But the income tax being a tax on the use of all his time spent on earning but not on the use of his time for leisure purposes might induce him to work less than he would otherwise have done (the substitution effect). Thus an inefficiency would have been caused by introducing a disincentive to work and effort.

But once a multiplicity of divergences between costs and values in the real world is allowed for, the possible effects of taxes on economic efficiency become very difficult to unravel. For the moment we can continue to think of a world in which there are no divergences between values and costs other than those caused by taxes. Suppose that an income tax has shifted people inefficiently from taxed work to untaxed leisure. Then a specially heavy tax which causes a specially high price relatively to costs for what may be called leisure goods, far from increasing inefficiencies, might increase economic efficiency. Thus a very high tax on mid-week football matches might deter people from taking extra leisure from work to watch the game. The high tax on football matches will have indirectly caused people to increase the supply of something else (namely work) whose social value is higher than its cost because of the divergence caused by the income tax. Thus the interplay of different taxes on economic efficiency can become very complicated.

The complications are compounded if it is taken into account that divergences between social values and costs can arise for other reasons (e.g. because of monopolistic factors or other forms of market imperfection, or because of social costs such as pollution and congestion which are not covered by the private costs of production).

In effect a tax change may cause many direct and indirect changes in the economy. Its net effect will be to decrease economic efficiency in so far as, on the average, it encourages activities with low marginal social values relatively to marginal social costs at the expense of activities with high marginal social values relatively to marginal social costs.

To give one particular example of this, let us revert to the effect of a poll tax causing the taxpayer to shift his purchases from the rich man's food, meat, to the poor man's food, potatoes. We have argued that this income effect did not directly imply any increase or decrease in efficiency; it was merely a symptom of the taxpayer's most efficient way of cutting his coat according to his cloth. But if for one reason or another the value of potatoes was higher than the value of meat relatively to their costs (e.g. because the production of meat caused some pollution of the environment), then the poll tax would indirectly have led to a more efficient use of resources; and vice versa, if it was the production of potatoes which caused the pollution.

Whether a given change in a tax is desirable or not cannot be judged solely by the efficiency effects described above. Such efficiency effects do not take into account possible direct and indirect effects upon the distribution of income between rich and poor; the measurement of efficiency effects depends upon the assumption that £1 of value and £1 of cost are comparable whether the £1 is the expenditure or the income of a rich man or of a poor man. A tax on any activity will, as we have argued, cause a divergence between value and cost, i.e. between the gross price paid by the buyer and the net price received by the seller. But whether the divergence is caused mainly by an absolute rise in the price paid by the buyer or an absolute fall in the price received by the seller will depend upon many other conditions. The tax will reduce the price to the seller (i) in so far as the buyer turns readily to the purchase of other things, and (ii) in so far as the supplier finds it difficult to turn to the production of other things; and if this is the case, it is the seller who bears the brunt of the tax burden. If the seller is a poor man, then the distributional effects will be undesirable.

Moreover, there may be indirect distributional effects. To revert to our example of a poll tax causing a taxpayer to buy less meat and more potatoes, if this indirectly caused the price of potatoes to rise and that of meat to fall, because it was difficult for producers to shift from the production of meat to that of potatoes, and if one set of producers was rich and the other poor, the tax would have caused an indirect redistribution of income.

Thus it is an impossible task to trace through the complete efficiency and distributional effects of a tax change in a complex economy in which there is a complicated network of market and productive inter-relationships between a large number of products and activities and in which there are many kinds of market imperfection and of environmental and similar side effects. In theory, almost every separate transaction should ideally be taxed at a special rate which takes into account all its direct and indirect efficiency and distributional effects.

Of course, nothing of that kind is feasible. All that can be hoped is to take account of a few of the most obvious and most probable direct and indirect effects of any given tax change. There are likely to be important differences of emphasis in this matter. Some will hope by greater use of more refined statistical data and techniques to make possible more and more helpful discriminations between tax rates on different economic activities, which take more and better account of the various direct and indirect effects upon efficiency and distribution which we have discussed in this appendix.

For reasons given in Chapter 3 (pp. 43–44) we incline to put more emphasis on the desirability of maintaining a rather straightforward non-discriminating set of taxes levied on one or two readily understood tax bases, although it is, of course, essential that those tax bases and the rates structures which are erected on them should be well chosen from the point of view of their most obvious and direct effects upon efficiency and distribution.

Note on the Distinction between a Tax-inclusive and a Tax-exclusive basis for Rates of Taxation

Much confusion can be introduced into discussions about taxation unless care is taken to distinguish between a rate of tax reckoned on a tax base inclusive of the tax itself and the corresponding higher rate of tax reckoned on a tax base exclusive of the tax itself. A tax on income, such as the income tax, capital gains tax and corporation tax, is normally reckoned on the former or tax-inclusive basis. An expenditure tax, like the present VAT, is normally reckoned on the latter or tax-exclusive basis. Suppose that from an income of £100 the taxman takes £40, leaving £60 to be spent on consumption. This represents a rate of income tax of 40 per cent reckoned on a tax-inclusive basis. The corresponding rate of VAT reckoned on a tax-exclusive basis would be $66\frac{2}{3}$ per cent, since a tax at this rate must be levied on £60 worth of cost price goods in order to raise £40 in VAT to make up £100 worth of consumption goods reckoned at prices inclusive of the tax.

The conversion of tax-inclusive rates into tax-exclusive rates and vice versa follows the simple formulae

$$t_e = \frac{t_i}{1-t_i} \quad \text{and} \quad t_i = \frac{t_e}{1+t_e}$$

where t_i is the tax-inclusive rate and t_e the tax-exclusive rate. The following is an illustrative conversion table:

Rate of tax on a tax-inclusive basis, t_i (%) (e.g. rate of income tax)	Rate of tax on a tax-exclusive basis, t_e (%) (e.g. rate of VAT)
35	54
40	$66\frac{2}{3}$
50	100
75	300
83	488
98	4,900

Any given tax can be expressed in either of these two ways. Consider (from the fourth line in the above table) someone who devotes a pre-tax income of £100 to expenditure on consumption, being taxed £75 in the process, so that he can spend £25 on consumption goods at prices exclusive of the tax. It may make a psychologically dramatic difference if it is said that he is taxed at a rate of 75 per cent (on his expenditure inclusive of tax) or at 300 per cent (on his expenditure exclusive of tax), although these are only two ways of expressing exactly the same real state of affairs.

Administratively it may be necessary to apply a given tax on only one of the two possible bases. To continue the example in the last paragraph, if the tax were administered as an excise duty it would be administratively necessary to *apply* a given rate of tax to the value of the pre-tax goods bought, i.e. to apply a 300 per cent rate of excise duty to £25 worth of goods before tax. But it would always be possible to *express* the tax in language which used a tax-inclusive base, i.e. to state that the purchaser of the goods was liable to pay a tax equal to 75 per cent of the value of the goods inclusive of tax. In this case the tax liability of 75 per cent expressed on a tax-inclusive basis would, for administrative application, have to be converted into a tax of 300 per cent on a tax-exclusive basis.

Throughout this Report we go out of our way – perhaps at the expense of some tedious repetition – to state whether we are talking of a tax on a tax-inclusive or a tax-exclusive basis whenever there could be any possibility of confusion about the tax base.

3 The Tax Base

We turn now to examine, in the light of the issues raised in the preceding chapter, some of the main considerations which affect the choice of tax base for a system of direct taxation. We do not cover all the relevant factors in this chapter. For example, we postpone for more detailed consideration in later chapters the administrative problems involved in operating the different tax systems and the transitional problems involved in moving from one base to another. Furthermore, we postpone until Chapter 6 all consideration of the very important differences which inflationary conditions may have on different tax bases. Our present concern is with some of the basic issues of principle; and we confine the analysis in this chapter to the economic considerations which would be relevant in the absence of any serious price inflation.

INCOME AS THE TAX BASE

A taxpayer's *income* is an obvious candidate to serve as the base for his tax liability; but there are unfortunately difficulties in establishing what in principle is meant by a taxpayer's income, quite irrespective of any practical difficulties of ascertaining and measuring his income when it has been defined. A natural and commonsensical approach is to draw a distinction between a man's capital and his income by regarding his *capital* as the stock of resources from which the flow of income proceeds; in terms of the familiar analogy, the tree is the capital from which the annual income of the fruit crop is derived.

But on examination this distinction is found to involve many difficulties. Should the whole of the fruit crop be counted as taxable income if the fruit trees are ageing and depreciating in value, so that part of the proceeds of the crop must be used to maintain the productive power of the orchard? Or to take an example at the other extreme, if a forester is growing trees from which there is no annual crop but which are ultimately cut down and sold for timber, does he have no income at any time but only a realisation of the gain in the capital value of his trees when he cuts them down and sells them? Or consider two Government bonds both of which are issued at a price of £100, the difference being that on bond A the government undertakes to pay no interest but to redeem the bond at a price of £110 in a year's time, whereas on bond B the government undertakes to redeem the bond at its issue price of £100 in a year's time but meanwhile to pay £10 in interest on its borrowing. Is there no income but only gain in capital value on bond A, while there is income but no capital gain on bond B?

The above are only some extremely simple and obvious examples of the relationships between gains and losses in capital values on the one hand and net income on the other. As rates of income tax have risen to their present high levels, the distinction between income and capital gains has become more and more important; more and more sophisticated ways have been devised by taxpayers to turn highly taxable income into less highly taxable capital gains; and the importance of finding, if it is possible, a definition of income which does not permit these uncertain and often irrelevant distinctions to continue has correspondingly increased. Two such definitions of income are in principle possible, which we shall call definition A and definition B.

DEFINITION A OF TAXABLE INCOME

In the first of these two definitions it is argued that the proper measure of a taxpayer's income in any one year is the value of what he could have consumed during the year without living on and so diminishing his capital wealth in the process. This comprehensive measure would take account of any capital gains or losses which had accrued in the course of the year and would include any other windfall receipts in addition to more narrowly defined income receipts from wages, dividends, rents, profits, etc. This measure, it may be argued, is the fairest one for tax purposes, because whatever the taxpayer may choose to do with these resources they constitute a true measure of the total economic opportunity accruing to him in the year in question.

We call this definition A. To accept definition A of income for the principal or sole measure of an individual's taxable capacity could lead to some very strange results. Consider a millionaire whose £1 million is invested at 10 per cent in a way which ensures an annual flow of £100,000 in interest. If in one year the market rate of interest rises from 10 per cent to $11\frac{1}{9}$ per cent, so that the capital value of his investment falls by £100,000 in the course of the year, his taxable income will be zero. His capital loss will have offset his receipt of interest or dividends, and he must save the whole of his receipt of interest of £100,000 in order to restore the value of his capital investment to £1 million. If income so defined were strictly used as the sole measure of riches or poverty for fiscal purposes, the millionaire, worth £900,000 at the end of the year and with the certain prospect of a future flow of interest of £100,000 a year, would be poverty stricken and would presumably qualify for supplementary benefit.

DEFINITION B OF TAXABLE INCOME

There is, however, an alternative principle upon which income may be defined for fiscal purposes, which does not lead to unacceptable results of the kind described in the previous paragraph. This is to define an individual's income not as the amount which he could consume in any one year without diminishing his capital wealth in the course of that year, but as the amount which he could consume in any one year and yet be left with the resources and expectations at the end of that year which would enable him to maintain that same level of consumption indefinitely in the future. Let us call this definition B of income as a tax base. In this case the millionaire's income is defined as £100,000.

Unfortunately this definition of income would be a quite impracticable criterion for tax purposes, because it depends essentially upon future expectations. The level of consumption expenditure which any individual can enjoy this year and expect to enjoy indefinitely in the future depends upon what his future earnings will in fact turn out to be, upon what will happen to the rate of interest in the future, and upon all such things as may affect what he should save this year in order to maintain his future spending power. It is not easy to envisage the tax inspector agreeing with each taxpayer upon what may reasonably be expected to constitute a maintainable level of consumption.

For this reason when it is suggested that comprehensive income should be chosen for the tax base, this is usually taken to imply the use of definition A, which – difficult as it may be to make the necessary valuations – does in principle rest on hard historic facts about what happened in the year in question, rather than definition B, which involves choosing between different expectations about the future.

In spite of the impracticability of making use of definition B it is helpful to an understanding of the problems involved to consider some of the implications of the choice between definitions A and B.

The difference between the two definitions of income can be illustrated by considering their implications for the treatment of capital gains, which may fall into at least three different categories:

1   A capital gain may be a change of the kind which occurred to the million-aire discussed above as a result simply of a fall in the rate of interest, which altered the present value of his constant assured stream of future purchasing power. On definition A the capital gain must be added to his other income, while on definition B it has no effect upon his taxable income.
2   But a capital gain might indicate that there was a once-for-all unexpected improvement in the efficiency of the company in which the taxpayer had invested his money, so that, for example, with a constant 10 per cent rate of interest the millionaire's property rises in value from £1 million to £1·1 million because the prospect of assured annual future return on the property has risen from £100,000 to £110,000. The capital gain is £100,000; and on definition A his income in the year in question has been increased by £100,000, while on definition B the rise in his income is £10,000.
3   But there is another possibility. Our millionaire may have invested his money in a concern which makes £100,000 profit each year, distributes none of this in dividend, but adds £100,000 to the value of its own assets each year. If the value of the millionaire's investment rises similarly by £100,000 a year, he will make a capital gain equal to this sum, the whole of which on definition B should be included in his taxable income. He can indefinitely realise and spend £100,000 worth of his shares at the

end of every year and maintain his consumption at that level without impairment. In this case the capital gain should be included in taxable income on both definitions.

Or consider the treatment of a windfall or exceptional receipt – e.g. the receipt of £100,000 from the winnings in a football pool, or from an author's sale of the copyright of a best-seller, or from an inventor's sale of a patent right. Suppose further that there is an assured return of 10 per cent on any long term investment. On definition A the lucky gambler, author or inventor has an income this year of £100,000, while on definition B he has an income of £10,000.

CONSUMPTION AS A TAX BASE

An alternative to taking income, whether defined on the A principle or the B principle, is to take expenditure on consumption as the essential base for personal taxation. A strong case can be made for this base in that it levies a tax on the claims which a taxpayer makes at any one time on the community's resources which he uses up for his own consumption purposes. If he saves his income instead of consuming it, he is putting resources back into the productive pool; if he dissaves, he is taking resources out of the productive pool in addition to his other income. His relatively low consumption in the case of savings and his relatively high consumption in the case of dissavings are measures of what he is appropriating at any one time for his own personal use.

This expresses what is normally regarded as the essential case for the choice of expenditure on consumption as the base for progressive personal taxation. A *progressive expenditure tax* (as it is usually called) falls more heavily than progressive income tax on the wealthy who are financing high levels of consumption out of capital resources, but at the same time it gives much greater opportunity than does a progressive income tax for the finance of the development and growth of private enterprises out of private savings.

The implications of this difference are very far reaching. With a progressive income tax a wealthy man with a high marginal rate of income tax of 83 per cent will be able to use only £17 out of £100 of profit for the development of his business, whereas with a progressive tax on expenditure he could use all his profit to develop his business. At the same time with the income tax a wealthy man could live on his capital without paying any tax, whereas with a progressive expenditure tax he could purchase only £17 worth of additional consumption out of each additional £100 of his capital which he realised. A progressive expenditure tax is the one form of tax which could have the political appeal of encouraging enterprise and economic development and at the same time heavily taxing high levels of consumption expenditure which at present, if it is financed out of capital, goes untaxed.

INCOME, CONSUMPTION AND CAPACITY TO PAY

It may, however, be asked whether it is fair and equitable to tax rich Mr Smith who chooses to save a large part of his income very much less heavily than equally rich Mr Brown who chooses to spend his income. Both have the same power of command over resources. Can the fact that Mr Smith chooses to use this power one way and Mr Brown in another way affect their present capacities to pay tax? If attention is confined to the immediate situation, the ability to pay of the two men is apparently the same, although their tax burdens are very different. The picture is, however, changed if the whole lifecycle of the two men is considered. Something will happen in the future to the wealth which Mr Smith is accumulating. If he spends it during his life time, he will pay tax on it and will then be subject to a heavier burden of tax than Mr Brown, who will not possess the same wealth to spend. Mr Smith may hand on his wealth to someone else by gift during his life or by bequest at his death; but according to the regime for the taxation of such capital transfers a tax will then be paid which Mr Brown will avoid, because he has no wealth to transfer. Over their lives Mr Smith's tax burden may well be considerably greater than Mr Brown's. However, it will be true that Mr Smith will have enjoyed the advantages of security, independence and influence which are associated with ownership of property over a period of his life, which Mr Brown will not have experienced. This fact, as we shall consider later, supports the case for some form of annual tax on the amount of a taxpayer's wealth, even if it is considered otherwise equitable to tax Mr Smith and Mr Brown on the basis of their lifecycle of consumption or giving rather than on the year-to-year basis of their capacities to save, to consume or to give.

SIMILARITIES AND DIFFERENCES BETWEEN CONSUMPTION AND INCOME AS A TAX BASE

The measurement of a taxpayer's actual consumption expenditure in any one year is, like income on definition A, a matter of historic fact and does not, like income on definition B, depend upon subjective views about the future. What the taxpayer does in fact decide to spend on consumption in any one year is, of course, likely to be much affected by his expectations about future events. If he expects his future income to fall in his old age, he is likely to reduce his consumption now in order to be able to maintain his future consumption out of his savings. But he makes the decision what to spend, and the tax inspector then inspects what he has in fact spent. This can be a troublesome task (as discussed in Chapters 9 and 22); but at least the tax inspector does not have to reach agreement about the future subjective expectations on which the taxpayer has based his action.

It would be one thing if definition B for income could be used as a tax base; but that is not a practical possibility. If, however, it was wished to use income on definition B as a tax base, it might be better to use consumption expenditure rather than income on definition A as the actual operative base. In the extreme case, if individuals always attempted to plan their affairs so as to maintain indefinitely a constant level of consumption expenditure, then consumption as a tax base would coincide with income on definition B as a tax base, provided that the tax inspector always accepted the taxpayer's views about the future.

In the light of these distinctions of principle it is of interest to compare the choice of income on definition A with the choice of consumption expenditure as the tax base for personal taxation.

There are a number of problems of definition which are common to both tax bases.

It is a well-recognised fact that to obtain a fair comparison of the comprehensive incomes of different taxpayers a decision must be made on how to handle benefits in kind and certain elements of real income which do not involve monetary transactions. A familiar problem of this kind is the need to distinguish between income and business costs. To what extent is the use of a company car provided for an employee of the company an addition to the personal comfort and standard of living of the employee, and to what extent is it merely a business expense like the cost of his office desk? If Mrs Smith goes out to work and uses part of her earnings to hire a babysitter while she is away from home, but Mrs Brown stays at home and looks after the children herself, is the Smith family income for that reason higher than the Brown family income, and, if so, by how much?

Exactly similar problems arise with the definition of consumption. How far does the use of the company's car increase the personal consumption of the user? Is Mrs Smith consuming the services of a babysitter, or is this a business expense which gives the family no net rise in its standard of consumption?

But some problems of definition which arise in the case of an income base are irrelevant in the case of a consumption base, and vice versa. Thus whether an increase in state pension rights should or should not be regarded as adding to the value of an individual's wealth and thus included in income or not is irrelevant for the definition of consumption; in either case it clearly is not an item of current consumption. On the other hand, there may be doubt as to whether an individual's expenditure on education should be included in his consumption or should be regarded as money which he saves and invests to yield a future return in the form of increased earning power. But this distinction is irrelevant for the definition of income: the expenditure comes out of his income whether it is regarded as consumption or savings.

INCOME TAX, EXPENDITURE TAX AND THE RETURN ON SAVINGS

A basic difference between an income base and a consumption expenditure base for personal taxation is to be found in their effects upon the return to the taxpayer's savings. This is illustrated in Table 3.1. We assume that Mr

Brown has earned £150 and that there is a tax either (i) on his income, or (ii) on his expenditure on consumption. We illustrate this with tax at a (tax-inclusive) rate of $33\frac{1}{3}$ per cent in section 1 of the table and at a (tax-inclusive) rate of 50 per cent in section 2 of the table. We assume that Mr Brown can invest any savings which he makes in machinery or some other form of physical investment which produces a return of 10 per cent on the investment.

Table 3.1 *The difference between an income base and an expenditure base (in £s)*

	Section 1 Tax rate $33\frac{1}{3}\%$ (tax-inclusive)		Section 2 Tax rate 50% (tax-inclusive)	
	(i)	(ii)	(i)	(ii)
	IT A	ET B	IT C	ET D
Earnings spent				
Earnings	150	150	150	150
Less IT	(50)	—	(75)	—
Less ET	—	(50)	—	(75)
Consumption	100	100	75	75
Earnings saved				
Earnings	150	150	150	150
Less IT	(50)	—	(75)	—
Less ET	—	nil	—	nil
Savings invested	100	150	75	150
Annual yield	10	15	7·50	15
Less IT	$(3\frac{1}{3})$	—	(3·75)	—
Less ET	—	(5)	—	(7·50)
Annual consumption	$6\frac{2}{3}$	10	3·75	7·50
Rate of return on postponed consumption (% a year)	$6\frac{2}{3} \div 100$ $= 6\frac{2}{3}\%$	$10 \div 100$ $= 10\%$	$3·75 \div 75$ $= 5\%$	$7·50 \div 75$ $= 10\%$

Section 1 of the table makes it clear that, with a $33\frac{1}{3}$ per cent tax rate, under the income tax (IT) regime Mr Brown has the choice of spending on consumption either a single lump sum of £100 or £$6\frac{2}{3}$ a year thereafter, and under the expenditure tax (ET) regime a choice of spending on consumption either a single lump sum of £100 or £10 a year thereafter. Thus if Mr Brown decides to save rather than to spend, he will obtain a return of only $6\frac{2}{3}$ per cent on his postponed consumption under the income tax regime but a full 10 per cent on his postponed consumption under an expenditure tax regime.

From section 2 of the table it is clear that, with the higher tax rate of 50 per cent Mr Brown has the choice under the income tax regime between consumption this year of £75 or £3·75 a year hereafter and under the expenditure tax regime between £75 this year or £7·5 a year hereafter. In this case under the income tax regime he can now obtain a rate of return of only 5 per cent on his postponed consumption, whereas under the expenditure tax regime he can still obtain the full 10 per cent return. Of course, the higher the rate of expenditure tax, the lower his consumption. In section 1 he can consume £100 now or £10 a year hereafter, while in section 2 he can consume only £75 now or £7·5 a year hereafter. He can consume less in section 2 than in section 1, but the rate of return on postponed consumption is the full 10 per cent in both cases, whereas with the income tax the higher the rate of tax, the lower the level of consumption *and* the lower the rate of return on any postponed consumption.

It is indeed the characteristic feature of an expenditure tax as contrasted with an income tax that, at any given constant rate of tax, the former will make the rate of return to the saver on his reduced consumption equal to the rate of return which can be earned on the investment which his savings finances, whereas the income tax will reduce the rate of return to the saver below the rate of return which the investment will yield.

In later chapters of this Report we shall frequently use this phenomenon as a basic criterion. We shall treat a tax regime as being equivalent to an expenditure tax if, at a constant rate of tax, it leaves the yield to the saver equal to the yield on the investment. Although we shall use this as our test, there is no implication that this is the sole reason why an expenditure tax regime may be preferred to an income tax regime; there are many other considerations (discussed in this chapter and in Chapter 6 on the effects of inflation on the two bases).

The equality between the rate of yield to saver and the yield on the investment is, however, more than just a test of the existence of an expenditure tax regime, since it does mean that there is no marginal tax incentive inducing taxpayers to substitute at the margin present consumption for future consumption simply because the future yield on savings has been reduced below the true yield.

But the equality between yield to saver and the yield on investment will rule only if the rate of expenditure tax is constant. If the rate of tax is lower at the time of saving than it will be at the future time when the yield on the saving is itself consumed, then the net rate of yield to the saver will be reduced below the rate of yield on the investment.[1]

---

[1] In the example in section 1 of Table 3.1, if the rate of expenditure tax on the yield of £15 had risen to 40 per cent, the saver would have had only £9 instead of £10 to spend – a rate of return of only 9 per cent on his initial abstinence from consumption of £100.

Thus with a progressive expenditure tax there will be a tax incentive to even expenditures out over time, even though, because of concentrated needs or otherwise, lumpy concentrations of expenditure would in the absence of tax considerations have been preferred, just as under a progressive income tax there is a tax incentive to even income receipts out over time.

THE EVEN SPREADING OF INCOME AND OF CONSUMPTION

With a consumption, instead of an income, base for taxation the distinction between once-for-all windfall receipts and regular income receipts becomes less important. If Jones wins a football pool or if author Smith sells his single best-seller in one year for a large lump sum, the individual concerned can, with a consumption tax base, spread the consumption of the windfall over a number of future years; and he will therefore not be liable to tax at the high progressive rate to which he would be liable if the windfall was treated as part of the single year's income. It may be regarded as a desirable feature of an equitable tax system that liability to tax should depend upon a taxpayer's average standard over his lifetime rather than on a current year-by-year standard. With a tax system with progressively higher marginal rates of tax, a fluctuating base will involve a heavier tax burden than a steady base. Thus if the average tax rate on an income of £3,000 were $33\frac{1}{3}$ per cent but on an income of £6,000 were 50 per cent, a taxpayer with a year's income of £6,000 followed by a year's income of zero would pay £3,000 in tax, whereas a taxpayer with two years at a steady £3,000 would pay only £2,000 in tax.

But this consideration tells in favour of a tax on consumption only if a taxpayer's consumption is likely naturally to be spread more evenly over his lifetime than is his income. If his consumption were more variable than his income, this particular argument would tell in favour of an income tax. We can in fact give the same example as in the previous paragraph, simply substituting 'consumption' for 'income'. 'If the average tax rate on a consumption of £3,000 were $33\frac{1}{3}$ per cent but on a consumption of £6,000 were 50 per cent, a taxpayer with a year's consumption of £6,000 followed by a year's consumption of zero would pay £3,000 in tax, whereas a taxpayer with two years at a steady £3,000 would pay only £2,000 in tax.' The balance of advantage will depend very much on what is regarded as consumption. We discuss later how owner-occupied houses should best be treated for such tax purposes. If the purchase of a house were itself treated as an item of consumption expenditure, there clearly could be much greater fluctuations in consumption expenditures than would be the case if the purchase of a house were considered as an act of saving not liable to a tax on consumption, and if instead a regular annual value imputed to the house were regarded as the value of the annual consumption of dwelling space. Equity in progressive taxation as between taxpayers with a steady and taxpayers with a fluctuating tax base requires some arrangements for averaging lumpy tax liabilities over a period of years in both the cases of an income tax and of a consumption tax. The need may be less under a consumption tax depending upon the definitions of consumption used for the purpose of the tax.

THE DIFFERENCE BETWEEN EARNED AND INVESTMENT INCOME

For income tax purposes there is an important difference between earned and investment income. Earned income is neither relieved of tax on its decay nor is it taxed on any capital gain in the human capital which produces the income. Thus no allowance is made for deduction from earnings of a depreciation allowance which will make up for the fact that in old age and by death an earner will lose his power of earnings, although his income will have disappeared in old age and he cannot hand on his earning power to his heirs. On the other hand, if a worker receives an unexpected promotion and increase in his earning power, the present capital value of his future earnings (suitably discounted) will rise; but he will not be taxed on this capital gain.

Investment income may or may not be relieved of tax on its decay and may or may not be taxed on any underlying capital gain. Thus a machine will wear out and lose its productive power, and it is normal to take this into account by refraining from taxing the gross profit on a machine and permitting deduction of some allowance for depreciation from the gross return before assessment of liability to tax. But such allowance for the decay of investment income is not always made. An outstanding example of this occurs in times of rapid inflation (a phenomenon discussed fully in Chapter 6) if in the case of the interest and capital of a money debt no allowance is made for the fact that its real value is being eroded by price rises. Thus a man who owns £100 of government debt with, say, a nominal annual interest of £10 on it will be receiving no allowance for the falling real value of his income if he is taxed on the whole of the £10 of interest. On the other hand, real capital gains on investments sometimes are and sometimes are not liable to income tax or a capital gains tax. The existing differentiation in favour of earned income, previously implemented through the earned income allowance and now through the investment income surcharge, is largely based on the principle that earned income is not lasting, since it will inevitably disappear with old age and death, whereas investment income is normally lasting if proper depreciation allowances are made. But for the reasons discussed above this is an oversimplification of the situation, particularly in times of rapid price inflation, the effect of which (as argued in Chapter 6) greatly complicates this issue.

But this set of problems simply does not arise if consumption rather than income constitutes the tax base. The taxpayer would, of course, prefer an income which was expected to last or better still to rise rather than an income which was expected to be eroded by old age or inflation. He will take his expectations into account when he makes his decisions as to how much he should save and how much he should spend. He can put aside out of earned or investment income in his savings whatever he considers necessary to maintain his position, and with an expenditure tax he will not be taxed on these savings. He can, as it were, decide on his own depreciation allowance and avoid all tax on it. He will be taxed only on what he consumes. Thus if Smith has an income of £5,000 a year which he expects to decline (e.g. because it is an earned income and he is ageing), while Jones has an income of £5,000 a year which he expects to be permanently maintained (e.g. because it is derived from a company whose profits are expected to be maintained in real terms), Smith will not be in a position to maintain as high a standard of consumption as Jones. With a consumption tax their differing abilities will be automatically recognised. In so far as Jones consumes more because he can afford to consume more, he will automatically pay more in tax.

Differences in lasting power are not, however, the only relevant differences between earned and investment incomes. Investment incomes are compatible with a life of leisure or can be supplemented by earnings. Earned incomes are derived from work and do not give the same opportunities for leisure or for a further supplementation of incomes. It is therefore not unreasonable with a consumption tax regime to give some differential treatment to earned income over investment income as alternative sources of purchasing power for the finance of consumption. The case for such differentiation and the degree to which it should be carried is, however, much less with a consumption tax than with an income tax.

WEALTH AS A TAX BASE

Moreover, apart from providing a source of income which is compatible with a life of leisure, wealth gives opportunity, security, social power, influence and independence. For this reason it may be argued that, however well a system of taxation of income or of consumption may be devised, equity requires that wealth itself should be included in the base for progressive taxation. On these grounds a surcharge on investment income may be justified as a proxy for a tax on the wealth which produces the investment income. But in order not to favour those who hold large wealth in forms which yield little or no income, it may be argued that it is wealth itself rather than investment income from wealth that should form the tax base.

THE TREATMENT OF GIFTS AND INHERITANCES

So far we have said nothing about the treatment of transfers of wealth or spending power from one taxpayer to another by way of gifts *inter vivos* or of inheritances on the occasion of death.

We consider the matter first in terms of a comprehensive income base for taxation. Smith gives some money to Jones. In an obvious sense this can be regarded as increasing Jones's economic opportunities and thus his taxable capacity. But does it reduce Smith's taxable capacity? There are two quite reasonable ways of answering this question: one is to regard the gift simply as a transfer of economic opportunities from Smith to Jones, in which case total taxable income has not changed since, while Jones's has risen, Smith's has fallen; the other is to regard Smith's gift as one way in which he chose to use his economic opportunities (i.e. his income) and at the same time to recognise that Jones's opportunities have thereby also been increased, in which case there are two personal incomes to be taxed.

With consumption as the tax base exactly the same issue arises. When Smith gives money to Jones to spend, is this merely a transfer of consumption from Smith to Jones or is the gift by Smith one of the ways in which Smith decides to enjoy and consume his resources, so that the transfer should be included in Smith's consumption base as well as in Jones's consumption base if and when Jones uses the funds for his own consumption?

There are in fact three possible social philosophies which may be adopted in this connection.

1   At one extreme it can be argued that the gift by Smith to Jones is a mere transfer from one taxpayer's base to another. It should be subtracted from Smith's income base or omitted from his expenditure base, but it should be included in Jones's income base or, when he spends it on himself, included in his expenditure base.

2   It may be regarded as appropriately included in the tax base of both Smith and Jones. In the case of the income base, the source from which Smith obtained the funds to give away is taxed as part of Smith's income and the receipt of the gift is taxed again as part of Jones's income. Or in the case of an expenditure tax, the gift is treated as part of Smith's consumption when he chooses to enjoy himself by giving money to Jones and subsequently also as part of Jones's consumption when he spends it on himself or decides to enjoy himself by passing it on again to Robinson.

3   The view may be taken that when Smith transfers part of his taxed income to Jones the mere transfer should not be taxed again as part of Jones's taxable income. But at the same time it may be believed that the transfer itself is an appropriate base for a separate tax, levied perhaps on a different principle. And similarly with an expenditure tax.

The resulting treatment of gifts under each of these three principles is summarised in Table 3.2.

The first of these three principles may be neglected, since there is a general consensus that gifts and bequests are a proper subject for tax.

We shall examine the implications of the adoption of the second principle when we come to examine a comprehensive income tax base and a comprehensive expenditure tax base in more detail in Chapters 7 and 9. Among other things it is clear that since gifts and, in particular, bequests on death may be made in large lump sums, the problem of averaging tax liabilities under a progressive tax system which we have already noticed (pp. 38–39 above) would be especially relevant if this treatment for gifts were adopted.

Table 3.2   *The treatment of gifts*

Principle	IT treatment		ET treatment	
	Donor	Donee	Donor	Donee
1	Deduct from income	Add to income	Omit from expenditure	Include in expenditure when spent on personal consumption
2	Do not deduct from income	Add to income	Include in expenditure	Include in expenditure when spent on personal consumption or when passed on as gift to a third party
3	Do not deduct from income	Do not add to income	Do not include in expenditure	Include in expenditure only when spent on personal consumption
	but apply a separate transfer tax		but apply a separate transfer tax	

CAPITAL TRANSFER AS A TAX BASE

The adoption of the third principle means that, in addition to the consideration of income or expenditure as a tax base and of wealth as a tax base, a third possible independent tax base is added, namely the giving or the receipt of wealth on the transfer from a donor to a donee – a tax which need not be progressively related to the level of the donor's or the donee's current income or expenditure.

THE EFFECT ON REVENUE

In Table 3.1 we have compared the fortunes of Mr Brown under an income tax regime and under an expenditure tax regime, both with the same rate of tax. But if on balance in the economy as a whole some part of the net national income is continually being saved, income will exceed expenditure and a given rate of income tax will raise more revenue than a given rate of expenditure tax. It may thus be proper to compare a given rate of income tax with a somewhat higher rate of expenditure tax. This comparison can be illustrated in an exaggerated form by comparing columns A and D of Table 3.1. Column A, which illustrates the effects of an income tax at a $33\frac{1}{3}$ per cent tax-inclusive rate, shows that in this case Mr Brown out of an earnings of £150 has a choice between consuming £100 this year or £6$\frac{2}{3}$ a year hereafter. Column D, which illustrates the effect of an expenditure tax at a 50 per cent tax-inclusive rate, gives Mr Brown the choice between £75 this year or £7·5 a year hereafter. Which of these regimes will have the worse efficiency effects is not at all certain. In so far as Mr Brown continues to earn £150 under both regimes, the expenditure tax will give better results; it allows Mr Brown to choose between jam today and jam tomorrow at a rate which corresponds to the true yield on his savings.[2] But will the 50 per cent rate of expenditure tax reduce Mr Brown's incentive to earn more than does the $33\frac{1}{3}$ per cent rate of income tax? If Mr Brown is concerned primarily with his immediate ability to consume, he gets less net return from his work under the expenditure tax (75 units of consumption) than under the income tax (100 units). But in so far as he is concerned with earning now in order to be able to consume in his old age, he gets a better return under the expenditure tax (£7·5 a year) than under the income tax (£6$\frac{2}{3}$ a year). The outcome is not certain, although, if people are concerned above all with immediate returns, it is possible that with an expenditure tax the improved incentives in the capital market (which is an outstanding feature of the tax) may be bought at the expense of somewhat worsened incentives in the labour market.

THE CASE FOR A SIMPLE SET OF TAX BASES

Considerations of this kind lead finally to the general question whether it is sensible to seek any one general tax base or simple set of tax bases for personal taxation. Perhaps it would be best to tax Mr Brown at one rate on his consumption and at a different rate (which might be higher or might be lower) on his saving. To decide on the ideal rates we would need to know the difference in his response to immediate and to future returns. Indeed a very strong case can be made in principle for a large range of different rates of tax on different types of transaction. In theory there is in fact a distinct optimum rate of tax for each and every separate transaction. The ideal system of taxes would impose high rates wherever the combination of incentive and distributional effects (both horizontal and vertical) was favourable and low rates wherever it was unfavourable.[3]

This principle may be illustrated by a single greatly oversimplified example. If land were not only fixed in amount but always let out for use in the

---

[2] See the example given on pp. 8–9 of Chapter 2.
[3] See Appendix 2.2.

occupation which yielded the highest possible post-tax rent, then a tax on land would fall solely on the landowner, the uses of land would not be affected, and no inefficiencies would be introduced. If at the same time all landowners were rich, then the tax might be welcomed from the point of view of vertical redistribution. If finally all rich persons invested to the same degree in land, there would be no horizontal inequity involved. A specially high tax on land would be indicated.

But to base a tax structure on the principle of considering each rate of tax on each specific type of transaction separately is to invite distortions through the influence of pressure groups of particular interests, each ob-taining some specific exemption or other advantage until the whole structure becomes a shambles of irrational special provisions. A complex system which was devised and administered by a committee of wise philosopher kings, advised by a group of omniscient economists and subject to no democratic pressures from well organised special interests, might be pre-ferable to any one more simple system which was debarred from making many specific and detailed provisions and exceptions which would in fact be improvements. But the latter would also be debarred from making many undesirable special provisions, and in the world as it is the acceptance of a simple system based on one or two easily understood, clear rules (provided, of course, that they were well chosen rules) would almost certainly be pre-ferable. There will, of course, inevitably be some special exceptions and exemptions; but it is desirable to start from some simple, reasonable, clearly understood general set of rules, from which only a limited number of very special exceptions are permitted.

In this chapter we have considered some of the general principles which should guide the choice of the set of rules. But there are many problems of detailed application which must influence the final choice. The effects of inflation on the tax base must be taken into account and the tax bases must be capable of application without excessive cost of administration or com-pliance. We examine in more detail the income base in Chapter 7, the con-sumption and expenditure base in Chapters 8, 9 and 10, the capital transfer tax base in Chapter 15 and the wealth tax base in Chapter 16.

CONCLUSIONS

There are serious difficulties in defining an individual's income satisfactorily for tax purposes and in particular in finding the appropriate treatment for windfall receipts and for different kinds of capital gain. Taking expenditure on consumption in place of income as a tax base raises less acute problems of definition; it taxes what a person takes out of the economic production system rather than what he puts into it; it combines greater opportunities for economic enterprise with heavier taxation of high levels of consumption financed out of the dissipation of wealth; and it avoids problems arising from the distinction between earned income and investment income. On the other hand it may involve somewhat higher rates of tax.

In addition to income or consumption as the main base for direct taxation, there is a case for direct taxes based on the amount of wealth owned by the taxpayer and (if gifts are not treated as taxable income or taxable consumption) on the amounts of wealth transferred by way of gift or inheritance.

While a strong case can be made out in theory for a multiplicity of different rates of tax on a large number of different types of transaction, we see merit in confining direct taxes to one or two well defined bases whose nature can be readily appreciated by the taxpayer.

PART TWO DEFECTS OF THE PRESENT SYSTEM

In this Part we describe what we regard as certain fundamental inconsistencies and anomalies in the existing structure of direct taxes in the United Kingdom, including the marked distortions which the rapid inflation of money prices has had on certain aspects of the tax structure.

4 · The Existing Base for Direct Taxes in the United Kingdom

In the two preceding chapters we have discussed the principles and objectives which should underlie a country's tax structure. In this and the following chapter we describe and analyse in the light of these principles two important aspects of the present structure of direct taxes in the United Kingdom. In the present chapter we analyse the extent to which income or expenditure constitutes in fact the effective base for direct taxation in this country. In the following chapter we consider the structure of effective marginal and average rates of direct taxation in this country. There are, in our opinion, in both of these respects some major anomalies in the present UK structure of direct taxation.

In both these instances anomalies have been much exacerbated, indeed in some cases mainly caused, by the rapid inflation of money prices in recent years; but in this and the following chapter we discuss these anomalies without reference to problems due to the inflation of money prices, leaving a discussion of these problems over to Chapter 6.

INCOME OR EXPENDITURE AS THE EFFECTIVE TAX BASE

In the United Kingdom there are three important direct taxes – namely the income tax, the capital gains tax, and the corporation tax – whose base purports to be income or some closely related element such as capital gains or company profits. But modifications and special provisions in the application of these taxes have been made in such a way that it is difficult to consider them any longer as straightforward income-based taxes. Many of these modifications have moved this part of the tax structure from an income base towards what is in effect a consumption expenditure base. Indeed in some cases the combined effect of these modifications is to overshoot the mark and to move the tax structure beyond the consumption expenditure base in ways which we explain below.

1 INCOME TAX (IT)

RELIEF TO SAVINGS

Some modifications of the income tax giving relief from tax on particular forms of saving introduce clear elements of a consumption expenditure tax into the system.

Thus, subject to certain limitations, savings out of the earnings of an employed person which are contributed to an approved pension scheme (including contributions made on his behalf by his employer) are not subject to tax. In the case of a self-employed person, subject to a different and more restricted set of limitations, savings for the purchase of an approved retirement annuity are similarly exempt from income tax. Moreover, the investment income which accrues to the pension or retirement annuity fund on the amounts so saved is not taxed. Tax is, however, charged on the full amount of the pension or annuity, treated as earned income, when ultimately received by the retired person. In so far as the sums so received are spent on consumption in the retired person's old age, there is a clear application of the expenditure base; income is not taxed when saved, but income and capital are taxed when spent.

Even in this clear case there is one obvious overshoot of the mark. About one-quarter of the total value of an individual's retirement benefits under some approved schemes may be commuted for a lump sum which is tax-free. This lump sum comes from untaxed savings and can in turn be spent without paying tax. This would remain a clear and unjustifiable anomaly even if it were desired to change the income tax into an expenditure tax.

A less clear-cut case is provided by the treatment of savings through premiums for life assurance, which, again subject to certain limitations, in effect enjoy partial remission of tax. The net effect of these arrangements[1] is that the initial savings through this medium are charged to half the basic rate and any higher rate tax but are exempt from the other half of the basic rate tax, while the investment income received on the fund so saved is exempt from higher rate tax but is charged to tax at a rate not much different from the basic rate of tax.

CAPITAL ALLOWANCES

Pension schemes and life assurance arrangements are examples of movements from an income base in the direction of an expenditure base effected through remission of tax on certain amounts of *savings*. A similar result is in fact achieved by remission of tax on the savings, not at the moment when they are saved, but when they are spent on *investment* in physical plant and machinery or stock in trade. In Chapter 8 and Appendix 8.2 we shall analyse in some detail the effects of remissions of tax on investment in real capital equipment. For the purposes of the present chapter it is necessary only to consider the broad similarity between remissions of tax on savings and remissions of tax on the investment of savings.

We can illustrate this by the simple example in Table 4.1. In column A Mr Smith earns £200 and, when he saves it, pays no tax. Mr Brown borrows the £200 from Mr Smith and spends it on the purchase of a machine. In column B we assume that there is no remission of tax on savings and that there is an income tax at a 50 per cent (tax-inclusive) rate. Mr Smith has only

[1] See section 1 of Appendix 4.1.

a net £100 after tax to lend to Mr Brown. But we assume now that Mr Brown can in the year in which he purchases the machine set the whole of his capital expenditure as a cost against his liability to tax on his own profits. In this case he can spend £200 on machinery, financing £100 from his borrowings from Mr Smith and £100 from his savings of his own tax bill, since with a 50 per cent rate of tax an increase in his 'costs' of £200 will reduce his tax bill by £100 below what it would otherwise have been. In effect Mr Smith's payment of £100 of income tax has been offset by letting Mr Brown off £100 of tax.

Let us suppose that Mr Brown's machine will give a net yield after depreciation of 10 per cent, so that at the end of the year it together with its product is worth £220. Suppose now that Mr Smith withdraws his savings from Mr Brown at the end of the year and that Mr Brown has to sell his machine and its product for £220 in order to pay off his debt. If column A of the table is taken to represent the expenditure tax treatment of a pension fund, Mr Smith will receive his pension of £220 but (with our illustrative tax-inclusive rate of tax of 50 per cent) will have to pay £110 in tax, leaving him with £110 to spend. As far as column B is concerned, Mr Brown has been allowed to write off the whole value of his machine when he bought it and he will therefore be liable when he sells the machine and its product to pay tax at a 50 per cent (tax-inclusive) rate on the whole of the proceeds of £220. He will be able to pay the remaining £110 to Mr Smith, who can then spend the whole sum on consumption. The ultimate effect of the two arrangements is the same.

Table 4.1   *Remission of tax on savings and on investment*

	A *Remission of tax on savings*	B *Remission of tax on investment*
Mr Smith earns	200	200
Mr Smith pays tax	nil	100
Mr Smith saves	200	100
Mr Brown borrows	200	100
Mr Brown invests	200	200
Mr Brown receives remission of tax	nil	100

We have told the above story as if there were no imperfections in the capital market. In the case both of the remission of tax on savings and of the remission of tax on investment we have analysed the effects as if Mr Smith received the whole of the available return on his savings while Mr Brown made no net profit or loss. In fact imperfections in the capital market may affect the outcome.

In this connection there is one very important difference between the two columns of Table 4.1. In both cases Mr Smith receives a 10 per cent return on his savings. In column A he receives £220 in repayment of his savings of £200, and in column B he receives £110 in repayment of his savings of £100. But the 10 per cent of column A is the market rate of return on the loan before payment of any tax, which is only incurred when Mr Smith spends the money on consumption, whereas the 10 per cent of column B is the market rate of return on the loan *after deduction at the source of the 50 per cent (tax-inclusive) rate of income tax*, which Mr Smith must pay, or have had paid on his behalf, when he receives the money. The pre-tax market rate of interest in column B would have to be 20 per cent and not 10 per cent to give the same real result as column A. We will return to some of the important consequences of this distinction at a later stage in our Report. For the moment we wish only to stress the point that, if the market rate of interest offered by Mr Brown in column B were not doubled because of the 100 per cent (tax-inclusive) rate of tax subsidy which he is offered on this investment, then the results of the two types of tax remission would not be the same. If the pre-tax market rate of interest in column B were less than 20 per cent, then Mr Smith would not obtain the whole of the net yield on the investment; Mr Brown would share in the profit.

It is not our contention that in fact the two outcomes will be precisely the same in the real world in the two cases. But it is our contention that there will be strong underlying influences at work which will tend to make the outcomes of the two processes converge. A proportionate income tax with 100 per cent capital allowances is much more nearly akin in its real effects to a proportionate expenditure tax than it is to a proportionate tax on income reckoned only after allowance for true economic depreciation. In the rest of this chapter it is this underlying tendency which we shall be examining, even though imperfections in the capital market may cause some divergences, particularly in the share-out rather than in the level of any yield on investment.

The effect illustrated in column B of Table 4.1 is now an extremely important feature of the UK tax system, since both for income tax and for corporation tax businessmen are permitted to set 100 per cent of the value of many forms of capital investment as a cost against their tax base of income or profit. Not all forms of investment in real capital may be treated in this way. There is at present a differentiation in the treatment of the costs which are allowed to be deducted from taxable profits in respect of various types of asset.[2] But the allowance of the full 100 per cent of the cost of a real asset is now of great importance. It covers some 75 per cent of all capital allowances, and this accounts for approximately 50 per cent of the country's gross domestic capital formation.

In this respect the history of the income tax in the United Kingdom is of considerable interest. At first no allowances were made for the depreciation

---

[2] These range from 100 per cent allowance of costs immediately upon investment in the asset, through depreciation allowances which correspond more or less to the economic depreciation of the asset, to the disallowance of depreciation on investment in certain assets. See section 2 of Appendix 4.1.

of any fixed assets. By any reasonable definition of income this was, as it were, to overshoot the income base for the tax. To maintain indefinitely the income from any asset which wears out or becomes obsolescent it is necessary to set some depreciation allowance aside to accumulate a fund for its eventual replacement; the whole gross yield cannot be consumed if the yield is to be maintained (cf. definition B of taxable income, Chapter 3, pp. 31–32). Or alternatively (in terms of definition A on p. 31), the value of the capital asset will decline as the years pass, and this fall in value must be regarded as a reduction in the owner's income.

To allow nothing for depreciation was thus to tax more than the current income. A strict application of the income base principle would allow each year as a depreciation cost against current profit a sufficient amount to maintain indefinitely the yield of the asset (definition B) or to maintain the current value of the asset (definition A). To allow the whole of the cost of the asset in the first year is thus a clear movement away from the principle of the income base in the direction of the remittance of tax on invested savings, i.e. in the direction of the expenditure base.

SIMILARITY BETWEEN SAVINGS RELIEF AND CAPITAL ALLOWANCES

A corollary of the 100 per cent capital allowance is that any proceeds from the subsequent sale of the asset itself, as well as from the sale of whatever it may currently produce, are taxable, since the whole of the expenditure on the purchase of the asset will have been allowed against the profits of an earlier year. Here the analogy with the treatment of savings in approved pension funds is clear. In the latter case the accumulated savings are free of tax, but the whole of the pension (capital and income) is taxed when it is later received and spent. In the case of fixed assets qualifying for 100 per cent capital allowances the sums invested are free of tax, but the whole of the proceeds of sale of the fixed asset and its products (capital and current product) is taxed when it is realised. If these proceeds are spent, they are thus taxed; if they are reinvested in assets which qualify for 100 per cent capital allowances, they are once more freed from the tax. The expenditure base principle is clearly evident.

Under the UK system it is possible to overshoot the mark by granting tax remission on savings when they are saved and once again tax remission on the investment financed by the same savings where both reliefs are effectively given against a single tax.[3] This double relief from tax on savings investment will occur in the case of an approved pension fund which puts its capital into the purchase of shares in a company which uses the proceeds for investment in assets which in turn qualify for 100 per cent capital allowances. The pension fund will be receiving, as it were, expenditure-based treatment twice over. We return to this problem later.

---

[3] The imputation system of corporation tax at present operating in the United Kingdom has this effect of making personal tax and corporation tax a single tax on dividend income.

DURABLE CONSUMPTION GOODS

The treatment of durable consumption goods presents some problems under an income-based tax system. In strict theory it can be argued that pictures, jewellery, furniture, cars, etc. should be regarded as capital goods, which produce a yearly product of culture, splendour, comfort, mobility, etc. On this basis the correct procedure would be to levy income tax on the annual value of the income which they produce for the owner, even though the objects themselves have been purchased out of taxed income. Since the owner of a picture which he lets out on hire would have bought the picture out of taxed income and would also be liable for tax on the net rental earned on the picture, it may seem only fair that the owner of a picture used for his own enjoyment should be treated as a man who rents his picture to himself.

THE SPECIAL CASE OF HOUSING

This principle is not observed in the UK income tax; and as a practical proposition it would seem pedantic to demand its observation in the case of a wide range of ordinary consumer durables. But there is one case, namely that of owner-occupied dwellings, in which the principle cannot be cavalierly brushed on one side. In most European countries tax is levied on a notional annual value of dwelling houses; and such a tax used to be levied in this country under schedule A of the income tax. But in 1963 the UK tax was abolished. However, dwelling houses are in fact capital assets of great importance which have long lives over which they provide dwelling space, shelter, warmth, etc., which constitute a large fraction of a normal family's total consumption. They are, moreover, capital assets which are not only enjoyed directly by their owners but also commonly rented out by their owners for the use of others; and, for many classes of person, living in rented accommodation may be a much more practical arrangement than owning a house. In this latter case the rental value of the annual produce of house shelter will be taxed as it is received by the owner; to exempt from tax the annual produce of house shelter in the case of the owner occupier is to give a very valuable tax advantage to owner occupation over tenancy.[4]

DEDUCTIBILITY OF INTEREST PAYMENTS

If it were wished to treat taxable income as the amount which the taxpayer could spend on consumption without eating into the value of his capital wealth (definition A) or as the value of the consumption expenditure which he could maintain indefinitely (definition B), it would follow that any interest

[4] The market for housing in the United Kingdom is, however, complicated by the facts that local authority houses are heavily subsidised, that special tax arrangements apply to owner occupiers, that private rents are controlled, and that all dwellings are in any case already subject to the imposition of local rates. For these reasons we relegate our discussion of the present tax treatment of housing and of possible reforms of such treatment to a special chapter (see Chapter 11).

which the taxpayer had to pay on any past debt which he had incurred should be deducted from his gross income before assessment of the net income to tax. A man who borrowed at an interest cost of £5 a year in order to invest in an asset which yielded £6 a year would have an addition to his power to consume or to add to his savings of only £1, not £6.

This principle would seem unexceptionable, provided always that the £6 in the above example were included in the taxpayer's tax base; in that case his total tax base would be increased by £1 (namely £6−£5) as it should be. If for any reason the £6 were not included in his tax base, then the £5 interest cost should not be deducted from his tax base; otherwise his tax base would actually be reduced by £5 instead of increased by £1.

It may be questioned whether it is desirable to allow as a deduction from taxable income the interest on a debt which is incurred solely for the purpose of financing an excess of current consumption. The disallowance of such a deduction does, however, differentiate between Mr Smith who for one reason or another borrows for this purpose (thereby incurring an annual debt interest of, say, £50) and Mr Jones who for the same purpose sells securities which he owned (thereby losing £50 a year of dividends or interest). In the absence of tax both would thereby have reduced their future spendable incomes by the same amount. But if tax were deducted from the dividends or interest on Jones's securities while the interest payable by Smith could not be set against his taxable income, Jones would lose only what remained of the £50 after deduction of tax but Smith would lose the full £50.

The UK arrangements provide examples of every possible treatment of interest.

1   In the case of owner-occupied dwellings financed by loan the owner may deduct the interest cost of the loan up to a limit of a capital sum of £25,000 from his taxable income, even though, as we have seen, he is not liable to income tax on the annual value of the house itself. In terms of the above example, he reduces his net tax base by the full £5 instead of increasing it by the £1 by which the annual value of the house exceeds his debt interest.

2   In the case of consumption goods the interest on a loan used for their purchase cannot be deducted from the tax base, while in turn the value of the annual yield on such goods as are durable is not taxed.

3   In the case of business assets which yield a taxable rent or profit (including houses let out to tenants at a rent), the interest cost may be deducted against the taxable gross yield of the asset.

4   In the case of other assets, such as stock exchange securities financed by loan, the interest cost may not be deducted from the tax base, although the yield on the asset is liable to income tax or to capital gains tax.

Two views may be held about the appropriateness of case 2. We have argued above that in principle it would seem proper to deduct interest from taxable income; but we have also argued that in principle (although not in practice) tax should be levied on the notional annual return enjoyed from the use of durable consumption goods. If such a tax were levied, then the interest on the loan used to finance them should undoubtedly be deductible for tax purposes. If, however, no tax is levied on the annual value of the durable consumption goods, it may be argued that an appropriate offset to this is to disallow the interest on any loan used to finance their purchase to be deductible from other income for tax purposes.

This, however, is equivalent to levying a tax on persons who finance the purchase of such durable goods by loan finance but not to do so on those who acquire such goods out of their own savings. If Mr Smith borrows £500 at 10 per cent interest for the purchase of such a good and cannot deduct the interest of £50 a year from his taxable income, the use of the good will cost him £50 a year. If Mr Jones uses savings of £500 with which he could have purchased a security which would have earned a 10 per cent pre-tax yield of £50 a year, he will lose in income not the pre-tax yield of £50 but the post-tax yield of, say, £25. The use of the good will cost Jones £25 a year but Smith £50 a year.

Case 1 is anomalous unless (as discussed in Chapter 11) local rates are considered to be in fact a substitute for income tax on the annual value of dwelling houses.

Case 4 would also appear anomalous, although a partial justification for this case may be found when taxpayers who are liable to a high rate of income tax borrow to invest in securities which will produce their yield in the form of capital gain rather than of dividend or interest. Since capital gains are taxed at a maximum rate of 30 per cent – a limited tax liability which may itself be postponed until the asset is in turn sold – it would be possible for a high rate taxpayer to obtain relief on his interest cost at a high rate of income tax (e.g. 98 per cent) and to incur merely a potential future tax liability of 30 per cent on the yield from his security. But just as in case 1 the ideal way of removing any anomaly which is held to exist would be to make the annual value of owner-occupied dwelling houses liable to adequate tax, so the ideal way of removing the anomaly in case 4 might be to allow the deduction of the interest cost from the tax base and to assimilate the tax treatment of capital gains to the tax treatment of other elements of income.

It is in fact very difficult to set particular borrowings against particular uses of the money borrowed. Thus Mr Smith who has funds of his own available for the purchase of a house may be able to borrow on mortgage for the purchase of the house and invest his own funds in stock exchange securities. He is in effect borrowing to finance the purchase of securities and obtaining tax deductibility on such borrowing. Whether or not a borrower can successfully claim that the borrowing is used for a particular purpose that justifies deductibility of the interest for tax payments may be affected by the order in which by choice or by force of circumstances the raising of the loan and the making of the related expenditure takes place.

2 CAPITAL GAINS TAX (CGT)

There are a number of important ways in which the taxation under the

Capital Gains Tax of the yields on investments which accrue in the form of capital gains differs from the taxation under the Income Tax of yields which accrue in the form of ordinary investment income, such as dividends, interest or rents.

But before listing these differences it is useful to note one similarity. The increase in value of an owner occupier's principal residence is exempt from capital gains tax just as under the income tax the annual value of the dwelling is also exempt. Thus in the case of owner occupied dwellings the whole yield – the annual produce of shelter and eventual appreciation of capital value – is exempt from tax.

THE RATE OF TAX[5]

A first major difference is in the rates of tax. In the case of capital gains these cannot exceed 30 per cent, whereas under the income tax the charge on dividends, interest, rents, etc. (including the surcharge on investment income) can rise progressively to as much as 98 per cent. There is thus a marked incentive for the higher rate taxpayer to distort his affairs by seeking investment channels which may not be the most productive but which will produce their product in the form of a capital gain rather than of investment income.[6]

REALISATIONS VERSUS ACCRUALS

A second major difference, which reinforces the attractiveness of assets yielding capital gains over assets yielding a taxable investment income, is that the Capital Gains Tax is levied on gains only when they are realised, not when they accrue, whereas the income tax is levied on the investment income when it accrues even if it is saved, ploughed back, and added to the existing capital stock from which it proceeded. A simple numerical example will illustrate the principle. Consider an asset worth £100 initially with an annual yield of 10 per cent. If this yield takes the form of a capital gain, the value of the £100 after 10 years at a compound rate of growth of 10 per cent will be £259, giving a capital gain of £159, which after Capital Gains Tax at 30 per cent will leave a net gain of £111. Suppose, however, that the annual gain of 10 per cent takes the form of an investment income taxable at 30 per cent as it accrues each year. Then the owner can accumulate his fund at a compound post-tax rate of return of 7 per cent instead of 10 per cent. At the end of 10 years his fund will be worth £197, giving a net post-tax gain of £97 instead of the £111 achieved with the postponed Capital Gains Tax. This aspect of the Capital Gains Tax has a locking-in effect, in the sense that there is an

[5] See section 3 of Appendix 4.1.

[6] In the case of a yield of dividends from the distribution of a company's profit as contrasted with the capital gain in the value of a company's shares resulting from the ploughing back of undistributed profits, the difference between the 98 per cent rate of tax on dividends and the 30 per cent rate of tax on capital gains exaggerates the true situation, because the dividends will enjoy imputation relief from corporation tax while the capital gains from the rise in share prices will enjoy no such relief. See section 4 of Appendix 4.1.

incentive to postpone the realisation of an asset carrying a capital gain, even if otherwise there might be some increase in yield to be obtained by selling the asset in order to invest the capital in a more productive line.

REALISATION ON DEATH

A third major feature is that Capital Gains Tax is not levied on an asset which passes hands on the death of an owner, although the new owner (purchaser or beneficiary) will be liable to pay Capital Gains Tax only on any further increase in value after the change of ownership. Thus income received in the form of capital gains and retained in that form until the death of the owner is wholly exempt from the tax. This consideration greatly reinforces the locking-in effect in the case of assets carrying accrued capital gains which are in the ownership of the elderly.

EXEMPTION OF GOVERNMENT SECURITIES

A further important feature is that capital gains on gilt-edged securities held for more than a year are exempt from tax.[7]

3 CORPORATION TAX (CT)

The UK corporation tax is a charge, at present at a tax-inclusive rate of 52 per cent, on the profits of incorporated, as contrasted with unincorporated, businesses, the company's profits being calculated after deduction of the capital allowances discussed earlier in this chapter (pp. 50–53) and of interest payable on any indebtedness of the company.[8]

THE IMPUTATION SYSTEM

The shareholder would suffer (as in fact he did before 1973) a heavy double taxation if he were taxed at his full rate of personal income tax on the net company income left over for the payment of dividends after the payment of the full rate of corporation tax on the company's profits. In order to relieve the shareholder from some part of this 'double' taxation, some part of the

---

[7] The reader is at this point reminded of the fact that we have postponed all discussion of the effects of inflation upon the tax system until Chapter 6. In the case both of investment income and of capital gains there will in times of rapid inflation be a great difference between *money* incomes or capital gains and *real* incomes or capital gains. In this chapter we are abstracting from this inflationary distinction. In fact the present CGT is a tax on *realised monetary* gains; to make it operate as a tax on *accrued real* gains would be a complicated operation (considered in Chapter 7).

[8] Certain complicating features of the corporation tax which are not discussed in the main text of this chapter are outlined in section 5 of Appendix 4.1. Our object in the present chapter is to illustrate the complicated anomalies which result at present from the interplay between income tax and corporation tax; and an examination of the most straightforward cases of the operation of the corporation tax is quite sufficient for this purpose.

corporation tax paid on company income is imputed to shareholders as an income tax credit if the company's income is distributed to them in dividends. The tax credit thus imputed on the shareholder's dividend is, under the present law, imputed at the basic rate of Income Tax, i.e. at present at 33 per cent calculated on the dividend plus the tax credit.

The working of this arrangement can be understood from the following example:

	£
Company income	100
Less CT	(52)
Dividend	48
Tax credit imputed on dividend	
(i.e. 33% of £71·6)	23·6
Dividend + Tax credit	71·6

We suppose that a company has an income of £100, pays corporation tax (CT) of £52 and has £48 to distribute in dividend. The shareholder will have a tax credit of £23·6 imputed to him when he receives the dividend of £48, making in all an income of £71·6 (= £23·6+£48). The tax credit of £23·6 represents 33 per cent of £71·6, so that he is being treated as if he had received a dividend of £71·6 with tax deducted at the source at the basic rate of 33 per cent. He will be liable to income tax on the £71·6 at his full rate of tax, but will be charged as if he had already paid £23·6 in income tax.

The company, when it pays the dividend of £48, will be under an obligation to pay to the Inland Revenue an amount equal to the tax credit of £23·6. This amount is then treated as an advance payment of corporation tax (ACT) and is set against the company's ultimate tax liability of 52 per cent of the original company income of £100.

The net result of this arrangement is that the shareholder receives in effect an income of £71·6 (which will be subject to his full rate of income tax) when the company decides to distribute to him the proceeds of £100 of its income. There is thus an underlying rate of corporation tax of 28·4 per cent on company income which is distributed in dividends (= 100−71·6).

THE EFFECT ON DIFFERENT FORMS OF BUSINESS INCOME

This corporate tax structure means that the tax treatment of business income will differ materially according to whether the business is an unincorporated business (not liable to corporation tax) or an incorporated business and, in the latter case, whether the company's income is distributed or retained in the business as an undistributed profit. The position is illustrated in Table 4.2.

The table shows that the net advantage to a shareholder in a company from undistributed profits subject, if realised, to a Capital Gains Tax of 30 per cent[9] will be the same as the gain from distribution if the shareholder in question were subject to a personal rate of income tax (including investment income surcharge) of 53·1 per cent. If he is subject to income tax at a higher rate than this, he will be better off if instead company income is put to reserve so that he enjoys the resulting capital gain.

Table 4.2   *The taxation of business income (in £s)*

| | Company | | Unincorporated business |
	Income undistributed	*Income distributed*	
Income before tax	100	100	100
Less CT	(52)	(52)	—
Available for distribution or addition to reserves	48	48	100
Imputation of tax credit	—	23·6	—
Amount on which personal tax is paid	48	71·6	100
Less CGT at 30% on £48	(14·4)	—	—
Less IT (including investment income surcharge) at 53·1%[a] on £71·6	—	(38·0)	—
Less IT at 66·4%[a] on £100	—	—	(66·4)
Net income after tax	33·6	33·6	33·6

  [a] These rates of IT of 53·1% and 66·4% are chosen simply to illustrate at what rates of tax the net income after tax in the second and third columns of the table would be the same as the net income after tax in the first column.

This possibility has led to special restrictions on close companies, i.e. on any company which is under the control of its directors or of five or fewer persons (persons who are closely related or otherwise associated being treated as one for this purpose). If such companies distribute less than their investment income plus 50 per cent of their estate or trading income, then, unless it can be shown that any higher dividend would prejudice the requirements of the company's business, the tax affairs of the company and its

  [9] In Table 4.2 we assume that when the company ploughs back its post-tax profit of £48 instead of using this sum for distribution of dividends, the value of the company's shares to the shareholders is increased by £48. In fact, of course, share prices will not react in any such precise manner, being influenced by many other factors affecting the expectation of profit, although on the average the effect may be expected to be of this order of magnitude. In the table we also assume for illustrative purposes that the shareholder realises his capital gains as they accrue.

shareholders may be adjusted as if the required level of dividend had been paid.

Table 4.2 also illustrates the influence of these tax arrangements on the choice between incorporation of a business and its conduct as an unincorporated private business. In the case of the unincorporated business the £100 of business income will be free of corporation tax, but will be subject to the full rate of the owner's income tax whether it is distributed or retained in the business. If the owner's rate is low, there will be a clear tax advantage in remaining unincorporated and thus avoiding corporation tax. If his rate is higher than 66·4 per cent,[10] there may be a direct tax advantage in incorporation in so far as close company legislation does not prevent taking advantage of the lower joint rate of corporation tax and capital gains tax on undistributed income.[11]

COMBINED EFFECTS OF INCOME TAX, CAPITAL GAINS TAX, AND CORPORATION TAX

In the preceding sections of this chapter we have outlined some of the salient features of the income tax, the capital gains tax, and the corporation tax in the United Kingdom. The combined effect of these taxes is a complicated matter. They all have effects upon the post-tax yield which can be obtained from any savings which are invested in different forms of capital asset. In Chapter 3 (p. 37) we have explained that a criterion which could be used to judge whether a direct tax was income based or expenditure based was the relationship between the post-tax rate of yield to the saver and the pre-tax rate of yield on the investment which the savings served to finance. With constant rates of tax an expenditure-based tax system would equate these two rates of yield to each other, whereas an income-based system would reduce the rate of yield to the saver below the rate of yield on the investment.

Accordingly we shall illustrate the inter-relationships between the income tax, the capital gains tax, and the corporation tax in the United Kingdom by considering their combined effects upon these rates of yield on capital sums which are saved and invested.

The yield on any sum which is saved and invested depends in the first place upon the pre-tax yield of the asset in which the funds are ultimately invested, whether it be a government security, plant and equipment in industry, a dwelling house, and so on. We consider the case of the investment of savings directly or indirectly in some form of physical asset (plant, machinery, commercial building, land, stocks, etc.) used for some form of industrial or commercial activity. For illustrative purposes we shall assume that the pre-tax yield on the physical investment is 10 per cent a year after allowing for

[10] The relevant rate of tax would be 59·4 per cent in the case of a small business, which, if incorporated, would be liable to the reduced rate of corporation tax of 42 per cent.

[11] It is not implied that the choice between private and incorporated business is determined solely or even primarily on such tax advantage or disadvantage. The great attraction of incorporation is, of course, that it can carry with it the privilege of limited liability.

normal economic depreciation of the asset. We ask what the combined effect of income tax, capital gains tax, and corporation tax will be upon the post-tax yield for the saver who provides the finance for the investment. How far will it diverge from the 10 per cent pre-tax yield on the investment?

The answer is a complicated one since the tax effect depends upon the interplay of the following conditions:

1   The total income and so the marginal rate of tax on investment income to which the individual saver is liable.
2   Whether the body which invested the funds was an incorporated company or a private unincorporated business.
3   What was the tax regime for the writing down of the value of the particular asset in question (e.g. 100 per cent capital allowances, ordinary writing- down depreciation allowances, no depreciation allowances).
4   Whether any new funds raised from outside by the business concerned were raised in the form of new equity share issues or by new debt.
5   Whether the return on the investment is distributed to the shareholders or ploughed back into the business.

The following five tables (Tables 4.3 to 4.7) illustrate the various possible outcomes. Throughout these tables it is assumed (as a means of simple illustration of the factors at work) (1) that the rate of corporation tax is 52 per cent; (2) that the basic rate of income tax and so the imputation rate for tax credits on dividends and advance corporation tax is 33 per cent; (3) that the addition of undistributed profits to a company's assets leads to an equal capital gain on the company's shares and that this capital gain is realised and taxed as it accrues, the rate of capital gains tax being 30 per cent; and (4) that interest is deductible from profits before liability either to corporation tax or to income tax is assessed. The examples apply these rates (i) to the case in which 100 per cent capital allowance can be claimed against the cost of the new asset (e.g. a machine), in which case we assume that the taxpayer has other tax liabilities which are immediately reduced by the tax on the 100 per cent capital allowance; and (ii) to the case in which allowances which measure the true economic rate of depreciation may be set against profits for tax purposes.[12] The outcome is illustrated for four types of original saver: (a) a saver who for some reason is exempt from income tax and whose marginal rate of tax is therefore zero; (b) a taxpayer who is liable at the basic rate of 33 per cent but whose investment income is so low that he is not liable to investment income surcharge; (c) a taxpayer who is liable to the 33 per cent basic rate but whose investment income surcharge is 15 per cent, making a marginal rate of 48 per cent on investment income; and (d) a taxpayer who is liable to the top income tax rate of 83 per cent plus a 15 per cent surcharge on any investment income, making a

[12] In practice, of course, the measurement of true economic depreciation is a will o' the wisp; but we may take it as representing the case where the depreciation rule of thumb (e.g. straight line over ten years) more or less measures the true position.

marginal rate of 98 per cent on investment income. It should be noted that case (a) refers not only to some saver whose total income is so low as to bring him below the tax threshold, but also to all funds, such as approved pension funds and charities, whose investment income is exempt from tax.

EQUITY FINANCE BY AN INCORPORATED COMPANY

Table 4.3 shows the results in the case of equity finance raised by an incorporated company. The first two columns show the case in which profits are distributed and the last two columns the case in which profits are retained. Columns A and C refer to the case in which the funds are invested in an asset which attracts 100 per cent capital allowance, and columns B and D to the case in which the particular asset attracts true economic depreciation allowances.

The structure of the table can be explained by considering column A. Line 1 shows an initial saving of £100. This serves to finance an investment in machinery costing £208·3 (line 3), because the 100 per cent allowance on this £200 investment gives a remission of corporation tax of £108·3 on other profits (line 2), which can be used to help to finance the investment. It is assumed (line 4) that there is a 10 per cent yield on this investment, i.e. an additional pre-tax revenue of £20·8; but this after corporation tax (line 5) leaves £10 a year for distribution (line 6). With this dividend distribution there goes a tax credit of £4·9 (line 7), which gives the shareholder a taxable income of £14·9 (line 8). Lines 9 then show the income tax liabilities of various shareholders; and after deduction of these amounts of income tax lines 10 show the net returns to the savers on the original £100 of savings.

It is necessary to consider the treatment of depreciation in column A. The arithmetic as we have expounded it would clearly be valid if the investment worth £208·3 in line 3 did not depreciate but produced its yield of 10 per cent *ad infinitum* without any deterioration. But suppose that the machine involved did have a life of only ten years, over which it lost its real value each year by one-tenth of its original value, so that a straight-line annual depreciation allowance of £20·83 would be appropriate. Then the gross yield on the machine would have to be £20·83+£20·83 = £41·76 in order to cover depreciation plus net yield. But the whole of this gross yield would be subject to the 52 per cent rate of corporation tax, since the whole of the capital value of the machine would have been written off in the year of its purchase. The annual depreciation of £20·83 after deduction of the 52 per cent rate of tax would provide only £10 for investment in the concern's real capital equipment. But such investment would in turn attract 100 per cent capital allowances, so that, just as the original share purchase of £100 was sufficient to finance the purchase of the original machine costing £208·3, so the use of the net-of-tax depreciation allowance of £10 would be sufficient to purchase assets costing £20·83 in order to maintain the value of the concern's real capital equipment. It can thus be seen that column A with line 4 representing the net yield on the machine will cover the story whether the investment is an asset which depreciates rapidly, slowly or not at all.

Table 4.3 *Equity finance by an incorporated company (in £s)*

		Profits distributed in dividends		Profits ploughed back	
		A 100% capital allowances	B True economic depreciation	C 100% capital allowances	D True economic depreciation
1	Saving	100	100	100	100
2	Remission of CT at 52% on investment	108·3	nil	108·3	nil
3	Investment	208·3	100	208·3	100
4	Annual yield at 10% on investment	20·8	10	20·8	10
5	*Less* CT at 52%	(10·8)	(5·2)	(10·8)	(5·2)
6	Available for distribution or reserve	10	4·8	10	4·8
7	Tax credit at 33% on Dividend + Tax credit	4·9	2·4	—	—
8	Dividend + Tax credit	14·9	7·2	—	—
9	*Less* IT or CGT for taxpayer whose marginal rate of IT (including investment income surcharge) is: 0%	(0)	(0)	(0)[a]	(0)[a]
	33%	(4·9)	(2·4)	(1·7)[a]	(0·8)[a]
	48%	(7·2)	(3·5)	(2·4)[a]	(1·2)[a]
	98%	(14·6)	(7·1)	(3·0)	(1·4)
10	Post-tax return on £100 of savings to taxpayers whose marginal rate of IT (including investment income surcharge) is: 0%	14·9	7·2	10·0	4·8
	33%	10·0	4·8	8·3	4·0
	48%	7·7	3·7	7·6	3·6
	98%	0·3	0·1	7·0	3·4

[a] It is assumed that the taxpayer is in a position to take advantage of the option under the CGT whereby he pays at his marginal rate of IT on one-half of the gain (see section 3 of Appendix 4.1).

Column B repeats the calculations of column A with only true economic depreciation allowed on the investment. It will be observed that the net yields to the savers (given in lines 10) are in column B only 48 per cent of what they are in column A as a result of the 52 per cent rate of corporation tax.[13] It is perhaps of interest to note that, if the case of an investment which in fact depreciated but against which no depreciation at all was allowed were considered, the reductions of net yield with a 52 per cent corporation tax would be even greater than they are in column B. To give a net yield of £10 at line 4 the investment would have to produce a gross yield greater than £10; but the whole of this gross yield would be subject to the 52 per cent corporation tax, so that the tax deduction in line 5 would be greater than £5·2.

Columns C and D repeat columns A and B up to line 6, which shows the profit available for distribution, which is now, however, not distributed but ploughed back into the business. Lines 9 show the capital gains tax which would be payable by various taxpayers on our assumption (i) that the value of the company's shares rise by the amount of profit ploughed back, and (ii) that the shareholders concerned realise their capital gains as they accrue. Lines 10 then show the net post-tax return on the original £100 of savings.

There is a wide divergence of rates of yield in the various cases shown in lines 10 of Table 4.3. The following features are worth noting:

1   In any one column the return to the low rate taxpayer is higher than that to the high rate taxpayer. This result is not difficult to explain, although in the case of undistributed profits it depends upon the particular assumed capital-gains liabilities which are explained in the footnote to the table. It is more difficult to find any logical justification for the differences in net-of-tax yields obtained under the different columns by a taxpayer liable to the same rate of tax. Thus for a taxpayer with a zero marginal tax rate the yield varies from 14·9 to 4·8 per cent and for a taxpayer with a 98 per cent marginal rate from 7 to 0·1 per cent.

2   With a rate of corporation tax of 52 per cent the advantage of an asset which attracts 100 per cent capital allowance, as contrasted with one which attracts only a true economic depreciation allowance, is in every case to double (approximately) the post-tax rate of yield. This does not, of course, imply that in reality the yield to the saver on one type of asset will be twice that on another. The tables show what would happen if the two types of asset had the same pre-tax rate of yield of 10 per cent. The tax advantage conferred by 100 per cent allowances might well divert investment from the unfavoured type of asset to the favoured type until the pre-tax yield on the favoured type of asset had so fallen relatively to that on the unfavoured type of asset that the post-tax yield to the saver was more or less equalised.

3   It is to be observed that in column A, which represents a very important and general range of investment activities, the shareholder who is exempt from income tax (which may be the trustee of a pension fund, for example)

---

[13] The discrepancies from this rule in lines 10 are due to rounding errors.

receives a rate of return on the savings which is in excess of the yield on the investment. The net effect of the *tax* arrangements is to *subsidise* the rate of yield. The taxpayer whose rate of tax is equal to the rate used for the imputation of the tax credit obtains a post-tax yield on his savings which (at 10 per cent in our example) is equal to the rate of yield on the physical investment which his savings serve to finance.

4 There is an extremely wide divergence in the yield to the high rate income taxpayer between the case of a capital gain from the undistributed profits on an investment in an asset which attracts 100 per cent capital allowances (namely 7 per cent) and the case of the payment of income tax on the distributed profits from an investment which attracts only a true economic depreciation allowance (namely 0·1 per cent).

DEBT FINANCE BY AN INCORPORATED COMPANY

Table 4.4 shows the case in which an incorporated company raises the funds for its investment not by equity capital but by incurring debt. Lines 1, 2, 3 and 4 of this table merely repeat lines 1, 2, 3 and 4 of the previous table. We now assume in line 5 that the company is paying a rate of interest on its

Table 4.4   *Debt finance by an incorporated company (in £s)*

			A 100% capital allowances	B True economic depreciation
1	Saving		100	100
2	Remission of CT at 52% on investment		108·3	nil
3	Investment		208·3	100
4	Annual yield at 10% on investment		20·8	10
5	*Less* Interest on loan		(20·8)	(10)
6	Net profit subject to CT		0	0
7	Interest on loan		20·8	10·0
8	*Less* IT for taxpayer whose marginal rate of IT (including investment income surcharge) is:	0% 33% 48% 98%	(0) (6·9) (10·0) (20·4)	(0) (3·3) (4·8) (9·8)
9	Post-tax return on £100 of savings to taxpayer whose marginal rate of IT (including investment income surcharge) is:	0% 33% 48% 98%	20·8 13·9 10·8 0·4	10·0 6·7 5·2 0·2

debt which just absorbs the available profit on the investment, so that (line 6) there is no net profit subject to corporation tax. (To the extent that higher or lower rates of interest are paid, the difference would affect the rate of return to shareholders on their own investment.) Lines 7, 8 and 9 then show respectively the pre-tax interest, income tax on this interest, and post-tax interest of the various types of individual taxpayer. It is of interest to note that the person or fund which is exempt from income tax will, with a rate of corporation tax of 52 per cent, receive a rate of return which is more than double the yield on the physical asset if the asset attracts 100 per cent capital allowances but equal to the yield on the capital asset if the asset attracts only a true economic depreciation allowance.

SELF-FINANCE BY A PRIVATE BUSINESS

In Table 4.5 we consider an unincorporated business where the owner of the business finances a capital development out of his own savings. In the case of investment in an asset which attracts only a true economic depreciation allowance (column B of the table) the position is very straightforward. The owner's pre-tax income is the yield on the physical investment (line 4), and his post-tax return (lines 6) depends simply on his personal tax rate (lines 5). In the case of an asset which does attract an initial capital allowance (column A) the immediate saving of income tax due to the capital allowance (lines 2) will depend upon the owner's marginal rate of income tax. For example, if his rate of income tax is 33 per cent he will save tax of £49·3 on an investment

Table 4.5   *Unincorporated business: finance from owner's savings (in £s)*

		A 100% capital allowances			B True economic depreciation		
1	Savings	100	100	100	100		
2	Remission of IT for owner whose marginal rate of tax on earned income is: 0% 33% 83%	0	49·3	488·2	nil	nil	nil
3	Investment	100	149·3	588·2	100		
4	Annual yield at 10% on investment	10	14·9	58·8	10		
5	*Less* IT for taxpayer whose marginal rate of tax on earned income is: 0% 33% 83%	(0)	(4·9)	(48·8)	(0)	(3·3)	(8·3)
6	Post-tax return on £100 of savings for taxpayer whose marginal rate of tax on earned income is: 0% 33% 83%	10	10	10	10·0	6·7	1·3

of £149·3 (since £49·3 = 33 per cent of £149·3), which will enable him with an original saving of £100 to finance an investment of £149·3. But what he gains on the swings he loses on the roundabouts, since the yield on the grossed-up investment will be subject to his same marginal rate of tax (lines 5). As a result in all cases (lines 6) the post-tax rate of return on the original savings is equal (at 10 per cent in our example) to the pre-tax rate of return on the physical asset and will only deviate from that return if the taxpayer's rate of tax in the period when his investment cost is incurred differs from his rate of tax when the income flows.

DEBT FINANCE BY A PRIVATE BUSINESS

Finally in Table 4.6 we consider the case of the unincorporated business in which the owner borrows money from some outside source for the finance of his investment. Lines 1, 2, 3 and 4 of Table 4.6 simply repeat lines 1, 2, 3

Table 4.6   *Unincorporated business: owner borrows from outside source (in £s)*

			A 100% capital allowances			B True economic depreciation
1	Amount borrowed		100	100	100	100
2	Remission of IT for owner whose marginal rate of tax on earned income is:	0% 33% 83%	0	49·3	488·2	nil nil nil
3	Investment		100	149·3	588·2	100
4	Annual yield at 10% on investment		10	14·9	58·8	10
5	*Less* Interest paid		(10)	(14·9)	(58·8)	(10)
6	Net profit subject to tax		0	0	0	0
7	Interest		10	14·9	58·8	10
8	*Less* IT for lender whose marginal rate of IT (including investment income surcharge) is:	0% 33% 48% 98%	(0) (3·3) (4·8) (9·8)	(0) (4·9) (7·2) (14·6)	(0) (19·4) (28·2) (57·6)	(0) (3·3) (4·8) (9·8)
9	Post-tax return on £100 lent by lender whose marginal rate of IT (including investment income surcharge) is:	0% 33% 48% 98%	10·0 6·7 5·2 0·2	14·9 10·0 7·7 0·3	58·8 39·4 30·6 1·2	10·0 6·7 5·2 0·2

and 4 of Table 4.5. We now assume that interest is paid by the borrower (line 5), which absorbs the whole profit, so that he is not liable to any tax on the net profit. (To the extent that higher or lower rates of interest are paid the difference would affect the rate of return to the proprietor on his own investment.) Line 7, which repeats line 5, shows the interest received by the lender in each case, which after deduction of tax at his marginal tax rate (lines 8) leaves his post-tax return (lines 9). In the case of assets which attract only true economic depreciation allowances (column B) the result is very straightforward. The saver simply gets the rate of return on the physical asset after deduction of his personal rate of income tax. But in the case of investment in a physical asset which attracts 100 per cent capital allowances the result depends in a startling fashion on the combined results of the marginal rates of tax of the lender and the borrower. The lender (person or fund) who is exempt from tax can obtain a post-tax return of 58·8 per cent on money lent to a borrower with an 83 per cent tax rate, whereas the lender

Table 4.7 *Summary of post-tax rates on saving as shown in the last lines of Tables 4.3 to 4.6 (in %)*

		Saver's or lender's marginal rate of tax			
INCORPORATED BUSINESS		0%	33%	48%	98%
Equity finance					
(a) Profits distributed					
(i) 100% capital allowances		14·9	10·0	7·7	0·3
(ii) true economic depreciation		7·2	4·8	3·7	0·1
(b) Profits undistributed					
(i) 100% capital allowances		10·0	8·3	7·6	7·0
(ii) true economic depreciation		4·8	4·0	3·6	3·4
Debt finance					
(i) 100% capital allowances		20.8	13·9	10·8	0·4
(ii) true economic depreciation		10·0	6·7	5·2	0·2
UNINCORPORATED BUSINESS					
Finance from owner's savings		0%	33%		83%
(i) 100% capital allowances		10·0	10·0		10·0
(ii) true economic depreciation		10·0	6·7		1·7
Finance from borrowed funds		0%	33%	48%	98%
(i) 100% capital allowances with	0%	10·0	6·7	5·2	0·2
owner's (i.e. borrower's)	33%	14·9	10·0	7·7	0·3
marginal tax rate at:	83%	58·8	39·4	30·6	1·2
(ii) true economic depreciation		10·0	6·7	5·2	0·2

with a 98 per cent tax rate will receive a rate of return of only 0·2 per cent on a loan to a borrower with a zero marginal rate of tax – the same rate of return as he would have achieved by lending his money to any borrower to invest in an asset which attracted only a true economic depreciation allowance.

Table 4.7 simply summarises the net post-tax rates of return shown in Tables 4.3, 4.4, 4.5 and 4.6. There is a remarkably wide range and strange scatter of post-tax rates of return. On an income tax principle it is not difficult to understand a wide range of post-tax rates of return between persons or funds with low marginal rates of income tax and those with high marginal rates. But what is less easy to understand is the *raison d'être* of the wide divergences of post-tax rates of return to persons or funds with the same marginal rates of income tax, which result from the organisational or institutional way in which the funds are saved and invested and which can be observed by running an eye down any one column of Table 4.7. Still less is it easy to justify rates of return on savings which exceed the rate of return on the investment which the savings serve to finance.

CONCLUSIONS

There are important features of the present income tax (such as the treatment of pension funds and of much investment by industry) which make the effects of tax in some cases similar to those of an expenditure tax. The interplay between these and other effects of the income tax, the capital gains tax and the corporation tax cause the yield on different forms of savings used to finance different types of investment through different institutions to vary in what appears to be a totally arbitrary manner. The yield is much affected by such considerations as (i) whether the savings are used by a company or by an unincorporated business; (ii) what particular tax rules govern the depreciation of the particular asset in which the savings are invested; (iii) whether the savings are provided by equity capital or by fixed interest loans; and (iv) whether the yield on a company's investment is distributed in dividends and interest or is put to reserve and ploughed back into the business. Some combinations of these features result in a heavy taxation of the savings and investment; at the other extreme, some combinations cause the *tax* system to provide extremely generous *subsidies* to savings and investment.

Appendix 4.1 Notes on Direct Taxes in the United Kingdom

Section 1. Premiums for qualifying life assurance policies (broadly policies for ten years or more) attract a deduction from tax equal to half the basic rate of income tax on the premiums. Relief is limited to total premiums not exceeding £1,500 or one-sixth of total income. Life funds are charged at a maximum rate of corporation tax of 37·5 per cent on investment income.

Section 2. The main allowances applicable to current capital expenditure are as follows:

1 Plant and machinery: a first-year allowance of 100 per cent of cost or, at the taxpayer's option, a lower initial percentage with the balance written off at 25 per cent on the written-down cost; sales of such assets are effectively taxed as income.
2 Industrial buildings: an initial allowance of 50 per cent of the cost of the building (not the land), plus an annual allowance of 4 per cent of cost. The full cost is written off within twenty-five years regardless of subsequent sale proceeds, although during the twenty-five years adjustments are made on sale to equate allowances to actual expenditure suffered.
3 Agricultural buildings and works: cost written off at 10 per cent per annum for ten years with no adjustments on subsequent sale.
4 There are a number of assets, including commercial buildings and rented houses, on which no depreciation allowance is permitted.

Section 3. Capital Gains Tax is at a proportional rate of 30 per cent, unless a charge to income tax of half the gain up to £5,000 plus the whole of any excess over £5,000 would give a lower charge. Tax charged on disposals of holdings in unit and investment trusts is reduced by a credit of 17·5 per cent of the gain.

Section 4. Consider a taxpayer with a tax rate of 98 per cent on investment income and a tax rate of 30 per cent on capital gains. Consider the case in which his income or capital gain is obtained from the ownership of shares in a company, the profits of which are used either (i) to finance a dividend, or (ii) to put to reserve with a consequential capital gain in the value of the company's shares. In case (i), of any £100 of profit the taxpayer will receive £71·6 in dividends plus tax credit, leaving £1·432 after tax at 98 per cent, which represents a tax rate of 98·568 per cent on the original profit:

	£
Company profit	100
Less CT	(52)
Dividend	48
Tax credit (i.e. 33 % of £71·6)	23·6
Dividend + Tax credit	71·6
Less Tax at 98 %	(70·168)
Dividend after tax	1·432

In case (ii) he will receive a capital gain of £48, leaving £33·6 after tax at 30 per cent, which represents a tax rate of 66·4 per cent on the profits:

	£
Company profit	100
Less CT	(52)
Capital gain	48
Less Tax at 30%	(14·4)
Capital gain after tax	33·6

The difference is illustrated by the contrast between the outcomes of columns A and C (or B and D) of Table 4.3.

Section 5. In addition to the main features of the corporation tax (explained on pp. 58–61 of the main text), the following special features may be noted:

1 The rate of corporation tax of 52 per cent is reduced to 42 per cent for companies with incomes below £40,000, with marginal relief where income is between £40,000 and £65,000.
2 The imputation arrangements described in the main text (pp. 53–59) apply only to distributions from the company's income and not to distributions from a company's capital gains. In that case there will be an underlying rate of corporation tax of the 30 per cent tax on the company's chargeable gains. This is illustrated by the following example, where the whole of the dividend, plus tax credit, of £70 is liable to income tax:

		£
Chargeable gain		100
Less Corporation tax		(30)
Dividend	46·9	
Tax credit thereon (i.e. 33% of £70)	23·1	
Dividend + Tax credit	70	70

Although the company accounts for ACT on such a dividend, it cannot recover the ACT by setting it off against its mainstream corporation tax liability since gains do not constitute part of its income.
3 There is, in addition, a limit to the amount of ACT which a company may set against its liability to corporation tax, this limit being set at 33 per cent of its income. This limitation can affect a company which distributes in dividends in any one year more than can be financed out of the income earned by it in that year. Thus suppose that a company (as in the example given on p. 59 of the main text) distributed £48 in dividends with a tax credit of £23·6, but had a current income of only £50 instead of the £100 needed to finance the distribution. On its income of £50 it would be liable to corporation tax of £26, but against this it could set off an ACT of only £16·5 (namely, 33 per cent of its income of £50).[1] Thus it would have to account to the Inland Revenue for the full tax

credit of £23·6 but could deduct only £16·5 of this against its current liability to corporation tax. It would be allowed to recover the remaining £7·1 against its mainstream corporation tax liability of the two previous, and all future, years.

NOTE

1 In this case the underlying rate of corporation tax on its current income is 19 per cent, since the corporation tax of £26 less the maximum permitted deduction of ACT of £16·5 (namely £9·5) represents 19 per cent of its income of £50.

5 The Direct Tax Burden and its Distribution

In the previous chapter we showed how at present in the United Kingdom the interaction of various separate taxes (income tax, capital gains tax and corporation tax) leads to serious anomalies in the capital market. Serious anomalies are also caused in the labour market through the interaction of a number of separate and unco-ordinated subsidies to, and charges on, personal incomes.

This phenomenon is especially marked at the lower end of the income scale because of the interaction of the income tax with the various arrangements for the relief of poverty by means of national insurance and of means-tested benefits. In order to gain a true picture of the situation it is necessary to treat social benefits of one kind or another as forms of 'negative income taxes' or 'income subsidies' with their own implied marginal rates of tax. For example, suppose that when a wage earner adds £2 to his earnings he loses £1 of some means-tested social benefit. In this case the means test has introduced a marginal rate of 'implied tax' of 50 per cent; he has in fact been charged 50 per cent of his additional earnings in reduction of the subsidy to his income. The great variety of measures for the taxation or subsidisation of personal incomes may be classified under the four following headings:

1 There is the levying of the income tax itself upon personal incomes after deduction of various personal allowances which permit a first slice of income to remain untaxed.
2 There are national insurance contributions, which are payable by employers and employed on the wages paid to employees.
3 There is a large corpus of social security benefits which are paid without subjection to any means test but upon certain other conditions, such as old age, sickness, unemployment and parenthood. In some cases these benefits are, and in some cases they are not, conditional upon past national insurance contributions. Although the receipt of these benefits is not subject to any special test of the means of the recipient, some of them are affected by the recipient's means in that they are subject to income tax, while others are exempt from income tax.
4 There is a large number of other schemes for the subsidisation of relatively low personal incomes, each of which is subjected to its own special means test, some of these schemes being of great importance quantitatively. The fact that there are marked differences in the arrangements for the testing of the recipient's other means implies that there are in fact a whole number of separate income tax systems operating simultaneously, often on the same persons and not infrequently in a somewhat inconsistent manner.

INCOME TAX

Under the income tax the taxpayer is allowed a first slice of income (his personal allowances) free of tax; there is then a large range of income subject to the basic rate of tax, which in 1977/78 stood at 33 per cent; and for incomes above this range there is a structure of higher tax rates rising progressively to 83 per cent. In addition there is a set of surcharges on investment income.[1]

PERSONAL ALLOWANCES

An outstanding feature is the great variety of the personal allowances. Some (such as the single person's allowance, married man's allowance and wife's earned income allowance) are clearly of the first importance quantitatively; others (such as the allowance for the services of a daughter resident with and maintained by the taxpayer) are of quite subsidiary importance but nevertheless cause considerable complexity in the administration of the system. Indeed, the arbitrary and detailed complexity of this structure of allowances may well be regarded as constituting in itself something of an anomaly.

THE TREATMENT OF MARRIED WOMEN

There is in any case one outstanding and quantitatively very important anomaly in this structure of personal allowances. A married man receives a personal allowance which is approximately 50 per cent higher than that received by a single adult. If his wife is earning an income as well as himself, the couple enjoy not merely two single person allowances but a married allowance plus a single person's allowance against the wife's earnings. Since the married allowance has been justified in part on the grounds that the husband is responsible for his dependent wife, it would appear anomalous that he should continue to enjoy this married allowance when his wife is no longer dependent and is enjoying a personal allowance against her own independent earnings. We shall return to this problem in Chapters 13 and 18 when we come to discuss social security and the tax unit in more detail.

THE VALUE OF PERSONAL TAX ALLOWANCES

There are important consequences (examined later) which result from the interaction between the personal allowances under the income tax and the other methods (by social benefits with or without means test) of giving help and relief to low incomes; and it is important to note the different effects of choosing the one method or the other. Thus a marked feature of the system of personal allowances under a progressive income tax, which distinguishes it from a system of social benefits, is that the allowance is worth more to the higher rate taxpayer than to the basic rate taxpayer, since an increase in a

---

[1] See sections 1 and 2 of Appendix 5.1 for an account of the personal allowances and rates of tax.

personal allowance means that there is so much less income taxable at the highest marginal rate to which the taxpayer is liable. At the other extreme of the scale, a taxpayer whose personal allowances already exempt the whole of his income will gain nothing from an additional personal allowance. This effect is illustrated in the top half of Table 5.1.

Table 5.1   *Personal tax allowances and retirement pensions*

	Annual amount	Weekly cash value (in £s) at marginal tax rate of:		
	£	33%	50%	83%
Personal tax allowances, 1977/78				
Single person	805	5·11	7·74	12·85
Married man	1,225	7·77	11·78	19·55
Married man with wife's earned income	2,030	12·88	19·52	32·40
Retirement pensions, November 1976				
Single person	796	10·26	7·65	2·60
Married couple	1,274	16.42	12·25	4·17
Married couple (if wife is a contributor)	1,592	20·52	15·30	5·20

THE TREATMENT OF INVESTMENT INCOME

There is in the UK income tax a differentiation between the treatment of earned income and of investment income, such as interest, dividends, rents, etc. Income after deduction of personal allowances is liable to income tax first at a basic rate and then on a progressive scale rising to 83 per cent, whether it be earned income or investment income. But an additional charge, called the *investment income surcharge*, is levied on investment income above £1,500 a year, first at a rate of 10 per cent, but on investment incomes above £2,000 a year at a flat rate of 15 per cent.[2]

This flat rate charge might at first sight suggest a constant differentiation against investment income of this same order of magnitude; but in fact the addition of this flat rate surcharge on top of the progressively rising rate of income tax makes the value of investment income relatively to the value of earned income diminish very greatly as the taxpayer goes up the income scale. Thus to obtain £1,600 after tax requires an investment income which is only 4 per cent greater than earned income; but to obtain £7,500 after tax requires an investment income which is 100 per cent greater than the equivalent earned income.[3]

[2] See section 2 of Appendix 5.1.
[3] See section 3 of Appendix 5.1.

We have discussed in Chapter 3 the reasons for charging investment income at a higher rate than earned income. It is a matter for political decision whether this pattern of differentiation which results from the addition of a flat 10 or 15 per cent to a highly progressive scale of income tax represents the appropriate weight to be given to the relative tax burdens on earned and investment incomes at different levels.

NATIONAL INSURANCE CONTRIBUTIONS

In addition to the income tax, national insurance contributions are payable in respect of employed and self-employed persons. In the case of employed persons the employer pays a contribution of 10·75 per cent and the employee a contribution of 5·75 per cent on total earnings up to a limit of £105 a week. Self-employed persons pay a fixed weekly contribution plus 8 per cent of their profits within the range between £1,750 and £5,500 a year.[4]

SOME INTERNATIONAL COMPARISONS

Before proceeding to examine social security benefits, some broad international comparisons may be helpful in putting the UK tax system in perspective. Detailed comparisons of the overall level of taxation, of the composition of tax receipts, and of minimum, maximum and average rates of income tax are included in Appendix 5.2. A word of warning is necessary, however: international comparisons are fraught with difficulties, especially as regards coverage and comparability. For example, countries differ in the extent to which they provide benefits by tax concessions or cash payments (e.g. a child tax allowance, or a cash grant like the UK family allowance or new child benefit scheme); yet for the same cost in revenue terms, the second method requires higher tax levels than the first. The extent to which social security benefits are financed from social security contributions varies greatly. Again, in comparing income tax rates between countries it is necessary to take account of local income taxes, which may be used to finance expenditures which in other countries are met from central government funds. And so on. But there is no doubt about the general characteristics of the UK tax system as compared with other similar countries.

First, when overall tax revenue (including social security contributions) is expressed as a percentage of gross national product, the United Kingdom is far from being, as is often thought, the most heavily taxed country. Indeed, in 1974 (see Appendix 5.2, Table 5.14) the United Kingdom was well down the list of industrialised countries and eleventh out of the twenty-two countries included in the table by the Organisation for Economic Co-operation and Development (OECD). This could be misleading as a guide to the present, however; 1974 is the latest year for which OECD figures are available, but it showed an unusually low position for the United Kingdom.

4 See section 4 of Appendix 5.1.

In 1970 the United Kingdom was fifth in the OECD league table, and the effective increases in taxation since 1974 must have pulled the country well up the table again.

The United Kingdom does have the distinction of being first in other respects. It has the highest starting rate and the highest maximum marginal rate of national income tax on earned income for comparable industrialised countries. (It also has the highest income tax on investment income, but this is misleading because a valid comparison must take account of the annual wealth tax in some European countries, which is an alternative to the UK investment income surcharge, and this cannot be done on any simple basis.)

The resolution of the paradox that the United Kingdom is far from being the most heavily taxed country, but yet has the highest starting rate and highest maximum rates of income tax, is to be found in other characteristics of the tax structure. The United Kingdom is unique in having a wide band of income taxed at a constant marginal rate of tax, as compared with the steadily progressive national income taxes which are normal elsewhere. Further, the United Kingdom raises a rather smaller proportion of tax revenue from taxes on goods and services than the average for OECD countries (27·1 per cent as compared with 29·3 per cent) and a very much smaller proportion of revenue from employees' and employers' social security contributions, especially the latter, than most of the OECD countries (see Appendix 5.2, Table 5.15). We shall return in Chapter 17 to a discussion of some of the implications of the relative weight of employers' security contributions and of payroll taxes in the tax structure.

SOCIAL BENEFITS NOT SUBJECT TO TESTS OF MEANS

Some support to incomes takes the form of the provision of social benefits which are not subject to special tests of the recipients' means. The basic element in this structure in the United Kingdom, introduced after World War II as a result of the Beveridge Report, is the system of national insurance, which provides benefits to persons who for certain specified reasons are not in work, subject to contribution and other conditions (such as availability for work in the case of the unemployed).

Benefits payable under the national insurance scheme include unemployment benefit, sickness benefit, retirement pensions, widows' pensions and allowances, maternity benefits and industrial injury benefits. These basic benefits are fixed in amount for all recipients; but in addition there are in certain cases earnings-related supplements to the flat rate benefits for sickness and unemployment.[5]

THE TAX TREATMENT OF VARIOUS BENEFITS

Some of these benefits are subject to tax and thus of less benefit to those with high marginal rates of income tax than to those with lower marginal rates.

[5] The scale of the national insurance benefits is given in section 5 of Appendix 5.1.

But some are not subject to tax and thus of the same net benefit to all recipients regardless of their other income. For example, the retirement pensions are included in taxable income for income tax purposes, and the marked contrast of this case with the effects of personal tax allowances of a similar magnitude is illustrated in Table 5.1. But on administrative grounds sickness and unemployment benefits were exempted from income tax shortly after the introduction of the national insurance scheme. These benefits remain exempt from tax in spite of the fact that with their earnings-related supplementations they can represent a substantial income.

The fact that unemployment benefit is not subject to tax can give rise to a particular anomaly, whereby a worker who would be better off in employment for a whole year than on unemployment benefit for a whole year may nevertheless be still better off if he spends part of the year in employment and part unemployed. Consider a man whose pre-tax weekly take-home pay exceeds the rate of unemployment benefit, but by less than the basic rate of income tax. When account has been taken of his personal allowances under the income tax, which give him a slice of annual earnings which is not subject to tax, he may well be better off with a full year's earnings than with a full year's unemployment benefit. But when he has worked for a sufficient number of weeks to have earned in total an amount which accounts for the whole of his tax-free personal allowances for the year, he will be better off for the rest of the year to receive untaxed unemployment benefit rather than his weekly earnings, which will now be subject to the basic rate of income tax. The cases in which this anomaly leads to serious reduction of work effort are no doubt limited; but it is nevertheless an undesirable feature of a tax system that it should make it more advantageous financially to be unemployed than employed.

FAMILY ALLOWANCES AND CHILD BENEFITS

The tax and social benefit treatment of children is in the process of radical change. In 1976/77 the position was as follows. There was an independent system of family allowances of £1·50 a week payable in respect of all children excluding the first child, except in the case of one-parent families, which were entitled to an allowance for the first child as well as for the other children in the family. These family allowances were included in taxable income for income tax purposes, and in addition there was an arrangement whereby a taxpayer's annual personal tax-free allowance was reduced by £52 for each family allowance which he received; the object of this arrangement when it was introduced was to 'claw back' from the richer parents the benefit which they would otherwise have enjoyed from an increase which was at that time being made in the family allowance. The taxpayer thus paid his marginal rate of tax both on the family allowance and on the £52 of loss of personal allowance. In the case of a parent liable to a sufficiently high marginal rate of tax, this combined amount would exceed the family allowance and it would pay not to take up the family allowance.

In 1975 a Child Benefit Act was passed which provided for the eventual replacement of these previously taxable family allowances paid in respect of second and subsequent children and of child income-tax allowances by a new tax-free child benefit. The ultimate effect of such a change will be to provide a cash benefit (i) which will have the same money value to all parents (unlike the present tax allowances, which are of greater value to the taxpayer with a higher marginal rate of income tax and of no value to the parent whose income would in any case have been below the tax threshold), and (ii) which will be received in respect of all children (unlike the previous family allowances, which, except in the case of the one-parent family, excluded the first child in the family). A further effect in many families will be to transfer cash from the wage-earning husband's pay packet (because of the loss of the child tax allowance) to the mother's receipt of cash benefits (as the enlarged child benefit replaces the previous smaller family allowances).

The first phase of the child benefit scheme has been introduced for 1977/78: a tax-free child benefit of £1 for the first child is now paid in addition to a tax-free benefit of £1·50 for subsequent children, which replaces the previously taxable family allowance of the same amount. At the same time child allowances for income tax purposes have been reduced, so that, in respect of children other than the first, basic rate taxpayers are neither better nor worse off than under the previous family allowance system. Higher rate taxpayers for whom previously it paid to waive family allowances will be slightly worse off. Families below the tax threshold will enjoy the whole of the new benefit of £1 a week paid in respect of the first child; but the reduction in the child tax allowance will mean that families paying the basic rate of tax will be better off by approximately 33p a week, while families with a marginal rate of tax in excess of 50 per cent will be worse off.

MEANS-TESTED BENEFITS

SUPPLEMENTARY BENEFITS

We turn next to the structure of means-tested benefits. The system of national insurance and of family allowances, overcomplicated though it is, needs to be backed by a number of means-tested benefits under which those whose incomes fall below certain prescribed levels receive additional help. For those not in full-time employment the deficiency is supplied by the payment of supplementary benefit.[6]

The supplementary benefit scale is generally taken to represent the minimum level of the standard of living necessary for the avoidance of poverty. But poverty is a relative concept, and the scale of supplementary benefits has been adjusted over the years, rising in real terms as average earnings have risen. National insurance benefits and family allowances have not risen to the same extent; and the system of national insurance and family allowances

---

[6] The scale of payments is given in section 5 of Appendix 5.1.

has thus become increasingly inadequate to cope with the problem of poverty as measured by the scale of supplementary benefits.

The scale of supplementary benefits does not cover the claimant's rent and rates, allowances for which are paid in addition, it being impossible with the present arrangements for housing to fix on any one allowance for rent and rates. This fact is of great importance in making a comparison between the rates of supplementary benefit and those for national insurance, to which no addition is made for rent and rates; and when allowance has been made for this fact it is apparent that the scale for national insurance benefits is markedly below the scale for supplementary benefit.

For a number of reasons even national insurance backed by the supplementary benefit system leaves a number of families below the poverty line, as measured by the supplementary benefit scale. One reason is the failure of persons eligible for supplementary benefit to take up their entitlement to benefit either through ignorance of the scheme or else through the stigma of poverty which attaches to it. Another reason is that persons in work are not eligible to apply for supplementary benefit. The low wage earner with a large family to support will thus be below the poverty level.

FAMILY INCOME SUPPLEMENT

The family income supplement scheme was introduced in order to help such families. Under this scheme a family supplement is paid equal to 50 per cent of the deficiency of the family's income below a 'prescribed amount', which increases with the size of the family.[7]

RENT AND RATE REBATES AND ALLOWANCES

In addition there are schemes for rent and rate rebates and allowances, which grant families some relief from payment of rent and rates, the relief depending upon (i) the amount of rent or rates payable, (ii) the size of the family, and (iii) the income of the householder.[8]

OTHER MEANS-TESTED BENEFITS

There are in addition a multitude of further means-tested benefits, including: free milk and vitamins; prescriptions, dental and optical charge exemptions; free school meals; education maintenance allowances; school uniform grants; legal aid; hospital travelling expenses; residential accommodation for the elderly; day nurseries; and home helps. There is much variety in the rules and tests for these various means-tested benefits.

[7] See section 6 of Appendix 5.1 for the scale of payments.
[8] See section 7 of Appendix 5.1 for the scales of rebates and allowances.

THE COMBINED EFFECTS OF INCOME TAX AND SOCIAL BENEFITS

Since these schemes all depend upon the assessment of a citizen's income in order to determine how much tax he should pay (in the case of income tax and national insurance contributions) or how much benefit he should lose (in the case of means-tested benefits), the situation is one in which there are, as it were, a host of separate income-tax systems running concurrently, administered separately and having their cumulative implied tax rates unco-ordinated.[9]

This is especially important in the case of the family income supplement scheme and of the schemes for rent and rate rebates and allowances. These schemes can bring quantitatively extremely important additions to family incomes.[10] But each has its own special arrangement for relating benefits to the family income, the family income supplement scheme implying a marginal rate of tax of 50 per cent, the rent rebate scheme one of 17 or 25 per cent, and the rate rebate scheme one of 6 or 8 per cent.

The sort of position which can result from the unco-ordinated combination of these schemes may be illustrated by a two-child family where the father earned £35 a week in July 1977. He would be paying income tax and national insurance contributions, receiving family income supplementation, receiving a rent rebate and entitled to free school meals. Each involves a separate form and different criteria. Incidentally, if the father were so exasperated by all this form filling that he assaulted one of the officials, he would then be eligible for legal aid.

Moreover, the problem is not one simply of duplication of administration. The implied marginal tax rates (i.e. the amount deducted from an extra £1 of earnings) are cumulative. In the above case, with a 33 per cent basic rate of tax, a 5·75 per cent national insurance contribution and a 50 per cent loss of family income supplementation, the father would find that of any increase in his earnings he would lose 90 per cent under the three heads above. When possible loss of rent rebate and free school meals is added, his implied marginal rate of tax could well be more than 100 per cent.

In considering the effect of these high marginal rates of tax on incentives it is important to remember that means-tested benefits are awarded for a period and not reassessed at once. For example, entitlement to family income supplementation is granted for a year on the basis of an assessment of the family's income over the past two months. Thus short-term changes in earnings (e.g. overtime for a limited duration) may not lead to withdrawal of benefit. Moreover, in so far as permitted income levels are liable to annual uprating an immediate increase in earnings may not lead to any reduction in benefit when the time comes for reassessment. The effects of high marginal tax rates of the kind described will thus be mitigated; but they will still be

---

[9] The bewildering variety of conditions and scales of benefit attached to the various schemes is illustrated in sections 8 and 9 of Appendix 5.1.

[10] See sections 6 and 7 of Appendix 5.1.

operative and will probably be most serious in the case of decisions leading to a permanent change in earnings relatively to the average: decisions about participation in the labour force and about choice of job.

THE NATURE OF THE POVERTY TRAP

In the above discussion of the interaction between the various schemes for income support and taxation at the lower end of the income scale we have concentrated attention upon the direct disincentive effects of the excessively high marginal rates of implied tax that may result. But disincentives to earn more are not the only results of the 'poverty trap', as it is often called. It undermines the effects of income policies designed to help the low paid; it has the depressing effect of making it difficult for the poor to pull themselves out of poverty by their own efforts; and it involves much administrative work in giving and taking funds to and from the same people. Moreover, there is something ludicrously inconsistent about a situation in which people who are receiving assistance from some public authorities to keep them above what those public authorities presumably judge to be a poverty level should find that their spendable incomes are actually reduced when they earn more – a result which can follow in those cases in which the marginal rate of implied tax exceeds 100 per cent.

IMPLIED AVERAGE AND MARGINAL TAX RATES

Table 5.2 illustrates the meaning and method of calculating implied average and marginal tax rates. We take as an illustration the case, as at July 1977, of

Table 5.2 *The calculation of implied average and marginal rates of tax*

	£	£
Unadjusted earnings	35·00	36·00
Child benefit	2·50	2·50
Less Tax	(1·45)	(1·78)
Less National insurance	(2·01)	(2·07)
Family income supplement	5·00	4·50
Rent rebate	3·60	3·47
Rate rebate	1·40	1·36
Free school milk and meals	1·50	1·50
Earnings after adjustment for direct taxes and subsidies	45·54	45·48

Effective tax = Unadjusted earnings minus adjusted earnings	= −£10·54	−£9·48
Average tax = Effective tax as a percentage of unadjusted earnings	= −30·1%	−26·3%
Marginal tax = Increase in effective tax as a percentage of increase in unadjusted earnings	=	+ 106%

a married couple with two children aged 4 and 6 with only the husband earning; we examine the effect of an increase in his earnings from £35 to £36 a week. We measure his effective average tax rates by comparing his earnings adjusted for direct taxes and subsidies with his unadjusted earnings of £35 or £36; and we can establish the effective marginal tax rate which he faces by noting the change in his adjusted earnings which occurs when he increases his unadjusted earnings by £1 from £35 to £36.

Table 5.3　*Average and marginal tax rates[a] at July 1977 on earned income*

	Single adult		Married couple with 2 children aged 4 and 6; wife not earning	
	(1)	(2)	(3)	(4)
Earnings per week (£)	Average rate of tax (%)	Marginal rate of tax (%)	Average rate of tax (%)	Marginal rate of tax (%)
25	4·4	62	−74·2	73
30	14·0	62	−52·0	86
35	20·8	62	−29·0	106
40	25·8	39	−13·6	101
50	26·5	39	6·9	137
60	26·9	39	17·5	45
70	27·2	39	20·7	39
80	27·4	39	23·0	39
90	27·5	39	24·8	39
100	27·6	39	26·2	39
150	34·5	45	28·9	40
200	38·2	55	32·9	50
300	46·5	70	42·1	70
400	53·3	75	49·9	75
500	59·0	83	55·9	83

[a] It should be remembered that (as described on pp. 82–83) the part of the implied tax rates which is represented by changes in means-tested benefits is likely to operate only after the lapse of a period of time when the benefits will be adjusted to the changed family circumstances. Many of the highest rates of tax in the table will therefore not make an immediate impact.

NOTES

Benefits included: Child benefit; Family income supplement; Rent and rate rebates; Free school milk and meals.
Taxes include: Income tax; national insurance at employed earner's rate.
Assumed weekly rent: Single £4·70; married with 2 children £5·60.
Assumed weekly rates: Single £1·85; married with 2 children £2·20.

In Table 5.3, using the method of Table 5.2, we give a comprehensive view of the way in which the combination of these means-tested schemes with the income tax will affect taxpayers in different family circumstances and with different pre-tax presubsidy earnings. The table outlines the result (i) for a single adult, and (ii) for a married couple with two children. The table shows in columns 1 and 3 the taxpayer's average rate of tax; and this average rate of tax is negative (i.e. he will receive a net subsidy) in those cases in which he receives more in benefit than he pays in tax. In columns 2 and 4 the table shows the taxpayer's implied marginal rate of tax, namely the proportion of any additional £1 of earnings which he would lose in additional tax or reduction of means-tested benefits.[11]

The tax rates in Table 5.3 are based upon the assumption that the earned incomes are not supplemented by an investment income. The marginal tax rates on additional earnings could thus be higher than is shown, since under the progressive income tax system the tax rate on earnings will depend upon the total income and not merely on the amount of earned income. For this reason the marginal tax rates on some of the higher earnings are likely to be underestimated. In particular the aggregation of a wife's investment income with the income (both earned and unearned) of the husband can result in a high marginal rate of tax on the husband's earnings. Moreover, the test of parents' incomes used for the payment of student grants can also result in important additional implied marginal rates of tax (amounting to 10 or 20 per cent) on those in the middle range of incomes.

THE EFFECT ON MARRIED WOMEN'S EARNINGS

The aggregation of husband's and wife's incomes for purposes of both income tax (subject to the right to elect for separate treatment of earned income) and of means-tested benefits means that the implied tax rates faced by a married woman who chooses, or has to, work in addition to her husband may be particularly high. This is in spite of the additional personal allowance for working married women under the income tax and the exemption of a proportion of earning under means-tested benefits. Table 5.4 shows the average rates faced by a married woman contemplating taking a job at either £20 or £40 a week (i.e. the proportion of the £20 or £40 which failed to lead to a net increase in the family's adjusted income), and the marginal rates faced on any further increase beyond the earnings of £20 or £40 a week.

---

[11] For the lower end of the income scale it has been estimated that, in December 1975, the following number of families (with children and with the head in full time employment) theoretically entitled to benefits faced the effective marginal tax rates shown:

No. of families	Marginal tax rate (%)
50,000	above 100
40,000	76–100
200,000	51–76

Source: Hansard, vol. 919, col. 1006.

Table 5.4 *Implied tax rates[d] at July 1977 on the earnings of a married woman with two children, according to the earnings of her husband*

Husband's weekly earnings (£)	Average tax rates[a] at wife's weekly earnings of:		Marginal tax rates at wife's weekly earnings of:	
	£20 (%)	£40 (%)	£20 (%)	£40 (%)
25	68·6	69·7	76	39
30	68·6	63·0	62	39
35	55·7	53·7	62	39
40	47·6	46·8	62	39
50	30·0	34·4	62	39
60	14·1	26·4	45	39
70–100	13·2	26·0	39	39
150	14·8[b]	31·4[b]	46[b]	51[b]
200	17·3[b]	36·1[c]	61[b]	39[c]
300	21·6[b]	39·1[c]	76[b]	39[c]
400	22·7[b]	41·2[c]	81[b]	39[c]
500	24·5[b]	42·8[c]	89[b]	39[c]

[a] It is assumed that national insurance contributions are paid at the full employed earner's rate.

[b] These rates arise from the aggregation for IT purposes of husband's and wife's earnings.

[c] Assuming that disaggregation of husband's and wife's earnings is opted for. The average tax rate includes additional tax payable as a result of the reduction of the married man's allowance to that of a single person.

[d] For the reasons given in note *a* to Table 5.3, many of the high rates of implied tax on the wife's earnings are unlikely to have an immediate impact.

These high rates of implied tax on a wife's earnings are particularly disturbing, because such evidence as there is on the effects of high tax rates in discouraging work and effort suggest that it is the incentive for women to supplement the family income from their earnings which is most sensitive to such tax disincentives.

CONCLUSIONS

Income tax, national insurance contributions and various social benefits (some subject to means tests and some not, some liable to income tax and some not) together constitute an unco-ordinated system of tax and subsidy on personal incomes. The system is extremely complicated, but even so is not fully effective in the relief of poverty. Moreover, it can result in what are in effect extremely high marginal rates of tax at the lower end of the income scale, so that by earning more a worker may add little or nothing to his spendable income (the poverty trap); indeed in certain extreme cases he may actually reduce his spendable income when he earns more. Very high marginal rates of tax are incurred also at the top end of the income scale. High marginal rates of tax involve the danger of disincentive effects, which may be particularly severe in certain cases where the system leads to very high marginal rates of tax on a wife's earnings.

Appendix 5.1   Rates of Direct Taxation and of Social Security Contributions and Benefits in the United Kingdom

Section 1.

Table 5.5   *Personal allowances under the income tax*

Type of personal allowance	1976/77 (£)	1977/78 (£)		Cost in 1976/77[h] (£ m)
		first child	subsequent child	
Single person	735	805	(945)[a]	2,480
Married man	1,085	1,225	(1,455)[a]	4,780
Person 65 or over: single	1,010[b]	1,080	(1,250)[a]	80
married	1,555	1,695	(1,975)[a]	140
Additional allowance in respect of wife's earned income – the amount of the earnings up to	735	805		1,300
Children – age at 6 April: under 11	300[c,f]	196	170	930
11–16	335[c,f]	231	205	450
over 16 and in full-time education	365[c,f]	261	235[g]	130
Housekeeper – for widow(er) in respect of female housekeeper	100	100		⎫
Female relative caring for claimant's brother or sister	100	100		⎬ 1·5
Additional allowance for single parent entitled to child allowance	350	420	(510[a])	40
Dependent relative maintained by: single woman	145[d,f]	145		⎫
others	100[d,f]	100		⎬ 35
Services of daughter resident with and maintained by claimant	55	55		⎭
Blind person	180[e]	180		1·5
Total reliefs reduced, for each family allowance received, by	52			−110

[a] The bracketed figures for personal tax allowances for 1977/78 are those which result from the Chancellor's decisions announced in July and October 1977. The unbracketed figures are those proposed in the Chancellor's original budget statement and have been used in all the examples given in this report.

[b] Relief reduced by £2 for every £3 of income over £3,250 but not so as to reduce the allowance below that given to persons under 65.

[c] Relief reduced by the excess of child's income over £350 in the case of a child over 18; and by the excess of investment income over £115 in the case of younger children with earnings (if any) not exceeding £235.

[d] Relief reduced by the excess of relative's income over basic retirement pension.

[e] Relief reduced by the amount of tax-free disability receipts.

[f] These allowances are apportioned if two or more persons support the child or dependent relative.

[g] Children over age 19 in full-time education in 1977/78 and the two following years attract an allowance of £365.

[h] Estimated revenue foregone. The separate estimates for the individual allowances cannot be simply added. If a number of the allowances were simultaneously removed, the taxpayers concerned might as a result move into higher tax brackets, so that the revenue foregone would be underestimated by a simple addition of the estimates taken separately. Moreover, the removal of an allowance might affect behaviour; e.g., the removal of a wife's earned income allowance might cause fewer married women to go out to work, with an additional loss of revenue.

Section 2.

Table 5.6   *Rates of income tax levied in 1977/78 on the various slices of personal income remaining after the deduction of personal tax allowances*

Rate of IT	Slice of income after allowances (£)	Rate (%)
Basic rate	0–6,000	33 (34)[a]
Higher rates	6,001–7,000	40
	7,001–8,000	45
	8,001–9,000	50
	9,001–10,000	55
	10,001–12,000	60
	12,001–14,000	65
	14,001–16,000	70
	16,001–21,000	75
	21,000 and over	83
Additional rate[b] on investment income	0–1,500	nil
	1,501–2,000	10
	2,001 and over	15

[a] The bracketed figure of 34 per cent is the rate set in July 1977 for 1977/78. The unbracketed figure of 33 per cent is that which the Chancellor envisaged in his original budget statement and has been used in all the examples given in this Report.

[b] The nil rate base is increased to £2,000 for those over age 65.

Section 3.

Table 5.7   *A comparison, at the rates of tax ruling in 1977/78, of levels of investment income (column 1) with the level of earned income (column 2) needed to obtain the same given net-of-tax income (column 3)*

(1) Investment income (£)	(2) Net income after tax[a] (£)	(3) Earned income necessary to produce (2) (£)	(4) (1) as % of (3) (%)
2,000	1,620	1,925	103·9
3,000	2,140	2,701	111·1
4,000	2,660	3,478	115·0
5,000	3,180	4,254	117·5
6,000	3,700	5,030	119·3
7,000	4,220	5,806	120·6
8,000	4,770	6,627	120·7
9,000	5,070	7,083	127·1
10,000	5,420	7,667	130·4
11,000	5,720	8,182	134·4
13,000	6,220	9,100	142·9
15,000	6,620	9,900	151·5
17,000	6,920	10,778	157·7
22,000	7,420	11,750	187·2
26,000	7,500	11,950	217·6

[a] Assuming allowances of £1,000 and a taxpayer aged under 65.

Section 4.
National insurance contributions must be paid in respect of all employed persons earning more than £15 a week, the employee's contribution being 5·75 per cent and the employer's contribution 10·75 per cent on total earnings up to £105 a week. Women may pay a reduced employee's contribution of 2 per cent if they so elected before May 1977, after which date the possibility of electing to pay the lower rate ceased. Self-employed persons with an income in excess of £775 a year must contribute £2·66 a week in the case of men and £2·55 a week in the case of women, plus 8 per cent of their profits in the range between £1,750 and £5,500 a year.

Section 5.

Table 5.8   *Weekly rates for certain principal national insurance benefits at July 1977*

Unit	Retirement pension (£)	Sickness and unemployment benefit (£)
Couple	24·50[a]	20·90
Single person	15·30[a]	12·90
1st child	7·45[b]	4·05
Additional children	5·95[b]	2·55

[a] Age addition of 25p at 80 or over.   [b] Including family allowance.

Table 5.9   *The scale of supplementary benefits at July 1977*

Unit	Ordinary (£)	Long-term[a] (£)
Couple	20·65	24·85[b]
Single householder	12·70	15·70[b]
Any other person, aged:		
18 or over	10·15	12·60[b]
16–17	7·80	
13–15	6·50	
11–12	5·35	
5–10	4·35	
under 5	3·60	

[a] If a person is under retirement age and has received supplementary benefit for less than two years, or has to register for work, then the ordinary rate applies.

[b] With supplement of 25p if the claimant or wife is over 80.

The rates of supplementary benefits do not cover the claimant's rent and rates, which are paid in addition to the above scale. An average supplement for rent and rates for a couple with two children might be about £5·50 a week. This fact is of great importance in making a comparison between the rates of supplementary benefit and those for national insurance, to which no allowance for rent and rates is added.

Section 6.

Under the family income supplement scheme as operating at July 1977, a family supplement is paid equal to 50 per cent of the deficiency of the family's income below a 'prescribed amount', which increases with the size of the family, starting at £41·50 a week where there is one child in the family. There is a maximum supplement of £8·50 a week, which may be paid to the one-child family, this maximum rising by 50p for each additional child. The effect of this system in supplementing the incomes of families is illustrated in Table 5.9.

Table 5.10   *Family income supplement payable to families with different numbers of children and different weekly incomes*

No. of children in family	'Prescribed amount' (£)	Family income supplement (in £s) where the family weekly income[a] is:			
		£25	£35	£40	£50
1	41·50	8·25	3·25	0·75	nil
2	45·00	9·00[b]	5·00	2·50	nil
3	48·50	9·50[b]	6·75	4·25	nil
4	52·00	10·00[b]	8·50	6·00	1·00
5	55·50	10·50[b]	10·25	7·75	2·75
6	59·00	11·00[b]	11·00[b]	9·50	4·50

[a] Income including family allowances but before tax.

[b] The maxima permitted for families with the given number of children.

Section 7.

The schemes for rent and rate rebates and allowances grant to some families part relief from payment of rents and rates, the relief depending upon (i) the amount of rent or rates payable, (ii) the size of the family, and (iii) the income of the householder. The rent rebate is operated on the following principle. The starting point is the 'needs allowances', which at July 1977 is £23·05 a week for a single individual and £32·75 for a married couple, with an extra £5·35 for each dependent child. If the household's income equals the needs allowance it usually gets a rebate of 60 per cent of its rent. The rebate is then increased by 25p for every £1 by which its income is less than the needs allowance and decreased by 17p for every £1 above it.

The structure of the rate rebate scheme is similar. The basic rebate is 60 per cent of the rates. Then the ratepayer receives an additional rebate equal to 8 per cent of any excess of his needs allowance over his actual income, or suffers a reduction in the rent rebate equal to 6 per cent of any excess of his actual income over his needs allowances.

Table 5.10 illustrates for a married couple with two children at July 1977 the value of the weekly rent and rate rebates that would result at different levels of family income and of the rent and rates for their dwelling house. It is clear that such rent and rate rebates have become important features of society.

Table 5.11   *Rent and rate rebates for a married couple with two children at July 1977*

| | Weekly income of married couple with two children: | | | |
	£25	£35	£40	£50
Weekly rent	Weekly rent rebate or allowance (£)			
£2	2·00	2·00	2·00	nil
£5	5·00	5·00	3·86	1·89
£8	8·00[a]	6·91	5·66	3·69
Weekly rates	Weekly rate rebate (£)			
£1	1·00	1·00	0·88	0·21
£2	2·00	1·88	1·48	0·89
£3	3·00[b]	2·48	2·08	1·41

[a] The maximum rent rebates normally allowed are £6·50 generally and £8·00 in London.
[b] The maximum rate rebates normally allowed are £2·50 generally and £3·00 in London.

Section 8.

Table 5.12 *The varieties of conditions which attach to different means-tested benefits at July 1977*

Scheme	Tax unit	Period of assessment of resources	Items which may be ignored in computing the total resources of the claimant in assessing eligibility for benefit	Is income tax deductible in assessing the total resources of the claimant?	Effective marginal tax rate on any additional earnings (%)	Treatment of savings or capital in computing the total resources of the claimant
Supplementary benefit	Individual or couple, distinguishing between householders and non-householders; children under 16 included	1 week for current benefit	Disregards certain part-time earnings, disability pensions and certain other income up to £4 in total	Yes	100	Assumed rate of return. If capital amounts to £1,250 or more a weekly income of 25p is assumed for every complete £50 over £1,200
Family income supplement	Family including children	5 weeks[a] (or 2 months)[b] for 52 weeks' benefit	Disregards certain income: e.g. attendance and mobility allowance, first £4 of disability pension, children's resources, rent allowance	No	50	Actual interest received
Rent and rate rebates	Householders, children included	5 weeks[a] (or 2 months)[b] for 26 weeks' benefit (non-pensioners) or 52 weeks' benefit (pensioners)	Typically disregard the first £5 of wife's earnings, working children's pay, £4 of any war or disablement pension received, attendance allowance	No	Rent 17–25 Rates 6–8	Actual interest received

Table 5.12 *continued*

Scheme	Tax unit	Period of assessment of resources	Items which may be ignored in computing the total resources of the claimant in assessing eligibility for benefit	Is income tax deductible in assessing the total resources of the claimant?	Effective marginal tax rate on any additional earnings (%)	Treatment of savings or capital in computing the total resources of the claimant
Free prescriptions	As for supplementary benefit	Benefit paid for 3 months	Disregards national insurance contributions, rent and rates, working expenses, hire-purchase payments, and first £4 of other income	Yes	—	As for supplementary benefit
Free school meals	Family	3 weeks for 52 weeks' benefit	Disregards national insurance contributions, rent and rates, working expenses, life assurance premiums, superannuation, cost of necessary daily help	Yes	—	Actual interest included

[a] If paid weekly.
[b] If paid monthly.

Section 9.

Table 5.13   *Comparison of the levels of various benefits and of the tax thresholds (in £s per week) at July 1977*

Unit	Tax[a] threshold		Pensions	Sickness and[f,g] unemployment benefits	Supplementary benefit[b]		Rent and rates rebates: needs level	Family income supplement: prescribed amount	School meals: needs level
	Under 65	Over 65			Short term[e]	Long term[i]			
Single person	15·48	20·77	15·30	12·90	10·15	12·60	—	—	—
Single household	15·48	20·77	15·30	12·90	12·70	15·70	23·05	—	—
Couple	23·56	32·60	24·50	20·90	20·65	24·85	32·75	—	—
Couple and 1 child	28·33 c,d to 29·58	37·37 c,d to 38·62	31·95 h	24·95 h	24·25 c,h to 28·45	28·45 c,h to 32·65	38·10	41·50	27·55
Additional children	4·77 c,d to 6·02	5·77 c,d to 7·02	7·45 h	4·05 h	3·60 to	7·80 c,h	5·35	3·50	6·15

[a] Tax threshold represents: the weekly level of tax-free income calculated on the basis of personal allowance.
[b] To supplementary benefit levels should be added an allowance for rent and rates.
[c] Levels depend on the age of children.
[d] Child allowances have been increased by the tax-free child benefits of £1·80 for the first child and £1·50 for additional children.
[e] Short term benefit applies to those under retirement age who have received benefit for less than two years and to those required to register for work.
[f] Where applicable, those receiving these benefits may also receive supplementary benefit to raise their income to supplementary benefit level.
[g] Earnings-related supplements may also be received for the first six months.
[h] These levels of benefits include child benefits of £1·00 for the first child and £1·50 for additional children.
[i] With a supplement of 25p if the claimant or wife is over 80.

Appendix 5.2　An International Comparison of Rates of Direct Taxation and of Social Security Contributions and Benefits

Table 5.14　*Ratio of tax receipts from all taxes (including social security contributions) to gross national product, 1974 (in %)*

Country	Ratio	Country	Ratio
Denmark	46·7	Canada	34·8
Norway	45·3	New Zealand	32·7
Netherlands	45·2	United States	28·9
Sweden	44·2	Australia	27·2
Luxembourg	40·8	Switzerland	26·2
Austria	38·1	Japan	22·2
Belgium	38·1		
West Germany	37·6	*Non-Europe average*	28·7
France	37·5		
Finland	36·3		
United Kingdom	35·6	Greece	22·4
Ireland	32·4	Portugal	22·3
Italy	31·9	Spain	18·8
Industrialised Europe average	39·2	*Developing Europe average*	21·2

Source: Revenue Statistics of Member Countries, 1965–74 (Paris: OECD, 1976) to which reference should be made for details of definition and coverage.

Table 5.15 Ratio of tax receipts from various sources to total tax receipts, 1974 (in %)

Country	Goods and services taxes	Income taxes		Social Security taxes		Property taxes		Wealth taxes	Gifts and inheritance taxes
		Personal	Corporate	Employee	Employer	Household	Corporations		
Austria	35·8	24·2	4·2	11·5	12·5		6·8	1·0	0·2
Belgium	28·3	29·4	7·8	9·0	20·6	—	—	—	0·7
Denmark	31·7	53·4	3·2	0·5	0·8	—	—	0·4	0·3
Finland	36·1	42·6	4·8	4·1	10·1	—	—	0·7	0·2
France	33·7	10·8	8·3	7·6	32·0	0·2		—	0·6
West Germany	25·3	30·5	4·7	13·5	21·4	0·6	0·4	1·3	0·1
Ireland	47·7	22·9	6·5	0·5	6·7	8·3		—	1·7
Italy	33·8	15·2	5·2	0·8	33·8	0·1		—	0·3
Luxembourg	18·4	26·1	21·3	10·9	15·3	0·6		2·5	0·4
Netherlands	23·3	27·6	6·7	18·8	18·0			0·6	0·5
Norway	36·6	27·5	3·4	11·2	18·5	0·4		1·8	0·3
Sweden	27·0	45·0	3·4	2·7	15·8			0·4	0·3
Switzerland	21·4	34·7	8·1	14·1	10·1	0·6		4·8	0·7
United Kingdom	27·1	35·2	8·1	6·9	9·5	4·7	5·7	—	1·3
Canada	32·2	35·0	12·8		9·1	8·1		—	0·3
New Zealand	22·0	54·5	14·4			6·5		—	1·3
United States	18·2	34·0	11·0	9·3	13·0	7·5	4·6	—	1·6
Australia	29·3	40·1	14·7			5·2		—	2·0
Japan	16·9	24·2	23·3	7·8	10·6			—	1·0
Greece	36·0	10·6	6·2	8·5	18·8			—	2·4
Portugal	37·2	8·3		8·8	18·8			—	1·2
Spain	26·9	12·9	8·5	8·8	35·9			—	0·9

Note: Dash indicates zero rate; blank spaces are where figures were not available.
Source: As Table 5.14

Table 5.16   *Comparison of income tax thresholds and marginal rates on earned income for a married man with two children, tax year beginning 1975*

Country	Tax threshold[a] (£)	Initial rate (%)	Maximum rate (%)
Belgium	1,290	14·0 (14·8)[b]	72·0 (75·6)[b]
Denmark	1,670	14·4 (35·0)[b]	39·6 (60·2)[b]
France	3,120	5	53·5
West Germany	1,800	22	56
Ireland	1,410	26	70
Italy	1,320	10	72
Luxembourg	3,740	18	57
Netherlands	2,300	20	72
United Kingdom	1,383	35	83
Sweden	1,150	7 (30)[b]	56 (79)[b]

[a] Based on exchange rate at 8 March 1976.
[b] Rates in brackets include local taxes.
Source: Hansard, vol. 908, Written Answers, col. 247 (25 March 1976).

Table 5.17   *Comparison of average tax rates (including employee social security contributions) on the income of a married man with two children, tax year beginning 1975 (in %)*

Country	Income levels in terms of UK average earnings[a]		
	Average	2 × average	3 × average
Belgium	17·16 (17·59)[b]	24·42 (25·4)[b]	29·18 (30·58)[b]
Denmark	6·69 (16·52)[b]	15·02 (31·13)[b]	23·96 (42·6)[b]
France	8·34	11·28	13.78
West Germany	22·20	26·38	28·45
Ireland	20·83	32·43	43·54
Italy	15·60	22·30	26·42
Luxembourg	8·34	15·91	22·71
Netherlands	23·56	29·26	33·98
United Kingdom	25·75	32·30	39·89

[a] Average earnings as estimated for August 1976 converted at exchange rates for 26 October 1976.
[b] Rates in brackets include local taxes.
Source: Hansard, vol. 918, Written Answers, col. 689 (4 November 1976).

6 Indexation for Inflation

THE CASE FOR INDEXATION

In any modern developed economy transactions take place through the medium of money, values are expressed in monetary terms, and – like all other transactions – tax bases are measured and taxes are levied in monetary forms and expressed in monetary values. No intolerable problems arise as a result provided that the general level of money prices – i.e. the real value of the monetary unit in terms of goods and services in general – is reasonably constant. But when the general level of prices is rapidly inflated (and in particular when the future rates of inflation are difficult to predict) very important inefficiencies and inequities can result. The resulting distortions to the tax system are only a part, though an important part, of this process. In the introduction to their Final Report in 1955, the Royal Commission on the Taxation of Profits and Income[1] emphasised this point in the following way:

'One point upon which we must make our position clear is the question of monetary inflation. It lies at the base of our whole subject and it directly affects several of the topics with which we deal. We have taken it as our general premise that there will not be any marked decrease or increase in the purchasing power of money in the United Kingdom. It would be absurd to assume a complete stability of purchasing power in the future, nor do we need to do so for any recommendations that we make. Nor again do we require to assume that there will be no sudden and temporary variations. But if we could not take it as our premise that stability in purchasing power is the normal thing to be expected, we think that our review would be beating the air, for there would be lacking a condition that is a necessary assumption upon which to build either a satisfactory tax structure or a satisfactory distribution of the total burden of tax.'

The monetary unit in the United Kingdom has in fact lost half its real purchasing power in the five years since 1972. With the rates of monetary inflation that have recently been experienced in all modern developed economies, and in a particularly marked degree in the United Kingdom, it is no longer sensible to consider the tax structure on the Radcliffe Commission's assumption of a basic constancy of the general level of prices. A reasonable tax structure must be considered in real terms and not in monetary terms, and this implies adjustment of the monetary value of any tax base in such a way as to measure the real value of the tax base.

In Chapters 4 and 5 we have considered some anomalies in the UK tax structure which would exist even if the general level of prices were more or

---

[1] Royal Commission on Taxation of Income and Profits (Chairman, Lord Radcliffe), Cmd. 9474, HMSO, 1955.

less constant. Some of these anomalies are compounded, and other anomalies are introduced, when the tax structure is set in terms of a monetary unit which is rapidly losing its real value.

Accordingly, in this chapter we shall consider (i) the general nature of the problems involved in the indexation of a tax structure to allow for price inflation; (ii) the present relationships in the United Kingdom between the tax structure and the inflationary process; and (iii) the measures which would have to be taken to remove the existing tax anomalies which are due to price inflation.

There are two quite separate types of problem involved in designing any system of indexation of a tax structure against the ravages of inflation. We shall call these the problems of *'bracket indexation'* and *'indexation for capital–income adjustment'* respectively.

BRACKET INDEXATION

TAXES ON CONSUMPTION AND WEALTH

The need for bracket indexation arises in the case of a progressive tax system once the monetary value of the tax base is clearly defined. We shall illustrate the problem in the case of a progressive tax on consumption expenditure or of a progressive tax on the holding of wealth. In both cases the fact that the price level is higher this year than last year does not basically affect the monetary measurement of the tax base.

If Mr Smith spends £2,000 on consumption goods this year, his consumption expenditure this year is £2,000 regardless of the fact that prices this year may be higher this year than last year. But the real value of his £2,000 of consumption does depend upon the price level. If a unit of consumption goods costs £1, his real consumption is 2,000 units; if the price of consumption goods has risen to £2 a unit, then his real consumption is only 1,000 units. If the tax on consumption expenditure is at a constant proportionate rate, no problem arises. If a 10 per cent tax is to be paid on the consumption whatever its level, then it makes no difference whether the tax base is reckoned in money terms or in real terms; in both cases Mr Smith will have to give up 10 per cent of his potential consumption.

But if the tax is a progressive one, then the tax base needs bracket indexation. Suppose that in year 1 there is a tax threshold for the consumption expenditure tax of £1,000 and that between year 1 and year 2 the price of consumption goods goes up by 10 per cent. Then in year 2 the first £1,100 of consumption expenditure must be exempt from tax in order to provide the same tax threshold in terms of the real volume of consumption that is exempt from tax. Each bracket point at which tax starts or at which one rate of tax gives place to a higher rate of tax must be multiplied by some general price index in order to maintain an unchanged rate of progression of the tax in real terms.

Another tax base which would need only bracket indexation of this kind is a progressive tax on the ownership of wealth. If Mr Smith's wealth is worth £100,000 at this moment, it is worth £100,000 regardless of what the price level was a year ago. The amount of real goods that it is worth now will depend upon the present price level; and if it is desired to have a progressive rate structure which applies higher rates of tax to those with larger amounts of wealth, then, to maintain this progressive rate structure in real terms, tax brackets in the schedule for different rates of wealth tax must be multiplied each year by some general price index.

TAXES ON TRANSFERS OF WEALTH

In Chapter 3 we have referred to the possibility of using as a tax base not the amount of wealth held but the amount of wealth transferred by gift or inheritance from one owner to another. If the tax is a progressive tax, then bracket indexation will be needed in order to maintain the progressive structure of the tax schedule in real terms, just as it will be needed for a progressive tax on consumption or on the holding of wealth. But the progression in a tax on the transfer of wealth may be based on the cumulative total amount of wealth which the donor has given away up to date over the whole of his life (as in the case of the present UK capital transfer tax) or on the cumulative total amount of wealth which the donee has received up to date over the whole of his life (as it would be with an accessions tax of the type discussed in Chapter 15). If there were a progressive tax of this kind, then when a capital transfer is made the cumulative total of past gifts made by the donor (or received by the donee) must be multiplied by the rise in the price index since those gifts were made, in order to calculate what is the present monetary value of the past gifts made; and the tax brackets in the scale of progression of the tax must also each year be subject to bracket indexation.

This is a special form of bracket indexation. There is no doubt of the tax base. On the occasion of each gift it is the amount of that gift; and if the tax were a proportionate one there would be no occasion for any indexation. If 10 per cent of every gift were to be taken in tax, that would be the end of the problem. But if the tax were a progressive one based on the cumulative total of gifts made, the bracket into which any new gift should fall for the purpose of the progressive scale would depend not only upon the present real value of the gift itself but also upon the present real value of money gifts made in the past. These must also be the subject of bracket indexation, i.e. be multiplied by the rise in the general level of prices between the dates of the past gifts and the time of the new gift.

INDEXATION FOR CAPITAL–INCOME ADJUSTMENT

When an income base (as distinct from an expenditure base) is considered for progressive taxation, bracket indexation is still needed in order to ensure that, once the taxpayer's monetary income has been satisfactorily measured, any tax threshold or any tax brackets for higher rates of a progressive income tax are measured in real terms. But there is in this case another problem of indexation which must first be tackled in order to determine in inflationary conditions what is the proper measure of money income to act as the tax base to which the rate schedules as adjusted by bracket indexation should be applied. We call this previous process 'indexation for capital–income adjustment'. The need for it arises whether the tax system is a proportionate one or a progressive one; it is a question of what is the proper size of the income which should form the tax base itself.

In Chapter 3 we have described two principles on which a taxpayer's income might be defined, namely definition A and definition B. The problem of indexation for capital–income adjustment can most readily be explained in terms of definition A, which defines a man's income in any year as the amount which he could spend on consumption during the year without subtracting from or adding to his capital wealth in the process. If it is wished to think in real, as contrasted with monetary, terms, then the proviso in the above definition must read 'without subtracting from or adding to his *real* capital wealth in the process'.

MONEY DEBTS

Consider Mr Smith who has £1,000 in money deposited with a bank or building society on which he is paid £150 a year in interest (i.e. a rate of interest of 15 per cent). If the price of the goods which he purchases is constant, then he can spend £150 this year and end up with an unchanged capital sum of £1,000 with an unchanged real value. But if prices rise by 10 per cent in the course of the year, he must end up with £1,100 on deposit at the bank or building society in order to have maintained the real value of his capital intact. Of his interest of £150 he must save £100 for addition to his deposit account in order to maintain his real capital intact, so that the amount which he could then spend is only £50 and not £150. After this indexation for capital–income adjustment Mr Smith's money income on definition A is only £50; and this is the sum which should be taxed on a rate schedule, which in turn needs to be adjusted by bracket indexation in order to express the relevant real values for any progressive income tax.

This indexation for capital–income adjustment will, of course, operate in reverse if Mr Jones, instead of lending £1,000 at 15 per cent interest, has borrowed £1,000 on a house mortgage at 15 per cent interest. During the year Mr Jones will pay £150 in money interest. If he does not repay any of the money capital sum, he will still owe £1,000 at the end of the year. But if all prices rise by 10 per cent, his real debt will remain unchanged only if he increases his money debt from £1,000 to £1,100. In effect he is relieved of £100 of real debt by the rise in prices. His net real capital wealth (after the deduction of real debt) rises by this amount. Of the £150 interest paid to the building society only £50 is a cost against his real income; the other £100 is offset by a real addition to his income, which is saved and used to reduce his real indebtedness.

Thus in the circumstances described in this example the interest received by the creditor Smith and the interest paid by the debtor Jones after indexation for capital–income adjustment is not £150 but only £50.

We have illustrated the principle of indexation for capital–income adjustments for the assessment of the true interest on money debts.[2] But wherever income from capital is involved, a similar problem of adjustment may arise. We enumerate three more cases in which such adjustment is typically necessary.

1 Capital gains

The first case is for making a distinction between real capital gains and monetary capital gains for the purpose of a capital gains tax. Suppose, for example, that Mr Brown owns stock exchange securities that have gone up by 20 per cent in value in the course of the year. If the general level of prices of goods and services has gone up by 10 per cent over the same period, then the first 10 per cent in the appreciation of Mr Brown's securities is needed in order to maintain the real value of his capital. Only the remaining 10 per cent is a taxable capital gain after indexation for capital–income adjustment.

2 Stocks

Or suppose that Mr Brown is a businessman and it is the value of his stock in trade that has gone up by 20 per cent. If, as before, the general level of prices of goods and services has risen by 10 per cent, then the first 10 per cent in the increased value of the stock in trade is needed to keep the real value of Mr Brown's capital intact. Only the other 10 per cent of the increased value of stocks is to be regarded as part of his business income or profit after

[2] A rather special case of the absence of capital–income adjustment for debts occurs in the UK tax system in the difference between the treatment of income tax under Schedule E (in which case, as a result of the pay-as-you-earn (PAYE) scheme, tax is levied on income as it is received) and under Schedule D Case I and II (in which case the tax payable on 1 January and 1 July in any year is based on profits made in the accounting year which ended during the tax year to the previous 5 April). However, when a trade or profession commences, the profits of one accounting year serve as the basis for two tax years. Because of this, when incomes are unchanged from year to year, the measure of the deferment enjoyed by the Schedule D taxpayer compared with a Schedule E taxpayer, whose income accrues evenly throughout the year, is only the difference between the average payment dates of approximately 30 September in one case and 1 April following in the other, i.e. approximately six months. It should, however, be remembered that Schedule D profits are in general computed on an accruals basis, so that the Schedule D taxpayer may not receive his income as early as the Schedule E taxpayer in receipt of a steady income. The deferral effect is more marked when incomes fluctuate, because the Schedule E taxpayer will experience the change in tax payable as those fluctuations occur whereas the Schedule D taxpayer will not feel the change until some time later (e.g. if the accounting year ends on 31 March, at 1 January and 1 July – nine and fifteen months later respectively; if it ends on 30 April, at 1 January and 1 July – twenty and twenty-six months later respectively).

Thus, comparing Schedule D and Schedule E taxpayers with like income, when income is steady there is up to six months' deferment of tax on the whole amount; when there is an increase in income there is in addition deferment of tax *on the increase* (but not on the principal); when there is a decrease in income there will be delay before the Schedule D taxpayer's tax payments are reduced. To the limited extent that there is such deferment, there is an interest benefit to the Schedule D taxpayer.

indexation for capital–income adjustment. It is, moreover, worth noting that this is in principle true whatever may be the reason for the 20 per cent increase in the money value of Mr Brown's stock in trade. It may be, for example, that the volume of Mr Brown's stocks has remained constant but that the price of the goods that he stocks has risen by 20 per cent whereas the prices of goods and services in general have risen only by 10 per cent. In that case Mr Brown has made a real profit because his goods have gone up in value relatively to the value of the generality of real goods and services. He could in fact have consumed or run down the volume of his stocks and still have maintained the real value of his wealth intact in terms of its purchasing power over the generality of goods and services.

3 *The depreciation of fixed capital*
If a businessman has invested in the purchase of a machine which loses its value because of wear and tear or obsolescence, he must deduct from the annual yield on the machine an allowance for the depreciation in its value before calculating his true net profit. Capital–income adjustment requires that from the gross *money* yield or profit on the machine there should be deducted an amount of *money* which, when it has been reinvested in some new asset, will maintain the *real* value of the assets of the business intact. In the absence of inflation this allowance for true economic depreciation may be approximated by deducting in each year either a given sum (straight line depreciation) or a given proportion of the remaining value of the machine (diminishing balance depreciation). The result will be a series of annual depreciation allowances which in the absence of inflation are related to the historic money cost of the machine. If, however, the general level of prices is rising by, say, 10 per cent a year, this series of annual money depreciation allowances must itself be multiplied by the general price index, which is rising by 10 per cent a year, in order to restore each year the given loss of real value due to the machine's depreciation. Thus in times of a general inflation of prices depreciation on an historic cost basis will overestimate the businessman's profit (i.e. the income from his business which he can take out and spend on consumption without impairing the real value of his business assets). Some form of depreciation which makes allowance for the rising money value of the real cost of depreciation must be adopted. If true economic profit is to be the basis for an income tax or a corporation tax, indexation of some kind for capital–income (in this case for capital–profit) adjustment is necessary.

TWO ALTERNATIVE DEFINITIONS OF INCOME

We have so far considered the problem of indexation for capital–income adjustment in terms of taxable income defined on what in Chapter 3 we have called definition A. But in that chapter we have also described an alternative principle for defining a person's taxable income (definition B), namely the amount which he could in any year spend on consumption and leave himself at the end of the year in a position to maintain that level of consumption indefinitely in the future. We argued that this would be in principle a much better tax base if it were feasible. But (as pointed out in Chapter 3) the level of this year's income on definition B depends essentially upon expectations about future developments.

The application of indexation for capital–income adjustment would in the case of definition B involve some process whereby a calculation was made of the amount of *money* which a taxpayer could spend on consumption this year and leave himself at the end of the year with sufficient capital to maintain indefinitely in the future a corresponding *real* level of consumption; and for this purpose expectations of the future rate of inflation and not merely the current rate of inflation would be of crucial importance.

In Appendix 6.1 we give a numerical example of a man who has a fixed annual interest of £150 in conditions in which the current rate of price inflation is 10 per cent a year. In our numerical example, if this rate of inflation is expected to continue indefinitely, his taxable income this year on definition B turns out to be £50; but if the inflation rate is expected to fall to zero in the near future, his taxable income this year is £137. The difference is very marked, and the reason for it is easy to understand. If the rate of inflation is expected to continue, the taxpayer must plan to save a substantial fraction of his interest every year in the future in order every year in the future to allow for the erosion by inflation of the real value of his interest. If, however, the rate of inflation is expected to fall to zero, then the taxpayer will in future years be able to spend the whole of his interest on consumption without any further decline in its real value. Thus he need save out of his original interest this year only an amount which is sufficient to cope with one year's erosion of the value of his original interest of £150.

The conclusion is, we believe, inescapable that uncertainties about future rates of price inflation greatly increase the difficulties of applying anything in the nature of a definition B income principle for the calculation of a tax base. Expectations of the real levels of consumption which taxpayers in different situations could hope to maintain indefinitely become hopelessly uncertain when future rates of inflation are uncertain. Indexation for capital–income adjustment for a definition A income principle for the calculation of a tax base involves a number of complications which we shall consider in later chapters when we come to deal with particular taxes, but it is not a hopeless matter. Inflationary considerations thus reinforce the conclusion reached in Chapter 3 that the real choice lies between a definition A income-tax base and a consumption-expenditure tax base rather than between a definition B income-tax base and a consumption-expenditure tax base. Some reasons have been given in Chapter 3 for preferring, if this were the choice, the consumption-expenditure tax base; and these reasons are reinforced by the fact that, whereas a definition A income-tax base would require indexation for capital–income adjustment as well as bracket indexation, the consumption-expenditure tax base requires only bracket indexation.

THE PRESENT POSITION IN THE UNITED KINGDOM

We turn now to a short account of the present relationships between tax structure and inflation in the United Kingdom.

DEPRECIATION ALLOWANCES

As far as depreciation allowances for fixed capital equipment are concerned, no capital–income adjustments are made in those cases in which depreciation allowances are still reckoned for tax purposes on conventional accounting principles. But (as explained in Chapter 4) the introduction of 100 per cent capital allowances has relieved the situation in respect of plant and machinery; and these allowances are now of great importance, representing some 75 per cent of all capital allowances in 1975. In these cases the whole of the cost of the machinery or plant is written off immediately for tax purposes, leaving no time for inflation to create a disparity between historic cost and current cost. In fact, these 100 per cent capital allowances turn the income base for tax into what is effectively an expenditure base in the way discussed later in Chapter 8 (pp. 154–159); and (as we have seen) capital–income adjustment is not needed in the case of an expenditure-based tax.

STOCKS

Special measures have been taken to cope with the increases in stock values which arise only through inflation. This is presently achieved by arbitrarily regarding part of the increase in stock values as representing additional investment to the extent of a fixed percentage of profit; the balance is then deducted from profit as representing the adjustment for inflated stock prices. Relief in this form is only temporary, although the principle of the relief is to be maintained.

OTHER CAPITAL–INCOME ADJUSTMENTS

But no other capital–income adjustments for inflationary effects have been introduced. Thus capital gains are still calculated in terms of money gains, and no inflation allowances are made to convert rates of money interest on debts into rates of real interest.

MONEY DEBTS

The potential importance of this failure to make capital–income adjustment is illustrated in Table 6.1. In line 1 we give the level of the bank rate or of the Bank of England's minimum lending rate on the average over each year for 1971 to 1976. In lines 2 we give these levels of money interest after deduction of income tax (including investment income surcharge) at tax rates of 0, 45 and 98 per cent. In line 3 we show the percentage increase in the general level of prices over the year, so that to maintain the real value of any money asset intact a percentage of the initial capital value equal to the percentage in line 3 would have had to be saved and added to the nominal money value of the asset. The real rate of return after tax on the nominal money interest, and after allowing for the reduction in the real value of the asset due to inflation, is therefore shown by the figures in lines 4, i.e. by the figures in lines 2 minus the figure in line 3.

Table 6.1　*Money and real rates of return on money debts, 1971–76 (in % a year)*

		1971	1972	1973	1974	1975	1976
1	Bank rate or minimum lending rate	5·92	5·91	9·86	11·93	10·79	11·77
2	Post-tax money rate of return to taxpayer whose marginal rate of IT[a] (including investment income surcharge) was: 0%	5·92	5·91	9·86	11·93	10·79	11·77
	45%	3·26	3·25	5·42	6·56	5·94	6·47
	98%	0·12	0·12	0·20	0·24	0·22	0·23
3	% increase in the retail price index during the year (1st quarter on 1st quarter)	8·6	8·0	8·0	12·8	20·3	22·5
4	Post-tax real rate of return to taxpayer whose marginal tax rate[a] was: 0%	−2·68	−2·09	+1·86	−0·87	−9·51	−10·73
	45%	−5·34	−4·75	−2·58	−6·24	−14·36	−16·03
	98%	−8·48	−7·88	−7·80	−12·56	−20·08	−22·27

[a] The tax rates of 45 and 98 per cent are used for illustrative purposes only and do not reflect the rates actually ruling in each particular year.

The real post-tax rates of return in lines 4 show frighteningly high *negative* figures. These figures are, of course, calculated on a definition A income base. As we have seen (p. 105), *if the rate of inflation were expected to be only temporary*, the adoption of the more reasonable, but impracticable, definition B for the income base would show a very much smaller effect of a given rate of inflation in depressing the real rate of return. The situation revealed in Table 6.1 is thus a truly disturbing one, unless present rates of inflation are expected to be rapidly reduced to very moderate levels.

BRACKET INDEXATION

In the United Kingdom there has been no formal bracket indexation for the personal allowances or other tax brackets under the income tax scheme, although as a matter of fact personal allowances under the income tax have been raised during the recent inflationary years. In Chapter 5 we have discussed some of the relationships between personal tax allowances and tax rates under the income tax on the one hand and the whole range of social security and similar benefits, whether means-tested or not, on the other hand; and we have considered some of the reasons why the income tax arrangements and the system of social security benefits must both be regarded as parts of a single general tax system (a theme developed further in Chapter 13). What we have called bracket indexation is in fact just as relevant for social security benefits as it is for tax allowances. If it is desired to maintain the real tax threshold constant, this must be adjusted by a general price index; and similarly, if it is desired to keep the real value of, say, unemployment benefit constant, this must be adjusted by a general price index. In fact social security benefits have of recent years been more or less formally indexed, in the sense that they have been subjected to regular periodic review for adjustment to offset the effects of inflation.

PRICE MOVEMENTS

Table 6.2 illustrates some of the developments in the United Kingdom which relate to this problem of bracket indexation. The first section of the table shows what has happened to certain price indices over the ten years from 1966/67 to 1976/77. The first three of these indices all show that prices in general have risen by between 166 and 182 per cent over these ten years. Later in this chapter we shall return to the differences in the movements of these three indices. For the moment it is sufficient to stress the general order of magnitude of the price change which they all disclose.

The fourth price index shown on Table 6.2, namely the average money earnings of men in manufacturing, may be taken to represent changes in the money price of a unit of labour. This money price has risen by a quite different order of magnitude, namely by 240 per cent, over the ten-year period since 1966/67. There is a very easy, straightforward explanation of this phenomenon. Suppose that real output per head were rising by 2 per cent a year. Then it might be expected that real earnings in terms of final product would rise by 2 per cent a year or, in other words, that money earnings relatively to the price of the final product would rise by 2 per cent a year. If this had happened over the ten years from 1966/67 to 1976/77, the prices of final products and the money earnings of wage earners would have moved relatively to each other by more or less exactly the degree indicated in the first section of Table 6.2.

TAX ALLOWANCES AND SOCIAL BENEFITS

The second and third sections of Table 6.2 show the extent to which the main

Table 6.2 *Prices, tax allowances, and social benefits: values in 1976/77 as percentage of values in 1966/67*

	%
Prices	
Retail price index	266
Pensioner price index (1-person household)	282
Price of gross domestic product at factor cost	274
Average monthly earnings (male; manufacturing industry)	340
Income tax allowances	
Single person (earned income)	260[a,b]
Married couple (earned income)	248[a,b]
Child: under 11	203[a]
11–16	186[a]
over 16	172[a]
Starting level for higher rates of tax (single person; earned income)	115
Social benefits	
Unemployment benefit: single adult	323
married couple	322
Retirement pension: single adult	383
married couple	377
Supplementary benefit (standard rate): single adult	314
married couple	311

[a] The base figures for 1966/67 have been taken as $\frac{9}{7}$ of the actual personal tax allowances in order to incorporate the allowance of $\frac{2}{9}$ of earned income.

[b] In 1969 and 1970 there were sharp increases in these personal allowances in order to offset some part of the effect of the elimination in those years of the reduced rates of tax for the lower bands of income. Part of the increase in these allowances between 1966/67 and 1976/77 should be ascribed to this cause rather than treated merely as a response to price inflation.

personal allowances under the income tax and some of the main social security benefits have moved. There is one very notable feature of this table. The tax allowances have moved more or less in line with the price indices of finished products; they have fallen behind a little, but not by very much. The social security benefits on the other hand have moved more or less in line with average earnings. The personal tax allowances have thus become lower relatively to average earnings or average income per head of the population,[3] even though they have been virtually indexed to keep their

[3] It has been estimated that the tax threshold as a percentage of average male earnings in manufacturing industry has moved in the following way since the end of World War II:

Year	Single male	Married couple with 3 children (%)
1949/50	39·4	123·5
1966/67	26·8	86·5
1976/77	21·9	57·1

Source: Hansard. vol. 911, Written Answers, col. 568 (19 May 1976).

absolute real value; and the result has been that an increasing proportion of the population has been brought into the income tax net.[4] As to social security payments, the fact that over the ten years to 1976/77 the levels of supplementary benefits, and indeed of the other main benefits, have been kept more or less in a constant relation to average earnings is perhaps an indication that poverty is regarded as a relative matter.

One very significant tax problem has arisen as a result of these divergent movements. The levels of social security benefits have in some cases now overtaken the levels of the tax thresholds for persons otherwise in similar circumstances. We illustrate by taking what is perhaps an extreme example. In 1976/77 the long term rate of supplementary benefit for a married couple (i.e. for a couple which had been on such benefit for more than two years) was £24·85 a week. This excludes the cost of the couple's rent and rates, which might amount to some £5 a week, making a total of the order of £30. At the same time the tax threshold for a married couple was £20·90 a week. Such couples, if they were earning, might well be receiving some tax-free benefits (e.g. rent and rate rebates or family income supplement), but even so some would start paying tax at an income level which, by the supplementary benefit criterion, would be considered markedly below the poverty line.

This phenomenon has become a notable and important feature of the present tax structure in the United Kingdom; but it is basically a phenomenon not of inflation but rather of economic growth. Even if the cost of living had remained absolutely constant, nevertheless increased output per head at 2 per cent a year would naturally have been associated with a rise in money earnings of 2 per cent a year. If personal tax allowances had remained unchanged (because they were geared to the constant cost of living) while social security benefits had risen consistently at 2 per cent a year (because they were geared to average earnings), benefits would sooner or later inevitably have overtaken the tax thresholds. Nevertheless this phenomenon is in one respect extremely relevant for the problem of indexation against inflation. Later in this chapter we shall consider which price index should be used for such indexation; and it is clear from the present discussion that trouble can arise if different indices are chosen for the indexation of different parts of the economic and tax structures.

SPECIFIC EXCISE DUTIES

There remains, however, one other marked change of tax structure in the United Kingdom which has occurred in recent years, basically as a result of inflation and not of economic growth, and which does raise a problem of bracket indexation of a fairly straightforward kind. Many of the most important indirect taxes in the United Kingdom – such as the duties on beer,

---

[4] The number of tax units paying income tax has risen from 19·69 million to 20·8 million, and the number liable to higher rates (surtax or higher rates of income tax) from 402,000 to 1·4 million over the ten years between 1966/67 and 1976/77.

wines, spirits and tobacco, which are important revenue raisers – are imposed as specific duties and not as *ad valorem* duties. That is, the tax is at a rate of so-and-so many pence per physical unit (i.e. per gallon or per pound in weight) rather than at a given percentage of the value of the commodity in question. If the specific duty is not raised but the general level of all other money prices is inflated, then the real burden or incidence of the specific duty is reduced.

Table 6.3 shows how some of the main specific duties have changed over the ten years from 1966/67 to 1976/77. The table shows that these duties have risen over this ten-year period considerably less than the general level of money prices; and as a result the proportion of total tax revenue raised by these indirect taxes[5] has fallen from 30 to 19 per cent over the period.

Table 6.3   *Specific duties on tobacco, beer, spirits and petrol compared with retail price index: values in 1976/77 as percentage of values in 1966/67*

	%
Tobacco (basic duty per lb)	193[a, b]
Beer (duty per pint)	226[a]
Spirits (duty per proof gallon)	192[a]
Petrol (duty per gallon)	188[a]
Retail price index[c]	266

[a] Allowing for the reduction in duties on the introduction of VAT by adding that reduction back to existing duties.

[b] Allowing for the reduction in duty on the introduction of the tobacco products duty (20 per cent of the retail price on cigarettes) by adding that reduction back to the existing duty.

[c] See Table 6.2.

It would be possible to deal with this phenomenon either (i) by subjecting these specific duties to what we have called bracket indexation, or (ii) by the alternative process of transforming these specific duties into *ad valorem* duties which levied a charge as a percentage of the value of the commodities themselves. These two procedures would have the same real results if the prices of these commodities as a result of inflation rose in step with the general level of prices. But the duties on these products make up a very large part of the total cost of the commodities to the consumer; and as a result of this a change in the cost of these commodities relatively to other money prices and costs would have a very different effect on the consumer according to whether the duty was expressed at an *ad valorem* rate or as an indexed specific duty. For example, a small rise in the cost of producing beer relatively to the price of other commodities would cause a much smaller rise in the

[5] Total customs and excise duties, excluding purchase tax, VAT, import deposits, import levies, and EEC agricultural levies.

price of beer to the consumer if an indexed specific duty rather than an *ad valorem* duty were charged. It might well be preferable to impose on the consumer in such a case a tax which remained fixed in terms of the generality of goods consumed (the indexed specific duty) rather than a tax which was fixed in terms of the particular good itself (the *ad valorem* duty). Moreover, the tax revenue would in this case be much less sensitive to accidental specific factors which affected the costs of these particular products.

FUTURE POSSIBILITIES

In the light of the preceding analysis of the nature of the problems involved in indexation for inflation and of the present position in the United Kingdom, we turn to a consideration of what further developments of policy are desirable to cope with these problems.

THE CONTAINMENT OF INFLATION

We start by emphasising the desirability of putting an end to general price inflation in the interests of the tax structure. It is not part of our task to consider by what means and how quickly general price inflation can be contained; but it is part of our task to emphasise the important difficulties which stand in the way of designing an efficient and just tax structure as a result of continuing inflation and, in particular, of uncertainties about the future rate of inflation. A currency with more or less stable purchasing power is important for many other reasons; but one important reason is, as the Radcliffe Commission emphasised, that it provides a firm foundation for building a reliable tax structure.

A SHIFT TO ALTERNATIVE TAX BASES

A second general conclusion is that, if we have to learn to live with inflation or the possibility of inflation, then tax bases (such as consumption expenditure or the holding or transfer of wealth) which do not raise the problems of indexation for capital–income adjustment have an added attraction in comparison with tax bases (such as income) which do require such indexation.

We have already outlined the general nature of the main measures which it would be necessary to introduce for capital–income adjustment if an income base were selected for direct taxation. We discuss these measures in detail in later chapters of this Report as they become relevant in our consideration of the different taxes, and in particular in Chapter 7 when we consider the problems involved in designing a comprehensive income tax. But there are some matters not of detailed application to particular taxes but of general importance which are worth noting in this chapter.

WEALTH AS A PROXY FOR INVESTMENT INCOME

The need for indexation for capital–income adjustment arises, as we have seen, from the fact that some part of the nominal money yield from an asset may be needed to be saved and put aside to maintain the real value of the asset or to maintain its real yield in the future, if the asset is one whose capital value is not expected itself to rise automatically *pari passu* with the rate of general price inflation. If it could be assumed that the real rate of return on all forms of wealth (i.e. the rate of return after any necessary capital–income adjustment) was more or less the same, that this real rate of return would remain more or less constant in the future, and that it would not itself be much affected by the rate of price inflation, and if in addition reliable current money values could be ascribed to all capital assets, it would be possible to devise a workable approximation to the present money value of the real income which could be permanently enjoyed for any given asset. This could be achieved by taking the current money value of the asset and multiplying it by the assumed real rate of yield. Thus if a man's wealth were £100,000 and the real rate of return on capital were estimated to be 3 per cent a year, then the current value of the real amount that he could expect to be able to consume permanently year after year as a result of the ownership of this wealth would be estimated at £3,000.

We hesitate to recommend the adoption of this method for the assessment of all personal investment income, although in spite of all its difficulties and its unfamiliarity it might provide a better base in times of rapid and, above all, uncertain inflation, which affects the nominal yields on different assets differently. But there are certain particular cases where the method might well be adopted.

INVESTMENT INCOME SURCHARGE

For example, if it is desired for the reasons discussed in Chapter 3 to tax investment income more heavily than earned income, then to assess the tax on the value of the assets (by way of a tax on wealth) rather than on the nominal yield on the assets (by way of an investment income surcharge) is equivalent to adopting the suggested method of assessing the true income yield.

DWELLING HOUSES

Another example might arise in the special case of housing (discussed in Chapter 11). We there suggest that if it were decided to tax the annual value of dwelling houses, the best measure of such an annual value in present circumstances would be achieved by assessing the capital value of the house and multiplying this by some real rate of return, say 3 per cent a year. If this method were adopted, the capital value of the house in money terms would need to be updated from year to year in order to achieve proper capital–income adjustment.

PIECEMEAL INDEXATION BY STAGES

If other methods of indexation for capital–income adjustment are to be introduced into the UK tax system, the question arises how far it is desirable, or indeed feasible, to do so in a piecemeal fashion.

A simple illustration of this problem arises in the case of adjustment for money debts. We have already described an example in which Smith lends Jones £1,000 at 15 per cent interest in a period of price inflation at 10 per cent a year. We gave reasons for believing that the interest received by Smith and payable by Jones should be reckoned not at £150 but at £50 after indexation for capital–income adjustment. If Jones runs a business from the profits of which interest may be deducted as a cost before his assessment to tax, and if Smith and Jones both pay the same rate of tax, it makes no difference to the total tax revenue whether the capital–income adjustment is made or not, provided it is either made or not made for both creditor and debtor. Smith is taxed on the same amount on which Jones receives remission of tax. But if the adjustment is made for creditor but not for debtor, tax revenue is lost; and if the adjustment is made for debtor but not for creditor tax revenue is gained.

It is clear that, if the adjustment is made for one party, it should be made for the other. In particular, in the present UK situation, if, as is often proposed, business profits should include for tax purposes the real profit made by the erosion of the real liability of the business's money debts resulting from inflation, then the persons or institutions which have invested in such monetary assets should receive a corresponding relief. At first sight it may appear satisfactory to let sleeping dogs lie and to make no adjustment for either creditor or debtor. Smith and Jones together will neither lose nor gain, and by fixing the terms of the loan appropriately they can distribute the tax loss-cum-gain from inflation between themselves appropriately.

There are a number of reasons for dismissing this solution:

1   Smith and Jones may well not be subject to the same rates of tax, and the fair total burden of taxation may thus depend upon making the capital–income adjustment for both parties.
2   Many monetary assets take the form of government debt, and in this case the failure to make the capital–income adjustment is wholly one-sided – a loss to the taxpayer.
3   Many contracts may be made in circumstances in which the actual rate of inflation may turn out to be quite different from that which was expected when the contract was made, so that the distribution of the burden between debtor and creditor will be uncertain and disturbed.
4   Subsequent unexpected changes in the rate of tax may cause an unfair redistribution of tax burden. Something approaching universal application of indexation for capital–income adjustment for tax purposes seems to be required.

The problem is in fact even more far reaching. If tax liabilities are indexed for capital–income adjustment, it may well prove necessary that other non-tax liabilities between creditors and debtors should be indexed also for capital–income adjustment. We give an example from the market for house mortgages in Chapter 7 (p. 136). In recent years the real rate of interest has been negative. If the interest on an owner-occupier's mortgage liability had been indexed for capital–income adjustment, far from having any positive interest liability to deduct from his current tax base he would have had a negative interest which he should have added to his tax base. With mortgage interest and capital liability fixed in terms of money, the owner-occupier – through no choice of his own – would have been gaining much from inflation, which was in fact rapidly paying off his capital debt for him. But this gain was to be enjoyed in the future; for the moment he would have had to meet an unchanged money liability on his mortgage and an increased tax liability out of his present uninflated money earnings. Capital–income adjustment would have pinched him hard in the present in return for a still more valuable gain in the future.

The position would be relieved if the mortgage liability were itself indexed, so that a lower rate of interest was applied to a liability which increased year by year in line with inflation. In that case, instead of facing a constant money liability for interest and repayment of debt which would in the future be eroded by inflation, the owner-occupier would be faced with a lower money liability in the present, but one which would rise in money terms with future inflation. His present position would be tolerable. But it is doubtful whether the building societies could index their mortgage loans unless they simultaneously indexed their deposit liabilities, so that their current liabilities to their depositors were reduced immediately to correspond with the immediate reduction of their receipts from their mortgage loans, with deposit interest and mortgage interest rising together in money terms in the future.

The above is only one example of the difficulties of piecemeal indexation for capital–income adjustment. If inflation is likely to continue at an appreciable rate and if an income-based tax system is continued, widespread indexation for capital–income adjustment becomes desirable. We believe also that, on the one hand, difficulties arise from piecemeal introduction of such indexation but that, on the other hand, the process must as a practical matter be undertaken by stages. This is a problem which merits much more detailed study than we have been able to give to it in the time at our disposal.

THE CHOICE OF PRICE INDEX

A shift from an income base to an expenditure base for direct taxes would remove all need for capital–income adjustment; but the need for bracket indexation would remain so long as inflation continued, for the progressive scales of any direct taxes, for social security benefits and for specific excise duties. It is necessary to consider what is the best general price index – or what are the best price indices – to use for indexation purposes.

RETAIL PRICE INDEX

An obvious candidate for this role is the retail price index, whose movement over the ten years from 1966/67 to 1976/77 is shown in Table 6.2. This index measures the movements in the general level of prices paid by consumers for the goods and services which they consume. Two possible difficulties with this measurement of price changes for bracket indexation may be mentioned.

(1)   The retail price index includes in prices the indirect taxes levied on the goods and services which it covers. This means that, if the government raised or lowered the level of indirect taxes (such as VAT or the specific duties on beer, tobacco, petrol, etc.), the consequential rise in the retail price index would set in motion the bracket indexation of all the direct taxes. Thus if indirect taxes were raised in order to raise more tax revenue, there would automatically be a reduction in the tax base and yield of income tax or of other direct taxes whose brackets were indexed on the retail price index. It would seem more sensible to select for bracket indexation some other index which would not rise or fall with rises or falls in indirect taxes; such taxes could then be used as fiscal instruments whose rise or fall was intended to raise more or less revenue which would not be partially offset automatically by counterbalancing changes in the tax brackets for other taxes.

(2)   A similar consideration arises in the case of changes in the international terms of trade. Suppose, for example, that the world price of goods imported into the United Kingdom for consumption or for the production of consumption goods (such as oil) goes up relatively to the world price of goods produced in the United Kingdom. When the price of such imported goods goes up, the retail price index will go up as a consequence. But in this case the average standard of living in the United Kingdom must be reduced *pro tanto* because it is possible to buy less of the imported goods for each unit of UK goods which is exported and sold on the world market. It may seem somewhat anomalous automatically to raise tax brackets and to reduce tax liabilities for all UK taxpayers in order to offset a rise in price which is a symptom of a real fall which must occur in the standard of living. Of course, it may be desired to make particular changes in the tax burdens of particular groups of persons to meet a general and inevitable real burden on the standard of living. But this can be done by *ad hoc* adjustments of particular tax rates. It would not seem appropriate to start with the pretence that everyone can be relieved automatically from any extra tax burden. It might be more suitable for coping with the problem of a general domestic inflation of money prices and costs to take a measurement of changes in the money prices of domestically produced goods and services.

THE PRICE OF THE GROSS DOMESTIC PRODUCT AT FACTOR COST

The price of the gross domestic product at factor cost, whose movement over the ten years from 1966/67 to 1976/77 is also shown in Table 6.2, both excludes indirect taxes from the prices of the goods and services covered and also refers only to domestically produced goods and services. But it differs in two further important respects from the retail price index in that it covers, in addition to the prices of goods and services bought by individuals for their personal consumption, also (i) the prices of capital goods (e.g. plant and machinery) bought for purposes of capital investment, and (ii) the prices of goods and services (e.g. the services of civil servants) bought by the government for public use.[6] It may well, however, constitute the best general index of the general inflation of money prices and costs in the United Kingdom.

AVERAGE EARNINGS

But is a general index of the prices of finished products what is needed for bracket indexation? We have still to consider the index of average earnings, whose movement over the ten years from 1966/67 to 1976/77 is also shown in Table 6.2. In the absence of any bracket indexation there is the phenomenon of 'fiscal drag', namely that when money incomes per head go up then, with a progressive tax system, the proportion of the total national income which is levied in direct taxes automatically goes up. This occurs because, with a general rise in money incomes per head, taxpayers automatically move from lower to higher income brackets and thus, with a progressive scale of taxes, from lower to higher tax rates. But money incomes per head may rise either because money prices have risen or else because real output per head has risen. Fiscal drag may be due to either of these phenomena, which we will call *monetary fiscal drag* and *real fiscal drag* respectively.

The use of an index of the prices of finished products (such as the price of the gross domestic product) will remove monetary fiscal drag; but it will not remove real fiscal drag. If money income per head goes up because real income per head has gone up, there will be no adjustment of tax brackets if prices have remained constant.

But using an index of average earnings will remove both monetary and real fiscal drag. Tax brackets will be adjusted when earnings per head go up whether this is due to a rise in real output per head or in the monetary price of an unchanged output per head. There are two reasons why such a result may be welcomed:

1 If real output is growing because of increased productivity, it may be considered better to have a tax system which, in the absence of planned

---

[6] Thus (i) a fall in the real value of indirect taxes, (ii) a reduction in the price of imported goods relatively to domestically produced goods, (iii) a rise in the price of capital goods relatively to consumption goods, or (iv) a rise in the price of goods and services bought by the government relatively to the price of goods and services bought for private consumption would cause the price of the gross domestic product at factor cost to rise relatively to the retail price index. Between the first quarter of 1973 and the first quarter of 1976 the two price indices rose both by the same amount, namely 66 per cent. In so far as there was a serious rise in the relative prices of imports, the retail price index might have been expected to show a greater rise. But at the same time, as we have seen, the money value of the specific duties rose by a below average amount, and average earnings (which play an above average role in government consumption where the services of civil servants make up a large part of expenditure) rose by an above average amount. Both of these two factors would cause the retail price index to rise less than the price of the gross domestic product.

changes in the tax schedule, shares the gain more or less equally between the private and the public sectors of the economy (which will be the result of tax brackets which are indexed on average earnings) rather than a tax system which automatically raises the proportion of resources which accrue to the government in taxes.

2   As we have already argued, there may be social reasons for thinking of many of the brackets (e.g. the value of the tax threshold for low wage earners or the value of social security payments) in relative terms, i.e. as properly bearing a certain relationship to average earnings.

Average earnings are likely to move very much in line with money incomes per head of the population. The correspondence may not be exact because the proportion of the national product which goes not to earnings but to profits or other investment income may change, although with the very high proportion of the national income which now goes to earnings any discrepancy due to this cause is likely to be of minor significance. There is, however, another and much more important reason for a discrepancy, namely variations in the level of employment. If unemployment rises and total output is reduced, the value of output per head of the population will fall even if the value of output per person employed remains unchanged.

This phenomenon presents an important argument for using an index such as average earnings rather than an alternative index of money income per head, such as the value of the total national income (e.g. of the gross domestic product) divided by the total population. In times of recession in the level of real output and employment the latter index would have a perverse destabilising effect. When real output and employment fall, it is desirable to reduce rather than to raise the average level of taxes in order on Keynesian principles to maintain total effective demand. If, however, in times of trade recession the fall in the value of real output per head of the population were used as the index for the adjustment of tax brackets, the money value of social benefits, of tax thresholds and of other tax brackets would be reduced, a higher proportion of incomes would be levied in tax, and effective demand would be reduced. The use of an index of average earnings of persons in employment avoids this destabilising effect.

THE SIMULTANEOUS USE OF MANY INDICES

It may be questioned whether it is essential that the same index should be used in all cases of indexation. In fact, as is shown in Table 6.2, there already exist separate retail price indices for pensioners. Persons in different conditions and, in particular, with different levels of spendable incomes purchase different collections of goods. The cost of a basket of the particular goods which retirement pensioners purchase has, as is shown in Table 6.2, gone up over the ten years to 1976/77 rather more than has the price of the average basket of goods bought by all consumers. Special price indices for pensioners have therefore been devised for use in the periodic review of the appropriate money levels for retirement pensions. But there are some serious difficulties in using different indices for the bracket adjustment of different elements in the tax structure. We have already explained (p. 110) how the fact that tax thresholds have moved more or less in line with the retail price index, whereas social security benefits have moved more or less in line with the index of average earnings, has led to an inappropriate relationship between the two elements. This particular clash might be removed by gearing the tax threshold to the same index as the social security benefits, although it should be noted (as shown in Chapter 13) that the initial step of raising tax thresholds sufficiently to bring them back once more into appropriate relationship with the social security benefits would be costly in revenue.

But bringing tax thresholds into, and keeping them in, an appropriate relationship with social security benefits would not be the end of the matter. Suppose it were desired to relate standards at the lower end of the scale of living standards (i.e. for social security benefits and for tax thresholds) to one index and to use another index for the taxation of those at higher levels (e.g. for the higher rates of income tax). Then it would not be a matter simply of using different indices to adjust the different tax brackets. If the indices moved in different ways the whole rate structure, including marginal rates of tax, would have to be appropriately adjusted.

The simple numerical example in Table 6.4 will make the point clear. We start in case (i) with a tax threshold of £1,000 and with a basic rate of income tax of 33 per cent between the tax threshold of £1,000 and the £5,000 level at which the higher rates of income tax are assumed to start. The taxpayer with £1,000 has £1,000 to spend. The taxpayer with £5,000 has £3,680 to spend.

Table 6.4 *Tax brackets and marginal rates of tax*

	Personal tax allowance (£)	Standard rate of tax on incomes between £1,000 and £5,000 (%)	Pre-tax income (£)	Tax (£)	Post-tax income (£)
Case (i)	1,000	33	1,000	nil	1,000
			5,000	1,320	3,680
Case (ii)	1,100	33	1,100	nil	1,100
			5,000	1,287	3,713
Case (iii)	1,100	33·8	1,000	nil	1,100
			5,000	1,320	3,680

We suppose then that the cost of the goods bought by those at the tax threshold rises by 10 per cent whereas there is no rise in the price of goods bought by those at the higher level. In case (ii) we react by raising the personal tax allowance (the tax threshold) by 10 per cent to £1,100, leaving the next tax bracket unchanged. The taxpayer with £1,100 will now have £1,100 to spend.

But the taxpayer with £5,000 (whose cost of living has not changed) will also gain from the rise in the personal tax allowance and will have £3,713 instead of only £3,680 to spend. As case (iii) shows, in order that the taxpayer with an income of £5,000 should be left in the same position it is necessary not only to leave unchanged the tax bracket of £5,000 at which higher rate tax starts but also to raise the basic rate of tax on incomes between £1,100 and £5,000 from 33 to 33·8 per cent. Thus using different indices for different tax brackets involves restructuring the whole pattern of marginal tax rates.

A possible solution to this problem would be to have one single index (such as the price of the gross domestic product at factor cost, or average money earnings) which is applied more or less automatically in all cases of bracket indexation. This would not imply that there should never be any changes in the relative levels of tax brackets, social security benefits and specific excise duties, since the operation of the automatic indexation could be readjusted by specific *ad hoc* adjustments made from time to time in the annual budget or other periodic reviews. On the occasions of such adjustments of the relative values of particular tax brackets and social payments the whole structure of tax rates would have to be appropriately reconsidered.

SOME REMAINING PROBLEMS

The problems of time lags and of automatic adjustment would still remain.

TIME LAGS

There are time lags between (i) the movement of the relevant prices, (ii) the construction of the resulting price index, and (iii) the application of the index to the adjustment of tax brackets, excise duties and social security payments. There may be a six-month lag between the actual movement of prices and the publication of the resulting price index; and if the automatic adjustment of tax brackets took place only once a year at the time of the budget, this would mean, for example, that the tax brackets operative between April 1977 and April 1978 would be determined on the basis of price movements up to September 1976 – an average time lag of twelve months. In times of rapid and uncertain rates of inflation such a time lag would be undesirable. If more or less automatic indexation were to be taken seriously, it would be worthwhile to put extra resources into the rapid collection of the data necessary to make at least provisional estimates of the relevant price movements. Another way of reducing the time lag would be to make the indexed adjustments more frequently than once a year; but this solution would seem to be ruled out without a complete recasting of administrative arrangements.

AUTOMATIC ADJUSTMENT

Next, what is meant by 'automatic adjustment'? In this connection there is a basic distinction between indexation for capital–income adjustment and bracket indexation. The former is a matter for permanent and continuing legislation, which defines the tax base in an appropriate manner, e.g. by defining the tax base for capital gains tax as the difference between sale proceeds and acquisition cost multiplied by the movement in a defined price index since acquisition. Bracket indexation, on the other hand, is a matter of choosing the appropriate level for personal allowances and other tax brackets annually on the advice and recommendation of the Chancellor in view of the general economic situation, the requirements of revenue and the views of the government about tax equity. The situation might perhaps be met if the House of Commons required the Chancellor every year to declare not only the tax brackets which he proposed in his budget but also what those tax brackets would be if last year's brackets were adjusted by the general index which had been selected for this purpose.

OTHER APPLICATIONS OF INDEXATION

In this chapter we have confined our attention to the problems of indexation which arise if it is desired to preserve the real structure of the tax system unaffected by the ravages of general price inflation. We are in favour of such indexation; in its absence the rate of inflation becomes a major and arbitrary form of taxation. But we have not considered many other important aspects of indexation. For example, we express no view on the important question whether the indexation of wage rates would increase the dangers of rapid inflation by increasing the speed with which wages chased rising prices or would damp down inflation by reducing the need for the current wage rate fixed at the time of any wage bargain to anticipate future inflation. We have confined our attention to what is necessary in order to maintain the real structure of a tax system.

CONCLUSIONS

Unless rates of price inflation can be brought down to very low levels and can be confidently expected to remain at such levels, indexation of taxes against inflation is essential in order to prevent the rate of inflation from acting as an important but wholly arbitrary method of raising revenue. We are for this reason in favour of adopting an effective indexation of the tax system.

In the case of taxes assessed on an income or similar base, two quite separate types of indexation are necessary. In the first place, it is necessary to make adjustments for changes in the real values of capital assets and liabilities in order to distinguish between capital and income in real terms; this involves adjustments for such items as money loans, depreciation, stocks and capital gains. In the second place, if the structure of tax rates is a progressive one, an additional form of indexation is needed; the brackets in any schedule of progressive tax rates must be indexed.

In the case of taxes assessed on the base of expenditure or of capital wealth there is no need for indexation of the former kind; only the indexation of the brackets in any schedule of progressive tax rates is needed. This constitutes an important advantage of expenditure or wealth over income as a tax base in inflationary conditions.

In the United Kingdom the failure over recent years to keep tax thresholds and social security benefits in line with each other has been a major cause of tax anomalies for the lower ranges of income; and in inflationary conditions it is important to index both tax thresholds and cash benefits in such a way as to keep them in line with each other.

Appendix 6.1   The Effect of Expectations of Inflation on Taxable Income on Definition B

Suppose Mr Smith owns $2\frac{1}{2}$ per cent Consols of a nominal amount of £6,000, which will bring him in a constant pre-tax annual interest of £150.

Case (i).
Suppose that the long term rate of interest is 15 per cent, that the rate of price inflation is 10 per cent a year, and that the rate of interest and the rate of price inflation are expected to remain unchanged for an indefinite future. Then Mr Smith's Consols will be worth £1,000 in the market. The amount which he can spend each year and maintain his consumption indefinitely at the same constant rate will be £50, £55, £60·5, etc., i.e. starting this year at £50 and rising by 10 per cent each year to keep in line with the price inflation. If he spends £50 this year, he will save £100 and have £1,100 worth of Consols at the end of the year. Next year he will have £1,100 ×0·15 = £165 in interest, of which he can spend £55 and add £110 to his savings. By this process he will each year increase his consumption, his savings, the value of his capital holding, and his interest income each by 10 per cent in money terms. His real consumption will remain constant.

Case (ii).
Suppose, however, that while price inflation of 10 per cent is expected this year, the rate of price inflation is expected to fall to zero after this year. As a result the long term rate of interest is expected to be only 5 per cent from next year onwards, since a 5 per cent money rate with no inflation gives (approximately) the same real return as a 15 per cent constant rate of interest with a 10 per cent constant rate of rise of prices. Since the long term rate of interest will be constant at 5 per cent from next year onwards, Mr Smith's Consols will be worth £3,000 from next year onwards. Suppose that out of his interest of £150 this year he spends X and saves (£150$-X$). Then next year he will own Consols worth (£3,000$+$£150$-X$). The 5 per cent yield on this sum will produce [(£3,150$-X$) ×0·05] in interest, which he can then consume indefinitely without any further saving since there will be no further inflation. But this future constant stream of consumption must be worth $1·1X$ in terms of money if it is to have the same real value as this year's consumption of X. It follows that (£3,150$-X$) ×0·05 = $1·1X$ or X = £137.

On definition B, Mr Smith's income this year is £50 in case (i) and £137 in case (ii).

PART THREE SOME RADICAL RESTRUCTURINGS OF THE SYSTEM OF DIRECT TAXES

In this Part we examine from first principles what would be the nature of certain alternative radical restructurings of the system of direct taxes. We examine in some detail the economic and administrative implications of each of these new structures. The purpose of these chapters is not to make precise recommendations on specific issues, but to show in sufficient detail the sort of problems which would arise in replanning the tax structure on certain clearly defined alternative principles.

7 A Comprehensive Income Tax

In Chapter 3 we discussed at some length the relative merits of income or consumption as the tax base. In this chapter we shall describe the tax structure which would be needed if a truly comprehensive income tax (CIT) were to be introduced into the United Kingdom.

THE CANADIAN CARTER COMMISSION

The problems of such a CIT have been analysed in great detail in the six volumes of the Report of the Canadian Carter Commission.[1]

The Carter Commission presented a masterly analysis of these problems, with one exception. They recognised the existence of inflation, but they stated that they were 'opposed to automatic adjustments tied to price indices, for this would impair the power of the tax system to stabilise the economy'. For the reasons which we have given in Chapter 6 we take the view that adjustment for inflation is an essential feature for the UK tax structure unless we are ready to accept inflation as an extremely powerful but inefficient and unjust revenue raiser. If it were only a question of moderate rates of inflation or deflation, the argument of the Carter Commission would be acceptable. In the ways described in Chapter 6, inflationary price rises cause an unintended increase in the proportion of income taken in tax and impose an unintended tax on some forms of capital in the guise of a tax on income; this damps down private spending, restrains the inflationary demand and thus helps to stabilise the economy. But with the great and continuous rates of inflation which have been recently experienced the disturbing structural effects of an unadjusted income tax system are in our opinion so serious that they cannot be neglected.

The administration of a CIT becomes incomparably more complicated if a system of automatic adjustments for inflation must be introduced into it. In this chapter we shall consider rather briefly many of the points which have been so exhaustively and effectively analysed by the Carter Commission; but we shall put much stress on the problems involved in indexing such a structure for inflation. The resulting system, while it might conceivably be feasible, would impose such a strain on administration by the authorities and compliance by the taxpayer that, for that reason alone, we consider it to be ruled out in present circumstances.

THE NATURE AND PURPOSE OF A CIT

The basic idea of a CIT is to tax opportunities (the 'accretion of economic

[1] Report of the Royal Commission on Taxation (Ottawa: Queen's Printer, 1966).

spending power') rather than the actual use of such opportunities, which may be better measured by consumption expenditure. There are a number of ways in which income may be defined. The existing UK system draws a distinction between income and capital gains. But any definition of income which purports to measure 'accretion of purchasing power' must bring income and capital gains under the same umbrella. For this purpose (as shown in Chapter 3) there are at least two main ways of defining income. To measure income as the level of consumption which the recipient could maintain indefinitely (what we have called definition B), however desirable in principle, is in practice not an operative measure, since it depends upon subjective views about future developments. The measurement of income as current consumption plus the current addition to the taxpayer's net capital worth (what we have called definition A) is a feasible operative criterion, provided there are enough markets in which the most important assets can be valued. It is this definition of income which, probably for this reason, normally lies behind the concept of *'comprehensive income'* as a tax base; and it is this concept which we accordingly adopt in this chapter, although we would stress that there is plenty of room for disagreement as to whether it is in fact the best criterion of what actually constitutes 'income'.

One of the aims of a CIT is to promote what is sometimes termed 'horizontal equity' by taxing all kinds of income under a single schedule. In this way, so it is argued, individuals with a given level of income would be treated in the same way regardless of the form in which their income accrued. This would also help to prevent resources from being wasted by attempts to convert one kind of income into another in circumstances where different kinds of income were taxed at different rates (e.g. dividends and capital gains). In addition, if the tax base of a CIT were larger than the current tax base, then a change to a CIT might enable a reduction in marginal tax rates to be made, which would reduce the disincentive effects on work decisions. And since, in its pure form, receipts of windfalls and inheritances would be included in the tax base, the CIT would make it possible to do without any separate system of tax on capital transfers and yet at the same time to tailor the rate of tax on gifts and inheritances received to the income of the recipient. But this would be at the expense of abandoning the cumulative principle.

The major differences between the current income tax and the CIT are that the latter would include in the tax base real capital gains (net of losses), and gifts and inheritances received, and that there would be no special tax reliefs on savings and investment. In addition, to be theoretically consistent an annual CIT should include in its tax base the change each year in the present value of all assets owned by an individual. Severe problems arise where these assets cannot be marketed. Three cases which deserve particular mention are (i) the change in the current value of pension rights, (ii) the change in the value of the assets of closely owned businesses, and (iii) the change in the present discounted value of future earnings. There are no current markets to provide a valuation for these items, and, although in the case of (i) and (ii) values might be established by pragmatic methods, we are of the opinion that items (i) and (iii) should not be included in the tax base.

We proceed to a consideration of the principal problem areas which would require attention if we were to move towards a CIT.

THE TREATMENT OF CAPITAL GAINS

REALISATION VERSUS ACCRUALS

Under a CIT, capital gains would be subject to ordinary personal tax rates. Moreover, in principle they would be taxed as they accrued, not, as at present, only when the gains were realised. Clearly the taxation of such holding gains could put heavy strains on the cash position of closely owned businesses. But above all they would pose serious valuation problems. It might be possible to use observed market values to estimate accrued capital gains each year for some assets which are homogeneous and for which there are large markets (e.g. ordinary shares), but for a wide range of assets this would be inordinately costly and difficult to implement. It might be argued that, if a wealth tax were operated in conjunction with a CIT, the information produced by returns for wealth tax would provide a source of data to estimate accrued capital gains. We are not happy with this argument, because (i) the wealth tax returns would have to cover all assets and all individuals with capital gains liable to CIT, and (ii) the data for wealth tax purposes might be considered as acceptable for measuring the level of wealth but not for estimating annual changes in wealth. Hence we conclude that all capital gains should be taxed on realisation. Given this, we suggest later a way in which the tax on capital gains could be adjusted to approximate the taxation of accrued gains but where the tax is collected on realisation.

CAPITAL LOSSES

A further difficulty with the idea of taxing capital gains as income is that some individuals might have very large negative incomes arising from capital losses. Since averaging provisions of some kind would certainly be necessary under a CIT (see below), these would have to provide for the averaging of losses as well as of gains. In principle this is quite just, but it might lead to misunderstanding if the media were able to claim that some individuals receiving large amounts of 'income' (e.g. earned income) were paying no tax because of the deduction against that income of capital losses. With the fall in stock exchange prices, in some recent years many wealthy taxpayers would have been exempt from all tax. If this were to seem unfair to members of the public then it would reflect a belief that 'comprehensive income' was not the appropriate tax base.

REALISATION ON THE OCCASION OF GIFT, DEATH OR EMIGRATION

Gifts and death would be events constituting deemed realisation of capital gains. This would require the restoration of capital gains taxation on death, which was abolished in 1971; the tax on capital gains would be at a rate related to the income of the previous owner, and the beneficiary would pay tax at his own rate on the net amount which he received. We would suggest also that emigration should constitute deemed realisation. We would define emigration to be a change in status from resident to not ordinarily resident. The value of the asset would be the value on some arbitrary date in the fiscal year during which the change in status occurred, say 6 April. Similar problems in reverse would arise with immigration.

SOME ARGUMENTS FOR SPECIAL TREATMENT

Some might challenge the assumption that capital gains should be taxed as income, and there are two sets of arguments for taxing capital gains at concessionary rates:

1 It is often maintained that capital gains of £X are not equivalent to £X of 'regular' income, whether the 'regular' income be earned or unearned income. At first sight this argument looks attractive, but it seems to us that it is not an argument for taxing capital gains at concessionary rates. If once-for-all capital gains and other windfalls are to be treated differently from receipts of regular income, then (as argued in Chapter 3) this is rather an argument for abandoning income in favour of consumption expenditure as the tax base.
2 Another set of arguments for the special treatment of capital gains asserts (i) that the definition of taxable capital gains does not allow for inflation, and if purely nominal gains are to be taxed then the tax rate should be lower; and (ii) that if the constraint that gains can be taxed only on realisation were accepted, then realised gains in any one year could be very large (reflecting accrued gains for a succession of years prior to realisation) and under a progressive tax system this might increase the tax liability because of the rather artificial bunching of taxable gains.

Against these considerations is the argument that taxing gains only on realisation enables the taxpayer to defer his tax liability until the date of realisation, which is equivalent to a reduction in the effective rate of tax on the accrued gain.

There is no reason to believe that these different factors will offset each other, leading to some sort of rough justice. The loss through taxing nominal gains is a function of the acquisition cost and the rate of inflation. The benefit from deferral depends upon the period, the size of the gain, the tax rate and the interest rate.

If all assets could be valued annually, it would be relatively easy to design a tax system which in principle would tax accrued gains in real terms. The values of the previous year would be marked up by some inflation factor chosen by the government. Clearly, this is impracticable. So we have to consider whether it is feasible to design a capital gains tax which will both (i) allow for inflation, and (ii) allow for the benefit of deferral, in such a way that a value for 'taxable real capital gains' is obtained, which can then be taxed under a separate schedule or added to other income for tax purposes.

ADJUSTMENT FOR INFLATION

The adjustment for inflation is straightforward in principle. It represents a clear case of what in Chapter 6 we have described as 'indexation for capital–income adjustment'. The acquisition cost must be increased by the rate of inflation in the period between acquisition and realisation.

Suppose that in period 1 the price index used for purposes of indexation is 1. In period 2 it is $(1+p)$ where p is the rate of inflation over the period. Call the value of $(1+p)$ the 'inflation factor'. The government then constructs and publishes a table of inflation factors such as Table 7.1, where the numerical entries are by way of example.

Table 7.1   *Example of a table of inflation factors*

Sale date	Purchase date			
	1	2	3	4
1	1·0			
2	1·03	1·0		
3	1·07	1·04	1·0	
4	1·11	1·07	1·03	1·0

For an asset purchased in period 1 and sold in period 2, the acquisition cost is multiplied by 1·03 (because there was 3 per cent inflation over the period). The taxable gain is equal to the sale value minus the adjusted acquisition cost.

How long should 'the period' be? A fiscal year seems rather long with current rates of inflation. For equities the monthly stock-exchange accounting period seems more natural, but this would require a monthly price index. A suitable compromise might be one-quarter, then in the table the periods would be labelled not 1, 2, 3, 4 etc. but rather 1976 I, 1976 II, 1976 III, 1976 IV and so on. There may be administrative arguments for extending the period to a year, which in any case would be appropriate in more stable conditions.

The table is easy to update. Each period the government announces the latest inflation factor, and a new row is entered. For example, if at the end of period 4 (or at some later date) the government announces that the rate of inflation between periods 3 and 4 was, say, 3 per cent, each number in row 3 is then multiplied by 1·03 to give the entries for row 4.[2]

---

[2] We have discussed in Chapter 6 the considerations affecting the choice of price index for the calculation of the inflation factor.

ADJUSTMENT FOR DEFERRAL OF TAX

At present capital gains or losses are taxed or relieved only on realisation, with the option through 'bed and breakfast' deals to take such gains or losses on an accruals basis if that is to the advantage of the taxpayer.[3] In the limit, current legislation permits total avoidance of the tax when assets are transmitted on death. There seems little reason to continue with this provision, and we suggested above that constructive realisation should take place on death, on the transfer of assets by gift and on emigration.

The benefit of deferral is a loan free of interest of an amount equal to the tax liability on accrued gains. Thus suppose that a gain of £100 accrues in 1975 and is realised in 1977. With a rate of tax of 30 per cent, £30 in tax is paid on a realisation basis in 1977 instead of in 1975. The taxpayer has kept the £30 for two years free of interest. If the tax paid in 1977 is to reflect this fact, then the £30 should be grossed up at compound interest for two years. To achieve this result it would be necessary to mark up the deferred tax liability by an interest rate factor. This process can be contrasted with the allowance for inflation, where it is necessary to mark up the acquisition cost by an inflation factor.

To mark up for interest a tax liability from one period (when the liability properly accrued) to a later period (when the tax is actually paid) would require a set of interest factors similar to the set of inflation factors already described in Table 7.1. If in Table 7.1 the rate of inflation between any two periods is replaced by the operative rate of interest between those two periods, then the figures in Table 7.1 will represent the relevant interest factors for the adjustment of tax liability resulting from the deferral of the payment.[4]

As for the choice of interest rates for the construction of this table of interest factors, it is to the advantage of the taxpayer for the chosen rate to be as small as possible; and the interest rate used to construct the table should be a post-tax interest rate (to reflect the net rate of return which the taxpayer could have obtained on the postponed payment of tax). We feel that it would be hopelessly complex to allow the interest factor to reflect the taxpayer's own tax rate (formally, his tax rates in the years when the gains were accruing), and so we suggest using a tax rate equal either to the basic rate or to some arbitrary rate, say 50 per cent. The interest rate could be that on government securities of, say, five years' maturity. The nominal rate would be reduced by the chosen tax rate to give a post-tax interest rate, which

[3] A 'bed and breakfast' deal is one in which the owner of a security sells the security (thereby realising any capital gain or loss on it) and then promptly repurchases it (thereby incurring a new acquisition cost equal to its current market value).

[4] It is worth noting that both sets of tables would be necessary even in the absence of any proposal for taxing the benefit of deferral; the inflation factor table would be needed for general indexation purposes, and the interest factor table would be needed to mark up tax losses, which would then be carried forward (see below). Hence the requirement of two adjustment factor tables, one for inflation and one for interest, does not add to the complexity of the system, because they would be necessary under a CIT even if no attempt were made to tax the benefit of deferral.

would be used to construct the interest factor tables. The updating of these tables would be simple and equivalent to the updating of the inflation factor tables.

In principle the procedure should be to job backwards over the periods for which the asset has been held, in order to apply the interest factors to the deferred tax liabilities in the following way. First a value should be computed for the gain in each of the past years since acquisition; this gain should then be added to taxable income in each of those years; and on this basis the appropriate tax liability should be calculated for each year, and marked up by the interest rate factor since that year to give the current tax liability.

The drawback to this scheme is obviously its complexity, and it seems inconceivable that all the records could be kept. But if records were not kept, gains would have to be taxed at the individual's tax rate of the year when the gains were realised. Since people often have some freedom of choice as to when they realise their gains, this does not seem unreasonable. It would also be necessary to proceed as if the real gain accrued evenly over the period between acquisition and realisation. In one sense this would be the equivalent of averaging the gains over time, and if the taxpayer felt that this compulsory smoothing procedure was working against his interests, then, to the extent that he could control the timing of realisations, the remedy would lie in his own hands.

A FORMULA FOR ADJUSTMENT

On this basis it is possible to devise a formula for the taxation of capital gains when they are realised which reduces the tax burden appropriately according to the importance of the inflation factor and increases it appropriately for the interest factor. The derivation of the formula is given in Appendix 7.1. It results in treating the capital gain which would be subject to tax on the realisation of an asset as

$$(S-C_2)\left(\frac{\log\dfrac{S}{C_1}}{\log\dfrac{S}{C_2}}\right)$$

where S is the amount for which the asset is sold, C_1 is the acquisition cost of the asset multiplied by the inflation factor between the time of acquisition and realisation, and C_2 is the acquisition cost multiplied by the corresponding interest factor.

The *raison d'être* of this formula is unfortunately not likely to be apparent to the taxpayer, though it does in fact make a sound adjustment both for inflation and for the deferral of tax. Ugly and complex though it is, its actual application may not be as difficult as may at first sight appear. It involves (i) adjusting the acquisition cost of the asset by inflation factors and interest factors (tables of which would be published annually or quarterly), (ii) calculating the sale proceeds of the asset as a proportion of these adjusted acquisition costs, (iii) using tables to take the logarithms of these ratios, and then (iv) adjusting the excess of sale proceeds over the interest-adjusted acquisition costs by the ratio of these logarithms.

An example may help to illustrate the operation of the formula. An asset bought in 1970 for £100 is sold in 1974 for £200. The inflation factor published by the government is 1·446 (the price level, taken here to be measured by the consumers' expenditure deflator in the *Blue Book*, rose by 44·6 per cent over the period). The acquisition cost adjusted for inflation is 1·446 × £100 = £144·6. The interest factor is 1·275 (the rate of interest on government securities after 50 per cent tax rate over the period). The acquisition cost adjusted by the interest factor is £127·5.

1   Under the current tax system the taxable gain is simply the nominal gain of £100.
2   Under an indexed system the taxable gain would be the real gain of £200 − £144·6 = £55·4.
3   Under a system allowing for both inflation and deferral the taxable gain would be

$$(\pounds 200 - \pounds 127 \cdot 5) \times \left(\frac{\log \dfrac{200}{144 \cdot 6}}{\log \dfrac{200}{127 \cdot 5}} \right) = \pounds 72 \cdot 5 \times \left(\frac{\log 1 \cdot 3831}{\log 1 \cdot 5686} \right)$$

$$= \pounds 72 \cdot 5 \times \left(\frac{0 \cdot 1409}{0 \cdot 1955} \right)$$

$$= \pounds 72 \cdot 5 \times 0 \cdot 7207$$

$$= \pounds 52 \cdot 3$$

This is less than under system 2 because the rate of inflation was greater than the post-tax rate of interest, so that the real rate of interest was negative. The example suggests that, provided capital gains were indexed *and* charged to full income tax rates, the need to allow for deferral would arise only when real interest rates were significantly different from zero.

If this formula were applied, it would satisfactorily (i) index capital gains tax, (ii) remove the 'lock-in' effect of taxing realised gains, and (iii) yield a value for real capital gains which could be added to other income to give a CIT base.

Two further points should be noted:

1   The revenue implications are not clear. A change from the current system would reduce the tax base in so far as it was indexed for inflation; but it would increase the tax base in so far as it eliminated the advantages of deferral, and it would increase the rates of tax from a maximum of 30 per cent to the marginal tax rates of individual taxpayers.
2   If capital gains are taxed at normal income tax rates, the lock-in effect becomes even more serious than at present and the case for doing something about deferral more pressing.

One problem which remains is what happens when a partial sale is made. If the original purchase was made at a single moment, there is no problem; the appropriate acquisition cost is simply the original total acquisition cost multiplied by the physical proportion of the asset disposed of. If, however, purchases have been made over a period of time, a choice must be made between treating the sale as being made from that part of the holding which was acquired in the most distant past (the FIFO or first-in-first-out principle) or from that part which was acquired most recently (the LIFO or last-in-first-out principle). We prefer the former.[5]

INDEXING OTHER FORMS OF PROPERTY INCOME

It would be wrong to index capital gains but not other forms of property income, such as interest on building society deposits.

INDEXING MONEY BALANCES

In principle all kinds of property income could be indexed. This seems acceptable in the case of fixed-interest securities, but what about indexing money? Are holders of money to be allowed to deduct from their income for tax purposes the fall in the real value of their money balances? In the context of an income tax, the answer in principle must be yes. One argument for not extending indexation to money in various forms (e.g. current account deposits) is that the imputed income from holding wealth in this form is not taxed. Examples of this imputed income are the benefits from liquidity and the services provided by banks at charges below the market cost of supplying those services. But this is not convincing, because the value of these services to the investor is not necessarily correlated with the rate of inflation. In fact if the value of these services was equivalent to a constant real rate of return, the case for indexation would be very strong. Nevertheless, it is hard to believe that indexation would be granted to all forms of money. Indexation could be restricted to money held in certain institutional forms, such as deposits on which interest was paid, but would not be extended to deposits on which no interest was paid nor to coins and notes. Thus real losses on cash would not be tax-deductible. This would provide an incentive for banks to

[5] An alternative would be to effect a compromise between the FIFO and LIFO principles by updating the acquisition cost each time a purchase is made. When a purchase is made the adjusted taxable gain on the existing holding is calculated in accordance with the formula described on p. 133 above, on the assumption that the existing holding has been sold at the purchase price. Call this *G*. The existing holding is revalued at the purchase price, and from this the adjusted gain *G* is subtracted to give a new adjusted acquisition cost for the whole of the existing holding. The total acquisition cost of the new holding is found by adding the value of new purchases. Then when a subsequent sale is made it is not necessary to bother with a FIFO or LIFO rule; the whole of the holding can be treated as having been acquired at the date of the last purchase. This procedure would, however, become very laborious if new purchases were made frequently, e.g. in the case of a unit trust saving scheme under which a given number of units may be purchased each month at the ruling price.

pay interest on their current accounts (to enable their customers to claim the benefit of indexation) and to charge for the services provided.

INDEXING INTEREST

Indexation can be granted on capital (as discussed above for capital gains) or on income. The former approach is not suitable for assets such as bank or building society deposits, or the holdings of a wide range of financial assets, because it requires knowledge of the average balance or holding over a period of time. If changes are made very frequently, this becomes very difficult for the Inland Revenue to monitor. An alternative is to base indexation on receipts of interest income, which will measure the average balance over the period; receipts of interest income are then multiplied by the nominal rate of interest minus the rate of inflation, all divided by the nominal rate of interest. This figure of 'adjusted interest receipt' would be the figure for tax purposes. The Revenue would need to know the interest rate paid.

An example may help to explain the process. A taxpayer declares, as at present, that he has received £100 of income on a deposit account. The government has been told by the bank that over the period concerned it paid an interest rate of 12 per cent, and the inflation tables published by the government show that in the same period the inflation rate was 15 per cent. Then taxable income is defined as $£100[(12-15)/12] = £100(-0.75) = -£25$; i.e. the taxpayer may deduct £25 from his other taxable income. With the rate of inflation higher than the rate of interest the taxpayer has in fact received a negative real rate of interest on his deposit (cf. Table 7.1). Strictly speaking, this method would require a fresh calculation every time interest rates changed.

Since indexation can be given either on capital or on income, it would be necessary to construct rules stipulating which assets were eligible for indexation as capital and which as income. The most obvious classification is to list assets which at the moment give rise to a liability for CGT as capital, and for other assets to give indexation on income. Assets for which there are markets are better given indexation on capital because the interest rates received on these assets change more frequently than those for other assets.

The same inflation adjustment would be made for interest payments which were deductible for tax purposes. Only the real component of interest payments would be an allowable deduction. In recent years, when inflation rates were higher than interest rates, this would have had the consequence that owner-occupiers with mortgages would have had a net addition to their taxable income instead of a net subtraction. Mortgage interest relief would have been negative. Such a change would almost certainly require a new pattern of mortgage finance, with repayments increasing over time instead of staying constant each year in money terms. Only in this way could current holders of mortgages continue to meet their commitments. (See Chapter 6, p. 115.)

Indexing of the tax system would thus require changes in the capital market, but the problems associated with this would be of a transitional nature. These considerations serve to illustrate the point made in Chapter 6, namely that indexation against inflation raises more difficulties with an income-based tax than it does with an expenditure-based tax. Indeed, for a truly comprehensive CIT indexation for capital–income adjustment would be very onerous indeed. We have tried in this section of our Report to describe what would in principle be needed; but we doubt whether a properly indexed truly comprehensive income base is a practical proposition.

GIFTS AND BEQUESTS

Gifts and bequests received would be included in the base of the CIT, which adds to the need for adequate averaging provisions. In theory, it would be perfectly possible to have an additional transfer tax to reflect the circumstances of the donor, although we find it hard to believe that the case for this would be very strong, except perhaps at the very top end. The extra tax would probably be a transfer tax rather than an accessions tax.

AVERAGING

Under a CIT the value of taxable income will fluctuate markedly from year to year for a limited number of persons, and if the tax is progressive then the marginal tax rate will be a function of income. As a result, major averaging provisions will be required. We outline three methods of averaging which could be used with a CIT.

1 TAX RESERVE CERTIFICATES

The first method is to allow individuals to purchase tax reserve certificates, the purchases of which would be tax-deductible and the sales of which would be added to taxable income. There would be no limit on these purchases. This would enable a taxpayer to average forward over time and would help people (such as pop stars) with very high current incomes which were expected to be only temporary. Of course, this idea is very similar to the use of an expenditure tax to smooth a tax liability in cases where incomes fluctuate greatly. No interest would be payable, however, on the tax reserve certificates. If interest were paid, then anybody would be able to save tax-free even if their incomes did not fluctuate, and this would be the equivalent of giving full expenditure-tax treatment to saving. It would also seem impossible to index the value of the certificates unless other government securities were available which were indexed and thus offered guaranteed positive real rates of return. Even if the tax system itself is indexed in the ways described, real rates of return will remain negative so long as the rate of inflation exceeds the money rate of interest; indexation of the tax system merely means that the real loss of capital value can be set against income for tax purposes. It would thus be anomalous to issue in unrestricted amounts tax certificates which were indexed against all real loss while other government securities were not so indexed.

2   BLOCK AVERAGING

The second method is to allow individuals to average backwards by a system of 'block averaging' as proposed by the Carter Commission. In any year an individual could elect to spread his current income over both the current year and a sequence of preceding years, subject to the following constraints:

1   The averaging period must consist of *consecutive* years.
2   The maximum number of years used is five.
3   Once a year has been used in an averaging calculation, it cannot be used again.

An example: suppose that the tax years are calendar years and that an individual's receipts are as follows:

Year	Income (£)
1970	2,000
1971	4,000
1972	4,000
1973	8,000
1974	20,000
TOTAL	38,000

In the years 1970–73 the individual pays tax on his current income. In 1974 he finds that his income is unexpectedly large, so he elects to average. He is entitled to divide the £20,000 between the years 1970–74 in any way he wishes, subject to the constraints given above. For example, the amounts allocated and the new levels of taxable income in each year might be:

Year	Amount allocated (£)	New income (£)
1970	4,000	6,000
1971	3,000	7,000
1972	3,000	7,000
1973	1,000	9,000
1974	9,000	9,000
TOTAL	20,000	38,000

Given the tax schedules for each year, the total liability for each year is calculated and the difference between the new liability and the amount paid in the past is collected. The effect of the constraints is:

1 Although the taxpayer might wish to exclude 1973 in the hope of using that year for averaging purposes in later years, this is forbidden. Year 1973 must be included as the averaging period must consist of consecutive years.
2 The averaging cannot go back beyond 1970.
3 In any future averaging calculation, the first year will be 1975. Thus no averaging can take place until 1976, when an average of 1975 and 1976 can be used. It will be 1979 before another averaging period of five years is available.

3 AVERAGING BY ANNUITY VALUES

A third method could be used to tax large capital receipts. The idea is to approximate averaging over the lifecycle. Theoretically, a lifetime cumulative CIT could be envisaged. This would be extremely complex administratively.[6] But for large capital receipts we suggest for consideration a scheme of forward averaging over the expected remaining lifetime.

The principle of the scheme is that the capital receipt is converted into an annuity value corresponding to (i) the individual's expectation of life, and (ii) an interest rate announced by the government. Theoretically this should be a post-tax interest rate, and it could be constructed on the same principles as the interest rate used in the capital gains calculations described above, except that it is a forward looking interest rate, not a rate obtaining over a specified period of time in the past.

The annuity value is added to current income and is deemed to be the marginal addition. The extra tax payable due to the addition of the annuity value is converted into an average rate on the annuity. The value of this rate is then applied to the whole capital receipt. The tax is paid at the time of the receipt, but the amount is determined by this method of lifetime averaging.

To calculate the annuity value the government would publish a set of tables corresponding to (i) different lengths of time for the horizon of the annuity, and (ii) different interest rates. Then each year the government would publish (i) the interest rate to be used and (ii) tables of expectation of life by sex and age group. There would be a *de minimis* provision to ensure

---

[6] Theoretically this could be done by applying, as it were, a pay-as-you-earn (PAYE) system, not merely over a year's income as it accrued week by week, but over a lifetime's income as it accrued year by year. Thus each year cumulative totals would be struck for the total income which the taxpayer had received and for the total tax which he had paid over his whole life up to date. A calculation could then be made of the tax which he would have paid if each year he had received the average of this total income evenly over his life up to date. He would then be liable to pay additional tax (or to receive a tax rebate) equal to the excess (or deficiency) of this calculated lifetime tax liability over the total tax which he had actually paid to date. Such a system of lifetime averaging was described by Professor W. Vickrey in his *Agenda for Progressive Taxation* (New York: Ronald Press, 1947), ch. 6.

that the method could be used only if the tax saving exceeded a certain minimum amount.

Such a procedure would apply only to capital receipts. It could not apply to the pop star's large earnings because the equivalent capital receipt – the increase in the value of human capital – is not taxed at all. Clearly, there would again be the unfortunate distinction between capital and income.

It is apparent that under a CIT averaging could be troublesome, though it would affect only a limited number of taxpayers; but this seems to be a price which one would have to pay for the advantages of a tax on comprehensive income.

PENSION FUNDS AND LIFE ASSURANCE POLICIES

LIFE ASSURANCE POLICIES

Under the existing regime, qualifying life assurance policies (broadly speaking, those involving regular annual premiums) are privileged in three ways:

1 On premiums which do not exceed one-sixth of total income the taxpayer paying the premiums gets relief at half the basic rate.
2 The rate of tax on income and capital gains received by insurance companies that are earmarked for the benefit of policyholders is restricted to 37·5 per cent.
3 Policyholders do not pay higher rate tax on the 'income' content of policy proceeds. (The amount paid on maturity of a life assurance policy can be regarded as a return of premiums plus income and capital gains earned thereon during the currency of the policy, less the cost of providing for the risk that the policyholder may die before his normal expectation of life and less also the insurance company's expenses of management and profit.)

The treatment of a single premium and other non-qualifying policies is less favourable since they do not attract the relief at (1) above, and the excess of policy proceeds over premiums (unindexed) may be liable to higher rate tax in the hands of the taxpayer. Term insurance cover (under which nothing is payable by the insurance company if the taxpayer survives to a stipulated date) attracts all three privileges set out above.

If the tax treatment of life assurance policies is to be assimilated to that of normal savings, it would seem to be necessary to make arrangements on the following lines:

1 No relief is to be given to the policyholder on premiums paid by him.
2 The insurance company is to be liable at basic rate on income and capital gains earmarked for policyholders.
3 Policyholders liable to higher rate tax are to pay that tax on the excess of policy proceeds over indexed premiums. The excess would be grossed

up at the basic rate (since the insurance company will have borne basic rate tax on its income and capital gains), and the amount of the grossing up would be credited against the higher rate tax. Since in most cases the excess will have accrued over a long period, it would almost certainly be necessary to give averaging relief of some kind. (But on the other hand there would be the benefit of deferral.)

4 Since insurance company taxation is a highly specialised subject, we have not thought it necessary to consider it in detail. But in principle it seems to us that under a CIT a life insurance company should have its profit based on actuarial principles and not on its investment income and capital gains less management expenses as at present. The profit as thus computed would then be dealt with in the same way as for other companies.

The problems involved in making changes of this magnitude would be enormous. There would be very great pressure to continue existing privileges for policies taken out before the appointed day. If that was done, the accounting and tax treatment of life assurance companies would become extremely complicated. The computation of indexed premiums referred to at (3) above would be an additional burden for insurance companies, although perhaps not an impossible one since most are highly computerised. Under the altered treatment there would be no distinction between qualifying and unqualifying policies, and premiums paid on term insurance cover would attract no tax relief.

PENSION FUNDS

Under a CIT the logical treatment, as with life assurance policies, would be to withdraw the existing concessions whereby contributions to pension funds (within certain limits) are tax-deductible, the income and capital gains of approved pension funds are tax-free and approved lump sums are tax-free. This would not be easy. For example, in many pension schemes, both contributory and non-contributory, employers' contributions are frequently not related to individual employees. In many cases the allocation of such contributions among employees (and in some cases among pensioners) could only be done on a fairly arbitrary basis. In addition, if employers made substantial 'topping-up' payments into a pension fund, individuals would find themselves facing problems of lumpiness in tax payments.

What would have happened to civil servants in recent years? In fact the case of civil servants illustrates the difficulty of implementing a pure annual CIT. First, no actual pension fund exists, only a 'notional' fund; but the promise of inflation-proofed pensions is a real one, and presumably the tax authorities would have to calculate the implicit contribution. Moreover, in 1975 civil servants would have faced enormous tax bills if these implicit contributions had been taxed. Even if only the real increase in the value of pension rights were taxed, the amounts involved could be substantial. If civil servants were not taxed on any increase in the value of their pension rights due to their being inflation proofed, then horizontal equity would suggest that there should be some form of tax relief for those persons with pension rights which were not so protected.

If the investment income and capital gains of pension funds are not to be exempt, then there are problems about allocating them among pension fund members.

Some of these difficulties result from the attempt to implement an annual CIT. If the lifecycle is seen as a more appropriate period over which to measure income, then there is a case for allowing individuals to save tax-free for consumption in retirement. Thus it is possible to justify within a CIT some relief on pension contributions (and a relief of this sort was embodied in the proposals of the Carter Commission).[7]

The CIT treatment of pension funds would seem to require something on the following lines:

1   Abolishing the relief on employees' contributions.
2   Attributing employers' contributions to members of the fund and assessing them on their share.
3   Abolishing the income tax and capital gains tax exemption of pension funds and apportioning those amounts among members of the fund in proportion to their interest in the fund.
4   Dividing pensions into two parts, one of which was taxable and the other tax-free, along similar lines to those currently used for purchased life annuities. The tax-free element would derive from employers' and employees' contributions and from income and capital gain during the build-up period, while the taxable amounts would represent income and capital gain during the pension payment period.

It might be possible to avoid attributing income and capital gain during the build-up period to members of the fund by increasing the taxable part of the pension referred to in (4) above. But it is not clear where the balance of advantage would lie, in view of the difficulty of allowing for the differing lengths of the build-up period and of the rate of contributions during those periods.

Clearly, these changes would present formidable problems, particularly as the old and the new treatment would have to march in parallel for many years.

These difficulties, coupled with the lifecycle argument mentioned in an earlier paragraph, seem to us to justify retention of the current tax treatment

[7] If relief of tax on savings for retirement is limited in amount, any savings above this amount will be taxed. For any taxpayer who is saving more than the restricted tax-free amount, the relief will, therefore, not affect his incentive to save; he will pay tax as before on any additional £1 which he saves. The relief must be regarded primarily as a device for the equitable distribution of tax burdens for those whose incomes fluctuate over years of earning and years of retirement rather than as a removal of any tax disincentive on savings, such as would result from a full expenditure tax principle.

except that lump sum benefits would become taxable, probably with averaging relief.

BUSINESS INCOME

DEPRECIATION, STOCKS AND MONEY LIABILITIES

To obtain a true estimate of income derived from business activities, it would be necessary to abolish 'free' or accelerated depreciation on plant and machinery, and on other fixed and working assets, and to replace it by 'true' economic depreciation. Depreciation rates intended to spread the cost of the asset over its useful working life would be applied to original cost (if the straight line method were used) or to written down value (for the reducing balance method). But each year the original cost or written-down value (as the case may be) would be increased by an inflation factor corresponding to the *average* rate of inflation, and not to a price index for the particular asset in question. In this way depreciation would be given not at historic cost but at indexed cost, and *real* holding gains on assets would be counted as income for tax purposes as and when they were realised.

In the case of stocks, the increase in the real book value of stocks would be taxed by subtracting from the closing value the opening value multiplied by the inflation adjustment factor.

Businesses could be allowed to deduct from their tax base all nominal interest payments, but in this case the fall in the real value of their net monetary liabilities would be added to taxable earnings. This would be done by applying the standard inflation adjustment factor to the opening value of net monetary liabilities on the balance sheet.

Capital gains would be treated in the way described above.

Unutilised tax losses would be carried forward marked up by the interest factor derived from a published table of the kind already discussed.

INTEGRATION OF COMPANY TAXATION AND PERSONAL INCOME TAX

This leaves open one major problem, namely the treatment of undistributed company profits. The treatment which would be most in harmony with a true CIT would be to allocate to each shareholder for inclusion in his tax base his *pro rata* share of the equity earnings of the company which had not actually been paid out to him in dividends. The basic idea would be to tax the company as if the shareholders formed a partnership. This has the great advantage that the need for special legislation to treat close companies differently from other companies would disappear.

Taxable profits would be defined by subtracting from receipts costs and appropriate allowances for depreciation, as described above. Capital gains by companies would be regarded as normal income, and no restriction would be placed on their distribution. Taxable equity earnings would be defined as taxable profits minus nominal interest payments. The latter would be made after a deduction of a withholding tax, which would represent a prepayment of personal income tax. The rate of withholding tax would be the basic rate of income tax.

A flat rate of corporation tax would be levied on taxable equity earnings. This rate could be either the basic rate of income tax or a special rate for corporate businesses. Dividends would be paid out as under the current system with a tax credit, and the taxable income associated with the dividend would be the dividend received plus the tax credit. The rate of imputation would be 100 per cent of the rate of corporation tax. Along with the dividend would go another piece of paper giving the amount of the 'non-distributable dividend' and associated tax credit, which would be a statement of the shareholder's proportion of taxable equity earnings minus dividends. The non-distributable dividend plus tax credit would be added to his taxable income. The shareholder's personal CIT liability would be calculated, and the two tax credits would be available to offset this.

A number of administrative problems arise. First, the allocation of retained earnings to shareholders need not be tied in with the payment of a final dividend, although the system would be easier to comprehend by all concerned if it were. There could be a rule requiring apportionment within six months of the end of the accounting period. Secondly, final profit figures would not have been agreed between the company and the Revenue when the apportionment was made. Companies would have to use estimated figures, and differences between those estimates and finally agreed figures would have to be adjusted when making the apportionment for later years.

Capital gains on a company's shares may arise because profits have not been distributed but have been put to reserve with a corresponding increase in the value of the assets and of the shares of the company. Since with the system described above shareholders will have paid full tax at their personal marginal rates of tax on all capital gains which are directly due to the ploughing back of profits, such capital gains must not be taxed again. For this purpose the acquisition cost of an individual's shareholding would be increased each year by the amount of his non-distributable dividend. This system would mean that the non-distributable dividend vouchers would have to be produced in order to confirm the adjusted acquisition cost of a taxpayer's shares when he realised them. The onus of keeping and producing for later inspection the non-distributable vouchers would rest with the taxpayer.[8]

This arrangement would operate in a straightforward manner so long as there was no change in the ownership of the shares. It is a matter for further consideration whether any special rules would need to be devised for dealing with a change of ownership of shares in the course of the company's accounting year, or between the close of the accounting year and the date when the non-distributable dividends in respect of that accounting year were issued to the shareholders.

---

[8] A similar scheme, which required holders of unit trusts to retain vouchers showing their share of the capital gains tax paid by unit trusts, proved cumbersome and was withdrawn.

In any case the rules should be such as to ensure that capital gains over and above those which corresponded to the amounts of profit ploughed back into the business (e.g. capital gains due to a fall in the rate of interest at which company profits were capitalised, or those due to some unexpected change in the company's profitability) would be liable to tax on realisation in the way already discussed. If capital gains were indexed there would be a problem in indexing these 'equivalent acquisitions', and this would make for a very complicated calculation on disposal of shares.[9]

OTHER FORMS OF CORPORATION TAX

It is important to recognise that the arrangements just described do not result in any extra taxation on corporate, as contrasted with unincorporated, businesses. They constitute simply a method of submitting to a shareholder's own personal rate of income tax his *pro rata* share of the profits of the enterprise that have been ploughed back into the business. If it is desired to levy a special additional tax on the profits of corporate businesses (e.g. in payment for the benefits of limited liability), then some further additional tax on companies will be necessary.

There are in fact two quite separate reasons for advocating the institution of a special corporation tax regime in addition to the personal income tax regime.

The first is, as we have just mentioned, the desire to tax corporate business more heavily than unincorporated business.

The second reason arises if it is considered impossible to integrate the taxation of undistributed company profits into the regime for the taxation of the individual shareholders' personal incomes in the way outlined. In this case corporate undistributed profits must be taxed at some arbitrary rate. In choosing that rate, even if there is no desire to tax corporate business more heavily than unincorporated business, it may well be considered proper to set a special rate which is higher than the basic rate of income tax on the grounds that the average shareholder is likely to be a higher rate taxpayer. We return to these possibilities in Chapter 12 when we discuss the corporation tax.

OTHER REMAINING PROBLEMS

TRUSTS, HOUSING AND ADMINISTRATION

There are a number of other important problems that arise in connection with the operation of a CIT, but we shall discuss these later in chapters devoted to these specific problems. In particular we relegate the discussion

---

[9] An alternative, equally complex method, would be to revalue the acquisition value of a holding of shares each year. This would correspond with the proposals described in footnote 5 (p. 135) as a way of avoiding a FIFO or LIFO rule for capital gains.

of the tax treatment of housing to Chapter 11, of trusts to Chapter 19 and of administration to Chapter 22.

TAX RELATIONS WITH OTHER COUNTRIES

In Chapter 21 (pp. 430–433) we shall discuss tax relations with other countries under a CIT. The problems raised by these relations are less acute than those which would arise if the United Kingdom had an expenditure tax while other countries had an income tax.

REVENUE EFFECTS

We make no attempt in this chapter to assess the effect which a change from the present UK income tax and corporation tax arrangements to a full CIT might have on the tax base and so on the amount of tax revenue. It is not certain that the amount of tax revenue would be greater than at present, since full indexation for capital–income adjustment against inflation would cause a reduction in revenue, while the extension of the real base in other ways would increase the revenue. In Chapter 23, however, we shall consider certain extensions of the tax base in the direction of a CIT, but without the introduction of any indexation for capital–income adjustment. Such extensions would increase the tax revenue, and tentative estimates of their effect will be given in Chapter 23.

CONCLUSIONS

The principal advantages that we see in a CIT are the following:

1 The effect on the yield of tax revenue of a full CIT combined with full indexation against inflation is uncertain. But without indexation against inflation some extensions of the tax base in the direction of a CIT should make it possible to raise the same revenue as at present with lower marginal rates of tax (see Chapter 23).
2 The idea of taxing gifts and inheritances to CIT offers the possibility of removing the need for a separate capital transfer tax and yet at the same time setting a rate of tax on gifts and inheritances received which was progressively related to the recipient's income. But this would be done at the cost of abandoning the cumulative principle for gifts and bequests.
3 It removes the incentive to convert one kind of income into another simply to avoid tax.

The principal disadvantages that we see in a CIT are as follows:

1 It is difficult to produce a satisfactory measure of income for tax purposes. The example of pension contributions discussed above demonstrates that the pure annual CIT is almost impossible to achieve, and in practice

the CIT treats human capital differently from money or physical capital.

2 The changes required to index the tax for inflation would be extremely complex, with heavy administrative and compliance costs.

3 The changes in the corporation tax would also be burdensome and complex.

4 The averaging provisions needed would also be complex, as well as costly both to administer and to comply with.

Appendix 7.1   Mathematical Appendix on Inflation, Deferral and Capital Gains Taxation

Assume an asset is acquired at a cost A, held for n years and sold for a value S. The average real rate of capital gain is g, and

$$e^{gn} = \frac{S}{AI}$$

where I is the general level of money prices at the end of the period as a ratio of its level at the beginning of the period. Hence

$$g = \frac{1}{n} \log \frac{S}{AI}$$

The average nominal rate of capital gain is $(g+p)$ where p is the rate of inflation, so that

$$e^{(g+p)n} = \frac{S}{A}$$

At time t the real gain is

$$gAe^{(g+p)t}$$

But the taxable real gain at time n accruing at time t is the real gain at time t marked up by the interest factor $e^{r(n-t)}$ where r is the interest rate used. Hence the total taxable real gain at realisation date n is

$$\int_0^n gAe^{(g+p)t} e^{r(n-t)} dt = \frac{gAe^{rn}}{g+p-r} (e^{(g+p-r)n} - 1)$$

$$= \frac{gA}{g+p-r} (e^{(g+p)n} - e^{rn})$$

Since the rate of interest should be the post-tax rate of interest, $r = (1-m)i$ where i is an appropriate market rate of interest and m is the individual's marginal rate of income tax. Hence

$$e^{rn} = e^{(1-m)in} = R^{1-m}$$

where R is the published interest factor for the period from time 0 to time n. Hence the taxable gain is

$$\frac{gA}{g+p-r} \left(\frac{S}{A} - R^{1-m} \right)$$

Now

$$\frac{g}{g+p-r} = \frac{\dfrac{1}{n} \log \dfrac{S}{AI}}{\dfrac{1}{n} \log \dfrac{S}{A} - \dfrac{1}{n} (1-m) \log R}$$

Therefore the taxable gain on realisation expressed in terms of variables either directly observed or published by the government is

$$\left(\frac{\log S - \log A - \log I}{\log S - \log A - (1-m)\log R} \right)(S - AR^{1-m})$$

If A is actual acquisition cost, C_1 is acquisition cost adjusted for inflation ($= AI$), and C_2 is acquisition cost adjusted by the interest factor ($= AR^{1-m}$), then

$$\text{taxable gain} = \frac{\log \dfrac{S}{C_1}}{\log \dfrac{S}{C_2}}(S - C_2)$$

8 Forms of Expenditure Tax

In Chapter 3 we have considered a number of the general qualities of a system which relied upon consumption expenditure rather than income as the tax base. We do not intend in this chapter to repeat that discussion of the general merits and demerits of such a tax system; rather we intend to consider the different ways in which it might be applied.

THE *MODUS OPERANDI* OF A PROGRESSIVE EXPENDITURE TAX

If it were desired to levy a rate of tax which rises progressively with a taxpayer's consumption, some means would have to be found to estimate each year for each separate taxpayer his total expenditure on consumption. The only possible way of setting about this estimation would be to calculate the taxpayer's consumption indirectly. His total receipts in the course of the year on both capital and current account would be the starting point, and from these total 'incomings' it would be necessary to deduct all his 'outgoings' on everything other than the consumption items which it was desired to tax. Total incomings less total non-consumption outgoings would necessarily leave total consumption outgoings as a balance. The method is illustrated in Table 8.1.

This table does not purport to give at this stage more than a general idea of the method of calculation. Indeed much of the next chapter will be devoted to a more detailed discussion of what items should be included and what should not and of the methods of keeping track of the various relevant items. But the principle is clear. All receipts should be included in items 1, 2 or 3 of the table, and item 4 should include all those expenditures which it is desired to treat as not being taxable consumption expenditures.

Thus, for example, if it is desired to submit the making of gifts to expenditure tax, gifts should not be included in item 4 (see Chapter 3, p. 41).

The other item which, even at this stage, we have queried in Table 8.1 as an uncertain candidate for inclusion in the non-consumption outgoings of item 4, is direct taxes paid by the taxpayer in question. If the expenditure tax paid is included in item 4, consumption expenditure in item 5 will be estimated exclusive of expenditure tax; if the expenditure tax paid is not included in item 4, then consumption in item 5 is estimated inclusive of expenditure tax. In the former case expenditure tax must be applied on a tax-exclusive basis to estimated consumption, but in the latter case it must be applied on a tax-inclusive basis. The basic outcome is not affected by the choice between the two methods, the differences between which are discussed in Appendix 8.1. We shall conduct our description of the expenditure tax for the most part in the rest of this Report on the assumption that the tax-exclusive basis is adopted.

It can be seen from Table 8.1 that this calculation of a taxpayer's total expenditure on consumption starts in item 1 by taking what under income tax would be his personal taxable income, and then adds to this items 2 and 3 minus item 4, namely the difference between his capital and windfall receipts and his non-consumption outgoings. In what follows we shall call the sum of items $(2+3-4)$ the '*expenditure tax adjustment*'. It represents what must be added to the taxpayer's income if he is spending on consumption

Table 8.1   *Computation of the assessment of liability to a comprehensive expenditure tax*

ADD		
1 *Personal incomes*		
Wages	XXX	
Salaries	XXX	
Dividends	XXX	
Interest	XXX	
Rent	XXX	
Profits	XXX	
Royalties	XXX	
	———	XXX
2 *Capital receipts*		
Realisation of capital assets	XXX	
Amount borrowed	XXX	
Receipt of repayment of past loans	XXX	
Reduction in money balances	XXX	
	———	XXX
3 *Windfall incomings*		
Inheritances	XXX	
Gifts received	XXX	
	———	XXX
Total chargeable items		XXX
DEDUCT		
4 *Non-consumption outgoings*		
Acquisition of assets	XXX	
Amount lent	XXX	
Repayment of past borrowings	XXX	
Increase in money balances	XXX	
(? Gifts made)	XXX	
(? Direct taxes paid)	XXX	
	———	(XXX)
Total allowable deductions		(XXX)
5 *Chargeable balance*		
(Representing Expenditure on consumption)		XXX

more than his income or what must be subtracted from his income if he is spending on consumption less than his income. Thus, if there were no gifts or windfalls, the 'expenditure tax adjustment' would consist simply of (i) the addition to the taxpayer's taxable personal income of his net dissavings, or (ii) the subtraction of his net savings. We shall call this the '*income adjustment method*' of applying the expenditure tax principle.

ALTERNATIVE METHODS OF APPLYING A PROPORTIONATE EXPENDITURE TAX

We have explained in Chapter 3 (p. 37) that we would test whether an expenditure tax principle was or was not in operation by asking whether, given constant rates of tax, the tax system did or did not lead to an equality between the rate of return on an individual's savings and the rate of yield on the investment which was financed by those savings. On this criterion there are a number of ways in which a constant rate of expenditure tax might be applied. Table 8.2 illustrates the basic possibilities.[1]

As in Chapter 3 (p. 36), we take as an illustration the case of Mr Brown who earns £150 and is faced with a tax at a (tax-inclusive) rate of $33\frac{1}{3}$ per cent either (i) on his income, or (ii) on his expenditure on consumption, and who has the opportunity of investing his savings in some line of activity which will produce a steady annual pre-tax yield of 10 per cent after economic depreciation. The first two columns of Table 8.2 merely reproduce the figures in the first two columns of Table 3.1 (p. 36).

Column B of Table 8.2 can represent the effect of a proportionate expenditure tax at a (tax-inclusive) rate of $33\frac{1}{3}$ per cent, levied through the 'income adjustment method' just described, by making an 'expenditure tax adjustment' to personal income in order to calculate the tax base. But column B of the table can equally well represent the effect of a uniform and universal tax on value added at a (tax-inclusive) rate of $33\frac{1}{3}$ per cent, levied on all consumption goods and services, any such tax previously paid on the purchase of the inputs of raw materials, capital goods, etc. being repaid to the producer of the consumption goods and services.[2]

As we have already explained, the income tax regime of column A causes the return to the saver (at $6\frac{2}{3}$ per cent) to fall below the rate of yield on the investment (at 10 per cent), whereas the VAT type of regime of column B causes the return to the saver (who obtains an annual consumption of £10 as a result of an initial once-for-all reduction in his consumption by £100) to be equal to the 10 per cent yield on the investment.

---

[1] Some rather more complicated examples, which apply the principle to corporation tax as well as to income tax, are discussed in Appendix 8.2.

[2] Such a uniform and universal tax on value added would differ from the present VAT in two essential respects. In the first place, no goods or services would be exempt from the tax; and in the second place, all goods and services would be taxed at the same rate, namely at a 50 per cent (tax-exclusive) rate in our example.

Table 8.2 *Income tax contrasted with different expenditure tax methods (in £s)*

	A	B	C	D
		Tax on value added or proportionate	IT with 100% capital	IT with remission of tax on the yield on
	IT	ET	allowances	investment
I Earnings spent				
1 Earnings	150	150	150	150
2 *Less* IT	(50)	—	(50)	(50)
3 *Less* Tax on value added or ET	—	(50)	—	—
4 Expenditure on consumption	100	100	100	100
II Earnings saved				
5 Earnings	150	150	150	150
6 *Less* IT	(50)	—	(50)	(50)
7 Savings	100	150	100	100
8 Remission of IT	—	—	50	—
9 Investment	100	150	150	100
10 Annual yield[a]	10	15	15	10
11 *Less* IT	$(3\frac{1}{3})$	—	(5)	—
12 *Less* Tax on value added or ET	—	(5)	—	—
13 Annual expenditure on consumption	$6\frac{2}{3}$	10	10	10

[a] The annual yield is the net yield after economic depreciation. For the purpose of illustrating the arithmetic in column C, suppose that the machine costing £150 has a gross annual yield of £30, of which £15 are needed as a depreciation allowance available for reinvestment in machinery in order to make up for the fall in value of the original machine. This gross yield of £30 will be liable to tax of £10. Of the remaining £20, £10 will be needed to pay the yield of £15 to the shareholders free of their income tax liability of £5. This leaves only £10 to offset the £15 depreciation of the machine. But this £10 net-of-tax depreciation allowance will upon reinvestment in a real asset itself attract a 100 per cent capital allowance. It will thus be sufficient for the purchase of real assets worth £15 and suffice to maintain intact the value of the concern's total of real assets.

154   *The Structure and Reform of Direct Taxation*

Columns C and D show two other ways in which this result could be brought about.

In column D the income which is saved and invested is taxed, but the yield on the investment is not taxed; and once again by refraining from consuming £100 in the initial year Mr Brown obtains an annual flow of consumption of £10.

THE EFFECT OF 100 PER CENT CAPITAL ALLOWANCES[3]

Column C of Table 8.2 is of great importance. It demonstrates how the system of 100 per cent capital allowances against investment expenditures (explained in Chapter 4, pp. 50–53, when we were describing the present arrangements in the United Kingdom) has a similar effect. Mr Brown earns his £150 (line 5), pays £50 in income tax (line 6) and saves £100 (line 7). He purchases £100 worth of shares in Smith and Co. Ltd. The company is under an obligation to deduct tax at $33\frac{1}{3}$ per cent (tax-inclusive rate) on its profits before it distributes net-of-tax dividends to Mr Brown; but as a result of a system of 100 per cent capital allowances it is enabled to set all of its expenditure on new machinery as an expense against the profit it is making on other activities before reckoning this tax liability. As a result Smith and Co. Ltd in the year in which it receives Mr Brown's £100 can use this sum to purchase £150 worth of machinery (line 9), the balance of £50 (line 8) coming from the saving in its tax bill due to the allowance of £150 as a cost against its taxable profits of that year.[4] The machine yields £15 a year (line 10), on which Smith and Co. Ltd deduct income tax at the source of £5 (line 11) leaving Mr Brown with a post-tax yield of £10 (line 13).

A COMPARISON OF THE EFFECTS OF A UNIFORM AND UNIVERSAL TAX ON VALUE ADDED AND OF A PROPORTIONATE INCOME TAX WITH 100 PER CENT CAPITAL ALLOWANCES

A comparison of the effects of a uniform and universal tax on value added (column B of Table 8.2) and of a proportionate income tax with 100 per cent capital allowances (column C) shows that they are very similar in their effects, both passing the expenditure tax test of making the rate of return to the saver equal to the rate of yield on the physical investment so financed. As noted in Chapter 4 (p. 52), the exact correspondence between the real effects of the two taxes is likely to be modified by imperfections in the capital market, but the underlying real forces at work are similar. But while the ordinary taxpayer might recognise the tax on value added as being a

[3] In order to illustrate the basic effect of 100 per cent capital allowances in its simplest form we assume that there is no separate corporation tax but that all businesses, whether incorporated or not, are taxed on their profits after deduction of 100 per cent capital allowances at the same proportionate rate of income tax of $33\frac{1}{3}$ per cent (tax-inclusive).

[4] It is assumed that Smith and Co. Ltd have a sufficiently large tax liability on the rest of their turnover to be able to make use of the tax remission on their investment, or else that tax losses can be carried forward with interest to be set against their tax liabilities in future years.

tax levied on consumption expenditure, it is doubtful whether he or she would recognise that an income tax with 100 per cent capital allowances has essentially the same expenditure tax effects.

In fact the proportionate rate of income tax will be levied only on personal incomes after deduction of a tax allowance which relieves the first slice of personal incomes from tax. A uniform and universal tax on value added would raise the price of all consumption goods, so that to reach the same result the personal allowances under the income tax would have to be replaced by some form of tax credit to cover the decreased purchasing power of the first slice of personal incomes (see p. 172 of Appendix 8.3).

With this adjustment the real effects of a uniform and universal tax on value added and of a proportionate income tax with 100 per cent capital allowances would tend to be the same. But there would remain two marked differences in their monetary effects.

In the first place, if the pre-tax nominal money wage rates remained the same (at £150 for Mr Brown in both columns B and C), market prices and the money cost of living would be higher with the tax on value added (raised from £100 to £150 inclusive of the tax), but there would be no deduction of income tax from earnings. With the income tax arrangement, take-home pay would be reduced by income tax from £150 to £100, but the cost of living would not be raised above £100.[5]

A shift from a proportionate income tax with 100 per cent capital allowances to a uniform and universal tax on value added would thus have implications for wage settlements, if the increase in the cost of living were not regarded by wage earners as offset by a reduction of equal value in the basic rate of income tax. Perhaps understanding of the meaning of such a shift has been made easier by the bargaining process which has gone on between the Chancellor and the trade unions in 1976 and 1977 about the relationship between earnings, levels of taxation and prices.

THE EFFECT OF 100 PER CENT CAPITAL ALLOWANCES ON THE RATE OF INTEREST

But there is a second and less obvious distinction between the monetary effects of a uniform and universal tax on value added and of a proportionate income tax with 100 per cent capital allowances. With the tax on value added (column B) the market rate of interest or the market rate of dividend yield on shares should be lower than with the income tax with 100 per cent capital allowances (column C).

With the tax on value added, Mr Brown's savings, i.e. the amount of

---

[5] If, as with the present VAT, exports were exempt from tax and imports were subject to the tax on value added, any rise in market prices due to a rise in the tax should not in itself have any significant effect upon foreign trade. The price in sterling which the foreigner could get for his exports or which he would have to pay for his imports from the United Kingdom would depend upon sterling prices exclusive of the tax on value added. If, however, the tax were not remitted on exports or imposed on imports, any rise in sterling prices due to a rise in the rate of tax on value added would need to be offset by a depreciation in the foreign exchange rate.

money which he puts into Smith and Co. Ltd, is £150 (line 7 of column B) and his annual return is £15 (line 10), giving a market rate of yield of 10 per cent. With the income tax arrangement, the amount which Mr Brown puts into Smith and Co. Ltd is only £100 (line 7 of column C) but he gets a *pre-tax* return of £15 (line 10), giving a market rate of yield of 15 per cent; in this case it is the *post-tax* yield of 10 per cent which corresponds to the rate of yield on the physical investment. It is this phenomenon which will obscure the real working of the system from the ordinary taxpayer; Mr Brown will be well aware that the income tax is reducing the yield on his savings from 15 per cent to 10 per cent; he is unlikely to appreciate the fact that it is the 10 per cent and not the 15 per cent which is linked to the yield on the physical investment which he has financed.

This difference could have important international repercussions. If, as is the case under many double taxation treaties, the foreign investor receives the pre-tax market rate of interest without deduction of UK tax, there may be a greater attraction for the foreigner to invest in the United Kingdom under the income tax arrangement of column C than with the tax on value added of column B. In other words, an income tax with 100 per cent capital allowances, by subsidising the market rate of return on capital, might attract funds into the country in a way in which a tax on value added or a tax levied directly on consumption expenditures would not do. But if tax arrangements were such that the foreigner, like the UK taxpayer, was liable to pay the basic rate of income tax on his investment income, and if this were not offset by double taxation relief against tax payable in his own country, this attraction of foreign capital funds would disappear. (See Chapters 20 and 21 for a further discussion of the international repercussions.)

A PARABLE ILLUSTRATING THE SIMILARITIES AND DIFFERENCES BETWEEN VARIOUS FORMS OF EXPENDITURE TAX

Consider the following parable:

1   At the start there is a set of independent excise duties, administered by Customs and Excise, levied at 50 per cent on all individual purchases of consumption goods and services. In other words, of every £100 of income used to purchase consumption goods and services, £33⅓ go in excise duties.

2   Someone has the bright idea that this system can be more readily administered as VAT is at present. Every producer adds a 50 per cent rate of VAT to his selling prices, but he is able to claim back the VAT that has been charged on all his purchases of goods used for the production of other goods. The result is administratively different from method 1 but has the same effect as a 50 per cent tax on all consumption goods.

3   Someone in Customs and Excise then has the bright idea (the reader is

warned against taking too seriously the administrative aspects of the present parable) that this VAT may be better operated on an annual accounts basis rather than on the present quarterly invoice method. Producers now have to pay each year a tax on value added equal to $33\frac{1}{3}$ per cent of their revenue from sales (at prices inclusive of tax) after the deduction of their expenditures (at prices inclusive of tax) on goods purchased for their productive purposes. The result is still the same as method 1.

4   There is a takeover bid from the Inland Revenue, which administers the arrangements under method 3. Each producer is taxed annually at a $33\frac{1}{3}$ per cent (tax-inclusive) rate on his total revenue from sales after deducting the cost of his purchases of intermediate products such as raw materials, machinery, etc. (which have been taxed at $33\frac{1}{3}$ per cent when supplied by their producers) but without deducting the cost of payments such as wages and salaries to employees, interest to creditors and rents for the use of land (which are paid free of tax and have not been taxed at $33\frac{1}{3}$ per cent when their services were supplied by their owners).

5   The Inland Revenue, remembering the good old days of the income tax, remodels the arrangements under method 4 in the following way. The services provided by employees and owners of other resources, which are remunerated by payments of wages, salaries, interest and rent, are made subject to the $33\frac{1}{3}$ per cent (tax-inclusive) rate of tax; and at the same time their payment by their employers is allowed as a deduction from the tax base of those employers. The purchase of the whole range of a producer's inputs is now treated in the same way; the tax base is revenue from sales less the cost of all inputs (including the cost of services of labour, of borrowed capital or of land, as well as the cost of purchases of raw materials and machinery, regardless of whether those are used for current replacement or for addition to capital stocks). What started under method 1 as an unambiguous proportionate tax on all consumption expenditures has ended at method 5 as a proportionate income tax with 100 per cent capital allowances. The real effect is the same.

THE ADVANTAGES OF METHOD 4

For the application of a proportionate expenditure tax there is much to be said in favour of the ultimate adoption of method 4 in the above parable, which we may call an *income tax form of value added tax* (or ITVAT). The advantages of ITVAT over the VAT methods 2 and 3 would be administrative in that the collection of tax would be through the Inland Revenue's existing machinery for direct taxation on an annual accounts basis rather than through the present more laborious quarterly invoice method. Moreover, the possibilities of evasion with ITVAT would almost certainly be less than with an extension of VAT. A tax-exclusive rate of VAT of 50 per cent would be needed to replace a tax-inclusive rate of ITVAT of $33\frac{1}{3}$ per cent. It may be questionable whether the existing quarterly invoice method of levying VAT could cope with rates of tax of 50 per cent or more, whereas the income tax machinery is well accustomed to coping with rates of $33\frac{1}{3}$ per cent or more.

The advantages of ITVAT over method 5 are of a different kind, namely that ITVAT can be much more readily perceived for what it is (namely a proportionate tax on consumption expenditure) than can an income tax with 100 per cent capital allowances. We have already explained the relevant differences in comparing the effects of a uniform and universal tax on value added with those of an income tax with 100 per cent capital allowances (pp. 154–155 above). In brief, with ITVAT, as with any tax on value added, wages would be free of any income tax and the tax would appear as something which raised the money prices of the goods which the wage earner bought relatively to his money wage earnings, whereas with an income tax with 100 per cent capital allowances the nominal money wage would be subject to tax but the tax would not raise the money price of goods relatively to the nominal money wage earnings. The effect on interest rates is equally important for an understanding of what is really happening. In the case of ITVAT the nominal rate of interest on debt or yield on shares (which would not be subject to tax) is directly linked to the rate of return on real resources used for productive investment, whereas with an income tax with 100 per cent capital allowances it is not the nominal rate of yield, but the nominal rate of yield after deduction of the tax to which it would in this case be subjected, which is linked to the rate of return on the resources used for productive investment. [6]

CAPITAL GAINS UNDER AN INCOME TAX WITH 100 PER CENT CAPITAL ALLOWANCES

A further question may be raised, namely whether, if what is essentially a proportionate expenditure tax is administered as an income tax with 100 per cent capital allowances, this income tax should or should not be accompanied by a capital gains tax at the same proportionate rate. In principle it would seem that there would be no stronger case for a capital gains tax to accompany an income tax with 100 per cent capital allowances than there would be for such a tax to accompany a tax on value added.

We shall consider this problem with the numerical example of columns B (the regime of a tax on value added) and C (the regime of income tax with 100 per cent capital allowances) of Table 8.2. Suppose that in either case for some reason or another an investment in machinery of £150 (line 9) turns out to be exceptionally profitable. The real capital assets become worth 10 per cent more than their cost (i.e. are valued at £165 instead of £150). We may expect as a result of this that in column B Mr Brown's shares will be worth £165 instead of £150 (line 7). If Mr Brown realises the capital gain of £15 and spends that sum on consumption, he will, after payment of tax on

---

[6] The *modus operandi* of ITVAT is considered in more detail in Appendix 8.3.

value added (line 12), have an additional £10 to spend on consumption (line 13).

In column C it cannot be expected that Mr Brown's shares, which are initially worth £100 (line 7), will appreciate by the full £15 capital gain in the value of the machine. Since the purchase of the machine has enjoyed 100 per cent capital allowances, the revenue from any sale of the machine itself as well as from the sale of its annual product will be subject to income tax at $33\frac{1}{3}$ per cent (tax-inclusive).

The asset is subject to a tax liability. Just as an issue of £100 of shares together with remission of tax has financed machinery costing £150, so a machine worth £165 is only worth £110 after meeting the tax liability on it. In this case Mr Brown will have a capital gain on his share value of £10, which he can spend on consumption.[7]

Therefore, if there were no case for combining a capital gains tax with a tax on value added, there would equally be no case for combining a capital gains tax with an income tax with 100 per cent capital allowances. They are both (as we have shown) forms of tax on the purchase of final consumption goods. This is more apparent in the case of a tax on value added, which raises the price of consumption goods relatively to spendable incomes directly; it is less apparent in the case of an income tax with 100 per cent capital allowances, which raises the price of consumption goods relatively to spendable income not by raising the price of consumption goods but by levying tax on incomes before they can be spent. If, of course, it were desired not merely to tax expenditure on consumption goods, however financed, but also to levy a special tax on windfall profits, then a tax on some forms of capital gain would be appropriate. But this would be equally valid for a tax on value added as it would be for an income tax with 100 per cent capital allowances.

Once again the question arises whether the situation would be comprehended by the ordinary taxpayer. In principle there may be no more logic in taxing capital gains under an income tax with 100 per cent capital allowances than there would be under a tax on value added; but this is unlikely to appear obvious to the man or woman in the street.

The exact similarity in their real effects between a tax on value added and an income tax with 100 per cent capital allowances is liable to break down if the capital market is imperfect. The story as we have told it depends upon the price of shares following the value of assets net of contingent tax liability. If, in the example just used, Mr Brown's shares in column C of Table 8.2 appreciate by more than the gain in the value of the underlying assets net of contingent tax liability, then Mr Brown will in fact gain more from a windfall profit under an income tax with 100 per cent capital allowances than under an equivalent tax on value added. The tax on value added is not merely capable of being more readily perceived as a tax on consumption; it is in fact a more reliable route to that end.

[7] See pp. 236–237 of Chapter 12 on the corporation tax, where this relationship between share values, asset values and tax liabilities is discussed in somewhat more detail.

THE DISTINCTION BETWEEN A UNIVERSAL EXPENDITURE TAX (UET) AND A TWO-TIER EXPENDITURE TAX (TTET)

We have outlined four different methods of applying the expenditure tax principle, which may be called (i) the income adjustment method, (ii) the value-added method, (iii) the method of 100 per cent capital allowances, and (iv) the method of tax remission on yield.

The first of these methods is the only one which makes possible a progressive schedule of expenditure tax rates, since it is the only feasible method by which the level of any individual taxpayer's total consumption can be estimated. If this method of assessment of tax liability is applied to every potential taxpayer, rich or poor, the tax will be what we shall call a *universal expenditure tax* (UET).

It would, however, be possible to combine method (i) with methods (ii), (iii) and/or (iv). In particular, a single rate of tax on value added (method (ii)) and/or a single basic rate of income tax with 100 per cent capital allowances (method (iii)) could be used to levy a proportionate rate of expenditure tax over a wide range of expenditure levels, while method (i) replaced only the higher rates of income tax and was used as an additional tax on a limited number of taxpayers to levy a progressive surcharge on expenditures above a predetermined level, comparable to the level at which higher rates of income tax are imposed under present income-tax arrangements. Such a combination of taxes we shall call a *two-tier expenditure tax* (TTET).

It is, however, important not to be misled by these two levels of taxation. The expenditure tax principle is not confined to the additional tax at the higher levels. Even if the income tax method (iii) were employed, the existence of 100 per cent capital allowances would mean that the expenditure tax principle would be in operation throughout the whole range of tax, although this might not be apparent to the ordinary taxpayer. In so far as TTET employed a tax on value added for the standard rate of tax, it would probably be recognised as applying the expenditure tax principle to everyone; but in so far as it made use of an income tax with 100 per cent capital allowances, its true nature would not be readily understood.[8]

CONCLUSIONS

We have considered four possible ways of applying an expenditure tax:

1   The taxpayer's total consumption may be calculated indirectly by taking his total receipts of funds and subtracting from that total any payments that he makes for purposes other than consumption (the income adjustment method).

---

[8] Under an income tax regime persons with low incomes can be relieved from tax by means of personal tax allowances. With a tax on value added some other method must be adopted for the relief of the first slice of income from tax. (See Appendix 8.3, p. 172, and Chapter 10, p. 209.)

2 A proportionate expenditure tax can be applied by means of a universal and uniform rate of tax on value added (the value-added method).
3 A similar result can be achieved by means of a basic rate of income tax with 100 per capital allowances (the method of 100 per cent capital allowances).
4 Relief from tax can be allowed on the yield from an investment instead of on the income by which the investment is financed in the first place (the method of tax remission on yield).

If it is desired that the schedule of expenditure tax rates should be progressive, method 1 must be employed. If this method is used to cover all levels of expenditure, the tax system is called a universal expenditure tax (UET), which we shall examine at length in Chapter 9.

If, however, a long band of expenditure is to be taxed at a single basic rate, method 2 or 3 can be used for the basic rate of tax. Method 1 can then be confined to use as a progressive surcharge on the higher levels of consumption. Such a combination, of method 1 for the surcharge with method 2 or 3 for the basic rate of tax, is called a two-tier expenditure tax (TTET), which we shall examine at length in Chapter 10.

Appendix 8.1   The Choice between a Tax-inclusive and a Tax-exclusive Base for an Expenditure Tax

If the tax that an individual pays in any year is always equal to the tax for which he is liable in that year, then it is never a matter of importance to him or to the Revenue authorities whether the base of the tax is tax-inclusive or tax-exclusive. Consider someone who is liable to tax at a rate of 75 per cent (tax-inclusive) or 300 per cent (tax-exclusive). His annual income is £160, and his normal savings are £40. Then his tax assessment appears as follows:

Tax-inclusive Base	£	*Tax-exclusive Base*	£
Income	160	Income	160
Less Savings	(40)	*Less* Savings	(40)
	—	*Less* Tax	(90)
Taxable expenditure	120		—
Less Tax	(90)	Taxable expenditure	30
	—		
Consumption	30		

Tax due = 75% × £120 = £90   Tax due = 300% × £30 = £90

Thus a problem can arise only if in some particular year payments and liabilities are not equal. Suppose for some reason that only £80 instead of £90 is paid in tax in one year. Then in order to complete the flow-of-funds statement the unpaid tax must be accounted for: it may be saved, consumed or partly saved and partly consumed.

We shall consider the two extreme cases. In case 1 below we assume that the taxpayer maintains his consumption each year at the equilibrium level of £30 and allows any difference between tax paid and tax due to fall on his savings. In case 2 we assume that he maintains his savings each year at the equilibrium level of £40 and allows any difference between tax paid and tax due to fall on his consumption.

CASE 1:   CONSUMPTION MAINTAINED AT £30

With a tax payment of £80 instead of £90 the position will be as follows:

Year 1

Tax-inclusive Base	£	*Tax-exclusive Base*	£
Income	160	Income	160
Less Savings	(50)	*Less* Savings	(50)
	—	*Less* Tax paid	(80)
Taxable expenditure	110		—
Less Tax paid	(80)	Taxable expenditure	30
	—		
Consumption	30		

Tax due = 75% × £110 = £82·5   Tax due = 300% × £30 = £90

On the inclusive base the tax due (£82·5) falls below the taxpayer's long run liability

(£90). On the exclusive base, the tax due (£90) is the same as the long run liability (£90). On the inclusive base the taxpayer has an unpaid liability of £82·5−£80 = £2·5; with the exclusive base he has an unpaid liability of £90−£80 = £10.

If in year 2 the taxman manages to put in a bill for the overdue tax and at the same time to make a correct assessment for the year 2 liability, then the year 2 assessments will be as follows:

Year 2

Tax-inclusive Base	£	*Tax-exclusive Base*	£
Income	160	Income	160
Less Savings	(30)	*Less* Savings	(30)
		Less Tax paid	(100)
Taxable expenditure	130	Taxable expenditure	30
Less Tax paid	(100)		
Consumption	30		

Tax due on year 2 = 75% × £130 = £97·5   Tax due on year 2 = 300% × £30 = £90

Tax underpaid in year 1 = £2·5   Tax underpaid in year 1 = £10

Total tax due = £100   Total tax due = £100

In both cases the tax paid over the two years is the same (£180) and is correct, given the long run liability of £90 a year. Equilibrium has now been restored; and in each future year, unless and until there is another disturbance, tax liability and tax paid will be £90 and savings will be £40 under both systems.

Problems will arise in year 2 only if the tax paid is once more different from the amount due. One way in which this may happen is if the taxman is always working one year in arrears. In that case, since in year 1 the tax liability was £82·5 under the tax-inclusive system and £90 under the tax-exclusive system, the position in years 2, 3 and 4 will be as follows:

Year 2

Tax-inclusive Base	£	*Tax-exclusive Base*	£
Income	160	Income	160
Less Savings	(49·5)	*Less* Savings	(40)
Taxable expenditure	112·5	*Less* Tax due in year 1 and paid in year 2	(90)
Less Tax due in year 1 and paid in year 2	(82·5)		30
Consumption	30		

Tax due = 75% × £112·5 = £84·4   Tax due = 300% × £30 = £90

Year 3

Tax-inclusive Base		*Tax-exclusive Base*
	£	
Income	160	As in year 2.
Less Savings	(45·6)	
Taxable expenditure	114·4	
Less Tax due in year 2 and paid		
in year 3	(84·4)	
Consumption	30	

Tax due $= 75\% \times £114\cdot4 = £85\cdot8$

Year 4

Tax-inclusive Base		*Tax-exclusive Base*
	£	
Income	160	As in year 3.
Less Savings	(42·2)	
Taxable expenditure	115·8	
Less Tax due in year 3 and paid		
in year 4	(85·8)	
Consumption	30	

Tax due $= 75\% \times £115\cdot8 = £86\cdot8$

Thus in this case, on the tax-exclusive base equilibrium is restored at once in year 2; whereas with the tax-inclusive base equilibrium is approached only gradually over the years, savings falling gradually back to £40 and tax payments rising gradually up to the equilibrium level of £90.

CASE 2: SAVINGS MAINTAINED AT £40

We turn now to the possibility that any discrepancy between tax payments and tax liabilities is met by the taxpayer not through adjustment of his savings but through adjustment of his consumption. He saves every year £40 out of his income of £160 and simply spends on consumption what is then left over after his actual payment of taxes in the year in question. In year 1, when, as we assumed for case 1, for some reason he pays only £80 instead of £90 in tax, the position will be as follows:

Year 1

Tax-inclusive Base		*Tax-exclusive Base*	
	£		£
Income	160	Income	160
Less Savings	(40)	*Less* Savings	(40)
	——	*Less* Tax paid	(80)
Taxable expenditure	120		——
Less Tax paid	(80)	Taxable expenditure	40
Consumption	40		

Tax due = 75% × £120 = £90   Tax due = 300% × £40 = £120

In this case it is the inclusive basis which continues to measure the tax liability correctly, and it is the exclusive basis which is erratic. The error is now much larger, because it is multiplied by 300 per cent instead of 75 per cent.

Again, however, the position can be retrieved in year 2 if the taxman puts in a claim for tax underpaid in year 1 and also at the same time correctly assesses the liability for year 2:

Year 2

Tax-inclusive Base		*Tax-exclusive Base*	
	£		£
Income	160	Income	160
Less Savings	(40)	*Less* Savings	(40)
	——	*Less* Tax paid	(100)
Taxable expenditure	120		——
Less Tax paid	(100)	Taxable expenditure	20
Consumption	20		

Tax due on year 2 = 75% × £120 = £90   Tax due in year 2 = 300% × £20 = £60

Tax underpaid in year 1 = £10   Tax underpaid in year 1 = £40

Total tax due = £100   Total tax due = £100

In year 3 under both systems consumption can be restored to the equilibrium level of £30, and the tax payable will in both cases be £90.

If, however, the tax actually paid in any one year is equal to the tax due from the previous year, under the tax-inclusive base equilibrium will be restored in year 2, but the tax-exclusive base will result in more extreme fluctuations. Since in year 1, as we have shown, tax due was £90 with the inclusive basis but £120 with the exclusive basis, the position in years 2 and 3 will be as follows:

Year 2

	Tax-inclusive Base	£		Tax-exclusive Base	£
Income		160	Income		160
Less Savings		(40)	*Less* Savings		(40)
		—	*Less* Tax due in year 1		
Taxable expenditure		120	and paid in year 2		(120)
Less Tax due in year 1					—
and paid in year 2		(90)	Taxable expenditure		nil
		—			
Consumption		30			

Tax due $= 75\% \times £120 = £90$ Tax due $= 300\% \times$ nil $=$ nil

Year 3

Tax-inclusive Base		Tax-exclusive Base	£
As in year 2.		Income	160
		Less Savings	(40)
		Less Tax due in year 2	
		and paid in year 3	nil
			—
		Taxable expenditure	120

Tax due $= 300\% \times £120 = £360$

The figures which result from the tax-exclusive base – and the behaviour on which they are based – are clearly ludicrous. But they do serve to illustrate the potential instability of the tax-exclusive base. The explosive result rests, however, upon three assumptions: (i) the automatic passing through of increased or decreased tax payments on to consumption; (ii) the existence of tax-exclusive rates in excess of 100 per cent; and (iii) the levying of tax on a continuing preceding-year base. If in each year payments of tax can be made to approximate to tax liabilities, there will be no continuing problems. The tax-exclusive base is, however, liable to be less stable than the tax-inclusive base; but if the taxpayer is sufficiently alive to the situation to adjust his behaviour so as to maintain his real sustainable consumption, any instability produced by the preceding year basis for tax collection will not arise.

The analysis suggests that if taxpayers meet divergences between tax payments and tax liabilities by adjusting their savings, the tax-exclusive basis leads more surely to the equilibrium position. In so far, however, as such adjustments fall on consumption rather than savings, it is the exclusive method which will lead to error; and these errors could be seriously unstable in the restricted number of cases where tax-exclusive rates are more than 100 per cent (tax-inclusive rates more than 50 per cent).

We consider that the balance of these factors does not point decisively in the one direction or the other. In the main text of our Report we normally use the tax-exclusive method. This choice may be justified on two grounds:

1 Taxpayers are in fact more likely to meet discrepancies between tax payments and tax liabilities through their savings rather than through their consumption.
2 The tax-exclusive method, which makes actual expenditure on consumption rather than income less savings the tax base, is a more straightforward way of bringing home to taxpayers the essential nature and purpose of the tax.

Appendix 8.2 Some Further Numerical Examples of the Expenditure Tax Principle

In Table 8.2 (p. 153) are displayed three ways in which an expenditure tax principle might be applied in the case of a proportionate tax. Column B illustrates a uniform and universal tax on value added; column C illustrates the operation of a proportionate income tax with 100 per cent capital allowances; and column D represents the case in which saved income is taxed but the yield on the investment is not taxed. In addition to the obvious method of simply neglecting the yield for tax purposes, a partial or total remission of tax on the yield can be achieved by means of an imputation system. Table 8.3 here sets out the possibility. It takes up the story from line 10 of Table 8.2 by starting with a yield of £10 on an investment of £100, and in columns D(i) and D(ii) it sets out in a formal manner two methods of exempting this yield of £10 from tax.

Table 8.3 *Remission of tax on the yield on investment*

		IT with remission of tax on the yield on investment	
		D(i) Direct	*D(ii)* Imputation
1	Annual yield	10	10
2	Imputed tax credit	—	5
3	Annual return subject to tax	10	15
4	*Less* IT on (3)	—	(5)
5	Available for consumption after tax	10	10

The direct exemption of yield is shown in column D(i). It may be noted that the deductibility of interest payments from a company's profits before assessing the charge to corporation tax results in the exemption from corporation tax of the yield on a company's assets in so far as that yield is devoted to the payment of interest on the company's loan capital.

Column D(ii) shows the imputation method of achieving the direct exemption of column D(i). In column D(ii) Mr Brown, who has spent his £100 on the purchase of an ordinary share, receives – together with his dividend of £10 (line 1) – a tax credit imputed on this dividend at the proportionate rate of tax of $33\frac{1}{3}$ per cent (line 2). But he is liable to tax at this rate on the grossed-up value of the dividend (line 3), and after satisfying this tax liability (line 4) out of his tax credit (line 2) he is left with a net £10.

It should be noted that all modifications of the taxation of income illustrated in these tables are operative in the present UK tax system. Amounts saved are exempt from income tax in the case of approved pension schemes (column B of Table 8.2); 100 per cent capital allowances are permitted for income and corporation tax in the case of a range of business investments in real capital equipment (column C of Table 8.2); in the case of housing, a man who buys a house out of taxed income does not pay any tax on the imputed real yield from that investment (column D(i) of Table 8.3); in the case of loan capital, interest may be deducted from profits before liability to corporation tax is assessed (a special instance of column D(i) of Table 8.3); and a credit is imputed to relieve liability to the basic rate of income tax on dividends paid by corporations (column D(ii) of Table 8.3).

It is important to note which combinations of these various reliefs are compatible with the maintenance of equality between the rate of return to savers and the rate of yield on the investment which the savings are used to finance. The basic principle is clear. In order to make the rate of return to the saver equal to the rate of return on the investment, there must be set against every individual tax one, and only one, of the three basic reliefs: *either* tax exemption of the amount saved, *or* tax subsidisation of the amount invested, *or* tax exemption of the yield. It is possible to have a system of many individual direct taxes in combination (e.g. an income tax, an expenditure tax and a tax on corporate profits); but provided that one, and only one, separate relief is given exclusively against each tax, the final outcome will leave the yield to the saver unaffected.

Table 8.4 gives an example of three such taxes, each with one relief:

1   There is a corporation tax at a 50 per cent (tax-inclusive) rate with relief in the form of 100 per cent capital allowances.
2   There is an expenditure tax at the rate of 25 per cent (tax-inclusive) with its tax relief on savings.
3   There is an income tax at a rate of $33\frac{1}{3}$ per cent (tax-inclusive) with an imputed tax credit at this rate on distributed dividends.

Such a system will give an expenditure tax outcome for savings invested in a company's ordinary shares whose yield is distributed in dividends. But, of course, care must be taken to ensure that the tax reliefs cover properly each form and channel of savings-investment. For example, the reliefs for loan finance might differ from those for equity finance; but in each case the basic question would remain: 'Is there one appropriate relief against each individual tax in the case of the particular type of savings-investment yield flow that is being considered?' It is important not only to have as many reliefs as there are separate taxes, but also to set each relief separately and appropriately against each tax. Table 8.4 gives a case in which this principle is illustrated.

We now consider (Table 8.5) lending on loan for interest yield to a company rather than investing in equity shares for dividend yield. In each of the three cases illustrated there is a combination of expenditure tax, corporation tax and income tax with three reliefs. But in column A two of the reliefs are set against corporation

Table 8.4   *Saving for the purchase of a company's shares to yield a dividend*

1 Corporation tax (CT) at 50% with 100% capital allowances	
2 Income tax (IT) at $33\frac{1}{3}$% with imputation of tax credit on dividends	
3 Expenditure tax (ET) at 25%	

(All taxes on a tax-inclusive basis)	£
Economy in consumption	100
Saving of ET at 25% on £$133\frac{1}{3}$	$33\frac{1}{3}$
Total saving	$133\frac{1}{3}$
Saving on CT through 100% capital allowances at 50% on £$266\frac{2}{3}$	$133\frac{1}{3}$
Total investment	$266\frac{2}{3}$
Annual yield at 10% on £$266\frac{2}{3}$	$26\frac{2}{3}$
Less CT at 50% on £$26\frac{2}{3}$	$(13\frac{1}{3})$
Dividend	$13\frac{1}{3}$
Tax credit at $33\frac{1}{3}$% on £20	$6\frac{2}{3}$
Dividend grossed up by $33\frac{1}{3}$% rate of IT	20
Less IT payable at $33\frac{1}{3}$% on £20	$(6\frac{2}{3})$
Available for expenditure	$13\frac{1}{3}$
Less ET at 25% on £$13\frac{1}{3}$	$(3\frac{1}{3})$
Annual consumption	10

tax and there is no relief against income tax; whereas in column B one relief is set against each tax. The result is too high a yield in column A because two of the reliefs are set against corporation tax (whose tax rate is high) and none against income tax (whose tax rate is relatively low).

The same end result as in column B can be achieved if the interest relief against income tax is in fact administered as an extra relief against corporation tax. In this case the company will pay so much the less in tax, but will pay interest to the individual lender, which will be subject to income tax. This administrative arrangement is shown in column C. Liability to corporation tax is now £$6\frac{2}{3}$, which is made up of corporation tax at 50 per cent on the annual yield (i.e. tax of £$13\frac{1}{3}$) *less* relief at $33\frac{1}{3}$ per cent on the interest of £20 (line 10) (i.e. less tax of £$6\frac{2}{3}$). The individual lender is then liable (line 11) to pay this income tax on his interest, which is now paid subject to tax. His final position is the same as in column B.

In column B the lender receives interest of £$13\frac{1}{3}$ (line 10) on his savings of £$133\frac{1}{3}$ (line 3), which represents a rate of interest of 10 per cent. In column C he receives interest of £20 on his savings of £$133\frac{1}{3}$, a rate of interest of 15 per cent. The difference is due to the fact that in column B the rate of interest is net of the basic rate of income tax, whereas in column C it is the rate before tax. At a market rate of interest of 15 per cent in general, subject to an income tax rate of $33\frac{1}{3}$ per cent, the arrangements of column B and column C would give equal results. A system of the kind described in column C means that the market rate of interest will tend to be higher than the rate of real yield on physical assets by the basic rate of income tax. It is the net rate of interest after deduction of income tax at the basic rate which will tend to measure the rate of real yield on physical assets.

Table 8.5   *Lending at interest to a company*

1   CT at 50% (tax-inclusive).
2   IT at $33\frac{1}{3}$% (tax-inclusive).
3   ET at 25% (tax-inclusive).

Column A: 100% capital allowance and interest deductibility against CT; no relief against IT; savings relief against ET.
Column B: 100% capital allowance against CT; interest relieved from IT; savings relief against ET.
Column C: 100% capital allowance with interest deductibility at IT rate allowed against CT; no relief against IT; savings relief against ET.

		A (£)	B (£)	C (£)
1	Economy in consumption	100	100	100
2	Savings of ET	$33\frac{1}{3}$	$33\frac{1}{3}$	$33\frac{1}{3}$
3	Total savings	$133\frac{1}{3}$	$133\frac{1}{3}$	$133\frac{1}{3}$
4	Savings of CT	$133\frac{1}{3}$	$133\frac{1}{3}$	$133\frac{1}{3}$
5	Total investment	$266\frac{2}{3}$	$266\frac{2}{3}$	$266\frac{2}{3}$
6	Annual yield	$26\frac{2}{3}$	$26\frac{2}{3}$	$26\frac{2}{3}$
7	*Less* Interest (from line 10)	$(26\frac{2}{3})$	—	—
8	Subject to CT	0	$26\frac{2}{3}$	$26\frac{2}{3}$
9	*Less* CT payable	(0)	$(13\frac{1}{3})$	$(6\frac{2}{3})$
10	Available for interest	$26\frac{2}{3}$	$13\frac{1}{3}$	20
11	*Less* IT payable	$(8\frac{8}{9})$	—	$(6\frac{2}{3})$
12	Available for expenditure	$17\frac{7}{9}$	$13\frac{1}{3}$	$13\frac{1}{3}$
13	*Less* ET payable	$(4\frac{4}{9})$	$(3\frac{1}{3})$	$(3\frac{1}{3})$
14	Annual consumption	$13\frac{1}{3}$	10	10

Appendix 8.3   The Operation of an ITVAT

We shall illustrate the analysis of the implications of an ITVAT by assuming a rate of 50 per cent (tax-inclusive base) or 100 per cent (tax-exclusive base).

All businesses would be required to pay the 50 per cent (tax-inclusive) rate of ITVAT on all their receipts from the sale of goods and services less their payments for purchases of goods and services other than payments of wages, interest and dividends. The dividing line between the payments which they could and those which they could not deduct from their sales would be drawn between those goods and services on which ITVAT had been charged and those on which ITVAT had not been charged on the occasions of their sale to the business in question. This would be equivalent to the operation of VAT, but on an accounts basis and with the rate of tax expressed on a tax-inclusive base.

In the case of an employee who was engaged to provide personal services to a private employer rather than to produce goods and services for sale by a business employer, the employer would be under an obligation to pay ITVAT at the tax-exclusive rate of 100 per cent on the wages which he paid to servants (subject to any remission from tax discussed on pp. 172–173 below).

The treatment of dwelling houses would be subject to the considerations discussed in Chapter 11 for the taxation of housing under an expenditure tax regime.

With an income tax combined with 100 per cent capital allowances, it is the rate of interest after deduction of the basic rate of tax which is linked to the real rate of return on investment, whereas with ITVAT the market rate of interest should be that much lower and should itself be linked to the real rate of return on investment (see Chapter 8, pp. 155–156). From the point of view of any debtor who is paying interest on borrowed funds, this difference is offset by the fact that with the income tax arrangement interest is in general properly deductible as a cost before the debtor's tax base is assessed, whereas with ITVAT interest is not so deductible. The effect on the debtor is the same.[1]

For the same reason problems relating to the tax positions of pension funds, charities and persons below a tax exemption level would be easier to handle with ITVAT than they are with an income tax with 100 per cent capital allowances. Under the income tax regime the investment income of pension funds and charities should not remain exempt from the basic rate of income tax. With 100 per cent capital allowances extended to all items of real capital investment it is the post-tax and not the pre-tax rate of interest which is the better measure of the real social return on capital (see pp. 155–156 above). With exemption from the basic rate of income tax on all contributions into a pension fund but with all payments from the fund (whether of a capital or of an income nature) subject to that tax, the pensioner is in fact getting full expenditure tax treatment, provided that the net yield on the investments in the fund is at the post-basic-rate-of-tax yield. If the pensioner has benefited from a pre-tax yield on the capital held in the pension fund, he is in fact receiving something more favourable than expenditure tax treatment.

In principle, for exactly the same reason there ought not in these circumstances to be any return of income tax on investment income to taxpayers whose income was below the exemption level. It is the post-tax yield on these investments which corresponds to the full free-of-tax social return on the investments in real assets financed by the taxpayer's capital funds. It is doubtful, however, whether the logic of this situation would be at all apparent to the taxpayers concerned. With ITVAT interest and dividends are not taxed in the hands of any recipient, however rich or poor; they, like wages and other personal incomes, are paid after deduction of ITVAT from the sale proceeds of the goods and services which the labour and capital serve to produce. The relief from ITVAT for those with low incomes must take a different form, which we shall discuss below.

In the case of trusts, tax problems would still exist in so far as capital taxes (whether on the holding of wealth or on the transfer of wealth) were concerned. But the problems of ITVAT would be minimal. There would in general be no ITVAT liability on the trustees. The beneficiaries would in fact be paying ITVAT when they spent on consumption any capital or income which they received from the trust funds. Liability to ITVAT would arise only if the trustees owned a dwelling house or any other asset whose use by a beneficiary provided a direct consumption benefit the value of which was to be subject to ITVAT.

There would be no need for special restrictions on close companies. Persons who drew funds from such companies, whether by way of salary, dividends or capital repayments, would in fact pay ITVAT as and when they spent those funds on consumption. For similar reasons there would be no need for any tax on capital gains.

The administration of the existing VAT and of the existing income tax could be amalgamated into a single process.

Appropriate arrangements would have to be made to deal with social benefits and personal tax allowances.

As far as 'conditional benefits' (such as unemployment benefits, sickness benefits, old age pensions and child benefits) are concerned, there would be no additional problems, except that the rates of benefit would have to take into account the cost of living inclusive of ITVAT.

But problems would arise concerning 'unconditional benefits' or tax credits or personal tax allowances. In Chapter 13 we shall discuss the choice between (i) a universal system of unconditional benefits or tax credits (whereby each individual or married couple receives a certain weekly unconditional benefit), and (ii) a system of personal tax allowances (whereby each tax unit receives an appropriate set of personal allowances against its income). In that chapter and in Chapter 18, in discussing the tax unit, a preference is expressed for a system of personal tax allowances.

The adoption of the system of unconditional benefits or tax credits would be easier to operate with ITVAT than would the system of personal tax allowances. It would involve each tax unit receiving directly through the Post Office or indirectly in the wage packet its appropriate unconditional benefit or tax credit, the level of which, as in the case of the conditional benefits, would have to take into account the cost of living inclusive of ITVAT. The rates of conditional benefit would then be set at the level which was necessary to top up the unconditional benefits in the case of unemployment, sickness, etc.

But the system of unconditional benefits or tax credits raises the problems connected with the tax treatment of dependent wives and of working wives, which we shall discuss at some length in Chapters 13 and 18. If it is desired, for example, to have a system under which a second member of a married couple is entitled to a personal allowance which can only be set against that second member's own earnings, it is necessary to devise a system which does not rely solely on social benefits, whether conditional or unconditional, but rather allows for a personal tax-free allowance to be set against certain earnings.

If, then, it were desired to operate a system of personal allowances against tax rather than a system of unconditional benefits or tax credits, the arrangements under an ITVAT regime would have to be of the following kind. With ITVAT all wages (as well as investment incomes) are paid free of tax. What is required to correspond with a personal tax allowance is a system which adds ITVAT (at a tax-exclusive rate) to the first slice of a taxpayer's income. The details of the arrangements which would be necessary for this purpose would depend upon the choice for the definition of the tax unit, which we shall discuss in Chapter 18. But we may at this point illustrate the general principle by considering the case in which a wage earner under the corresponding income tax regime would be granted the first £X of his earnings free of tax. The corresponding arrangement under ITVAT would be for the employer to add to the first £X a week of each employee's wage a second £X (since we take ITVAT at a 100 per cent tax-exclusive rate for purposes of illustration), this second £X being deducted by the employer from his liability to ITVAT.

Self-employed persons would similarly have to have their ultimate ITVAT liability reduced by a corresponding amount.

Any family which through the above arrangements had not received a refund of ITVAT on its total income which was equivalent to the personal allowances to which it would have been entitled under the corresponding income tax regime, would have to be able to claim the additional refund.

It should be noted that a change from an income tax regime to an ITVAT would shift the tax burden from the pay packet to the housekeeping purse. It would require appropriate adjustment of arrangements within the family.

Finally the question arises how to treat foreign trade for the purpose of ITVAT. There is a choice between two principles:

1   the *'destination principle'*, under which imports would be subject to ITVAT but ITVAT would be remitted on exports; and
2   the *'origin principle'*, under which ITVAT would not be levied on imports and would not be remitted on exports.

With the 'destination principle' (which is the principle on which the present VAT is levied) any rise or fall in domestic prices which is due to a rise or fall in the rate of tax on value added has no immediate effect on foreign trade. The foreign exporter to the United Kingdom can obtain the same sterling price as before, since he obtains for his exports to the United Kingdom a net sterling price exclusive of the tax on value added; the UK exporter to foreign countries can sell at the same sterling price as before, since his exports are exempt from the tax on value added. If the 'origin principle' were adopted, any change in domestic sterling prices due to a rise or fall in the rate of tax on value added would be reflected in the sterling price which foreign exporters to the United Kingdom could receive for the sale of their goods in this country and in the sterling price which UK exporters to foreign countries would have to charge to the foreign importers. Such price changes would, if necessary, have to be offset by changes in the rates of exchange between sterling and foreign currencies.

There are, however, three possible advantages in the imposition of an ITVAT on the 'origin principle' rather than on the 'destination principle'.

(1) It is in fact difficult and indeed in some cases impossible to levy a tax on value added on all goods and services consumed by UK residents. The present VAT, for example, is levied on foreign goods imported into the United Kingdom; but a UK resident who goes abroad for a holiday and buys with wages earned in the United Kingdom foreign goods and services while he is abroad cannot be charged to UK VAT on those goods and services, although the effect on the economy is the same as if he had stayed at home and had imported the foreign goods and services for consumption in the United Kingdom. With the 'destination principle' the UK exports which have indirectly earned the foreign exchange which the UK tourist abroad is spending on foreign goods have themselves been exempt from UK tax, as well as the foreign goods and services which the UK tourist buys abroad. With the 'origin principle' the UK exports which indirectly financed the foreign holidays of the UK tourist would themselves have borne the tax.

(2) The income tax is in fact an origin-based tax. Income tax is not remitted on exports or charged on imports. An ITVAT on an 'origin principle' would thus be more similar to existing income tax than would be an ITVAT on a 'destination principle'. The shift from the present income tax to an ITVAT on an 'origin principle' would for this reason cause less upheaval and be more readily understood than a shift to an ITVAT on a 'destination principle'.

(3) With the 'destination principle' the cost of living to a consumer resident in a country which has a high rate of tax on value added will (at the current rate of exchange) be raised relatively to the cost of living to a consumer resident in a foreign country which has an income tax with no tax on value added or has a much lower rate of tax on value added. Thus suppose that the United Kingdom had an ITVAT with a tax rate of 100 per cent (tax-exclusive) or 50 per cent (tax-inclusive) on the 'destination principle', while other countries had an income tax with a similar tax rate of 50 per cent (tax-inclusive) on an 'origin principle'. Foreign goods imported into the United Kingdom would receive no remission of foreign income tax but would have their price in this country doubled by the 100 per cent (tax-exclusive) rate of ITVAT. The price charged to domestic consumers of UK goods would be cut in half when these goods were exported and sold to foreigners with remission of UK ITVAT and with no charge to income tax in their foreign destination. The cost of living at the current rate of exchange would tend to be twice as high in the United Kingdom as in foreign countries. This would give a marked incentive for UK residents who had saved for their retirement out of their earnings during their working life in the United Kingdom to emigrate with their saved capital in order to spend it in their retirement at a lower cost of living in some foreign country. With ITVAT on an 'origin principle' this would not occur. Foreign goods would not be raised in price to UK consumers by submission to ITVAT on importation into the United Kingdom nor would the domestic price of UK goods be reduced to foreign importers by the remission of ITVAT on their export from the United Kingdom. We shall return to this important aspect of the distinction between the 'origin principle' and the 'destination principle' in Chapters 20 and 21.

NOTE

1   Consider a debtor whose receipts are £1,000 with an income tax or ITVAT rate of tax of 50 per cent (tax-inclusive) but whose interest payments are £200 under the income tax arrangement but only £100 under the ITVAT arrangement. In both cases he will be left with an income of £400 after meeting his tax liability and the interest on his debt:

	IT with 100% capital allowances (£)	ITVAT (£)
Tax base	800[a]	1,000
Tax at 50%	400	500
Receipts	1,000	1,000
Less Tax payable	400	500
Income net of tax	600	500
Less Interest payable	(200)	(100)
Income net of tax and interest	400	400

[a] Tax base = Receipts *less* Interest payable = £1,000—£200 = £800.

9   A Universal Expenditure Tax

We turn now to consider in more detail the characteristics and problems of a universal expenditure tax (UET). Our discussion of these matters will fall into two separate parts. We shall first consider how a UET might be operated if all transitional problems had long been solved and the system was in full running order. We shall then turn to a consideration of the transitional problems involved in moving from an income tax regime to a UET regime, for these transitional problems are very real and the adoption of a UET might depend upon their solution.

THE TREATMENT OF ASSETS UNDER A UET

A progressive UET must be operated on what we have called the income adjustment method of an expenditure tax. This means in principle that all purchases of assets should be deducted from the tax base (item 4 of Table 8.1), but all sales of assets (item 2) as well as the income yield on all assets (item 1) should be added to the tax base.

But it would clearly be impossible on administrative grounds to include literally all assets in the computation of the taxpayer's net saving or dissaving. To take two trivial items, it would clearly be foolish to attempt to assess as between the beginning and the end of any financial year the changes in the amount of coin in a man's purse or the amount of durable clothes in his wardrobe. It would be necessary to omit certain items solely for administrative convenience; and, as we shall argue, there may well be good reasons for excluding a larger class of assets.

REGISTERED AND UNREGISTERED ASSETS

Thus for the purpose of a UET assets could be divided into two distinct classes according to the nature of the asset itself. Certain specific assets would be classed as *'registered assets'*, with all unspecified assets classed as *'unregistered assets'*.[1] Only transactions in registered assets would be debited to, or credited against, taxable income under items 2 and 4 of Table 8.1, so that the 'expenditure tax adjustment' would include disposals less acquisitions of registered assets but not of unregistered assets. All transactions in unregistered assets would be omitted from the calculation. The income yield on such assets would, however, normally be included in the tax base (item 1

---

[1] The terms 'registered' and 'unregistered' are used solely to distinguish between the tax treatment given to the two types of asset. They do not imply that there would be any formal register of certain assets.

of Table 8.1), in which case unregistered assets would receive the normal income tax treatment; any income from which they were purchased would be subject to tax, the income yield on them would be subject to tax, but the capital proceeds from their sale would not be subject to tax.

One apparently fatal flaw in this arrangement may be discounted at once. It would appear that a rich man who held a large fund of unregistered assets could avoid all tax liability indefinitely simply by disposing of his unregistered assets (on which he would incur no tax liability) and shunting the proceeds into registered assets (on which he would obtain a tax credit which he could set against any tax liability on the rest of his year's transactions).

The danger, however, is more apparent than real. It may be asked why anyone should choose in the first place to put any of his new savings into unregistered assets. When his assets were first acquired or accumulated, his decision to invest in unregistered assets instead of registered assets was in fact a decision to anticipate a tax liability which could have been postponed by investment in registered assets. When he converts back into registered assets he is in fact recalling from the Inland Revenue an interest-free loan which he has voluntarily extended to them. If it proved possible to cope with the transitional problems, the holding of unregistered assets could properly be regarded as the holding of assets on which tax payment had been anticipated.

The distinction between registered and unregistered assets could bring administrative simplification. Taxpayers would have to add or subtract from their income tax base simply disposals or acquisitions of specified categories of assets; and for tax purposes no regular track would have to be kept of other assets. We shall proceed to review the various considerations which are relevant to the choice of assets for registration, leaving aside at this stage the problems of the transition which will require the widest degree of registration in order to limit opportunities for subsequent expenditure without incurring a charge to tax. The special problems of the transition, which we do not underrate, are discussed below (pp. 187–192).

UNREGISTERED ASSETS AS AN AVERAGING DEVICE

The income yield on registered assets would be included in the individual's tax base (as would all receipts, whether of 'capital' or 'income', derived from the asset). For unregistered assets it might be decided that they should continue to be taxed broadly as assets generally are now – with no tax relief on their purchase and no income tax liability on their sale, but with the yield subject to tax. Alternatively, the view might be taken that since no relief had been given on the cost no tax should be levied on the proceeds.

This would imply that the income from unregistered assets (even unregistered financial assets) should be tax-free.[2] If this latter procedure were adopted, then for someone whose marginal tax rate was constant and was

[2] This would be an example of what in Chapter 8 (p. 160) we have called method (iv) for the application of an expenditure tax principle, namely exemption from tax on the yield on an investment instead of exemption from tax on the purchase of the investment.

expected to remain constant there would be no advantage or disadvantage in choosing registered rather than unregistered assets.

Whichever of these two procedures was adopted, the attraction of unregistered assets would be that under a progressive tax regime they could be used as a method of averaging out tax liabilities on lumpy expenditures.

Consider the case of a taxpayer who is saving up for some future element of lumpy expenditure, e.g. a family holiday, education, furnishing a house, purchasing a car, etc. With a progressive expenditure tax such concentrated elements of expenditure might bring the taxpayer into a higher tax bracket and thus impose an exceptionally high tax upon him simply because his expenditure was to be concentrated in one year. By the purchase of unregistered assets now, he could build up a fund which would be subject to tax now at a moderate rate of tax rather than incur his tax liability at a higher marginal rate when his level of expenditure was concentrated at a high level. By so doing he would, of course, lose the gain from the deferral of tax, which is a privilege confined to registered assets. The existence of unregistered assets would, however, enable him to avoid paying exceptionally high rates of tax on lumpy expenditures which must be concentrated at particular times; and it may be regarded as desirable that such a person should be taxed on his average level of consumption over a period of years rather than be penalised under a progressive tax system because his expenditure had to be concentrated in time.

However, this treatment is unsatisfactory in the case of unregistered assets which might give rise to large capital gains. Since being taxed on what is put in is not at all the same thing, under a progressive tax system, as being taxed on what is taken out, the lucky (or successful) speculative purchaser of an unregistered asset would pay tax at a low rate in order to obtain freedom from the much higher rates to which his windfalls would be liable had they been gained on a registered asset. Clearly, it is not acceptable that people in this position should be so lightly taxed; and hence we conclude that assets which are likely to give rise to substantial capital gains should in all possible cases be registered.

These and other considerations lead us to the view that it would be better if the vast majority of financial assets were registered; and this suggests that the less favourable of the two treatments of unregistered assets described above would in fact be more appropriate. Where such assets gave rise to income that income would be taxed, so that the interest on unregistered bank accounts, for example, would be taxed in just the same way as now. If this were so, it would be disadvantageous to most investors to hold unregistered assets; they would always gain by putting their capital into registered assets which would qualify for tax relief. Only people with sharply variable tax rates would find it advantageous to buy unregistered assets for averaging purposes. Hence unregistered financial assets would exist and would be used by such people; but they would be limited in number and attractiveness, and financial institutions would have an incentive to ensure that their deposits and securities complied with whatever administrative conditions were involved in qualifying for registration.

REGISTERED AND UNREGISTERED BORROWINGS

We have explained the principle of distinguishing between registered and unregistered assets. Should the same distinction be applied to borrowings? In principle, it is possible to have both registered and unregistered borrowings. A registered borrowing would count as dissaving when it was raised, and the borrowing would be part of the expenditure tax adjustment. The whole of any repayment would then count as savings, so that the full payment (and not just the interest component) would qualify for tax relief. In effect, part of the borrowing would be re-lent to the Inland Revenue, who would then provide a corresponding share of the repayments. This would, we anticipate, be the normal treatment of business borrowings or borrowings for the purchase of registered assets.

UNREGISTERED BORROWINGS AS AN AVERAGING DEVICE

Unregistered borrowings, on the other hand, would not lead to any tax liability at the time of borrowing, but neither would they attract any tax relief either on principal as repayments were made or on interest. Thus the man who borrowed to buy a motor car would have no immediate UET liability but would gradually pay UET as he paid off his debt; and this would seem the normal treatment of consumption loans. Hire purchase agreements would be treated similarly, so that the purchase would not be the occasion of tax liability but the subsequent payments would be. The general principle to be applied is that, in all such transactions, if the costs are deductible the proceeds are taxable and vice versa.

POSSIBLE RESTRICTIONS ON UNREGISTERED BORROWING

If an individual borrows £100 on unregistered terms and invests this £100 in registered assets, he will obtain an expenditure tax credit, which he can use to meet any liability to expenditure tax due on the rest of his year's transactions. But this is not in fact the wide-open abuse which it may at first sight appear to be, for two reasons:

1 While the yield on the registered assets would be taxable, the interest payable on the loan would not be deductible as a credit against tax. This means that, in effect, the individual's tax liability is increased by an amount which corresponds to the interest on the amount of tax he has deferred.
2 Financial institutions would be reluctant to lend on unregistered accounts to the full amount of the security provided by registered assets, since such assets would carry with them a contingent tax liability on disposal.

But the final outcome would in the end depend upon the treatment of bequests of registered assets upon the owner's death, which we shall discuss later (pp. 183–185). If the tax treatment of such assets on transfer on death were on an appropriate scale, then the owner would be unable, merely by postponing tax until his death, to live at a higher standard of consumption during his lifetime without diminishing the net value of what he would leave to his heirs.

Nevertheless, however carefully the position was safeguarded the ability to postpone tax without legal limit by borrowing on unregistered account for investment on registered account would probably be unacceptable, for two reasons:

1 The safeguards surrounding it would not be understood by the man or woman in the street.
2 Postponing the receipt of revenue would mean that the government would have to increase its borrowing requirement during the period while the taxpayer accumulated funds to meet a future tax liability.

If borrowing on unregistered account were permitted on any considerable scale, there would probably have to be special arrangements designed to limit unregistered borrowing for the purpose of investment in registered assets. These might take the form of requiring those claiming tax relief on purchases of registered assets to declare that they had not borrowed more than, say, £1,000 on unregistered account. If they could not make such a declaration, then details would be required and the excess of such borrowings would be deducted from the total of registered asset purchases eligible for relief. Such a provision would, however, leave open the possibility of heavy borrowing on unregistered account in one year being used to purchase registered assets in the next year. It might therefore be necessary to put some limit on the total amount of unregistered borrowing outstanding at any one time, any excess being included in the tax base as it was incurred.

THE TREATMENT OF CAPITAL GAINS

So much for the treatment of borrowings. We return to a discussion of the considerations which should affect the choice of assets for registration.

In the case of registered assets the total proceeds from the sale of the asset would be liable to tax; there would be no distinction between the realisation (i) of the original cost of the asset, (ii) of any capital gain on it, or (iii) of any form of income yield on it. In so far as assets were registered, the capital gains tax could thus be abolished. It would be desirable, therefore, that all assets on which important capital gains might be made should be registered.

Suppose, then, that the capital gains tax were abolished, but that nevertheless there remained some unregistered assets on which a capital gain might be made. Consider Mr Robinson who invests £1,000 in some unregistered asset simply as an investment in expectation of a capital gain. Suppose that he is successful, that his investment of £1,000 becomes worth £10,000 and that the capital gain of £9,000 is not taxed. It is arguable that this is a tolerable situation on the grounds that it does not give such investment any better treatment than that given to any registered assets. Suppose that Mr Robinson is subject to a marginal rate of expenditure tax of 50 per cent (tax-inclusive). Out of an income of £2,000 he has originally paid £1,000 in tax and invested £1,000 on the assets concerned. If he had not been taxed, he could have invested £2,000 instead of £1,000 in them, in which case he would have made a capital gain of £18,000 instead of only £9,000. He has in effect been taxed at 50 per cent. This is an example of method (iv) of Chapter 8 (p. 160) of applying the expenditure tax principle. Mr Robinson's investment in the asset has been taxed, but the capital gain yield on it has not been taxed.

But with a progressive tax system it is not a matter of indifference whether the savings-investment is taxed and the yield exempted or the savings-investment is exempted and the yield taxed. If Mr Robinson is a man who starts in humble circumstances liable to a low rate of expenditure tax, speculates with modest sums in purchasing assets which appreciate very greatly in value, and then realises the proceeds so that he becomes relatively wealthy and subject to a high rate of expenditure tax, it will make a great difference to him whether he is taxed at the low rate on what he put in or at the high rate on what he takes out, and it will make a great difference to the average rate of tax which he pays. Clearly it is not acceptable that successful speculators are taxed at lower rates than individuals who achieve similar levels of expenditure out of earned income. This means that it is desirable to register all assets which are likely to yield appreciable capital gains.

THE TREATMENT OF PERSONAL CHATTELS

On administrative grounds, if for no other reason, it would be sensible to treat durable goods used for personal consumption purposes as unregistered assets. This would cover normal clothes, furniture, other household effects, cars for personal use, etc.

The problem, however, arises of the treatment of exceptionally valuable items, such as an individual's possession of a Rembrandt picture or of a collection of Ming china. If the capital gains tax is abolished and if such objects are treated as unregistered assets, Mr Robinson, whose speculative ventures we have examined in the last section, can make his planned investment for capital gain in objects of this kind.

For this reason it would be desirable that indexed capital gains on such assets should be taxed, subject to fairly generous roll-over provisions. A tax liability would therefore be imposed on the amount by which the proceeds of net disposals of such assets exceeded their cumulative indexed acquisition costs. This amount would simply be added to income as part of the expenditure tax adjustment and would therefore be taxed at the normal expenditure tax rates. The effect of this proposal is that an individual who collected Ming china would be subject to expenditure tax on the amount which he spent on the purchase of such items; and if by shrewd purchases and sales he accumulated an especially fine collection he would not be further taxed on that account alone. But to the extent that he made a realised profit from dealing in the china, which he used to finance expenditure on anything else (other than a registered asset), an additional tax charge would arise.

HOUSING AS A REGISTERED ASSET

While non-registration seems appropriate for most consumption goods, if registration were permitted for any asset which does yield consumption benefits it would be necessary to levy tax on the estimated value of these benefits. The durable asset most likely to come into this category is housing; but the treatment of housing poses a number of special problems, which we postpone for discussion in Chapter 11.

ADMINISTRATIVE CONSIDERATIONS

We have already noted the fact that certain assets, such as cash and ordinary personal consumption goods, would be excluded from the range of registered assets on the simple administrative grounds that for the taxpayer to record and for the Inland Revenue to attempt to check transactions in such assets would be a senseless administrative task. But there is a quite different set of issues which arise in the selection of categories of assets for registration, depending upon the method chosen for the administration of the tax.

Unless special measures are taken, it appears that a UET must involve for every taxpayer an end year review of his tax liability, since his tax base must be adjusted for his net sale or purchase of registered assets in the course of the year. If a system of self-assessment were introduced into the United Kingdom, whereby as in the United States every taxpayer records and assesses his own tax base and liability at the close of each fiscal year, there would be no insuperable obstacle to prevent the taxpayer from so recording and assessing not only his income but also items in his expenditure tax adjustment.

But at present in the United Kingdom, with the wide band of income tax at a basic rate of tax, with an extensive system of deduction of tax at this rate at source on many forms of unearned income, and with the cumulative pay-as-you-earn (PAYE) system which enables allowances and untaxed income to be adjusted against the tax deductions which are made from earned income, liability to tax for some 80–85 per cent of all employees is fully dealt with by deduction at source, and no return of income is required from 60 per cent of taxpayers except at intervals of five years.

We have considered whether it would be possible to administer a UET in a similar manner. For this to be possible there would have to be, as with the present income tax, a wide band of expenditure subject to the same basic rate of tax. In addition, there would be important implications about the selection of assets for registration. In theory, relief for continuing contractual savings (such as life assurance) could be given by adjustment of PAYE codings, in which case the assets thus acquired would be registered. But this method is from 1979/80 to be discontinued for the present tax relief on life assurance premiums in favour of giving relief by the payment of premiums after deduction of the relevant tax. This suggests that assets could be registered if it were possible to arrange for net dealings in them whereby (i) the individual seller of such an asset received from the sale of such an asset only the proceeds after deduction of the basic rate of tax, and (ii) the individual purchaser of such assets paid only this net amount on his purchase.

For sales and purchases of such registered assets, such a system would be the analogue of the deduction of the basic rate of tax at source in the case of the income tax. Assets which typically are bought and sold by large numbers of basic rate taxpayers would with this system be registered only if they were capable of being subjected to a regime of net dealings.

We have also considered arrangements to encourage the vast majority of basic rate taxpayers to put their savings either into unregistered assets or into special and limited forms of registered assets which could be readily dealt with on a net dealing basis, i.e. by deduction of tax at source. For this purpose no tax allowance would be granted for the first, say, £500 a year of net savings in registered assets,[3] unless these savings had been put into a limited number of specified assets which could be dealt with on a net dealing basis; but at the same time all dissavings of registered assets of all kinds would be liable to tax. With arrangements of this kind everyone would have a strong tax incentive to put the first £500 of their savings either into unregistered assets or into special categories of registered assets which could readily be handled on a net dealing basis.

Arrangements of this kind would, however, sacrifice one of the great attractions of a UET, which consists in freeing the capital market from various institutionalised discriminations. With present arrangements, which give special privileges for savings through insurance and pension funds, a large amount of personal savings is institutionalised. This inhibits, for example, the use of small personal savings for the development of new businesses. Arrangements which channelled the first £500 of personal savings into specified institutionalised assets would have similar disadvantages.

In Chapter 22 we shall examine in more detail the administrative problems involved in operating a system of net dealings in registered assets. The difficulties are very considerable, and we doubt whether it would be feasible. Moreover, the system would not be easily understood by a large number of taxpayers, and it is in any case applicable only if the structure of tax rates continues to rely upon a long band at a single basic rate of tax. If such a long band at a single basic rate of tax is to be preserved, an alternative approach (which we shall discuss in the next chapter) is to turn to a two-tier expenditure tax of the kind described at the end of the last chapter, which tackles the basic rate of tax by a different form of expenditure tax.

The position would be quite different if there were a system of self-assessment for tax under which every taxpayer would in any case be completing a form stating his or her income. In this case a statement of purchases and sales of all kinds of registered assets could be added to the form. We incline to the view that the introduction of a self-assessment system into the United Kingdom – a step which many persons favour on quite other grounds – is

---

[3] If houses were treated as registered assets (see Chapter 11), there would have to be an exception which gave unqualified relief on sums saved and used for house purchase.

a necessary precondition for the operation of a full-blooded UET.[4]

A SUMMARY OF CONSIDERATIONS AFFECTING THE SELECTION OF ASSETS FOR REGISTRATION

We have argued that it would be desirable to register all assets on which substantial capital gains might be made, but that durable goods for personal use should remain unregistered.[5] Admittedly there is some conflict between these desiderata. We have argued that valuable personal possessions should remain unregistered even though important capital gains can be realised on them; and for this reason we were led to the conclusion that they should be subject to tax on any capital gain.

The best arrangement would probably be that one group of assets should always be compulsorily registered (such as stock exchange securities, all business assets and perhaps houses[6]), that another group (such as personal chattels) should always remain compulsorily unregistered, but that some assets (such as bank accounts) might be offered in either form. For this last group it would be necessary to ensure that the institutions concerned (such as the banks) undertook the necessary obligations (such as reporting movements into and out of registered assets) to enable the system to be policed.[7]

THE TREATMENT OF GIFTS AND BEQUESTS

We have already described in Chapter 3 (pp. 40–42) the broad distinction between two treatments of gifts under an expenditure tax:

1 One method is to exclude gifts from the donor's taxable expenditure and to impose a quite separate transfer tax on the making of gifts.
2 The other method is to abolish any separate transfer tax, and to levy a tax on transfers of wealth by treating a gift as part of the donor's taxable expenditure as well as being part of the donee's expenditure when he in turn spends it or gives it away. We call this second method a Gifts Inclusive Expenditure Tax (GIET).

If the former of these treatments were adopted, questions would be left concerning the best form for a separate transfer tax (we shall return to this

---

[4] The introduction of a system of self-assessment into the United Kingdom is examined in detail in N. A. Barr, S. R. James and A. R. Prest, *Self-Assessment for Income Tax* (London: Heinemann Educational Books, for the Institute of Chartered Accountants in England and Wales and the Institute for Fiscal Studies, 1977).

[5] See Chapter 11 for a consideration of the question whether houses should be treated as registered assets.

[6] See Chapter 11.

[7] In the case of registered current accounts it would be necessary to report changes in cleared balances, in order to prevent the artificial boosting of balances at the end of the fiscal year by exchange of cheques between two taxpayers immediately before 5 April.

subject in Chapter 15).[8] If the second of these treatments were adopted, the system would work as follows.

All recipients of gifts would have to include their receipt in their tax base (item 3 of Table 8.1). When a donor transferred a registered asset to a donee, this would have to be recorded as a disposal of a registered asset by the donor (item 2) but as an acquisition of a registered asset by the donee (item 4). The result would be that the donor would be charged to expenditure tax on the gift, while the donee would not be charged (since his receipt of a gift would be offset by his acquisition of a registered asset) unless and until he disposed of the asset and spent it in consumption or on some unregistered asset, or in turn passed it on to some new donee.

When a donor transferred an unregistered asset to a donee, there would be no effect upon the donor's tax liability. But in this case the donee would be liable to tax, since the receipt of the gift (item 3) would increase his tax base without in this case any acquisition of registered assets to set against it (item 4).

The arrangement is a natural and logical one. The donor has not already paid tax on a registered asset, but he does so when he passes it on; and the donee also pays tax if and when he realises the registered asset and spends the proceeds. The donor has already paid tax on an unregistered asset, and the donee is now in turn required to do so when he receives it.

The inclusion of gifts in the UET base in this way would very greatly broaden the tax base, with consequent implications for average and marginal rates of tax. The possible revenue effects are very uncertain; but it is clear that the revenue impact of bringing into tax all gifts, including those which currently fall below the exemptions for transfer taxes, and of taxing them at the minimum of the basic rate of expenditure tax is potentially very large. Indeed if this treatment of gifts were adopted it would almost certainly be necessary to give some special treatment for small and moderate gifts by, for example, some annual exemption and perhaps in addition by some abatement (such as charging only a proportion of the gift) on a further slice of gifts made or received in any one year. Such exemption and abatement could, however, much reduce the revenue yield, e.g. as the ownership of the family house was transferred piecemeal by annual instalments from father to son.

In addition to the revenue potential a further attraction of the arrangement would be the possibility of abolishing completely the whole apparatus of a separate transfer tax.

The price to be paid for this would be a loss of flexibility of several kinds.

---

[8] One tiresome problem remains, however, for the UET itself, due to the problem of distinguishing between the treatment of gifts of registered assets and that of gifts of unregistered assets under a UET even when it is intended to exempt gifts from expenditure tax. Gifts of registered assets can be exempt from tax in a straightforward manner. But if a donor gives a valuable unregistered asset (e.g. a Rembrandt) to a donee, the question arises whether there should be no adjustment of the expenditure tax which the donor will already have paid on the Rembrandt, or whether the donor's expenditure tax on the picture should be refunded and the donee in place of the donor should be charged to tax on the picture. The treatment of UET under a system in which gifts are to be charged to a separate transfer tax is discussed in Appendix 9.1.

In particular, the rate structure of the transfer tax would be replaced by the rate structure of the expenditure tax; and the rate imposed on any particular transfer would be a function of the level of the donor's expenditure in that year rather than the cumulative total of such transfers made or received.

THE NEED FOR AVERAGING

Moreover, this UET treatment of gifts would raise in acute form the problem of averaging, since to include a large gift in the expenditure total of one year might raise a progressive rate of UET to an unacceptably high degree. This problem would be especially pronounced in the case of transfer at death. Depending on the rate structure of UET, it would almost certainly be necessary to have special arrangements for property left at death in order to avoid counting the whole of the deceased's property as part of his personal expenditure in the year of his death.

We have already noted that the problem of averaging tax liabilities is mitigated by the existence of unregistered assets (pp. 176–177) and of unregistered loans (p. 178). Even if gifts were not included in the tax base for UET, it might well be desirable to supplement these possibilities by some special arrangement for averaging specially lumpy concentrated expenditures. The inclusion of gifts in the UET tax base would make this requirement a certainty. For example, anyone incurring a single lumpy expenditure in excess of a fixed amount (say £1,000) might be permitted to spread the expenditure backwards or forwards over a number of years to avoid an excessive liability arising in any one year.

THE PRACTICAL MERITS AND DEMERITS

A UET involves making the expenditure tax adjustment to taxable personal incomes. The administrative complications would arise from the need to ensure that taxpayers added and subtracted the relevant items to or from their tax base. As we have indicated, the previous introduction of a system of self-assessment would certainly greatly ease this administrative task and may well be a necessary condition for its attainment.

But the administrative problems would in other respects be much eased if and when a UET system were in full running order.

For all registered assets, net amounts added to such assets would be exempt from tax and net amounts realised from the disposal of such assets would be liable to tax. If all assets held in a business, a trust or a pension fund are treated as registered assets, then it is only the net amounts drawn out of such funds which are liable to tax and the net amounts added to such funds which are exempt from tax.

Thus some difficult distinctions between capital and income would be avoided for tax purposes. In the case of a business which was not liable to corporation tax[9] it would make no difference to tax liability what method of depreciation of capital assets was adopted – whether straight line, diminishing balance, initial capital allowance, historical cost, replacement cost, etc. To take another example, an author or inventor can either sell his copyright or patent and invest the capital sum in other assets which earn an income, or he can hold on to his capital asset (the copyright or patent) and receive royalties on its use. With an income tax a decision has to be made on whether or not the author or inventor should be taxed twice in the former case (on the sale of the copyright or patent and on the income from his investment of the proceeds) but only once in the second case (on the receipt of royalties). With an expenditure tax the problem does not arise; whatever he may receive, by way of income or from the sale of a capital asset, the taxpayer pays tax only on what he spends.

Problems of accrued as contrasted with realised income would disappear. Problems connected with the correct rate of tax to be levied on profits or other income put to reserve in private businesses and partnerships would disappear. Close company legislation would become unnecessary. Since all savings would receive the tax treatment presently accorded to pension funds, there would be no reason to impose restrictions on contributions to such schemes or on the way in which disbursements from them were made. Regulation of pension funds by the Inland Revenue could therefore be abandoned, and the provisions governing private contributions to pension schemes for the self-employed could be repealed. The present tax treatment of life insurance would be drastically simplified; funds would become tax-exempt, while contributions would become fully deductible and proceeds fully taxable, except in so far as the proceeds were reinvested in registered assets. There would be no necessity for restrictions on the design of qualifying policies or the proportion of income which might be subscribed to them.

Capital gains tax would cease to be applied to all registered assets, since it would be the total sums realised by the sale of such assets (and not merely the realised gains on such assets) which would be subject to tax, while the total sums spent on the acquisition of such assets (and not merely any realised losses on such assets) would be exempt from tax. Realisations and acquisitions of such assets would still have to be recorded, but the past cost of such assets would become irrelevant. Questions about the double taxation of capital gains (in so far as business profits are subject to tax when they are accumulated and the shares are in addition subject to capital gains tax when their resulting increase in value is realised), or about the difference in rates of tax on income and on realised capital gains, would not arise.

One of the main advantages of a UET is that it would be immeasurably easier to cope properly with tax problems arising from inflation. As in any progressive tax system, some method of 'bracket indexation' would be appropriate; but problems of 'capital–income adjustment' would not arise (see Chapter 6). It would be current expenditure as such (regardless of

---

[9] We shall discuss in Chapter 12 possible treatments of corporation tax which would make the above claims relevant for incorporated as well as unincorporated concerns.

whether it was financed from income or capital and regardless of whether these were measured in real or in money terms) which would be the basis of taxation. In Chapter 7 we described the formidable problems which arise in trying to make a proper capital–income adjustment under a true income tax; these problems simply would not exist under a UET.

The administrative simplifications which would result when a UET was in full running order are thus by no means negligible. The problems arising from a transition from the present tax regime to a UET in full running order are, however, formidable and do involve a number of administrative headaches. It is to these that we now turn.

PROBLEMS OF THE TRANSITION

Serious problems would arise in the process of transition from the present tax regime to a UET. These problems fall into two closely related categories, namely problems of equity and problems connected with disturbances on the capital market.

TRANSITIONAL PROBLEMS OF EQUITY

Any taxpayer who had saved up for future consumption and had invested those savings in assets which were then registered would suffer the unexpected burden of having been taxed under the old income tax regime on the income which he saved and then taxed again unexpectedly under the new regime when the savings were used for expenditure on consumption.

There would be no problem of this kind with existing recognised pension schemes, which are already subject to an expenditure tax rather than an income tax regime; the contributions to such pension funds will have been exempt from tax and the pensioners will already be expecting to pay tax on the pensions when they are received. But persons who have saved for their old age in other ways would suffer unexpected double taxation on their savings when made under the income tax regime and on their savings once again when spent under the expenditure tax regime.

This problem would arise even if no distinction were made between different categories of asset, so that all assets were registered on D-day; but if some assets remained unregistered, the unfairness would be compounded by the fact that it would be confined to those who happened at the time of the change to hold assets which were thereafter designated as registered assets. Other persons who were otherwise in exactly similar conditions but happened at the time of the change to hold assets which were designated as unregistered assets would escape this new and unexpected tax burden.

The elderly citizen without any considerable pension rights who was just about to live in retirement on his past savings, who at the moment of change held only registered assets, and who had a high standard of living and therefore a high marginal rate of expenditure tax, would lose most heavily. But it would not be only the elderly unpensioned rich who suffered. Any taxpayer who had saved up for a future consumption expenditure (e.g. to furnish a home for the first time) would be liable to the new unexpected charge if the savings had been invested in registered assets.

DISTURBANCES ON THE CAPITAL MARKET

The taxpayer who held unregistered rather than registered assets on D-day would be at a great advantage. He would not merely avoid tax if he wished after D-day to finance consumption expenditures by the sale of his assets. He would be in a position after D-day to sell his unregistered assets and purchase registered assets with the proceeds, thereby reducing his current liability to tax on the rest of his year's transactions in the way noted on p. 176 above. If he invested in registered assets not only the proceeds of his sale of unregistered assets but also the saving of current tax which this shift would occasion, he would thereby permanently increase his annual investment income.

Prior to D-day there would thus be an incentive for the sale of registered assets in order to hold unregistered assets at D-day; and after D-day, whether the change had been anticipated or not, there would be an incentive to shift from unregistered to registered assets. Quite apart from any questions of equity, these shifts would cause unacceptable losses of tax revenue and disturbances in the capital market, the nature of which is described in more detail in Appendix 9.2.

PHASING-IN OF THE UET REGIME

One way of mitigating these disturbances would be to phase in the change gradually. As we have shown, an income tax is turned into a UET through the expenditure tax adjustment, which involves adding purchases and deducting sales of registered but not of unregistered assets to and from the income base. A phasing-in of the new tax regime might be arranged in the following ways. The full distinction between registered and unregistered assets would be made immediately upon the inception of the change. But the full impact of the expenditure tax adjustment would be applied only gradually over a period, say of ten years. In the first year of the change the tax base would be income plus one-tenth of the expenditure tax adjustment; in the next year it would be income plus two-tenths of the expenditure tax adjustment; and so on, until in the tenth year the UET was in full operation.

Such an arrangement would undoubtedly greatly mitigate any disturbances and inequities caused by the change in tax regime. The changes in prices and yields of various assets would be smaller and more gradual, and individual taxpayers would be given time to adjust their affairs to the new regime. But this type of solution is open to serious disadvantages.

(1)   There are bound to be some unregistered assets; and as a result there would still be an incentive immediately before each jump in the percentage applied to the expenditure tax adjustment for taxpayers to hold abnormally large amounts of unregistered assets for exchange into registered assets im-

mediately after the jump. The gain on each such shift would, of course, be much less than the potential gain which would arise from the 100 per cent application of UET at one clear stroke, and the costs of moving funds backwards and forwards between registered and unregistered assets would act as some discouragement. But the disruptive effects on capital markets would not be eliminated; they would in the main merely be spread more thinly over a longer period.

(2) One of the main attractions of a shift to a UET base is that it would impose a heavier tax on persons who maintained a high level of consumption by living on capital which they had inherited. The gradual phasing-in of a UET would mean that such taxation would not begin to bite for some time, during which a gradual shift of wealth from registered to unregistered assets might allow the main impact of the scheme to be permanently avoided.

(3) Many administrative advantages of a UET would have to be postponed. As we have already argued, a UET, while it would involve many administrative problems, would as a partial counterweight bring with it a number of administrative simplifications: the elimination of capital gains tax on registered assets, the end of close company legislation, the absence of any need for capital–income adjustment for inflation, the various simplifications which would arise in the tax treatment of pensions, patents, businesses and trusts because of the opportunity of disregarding for tax purposes many distinctions between income and capital payments. But so long as certain capital payments under a UET (i.e. the acquisition and disposal of registered assets) counted only as one-tenth or two-tenths or three-tenths as much as certain income payments, these administrative simplifications would have to be postponed. For some years the administrative difficulties of a UET would have to be faced without the administrative gains being reaped.

AN ALTERNATIVE SET OF TRANSITIONAL ARRANGEMENTS

Any acceptable set of arrangements for a transition to a UET at one clear stroke must cope effectively with two separate, but closely related, problems. It must (i) give some reasonable relief from expenditure tax to those who on D-day own in the form of registered assets sums which they have saved out of taxed income for future consumption purposes; and (ii) also remove or very greatly restrict opportunities for making a once-for-all gain by holding unregistered assets at D-day for subsequent shift into registered assets.

One method of proceeding is as follows:

(1) A scale for an upper limit of lump sum relief from expenditure tax on past accumulations of wealth would be fixed, the scale depending on the age of the taxpayer at D-day, so that those nearest retirement would obtain the greatest relief.

(2) On D-day as wide a range of assets as possible would be specified as registered assets. Taxpayers would have to declare the value of their holdings of unregistered assets in so far as they were above some exempt limit, such as £500; but there would be no requirement to include in the declaration the

value of such unregistered assets as normal furniture and other durable consumption goods.

(3) The value of taxpayers' unregistered assets under (2) would be deducted from their upper limit for lump sum relief under (1), and the balance would be recorded as their 'effective relief'. If the value of their unregistered assets under (2) exceeded the limit of their relief under (1), then the excess of such unregistered assets would have to be treated as registered assets and their 'effective relief' would be recorded as nil.

(4) After D-day, exemption from tax would be granted on a cumulative basis for disposals of registered assets up to the taxpayer's total of 'effective relief' under (3).

The upshot of these arrangements would be that any taxpayer could, free of tax, spend out of his D-day wealth on consumption, either from his unregistered assets under (2) or from his registered assets under (3), an amount up to his limit under (1).

(5) This arrangement would, however, be unduly favourable to those who enjoyed substantial pension rights as compared with those who after D-day had to finance their retirement from their own savings, since the pension rights will have been accumulated out of untaxed income and will therefore already have received expenditure tax treatment. This advantage from existing pension rights might be offset by treating the receipt of such pensions after D-day as a debit under (4) above against the taxpayer's 'effective relief'.

A similar problem would arise in connection with the treatment of accrued capital gains, if the capital gains tax were discontinued at D-day. Those persons to whom capital gains had accrued tax-free up to D-day would properly be taxed on the expenditure of those gains after D-day. They would be in the same position as persons with pension rights which had 'accrued' tax-free before D-day and the expenditure of which should properly be taxed after D-day.

This suggests that the realisation after D-day of capital gains accrued before D-day should, like the receipt of pensions, be treated as a debit under (4) above against the taxpayer's effective relief. Such a rule would involve, on the occasion of a realisation after D-day of an asset acquired before D-day, a valuation of any increase in value between the date of acquisition and D-day. As an alternative it might be considered that rough justice would be done by setting the relief under (1) on a low enough scale to take into account that some part of post D-day expenditure will be financed from accrued capital gains which had not been taxed.

The above arrangements would deal with the problem of relief to taxpayers who had accumulated savings out of taxed income to finance consumption after D-day. But they would not cope with the other major transitional problem, namely the killing which someone who owned substantial unregistered assets on D-day could make by shifting them immediately after D-day into registered assets. Such possibilities would be restricted in so far as it was possible under (2) to treat virtually all valuable assets as being registered on D-day. But if necessary, in order to remove opportunities for gains of this kind it would be appropriate to add some such additional provision as:

(6)   After D-day acquisitions of registered assets would not qualify for exemption from tax on a cumulative basis up to a total equal to the value of the unregistered assets declared by the taxpayer under (2) above.

This last provision would mean that no one would make a gain by shifting after D-day from unregistered to registered assets except to the extent that they reduced their holding of unregistered assets below £500 or whatever figure was set as the exemption level under (2). It would, however, also have the undesirable effect that a taxpayer would not be able to obtain tax exemption even on genuine post-D-day savings which he used to purchase registered assets, until he had done so on a sufficient scale to balance any D-day holdings of unregistered assets (above the £500 exemption) which, for one reason or another, he wished to retain after D-day. To meet this problem it might be possible to allow him the option of requesting that specified unregistered assets held at D-day should be treated as registered assets and thus liable on future disposal to UET. Even this device would not deal with the case of a taxpayer who wished to sell a Rembrandt which he owned at D-day in order to buy a Picasso; to meet that the Picasso would also have to be treated as a registered asset.[10]

RADICAL VERSUS CONSERVATIVE TREATMENT OF THE TRANSITION

This general treatment of the transition may be regarded as intermediate between what might be called a completely 'radical' treatment and what might be called a completely 'conservative' treatment of the problem.

With a completely radical treatment virtually all assets on D-day would be treated as registered assets; and taxpayers would merely be able to build up holdings of unregistered assets after D-day if, for one of the reasons discussed earlier in this chapter, they wished to anticipate tax payments in that way. This treatment would result from the arrangements suggested in the preceding section, if no lump sum relief under (1) were given so that under (3) all D-day unregistered assets were treated as registered. The result of this radical treatment would be that all wealth on D-day would become liable to UET if it were spent on consumption, but all future private savings would be exempt from tax in so far as the persons concerned chose to put their future savings into registered assets.

The completely radical transition would thus treat all D-day assets as registered but allow holdings of unregistered assets to be built up after D-day. The completely conservative transition would on the contrary treat all D-day assets as unregistered but allow holdings of registered assets to be built up after D-day. If a solution were sought on the latter lines, there would have

---

[10] Disadvantages of these transitional arrangements are the need under (2) and (3) above for a valuation of unregistered assets at D-day and the need for safeguards under (6) to limit the post-D-day acquisitions of registered assets. A suggested modification of the scheme, which requires the listing but not the valuation of unregistered assets at D-day and eliminates the need for post-D-day restrictions on the acquisition of registered assets, is outlined in Appendix 9.3.

to be strict limits to the speed with which post-D-day holdings of registered assets could be built up in order to prevent a flood of funds moving from unregistered to registered assets immediately after D-day, with catastrophic effects upon the tax revenue. Ideally it would be desirable to find a way of limiting the building-up of such registered holdings to true post-D-day net savings. This conservative treatment would result from the arrangements suggested in the preceding section if the lump sum reliefs under (1) were without limit and if under (6) suitable restrictions were imposed on the post-D-day build-up of registered assets. The result of such arrangements would be that no holdings of pre-D-day wealth were subject to UET on their expenditure on consumption, but new private savings would be exempt from tax.

By suitable adjustment of the limits to relief under (1) and the restrictions on tax privileges for post-D-day purchases of registered assets under (6), the transitional arrangements can be made to approach more closely either the full radical or the full conservative solution.

TAX RELATIONS WITH OTHER COUNTRIES

If the United Kingdom adopted an expenditure tax while other countries retained an income tax there would be several troublesome problems, of which the most severe would be these:

1   It would be necessary to retain an income tax code for persons receiving income from the United Kingdom who had little connection with the country, perhaps defining that group as those who were not ordinarily resident in the United Kingdom.
2   Some immigrants would be deterred if while in the United Kingdom they had to pay expenditure tax on dissaving out of wealth acquired before coming to the country.
3   On the other hand, people who expected to dissave either out of inherited wealth or out of savings which had been accumulated tax-free under an expenditure tax regime would have an incentive to emigrate to a country where there was an income tax and where indirect taxation of expenditure was not heavy.
4   The giving of relief on the cost of acquiring overseas investments as well as double taxation relief on the yield from those investments would result in a double allowance; one or the other relief should be disallowed.

These problems will be discussed in Chapter 21 (pp. 434–442), together with possible methods of dealing with them.

REVENUE EFFECTS

The revenue implications of a move to an expenditure tax are much smaller than might at first sight be expected from a reform that involves the exemption of savings from the existing income tax. The reason is that, as we have already noted, the present UK income tax is in many respects more akin to an expenditure tax and in some respects goes beyond it. Thus the three forms of saving (housing, pension funds and life insurance) that would receive no more (or in the case of housing, less) favourable treatment under an expenditure tax account for almost the whole of net personal saving – between 1971 and 1975 for some £23,356 million out of net non-business saving of £24,778 million; the outflow from other savings media is almost equal to the inflow. Precise figures depend upon the treatment of housing, which we shall discuss in Chapter 11. However, we estimate that, on the basis of unchanged behaviour and the same (tax-inclusive) rate schedule as for the present income tax, the revenue cost of opting for an expenditure base rather than an income base would have averaged £200 million over the period 1971–75, if housing had been brought fully within the expenditure tax system by treating houses as registered assets on purchase and sale and by imposing a tax on their annual value. If the tax treatment of housing had been left entirely unchanged, the revenue loss would have been £1,500 million for that period. These figures compare with an average revenue from income tax over the same period of £11,000 million (figures expressed at 1975 prices).[11] Such losses could be restored by a rise in the basic rate of tax of half of a percentage point (i.e. from 33 to 33·5 per cent) with these radical changes in the tax treatment of housing; a rise of four percentage points (i.e. from 33 to 37 per cent) would be needed if no change were made in the arrangements for taxing housing.

However, we do not expect unchanged behaviour. If there were an increase in saving as a result of the tax, then the revenue cost of the change would be greater. Paradoxically, however, the effect of this would be to permit lower rather than higher rates of tax. This is because a more appropriate criterion for neutrality of tax changes is a constant level of demand in the economy rather than a constant level of tax revenue; and an increase in aggregate saving would reduce aggregate demand by more than the amount of the tax revenue lost. If, less plausibly, the expenditure tax led to a fall in saving, the argument would operate in the opposite direction.

Two very important qualifications must be made to this. The calculations above assume a 'radical' transition, in which the UET is immediately applied to all existing wealth and savings. If, as we believe, more generous transitional provisions than this are required, then the revenue losses will be greater. However, it must also be considered that, except in the very short run, the increase in the effective return on savings means that withdrawals must rise relative to inflows. For example, the proceeds of life insurance policies must be greater than now, and hence the tax paid when they mature will be greater than the figures above would suggest. So our estimates overstate the revenue from an UET in the short run and understate it in the long run. Without far more detailed information about the pattern of responsiveness of savings

---

[11] See Appendix 9.4 for more detailed figures.

behaviour than we have – or anyone has – we cannot sensibly attach precise magnitudes to these effects.

CONCLUSIONS

To operate a general progressive expenditure tax it would be necessary to adopt the principle of adding dissavings to, and deducting savings from, the taxpayer's income in order to calculate his tax base. But assets would be divided into two classes: registered and unregistered. Only savings and dis-savings of registered assets would be included in the tax base. To treat some assets as unregistered would be necessary on administrative grounds, but it would also have the positive advantage of providing taxpayers with a means of averaging their tax liabilities over time. Borrowings could also be registered or unregistered, although it would probably be necessary to put some re-strictions on the use of unregistered borrowings. Capital gains tax could be abolished, but capital gains on unregistered assets would have to be included in the tax base.

For administrative reasons it would not be practicable to operate such a tax unless a system of self-assessment was first introduced into the United Kingdom.

The making of gifts and bequests could be treated as a part of the taxpayer's expenditure, in which case there would be no need for any separate tax on capital transfers. An alternative arrangement would be to exempt the making of gifts from the expenditure tax and to retain some separate form of tax on capital transfers.

The tax, once it was in full operation, would have many practical merits in simplifying the treatment of pensions, trusts and close companies, in making capital gains tax unnecessary for registered assets, in eliminating the need to make many distinctions between income and capital, and in greatly simplifying tax problems arising from inflation.

There would, however, be serious practical problems in avoiding in-equities and disturbances on the capital market during the transition to the new tax base. It would be necessary to treat virtually all assets as if they were registered at the time of transition but to make some allowance for future untaxed expenditure from such assets in order to avoid hardship for those who had saved out of taxed income in the past in order to make future un-taxed expenditures, e.g. on retirement.

Another set of difficult problems would arise in relations with other countries that maintained an income base for their tax structure, but these problems will be discussed in Chapter 21.

The shift from an income to an expenditure base would probably involve some moderate loss of revenue, the magnitude of which would depend very much upon the treatment of housing (discussed in Chapter 11).

Appendix 9.1   The Treatment of Gifts for UET Purposes in Combination with a Separate Transfer Tax

We shall consider two possible methods, which differ essentially in their treatment of valuable gifts of unregistered assets.

Under the first of these systems, which may be called the donee-based expenditure tax, small gifts below the transfer tax exemption level would presumably be treated as consumption of the donor and disregarded when they were received. Large gifts, however, would be excluded from the computation of the donor's taxable expenditure but included in the corresponding calculations for the recipient.

This is in many ways the most logical and flexible system. It is achieved by requiring that gifts (whether of registered or unregistered assets) which are above the transfer tax limits are deductible for UET purposes from the donor's income and added to the income of the donee. Gifts of registered assets are deemed to be disposals by the donor, while their receipts by the donee count as acquisitions. The following are some examples of the operation of this system:

1 A gives B a registered asset whose value exceeds the exemption limit. A receives a credit, which offsets his tax liability on disposal; B suffers a debit, which offsets his tax credit on acquisition. No tax other than transfer tax is paid until B sells the asset and spends it.

2 A gives B a registered asset whose value is below the exemption limit. A is taxed on disposal of the asset. If B continues to hold it, he receives a credit but will be liable for tax when he sells it; if B immediately disposes of the asset and spends the proceeds, the credit he receives on acquisition offsets his liability on disposal so that no tax will be payable by B.

3 A gives B an unregistered asset whose value is below the exemption limit. UET has already been effectively paid by A, and no notice is taken of the transaction for the purposes of any tax.

4 A gives B an unregistered asset whose value is above the exemption limit. In addition to liability to transfer tax, the donor will receive a repayment of UET and the donee will therefore incur a UET liability. Suppose, for example, that valuable chattels are unregistered. A buys a Rembrandt for £1 million in 1980, and in 1990, when it is worth £$1\frac{1}{2}$ million, gives it to B. He now has a tax liability on his £$\frac{1}{2}$ million profit from dealing in unregistered assets, but can offset against this a credit on £$1\frac{1}{2}$ million for the gift; his tax liability is therefore on a balance of minus £1 million. In effect he will be receiving a refund of the UET he has already paid without compensation for the ten-year delay; this is the tax he pays on the consumption services he has enjoyed over the period. To make this equitable it would be necessary to allow negative consumption to be set against tax which had been paid in the past when such negative consumption resulted from gifts made. B receives the gift and has a tax liability on £$1\frac{1}{2}$ million.

The principal disadvantage of this first system is case 4. It may be difficult to appreciate the good sense of the arrangement, even though in fact it represents a logical and defensible treatment of unregistered assets. The most difficult case is that in which a man receives a gift of an unregistered asset on which he pays a relatively low rate of expenditure tax because his standard of living and expenditure on consumption are relatively low at the time of the receipt of the gift; later, when he is much better off and living at a much higher standard of consumption, he gives the asset away again, so that he receives a refund at a higher marginal rate than he paid.

A second possible system would be to ignore gifts entirely for expenditure tax purposes. This system would operate in the following way. In Table 8.1 (p. 151) no debit item or credit item would appear either under the donor's or the donee's tax computation in respect of the transfer of either registered or unregistered assets. In particular, the gift of a registered asset would not appear as a debit disposal of a registered asset by the donor under item 2 of the table; nor would its acquisition appear as a credit under item 4 of the table for the donee. [1]

This second solution might well be the best to adopt, since it would be easier to understand and would avoid the difficulties described in case 4 above. But it is basically less logical because there is in fact a fundamental difference between gifts of registered assets and those of unregistered assets. A gift of a registered asset is a gift of something which has not yet been franked for expenditure tax; its conversion into cash for expenditure on consumption would entail a liability to expenditure tax. A gift of an unregistered asset, on the other hand, is a gift of something which has already been franked for expenditure tax; its expenditure on consumption entails no further tax. It would therefore appear at first sight that, with a progressive expenditure tax, the rich would always choose registered assets to give to the poor (thereby converting the rich man's liability to a high marginal rate of expenditure tax into the poor man's liability to a low rate) and that the poor (if they gave to the rich) would choose unregistered assets already franked for tax at the poor man's lower rate of tax.

But if the transfer tax, whatever its form, is also at a progressive rate and is applied to the nominal value of the transferred asset, whether it is a registered or an unregistered asset, this result is not certain. An unregistered asset (franked for tax) is more valuable to both donor and donee than a registered asset (not yet franked for tax). For this reason, to give something of equal real value, more must be given in nominal value in a registered form than must be given in an unregistered form. It follows that, if there is a progressive transfer tax related to the nominal value of the gift, the rate of transfer tax may be higher on a registered gift of a given real value than on an unregistered gift of the same real value.

Table 9.1 gives a numerical example of the problem. We suppose that a donor wishes to give £100,000 of stock exchange securities (a registered asset) to a donee who, after payment of whatever transfer tax is payable, wishes to retain and hold the balance of the stock exchange securities in the same registered form. Example 1 in the table shows the result of the straightforward transfer of the securities in registered form if the rate of transfer tax on the £100,000 is 25 per cent (tax-inclusive).

But the donor and donee have the option of transfer in an unregistered form. The donor can sell the £100,000 of securities for cash (an unregistered asset), transfer the cash to the donee, who can subsequently use the balance of the cash after payment of transfer tax to purchase the stock exchange securities. If this process is adopted, the donor will have to pay UET at his marginal rate on the sale of the securities, but the donee will be able to obtain a UET credit at his marginal rate of tax on the subsequent purchase of the registered stock exchange securities with unregistered cash.

In examples 2 and 3 of Table 9.1 we examine the case in which the donor's rate of UET is 100 per cent (tax-exclusive) so that he can obtain £50,000 in cash on the sale of his £100,000 worth of securities. We assume that the donee's rate of UET is less than the donor's and is either (a) slightly less than the donor's (namely 80 instead of 100 per cent), or else (b) greatly less than the donor's (namely 25 instead of 100 per cent).

In example 2 we suppose that the rate of transfer tax on £50,000 is the same as that on £100,000, namely 25 per cent (tax-inclusive). It is clear that in this case, with the donee's rate of UET lower than the donor's, it will pay to make the gift in its registered form.

But in example 3 we suppose that there is a progressive scale for the transfer tax and that in consequence the rate of transfer tax is reduced from 25 to 10 per cent when the nominal value of the gift is reduced from £100,000 to £50,000. The donee will therefore receive £45,000 in unregistered cash. If he uses this to invest in registered securities, (a) he can purchase £81,000 worth of securities if his rate of UET is 80 per cent (tax-exclusive), and (b) he can purchase £56,250 worth if his rate of UET is 25 per cent (tax-exclusive). In case (a) it will pay to make the transfer in the unregistered form (the gain on transfer tax will outweigh the loss on UET); but in case (b) it will pay to make the transfer in the original registered form (the gain on UET will outweigh the loss on transfer tax).

Table 9.1 *Gifts of registered and of unregistered assets*

	£
Example 1	
Gift of registered securities by donor	100,000
Less Transfer tax at 25 % (tax-inclusive)	(25,000)
Receipt of registered securities by donee	75,000
Example 2	
Gift of unregistered cash by donor	50,000
Less Transfer tax at 25 % (tax-inclusive)	(12,500)
Receipt of unregistered cash by donee	37,500
Purchase of registered securities by donee:	
(a) with UET at 80 % (tax-exclusive)	67,500
(b) with UET at 25 % (tax-exclusive)	46,875
Example 3	
Gift of unregistered cash by donor	50,000
Less Transfer tax at 10 % (tax-inclusive)	(5,000)
Receipt of unregistered cash by donee	45,000
Purchase of registered securities by donee:	
(a) with UET at 80 % (tax-exclusive)	81,000
(b) with UET at 25 % (tax-exclusive)	56,250

These complexities could in theory be removed if all gifts were reckoned for transfer tax at their values in unregistered form. The operation would, however, be an administrative nightmare. It would, to follow through the example 1 in Table 9.1, involve: (i) converting the donor's gift of £100,000 at the donor's UET rate into an unregistered value of £50,000; (ii) applying the relevant transfer tax rate to the £50,000; (iii) crediting the donee with an unregistered gift of £50,000 less this transfer tax; (iv) grossing up the resulting figure at the donee's UET rate to convert to a registered form; and finally (v) levying an actual tax on the registered assets equal to the difference between £100,000 and the value at (iv). Probably the tax lawyers and accountants would have to be left with that amount of profitable employment which the methods used in Table 9.1 would provide for them in advising their clients on the choice between registered and unregistered forms for gifts and bequests.

NOTE

1 Steps would have to be taken to prevent tax evasion through donees including in their credit item 4 of Table 8.1 acquisitions of registered assets by way of gift. It is possible that, purely for administrative purposes, all gifts should be reported and included both by donor and donee in both their debit items 2 and their credit items 4, instead of being omitted from both credit and debit items.

Appendix 9.2   UET: Transitional Effects in the Capital Market

After the change of tax regime there would, at current prices and yields of existing assets, be a shift of demand from unregistered to registered assets.

Suppose that, at the time of the change to a UET, bank deposit accounts earned 10 per cent a year interest and that there was a government bond which had the same 10 per cent yield. Suppose that the bank deposit remained unregistered but that the government bond became a registered asset. A taxpayer liable to a 50 per cent (tax-inclusive) rate of tax could shift £100 from his bank deposit and thereby purchase £200 worth of the government bond (since he would obtain remission of tax of £100 on his purchase of the £200 worth of registered assets), thereby increasing the annual yield of his assets from £10 to £20. There would thus be a shift of demand from unregistered to registered assets.

The effects of this on financial markets would depend on the methods by which the government financed the loss of tax revenue which this shift of demand would imply and on the extent to which various assets – registered and unregistered – were substitutes for each other. The increased demand for securities on the stock exchange would give a lift to security prices, offset to a greater or less extent by the issue of government securities to finance the losses of government revenue following on this shift in demand.

There could be other disturbances in the capital market. Suppose, for example, that building society deposits were unregistered. The increased attractiveness of registered assets might mean that building society interest rates would have to be raised so that the increased yield on such assets offset the tax advantage of shifting into registered assets. Persons who held pictures, jewellery, etc. as a form of investment might at existing prices wish to sell such assets in order to reinvest their funds in registered assets.

So much for the disturbances which might occur if the change to a UET regime were sudden and unexpected. But the change would probably not be wholly unexpected. Disturbances in the capital market would be likely to occur in anticipation of the change. In so far as the change of tax regime was anticipated, there would be an incentive to shift from assets which were expected to become registered assets into assets which were expected to remain unregistered assets, so that – when the change came – there would be the maximum scope for tax gain by shifting back from unregistered to registered assets. The anticipatory sale of registered assets would cause a fall in their prices, and the anticipatory purchase of any unregistered assets which were not fixed in money value would cause a rise in the prices. Stock exchange securities would slump; the price of pictures and jewellery would rise; the rate of interest on building society deposits (if they were expected to be unregistered) might well have to be reduced in order to curb the inflow of funds.

If the authorities wished to offset any deflationary effects of a slump in stock exchange prices, they would have to adopt an expansionary monetary policy, supplying the increased amounts of cash and money deposits which persons wished to hold in anticipation of the change of tax regime. But any such policy would compound the ultimate loss of tax revenue, since the greater the anticipatory shift from registered to unregistered assets and the shift back from unregistered to registered assets after the change, the greater the loss of government tax revenue.

There would be some loss of revenue even if the authorities did not adopt any monetary measures to offset the slump in the price of registered assets before the change and their subsequent boom after the change. If these price fluctuations were allowed to occur, there would be some tendency for the rich to sell registered assets to the less rich before the change and for the rich to buy registered assets from the less rich after the change. An extreme example may serve to illustrate the point. Mr Smith has a zero marginal rate of tax, and will therefore be interested solely in the market prices and yields of various assets without any regard for their future tax implications. When stock exchange securities slump in price before the tax change, with the prospect of a sharp rise in their price after the change, they will offer a very good buy for Mr Smith. Mr Brown, who is subject to a high marginal rate of tax, will have a tax incentive to sell securities before the change and to buy them back after the change. As a result, the change will take place at a time when Mr Smith's holding of securities and Mr Brown's holding of cash are abnormally high; and the government will lose revenue after the change when Mr Smith sells the securities back to Mr Brown.

Appendix 9.3   A Modified Set of Transitional Arrangements

1   At the appointed day all taxpayers would be required to schedule all their unregistered assets which had a value per unit (or per set in the case of such items as antique cutlery) in excess of £1,000. There would be no requirement for an independent valuation, but in the absence of such a valuation the taxpayer would be required to schedule items which in his opinion had a value in excess of £500. The assets thus listed would be known as 'scheduled assets'. Taxpayers would be required to account for the subsequent disposition of scheduled assets as if they were registered.

2   No assets of a financial nature (e.g. bank accounts) would be treated as unregistered assets until after the appointed day. At the appointed day all registered assets (including holdings of cash, bank notes etc. in excess of £200) would have to be listed, but not valued.

3   All taxpayers would be given a lump sum allowance which could be set against net sales of registered assets after the appointed day. The scale for the allowance would be related to the age of the taxpayer, so that those nearest retirement would obtain the greatest benefit.

4   After the appointed day the proceeds of the sale of any unregistered asset which (i) was owned on the appointed day or was purchased out of the proceeds of the sale of such assets owned on the appointed day and (ii) had a value at the time of sale of more than £1,000 per unit or per set, would be treated as if it were the proceeds of sale of a registered asset. This rule would apply whether the asset was scheduled or not. The figure of £1,000 should be regularly adjusted for inflation. The taxpayer would be permitted to deduct in his expenditure tax computation the cost of any unregistered assets having a cost of more than £500 per unit or per set which were bought wholly out of the proceeds of sale. Such replacement assets would become scheduled assets.

5   On a gift or bequest of unregistered assets having a unit or set value in excess of £1,000 and which were owned at the appointed day or bought in replacement of such assets, there would be an option between (i) the donor paying expenditure tax on the value of the gift and the donee treating it as an unregistered asset, and (ii) the donor paying no expenditure tax on the value of the gift but the donee treating it as a scheduled asset. Transfer tax on the gift would follow the rules of that tax.

6   Arrangements comparable to those outlined on p. 190 of the main text could be made to set the post-D-day receipt of occupational pensions and possibly also the post-D-day realisation of pre-D-day capital gains against the tax allowance mentioned at (3) above.

Appendix 9.4   The Revenue Implications of an Expenditure Tax

In this appendix are listed the principal changes which would be required to transform the present income tax system into a universal expenditure tax, and the estimated revenue effects of each change. It is assumed that the rate schedule remains unchanged, so that the 33 per cent basic rate of income tax would become a 33 per cent basic rate of expenditure tax (expressed on a tax-inclusive basis), with the same (tax-inclusive) rate bands as at present. It is further assumed, as a starting point, that all savings behaviour is entirely unaffected by these tax changes. The figures are given in Table 9.2 for the years 1971–75 inclusive; the rate structure assumed is that applicable in 1976/77. The estimates are of widely varying degrees of accuracy, and the worst are highly speculative. They are summarised in Table 9.3, positive figures being revenue gains.

The net cost of giving tax relief on net purchases of securities would be small, and in some years there would have been a net revenue gain. This is mainly because the private sector is, and has been for some time, a large net seller of company securities. In 1974 this was offset (exceptionally) by extensive purchases of local authority debt. (Note the low figures in the table for national savings and building societies deposits in 1974.) Nothing is included for the abolition of income tax on dividends; this is because such dividends are either spent (in which case they will continue to be taxed) or reinvested in some savings medium (in which case they are included under the appropriate heading).

Life insurance would be treated more generously under an expenditure tax but not enormously so. The existing relief on policies would be abolished; the whole of premiums paid would be deductible; the whole proceeds of policies would be taxable.

Table 9.2 *The revenue implications of an expenditure tax (in £ millions)*

Change required	1971	1972	1973	1974	1975
Securities					
1 Abolition of CGT	−150	−205	−280	−360	−380
2 Relief on net purchases of company securities	+438	+480	+800	+485	+482
3 Relief on net purchases of government securities	−173	+6	−282	−218	−358
4 Relief on net purchases of local authority debt	+82	+35	−177	−317	+56
Life insurance					
5 Abolition of present relief	+110	+120	+135	+190	+235
6 Relief on net payments to companies	−183	−346	−403	−384	−394
7 Abolition of tax on life funds and repayment of ACT on dividends to life companies	−124	−118	−164	−193	−208
Building societies					
8 Relief on net deposits	−412	−449	−460	−420	−872
Other savings					
9 Tax on net additions	−235	−312	−102	−25	−236
10 Relief on net deposits	−80	−150	−290	−307	+7
Housing[a]					
11 Treatment 1	+600	+850	+1,000	+1,000	+1,600
12 Treatment 2	+142	+70	+105	+25	+500
13 Treatment 3 – no revenue implications	—	—	—	—	—
Total: net revenue effect:					
with treatment 1 for housing	+60	−90	−220	−460	−60
with treatment 2 for housing	−400	−870	−1,100	−1,430	−1,160
with treatment 3 for housing	−540	−940	−1,200	−1,460	−1,660

[a] See p. 203 for a description of the three treatments of housing.
Sources: Own estimates based on the following published data:
 1 Inland Revenue Statistics, 1976, HMSO 1977.
 2 Financial Statistics, April 1977, HMSO 1977.
 3 Life Insurance in the UK 1971–75, The Life Officers Association, London 1975.
 4 National Income and Expenditure Blue Book 1965–1975, HMSO 1976.
 5 Royal Commission on the Distribution of Income and Wealth, Report No. 1, Initial
   Report on the Standing Reference, HMSO July 1975.

Table 9.3 *The revenue implications of an expenditure tax: summary*

	1971	1972	1973	1974	1975	Total
Net revenue effect at current prices:						
with treatment 1 for housing[a] (£ m)	+60	−90	−220	−460	−60	
with treatment 3 for housing[a] (£ m)	−540	−940	−1,220	−1,460	−1,660	
Income tax receipts at current prices (£ m)	6,184	6,365	6,929	8,975	13,788	
Net revenue effect at 1975 prices:						
with treatment 1 for housing[a] (£ m)	+99	−139	−316	−563	−60	−979
with treatment 3 for housing[a] (£ m)	−887	−1,453	−1,751	−1,787	−1,660	−7,535
Income tax receipts at 1975 prices (£ m)	10,260	9,860	9,900	11,000	13,788	54,808
Revenue effect as % of receipts:						
with treatment 1 for housing[a] (%)	+1·0	−1·4	−3·2	−5·1	−0·4	−1·8
with treatment 3 for housing[a] (%)	−8·6	−14·7	−17·7	−16·2	−12·0	−13·7

[a] See p. 203 for details of housing treatments.
Sources: As for Table 9.2.

The figures shown represent the initial impact of these changes; but they would subsequently decrease and could even change sign, since in the long term the net proceeds of policies would increase as a result of the removal of tax on the underlying funds.

Three possible treatments of housing are considered. Treatment 1 assumes that tax relief on mortgages continues as at present, but that householders (whether owner-occupiers or tenants) are taxed on the difference between an imputed rent of 3 per cent of the capital value of the house and the rent (if any) actually paid. The second treatment regards local authority rates as a substitute for basic rate income tax on income from housing, so that owner-occupiers are taxed only at higher rates and tenants receive relief at the basic rate on rent actually paid. In both these cases the net proceeds of the sale of houses are subject to expenditure tax, tax relief is given on the purchaser's equity in a house he buys, and the capital component of a mortgage, as well as the interest, attracts relief. Treatment 3 makes no change to the present position.

Net deposits in building societies would attract tax relief, and tax on interest received would end. As explained above, it is unnecessary to make explicit allowance for this latter item. Net additions to national savings would obtain tax relief. Interest rates on so-called 'tax-free' national savings media would have to be raised to competitive levels. If the proceeds of national savings are spent the excess will be recouped in expenditure tax, while if saved they are already accounted for; thus no entry for the cost of this is required, although it would be a necessary part of a move to an expenditure tax.

Tax relief would be given on net deposits with banks and related financial institutions. The figures cited probably represent an overestimate, for two reasons. First, it is not possible to distinguish persons from unincorporated business in the available statistics on bank deposits, so that these figures are likely to exaggerate the element relating to the personal sector. Secondly, the figure is highly sensitive to the rate of inflation: increases in bank deposits of around £3,000 million were required (and made) in 1974 simply in order to maintain the real value of transactions balances. The figures for 1973 and 1974 are therefore exceptional.

10 A Two-Tier Expenditure Tax

From the discussion of a universal expenditure tax (UET) in the preceding chapter it has become clear that, in the absence of a system of self-assessment for liabilities to expenditure tax, it would not be practicable to administer a UET unless there were a long band of expenditure liable to a single basic rate of tax, which covered a large proportion of all taxpayers. Even in this case there would be difficulty in avoiding an end-year review of virtually every taxpayer's tax liability, unless special measures were taken to ensure that the savings and dissavings of those taxpayers whose liability to tax remained in the basic rate band were in some way automatically adjusted for remission of tax on their savings and for deduction of tax on their dissavings. On pp. 181–182 of Chapter 9 two possible methods were outlined,[1] namely (i) dealing in assets net of tax, and (ii) giving a tax incentive for small savers to channel their savings through a restricted range of securities specially designed for the purpose of giving automatic basic rate relief to savings and imposing automatic basic rate tax on dissavings.

There is, however, an alternative approach to the problem, which is feasible provided that the long band for a single basic rate of tax is preserved. This is the method of a two-tier expenditure tax (TTET), which has been outlined briefly at the end of Chapter 8.

In that chapter four methods of applying the expenditure tax principle have been outlined, summarised on p. 160 as (i) the income adjustment method, (ii) the method of some form of universal and uniform tax on value added, (iii) the method of a basic rate of income tax with 100 per cent capital allowances, and (iv) the method of a basic rate of income tax with remission of tax on the yield on a taxpayer's savings. We have argued that, while a *progressive* expenditure tax could be administered only by method (i), a *proportionate* expenditure tax could also be administered by methods (ii), (iii) or (iv).

The TTET is a combination of what are in effect two separate taxes, namely (i) for the lower tier of a taxpayer's expenditure either an income tax with 100 per cent capital allowances or a form of universal and uniform tax on value added to cover the long basic rate band combined, for the upper tier of taxpayer's expenditure, with (ii) a surcharge on levels of expenditure above the basic rate band, liability to this surcharge being assessed by the income adjustment method that has been considered at length for a UET in Chapter 9.[2]

---

[1] These will be discussed in more detail in Chapter 22 on administration.

[2] We exclude method (iv) (i.e. the remission of tax on the yield on savings) from further consideration in this chapter on the following grounds. Its proper application would require that only true economic depreciation should be allowed against all forms of capital assets, so that all existing 100 per cent capital allowances would need to be scrapped. Otherwise taxpayers would be getting a double relief from tax on their savings. As the basic rate of the present income tax is at least halfway to a method (iii) type of proportionate expenditure tax, and as the present

THE PROGRESSIVE EXPENDITURE TAX SURCHARGE

As far as the upper tier of this tax system is concerned, the taxpayer's liability to progressive surcharge on his expenditure would be calculated at the end of the fiscal year on lines shown in Table 10.1.

Table 10.1   *Calculation of taxpayer's liability to expenditure surcharge*

1	Income		XXX
2	Expenditure tax adjustments:		
	Add Disposals of registered assets	XXX	
	Receipt of gifts and other windfalls	XXX	
	Deduct Acquisitions of registered assets	(XXX)	
	Gifts made during the year*a*	(XXX)	
	IT paid during the year	(XXX)	
	ET paid during the year	(XXX)	XXX
3	Expenditure during the year		XXX
4	*Less* Personal allowance for ET		(XXX)
5	Balance liable to ET		XXX

a Gifts made are excluded from the tax base for the upper tier of expenditure tax in this calculation, on the assumption that they would be separately taxed under some form of tax on capital transfer. If, however, it were desired to submit gifts made, like other forms of consumption, to ET instead of to a separate transfer tax (as in the case discussed for UET on pp. 183–185 above), this could be done by charging on gifts as they were made both the basic rate of tax on income or on value added and also, where relevant, the expenditure surcharge.

The personal allowance for expenditure tax at line 4 would be of the order of, say, £4,000 to correspond to the level of expenditure which could be met post-tax out of the income at which higher rates of income tax now start. The expenditure tax surcharge would be assessed on the balance at line 5 and would be on a progressive rate schedule which corresponded, on a tax-exclusive basis, to the excess of the higher rates of income tax over the basic rate of income tax. The tax thus computed would be compared with the payments on account already made and the difference paid to, or refunded by, the Inland Revenue. The tax would correspond in many ways to the old surtax on *incomes* above a given level; it is a surtax on *expenditures* above a given level.

VAT in many respects resembles method (ii), it is sensible to confine attention to these two possibilities. Moreover, the distributional effects of the introduction of method (iv) would be unacceptable. To allow the tax relief on all existing investment income would give a wholly unwarranted bonus to all existing owners of capital; and even if it were administratively possible to restrict the relief to the yield on new net savings, there would still be no new charge on expenditure on consumption out of existing capital.

ADMINISTRATION OF EXPENDITURE TAX SURCHARGE

The problems of administering this upper tier tax would in many ways be the same as those discussed at length in Chapter 9 in connection with a UET. The essential problem is to determine the items which should be included in the expenditure tax adjustment at line 2 in Table 10.1. This administrative problem would be on a much smaller scale in that the expenditure tax adjustment would have to be made for a much smaller number of taxpayers.

IDENTIFICATION OF THOSE LIABLE TO THE SURCHARGE

There would, however, be a tiresome and difficult problem in determining which taxpayers should have their affairs reviewed each year to discover whether they were liable to the upper-tier expenditure surcharge. The taxpayer would be liable himself to declare the fact if his expenditure (line 5 in Table 10.1) exceeded the exemption level for the expenditure tax surcharge. The Inland Revenue would be given the power to require any taxpayer to supplement his income tax return with the additional information needed to assess his expenditure tax adjustment, and would presumably automatically require such information from all taxpayers who had total incomes above a certain figure, from all taxpayers who had investment incomes above a moderate level, and – if there were an annual wealth tax in operation – from all persons who owned more than a certain amount of wealth. They could also, through the machinery of any tax on gifts and inheritances, require returns from any persons who received substantial capital sums in this manner. By processes of this kind it should be possible to pick out the majority of those who would be liable to the expenditure tax surcharge, but at the cost of demanding returns from a number of persons who would in fact turn out to have expenditures below the exemption level. The class of persons who would have the greatest opportunity to evade the tax would be those who had low incomes but lived at a high standard of consumption upon the sale of valuable assets (such as jewellery, cash, etc.) which yielded little or no taxable investment income.

TRANSITION TO THE EXPENDITURE TAX SURCHARGE

The transition to such an upper-tier expenditure surcharge could be made essentially on the 'radical' principle that virtually all assets (other than the general run of personal durable consumption goods) would be treated as registered assets on D-day. It would only be annual expenditure above the exemption level of, say, £4,000 which would be subject to the new tax charge, and the rate of new charge would be restricted to a surcharge which corresponded not to the whole of the higher rates of tax but only to the excess of those rates over the basic rate of tax. Thus the need for relief for those who had accumulated, out of past sources which were liable to income tax, funds which after D-day would be unexpectedly liable to expenditure tax would be much diminished.

POSSIBILITY OF PHASING IN THE SURCHARGE

If in addition the change could be phased in over a period of years in the way described on pp. 188–189 above, any hardships would be further mitigated. For expenditure tax purposes the higher rates of income tax would in the first instance be treated, like the old surtax, as a ₋rcharge on incomes above a certain level; but in computing the tax base for these surcharges one-tenth of the expenditure tax adjustment (i.e. net sales or purchases of registered assets) would be added or subtracted in the first year, two-tenths in the second year and so on, so that the full impact of the expenditure tax adjustment of the surcharge would not be felt until ten years after the change.

With arrangements of this kind it might well be considered unnecessary to make any further arrangements for relief from the expenditure tax surcharge on assets existing on D-day. But if it were considered necessary, transitional relief of the kind discussed on pp. 189–192 above for the UET might be devised.[3]

THE BASIC RATE TIER

So much for the progressive expenditure tax surcharge for the upper tier of a TTET. We now turn to consider the accompanying basic rate tax.

There would, of course, be nothing inherently absurd or basically inconsistent in combining a true income-tax system (which approximated as closely as possible to a comprehensive income tax regime) for the basic rate of tax with a true expenditure-tax surcharge on high levels of consumption. Everyone, rich and less rich, would be taxed at a proportionate rate on their income (above some threshold level); but those who were living at exceptionally high standards of consumption would be taxed progressively on their extra expenditure.[4]

On the general principles discussed in Chapter 3 we would, however, favour transforming the basic rate of tax as far as possible into an effective expenditure tax, either by extending the principle of 100 per cent capital allowances against liability to income tax to cover all or virtually all forms of capital expenditure on items of physical investment,[5] or else by extending the use of some form of tax on value added.

---

[3] There would in this case be a problem in connection with the assets existing on D-day of those persons who were not immediately thereafter chargeable to the upper-tier expenditure surcharge but who might later become so chargeable when their expenditures had risen above the threshold for the expenditure surcharge. It might be necessary to give to such persons on D-day the opportunity of recording their existing D-day assets, so that at a later date, if and when they lived on them to finance a high level of expenditure, they could obtain the appropriate relief.

[4] This was the general set of ideas which, with the support of Hugh Gaitskell, was advocated by Professor Lord Kaldor in his book *An Expenditure Tax* (Allen & Unwin, 1955).

[5] With parallel arrangements for corporation tax, which we shall discuss in Chapter 12.

THE TAXATION OF VALUE ADDED

Taxing value added would be much more clearly perceived by the taxpayer as being a tax on consumption than would taxing income with 100 per cent allowances on real investment. With the value-added base, taxpayers would receive their incomes free of any income tax but would be aware that the tax on value added was raising the price of what they were buying. In particular, with the tax on value added individuals would get a tax-free rate of return on their savings which was directly linked to the rate of return on real capital investment. With the income tax method they would not realise that it was the post-tax yield on their savings which was linked to the yield on real capital investment; they would inevitably think that the rate of income tax on the interest on their savings was a true tax on the yield from the use of their savings.

EXTENSION OF COVERAGE OF VAT

One way of moving in the direction of tax on value added would be to make use of the existing VAT, to reduce the range of goods and services which are exempt or zero rated, and to raise the rate of VAT as the basic rate of income tax was reduced. But some of the logical implications of any really radical shift in this direction would involve a number of unfamiliar ideas. Thus as the basic rate of income tax was reduced on the incomes of farmers and producers of books, and (if it were part of the income tax base) on the notional annual value of houses, so this reduction of income tax on such activities would need to be replaced by an equivalent rate of VAT on their outputs – on foodstuffs, books, and the consumption of dwelling space by owner-occupiers. It is, of course, possible with VAT to maintain some differences in the rates of tax on different products; but if the replacement of the income tax by VAT were to take place on a really large scale, it would be difficult to continue the zero rating or exemption for VAT of any branch of activity which had previously been liable to income tax. Moreover, any such large scale shift from income tax to VAT would strengthen the case on administrative grounds for operating the tax on value added by means of an annual tax on an accounts basis, of the kind which we have described in our discussion of ITVAT in Appendix 8.3.

A possible combination which might be regarded as the ultimate objective for the reform of this part of the tax system might be the transformation of the basic rate of income tax into a basic rate of tax on value added on the lines of the ITVAT described in Appendix 8.3, together with the retention of a supplementary VAT on a quarterly invoice basis, as we know it at present. The retention of the existing VAT would retain the possibility of making some distinctions in the rates of tax on different products. It would also enable the general level of taxation on value added to be changed at shorter notice than would be possible if the whole of such taxation were on an annual basis; and this might provide an important instrument of economic control if such variation were needed to regulate the general level of demand in the economy. Moreover, it might be desirable or even necessary, to retain the existing VAT for EEC purposes.[6]

TREATMENT OF SOCIAL BENEFITS AND TAX THRESHOLDS

If there were any extensive shift from income tax to the taxation of value added, the payment of social benefits would need to be adjusted to any rise in the cost of living due to the extension of the coverage and the rise in the rates of the tax on value added. Moreover, the reduction of the basic rate of income tax would reduce to all taxpayers the value of the income tax threshold, whereas the rise in the tax on value added would fall on all members of the community. This would imply that personal allowances under the income tax should be replaced by some form of *'unconditional social dividend'* (see p. 274 below), which would give to all potential taxpayers in the form of a personal social benefit something which had a value in real terms equal to the value of the former personal allowance to the payer of the basic rate of income tax. Or alternatively it would imply that some form of subsidisation of the taxpayer's income up to the previous threshold level should be devised to offset the tax on value added levied on that first slice of his consumption (see p. 172 of Appendix 8.3).

THE EFFECT ON MONEY PRICES

Any transition from a tax based on incomes to a tax based on value added would have the effect on money prices discussed on p. 155 of Chapter 8. If pre-tax money wages remained unchanged, earners would gain from the removal of income tax but would lose through the rise in prices which would result from superimposing the tax on value added on unchanged labour costs. Clearly the process of change raises problems for the fixing of money incomes and for the control of prices in any set of financial and economic policies designed to damp down an inflation of money prices and costs. The timing and pace of any shift from the one tax procedure to the other would clearly depend upon these considerations of short run policies for the control of inflation. The shift is designed as a long term measure to achieve quite different results. If the present VAT rules for exempting exports from tax on value added but levying the tax on imports were retained, the shift from income tax to tax on value added need have no effect upon the prices at which importers in the United Kingdom could deal with their foreign suppliers or customers; it would have no direct effect on the balance of payments or on foreign exchange rates. But if, for the reasons discussed in Appendix 8.3, there were no exemption for exports and no tax on imports, some adjustment of the foreign exchange rate would be necessary.

---

[6] Thus VAT could continue to be operated on the 'destination principle' (with the exemption of exports and the taxation of imports), even if, for the reasons discussed in Appendix 8.3, it were decided to operate ITVAT on the 'origin principle' (with no exemption of exports and no tax on imports).

THE EXTENSION OF 100 PER CENT CAPITAL ALLOWANCES UNDER THE INCOME TAX[7]

The alternative to a shift from income tax to some form of tax on value added would be to extend the range of 100 per cent capital allowances under the existing income tax regime. While this would have the very serious disadvantage of being a less direct form of tax on consumption and, above all, a less readily understood form of consumption tax, it would not raise short run problems for the control of inflation; and it would mean a smaller upheaval in the general tax structure. It would involve a gradual extension of 100 per cent allowances to cover virtually all forms of capital expenditure on real assets (e.g. stocks, land, buildings, etc.). However, its full and proper application would involve a number of other changes.

INVESTMENT INCOME OF PENSION FUNDS AND CHARITIES

First, the investment income of pension funds and charities ought not to be exempt from tax, since it is the post-tax return and not the pre-tax return which is linked to the rate of return on investment in real resources. The pensioner will be getting full expenditure-tax treatment if his contributions into the fund are exempt from tax, if the return on the capital in the fund corresponds to the rate of return on the real capital which it represents, and if the whole of the pension paid from the fund is taxed. If pension funds were treated in this way, there would in principle be no reason to restrict the extent to which they could be used. It is true that this would enable contributors, by putting unlimited amounts into the pension fund, to obtain apparently unlimited immediate remission of the basic rate of tax. But against this the interest in the fund as it accumulated and the whole of the ultimate outgoings from the fund to the pensioner would be subject to the basic rate of tax. The taxpayer and the Inland Revenue would both be postponing a tax liability which would itself be growing at compound interest.

INVESTMENT INCOME BELOW THE TAX THRESHOLD

Secondly, since it is the yield on savings after deduction of the basic rate of tax which corresponds most closely to the rate of return on the real capital financed by the savings, any exemption from the basic rate of tax on investment income for those below the tax threshold in fact represents a subsidy to the yield on such holdings of wealth and thus loses much of its justification.

---

[7] In our discussion of the effects of 100 per cent capital allowances in this chapter we neglect certain problems raised by the corporation tax. We discuss the matter as if there were no separate corporation tax, with all businesses, whether incorporated or not, being subject to the same basic rate of income tax. An exactly similar result would occur if corporation tax were at the same rate as the basic rate of income tax and tax credits were imputed to dividends at this basic rate of tax. In Chapter 12 (pp. 253–256) we shall consider the situation with corporation tax at a higher rate than the basic rate of income tax.

ANNUAL VALUE OF DWELLING HOUSES

Thirdly, if it were desired to tax the value of the consumption of dwelling space (the case for which is examined in Chapter 11), owner-occupiers would be charged the basic rate of tax on the annual value of dwelling houses. This would be offset by tax deducted from any interest payable on mortgage debt or any rent payable to a landlord. The purchase of a house would qualify for a 100 per cent capital allowance, but the sale of a house would be subject to a basic rate of tax.

ABOLITION OF SOME CAPITAL–INCOME DISTINCTIONS

The system would, however, bring with it a number of simplifications. Thus a number of capital–income distinctions would become irrelevant. The system of 100 per cent capital allowances itself removes the distinction between income and capital in that all purchases of capital goods (whether for current replacement or for new capital development) are treated alike, while all sales of goods (whether out of capital stocks or out of current production) are treated alike.

TREATMENT OF CAPITAL GAINS

It is, however, a troublesome matter to decide whether under this system it would be appropriate to retain a capital gains tax in order to tax capital gains at the basic rate of tax. As far as the higher rates of tax are concerned, under the expenditure tax surcharge the whole of the proceeds from the disposal of assets and not merely any capital gain on such assets would be liable to tax. But should such capital gains be liable to tax at the basic rate?

We have in Chapter 8 (pp. 158–159) given some theoretical reasons for believing that in principle no such tax need be maintained. That argument rests, however, upon an easy and precise working of competitive capital markets which adjust the post-tax rate of interest to everyone to the social yield on capital. This may be quite far from reality, and in fact there may be many cases where divergences of the actual outcome from this simple theoretical model may make the retention of a tax on capital gains desirable. In particular, it might be well to subject capital gains made on valuable chattels, such as pictures, jewellery, etc., to the basic rate of tax.

IMPERFECTIONS OF THE INCOME TAX WITH CAPITAL ALLOWANCES

The fact that, in actual outcome, imperfections and uncertainties in the capital market will not in fact in all cases equate the post-tax rate of yield to the saver to the social rate of yield on investments in real capital assets, weakens the desirability of relying upon the extension of 100 per cent capital allowances as a method of applying the expenditure tax principle to a proportionate basic rate of tax. It does not, of course, destroy the case. In spite of its imperfections, there is no doubt that a system of a basic rate of income tax with 100 per cent capital allowances will be a much closer approximation to the expenditure tax principle than will a basic rate of income tax without 100 per cent capital allowances. But the taxation of value added is a still more direct application of the expenditure tax principle.

UNUTILISED TAX LOSSES

As we have shown in Chapter 8 (pp. 154–156), an income tax with 100 per cent capital allowances has an effect similar to that of an expenditure tax only because the cost of investment in physical assets is reduced by an amount equal to the remittance of tax on the capital outlay. In order that this cost reduction should be effective it is necessary either (i) that the taxpayer should have other current tax liabilities against which the tax remittance can be set, or, in so far as such other tax liabilities are inadequate, (ii) that an amount equal to the balance of remitted tax should be paid by the Revenue to the taxpayer, or (iii) that the balance should be carried forward at an appropriate rate of interest to be set against future tax liabilities. We assume that effective arrangements on the lines of (ii) or (iii) would be made to cover the cases in which other current tax liabilities were inadequate. This is particularly important in order to avoid discrimination against the setting up of new businesses, in which case heavy initial investment might be necessary before any subsequent taxable profit could be enjoyed.

THE LIMITATIONS AND ADVANTAGES OF TTET

NEED FOR A WIDE BAND AT THE BASIC RATE OF TAX

A TTET, in contrast to a UET, would imply that there was a large range of incomes over which the same basic rate of tax was imposed. In so far as it was desired to use an income tax with 100 per cent allowances or a tax on value added as an indirect form of tax on consumption expenditure, the rate of tax could not be varied according to the level of the total consumption of the individual taxpayer. A TTET would thus have the disadvantage of restricting the degree of progressivity of the marginal rate of tax at the lower end of the scale.

DIFFICULTIES FOR POPULAR UNDERSTANDING

If the lower tier were operated by means of a basic rate of income tax with 100 per cent capital allowances, a TTET would be less readily understood by the general body of taxpayers. A UET could be readily explained and understood to be what it was, namely a method of progressively taxing expenditures on consumption by remitting tax on savings and imposing tax on dissavings. We have already discussed in Chapter 8 the fact that, while an income tax with 100 per cent capital allowances would in fact operate as a tax on expenditure, it would not readily be perceived as such. In particular we have argued that, except perhaps in the case of gains on valuable chattels such as pictures, jewellery etc., it might be appropriate to abolish capital gains tax if the object were to tax consumption (by means of an income tax with 100 per cent capital allowances) rather than income; but, as pointed out in Chapter 8, the reasons for holding this view would not be easily understood by the inexpert citizen.

One particular difficulty in the understanding of the tax would relate to the rate of interest. Since, as we have explained, it would be the post-tax rather than the pre-tax rate of interest which would correspond to the social yield on capital, it would in principle be wrong to allow remission of such tax on incomes below the tax threshold, and the income of charities and pension funds as well as all individual savers ought to be subject to the basic rate of tax. Whether or not the reason for this conclusion would be readily understood is quite another matter.

VALUE-ADDED TAXATION MORE READILY UNDERSTOOD

These problems of understanding the essential nature of the tax would not arise in so far as it was possible to replace the basic rate of income tax with a proportionate rate of some form of tax on value added.

RELATIVE EASE OF TRANSITION TO A TTET

A TTET has a marked advantage over a UET in that its introduction would present less formidable transitional difficulties than would the introduction of a UET. The number of persons whose tax treatment would be suddenly and drastically altered by the expenditure tax adjustment would be much smaller, and the change in their tax treatment would relate only to the excess of higher rates of tax over the basic rate. As we have shown, the obstacles to a radical transition would be much less severe, and the possibilities of a gradual phasing-in of the new tax regime for the limited number of persons would be greater.

But the possibilities of gradual change for the basic rate taxpayers would be even more marked. Capital allowances at 100 per cent could be extended by gradual stages to a wider range of assets; the imposition of the basic rate of tax on the investment income of pension funds and charities and, if the consumption of dwelling space were to be part of the tax base, the levying of the basic rate of tax on the notional annual value of dwelling houses could be introduced by gradual stages; and, if it were decided to so proceed, the extent of the replacement of the basic rate of income tax with a proportionate rate of some form of tax on value added could be undertaken by a gradual process of trial and error.

A TTET could itself be attained by a much more gradual process than could a full UET. Moreover, a TTET could be regarded also as a helpful first stage towards a full UET, in so far as the operation of the income adjustment method for the limited number of payers of expenditure tax surcharge would give experience, familiarity and practice in the administration of this method.

PROBLEMS OF TRANSITION FROM A TTET TO A UET

But it must not be imagined that there would be any very easy process of gradually turning a TTET into a UET by gradual reductions of the threshold for the expenditure tax surcharge combined with gradual reductions of the basic rate of income tax or of tax on value added and gradual increases in the rates of expenditure tax surcharge.

The reason is a simple one. In order to extend the expenditure tax surcharge regime to a limited number of taxpayers who were just below the existing threshold for the expenditure tax surcharge, without imposing on them any net additional tax burden, it would be necessary to reduce for them the basic rate of income tax or of tax on value added at the same time that they were made liable to an expenditure tax surcharge. But if the basic rate of tax were reduced for this narrow class of taxpayers, it would – since it is a basic rate – have to be reduced for all taxpayers. Those taxpayers who were already above the threshold for the expenditure tax surcharge before the downward extension of the tax could have their reduced liability to the basic rate of tax offset by a rise in the rates of expenditure tax surcharge. But those taxpayers who still remained below the new and lowered threshold for expenditure tax surcharge would enjoy a reduction of basic rate tax which would not be offset by any new or additional alternative tax liability.

Taxpayers in this latter group would thus all gain a tax bonus which it might not be desired to extend to them or which might be too expensive in revenue to contemplate. The alternative would involve raising the joint tax burden of basic rate of tax plus expenditure tax surcharge for all those tax brackets which it was wished to include in the expenditure tax surcharge regime after the change.

In fact the TTET regime can only be readily extended downwards in this way by taking in at each step of downward revision the whole class of taxpayers who are in the next lower tax bracket. Thus if the lower tier were being operated by means of an income tax with 100 per cent capital allowances, a TTET could be gradually converted into a UET, but only if one of the necessary conditions for a pure expenditure tax regime were first disregarded by breaking the wide band of incomes liable to the single rate of tax into a number of separate, gradually tapering tax brackets.

As a longer term prospect, the conversion of a TTET into a UET might perhaps be achieved through the following stages of reform: first, the introduction of a TTET of the kind described in this chapter, with the lower tier operated through a basic rate of income tax with 100 per cent capital allowances; followed next by turning to a process of self-assessment, which would allow a gradual substitution of tapering tax brackets over the lower range of basic rate taxpayers; and completed by a replacement of the income tax by a gradual process of extending the expenditure tax regime down the different brackets of the income tax. But this particular transitional process would suffer from the disadvantage of having to operate the lower tier of TTET by means of an income tax with 100 per cent capital allowances (which could be split into a number of brackets with different rates of tax) rather than by a tax on value added (which could not be split into a number of brackets which depended upon the individual consumers' incomes).

TAX RELATIONS WITH OTHER COUNTRIES

The international aspects of the expenditure surcharge would in principle be the same as those of a UET, but they would affect a much smaller number of taxpayers. Those of the basic rate tier would depend on whether that took the form of a VAT, ITVAT or an income tax with 100 per cent capital allowances. These issues will be discussed in Chapter 21 (pp. 442–446).

CONCLUSIONS

If the limitation of a long band of income or expenditure for tax at a single basic rate is acceptable, an expenditure tax could be operated by a combination of two taxes:

1   A progressive surcharge on expenditure above a fairly high limit, such as £4,000 a year, applied through an expenditure tax adjustment to income as the tax base.
2   A proportionate rate of tax at the basic rate, applied either through an income tax with 100 per cent capital allowances or through a tax on value added. A tax on value added would be a more readily understood and a more certain method than an income tax with 100 per cent capital allowances for applying a basic rate of expenditure tax, but it would involve a bigger change from present tax arrangements.

A TTET of the kind discussed in this chapter could be introduced in a more gradual manner and with less upheaval than could a UET of the kind described in Chapter 9; and it could be introduced as a first stage towards the latter type of tax.

11 Housing

In discussing the tax bases for an income or for an expenditure tax in the preceding chapters of our Report we postponed discussion of the tax treatment of dwelling houses for special treatment in a separate chapter. The market for dwelling houses is so distorted by various governmental interventions and regulations (including special tax provisions) that any changes in the tax treatment of housing present peculiar difficulties, which we attempt to outline in this chapter. There are, as we shall argue, a number of different approaches to this problem, the choice between which should not be allowed to affect the main thrust of the rest of our discussion of the choice between an income tax base and an expenditure tax base for other sectors of the economy.

THREE CATEGORIES OF DWELLING HOUSE TENURES

There are three major categories of dwelling house tenures, namely (i) rented houses owned by local authorities, (ii) rented houses owned by private landlords, and (iii) owner-occupied houses, each category being subject to its own distinct treatment in so far as governmental policies are concerned. These three categories account for approximately (i) one-third, (ii) one-sixth, and (iii) one-half respectively of UK housing.

DISTORTIONS IN THE MARKET FOR HOUSING

LOCAL AUTHORITY HOUSING

Local authority houses are subsidised and generally let at rents which are considerably lower than what would be necessary to yield a normal market rate of return on the capital values at which they would sell in the market. There is normally a waiting list of potential tenants seeking local authority housing, and the houses are allotted by each authority to particular tenants. Sitting tenants may therefore be reluctant to vacate their houses because of the uncertainty of obtaining another. This has a locking-in effect; and as a result tenants who would prefer a house in a different locality or of a different size (e.g. because their families have grown up and left home) may cling to their existing accommodation. As a result there may be a marked difference between the usefulness of such houses (and so their values) to the sitting tenants and their usefulness in a market which allowed freer movement.

PRIVATELY RENTED HOUSING

Houses rented out by private landlords are subject to rent controls with security of tenure for the existing tenants, with the result that such houses have a market value considerably lower than that of similar houses for sale with vacant possession. Rents for such houses are thus kept down, but not (as in the case of local authority houses) through governmental subsidisation. On the contrary, the landlord pays the full rate of tax on the rent which he receives, but the government loses tax revenue in so far as the landlord does not receive a full market rent. As in the case of local authority housing, these arrangements result in an unwillingness of existing tenants to move.

OWNER-OCCUPIED HOUSING

Owner-occupied houses are not subject to any tax on their annual value, although they are, as it were, houses which the owner as private landlord rents out to himself as tenant. Consider Mr Smith who has invested his money in securities and uses the interest on them to rent a house from Mr Brown. Smith can afford to pay Brown a rent which is equal only to the interest on the securities less the tax which Smith must pay on that interest. If Smith sells his securities to Brown and buys the house from Brown, Brown will get a yield in interest instead of rent and will have to pay tax in both cases. But Smith will now get a yield not in the form of interest, on which he would have to pay tax, but in the form of the rental value of his owner-occupied house, on which he pays no tax. The government will have lost just so much in tax revenue. If Smith were then to let his house to Robinson, he would once more pay tax on the rental yield on the house. Thus the failure to tax the annual value of a house which is owner-occupied while taxing the rent of a house which is let to a tenant constitutes a clear tax privilege on owner-occupied dwellings relatively to rented dwellings. But in spite of this fact the owner is permitted to deduct from his other sources of income any interest which he pays on debt (up to a capital value of £25,000) which he has incurred for the purchase of his house.

Quite apart from differences in tax treatment, the other governmental interventions in the market for housing are so great that the question arises whether there is much point in trying to remove tax anomalies so long as so many other basic distortions remain; and it may be argued that any serious tax changes in this field should wait until there are relaxations of the other governmental rigidities in housing.

We attempt in this chapter to see what would be implied by tax changes which would remove some of the anomalies in the housing market, in order to help towards an answer to the question whether, in view of the amount that could be so achieved and of the difficulties of making the changes, basic tax changes in this field are worth the effort unless and until other basic reforms of housing policies are introduced.

LOCAL RATES AND THE TAXATION OF HOUSES

There remains one further tax complication in considering this matter. Local rates are levied on the annual values of most forms of real property, including dwelling houses and commercial and industrial buildings. The question therefore arises whether in the case of dwelling houses the existence of these local taxes weakens the case for the imposition of a national tax. In the case of privately rented property the national income tax is levied in addition to local rates; in the case of owner-occupied houses it is not. Which of these two procedures is the better?

On this two views are possible. It may be argued that, while the income tax is a general national tax levied to raise revenue for general national purposes, local rates are not such a tax but are the way of charging the inhabitants of the locality for the services of roads, refuse collection, etc. which they enjoy. There is therefore no anomaly in charging a general tax on all income (including the actual or imputed income derived from housing) and at the same time making a separate additional local charge on householders to cover (in part at least) the cost of the local services provided for them.

Against this it may be contended that the link between a particular householder's charge to rates and the value of the local services which that particular householder enjoys is very tenuous. A cnildless family, for example, wiu pay rates which help to cover the locality's expenditure on education; and in general the link between what the individual householder pays in rates and the value to him of the local services which he himself enjoys is rather remote. It is therefore – so it is argued – more appropriate to regard local rates as a form of local tax gathered on the basis of means (measured by the householder's ratable value) for the purposes of financing general services to the whole local community. And if this view is taken of the matter, it may be asked whether it is desirable to subject to both national and local tax a form of necessity such as shelter. At the present time, as we have said, the owner-occupier pays the local tax but is exempt from the national tax. The landlord and tenant together pay both. There is clearly no case for giving further relief to owner-occupiei . But if the present position of the owner-occupier is justified on the grounds that the rental value of his house is subject to a local tax from which th   eld on other forms of wealth (e.g. stock exchange securities) is exempt, then there is a case on the same grounds for some similar remission of tax in the case of the rented dwelling. In this case some alternative source of revenue would have to be found.

A LOCAL INCOME OR EXPENDITURE TAX

If the local rates did not exist, the case for subjecting the annual value of ᵓll categories of housing to the national tax on income or expenditure would be greatly strengthened. Local rates would disappear if they were completely replaced by a comprehensive form of local income tax (LIT) or local expenditure tax (LET). The possibilities for an LIT have recently been exhaustively examined by the Layfield Committee.[1] They considered only an LIT which would partially replace local rates; and in any case they suggested an LIT

[1] Local Government Finance, Report of the Committee of Enquiry, HMSO, Cmd 6453, May 1976.

of a kind which did not in fact differentiate according to locality for the rate of tax on investment income but which differentiated in the rates of tax only on earned income and that only as between a limited number of local authorities. It is clear to us from their report that an LIT which truly submitted all income (whether earned or unearned) to an additional charge to tax which varied according to the main residence of the taxpayer and as between a really wide range of different authorities, would be possible only if some system of self-assessment to income tax were introduced. In that case each taxpayer on the occasion of assessing his liabilities to national tax would be required to add a surcharge whose rate depended upon the place of residence. A similar analysis would cover the case of adding an LET to a national universal expenditure tax. In assessing his liability to such a tax, the taxpayer would be required to add a local surcharge.

We have not studied the problems of local taxation in any depth, and we therefore hesitate to express any firm views on this subject. But on the face of it a local income tax or a local expenditure tax would appear to us to be a fairer and better measure of ability to pay than the annual value of a taxpayer's residence. But serious problems would continue so long as local rates were only partially replaced by an LIT; and in any case, even if local rates on dwellings were completely replaced, the question what to do about local rates on business properties would remain. If, however, local rates on domestic properties were ever replaced by an LIT or an LET, the case for submitting the annual value of all forms of housing to the appropriate national tax would become incontestable.

THE NATIONAL TAXATION OF HOUSING

We shall therefore proceed as follows: (i) we shall consider what steps would have to be taken to impose on all forms of housing a national income tax or a national expenditure tax, whether or not local rates were still levied; then (ii) we shall consider what additional steps would have to be taken if, after imposing such a national tax on all forms of housing, it were desired to introduce an appropriate relief from the national tax in order to remove the effect of the double taxation due to the incidence of local rates.

THE ASSESSMENT OF ANNUAL VALUES

The taxation of houses depends upon the possibility of imputing to each dwelling house an appropriate annual rental value, exclusive of the normal cost of repairs and maintenance. The present state of the housing market is so affected by rent controls and other special regulations that the assessment of annual values on the basis of the current levels of market rents is no longer possible. But there is still a relatively free market in which the capital value of dwelling houses is determined by the sale and purchase of houses; and notional capital values might thus be assessed for all houses. The Layfield Committee made the proposal, which the government has in principle accepted, that capital values of dwelling houses should be assessed for the purpose of levying local rates. Such values might also be used for the purpose of assessing imputed annual values for the purpose of national taxation.

For this purpose it would be necessary to apply to the capital value of a house an appropriate net rate of interest, in order to determine the annual imputed rental value, net of normal costs of repair and maintenance. The rate of interest selected should represent the *real* rate of return on capital investments and not any inflated *money* rate of return. The money return on a house is represented by its current rental value plus the expected rise in its money price. In so far as house prices and rental values are expected to rise in line with the general level of prices, the current rental value as a ratio of the current capital value of the house represents the real rate of return on the capital value. Thus the application of some real rate of return to an up-to-date assessment of the capital value would take care of the inflationary factor. Some fairly arbitrary, constant, moderate net rate of return in the region of 3 per cent a year might be appropriate, provided that there were regular updatings of the capital values on which such a return was being estimated. The Layfield Committee concluded that house values should be reassessed at regular intervals of not more than five years and preferably at three-year intervals. If these intervals were at all prolonged and if the general inflation of money prices were to continue at any appreciable rate, it would be necessary to adjust capital values between revaluations by means of appropriate price indices. The large discontinuous jumps in assessed values which would otherwise occur at each reassessment would be likely to be so disturbing as to make it difficult politically to maintain the system. With modern computerised techniques, regular updating by appropriate price indices should be feasible.

CHARGING ANNUAL VALUES TO INCOME TAX

With an income tax regime it is desired to tax the person who receives this net income. An owner-occupier may be regarded as the owner of a house who lets the house to himself at its full economic rent. The appropriate procedure would therefore be to add the net annual value of his house to his taxable income. The private landlord would simply pay tax on any actual rent which he received after deducting expenditures on repairs and maintenance. The intermediate class of what may perhaps be called the 'mixed tenant-owner' who paid a rent below the economic level because he was protected by rent controls or was privileged by subsidised local housing or had acquired a partial interest in the house through leasehold arrangements, would be taxed on the excess of the full economic rent (as represented by the annual value of the house) over any rent which he was paying for it (exclusive of any element in the rent paid for the landlord's obligation to carry out repairs and main-tenance). In these intermediate cases the tenant would thus be treated as himself enjoying that part of the real income from the house which was not being paid to the landlord in rent.

In the case of an income tax regime any owner of a house, whether owner-occupier or landlord, would be allowed to set against his liability to tax on the annual value of the house the interest on any mortgage or other debt incurred for the purchase of the house. But, since the annual value of the house would represent only the real value (excluding any inflationary capital appreciation), it would in inflationary conditions be proper to allow as a deduction from the annual value of the house only the same real rate of interest on the mortgage debt as had been used in deriving the annual value of the house from its capital valuation (e.g. the 3 per cent a year suggested above).

CHARGING ANNUAL VALUES TO EXPENDITURE TAX

A similar set of arrangements would be appropriate in the case of a national expenditure tax. In this case the object is to tax the occupier or consumer of the dwelling space on what he may be considered to be spending on that space. If no special modifications were made to the 'expenditure tax adjustment' of Table 8.1 (p. 151), the balancing item 5, which represents the base of the expenditure tax, would already include any rent which the occupier was paying and any expenditure on repairs and maintenance which he was undertaking. What ideally should be measured is the true net annual value of the dwelling to him plus an allowance for repairs and maintenance. Therefore, to the occupier's tax base must be added the difference between these two sums, which amounts to the excess of the net annual value of the house over the net rent paid by the occupier.[2] This is in fact the same rule as that laid down in the previous section for the case of an income tax regime, and it can be applied with equal generality to owner-occupier, tenant of a private landlord's house and tenant of a local authority house.

The difference of treatment as between an income tax and an expenditure tax would arise in connection with the tax treatment of the purchase and sale of houses and of any debt incurred for their purchase. If houses held as business assets by private landlords and owner-occupied houses were both treated as assets which produce an actual or notional annual return, it would be appropriate to treat all houses as registered assets. It would then be appropriate to treat mortgage debt as a registered liability. In this case, when a house was purchased the relief from expenditure tax on the purchase would be offset by increased expenditure tax in so far as the purchase was financed by borrowing or by the sale of registered assets; and when the house was sold the increased liability to expenditure tax would be offset by relief from expenditure tax on the repayment of any mortgage debt (or, of course, by the relief from expenditure tax on the reinvestment of the proceeds of the sale in another house or any other registered asset). The result of this arrangement would be that the purchase of a house or the payment of interest and repayment of principal upon a mortgage debt would be deducted from the tax-

[2] (Net annual value plus allowance for repairs and maintenance) minus (net rent paid by occupier plus additional rent paid to cover landlord's liability for repairs and maintenance plus repairs and maintenance carried out by occupier) = (net annual value) minus (net rent paid).

payer's tax base, while the sale of a house or the raising of the principal of a mortgage debt would be added to his tax base. As is normal with an expenditure tax, no indexation for capital–income adjustment would be needed to offset the effects of inflation.

CAPITAL GAINS ON HOUSES

Up to this point we have said nothing about the treatment of capital gains on dwelling houses. Such monetary gains as merely correspond to the inflationary rise in the general level of money prices can be ignored. But a further problem arises in the case of houses on which a real capital gain is enjoyed, i.e. in those cases in which the money value of the house rises more rapidly than the general level of prices. Compare two houses, A and B, which are exactly similar except that the value of house A is expected to rise more rapidly than the general level of prices whereas that of house B is expected to rise only at the rate of general price inflation. The current money value of house A will be greater than that of house B because, while both will provide the same annual service of dwelling space, house A will in addition represent an investment of capital for a real capital gain.

For a comprehensive income tax it will therefore be appropriate to tax the owner of house A on a higher real annual income than the owner of house B, since the owner of house A is enjoying an element of real income which he is saving and investing in the appreciation of the real value of his house. But it will not then be appropriate to charge the owner of house A a tax on any capital gain which he makes on the house when he sells it, since he will in fact have been taxed on the imputed capital gain each year as it accrued.

With a universal expenditure tax, however, the real current expenditure on dwelling space will be properly assessed by the process of multiplying the current capital value of the house by a fixed real rate of return only in the case of houses on which no real capital gain or loss is anticipated. In the example given above the owner of house A enjoys the same real current expenditure on dwelling space as does the owner of house B; and he should not be taxed on those of his savings which are invested in the real appreciation of his house. Thus in principle at least the formula for the assessment of annual value needs some modification in the case of an expenditure tax. In order to avoid any tax on real capital appreciation, the capital values on which the annual values are based should exclude any part which is due to the expectation of an appreciation in the real value of the house.

LOCAL RATES AS AN OFFSET TO NATIONAL TAX

So much for the case in which either local rates have ceased to exist or are to be disregarded in considering the application of a national income or expenditure tax to all categories of housing. We turn now to consider how an appropriate relief might be devised to allow some reduction in the national tax as an offset against the local tax.

Any suggestion that what a taxpayer paid in local rates might be simply deducted from his liability to national tax is to be rejected. It would mean that local authorities by putting up their rates would be putting the burden on to the national taxpayer and not on to the local ratepayer. No local authority would have any incentive to restrain local expenditure and local taxation.

On average, domestic local rates amount to about 1 per cent of the capital value of owned houses. If the real rate of interest used to calculate annual values on the basis of capital values were 3 per cent, the rates might be regarded as representing on the average a tax of $33\frac{1}{3}$ per cent on these annual values. In principle, the best arrangement might therefore be to proceed with the arrangements described above for the case in which local rates either did not exist or were ignored, but to allow relief against national tax equal to $33\frac{1}{3}$ per cent of the annual value of the dwelling. But $33\frac{1}{3}$ per cent is approximately equal to the present basic rate of income tax. To allow the relief always at the basic rate of tax on the annual value of the house would constitute an important administrative simplification of any scheme of this kind, and we shall therefore assume this measure of relief in what follows.

In Appendix 11.1 we shall describe in more detail the operation of such a scheme of relief. It can be summarised by saying that the appropriate rule for the relief of rates against national tax in the case both of an income t x and of an expenditure tax is in all cases (i) to add to the occupier's tax base an amount equal to the excess of the annual value of the dwelling over any rent paid by him (exclusive of any element of rent to meet the landlord's obligations for repairs and maintenance), and simultaneously (ii) to give the occupier a tax credit for the basic rate of tax on the annual value of the dwelling.

This rule would make good sense in present circumstances in the case of owner-occupiers. They would not be charged the basic rate of tax on the annual values of their houses, as the local rates would be regarded as the corresponding charge; but they would be charged higher rates of tax on their annual values, since these higher rates could not be regarded as offset by local rates.

In the case of privately rented houses the arrangement with a minor modification would also make good sense. In this case the full annual value of the house would, in the absence of any tax credit relief, be charged in fact both to basic rate tax and also to local rates, either in the hands of a privileged tenant or in the hands of the landlord. The relief at basic rate on the annual value of the dwelling would remove this duplication of tax. In the case of privileged tenants the rule would be operated by applying only higher rates of tax to any excess of the annual value of the dwelling over the rent actually paid and by granting the tax credit at basic rate only on the rent actually paid. But where rent control existed and the relief was given to the tenant, the arrangement would only make good sense if controlled rents were simultaneously raised by the amount of the tax credit to the tenant (i.e. by basic rate on the rent actually charged), subject to the rent not being raised above the annual value of the dwelling. The tenant is, as it were, already subsidised through rent control at the expense of the landlord who pays full taxes on the rent which he receives. It would be out of place in such conditions to use the tax relief for the sole advantage of the tenant.

A similar situation exists in the case of local authority housing. In this case the tenant is being subsidised at the expense mainly of the national taxpayer. It may be held that, just as in the case of controlled private rents the remission of tax should relieve the landlord who is subsidising the tenant, so in the case of local authority housing the remission of tax should relieve the national taxpayer who is subsidising the tenant. Or in other words, the remission would be out of place in that it would increase the net subsidy of the tenant by the national taxpayer.

The upshot is therefore that it would be reasonable to include in all occupiers' tax bases, for higher rates of tax but not for basic rate of tax, any excess of the net annual value of their dwellings over the net rent paid, and at the same time to give to private tenants a tax credit equal to the basic rate of tax on the rent actually paid, an appropriate part of this relief being passed back to the landlords in the case of controlled rents. The higher rate charges would raise revenue; the remission of basic rate on rents received by private landlords would be a charge on the national funds.

CONCLUSIONS

As a result of this analysis we may conclude that, as far as the taxation of houses is concerned, in the absence of radical reforms in the housing market which covered the much wider topics of rent control and housing subsidies, the choice would seem to lie between: (i) introducing a full scheme for taxing the annual values of all dwelling houses, ignoring the existence of local rates; (ii) introducing a scheme which would combine the effect of (i) with a tax credit to occupiers at the basic rate of tax on the annual value of the dwelling as an offset to local rates, the benefit of the credit being passed back to the landlord to the extent that the rent was subsidised or controlled; and (iii) making no change in existing tax arrangements except ultimately as part of a wider reform of housing policies.

Appendix 11.1 Offsetting Local Rates against the National Taxation of Dwelling Houses

The following are some detailed comments on the suggestion made in the main text for eliminating any duplication of national and local taxation on dwelling houses.

(1) The proposals would be appropriate only if the valuations for rating purposes corresponded with the annual values used for the purpose of national taxation. Otherwise the broad correspondence between the average rate burden and the basic rate of national tax on annual values would break down. In particular, it would be necessary to ensure that rent-controlled private dwellings and local authority houses were fully valued for rating purposes.

(2) It would be desirable that the same rate of relief, namely the basic rate of tax on the annual value of the dwelling, should be allowed in all cases and should not be varied in accordance with the rates charged by the particular local authority in question. For example, to allow as relief the rates actually paid with an upper limit of the basic rate of tax on the annual value of the house would invite every local authority whose rates were below this limit to raise them up to this limit at the expense of the national government's revenue.

(3) The question arises as to who should receive the relief. Should it be the person who actually pays the rates? Or should it be the tenant in all cases? Or the landlord? The owner-occupier is simultaneously tenant, landlord and ratepayer, so that no problem arises in his case. The cases of tenant and landlord (whether private or local authority) need further consideration.

Let us illustrate the analysis with a numerical example in which:

$$\begin{aligned} \text{annual value of the dwelling} &= \text{£}600 \\ \text{net rent actually paid} &= \text{£}500 \\ \text{rates paid} &= \text{£}200 \end{aligned}$$

On the assumption that the tenant paid the rates and that income tax or expenditure tax was levied at a tax-inclusive rate of $33\frac{1}{3}$ per cent, the tenant of such a house would need an independent income of £1,100 simply to meet the rent. His tax base would be £1,100 plus the £100 excess of the annual value of the house (£600) over the rent paid (£500); his liability to income or expenditure tax would be £400; and this would leave £700 (i.e. £1,100 − £400) to meet the rent of £500 and the rates of £200. The landlord would receive £500 in income, on which (in the absence of any savings) he would pay £166$\frac{2}{3}$ in tax. The position would be as follows:

	Tenant			Landlord			
Income	(£)	*Expenditure*	(£)	*Income*	(£)	*Expenditure*	(£)
Annual value *less* Rent	100	Annual value *less* Rent	100	Rent	500	Consumption	333$\frac{1}{3}$
Other income	1,100	Rent	500				
		Consumption on housing	600				
		Rates	200				
		IT or ET	400			IT or ET	166$\frac{2}{3}$
TOTAL	1,200		1,200		500		500

The tax credit of £200 would be allowed to the tenant, who in the absence of any adjustment of his rent would have just so much more available to spend on other consumption goods. If, however, the tenant's rent were kept down to £500 by rent control, it would seem appropriate that to the extent of £100 (which measures the extent to which the rent is controlled below the annual value) the remission of tax should be allowed to restore the landlord's rent. In this case the position would become as follows:

		Tenant				*Landlord*	
Income	*(£)*	*Expenditure*	*(£)*	*Income*	*(£)*	*Expenditure*	*(£)*
Other income	1,100	Rent	600	Rent	600	Consumption	400
		Rates *less* Tax credit	nil				
		Other consumption	$133\frac{1}{3}$				
		IT or ET	$366\frac{2}{3}$			IT or ET	200
TOTAL	1,100		1,100		600		600

12 Corporation Tax

THE PURPOSES OF A CORPORATION TAX

The corporation tax is a tax levied on corporate, as contrasted with un-incorporated, enterprises.[1] The following four considerations may be adduced as justifications for this differential treatment of corporate enterprise:

1 As we have already mentioned in Chapter 7 (p. 145), it may be thought that the privileges conferred by incorporation, and in particular the benefits of limited liability, justify the levy of an additional tax on such concerns.

2 As we have also mentioned in Chapter 7 (p. 145), there is the problem of the tax treatment of the undistributed profits of companies with a large number of independent shareholders. If the incomes of private businessmen are subject to a personal progressive income tax even when they are saved and ploughed back into the private business, then equality of treatment would require that company profits should be correspondingly taxed when they are ploughed back into the business. But if, for one reason or another, it is not feasible to allocate undistributed company profits for personal income tax to the individual shareholders in the manner described in Chapter 7, then some special tax on company profits will be required to approximate to this result as closely as may be feasible.

3 There is the straightforward revenue consideration. A tax levied on company profits at somewhat higher rates than on the corresponding personal incomes may be a convenient way of raising a considerable tax revenue.

4 The corporation tax already exists. It is possible that if one was starting from scratch one would wish to avoid any special tax on corporate enterprise. But in fact corporation tax already exists as an important element in the UK system of direct taxation; and this fact in itself constitutes a valid argument in favour of the continuation of some form of corporation tax. Its elimination would lead to substantial unexpected windfall gains for existing shareholders; and (as discussed in Chapter 2, pp. 13–14) there is an element of truth in the adage that 'an old tax is a good tax', in so far as people have adjusted their affairs in the expectation of the continuation of a tax, the elimination of which would bring unexpected windfall gains to a particular section of the community.

THE STRUCTURAL FORMS OF A CORPORATION TAX

The main structural features of a corporation tax can be considered under two heads: (i) the nature of the tax base, and (ii) the relationship between the

---

[1] The tax applies also to 'unincorporated associations' and to authorised unit trusts which are not incorporated.

corporation tax and the personal direct taxes on income or expenditure. These two features of a corporation tax can be illustrated from the present UK corporation tax. As explained in Chapter 4 (pp. 58–61), (i) the tax base is the profits of the company after the deduction of interest payments on the company's debts, and after the various arrangements for special capital allowances ruling for the income tax;[2] while (ii) the relationship between the corporation tax and the personal income tax is governed by the imputation system described in Chapter 4. There are, however, many other possible forms for the tax base and for the relationship between the corporation tax and the direct taxes on persons.

There is in fact a bewilderingly large number of possible structures. What the economic effects of a corporation tax will be will depend upon combinations of the following characteristics:

1 The nature of the tax base for the corporation tax.
2 The nature of the tax base for personal direct taxation.
3 The nature of the relationship between the two sets of taxes.
4 The relationship between the tax rates in the corporation tax system and in the personal tax system.

A number of the possible structures which could be built out of these elements may for one reason or another be regarded as obvious incongruities.[3] But many of the possible combinations are in no sense absurd, and the choice between them rests upon a consideration of administrative feasibilities and of what it is desired that the tax system should do.

In order to limit the scope of the inquiry we shall proceed as follows. First, we shall discuss three possible alternative bases for the corporation tax, which we shall call the *P* base, the *R* base, and the *S* base. Then we shall describe two possible systems for relating the direct taxation of companies with personal direct taxation, namely the classical system and the imputation system. Thirdly, in the light of these possible tax bases and relations with personal direct taxation, we shall consider in turn the types of corporation tax which in our view would harmonise best with each of the three main regimes for personal taxation discussed in Chapters 7, 9 and 10, namely a comprehensive income tax (CIT), a universal expenditure tax (UET), and a two-tier expenditure tax (TTET).

THE CHOICE OF TAX BASE

POSSIBLE BASES FOR A CORPORATION TAX

There are in fact a large number of possible bases for the taxation of corporations, including such bases as turnover, the value of total assets and so

---

[2] And after the inclusion of a part of a company's capital gains.

[3] We shall later give as an example of an incongruous system a corporation tax on a flow-of-funds base *plus* an expenditure base for personal direct taxation *plus* an imputation system (see pp. 248–249 below).

on. But we shall confine our attention to two types of base: a profits base and a flow-of-funds base. We do so for a number of reasons. Most corporation taxes start from a profits base, as indeed does the UK corporation tax; and in its pure form a profits base for corporation tax corresponds in many respects with an income base for personal taxation. The true profit of a corporation corresponds with the true income of an individual. But in the case of the UK income tax (as shown in Chapter 4) the base of personal tax has been modified in the direction of an expenditure base, e.g. by deducting the amounts saved through pension funds from the tax base and including receipts from the realisation of assets in a pension fund in the tax base. In a similar manner a profits base for corporation tax can be modified, and in the United Kingdom has in large manner been modified, in the direction of a flow-of-funds base, e.g. by deducting from the company's tax base capital expenditures on assets which are eligible for 100 per cent capital allowances and including in the tax base any revenue receipts from the later sale of such capital assets. With a pure flow-of-funds base, liability to corporation tax is based, not on true profit (i.e. on the excess of receipts on current account over costs on current account including true economic depreciation), but on the flow of the total of receipts from the sale of certain goods and services over the total of expenditure on the purchase of such goods and services, whether these transactions be on current or capital account.

A TRUE PROFITS BASE

We shall call a corporation tax based on a true profits base a *P*-based corporation tax. It is unnecessary at this point to describe the base in detail because it involves all the problems that have already been described in detail in connection with a CIT in Chapter 7. The base is the real current profits of the corporation, whether these be distributed or undistributed. It involves the deduction from gross profits of net interest on debt, an allowance for true economic depreciation adjusted for price inflation, a calculation of real accrued capital gains made by the company on its assets, and the adjustment for general price inflation of stock appreciation and of the value of monetary assets and liabilities. As shown in Chapter 7, the effective implementation of such a tax presents many difficulties.

THE PRESENT UK POSITION

The base for the corporation tax in the United Kingdom is clearly already far removed from a true *P* base of the kind described in the preceding paragraph. Its nature has been described in Chapter 4, and we do not repeat the detail here; but its divergences from a true *P*-based tax are of two main kinds. In the first place it has little of the necessary adjustments for inflation, and these, as we have shown, are difficult to implement. In the second place, with the very important range of 100 per cent capital allowances the UK corporation tax is half-way towards a flow-of-funds tax. The UK tax suffers from the disadvantages of being in this half-way house. It is still confronted with basic problems due to the need for capital–income adjustments to inflation, a need which (as we shall show) disappears with a true flow-of-funds base. On the other hand, the fact that some of its transactions are treated on a flow-of-funds basis and some are not creates a number of distortions, which have been discussed and illustrated in Chapter 4.

Finally there remains what may be considered the basic reason for considering a shift from a *P*-based tax to a flow-of-funds-based tax. The latter gives greater opportunity and incentive for capital development and investment. Just as an income tax reduces the rate of return to the saver below the rate of yield on the real investment which the savings finance, so, for the same reason, a corporation tax based on the true profit earned on an investment reduces the post-tax rate of yield to the company below the pre-tax rate of yield on the real investment. As we shall argue later in this chapter, a corporation tax based on a flow of funds does not have this effect but allows the company to retain the whole of the true yield on any new capital development which it undertakes.

A FLOW-OF-FUNDS BASE

We turn then to a more detailed consideration of a true flow-of-funds base for a corporation tax. The relevant flows of funds are shown in Table 12.1. On the flow-of-funds basis no distinction is made between transactions carried out on income account and transactions of a capital nature. But, as is illustrated in the table, a distinction may be drawn between the following:

1 Purchases and sales of real goods and services (the *R* elements in the table).
2 Inflows and outflows of cash on account of financial transactions other than transactions involving corporate shares (the *F* elements in the table).
3 Transactions in corporate shares and in dividend payments (the *S* elements in the table).
4 Payments of tax (the *T* elements in the table).

The two pure flow-of-funds bases which we shall examine in some detail are $(R - \bar{R})$, which we shall call the *R* basis, and $(\bar{S} - S)$, which we shall call the *S* basis.

AN *R* BASE

On the *R* basis, tax would be levied on the total receipts of the company from the sale of all real goods and services (whether these were currently produced items or sales out of capital stocks) less the total purchases of all real goods and services (whether these were for current productive use or for addition to stock or other real capital assets). Two significant changes in the present UK corporation tax would be necessary to convert the present base into a pure *R* base:

1 It would be necessary to extend 100 per cent capital allowances to all real assets (including stocks, land, commercial buildings, etc.) with the corollaries that (i) the whole proceeds of any subsequent sale of any real assets would be liable to corporation tax, and (ii) such arrangements would eliminate the need for any special treatment of a company's capital gains. If this were done all real sales (R) would be taxable and all real purchases ($\overline{R}$) would be deducted from the tax base.

2 It would be necessary to abolish the deductibility of net interest payments from the tax base and to exempt net interest receipts from tax.

Table 12.1 *Corporate flows of funds*

Inflows		*Outflows*	
Real items			
R_1	Sale of produce	$\overline{R}_1$	Purchase of materials
R_2	Sale of services	$\overline{R}_2$	Wages, salaries and purchases of other services
R_3	Sale of fixed assets	$\overline{R}_3$	Purchase of fixed assets
R		$\overline{R}$	
Financial items other than shares of corporate bodies resident in the UK			
F_1	Increase in creditors	$\overline{F}_1$	Decrease in creditors
F_2	Decrease in debtors	$\overline{F}_2$	Increase in debtors
F_3	Increase in overdraft	$\overline{F}_3$	Decrease in overdraft
F_4	Decrease in cash balance	$\overline{F}_4$	Increase in cash balance
F_5	Increase in other borrowing	$\overline{F}_5$	Decrease in other borrowing
F_6	Decrease in other lending	$\overline{F}_6$	Increase in other lending
F_7	Interest received	$\overline{F}_7$	Interest paid
F_8	Decrease in holding of shares in other corporate bodies not resident in the UK	$\overline{F}_8$	Increase in holding of shares in other corporate bodies not resident in the UK
F		$\overline{F}$	
Share items of corporate bodies resident in the UK			
S_1	Increase in own shares issued	$\overline{S}_1$	Reduction in own shares issued
S_2	Decrease in holding of shares in other corporate bodies resident in the UK	$\overline{S}_2$	Increase in holding of shares in other corporate bodies resident in the UK
S_3	Dividends received from other corporate bodies resident in the UK	$\overline{S}_3$	Dividends paid
S		$\overline{S}$	
Tax items			
T	Tax repaid	$\overline{T}$	Tax paid
$R+F+S+T$	Total inflows =	$\overline{R}+\overline{F}+\overline{S}+\overline{T}$	Total outflows

It can readily be appreciated that with a tax base of this kind the corporation tax in itself would not affect yields on new investment in such a way as to introduce any distortion into future financial decisions. The yield on the company's investment in financial assets would be wholly unaffected by the tax, since neither the investment nor the yield on the investment would be affected by the tax.[4] Investment in a real asset (e.g. plant or machinery or stocks) would involve tax computations, but in such a way that the rate of yield on such investment would not be affected. If the rate of corporation tax were 50 per cent (tax-inclusive), then a real capital asset costing £200 would require independent finance of only £100; the other £100 could be covered by the remission of corporation tax on the rest of the company's activities, since its tax base would be reduced by the £200 spent on the purchase of the asset ($\bar{R}$ = £200). If the asset produced a yield of 10 per cent and was then sold with its yield for £200 (R = £220), the company would have to pay corporation tax at 50 per cent on this £220, retaining £110 for its own purposes. On the £100 of independent finance which it had to raise in the first place for the purchase of the asset, the company would receive the full yield of 10 per cent on its investment, and this would be true whether the investment had been financed by the issue of new share capital, the raising of a loan or the ploughing back of undistributed profit.

Nevertheless, in spite of the fact that a corporation tax levied on this base would not in itself distort the rate of yield on any form of saving or investment, it would raise revenue. This it would do for two reasons. In the first place, when the tax base was first applied in this manner there would be many capital assets which had not enjoyed 100 per cent capital allowances when they were acquired in the past, but the sale of the produce of such assets or the sale of the assets themselves would hereafter be subject to the tax. *Existing* shareholders would thus continue to be subject to a tax burden even though no *future* financial decisions were distorted. In the second place, such a tax base would in effect mean that the government would receive a tax revenue from any profits made by companies on their real transactions in excess of the rate of interest on government debt. Suppose that the real capital asset which was assumed in the previous paragraph to cost £200, could be sold with its yield in the next year not for a mere £220 but for £300, even though the rate of interest on government debt was only 10 per cent. The investment would achieve a profit of £80 (i.e. £300−£220) over and above the pure rate of interest. With a rate of corporation tax of 50 per cent the company would have to pay £150 in tax on the sale of assets. The company would receive half the excess profit (i.e. £150−£110), and the government would receive the other half in the sense that, although the rate of interest on government borrowing was only 10 per cent, it received £150 in corporation tax on the sale of the asset while it remitted only £100 of

[4] In so far as the prices of real inputs and outputs are affected by the giving of trade credit, this would not be strictly true. In this case the yield on trade credit given would be taxed, since the giving of trade credit is in F_2 and the return is in R_1. Conversely, trade credit received is in F_1, and the interest cost is in $\bar{R}_1$. Thus there would be a tax advantage in taking as much trade credit as possible.

corporation tax in the previous year when the asset was first purchased.

In essence the government would be acquiring an equity stake in the company, sharing both the cost of investment (through free depreciation) and the resulting profits and losses. On the assumption that the rate of return on company activities was on average higher than the rate at which the government could borrow, the government would make a net revenue gain. The government's share in the transactions would be equal to the rate of tax that could be altered if the government so wished.

AN $(R+F)$ BASE

To base the tax on the excess of the inflows over the outflows of funds in respect of the purchase and sale of 'real' goods and services would involve drawing a distinction between transactions in 'real' goods and services and transactions in 'financial' services. As we have shown, this would imply disallowing the deduction of interest payments from the company's tax base and ceasing to include interest receipts in the tax base. This would cause some transitional problems for highly geared companies that had to make large interest payments which had previously been exempt from tax. But, more importantly, in the long run it would constitute a tax base which was not appropriate for financial institutions which did not sell 'real' goods and services but made their living through 'financial' transactions. The banks, for example, charge for their 'financial' services by charging higher interest rates on their loans to their customers than the interest which they pay on sums deposited with them. If the excess of interest receipts over interest payments were not taxable, the banks would be exempt from all corporation tax.

This result would be avoided if the tax base were not the excess of inflows over outflows of funds in respect only of 'real' transactions, but were the excess of inflows over outflows of funds in respect of both 'real' and 'financial' transactions, whether these transactions were on current or capital account. To reach this new base for corporation tax the base of the present corporation tax would have to be adjusted in two ways: (i) the flow-of-funds base for the 'real' sector would, as before, have to be completed by the extension of 100 per cent capital allowances to cover the purchase of all 'real' inputs; but (ii) the flow-of-funds tax for the 'financial' sector would have to continue to tax the excess of inflows over outflows of interest on debt but would have to be completed by adding the excess of inflows over outflows of debt finance on capital account as well. In terms of Table 12.1 the base would become $[(R+F)-(\bar{R}+\bar{F})]$.

AN S BASE

But for a company as a whole the total inflow of funds must be equal to the total outflow of funds; and from Table 12.1 it can be seen that

$$(R+F)-(\bar{R}+\bar{F}) = (\bar{S}-S)+(\bar{T}-T)$$

In other words, any net receipt of funds from 'real' and 'financial' transactions must go to the advantage of shareholders $(\overline{S}-S)$ or of the taxgatherer $(\overline{T}-T)$. Suppose, for example, that $[(R+F)-(\overline{R}+\overline{F})]$ were £10 million, that $(\overline{S}-S)$ were £5 million and that $(\overline{T}-T)$ were £5 million. Then it could be said either that the corporation was being taxed at a tax-inclusive rate of 50 per cent on the base $[(R+F)-(\overline{R}+\overline{F})]$ or that it was being taxed at a tax-exclusive rate of 100 per cent on the base $(\overline{S}-S)$. These are two ways of saying what is in effect the same thing. It makes no real difference whether tax is levied on a given excess of inflows over outflows of R and F funds or on the resulting necessarily equal excess of outflows over inflows of the balancing items S and T. An $(R+F)$ base can in many ways be more simply treated as an S base, the rate of corporation tax in this case being more suitably expressed on a tax-exclusive rate.

In this case the tax base is $(\overline{S}-S)$. This S basis levies tax on the net amount of cash flowing out of the corporate sector of the economy on account of share capital, i.e. the total of dividends paid to outside shareholders less the amount of new share capital raised from them. In other words, the tax is based on the net amount of cash which the shareholders take out of the corporate business.

The tax base $(\overline{S}-S)$ for any one corporation is not simply a tax on its own dividend payments less its own issue of new shares, i.e. the net amount of money which it pays out to its own shareholders. The tax base is the net amount of money which it pays out to its own shareholders plus any additional amount of money which it pays out to other UK corporate bodies on account of share capital (e.g. by purchasing the shares of another UK corporation). The addition of this term is simply a means of avoiding double taxation or double tax relief. In its absence there would exist obvious avoidance devices of the following kind. At the close of each tax year corporation A issues shares to corporation B, which issues shares to corporation A on a scale which would be sufficient to wipe out their tax liabilities if each corporation received a tax remission on its own newly issued shares without incurring a tax liability on its new holding of the shares of the other corporation. Thus properly applied an S-based tax makes a levy on the net amount of money which the corporate sector as a whole pays out to shareholders in the unincorporated sector of the economy.

The S base, like the R base, means that the rate of yield on any future forms of investment is unaffected by the tax. Any investment financed by debt is unaffected, since the interest payment on the debt is not taxed and the raising of loan finance attracts no remission of tax. As far as yield is concerned, the S base makes no distinction between finance raised from shareholders through the issue of new shares and finance raised from shareholders through the retention of profits which might have been distributed in dividends. With a corporation tax of 50 per cent on a tax-inclusive basis, the issue of £100 in new shares together with the tax relief which it would attract would serve to finance an investment of £200. If the investment were instead financed out of £200 of undistributed profits, this also would cost the shareholder only £100, since the £200 of profit, if distributed, would serve after tax to finance only £100 of dividends. In both cases the shareholder would give up £100 to finance the £200 of investment. But with a rate of yield on the investment of 10 per cent the shareholders would in both cases receive a 10 per cent return. The £200 investment with its yield of 10 per cent would be worth £220; but if this sum were in one form or another paid out to the shareholders, it would be subject to corporation tax and the shareholders would receive £110, giving a 10 per cent rate of yield on their original £100 contribution.

The *S* base would thus, like the *R* base, mean that the corporation tax did not cause any distortions of the rates of yield on different forms of future saving and investment. Nevertheless, like the *R* base it would raise revenue for two reasons:

1 On its introduction, existing shareholders who had received no tax remission when they subscribed to their shares before the introduction of the tax would nevertheless be subject to the taxation of their dividends after the introduction of the *S* base.
2 The tax would levy revenue on any additional profits made. In terms of the example used in the previous paragraph, suppose that an investment of £200 yielded £100 instead of a normal 10 per cent rate of return of £20. If the additional yield of £80 were distributed to shareholders, there would be a corporation tax liability of £40. The shareholders would receive one-half of the extra profit and the government would receive the other half.

It is to be noted that, whereas the *R* base would yield a tax revenue to the government only on the additional profits made on real capital assets ($\overline{R}$ items), the *S* base would yield a revenue on additional profits made on all forms of company investment, whether these investments were in real assets ($\overline{R}$ items) or in financial assets ($\overline{F}$ items). As with the *R* basis, the *S* basis means that the government shares the equity returns on corporate investment; and, on the assumption that the rate of return of profits in business will on the average be greater than the pure rate of interest on government debt, the government receives a net revenue on new investment by corporations.

DIFFERENCES BETWEEN AN *R* BASE AND AN *S* BASE

From Table 12.1 it can be seen that

$$R - \overline{R} = (\overline{S} - S) + (\overline{F} - F) + (\overline{T} - T)$$

In other words, the *R* base exceeds the *S* base by two elements: by the excess of financial payments over financial receipts ($\overline{F} - F$), and by the net amount of tax payments ($\overline{T} - T$).

The second of these elements – the tax liability – is due simply to the fact that the *R* basis is a tax-inclusive basis and the *S* basis is a tax-exclusive basis. In the first case the tax is being reckoned on something (the excess of real receipts over real payments) from which the tax must be deducted; in the second case the tax is being reckoned on something (the excess of payments to shareholders over receipts from shareholders) to which the tax must be added. There is in fact no effective difference involved. A tax of 50 per cent on the tax-inclusive basis corresponds to a tax of 100 per cent on the tax-exclusive basis.

The balance of financial flows $(\overline{F}-F)$ does, however, introduce an effective difference. It means that the R base will exceed the S base if there is an excess of financial flows out of the company, and that the S base will exceed the R base if there is an excess of financial flows into the company. The distinction may be illustrated by considering cases in which there are no financial transactions on capital account (i.e. no change in the net amount of debt or in the net amount of financial assets held by the company), but in which there are interest receipts and payments on old financial debts or assets. If there are net payments of interest by the company on existing debt, the R base will exceed the S base. With the R base, as we have shown, the deductibility of interest payments against profit for the assessment of liability to corporation tax is disallowed; but, by implication, with the S base such deductibility is still allowed. On the other hand, consider a financial institution (such as a bank) whose whole profit is made by providing financial services which it finances by borrowing at low interest rates and lending at higher interest rates. It may have no sales of real goods and services ($R = 0$), although it has some purchases of such real items (wages, purchase of stationery, etc.). With an unmodified R basis its tax base would be negative ($-\overline{R}$). With an S basis its tax basis would be positive ($F-\overline{F}-\overline{R}$); it would be taxed on the 'profit' which it makes by receiving high interest (F) after deduction of the low interest that it pays out ($\overline{F}$) and of the real items which it purchases ($\overline{R}$).

VALUATION OF ASSETS UNDER R AND S BASES

There is a corresponding important difference between the balance sheet positions of companies under an R-based and under an S-based corporation tax and, as a consequence, between the appropriate market valuations of their shares. Under an R base with a corporation tax of 50 per cent (tax-inclusive), any real asset which will sell in the market for £200 will have a value to shareholders of only £100, since its sale would lead to a tax liability of £100. The market valuation of the shares should thus be related to the market value of the company's assets less its potential liability to corporation tax on its real assets. With an S base, tax would be payable on distributions out of the realisation both of any real assets and also of any net excess of the market value of financial assets over that of financial liabilities. The appropriate market value of the shares would be affected by this potential tax liability.

The easiest way to see these relationships is to consider what would happen if the company were liquidated and the shareholders received the market value of the assets after the payment of any tax liability. But the effect of the relationship would not depend simply upon the anticipated possibility of liquidation. The normal operation of market forces on the stock exchange should cause share prices to take into account the potential tax liability on the company's underlying assets. Thus consider a company, under an *S*-based tax regime, which owned real physical assets worth £1 million before deduction of any tax liability. If the market valued the company's shares at the full £1 million, there would be great advantage in selling these existing shares for £1 million in order to invest them in £1 million worth of newly issued shares for the purchase of a similar set of real assets costing £1 million, since in addition to this set of real assets the newly issued shares would, at a 100 per cent (tax-exclusive) rate, enable dividends or other $\bar{S}$ items amounting to £1 million to be paid free of corporation tax. Thus in such a situation there would be a strong tax incentive to sell existing shares in order to purchase newly issued shares. But the general attempt to sell existing shares would in fact keep their price down to a value which was related to that of the underlying assets after, rather than before, deduction of potential tax liability, at which point this absurd tax incentive would disappear.[5]

There is another way of putting this point. As we have already explained, with an *R*-based tax the government is in effect taking an equity interest in all real investment by the company, and with an *S*-based tax an equity interest in all investment by the company, whether in real or financial assets. The gap between asset value and stock market value of the equity will represent the government's equity share, which takes the form of a contingent tax claim.

The importance of this share valuation effect can be illustrated by the following example. If share values reflected the market value of assets without regard to potential tax liabilities, then with an *S*-based corporation tax dividend distributions would be greatly discouraged and shareholders would rely on capital gains due to ploughed-back profits. Thus suppose a company had £100 of cash. If it distributed this cash in dividends, the shareholders would receive only £50 after payment of corporation tax at 100 per cent (tax-exclusive). If the company retained the cash and invested it in some form of assets and if the value of shares were increased by the full £100 increase in the market value of the company's assets, the shareholders would enjoy a capital gain of £100, which they could realise by sale on the stock exchange without any payment of corporation tax. In fact, however, as just shown, share values would not rise by the whole of the pre-tax value of the additional assets; and in so far as they reflected asset values after deduction of potential tax liabilities there would be no distortion in favour of retained profits.

Some further examples of the importance for company accounts of

---

[5] Share prices, which can be very volatile as a result of changes in confidence, expectations of profit and similar factors, are not, of course, precisely tied to the value of the company's underlying assets. All that is maintained in these paragraphs is that, in so far as an increase in a company's assets does affect the company's net worth and so the value of its share capital, the relevant factor will be the value of the assets after the deduction of any potential tax liability attached to them.

distinguishing between the pre-tax value and post-tax value of assets may be helpful.

In the case of an R-based corporation tax a reduction of financial assets and an increase in real assets (e.g. the investment of a bank balance in stocks of commodities) would bring an immediate reduction of tax. But the holding of the additional stock would carry with it a future tax liability (a liability which would itself rise at the same rate as the prospective yield on the stocks of commodities), whereas the holding of the bank balance would involve no future tax liability.

In the case of an S-based corporation tax an increase in equity finance (by the issue of new shares or the restriction of dividend payments) and the investment of the funds in real or financial assets would likewise bring an immediate reduction of tax. But the holding of the additional real or financial assets would carry with it a future tax liability, which (in the absence of increased dividend distribution and so of actual tax payments) would grow at the same rate as the prospective yield on these assets.

Or consider the issue of convertible stock with an S-based tax. So long as the stock retained the form of debt finance there would be no tax involved. However, when it was converted into an equity form there would be an immediate tax remission on the implied new share issue; but against this there would be a future tax liability on the future dividend payments.

A financial institution which invested its funds in shares would, under an S-based tax, incur a tax liability when it bought the shares; but against this it would enjoy a future tax credit when it sold the shares or when it received dividends on the shares. If it financed its investment in shares by the issue of its own shares, its tax liabilities and credits would cancel out; but if it financed its investment in shares by the issue of debt, its immediate tax liability would be offset by a future tax credit which would grow at the same rate as the yield on the shares which it had purchased. It is perhaps worth noting that, whereas a financial institution would incur an immediate tax liability if it raised loan capital in order to invest in ordinary shares, it would not do so if it financed its purchase of ordinary shares by the issue of its own preference shares, which, if so desired, could be redeemable.

UNUTILISED TAX LOSSES

With a flow-of-funds base for corporation tax, whether of the R type, the $(R+F)$ type or the S type, cases may arise in which the tax base is a negative figure. This is particularly likely to happen in the case of the setting up of new companies when (on the R base) heavy expenditure on the purchase of plant and machinery precedes the sale of any taxable product, or (on an S base) the issue of new shares precedes any profit available to be distributed in dividends. But the flow-of-funds corporation tax will preserve its distinguishing feature of not driving any tax wedge between the yield on new investment and the return on the underlying savings only if the remission of tax on real purchases (on the R base) or on share issues (on the S base) can be made effective. This requires that where the tax base is a negative figure the balance of tax remission due to the company should be either (i) paid by the Revenue to the company, or (ii) carried forward at an appropriate interest rate to be set against the company's future liability to corporation tax. This requirement is analogous to that discussed in connection with the operation of an income tax with 100 per cent capital allowances as an effective way of operating a proportionate expenditure tax for the lower tier of a TTET (see Chapter 10, p. 212).

THE RELATIVE MERITS OF AN *R* AND AN *S* BASE

We are now in a position to consider the relative merits and demerits of the adoption of an *R* base or an *S* base for a flow-of-funds type of corporation tax. This can be done under the four headings, as follows.

1 *Simplicity, familiarity and flexibility*
Ignoring for the moment the questions of the transition and of foreign investment, the *S*-based tax would be a simpler tax to administer. It would involve only the assessment of actual cash payments and receipts for transactions in shares and dividends over a given period. The *R*-based tax would involve a more detailed account of all particular transactions in real goods and services. One particular advantage of this greater simplicity would be that an *S*-based tax could be administered on a uniform fiscal-year basis; whereas this would present real difficulty in the case of an *R*-based tax, which would almost certainly have to be operated, as in the case of the existing UK corporation tax, on the basis of each company's normal accounting year. As we explain below, there are certain avoidance possibilities which are possible only if different companies have different tax years. These possibilities could be readily removed by the adoption of a uniform fiscal year for all companies in the case of an *S*-based tax.

On the other hand, an *R*-based tax would be a more familiar type of tax in that it could be perceived as a straightforward modification of the existing system achieved by extending 100 per cent capital allowances to a wider range of assets and by disallowing deductibility of interest payments against profits for the assessment of liability to the tax. The *S* base would appear to involve a much more radical, root-and-branch change of system. Moreover, in certain respects the *R*-based tax would be a more flexible tax, since the 100 per cent capital allowances would not need to be extended to all forms of real capital investment. Thus if it were desired to encourage investment in manufacturing plant and machinery rather than in land and commercial buildings, the full capital allowances could be denied to the latter; at present land and commercial buildings attract no depreciation allowances at all. Such discrimination against certain kinds of investment could be achieved under an *S*-based tax by treating the disallowed items as if they were $\bar{S}$ outgoings; but this would be a much less natural arrangement.

2 *Foreign investment*
In Chapter 21 (pp. 446–447) we shall discuss overseas aspects of corporation

tax, and there it is pointed out that the question of double taxation relief is of great significance both quantitatively and in terms of its influence on the extent and location of overseas investment. We shall argue that under the *R* or *S* base it would be inappropriate to give tax relief on overseas investment and in addition to give double taxation relief on the yield from that investment; one relief or the other should be disallowed. Past investment has been incurred in the expectation that the yield will attract double taxation relief, so that there would be a transitional problem if all double taxation relief ceased on the appointed day. On the other hand, to disallow relief on future overseas investment would raise other difficulties. Although (as made clear in Chapter 21) the *R* and *S* bases would raise rather different issues in respect to these problems of double taxation relief, there does not seem to be a strong balance in favour of the one basis rather than the other.

3   *Financial institutions*

One clear advantage of an *S*-based tax over an *R*-based tax is that the former could be applied to financial as well as to manufacturing and trading institutions, whereas the latter is not suitable for financial institutions. We have already pointed out the reason for this. Many financial institutions in fact receive payment for the services which they render by charging a higher rate of interest on the funds which they lend and paying a lower rate of interest on the funds which they borrow. Accordingly there is in their accounts no direct assessment of the value of the real services which they 'sell' to the public – i.e. no *R* on which to base a tax. If an *R* base were adopted for corporation tax, then either the accounts of financial institutions would have to be radically recast in order to disclose the value of the real services which they provide to the public,[6] or else some quite different base would have to be found for their tax treatment – a solution which would clearly present problems for borderline cases where financial, trading and manufacturing transactions were combined. In fact there are many cases where sale prices include an interest element (e.g. long term contracts and hire purchase sales, as well as the case of trade credit noted in the footnote on p. 232), so that this problem is a far-reaching one.

On the other hand, an *S*-based tax could be applied without modification to financial institutions, since the way in which the accounts of financial transactions were kept would not affect the questions of fact whether dividends on existing shares had been paid or whether new shares had been issued.

4   *Problems of avoidance and transition*

With an *R*-based tax there could be some possibility for a company to avoid tax by a temporary investment in stocks of otherwise unwanted materials or in other forms of real asset towards the end of its accounting year. If com-

---

[6] See Appendix 12.1 for a discussion of what this recasting would involve. The appendix makes it clear that the problem of the proper taxation of financial institutions arises in the case of income tax, expenditure tax and VAT, as well as corporation tax.

pany A's and company B's accounting years did not coincide, A could purchase stocks from B at the end of A's accounting year and resell them to B at the end of B's accounting year. In so far as this would involve a change only of ownership and not of the physical location of the stocks, the operation could be easily conducted between companies which had confidence in each other. But the device would be subject ultimately to a strict limitation, since to avoid tax year after year by this means would involve a company in *increasing* the scale of such avoidance adjustment at the end of any one year over the amount of such avoidance undertaken at the end of the previous year by the full amount of the taxable profit which was to be offset for the year in question. Ultimately the amount of *unwanted* real assets, the ownership of which would have to be accumulated in order to be shuffled around from company to company in this manner, would have to grow without limit if anything more than a once-for-all avoidance of tax were contemplated; and anti-avoidance legislation could deal with the problem if it became serious.

There would be a corresponding tax avoidance possibility for companies under an *S*-based tax. At the end of its accounting period company A could issue shares on a scale sufficient to offset A's taxable payments of dividends, these shares being purchased by company B. In return, company A could purchase shares issued by company B at the end of B's accounting year, this issue being on a scale sufficient to offset both B's previous purchase of A's shares and B's taxable payment of dividends to its shareholders. Year by year this artificial duplication of shares would have to mount up. The trick would, however, be impossible if A's and B's accounting periods coincided. In the case of an *S*-based tax the operation of the tax on the same fiscal year base for all companies should be possible, so that the *S*-based tax would be less open to this type of avoidance than the *R*-based tax.

With an *S*-based tax it would be necessary to prevent companies from issuing debt to their shareholders at abnormally high interest rates, so that the return on capital which had in fact been financed by share issues (on which remission of tax had been claimed) would be paid out as interest on debt (on which no tax was liable). A similar problem arises under the present United Kingdom corporation tax, since interest on debt can be deducted from profit for the assessment of the tax base. The present requirement that interest in excess of a commercial rate should be treated as a dividend distribution would have to be continued.

A change from the present corporation tax to an *R* base or an *S* base would raise some serious transitional problems, although it is questionable whether the changes would be more abrupt than those faced on the occasion of past restructurings of the tax. In what follows we describe the types of transitional effects which might occur, but we have not tried to assess the extent to which, or the form in which, special measures would be needed to offset any of these effects.

The main transitional problems on the introduction of an *R*-based tax would be due to the change in the treatment of interest receipts and payments. Net receipts of interest by a company would no longer be taxable;

and, as we have already said, this would cause banks and similar financial institutions to be exempt from tax unless they were required to cast their accounts in an appropriate new fashion or were taxed under some different system independent of the *R* base. In the case of highly geared manufacturing or trading concerns with a heavy excess of interest payments over interest receipts, the shift to an *R* base would increase the tax base by the amount of net interest payments. The scale of the effect must not be exaggerated, however, since (as shown in Chapter 4, p. 59) with the present imputation system the underlying corporation tax on dividend distributions is 28·4 per cent and not the full corporation tax rate of 52 per cent. If interest payments were treated in the same way as dividend distributions after the change to an *R* base, this 28·4 per cent and not the full 52 per cent would measure the extent to which the change would impose a tax burden on interest payments *relatively* to that on dividend payments. The *absolute* tax burdens both on dividend payments and on interest payments would depend upon what happened both to the rate of corporation tax and to the imputation system. Thus *either* if the rate of corporation tax remained at 52 per cent and imputation continued at 33 per cent *or else* if the rate of corporation tax were reduced to 28·4 per cent and imputation were abolished, there would be no absolute change for dividends but a 28·4 per cent additional tax in respect of interest payments. If, on the other hand, the rate of corporation tax remained at 52 per cent and imputation were abolished, the tax in respect of dividends would rise from 28·4 to 52 per cent and in respect of interest payments from 0 to 52 per cent.[7] Many intermediate solutions are obviously possible. Whatever solution was adopted, the change could impose a serious transitional burden on some highly geared companies, e.g. some property companies.

With the introduction of an *S*-based tax the boot would be on the other foot. Consider two companies A and B, otherwise similar except that A is highly geared having in the past financed a large part of its investments through the issue of debt, while B has done so through the issue of ordinary shares. Company B will have received no tax remission in the past on its share issues. After the introduction of an *S*-based tax company A could issue new shares and pay off its debts, thus restructuring its finances on the same lines as B; but if it did so it would, unlike B, receive a tax credit on its share issues.

A similar difference would arise between two financial institutions with portfolio investments which, according to their anticipations of stock exchange prospects, they were in the habit of shifting between shares and liquid financial assets. If, on the introduction of the *S*-based tax, financial institution A happened at that date to be liquid in financial assets while institution B was fully invested in shares, then A would bear the full rate of *S*-based tax

[7] We shall give reasons later (pp. 248–249) for the view that the imputation system is basically inconsistent with a flow-of-funds base for corporation tax combined with an expenditure base for personal tax, although we then go on to discuss arrangements which would allow a formal system of imputation to be continued if this were necessary for EEC harmonisation purposes.

when it reinvested its liquid fund in shares, whereas B would have no such tax to pay.

These divergences of fortune on the introduction of an S-based tax could lead to further serious transitional problems if the introduction of the S-based tax was widely anticipated in advance. Companies of every kind would have an incentive to issue debt or to run down their financial assets and to use the proceeds for heavy investment in existing shares, so that on the introduction of the tax they could enjoy the tax credit which would arise from the sale of the shares. Not only would widespread action of this kind greatly disturb stock exchange valuations; it could also lead to a large loss of revenue in so far as companies temporarily exchanged debt for shares with the unincorporated sector of the economy, selling the shares back to the unincorporated sector and redeeming the loans raised in that sector immediately after the introduction of the tax.

Under existing tax law, payments made to shareholders on the liquidation of a company are not treated as taxable distributions. With an S-based tax they would need to be so treated in order to prevent avoidance through the simple device of liquidation (which carries no tax liability) followed by re-incorporation through the issue of new shares (on which a tax credit would be obtained). But the question arises whether it would be fair so to treat liquidations occurring immediately after the introduction of the new tax, since the sums involved would be arising either from share issues on which no tax remission had been enjoyed or from undistributed profits which had been fully taxed under the previous regime. One possible form of transitional relief would be to give companies which liquidated within, say, five years of the introduction of the new tax base the option of paying tax in the period up to liquidation on the previous tax basis. On the other hand, an anti-avoidance provision would be required in order to deal with liquidations carried out in anticipation of the introduction of the S-based tax followed immediately after the introduction of the new tax base by incorporation. Such a provision might take the form of disallowing for S-based corporation tax the deduction of new issues made to acquire a business which had been a going concern before the introduction of the new tax base.

THE $(R+F)$ BASE AS AN ALTERNATIVE SOLUTION

From Table 12.1 it can be seen that

$$(\bar{S}-S) = (R-\bar{R})+(F-\bar{F})+(T-\bar{T})$$

Or in other words (as explained on pp. 235–236) the S base can be the subject of tax *either* by imposing a tax (at tax-exclusive rate) on $(\bar{S}-S)$ or by imposing a tax (at tax-inclusive rate) on $[(R-\bar{R})+(F-\bar{F})]$. Suppose that an S-based tax were administered indirectly by the latter of these two means. What would it imply?

In the first place, it would mean the extension of 100 per cent capital allowances on all investments in real assets. This part of the change would be exactly the same as would be necessary to achieve an R-based tax.

In the second place – and this is what distinguishes the S base from the R base – it would involve taxing all financial inflows (the F items) and remitting from tax all financial inflows (the $\bar{F}$ items), whether these inflows or outflows were on capital account or current account. In other words, interest payments would still be deductible and interest receipts taxable; but in addition all repayments by the company of any outstanding debts which it owed or the extension of new loans by the company to new debtors would be deductible for tax purposes, whereas all new borrowings by the company or repayments to the company of outstanding debts which were owed to it would be taxable. This approach to what would in effect be an S base would have a number of advantages:

1   It could be achieved gradually in a piecemeal fashion in a step-by-step process from the present position and would appear largely as a development of the present system rather than as a radical unfamiliar revolution. The system of 100 per cent capital allowances could be gradually extended, and the tax on the net excess of inflows over outflows of financial items on capital account might perhaps be phased in. This could help to relieve the transitional problems.
2   It would cover the taxation of financial institutions as well as of other types of company and would not impose a sudden extra burden on highly geared companies.
3   It would be possible to deny 100 per cent capital allowances on future overseas investment together with the continuation of double taxation relief on the yield on overseas investments, if this were the preferred method of dealing with the problems of double taxation relief (see Appendix 21.2, pp. 457–459).

It would, however, suffer from one major disadvantage in comparison with a direct tax on $(\bar{S}-S)$, namely the loss of administrative simplicity. As we have argued, the direct $(\bar{S}-S)$ base would involve the taxation only of net outpayments on account of share capital. This would be a relatively simple base to assess and could be operated on a fiscal year basis for all companies, thus eliminating many tax avoidance possibilities.

Perhaps the best policy would be to approach the S base gradually by the indirect way of a tax-inclusive rate on $[(R-\bar{R})+(F-\bar{F})]$. On completion of that indirect route, the system might thereafter for administrative simplicity be operated without any upheaval as a tax-exclusive rate on $(\bar{S}-S)$, provided that some means could then be found for continuing the solution of the problem of double taxation relief.[8]

---

[8] The ideal solution would be to persuade the rest of the free enterprise world to harmonise on an S-based tax without imputation or double tax relief. But the United Kingdom has a long way to go in putting its own house in order before it can hope to exert the necessary influence over the choice of international harmonisation policies.

THE EFFECT ON THE YIELD OF CORPORATION TAX

The revenue implications of a move to either the R or the S base (or to the $(R+F)$ base) will, of course, depend on how companies react to the new system. Nevertheless, it is possible to estimate the order of magnitude of the effect by calculating what the revenue would have been in the past under the proposed systems on the assumption that the real behaviour of companies would have remained unchanged. In fact the principal difficulty to be faced in comparing this potential revenue with the revenue actually raised in the past is that we have little information on the size of the tax benefit which companies have received in the form of double taxation relief. As we show in Appendix 12.2, the sums of money involved in double taxation relief are very large.

From what information we do have, however, it seems likely that both the R and the S bases would raise no less and perhaps more revenue than the corporate tax systems which we have had in the past, and considerably more than the current system raises when account is taken of stock relief. It is striking that tax revenues from the corporate sector have remained almost constant in money terms, at about £1,000 million, despite a continually rising price level, and that in recent years stock relief has virtually wiped out tax liability for many companies. It is not difficult to imagine that a reformed system would help to increase revenue from the corporate sector. We must also stress the importance in quantitative terms of the size of income from abroad, and hence the significance of double taxation relief. Hence the revenue implications of a change in the system are sensitive to any transitional or longer run change in the treatment of double taxation relief.

THE RELATION BETWEEN CORPORATION TAXES AND PERSONAL TAXES

We turn now to the second major feature of a corporation tax, namely its relationship with the system of direct taxes on individuals outside the corporate sector. There is a basic choice between two possible types of relationship, which we shall illustrate in terms of a tax structure in which corporation tax is levied on a company's profits (the P base) and in which personal taxation has been based upon the individual's income.

In the first place, the whole of the company's profits may be subject to corporation tax, whether those profits are undistributed or distributed in dividends, and the dividends may then in addition be subject to personal income tax in the hands of the individual shareholders. This system is often known as the *classical system*. Such a system subjects undistributed profits to corporation tax and distributed profits both to corporation tax and to personal income tax. This leads to a tax differentiation against the distribution of profits, except in so far as there is a fully effective capital gains tax (CGT) which is levied on the increased value of the company's shares due to the increase in its undistributed profits and so in its underlying assets.

In order to remove or partially to mitigate this possible tax differential against the distribution of profits, a second type of relationship is necessary. This may take any one of three possible forms:

1   A *two-rate system*, under which there is one rate of corporation tax on undistributed profits and another and lower rate on distributed profits.
2   An *imputation system* (such as the current UK system described in Chapter 4), under which all profits are in the first place taxed at a single rate of corporation tax but in which dividends are subsequently endowed with an imputed tax credit which can be set against the liability to direct personal tax.[9]
3   An *avoir fiscal system* (as in France), under which the recipient of cash dividends is once again endowed with an imputed tax credit (the avoir fiscal) but in which this tax credit is reckoned as a certain fraction of the corporation tax which has been levied on the profits used to pay the cash dividend, instead of being reckoned, as in the imputation system, simply as a given imputed rate of tax on the dividends.

All these three systems result in effect in a lower underlying rate of corporation tax on distributed than on undistributed profits. If the rates of tax under the three systems are suitably chosen, they can all three result in the same effective degree of tax differentiation in favour of distributed profits. In the rest of this chapter we shall restrict our discussion to a comparison between the classical system and the imputation system, treating the latter as a typical example of the group of systems which can be used to reduce the effective rate of corporation tax on distributed profits.[10]

We have now discussed three possible bases for a corporation tax (the P base, the R base and the S base) and two possible systems of relationship between the corporation tax and personal direct taxes (namely, the classical system and the imputation system). We are now in a position to consider what type of corporation tax structure would be most suitable for each of three possible bases for personal direct taxation, namely CIT, UET and TTET.

CORPORATION TAX AND CIT

In the case of a CIT for personal taxation, if there were no desire to impose any special extra tax on corporate as contrasted with unincorporated concerns, then the appropriate structure would be the full integration of the corporation tax with the personal income tax on the lines discussed in Chapter 7.

---

[9] As we have seen on p. 59 above, in the United Kingdom at present the result is that dividend payments are in effect subject to an underlying rate of corporation tax of 28·4 per cent and not of the full 52 per cent.
[10] In Appendix 12.3 we give a more precise account of the relationships between a two-rate system, an imputation system and an avoir fiscal system.

If, however, it were desired in addition to impose some extra tax on corporate activity as such, then some additional independent corporation tax would be appropriate. The easiest way to achieve this end would be to impose a corporate tax on profits in the way suggested in Chapter 7 (pp. 143–145). but to impute tax credits to shareholders on their entitlements to dividends and undistributed profits at a rate lower than the rate of tax on corporate profits. This is to levy the extra tax on corporate profits on a P base which corresponds exactly to the CIT base for individual taxpayers. But there would be no necessity to choose a P base for the additional tax on companies. An S base or an R base would be appropriate if it were desired to avoid any further divergence between returns to savers and yields on investment than was caused by the rates of personal tax. But whatever base was chosen for the additional corporation tax, there would be no case for any imputation system covering that additional tax; the additional charge on corporations should remain as such, and this implies a classical system of relationship between any additional corporation tax and personal tax.

Suppose, however, that full integration of corporation tax with personal income tax on the lines discussed in Chapter 7 was not feasible, but that nevertheless it was desired to approximate the total tax structure as nearly as possible to that of a CIT. If there were a fully effective CGT (which in principle would involve the taxation of capital gains as they accrued at the individual taxpayer's marginal rate of personal income tax), and if there were no desire to impose any special tax on corporations as such, then no corporation tax would be needed. Shareholders gain from undistributed profits only in so far as these lead to an increased value of their shares, and with a fully effective CGT this gain would be taxed as if it were part of their income. If it were desired to impose some special tax on corporate businesses as such, then some additional corporation tax would be appropriate. An imputation system would, however, be inappropriate, unless by a combination of full CGT on undistributed profits and imputation relief on distributed profits it were desired positively to give a tax advantage to the distribution of dividends.

Suppose, however, that there were no fully effective CGT. It would then be suitable to have a special corporation tax which would levy a charge on undistributed profits at a rate which would as nearly as possible make up for the deficiency of a CGT in representing the marginal rate of personal income tax of the typical shareholder. Such a tax could be levied either by a *two-rate corporation tax* which levied tax at this rate on undistributed profits and at a zero rate on distributed profits, or else by a system which levied tax at this rate on all profits and then imputed a tax credit at this rate on all dividend payments. Thus a corporation tax on a P basis with a 100 per cent imputation system would be appropriate.

The arrangement just described would be appropriate if the objective were to approximate as closely as possible to a CIT, if there were no fully effective CGT and if there were no desire to impose any special levy on corporate business as such. If it were desired in these conditions to impose some additional tax on corporate business as such, then the suitable modification of the above arrangement would be to continue to levy corporation tax on a P basis on all company profits, but at a higher rate than the rate which would otherwise be appropriate, and at the same time to continue to impute the tax credit to shareholders only at the restricted rate described in the previous paragraph.

CORPORATION TAX AND UET

We turn next to the case in which personal direct taxation takes the form of a UET of the kind described in Chapter 9. In this case, if it were not desired to impose any special tax on corporate business as such, there would be no case for any corporation tax. Persons would be taxed on what they took out of businesses to spend on consumption or on unregistered assets; there would be no case for taxing any company transactions except for the possibility of a straightforward withholding tax on payments by companies to individuals to be credited to the individuals concerned against their ultimate liability to expenditure tax.

If, however, for the reasons discussed above, it were desired to levy some charge on corporate activity as such, then a corporation tax on an R basis or an S basis would seem to be the most appropriate form to combine with personal taxation on an expenditure basis. The distinguishing feature of an expenditure tax is that the taxpayer receives a rate of return on his savings which is equal to the rate of yield on the investment which his savings serve to finance. The introduction of a P-based corporation tax into a personal expenditure tax system would, however, disturb this relationship in so far as savings and investment took place through a corporate business, whereas, as we have shown, a corporation tax on an R basis or an S basis would preserve this equality between rate of return on savings and rate of yield on investment.

THE INAPPROPRIATENESS OF IMPUTATION

But if a corporation tax on an R basis or an S basis is combined with personal taxation on a UET basis, then an imputation system is totally out of place. This can be shown by the simple example given in Table 12.2. We assume a rate of corporation tax of 100 per cent (tax-exclusive), on an S basis in the first column and on an R basis in the second column, combined with an imputation system which imputes a tax credit to dividends at a rate of $33\frac{1}{3}$ per cent (tax-inclusive). In both cases the company starts (at line 1) with £100 cash, uses this to distribute in dividends and simultaneously issues shares to take back what it has distributed.

In the case of the S-based tax the company pays £50 in corporation tax on the distribution (line 2). The shareholder receives a cash dividend of £50 (line 3), but on this he obtains a tax credit of £25 (line 4), giving a total of £75 (line 5). If company shares are registered assets, the shareholder will be exempt from tax on his purchase of new shares, so that (line 6) he can purchase £75 worth of shares. The company obtains relief from corporation tax from its new share issue (line 7), thus ending up with cash of £150 (line 8).

The case of an *R*-based tax is even more straightforward. The company uses its £100 cash (line 1) to distribute in a dividend (line 3) on which there is a tax credit of £50 (line 4). The shareholder purchases new shares worth £150 (line 6), financing this from his dividend plus tax credit (line 5), since he will be exempt from tax on the purchase of the new shares. The company has turned £100 cash into £150 cash simply by distributing the cash and then issuing new shares to take up the original distribution plus the tax credit.

Table 12.2   *Imputation and expenditure tax (in £s)*

		S *basis*	R *basis*
1	Cash in bank	100	100
2	*Less* Payment of CT	(50)	nil
3	Net dividends	50	100
4	Imputed tax credit	25	50
5	Dividend *plus* Tax credit	75	150
6	Purchase of new shares	75	150
7	Relief from CT	75	nil
8	Cash in bank	150	150

In these circumstances an imputation system would not merely mean that there was a tax advantage in distributing profits and raising funds by the issue of new shares rather than by the retention of undistributed profits. There would in fact be a definite tax subsidy on all investment financed by the issue of new shares; personal income used to purchase new shares would under an expenditure tax be exempt from tax, but the dividends issued on the new shares would receive a subsidy in the form of the imputed tax credit. A personal expenditure tax combined with a corporation tax on an *R* basis or an *S* basis requires a classical system rather than an imputation system for relating corporation tax with personal tax.

THE PROBLEM OF EEC TAX HARMONISATION

There would be no special difficulty in the way of adopting such a system in the United Kingdom, were it not for the problem of international tax harmonisation. The latest draft directive of the Commission of European Communities[11] suggests that the harmonisation of EEC corporation taxes should be on the basis of an imputation system, with tax credits extended to

[11] Proposal for a Council Directive Concerning the Harmonisation of Company Taxation and Withholding Taxes on Dividends, European Communities Commission, August 1975.

individual shareholders in other member countries. Any refunds due would be paid by the authorities of the country in which the underlying profits were taxed, not by the authorities of the country of residence of the shareholders. An additional withholding tax would be levied on dividends when paid to someone other than known residents of a member country or to residents of a country which had negotiated an appropriate double tax treaty. As far as rates of tax are concerned, it is proposed that (i) the rate of corporation tax must lie in the range 45–55 per cent, and (ii) the rate of imputation should be such that shareholder's tax credits would be between 45 and 55 per cent of the corporation tax paid on the gross profits underlying the dividend that he received.[12] This does in fact narrowly limit the imputation rate; e.g. with a 50 per cent (tax-inclusive) rate of corporation tax, the rate of imputation would have to lie between 31·03 and 35·48 per cent (tax-inclusive).

The question therefore arises whether there is any way in which the United Kingdom could operate personal taxation on an expenditure basis with a corporation tax effectively on an R basis or an S basis, and yet meet this EEC harmonisation requirement. There is in fact one way in which an expenditure tax could be combined with a modified, but nevertheless effective, S-based corporation tax and yet meet the strict requirements of the EEC draft directive. This would involve a modification of the tax base. With the unmodified form discussed so far, the tax base is all share outpayments such as dividends ($\overline{S}$) *less* all share inpayments such as new share issues (S). With the modified form only a proportion of share inpayments would be allowed as a set-off against share outpayments, so that the tax base would become $\overline{S}$ less a stated fraction of S. The effect of this modification can be seen in the example given in Table 12.3. The first column is merely a reproduction of the first column of Table 12.2 and shows how, with a corporation tax rate of 100 per cent (tax-exclusive) or 50 per cent (tax-inclusive) and an imputation rate of $33\frac{1}{3}$ per cent (tax-inclusive), the unmodified S-based tax would enable £100 of share outpayments to be converted at the expense of the tax revenue into £150 of share inpayments. The second column shows the position if only one-third instead of the whole of the share inpayments could be deducted from the tax base. The figures in the second column remain unchanged from those in the first column until line 7, where the relief from corporation tax due to the issue of new shares is reduced in such a way as to remove any tax gain from a mere distribution of cash and its subsequent recall by new share issues.

---

[12] This restriction can be understood most easily in terms of the French avoir-fiscal system described in Appendix 12.3, where α is taken to represent the proportion of the underlying corporation tax which is allowed as a tax credit on dividends. The restriction is that this fraction α should lie between 45 and 55 per cent. As it is shown in the appendix,

$$\alpha = \frac{m}{1-m} \div \frac{c}{1-c}$$

or the ratio of the imputation rate (on a tax-exclusive basis) to the rate of corporation tax (on a tax-exclusive basis). With $c = 50$ per cent and $m = 33\frac{1}{3}$ per cent, $\alpha = 50$ per cent, so that the requirement that α should lie between 45 and 55 per cent would be satisfied.

It can be seen that dividends worth £75 (line 5) can be financed out of £100 profit (line 1); or in other words, the effective rate of corporation tax on dividends is not 100 per cent (tax-exclusive) but only $33\frac{1}{3}$ per cent, because of the imputed tax which is credited to the shareholder, and is thus in effect set against the corporation's tax liability. In order, therefore, that the effective remission of corporation tax on new share issues should be at the same rate as the effective rate of corporation tax on dividend payments, it is necessary to allow only one-third instead of the whole of the new share issues to qualify as a deduction from the tax base. The whole arrangement then is equivalent to an unmodified S base without any imputation of tax credits at a rate of corporation tax of $33\frac{1}{3}$ per cent (tax-exclusive) or 25 per cent (tax-inclusive).[13] It would not be possible to use this method to achieve a harmless imputation with the R basis.

Table 12.3   *Expenditure tax and modified imputation (in £s)*

		Tax base	
		$(\bar{S}-S)$ basis	$(\bar{S}-\frac{1}{3}S)$
1	Cash in bank	100	100
2	*Less* Payment of CT	(50)	(50)
3	Net dividend	50	50
4	Imputed tax credit	25	25
5	Dividend *plus* tax credit	75	75
6	Purchase of new shares	75	75
7	Relief from CT	75	25
8	Cash in bank	150	100

An alternative possibility, if it were essential to combine an imputation system with a personal expenditure tax, would be to abandon the S base and the R base for corporation tax and substitute a P base for the tax. This combination would not remove the tax differentiation in favour of distribution of profits and of raising new capital by new share issues rather than by the retention of undistributed profits. The ability to pick up the imputed tax

[13] If $\bar{S}$ is the amount paid in dividends and m is the imputation rate, then $(1/[1-m])\bar{S}$ is the value of dividends plus tax credit to the shareholders. The tax credit is $(m/[1-m])\bar{S}$, so that with a corporation tax at a rate t (tax-exclusive) the amount of effective corporation tax paid on dividends is $t\bar{S}-(m/[1-m])\bar{S}$. If this is expressed as a proportion of $(1/[1-m])\bar{S}$ (i.e. of the full value of the dividends to shareholders), an effective rate of corporation tax on dividends of $t(1-m-m/t)$ is obtained. In order that the same effective rate of relief of tax should be allowed against new share issues, only the fraction $(1-m-m/t)$ of such share inpayments should be allowed against the tax base.

credits by paying dividends and simultaneously issuing new shares, which is illustrated for the *R* basis in the second column of Table 12.2, would be exactly the same with a *P*-based tax. There would in fact remain a tax incentive to make the maximum dividend distribution possible and to rely on new share issues for obtaining any desired capital finance.

But to combine a *P*-based corporation tax with a personal expenditure tax and an imputation system would remove the positive subsidy on all real investment financed by the issue of new shares which, as we have explained, would result with an *S*-based or *R*-based corporation tax. The difference is illustrated in Table 12.4. Throughout that table we assume a rate of corporation tax of 50 per cent (tax-inclusive) or 100 per cent (tax-exclusive), an imputation rate where relevant of $33\frac{1}{3}$ per cent (tax-inclusive), a rate of expenditure tax of 40 per cent (tax-inclusive), and a real yield on the company's investment of 10 per cent. As can be seen from the table, the return to an individual saver would be

S or *R* base:	with imputation	15%
	without imputation	10%
P base:	with imputation	7·5%
	without imputation	5%

Table 12.4 *Imputation and expenditure tax with a* P-*based corporation tax (in £s)*.

		S *or* R *base*		P *base*	
		Without imputation	*With imputation*	*Without imputation*	*With imputation*
1	Once-for-all reduction in consumption		60		
2	ET relief		40		
3	Savings		100		
4	CT relief	100		nil	
5	Total investment	200		100	
6	Yield		20	10	
7	*Less* CT liability		(10)	(5)	
8	Cash dividend		10	5	
9	Tax credit	nil	5	nil	2·5
10	Dividend + Tax credit	10	15	5	7·5
11	*Less* ET	(4)	(6)	(2)	(3)
12	Increase in annual consumption	6	9	3	4·5
13	Rate of yield to saver (i.e. line 12 ÷ line 1)	10%	15%	5%	7·5%

In the example in Table 12.4 we assume the rate of corporation tax to be the same with an imputation system as without an imputation system. But in order to obtain the same revenue, a lower rate of corporation tax would be needed in the absence of an imputation system, since without imputation the shareholders would be derived of their tax credits to set against their personal tax liabilities. But even if a lower rate of corporation tax than 50 per cent (tax-inclusive) were assumed in those columns of Table 12.4 which show the results in the absence of imputation, the following three rates of yield would still result:

S or *R* base:	with imputation	15%
	without imputation	10%
P base:	with imputation	7·5%

It is an *S* base or *R* base without imputation which equates the rate of yield to the saver to the yield on the rate of investment, whatever the rate of corporation tax may be. With imputation such a system subsidises investment by raising the rate of yield to the saver above the rate of yield on the investment by the rate of imputation, whatever the rate of corporation tax may be. With a *P*-based corporation tax the rate of yield to the saver is reduced below the rate of yield on the investment, although this discrepancy can be reduced by an imputation system. If there were full imputation, the rate of yield on dividends to the saver would be raised to the rate of yield on the company's investment, and the corporation tax would become simply a tax on undistributed profits; but since, as we have indicated, there would in any case be a strong tax incentive to reduce undistributed profits to the barest minimum, the tax would be largely ineffective as a revenue raiser. A *P*-based tax combined with an expenditure tax and partial imputation is, however, a possible combination and could be operated in such a way as to fulfil the strict requirements of the present EEC draft directive.

However, true tax harmonisation is in fact much affected not only by rates of tax and the choice between the classical and the imputation principles of relationship with personal tax; it is also much affected by the choice of tax base both for corporation tax and for personal direct taxation. The present EEC directive completely neglects these choices of tax base. In the United Kingdom the corporation tax has already been shifted very substantially from a *P* base towards an *R* base, and personal direct tax from an income base towards an expenditure base, in the ways described in Chapter 4. The problem has already become very relevant.

CORPORATION TAX AND TTET

A TTET is (as explained in Chapter 10) a combination of two taxes: (i) either a proportionate tax on value added, or a basic rate of income tax with 100 per cent capital allowances on all investments in real capital goods; and (ii) an expenditure tax levied on the expenditure-tax adjustment method at a progressive rate on all expenditures above a certain limit.

In this case (as in the case of the UET just examined) there is no need for any corporation tax unless it is desired for one reason or another to impose some additional charge on corporate as contrasted with unincorporated business.

If it were desired to impose some additional charge on corporate enterprises, then an R base or an S base would harmonise better than a P base with a TTET as with a UET, on the grounds that, like a TTET or a UET, neither an R-based nor an S-based corporation tax would cause the return on savings to diverge from the yield on investment.

If the lower tier of the TTET were operated by means of a basic rate of income tax with 100 per cent capital allowances, then to achieve the desired result with an R-based or an S-based corporation tax it would be necessary to allow imputation on dividends at the basic rate of income tax and, in the case of an R base, also to allow deductibility of interest payments against corporation tax but only at the basic rate of income tax.

Moreover, if the lower tier of the TTET were operated by a basic rate of income tax with 100 per cent capital allowances, there would be an apparent convenience in operating an R-based rather than an S-based corporation tax in so far as both the income tax and the corporation tax would in this case start from the same base, calculated after deduction of the 100 per cent capital allowances.

In Table 12.5 we demonstrate this particular combination. The desired result is achieved by: (i) imposing a rate of corporation tax which is somewhat higher than the basic rate of income tax; (ii) allowing imputation on dividends at the basic rate of income tax; and (iii) allowing deductibility of interest payments against the base for corporation tax, but allowing such deductibility not at the full rate of corporation tax but only at the basic rate of income tax. To illustrate this system in Table 12.5 we assume (i) a rate of corporation tax of 50 per cent (tax-inclusive), (ii) on an R base, i.e. with 100 per cent capital allowances against all expenditures on investment in real goods, (iii) with a basic rate of income tax on personal incomes of $33\frac{1}{3}$ per cent (tax-inclusive), (iv) with an imputation rate for dividends at the same rate as the basic rate of income tax, and (v) with deductibility of interest payments against liability to corporation tax at this same basic rate of income tax. We consider this system in the case of an individual saver whose standard of living is high enough to make him liable to an upper-tier expenditure surtax at 25 per cent (tax-exclusive); and we illustrate the effect in column A on the assumption that he invests his money in the company's shares, and in column B on the assumption that he lends the money at interest to the company. We assume that the company can earn a 10 per cent yield on any real investment.

Lines 1 to 10 of the table are the same for both columns. If the individual concerned were to earn £150 and were to spend this on consumption, he could purchase £80 worth of consumption goods (lines 1 to 4). If he were to save his earnings, he could lend £100 to the company after payment of his income tax liability on his earnings (lines 5 to 7). The company could finance £200 worth of investment (line 9), because the capital allowance against the £200 of expenditure on capital goods would, at a corporation tax rate of 50 per cent (tax-inclusive), lead to a reduction of tax of £100 on the rest of the company's transactions (line 8). The investment would at 10 per cent produce an annual yield of £20 (line 10).

Table 12.5 *A TTET with income tax with 100 per cent capital allowances and an R-based corporation tax (in £s)*

	Corporation Tax 50% *(tax-inclusive basis)* Income Tax $33\frac{1}{3}$% *(tax-inclusive basis)* Expenditure Tax 25% *(tax-exclusive basis)*	
	A Finance by share capital *(Imputation rate = basic rate of income tax)*	*B* Finance by loan *(Interest deductible at basic rate of income tax)*
Earnings spent		
1 Earnings	150	150
2 *Less* IT	(50)	(50)
3 *Less* ET	(20)	(20)
4 Consumption	80	80
Earnings saved		
5 Earnings	150	150
6 *Less* IT	(50)	(50)
7 Savings	100	100
8 CT remission	100	100
9 Investments	200	200
10 Annual yield	20	20
11 *Less* CT	(10)	(5)[a]
12 Dividend	10	—
13 Tax credit	5	—
14 Dividend+Tax credit	15	—
15 Interest	—	15
16 *Less* IT	(5)	(5)
17 *Less* ET	(2)	(2)
18 Annual consumption	8	8

[a] $(\frac{1}{2} \times 20) - (\frac{1}{3} \times 15) = 5$.

In the case of finance by share capital (column A) the company would be liable to pay £10 in corporation tax on the £20 yield, leaving £10 for dividend payment (lines 10 to 12). This dividend with imputed tax credit at the standard rate of $33\frac{1}{3}$ per cent (tax-inclusive) would give the shareholder a pre-tax dividend income of £15 (lines 13 to 14). After payment of income tax and expenditure surtax this would finance an annual consumption of £8 (lines 16 to 18). The return to the saver would be 10 per cent on his postponed consumption (line 18 as a percentage of line 4).

In the case of loan finance (column B) the company could offer £15 in interest (line 15). Its corporation tax liability would be only £5, because it could deduct from the 50 per cent (tax-inclusive) corporation tax on the profit yield of £20 the basic rate of income tax at $33\frac{1}{3}$ per cent (tax-inclusive) on the interest of £15, giving a net liability to corporation tax of £5, i.e. of 50 per cent of £20 minus $33\frac{1}{3}$ per cent of £15 (line 11). The recipient of the £15 of interest could spend £8 on consumption after payment of income tax and expenditure surtax (lines 15 to 18). Once again there would be a 10 per cent return on the savings.[14]

These arrangements may seem somewhat complex. But they have some important practical advantages.

1   They do not in fact involve such radical changes in the present corporation tax as some of the other arrangements discussed in this chapter. They involve an extension of 100 per cent capital allowances and a partial, but only partial, discontinuation of interest deductibility against corporation tax liability. Such deductibility would still continue at the basic rate of tax. They allow also for the present system of imputation of tax credits on dividends at the basic rate of tax.
2   They would be fully in accord with the EEC draft directive on the harmonisation of corporation taxes, since they would involve imputation at the basic rate of income tax and would be perfectly compatible with a rate of corporation tax in the range prescribed in the EEC directive.
3   Since they rest on an *R* base it would be easier to cope with the problem of double taxation relief by restricting 100 per cent capital allowances to domestic investment, if that were the preferred method of treatment (see Chapter 21).

The system is, however, a complicated one which is not straightforward and easy to understand. Moreover, it has the disadvantage of an *R*-based tax in that it does not satisfactorily cope with financial institutions. Moreover, the lower tier of the TTET may not be operated by means of a basic rate of

[14] It will be observed that the pre-tax return on savings, i.e. pre-tax dividends of line 14 or pre-tax interest of line 15, is 15 per cent of the individual's savings (line 7). This is a case in which it is the rate of return after payment of the basic rate of tax which measures the yield on the investment. As explained in Chapter 10 (p. 210), in this case persons or institutions who are at present exempt from tax (i.e. pension funds, charities, persons whose income is below the tax threshold) should nevertheless be liable to the basic rate of tax on their investment income.

income tax with 100 per cent capital allowances. If it were operated through some form of tax on value added, it would (as argued in Chapter 10) be more readily understood to be a tax on consumption expenditure.

In this case, with the disappearance of the income tax with 100 per cent capital allowances, the need for imputation of a tax credit to dividends at the basic rate of tax and, with an R base, for deductibility of interest payments at the basic rate of tax against corporation tax would disappear. Moreover, since the apparatus of 100 per cent capital allowances would no longer be needed for the operation of the TTET, any special reason for choosing an R-based corporation tax to accompany the lower tier of the TTET would also disappear. An S-based corporation tax, whether operated directly or approached indirectly through the $(R+F)$ basis described on pp. 233–236 above, would be just as appropriate to accompany a TTET as to accompany a UET. In the end, if the S-based tax could be operated directly on the base $(\bar{S}-S)$, there would be a simple straightforward tax system, the *raison d'être* of which would be easy to comprehend: a proportionate tax on value added and an expenditure tax surcharge to give a progressive tax on consumption, together with a corporation tax that levied a charge on the net amount which shareholders took out of business corporations.

CONCLUSIONS

The base of the present UK corporation tax is half-way between a true profits base and a flow-of-funds base. The final choice of base for corporation tax must be much affected by what happens to the base for personal taxation. If the UK tax on personal incomes were to move in the direction of a true CIT, this would strengthen the case for making true profits the base for corporation tax. But if UK personal taxation were to move in the direction of an expenditure base, we see merit in moving the corporation tax fully on to a flow-of-funds base.

Such a base could take more than one form:

1 The base could be the excess of the total proceeds from the sale of real goods and services over expenditures on the purchase of such goods and services by the company, whether on capital or current account.
2 The base could be the excess of the total amount paid out over the total amount received by the company in respect of dividends or of the capital value of the shares themselves, which would imply a tax on the net amount of funds that were taken by shareholders out of the corporate sector of the economy.
3 A result similar to (2) could be achieved by taxing the excess of the inflow over the outflow of funds in respect of all transactions (whether real or financial and whether on capital or current account) other than the inflow or outflow of funds in respect of the shares of UK companies. We are in favour of adopting this base for the UK corporation tax, at least in the first instance.

The combination of this base for corporation tax and an expenditure base for personal taxation makes very good sense; but it does not fit in readily with the system of imputing tax credits to dividend payments. However, if the imputation system must be preserved for the purpose of EEC harmonisation rules, ways can be devised for doing so.

There is no reason to believe that the shift of corporation tax on to a flow-of-funds base would involve a loss of revenue. The change of base does, however, raise important issues connected with double taxation relief (discussed in Chapters 20 and 21). The treatment of double taxation relief is quantitatively of great significance.

Appendix 12.1 The Taxation of Financial Institutions

Consider the following example. A bank pays its depositors 5 per cent and charges borrowers 13 per cent. It incurs expenses of £4 (per £100 of deposits), which we assume to be divided equally between wages and salaries on the one hand and inputs liable to VAT (such as paper clips) on the other hand. The 'pure' rate of interest is 10 per cent.

The fact that depositors can earn only 5 per cent although the 'pure' rate is 10 per cent suggests that they receive services (such as cheque clearing, safekeeping, book-keeping) which compensate them for the difference; and similarly the borrower can be assumed to receive services for which he is prepared to pay a premium of 3 per cent over the 10 per cent 'pure' rate.

To clarify the tax implications of this situation we set out in Table 12.6 a set of bank's accounts drawn on a conventional basis and contrast this with its accounts adjusted in such a way as to reveal the value of its real services to its customers.

Table 12.6 *The value of a bank's real service*

1 *Bank's conventional accounts*			
Income	(£)	*Expenditure*	(£)
Loan interest	13	Deposit interest	5
		Wages and salaries	2
		Paper clips etc.	2
		True profit	4[a]
	13		13

2 *Bank's adjusted accounts*			
Income	(£)	*Expenditure*	(£)
True loan interest	10	True deposit interest	10
Charge to borrower	3	Wages and salaries	2
Charge to depositor	5	Paper clips etc.	2
		True profit	4
	18		18

[a]Made up of net investment income £8 less trading loss £4 to give a true profit of £4.

Under the present system the bank pays corporation tax on its true profit of £4, being the sum of its net investment income of £8 and its trading loss of £4. Depositors pay income tax on £5, and borrowers can claim relief (where applicable) on £13. Thus if corporation tax and income tax rates are equal, the whole arrangement attracts relief on £4.

Under a CIT the bank might still pay corporation tax on its true profit of £4 (with a credit to shareholders on the lines discussed in Chapter 7). But the depositors on their personal accounts would pay tax on £10 (interest of £5 plus value of imputed service of £5), and borrowers on personal account would be able to deduct only £10 of interest (the balance of £3 being payment made for banking services). In so far as the bank accounts were operated for business purposes, the depositors might claim the £5 of imputed bank services as a business expense and borrowers might similarly claim the additional £3 of bank charges as a business expense.

Under an expenditure tax an individual's tax liability would be assessed by calculating his income and adding to it the net 'expenditure tax adjustment' as described in Chapter 8 (i.e. his net sales of registered assets). In the calculation of the income element in this assessment the same problems would arise as those discussed in the previous paragraph in connection with a CIT. The true profit of the bank would be assessed in so far as it was distributed to individuals in the form of dividends; the depositor would count £10 as income (£5 interest plus £5 imputed bank services); the borrower would treat only £10 as interest, deductible against his other income if the borrowing were on registered account (the remaining £3 being treated as payment for an imputed service); and the depositors and borrowers could then deduct the £5 and £3 imputed service charges only in so far as these qualified as true business expenses. The corporation tax treatment would depend upon the tax base chosen for this purpose. With the present corporation tax system the tax would be payable on net interest received (£8) less trading loss (£4); on an R basis it would be paid on the value of real services sold (£5 + £3) less purchases of real goods and services (£2 + £2); and on an S basis it would be charged on dividends paid (a potential £4).

Under the present VAT the bank's allowable inputs (£2 of paper clips) exceed its sales liable to VAT (nil). The bank is at present rated as 'exempt' from VAT, which means that it cannot obtain relief from VAT on its £2 of inputs liable to VAT; if it were not so rated, it would be able to obtain a net repayment of VAT on these inputs. The bank's true value added (profit plus wages and salaries) is, however, *plus* £6 and not *minus* £2. This value added would be taxed if the imputed charges on depositors and borrowers of £5 and £3 respectively were liable to VAT, against which the £2 of eligible inputs would be set.

With corporation tax, income tax, expenditure tax and VAT all involved in this way, the tax sums involved are very substantial. The corporation tax problem could be met by retaining the present system or by shifting to an S-based tax; but it would arise in an acute form if there were a shift to an R base, involving the elimination of net interest receipts from the tax base. But the problems for income tax, expenditure tax and VAT could not be easily met, unless banks could be required to alter their accounting methods for tax purposes from form 1 to form 2 outlined above, which would involve their being told what was to be treated as the 'pure' rate of interest. It is unfortunately necessary to justify a particular 'pure' rate, since the choice would in effect serve to distribute the burden of imputed bank services between borrowers and lenders. Perhaps use could be made of the current Treasury Bill rate. An alternative rule-of-thumb method would be to use the mean of the bank's average lending and borrowing rates (9 per cent in our example) rather than any outside reference level.

Appendix 12.2   The Revenue Yield of Corporation Taxes

In this appendix we discuss some estimates of the revenue which could have been expected from corporation tax in the period 1964–74 under the S and R bases, *given* the assumption that the 'real' behaviour of companies would have remained unchanged. 'Real' behaviour is defined as the level of output, the price at which that output was sold and investment in different kinds of assets. The assumption is clearly unrealistic, but it is a first step. The effect of making this assumption is probably to overestimate the potential revenue from the S and R bases in comparison with the revenue actually raised.

Our aim is to estimate the *tax-inclusive*[1] bases for the various systems discussed. A major part of corporate sector income consists of income from abroad, which is liable to UK corporation tax. This income may, and in general will, have borne foreign corporation tax, and part or all of the foreign tax paid will be available as a credit against the company's UK tax liability. How much of the foreign tax is available as a credit is a complex question which will depend upon the relationship between the foreign and the UK corporate tax rates and upon the circumstances of the individual company. Because of this we shall estimate the tax-inclusive bases before any credit is given for foreign tax. An upper limit to the credit is then given by the figure for foreign taxes paid. Although we have argued that under the S basis the appropriate solution may well be to abolish or restrict double taxation relief, these calculations enable the potential revenue to be compared with the revenue actually raised in the past.

To ensure consistency in the definitions of the tax-inclusive bases, it is helpful to employ the previous accounting framework of Table 12.1 and to assume (for the sake of simplicity) that there are no transactions in financial assets. In this case, the pure S basis and the pure R basis as discussed above are identical. The inflows and outflows of the firm are given by

Inflows	Outflows
R	$\overline{R}$
S	$\overline{S}$
I	T_{UK}
	T_F

where R, $\overline{R}$, S and $\overline{S}$ are defined as in previous discussions of the bases, I is income from abroad, T_{UK} is UK taxes actually paid (after whatever relief for foreign tax is granted) and T_F is foreign taxes paid. On a tax-inclusive basis the R basis is defined as $(I+R-\overline{R})$. The question is: what is the equivalent tax-inclusive S basis? In this example, the S and R bases are identical. Hence the tax-inclusive S basis is given by the accounting identity as above:

$$\overline{S}-S+T_{UK}+T_F = I+R-\overline{R}$$

This explains the layout of Tables 12.7 and 12.8.

Estimates are given for: (i) the S basis; (ii) an R_1 basis, which is the 'pure R' basis except that free depreciation is granted only on domestic investment; (iii) an R_2 basis, which restricts free depreciation to domestic investment on all assets which currently qualify for some kind of depreciation allowance (i.e. excludes commercial buildings and land); and (iv) an R_3 basis, which goes beyond R_2 in not giving free depreciation to investment in stocks. Tables 12.7 and 12.8 show the estimates, and their construction, of the tax bases for each year in the period 1964–74. The tax bases are all shown as tax-inclusive bases. In Table 12.9 are shown the arithmetic averages of the four bases for 1964–69, 1970–74 and 1964–74.

Table 12.7   *Potential revenue from the UK company sector, 1964-74: S basis (in £ millions)*

Year	(1) Ordinary and preference dividends[a]	(2) UK taxes (accruals)[b]	(3) Taxes paid abroad	(4) Share issues[c]	Tax-inclusive base = (1)+ (2)+(3)−(4)
1964	1,516	1,010	504	158	2,872
1965	1,741	678	543	63	2,899
1966	1,661	1,174	505	124	3,216
1967	1,607	1,065	561	65	3,168
1968	1,588	1,211	744	303	3,240
1969	1,693	1,234	838	183	3,582
1970	1,531	1,128	996	44	3,611
1971	1,704	958	1,282	160	3,784
1972	1,690	1,426	1,527	326	4,317
1973	1,753	2,310	2,166	107	6,122
1974	1,570	963	3,819	43	6,309
Averages					
1964–69					3,163
1970–74					4,829
1964–74					3,920

[a] For gross dividends until April 1973 and then for net payments.

[b] Includes ACT after April 1973; columns 1 and 2 are not consistent series over time taken separately, but the sum of the two is consistent. Taxes are defined net of receipt of investment grants.

[c] Issues of ordinary shares for industrial and commercial companies. There are no data on issues of preference shares (these were very small) nor, more importantly, on share issues by financial institutions other than banks. An upper limit of £200 million might be put on these.

Source: Blue Book (1975), Tables 32 and 83.

It shows that the S basis exceeded the R basis because, in the period concerned, companies were disposing of financial assets or incurring financial liabilities. This illustrates the point that cyclically the two bases have different effects, in that in a year when the company sector is in financial deficit (see the figures for 1974) the S basis is very much higher than the R basis; the figures for S for 1973 and 1974 seem to be 'atypical'.

Estimates of the revenue which would have been obtained from S, R_1, R_2 and R_3 are shown in Table 12.10 on the assumption that the tax rate would have been 50 per cent and, again of course, assuming unchanged behaviour. The potential revenue

Table 12.8 Potential revenue from the UK company sector, 1964-74: R basis (in £ millions)

Year	(1) Gross trading profits net of SA[a]	(2) Income from abroad	(3) Rent	(4) Investment in stocks	(5) Total GDFCF[b]	(6) Domestic investment excluding land and commercial buildings	Tax-inclusive base R_1 $=(1)+(2)+(3)$ $-(4)-(5)$	R_2 $=(1)+(2)+(3)$ $-(4)-(6)$	R_3 $=(1)+(2)+(3)$ $-(6)$
1964	4,306	1,281	179	654	2,467	1,859	2,645	3,253	3,907
1965	4,485	1,411	191	457	2,667	2,069	2,963	3,561	4,018
1966	4,308	1,335	205	267	2,706	2,149	2,875	3,432	3,699
1967	4,514	1,406	227	206	2,697	2,190	3,244	3,751	3,957
1968	4,800	1,728	254	389	3,050	2,483	3,343	3,910	4,299
1969	4,559	2,052	290	437	3,556	2,896	2,908	3,568	4,005
1970	4,538	2,287	331	396	3,955	3,249	2,805	3,511	3,907
1971	5,224	2,574	378	−129	4,038	3,364	4,267	4,941	4,812
1972	5,840	3,033	429	−149	4,395	3,644	5,056	5,807	5,658
1973	6,119	4,787	489	764	5,699	4,446	4,932	6,185	6,949
1974	4,822	6,643	601	1,066	7,020	5,655	3,980	5,345	6,411
Averages									
1964-69		1,535					2,996	3,579	3,981
1970-74		3,865					4,208	5,158	5,547
1964-74		2,594					3,547	4,297	4,693

[a] SA = Stock adjustment.
[b] GDFCF = Gross domestic fixed-capital formation.
Source: Blue Book (1975), Tables 13, 32, 60, 65 and 79.

Table 12.9 *Comparison of different tax bases (in £ millions)*

Years	S	R_1	R_2	R_3	Net disposal of financial assets minus overseas investment
Average 1964–69	3,163	2,996	3,579	3,981	134
Average 1970–74	4,829	4,208	5,158	5,547	1,049
Average 1964–74	3,920	3,547	4,297	4,693	550

Source: Tables 12.7 and 12.8 above; and *Blue Book* (1975), Table 33.

Table 12.10 *Comparison of potential revenue with 50 per cent rate (in £ millions)*

Years	S^a	R_1^a	R_2^a	R_3^a	Taxes paid abroad	Actual UK tax accruals[b]
Average 1964–69	1,582	1,498	1,790	1,991	616	1,061
Average 1970–74	2,415	2,104	2,579	2,774	1,958	1,060
Average 1964–74	1,960	1,774	2,149	2,347	1,226	1,061

[a] Before double taxation relief.

[b] Net of investment grants (as in Table 12.7) and net of ACT, which has been estimated at £701 million for 1973 and £785 million for 1974. Figures given before stock relief. Some of the investment grants should really be regarded as regional incentives and would thus be required under *S* and *R* bases to ensure a fair comparison.

Note: These figures assume unchanged behaviour. It is likely that the response of companies would lead to lower figures for the potential revenue from the *S* and *R* bases.

Source: Tables 12.7 and 12.8 above.

is given by the figure shown under the appropriate definition minus credit for foreign taxes paid. Although we have no means of knowing the exact figure for the value of double tax relief, we do know that the upper limit to this credit would be the figure for taxes paid abroad. Thus the figure for the revenue of each base minus taxes paid abroad can be compared with the revenue actually raised in the past to give an approximate idea of the revenue potential of each tax base.

The provisional conclusions seem to be:

1   *S* raises a little more revenue than R_1, but the difference is probably insignificant if 1973 and 1974 are ignored and the potential revenue for, say, 1964–69 is considered.
2   R_2 raises about £500 million more in 1976 prices.
3   R_3 would raise about £250 million more than R_2 in current prices and hence about £750 million a year more than *S* or R_1.

The calculations are subject to three reservations:

1 We cannot quantify the effect of the proposals made in Chapter 20 for dealing with overseas investment; but we can indicate the probable direction of the adjustments that arise:
   (a) The S base would be smaller than we show because some foreign tax would not attract double taxation relief and so would not enter the tax base.
   (b) Because we have disallowed overseas investment in arriving at the R base, double taxation relief would be continued in full against the tax due on that base. But since overseas investment has not been disallowed in arriving at the S base, there would under the S method be a disallowance of double taxation relief on the yield on post-appointed-day overseas investment.
   (c) If the company sector is in 'financial deficit' (i.e. if F exceeds $\bar{F}$), the S base will be larger, apart from the disallowance of overseas investment, than the R base. To that extent the amount of double taxation relief may be larger under the S than under the R method.
2 It would be possible, although perhaps inelegant, to disallow under the S basis expenditure on commercial buildings and land (corresponding to R_2) and also investment in stocks (corresponding to R_3).
3 The figures for the R basis make no provision for any special arrangements for taxing financial companies (e.g. maintaining the current system for financial companies).

Our discussion has been conducted in terms of the R and S bases, although the conclusions apply equally to the $(R+F)$ basis, which, we have argued, is a rather attractive compromise. In one sense the $(R+F)$ base is nearer to the S base because it taxes the profits of financial companies; but on the other hand the treatment of overseas investment and double taxation relief could follow that of the R base. Hence the revenue from the $(R+F)$ base would normally be larger than that produced by R, but its relationship to that yielded by S would depend upon the exact treatment of double taxation relief under the S basis. In any event the general conclusions about the revenue of S and R, would apply also to $(R+F)$.

NOTE

1 The natural base for the R method is tax-inclusive and for the S method tax-exclusive.

Appendix 12.3   The Formulae for Various Systems of Corporation Tax: Classical, Two-Rate, Imputation and Avoir Fiscal

We deal here with a corporation tax which is based on pure profit (P), so we can write

$$R = P - T - D$$

where R is cash put to reserve, P is pre-tax profit, T is tax paid by the corporation, and D is the cash value of the dividends to a taxpayer with a zero rate of personal tax. Thus T represents the total tax paid by the corporation to the Revenue less any withholding tax, tax credit or avoir fiscal which is credited to the recipient of the dividends. The equation is expressed as if the corporation paid this sum directly to shareholders as part of the dividend due to them before payment of personal tax, instead of paying it to the tax authorities who would then credit it to the shareholders.

1   *The classical system*

$$R = P - cP - D$$

where c is the rate of corporation tax levied on all profits.

2   *The two-rate system*

Let c_u be the rate of corporation tax on undistributed profits and c_d the lower rate on distributed profits. Undistributed profits are total profits less distributed profits; but there are two possible interpretations of the term 'distributed profits':

(a)   It could be defined as the amount of profit needed both to pay the cash dividend and to meet the corporation tax due on distributed profits, in which case distributed profits are gross of the corporation tax payable on them and are equal to $D/(1-c_d)$.

(b)   It could be used to mean the net cash dividend exclusive of the tax payable on it.

It is this latter interpretation which is applied in the West German two-rate system. But we illustrate both systems. Thus

$$\text{with method (a),} \quad R = P - c_u\left(P - \frac{D}{1-c_d}\right) - \frac{c_d}{1-c_d}D - D$$

$$\text{with method (b),} \quad R = P - c_u(P - D) - c_dD - D$$

3   *The imputation system*

Let m be the imputation rate, which in the United Kingdom system is equal to the basic rate of income tax. Then

$$R = P - (cP - mD) - D$$

where D is dividends plus tax credits and mD is advance corporation tax.

4   *The avoir fiscal system*

In the French system the corporation pays a tax equal to cP. The remainder of its profit it can put to reserve or distribute in a cash dividend. But the recipient of the dividend receives from the tax authorities a tax credit or 'avoir fiscal'. If A is this avoir fiscal, then $(D-A)$ is the cash dividend distributed by the corporation. The avoir fiscal A is expressed as a fraction of the corporation tax which has been charged on the profits used for the cash dividend. Thus if $(D-A)$ is the cash dividend, $(D-A)$ grossed up or $(D-A)/(1-c)$ is the pre-tax profit underlying the cash dividend, so that $[c/(1-c)](D-A)$ is the corporation tax incurred in respect of the cash dividends. If a proportion α of this is credited to the personal shareholder as a tax credit,

$$A = \frac{\alpha c}{1-c}(D-A) = \frac{\alpha c}{1-c(1-\alpha)}D$$

The French system can therefore be expressed as

$$R = P - cP - (D - A)$$

$$= (1-c)\left(P - \frac{D}{1-c(1-\alpha)}\right)$$

In each system the effective rate of corporation tax on profit used to put to reserve can be defined as

$$t_r = 1 - \frac{\delta R}{\delta P}$$

and the effective rate of corporation tax on profit used to distribute a dividend can be defined as

$$t_d = 1 - \frac{\delta D}{\delta P}$$

From the expressions connecting R, P and D under the various systems, the following values of t_r and t_d are obtainable:

		t_r	t_d
1	Classical system	c	c
2	Two-rate system: method (a)	c_u	c_d
	method (b)	c_u	$\dfrac{c_d}{1-c_u+c_d}$
3	Imputation system	c	$\dfrac{c-m}{1-m}$
4	Avoir fiscal system	c	$c(1-\alpha)$

The classical system (1) subjects both R and D to the same rate of underlying corporation tax, the distributed dividend being then in addition subject to personal tax.

The other systems differentiate between the two rates of underlying tax. But if their tax rates and other relevant parameters are appropriately chosen, they can each express the same real degree of differentiation. This can be shown by comparing each of the remaining systems (2(a), 2(b) and 4) with an imputation system (3) with the particular values of $c = c^*$ and $m = m^*$. In this case, if

$$\text{with system 2(a), } c_u = c^* \quad \text{and} \quad c_d = \frac{c^* - m^*}{1 - m^*}$$

$$\text{with system 2(b), } c_u = c^* \quad \text{and} \quad \frac{c_d}{1 - c^* + c_d} = \frac{c^* - m^*}{1 - m^*}$$

so that

$$c_d = c^* - m^*$$

and if

$$\text{with system 4, } c = c^* \quad \text{and} \quad c^*(1-\alpha) = \frac{c^* - m^*}{1 - m^*}$$

so that

$$\alpha = \frac{m^*}{1-m^*} \times \frac{1-c^*}{c^*}$$

or the ratio of the imputation rate on a tax-exclusive basis to the corporation tax rate on a tax-exclusive basis

then all the systems 2(a), 2(b), 3 and 4 will have the same real tax implications. With the present UK tax, $c^* = 52$ per cent and $m^* = 33$ per cent, giving $t_r = 52$ per cent and $t_d = 28\cdot4$ per cent. To obtain the same real result the following values would be needed under other systems:

under system 2(a), $c_u = 52\%$ and $c_d = 28\cdot4\%$
under system 2(b), $c_u = 52$ and $c_d = 19\%$
under system 4, $c = 52\%$ and $\alpha = 45\cdot5\%$

13 Social Security and Income Maintenance

In Chapter 5 we have discussed the provisions of the existing income tax, national insurance, family allowances and various forms of means-tested benefits such as supplementary benefit, family income supplement and rent and rate rebates. These provisions are designed to fulfil a number of different functions, but in this chapter we are concerned with the role they play in alleviating poverty where, for some reason or another, small resources and/or large needs would otherwise cause distress and hardship.

THE OBJECTIVES OF INCOME MAINTENANCE SCHEMES

This broad objective is not always expressed in a very precise manner, and in considering the present system and possible reforms we have applied the more explicit criteria outlined below. These will not necessarily command universal agreement, but they do, we feel, include those which have received most attention in public debate.

1 The system should aim at guaranteeing an adequate minimum income for everyone, a standard which we take to be represented by the present supplementary benefit level.
2 This minimum should be provided with dignity, so that the recipient perceives no loss of social esteem.
3 Subject to achieving objectives 1 and 2, the system should redistribute among the non-poor towards those only just above the poverty line.
4 The design of the benefits, and of the taxes necessary to finance them, should be such as to minimise any adverse effects on the incentive to work and save.
5 The whole system should be as simple, as easy to understand and as cheap to administer as possible.
6 The benefits from the system should be as little open to abuse as possible.

In our analysis of the present system in Chapter 5, we have shown that it fails to meet in full the objectives outlined above. It does not guarantee that no one falls below the full supplementary benefit level, a failure which is due to the shortcomings of national insurance (incomplete coverage and inadequate benefits) and to incomplete take-up of means-tested benefits. The low take-up of these benefits in turn reflects the stigma associated with them and the lack of information about entitlement. The system is far from simple, having grown up in a pragmatic and unsystematic manner. As a result there is at present a complex of overlapping arrangements, subject to some form of means test or assessment of income and other resources, and the whole structure is difficult to understand and expensive to administer. Finally, the system incorporates high implicit marginal rates of tax, with potentially serious disincentive effects, and is in some respects open to abuse. There is a widespread feeling, which we share, that some rationalisation and simplification of this whole apparatus is to be desired.

FOUR VARIETIES OF REFORM

A number of different forms of radical restructuring of the present complex have been put forward, and it is important to bear in mind the basic structural differences between the various types of scheme. This we shall do by first describing four possible types of scheme, which do not provide a comprehensive catalogue of all the proposals advanced in recent years but do include the most important varieties of reform:

1   A full social dividend.
2   A modified social dividend/minimum income guarantee.
3   A two-tier social dividend.
4   A 'new Beveridge' scheme.

In the first section of this chapter, we consider the basic differences between these schemes. For this purpose, we illustrate their operation in the case of a single adult person, unmarried and without children or other dependants. In fact the effectiveness and the cost of various schemes depends crucially upon the ways in which they deal with families or households of different compositions, the treatment of married couples, of children, of other dependants, of the joint earnings of husband and wife and of income other than earned income. These are important matters, to which we turn in the second section of the chapter, where we examine in more detail two of the schemes.

SECTION I

THE BASIC PRINCIPLES OF THE FOUR SCHEMES

We start with the simplest case of Mr Smith, an adult worker, unmarried, without dependants and without any income other than his wages. How will he be treated if in work or if, for one reason or another, he is out of work and so without any income? To illustrate the different treatments that he may get under the different schemes we make two further assumptions, solely for the purpose of illustrating the various situations. We assume (i) that the minimum income necessary to keep Mr Smith out of poverty is 40 per cent of the average income;[1] and (ii) that in all the schemes a basic rate of tax on income of 15 per cent is required to finance other expenditure.[2]

---

[1] The figure of 40 per cent would no doubt in fact be overgenerous for a single adult; but in our explanation of the basic principles of the various schemes Mr Smith must for the purposes of illustrating the cost of the schemes be taken to have the needs not of a single individual but of a typical family unit.

[2] For this purpose the income tax rate is taken to include employee national-insurance contributions. Employer contributions are assumed to be the same in all cases.

1 A FULL SOCIAL DIVIDEND

This is the simplest and most radical of the proposed solutions. Every family receives a tax-free social dividend at a level corresponding to the present supplementary benefit scale. The whole of the national insurance benefit system, a host of means-tested benefits and all personal allowances under the income tax are abolished. All incomes (other than the social dividend) are subject to a basic rate of income tax. The system is, however, quite compatible with the maintenance of higher progressive rates of tax on the higher slices of income and of a surcharge on investment incomes. These are separate issues.

How would this system score on the criteria set out above? It clearly has major advantages. It would effectively guarantee a minimum income; it would do so in a way in which no citizen was treated in a less dignified manner than any other citizen; it would be easy to understand and relatively easy to administer; and it would be relatively difficult to abuse. But it has two major disadvantages:

1   Under the social dividend scheme the benefit would not vary according to individual circumstances in the same way as the present supplementary benefit does. Even in the case of Mr Smith, blissfully unencumbered by dependants, the receipt of supplementary benefit at present depends upon his not being in employment. With the social dividend, however, the net payment would be related to his income but not to his employment status. The same net benefit would accrue to a single man with a given income whether or not he was working.

2   The second, and not unrelated, disadvantage of the full social dividend is that the basic rate of tax is likely to be high. This aspect of the scheme is illustrated for our single adult worker, Mr Smith, in Figure 13.1. Along

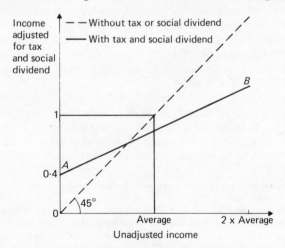

Fig 13.1   Income effect of a social dividend

the horizontal axis is measured unadjusted income – in this case Mr Smith's wages before deduction of tax or addition of social dividend. On the vertical axis is measured his income after adjustment by deduction of tax and addition of social dividend. If there were no tax or social dividend, adjusted income would be the same as unadjusted income, and Mr Smith would be on the broken line at an angle of 45 on which the height (the adjusted income) is the same as the horizontal distance (the unadjusted income). But in fact he is given a social dividend of 40 per cent of average income and is then taxed at a rate of 55 per cent on all his earnings.[3] He will now be on the line AB, since if his earnings were zero he would receive only the social dividend and would start at the point A. But he will in addition retain 45 per cent of his earnings (the line AB slopes upwards with the gradient of 45 units up for every 100 units along). So long as the line AB is above the 45 line, adjusted income exceeds unadjusted income, or, in other words, the social dividend which is received exceeds the tax paid. It is only when the line AB falls below the 45 line that any net tax is paid in excess of the social dividend received. (This occurs when earnings reach some three-quarters of average income.) The high tax rate is necessary to confine the net benefit to the lower income groups.

2   A MODIFIED SOCIAL DIVIDEND/MINIMUM INCOME GUARANTEE

If such a high basic rate of income tax were unattractive on political or other grounds, then it would be possible to modify the scheme to have a specially heavy rate of tax on the first slice of Mr Smith's earnings. In Figure 13.2(a) this possibility is illustrated by imposing a tax of 78 per cent on earnings up to 40 per cent of average income (i.e. effectively clawing back 78 per cent of the social dividend from those who are able to earn an amount equal to that dividend) and then imposing a standard rate of tax of 45 per cent on all earnings above that level. Such a scheme might be administered by the imposition of a basic rate of tax of 45 per cent on all earnings with, in addition, a national insurance contribution of 33 per cent on earnings up to the amount of the social dividend received.[4]

The extreme case of the modified social dividend is the minimum income guarantee. This type of scheme, which is illustrated in Figure 13.2(b) is designed simply to make every family's income up to the desired minimum level, neither more nor less. It could be administered as a social dividend scheme, under which in Mr Smith's case the first slice of his earnings up to

[3] With the assumptions made, the tax rate is 40 per cent (to pay for the social dividend) plus 15 per cent (to finance other expenditure).

[4] In broad terms around 30 per cent of total income falls into the 'deficient' category of personal incomes less than the social dividend level. Taxing this 30 per cent of total income at 78 per cent and the remaining 70 per cent of total income at 45 per cent raises 55 per cent of total income in tax revenue, which is sufficient to finance the 40 per cent universal social dividend and the 15 per cent needed for other purposes.

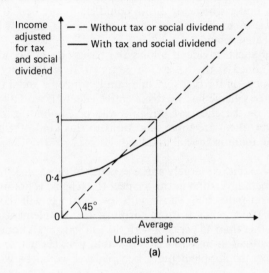

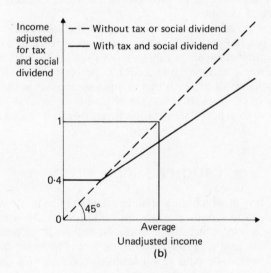

Fig. 13.2   Income effect of (a) a modified social dividend, and (b) a minimum income guarantee

an amount equal to his social dividend was subject to a marginal rate of tax of 100 per cent, the rest of his earnings being taxed at 35 per cent.[5] Alternatively, it could be administered as a single means-tested supplementary benefit scheme, under which Mr Smith could claim any benefit necessary to bring his income up to 40 per cent of average income, entirely regardless of the cause of the deficiency.

The modified social dividend allows the basic rate of tax to be reduced considerably. Indeed, if there were no administrative difficulty in imposing the 100 per cent tax on the first slice of a family's income and if the minimum income guarantee scheme had no disincentive effects, it would – more or less by definition – be the cheapest possible way of eliminating poverty completely. However, there are three objections to this kind of scheme, and to the less extreme, modified social dividend scheme:

1 The saving is achieved largely at the expense of those close to the supplementary benefit level, and in this respect the scheme is not in accord with objective 3 on page 269. Those with low earnings will receive only 22 per cent (or 0 per cent) of those earnings as a supplement to the social dividend, rather than 45 per cent with the full scheme. A comparison with the current situation may indeed show that workers whose earnings are not far above the supplementary benefit level would be worse off than at present.
2 The scheme is more complicated than the full social dividend in that it involves the administrative problem of raising a specially high tax on the first slice of incomes.
3 There are the possible adverse effects of the high marginal rate of tax of 78 per cent (or 100 per cent) on the incentives to work and save of those within the range of earnings subject to this rate. Although at present the implicit marginal rates may exceed 100 per cent, this only applies to those who take up all benefits, and in any case the fact is obscured by the multiplicity of schemes with varying eligibility criteria. It seems reasonable therefore to expect the effects on incentives to be more marked than at present.

3 A TWO-TIER SOCIAL DIVIDEND

The alternative way in which the social dividend may be modified is to relate the social dividend to labour market status. This could be done through a two-tier scheme, under which there would be two levels of benefit: a lower unconditional rate, and a higher conditional rate. The lower unconditional social dividend would be paid to all families regardless of their needs or employment situation. The higher conditional rates would be paid only to

[5] Taxing the deficient 30 per cent at 100 per cent and the remaining 70 per cent at 35 per cent raises in tax 55 per cent of total income, which is sufficient to pay the 40 per cent universal social dividend and the 15 per cent needed for other purposes.

those who were prevented by old age, involuntary unemployment, sickness or similar obstacles from earning a full time wage. For purposes of illustration we assume that for our single adult worker, Mr Smith, the rate of conditional benefit remains at 40 per cent of average income but that unconditional benefit is paid at half that rate. Mr Smith's position is now illustrated in Figure 13.3. If he is out of work, he receives the full social dividend. If he is earning, he receives a reduced social dividend and retains 58 per cent of his earnings.[6] It will be seen from Figure 13.3 that with this scheme if he is

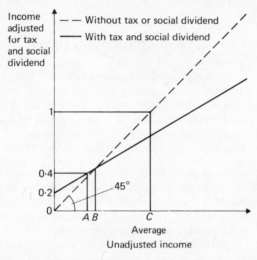

Fig 13.3   The income effect of a two-tier social dividend

in work he will have to earn at least 34 per cent of average income to keep himself above the poverty level (OA is 34 per cent of OC) but that he will receive more in social dividend than he pays in tax so long as he earns less than 48 per cent of average income (OB is 48 per cent of OC).

The two-tier social dividend would allow the basic rate of tax to be reduced. It has the advantage over the modified social dividend of avoiding the disincentive effects at the lower end of the income scale of a 78 per cent marginal rate of tax on additional earnings. However, there are disadvantages:

1   It would affect the incentive to seek employment. To the extent that Mr Smith can choose to remain unemployed (and receive the conditional credit) there will be a financial advantage to doing so if his earnings are less than 34 per cent of average income (i.e. less than OA in Figure 13.3).

[6] On the assumption that one-third of the population was receiving conditional benefits, the cost of the conditional and unconditional benefits would be $33\frac{1}{3}$ per cent of 40 per cent plus $66\frac{2}{3}$ per cent of 20 per cent $= 26\frac{2}{3}$ per cent of total income. This together with the 15 per cent needed for other public expenditure would require a tax revenue of approximately 42 per cent of total income.

2   Like the modified social dividend, it may do little to benefit those above
    but close to the supplementary benefit level. This only applies in the case
    of those in employment – in contrast to the modified social dividend
    scheme – but it may actually leave some persons earning unusually low
    wages somewhat below the poverty level.
3   It raises the administrative problem of distinguishing between those
    who are out of work because they are prevented from working by un-
    employment, sickness or other recognised cause and those who are not
    in fact willing to work.

4   A NEW BEVERIDGE SCHEME

We turn finally to a different general approach to the problem. This approach
does not involve merging social security and the income tax into a single
composite scheme, but is rather based upon a return to the principles of the
Beveridge Report of 1942 combined with modifications of the income tax
which will harmonise it with a revised social security scheme.

The Beveridge principles may be summarised under three heads:

1   The payment of social security benefits to those who are unemployed,
    sick, retired from work or otherwise incapacitated, on scales sufficient
    to meet the minimum needs of a single adult or of a married couple.
2   The payment of unconditional family allowances in respect of all children,
    on a scale sufficient to meet their minimum needs.
3   The provision of a system of means-tested benefits as a safety net to
    meet those infrequent occasions when for some special reason principles
    1 and 2 failed to maintain a level of income adequate to meet minimum
    needs.

The criterion of minimum needs is normally taken as being that which is set
by what Parliament considers to be the appropriate level for supplementary
benefit (previously national assistance). This concept of minimum needs can
change and is clearly a relative one. As the figures in Table 13.1 illustrate, the

Table 13.1   *Benefits as a percentage of average weekly earnings (figures for
single adult males)*

Year	Supplementary benefit or national assistance[a]	Sickness or unemployment benefit
1950	22	17
1960	22	17
1970	25	17
1976	23	16

[a] Including an average allowance for rent and rates.

supplementary benefit scale (inclusive of an average allowance for rent and rates) has over the years more than maintained its relation to average earnings.

The main reasons why the existing system has not prevented poverty as measured by the scale of supplementary benefit are that the social security benefits under principle 1 above and the family allowances under principle 2 above have been below the criterion of minimum needs as measured by principle 3, and that the safety net under principle 3 provided by the supplementary benefit system has failed to catch all families because of low take-up.

The new Beveridge reform would involve a return to all three principles and an extension of the scheme to cope with problems that have become more important in the past thirty-five years. Basically, it would mean an up-rating of all social insurance benefits to the supplementary benefit level, the payment of child benefit at the supplementary benefit level, the extension of coverage (to one-parent families, the disabled, etc.) and the introduction of a home responsibility payment. The income tax system would be retained, but co-ordinated with the social security benefits (in particular the tax threshold would be raised to the supplementary benefit level).

There are many possible variants of particular provisions which may be adopted in a new Beveridge scheme – how to deal with the single parent family, what particular disabilities and incapacities to compensate with special social benefits, what treatment to give to a wife's earnings, and what particular changes to make in the income tax in order to harmonise it with the revised social security system. We shall discuss these problems later in this chapter. For the present limited purpose of illuminating the scheme's basic structure, most of these complications can be disregarded, since we are dealing only with Mr Smith, a single adult with no dependants and no income other than his earnings. We assume that he obtains a social insurance benefit which is adequate to provide him with his needs of 40 per cent of average earnings if he is out of work, and that if he is in work he receives a personal tax allowance of 40 per cent of average earnings.

On these assumptions, with a basic rate of income tax of 40 per cent,[7] Mr Smith's position under the new Beveridge arrangements is illustrated in Figure 13.4. If he is in work he will need to earn 40 per cent of average earnings to keep himself out of poverty, and from this point on he will begin to pay a net amount in tax.

If the new Beveridge arrangements are compared with the two-tier social dividend, one similarity and one difference may be noted. The difference consists in the fact that, whereas the two-tier system gives a relatively low unconditional benefit to those in work but taxes the whole of their earnings, the new Beveridge scheme provides no such unconditional benefit. It makes

---

[7] In this case 70 per cent of income will be taxable. At a tax rate of 40 per cent this will raise 28 per cent of total income in tax. Of this 15 per cent is assumed to be needed to finance other public expenditure, leaving 13 per cent which is approximately the amount needed to cover the $33\frac{1}{3}$ per cent of the population receiving a benefit of 40 per cent of average income ($33\frac{1}{3}$ per cent of 40 per cent = $13\frac{1}{3}$ per cent).

up for this in part by maintaining in the income tax arrangements a tax allowance which permits a first slice of earnings to be kept tax-free, but it is inherently less generous and more open to objection on this account. The similarity is that in both cases there must be administrative machinery for distinguishing between (i) those who are eligible for the full rate of social benefit because they are prevented or excused from working by sickness,

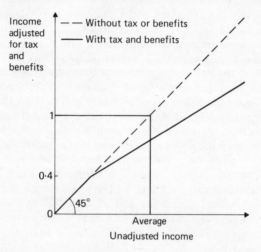

Fig 13.4   The income effect of a new Beveridge scheme

involuntary unemployment, old age, etc., and (ii) those who are not so prevented or excused and therefore do not qualify for any benefit under the new Beveridge scheme or qualify only for the lower unconditional benefit under the two-tier system. This machinery may, however, be different, if only in that the new Beveridge scheme may well retain some element of the rules that make the receipt of some of the benefits conditional upon previous payments of national insurance contributions.

THE FOUR SCHEMES COMPARED

No scheme can meet perfectly all the objectives set out at the beginning of this chapter. The full social dividend is effective, simple to understand and administer, but the basic rate of tax is likely to be so high as to affect incentives over a wide range and to give rise to political difficulties. The other schemes involve lower basic rates of tax at the expense of greater administrative complexity and other disadvantages. The modified social dividend/ minimum income guarantee shifts the incentive problem to the lower end of the scale; the two-tier and new Beveridge schemes are likely to create disincentives to entering the labour force. The modified social dividend is open to the criticism that it does little for those above but close to the supplementary benefit level; the two-tier and new Beveridge schemes do less for the low paid worker.

The final choice must therefore involve a trade-off between conflicting objectives. The position taken by the Committee is that the full social dividend with a high basic rate of tax is unlikely to attract sufficient political support for it to be worth considering further. In the case of the modified social dividend, the high rate of tax on the first band is considered to have potentially serious disincentive effects and to introduce major administrative difficulties. In view of this, the two schemes considered in more detail in the next section are the two-tier social dividend and the new Beveridge schemes.

SECTION II

DETAILS OF THE TWO-TIER SOCIAL DIVIDEND AND NEW BEVERIDGE SCHEMES

In the previous section we considered the schemes purely as 'ideal types'. Any actual legislation must, however, consider the details of the schemes and the transition from the present system. Of the two schemes considered more fully here, the new Beveridge (NB) is perhaps closest to the existing structure; it may indeed be seen as a natural evolution of the existing national insurance together with a rationalisation of the overlap with the tax system. The two-tier social dividend (TTSD) scheme would be a more radical departure; however, the tax credit scheme set out in the Green Paper of 1972,[8] and examined by a Select Committee, may be seen as a step in that direction. The credits, which would have replaced tax allowances, would have been equivalent to the unconditional dividend; and the retention of national insurance benefits would have corresponded to the second tier of dividend. In what follows, a number of the administrative details are based on those set out in the Green Paper and in the evidence to the Select Committee.

Some of the most important operational problems with the two schemes are considered below.

ENTITLEMENT

Both schemes relate the benefit received to employment status, and for this purpose individuals may be divided into the following three main classes:

1   Individuals below retirement age and in full time employment. We label such persons as being *in work* or I.
2   (a) Individuals exempt from work because of incapacity due to sickness or other forms of invalidity or because of being over the retirement age.
    (b) Individuals available for work but unemployed (where availability for work is subject to administrative tests such as signing on and accepting offers of suitable employment).

---

[8] Proposal for a Tax Credit System, Cmd 5116, HMSO, 1972.

We designate persons in categories (a) and (b) as *eligible for benefit* or E.

3 Persons below retirement age who may not seek paid work, e.g. because they have independent means from investment income or because they are supported (e.g. a wife by her husband). We designate such persons as *not seeking paid work* or N.

If this broad categorisation were used for the determination of the legitimacy of claims to benefits, there would be three implications which should be noted.

(1) This classification is much less detailed than that at present embodied in the national insurance system. The retirement pension, for example, is not strictly an old age pension. Between the ages of 65 and 70 it is subject to a retirement condition, which is enforced by the earnings rule by which the pension is reduced if earnings exceed a certain level. Similarly, the receipt of pensions and other benefits is dependent on contribution conditions. The measures which would be necessary to restore something corresponding to the present combination of benefits may be treated as later complications of the system.

(2) The three categories I, E and N make no distinction between the sexes in the determination of claims to benefit. The present UK system in fact makes many such distinctions. For example, in the case of unemployment benefit an unemployed man with a non-working wife to support will obtain the scale of benefit appropriate to a married couple; but a married woman who is unemployed may qualify for unemployment benefit (if she has paid full contributions) in her own right normally at a rate of £7·80 as compared with the rate for a man or single woman at £11·10. She may get the man's rate of £11·10 if the husband is (i) entitled to an invalidity pension, retirement pension or any unemployability supplement or allowance, or (ii) is incapable of self-support. It may be questioned whether in this day and age of equal treatment for men and women it is appropriate to distinguish in this way between the sexes.

(3) In the category N we have included a person who stays at home and does not seek work, whether or not he or she has children or other dependants in need of care at home. We have not included a housewife who stays at home to look after a family of children as being eligible for benefit (E). There is, however, a very real and relevant distinction in status between, for example, the young wife without children who elects to retire from work to keep house for her husband and the young mother who retires from work because there are young children at home needing care and attention. Whether or not the N–E distinction is the best way to deal with this difference of status is a question to which we shall return when discussing the treatment of children and of other dependants needing care in the home.

THE SINGLE ADULT

On the basis of the simple categorisation of individuals into I, E and N status, the treatment of Mr Smith, our single adult without dependants, is clear. He has a claim to conditional social dividend or social insurance benefit if he is

E; he has no such claim if he is I or N. But when considering the treatment of more complicated family or household groups – of married couples with or without children or other dependants needing home care, or of single parent families – the appropriate qualifications for claims to conditional benefits are by no means so clear, even if the simple categorisation of individuals into the three classes I, E and N is accepted.

THE MARRIED COUPLE

Let us turn then to the treatment of married couples with and without children under the two alternative schemes. The first question is to determine the basic benefit scales for married couples and for children as well as for single adults. The object of the schemes is to prevent families from falling below a stated poverty level, which we take to be represented by the scale of supplementary benefits. The precise scale has been described in Appendix 5.1, section 5; but for the purpose of illustrative exposition we take the following hypothetical scale:

	£ per week
Single adult	16
Married couple	24
Each child	4

This scale is a simplification in many ways. It does not differentiate between short term and long term benefits; it does not relate the scale of support payments for a child to the age of the child; and it does not refer to the problem of rents and rates. As explained in Chapter 5, with the present chaotic conditions in the housing market, the cost of rent and rates varies so much that supplementary benefits are paid on a fixed scale to cover needs other than housing costs, but the addition needed to meet the cost of rent and rates is assessed separately case by case. For the immediate purpose we proceed as if a scale which covered an average figure for rent and rates would meet all needs.

This scale can be taken as representing the main social benefits which would be paid conditionally under an NB scheme and a TTSD scheme. The two schemes are not, of course, identical. The NB scheme is likely to take account of a wider variety of circumstances when determining the case for benefit, and some linking of benefits to contributions may well be retained. For present purposes the structure of benefits under the two schemes may, however, be treated as being broadly the same.

The main difference is that the TTSD scheme would involve the payment of the unconditional social dividend, which we illustrate with the scales in Table 13.2.

We assume that the support for a child remains the same whether the parents are receiving unconditional or conditional benefits, but that for a single adult or a married couple the unconditional benefit is half the conditional benefit.

It remains, then, to decide which married couples would qualify for conditional benefit on the basis of our I, E and N categorisation of individuals. The answer is not in every case obvious, since one spouse may be in one category and the other in a different category. It is necessary to ask what combinations of individual categories would be eligible for a married couple's conditional benefit.

Table 13.2   *Conditional and unconditional benefits (in £s per week)*

Unit	Conditional benefits	Unconditional benefits
Single adult	16	8
Married couple	24	12
Child	4	4

It is clear that where neither partner is eligible for benefit (E), conditional benefit should not be paid; this covers categories II, NN and IN. It is equally clear that where both partners are eligible for benefit, conditional benefit should be paid; this covers the category EE. This leaves the categories IE and NE, where one but only one of the partners is eligible for benefit. Table 13.3 gives benefits to households one of whose members is E on the basis that a couple have benefits of three-quarters the sum of their individual benefits. This gives an EE household one and a half times the benefit of an E individual, which is consistent with the relationship between the benefits of a single adult and of a married couple as shown in Table 13.2.

Table 13.3   *Rates of benefit for married couples (in £s per week)*

Category	TTSD scheme	NB scheme
1 II	12	0
2 EE	24	24
3 NN	12	0
4 IN	12	0
5 IE	18	12
6 NE	18	12

The appropriateness of the benefit rates in lines 5 and 6 raises difficult issues, which are illustrated in the following examples.

The case in which one spouse is in work (I) and the other is eligible for benefit (E) might arise where both spouses had been in work and one of them – let us assume the one earning the chief part of the joint income – became unemployed or sick. If no conditional benefit were paid, the couple might be in serious need. On the other hand, a situation might arise of a wife becoming unemployed whose husband was earning a high income. It might seem excessive in such a case to pay the couple the full unconditional benefit.

The case in which one spouse is eligible for benefit (E) and the other is a non-worker (N) is perhaps the most troublesome of all. It might occur as the result of the loss of employment by a man who was earning a good wage and whose wife was at home keeping house. The immediate needs of a couple in such a case would be as great as those of a couple both parties of which were out of work. But should full benefit be paid to a couple one partner of which makes no effort to earn, although there are no children or other dependants needing care in the home? Moreover, the combination EN could arise starting from a couple with independent means, neither partner in which chose to seek paid work, if one of the partners registered for work but failed to obtain a post. It would appear extravagant to pay full benefit to such a couple; but on the other hand, if both parties had all along been registered and failed to obtain work they would presumably have been uncritically accepted as deserving benefit.

The present system has a number of provisions that deal with such cases:

1　The condition relating to the beneficiary's contribution record would disqualify an applicant who sought paid work for the first time; while an application for supplementary benefit by such a person with independent means would probably be ruled out on account of the wealth which had supported him thus far.
2　As noted above, the present system does not treat husbands and wives symmetrically; the E husband of an N wife receives the full benefit for an EE married couple (£24), whereas the E wife of an N husband receives the reduced benefit of £10.

All these provisions could be carried over into either the NB or the TTSD scheme, although the latter, if it were based on the final abolition of supplementary benefit, would probably have to err on the side of generosity. However, the asymmetrical treatment of husbands and wives might no longer be acceptable, in which case there would be two alternatives.

One solution would be to pay the intermediate benefits set out in lines 5 and 6 of Table 13.3. However, the full EE benefit rate of £24 is related to the minimum needs of a couple; thus to expect an NE couple to live on £18 (or £12 under the NB scheme) is not reasonable. A similar problem arises for the IE couple if one partner is in work (possibly part time) but earns very little. The present system gives the E husband in such a case the full £24 benefit (rather than an individual's £16) if the wife's earnings are below a specified level. While such a test could be incorporated into the NB scheme, at the cost of some extra administration, its complexity runs counter to the spirit of the TTSD scheme.

An alternative, also involving some extra administration, is to attempt to distinguish directly between principal and subsidiary earners rather than assuming all husbands to be principals and wives subsidiaries. In an EI couple the E party would be treated as the principal if either his or her previous earnings or his or her unemployment or sickness benefit over some specified previous period exceeded the working spouse's earnings. In an EN household the E party would be treated as the principal earner if either his or her previous earnings or his or her unemployment or sickness benefit over the specified previous period constituted more than half of the family's taxable income (or expenditure).

With this distinction we have to decide on the benefits for the four types of household covered by lines 5 and 6 of Table 13.3. In Table 13.4 a possible benefit structure for these cases is listed with the 'principal earner' first.

Table 13.4　*Benefits of principal and subsidiary earners (in £s per week)*

Category		TTSD scheme	NB scheme
5a	EI	20	16
5b	IE	16	8
6a	EN	24	20
6b	NE	12	8

Notice that in a number of cases a household in which the E party was initially classified as the principal earner would tend to progress from (a) to (b) as prolonged unemployment (or retirement) led to the party losing his 'principal earner' status. This feature seems reasonable in that, for example, the wife of a man who ceased to be able to work but was capable of doing quite a lot about the home might be expected to go out to work herself in due course, although the benefit over an initial period should not take this into account. In other TTSD variants it might be desired to build in explicitly a phasing-down of the benefits payable to EN households.

THE TREATMENT OF PARTICULAR GROUPS

We have described the general principles of entitlement to benefit; now we shall consider more concretely the application of entitlement to particular groups, especially those which could be classified as E or N. Under the present arrangements, this classification is based on a variety of information including:

> age
> medical evidence
> contribution record
> availability for employment
> period away from work

The procedure under the TTSD and NB schemes would presumably be similar, except that the former would not in its present form relate benefits to the contribution record. Indeed, the insurance principle is abandoned under this scheme. If the distinction between principal and subsidiary earner were to be embodied in the schemes, the classification of principal earner would require some earnings record, if not a contribution record. The compilation of such a record is part of the proposed state earnings-related pension system, and that information should be available for these schemes. Both schemes would, however, aim to extend coverage to groups not at present receiving national insurance. These include the following:

Long term unemployed
The dividend under the TTSD scheme would be payable to all those unemployed, so that the present twelve-month rule would cease to operate. Under the NB scheme the benefit would similarly be made unlimited in duration. But in both cases the unemployed erstwhile-principal earner might lose that status with the passage of time, as noted above.

Disabled
The social dividend under the TTSD scheme would be payable as a disability pension on the basis of medical evidence, with the rate possibly varying with the severity of disablement. The same would be achieved under the NB scheme by an extension of the non-contributory invalidity pension.

Single parent families
Under the TTSD scheme it would be possible to provide benefit to this group by treating the single parent as E, whether or not he or she worked. Under the NB scheme this could be done by introducing a home responsibility payment. Both of these possibilities are discussed below.

Self-employed
At present the self-employed cannot qualify for unemployment benefit. Under both schemes, benefit could be expanded to this group with appropriate conditions with regard to availability for work.

Other particular distinctions
In addition to determining eligibility, the characteristics listed above are used at present to determine the rates of benefit. Thus the retirement pension depends on the contribution record, date of retirement, age and past earnings. There are supplements for the blind, to assist mobility, for exceptional disablement, etc. Under the NB scheme these special provisions would presumably remain (although there is an argument for phasing out the short term earnings-related benefits), but the position under the TTSD scheme is less clear.

Finally, under each of the different categories listed above there is a considerable scope for varying the parameters of the scheme, and this may affect substantially the numbers categorised as E. The most obvious, and important, example is that of the minimum retirement age. There has been much recent discussion of this issue, and pressures to equalise treatment between men and women may lead to a uniform pension age. A common retirement age of 60 would, however, add very considerably to the cost of the conditional benefits. Other examples of parameters which affect eligibility are the grading of disability, waiting periods for benefit, age limits for child benefits, residence requirements, etc.

CHILDREN AND HOME RESPONSIBILITY PAYMENTS

We turn next to the treatment of children. It was one of the principles of the original Beveridge Report that family allowances should be paid on an adequate scale unconditionally in respect of (i) all children except the first in families where the father was in work, and (ii) all children in other families. Since that time, public thinking has moved in the direction of a unified child benefit combining both family allowances and tax allowances, payable for all children. This was embodied in the tax credit proposals and has now been enacted in the Child Benefit Act 1975. Both the TTSD and the NB schemes incorporate this principle, which we illustrate by assuming that a benefit of £4 per week is paid in respect of each child – although there would be nothing to prevent the adoption of the arrangement whereby the amount of the benefit depended upon the age of the child, on the grounds that the support of an older child involves more expense than that of a younger child.

There remains, however, the question referred to earlier, namely whether an adult who needs to make arrangements to look after children or other dependants needing home care should or should not be treated as eligible for benefit (E). Such a treatment would, for example, mean that a couple with children or other dependants in need of home care and with the husband in work would be treated as IE, whether the wife was also in work and making other arrangements for the necessary home care or whether she was herself staying at home to provide the care. With the arrangements for IE suggested in Table 13.3, both such groups would receive the intermediate benefit which is there proposed under the TTSD scheme. The treatment of an adult with dependants needing home care as E could also provide help under the TTSD scheme for the single parent family. The parent would qualify as E whether he or she arranged to go out to work or to stay at home, and he or she would therefore qualify for the adult unconditional benefit in addition to any child or other benefit. The couples with children or other dependants needing home care who would not gain under this arrangement would be those who would in any case have received the full conditional benefit (EE). This result might be acceptable if the child benefits were on an adequate scale and if both or at least one of the parents were able-bodied and qualified as E because of involuntary unemployment. But if both parents were classed as E because they themselves were sick or incapacitated, there would remain an unfilled need for aid to look after the dependants, which would need special arrangements for its satisfaction.

In the case of the NB scheme, the provision for those who have care of children or other dependants would be met not by treating them as E, but by introducing a special benefit, which we shall call a *home responsibility payment*. This benefit would be paid to all families in which there were children or other dependants needing home care, except those where the social insurance benefit included a dependent's allowance for the wife (EE).[9] In the case of children such a benefit could presumably be paid simply by paying an addition to the child benefit payable for the eldest dependent child in the family,[10] and it might be better presented in this way. The payment for the care of adult dependants would then be a separate benefit, a development of the present invalid care allowance.

THE TAX TREATMENT OF BENEFITS

We turn now to the question of the tax treatment of incomes under the two alternative schemes of a TTSD and an NB arrangement.[11]

The first question is whether the benefits themselves should be taxable. There are in fact three ways in which a benefit may be given: as a tax allowance, as a non-taxable benefit and as a taxable benefit. The difference is shown in Table 13.5, which illustrates the case of a progressive rate of tax with a zero marginal tax rate for those below a tax threshold, a 40 per cent basic tax rate and a 60 per cent higher rate of tax. We examine the effect of

Table 13.5   *The tax treatment of social benefits*

Benefit for child support	Value (in £s) to taxpayer with marginal rate of tax of:		
	0%	40%	60%
Child tax allowance of £500	0	200	300
Untaxed child benefit of £200	200	200	200
Taxable child benefit of £333⅓	333⅓	200	133⅓

[9] Depending upon the scale at which the universal home responsibility payment was paid, it would be a matter for decision whether the payment would need to be made at a specially enhanced rate in the case of single parent families.

[10] And reducing the national insurance benefit appropriately.

[11] In this chapter we discuss the tax problems in terms of an income tax and not of a general expenditure tax. The main issues revolve around the proper treatment of tax-free allowances. The problems remain essentially unchanged whether it is a tax threshold for an income tax or a tax threshold for an expenditure tax that is being considered.

such a progressive tax upon three different ways of giving such support for a dependent child as would in all three cases be worth £200 a year (i.e. approximately £4 a week) to the basic rate taxpayer.

It can be seen that the tax allowance method gives no help to those whose income is in any case below any existing tax threshold and gives more help to the higher rate taxpayer than to the basic rate taxpayer. The untaxed benefit (e.g. as proposed in the Child Benefit Act 1975) gives the same help to all taxpayers. The taxable benefit gives more help to the low rate taxpayer than to the higher rate taxpayer.

If a move is made from the present position towards a TTSD or NB arrangement, there is a strong case for making the benefits taxable. An essential feature of both schemes is to raise the conditional benefits to levels which are sufficient to maintain persons who have no other income and to pay these sums without means tests to all persons who qualify by the status of involuntary unemployment, sickness, old age, etc. This implies paying these benefits on a considerably more generous scale than at present to all who are in the qualifying categories, regardless of their other means. Subjecting the benefits to a progressive income tax would automatically apply to them that degree of 'means test' which is embodied for all citizens for all purposes in the progressive schedule of direct taxation.

In so far as social benefits are paid for the purpose of putting a floor to incomes in order to prevent poverty, this case for taxing benefits is incontestable. Those who are above the tax threshold (on the assumption that the tax threshold is at an adequate level) will not be in poverty and should be subjected to the income tax test of means on their benefits.

In the case of the present child benefits, which are currently untaxed, there is an argument on grounds of horizontal equity for continuing their exemption from tax, in so far as such benefits are regarded not only as one means for setting a floor for the avoidance of poverty but also as a means of discriminating at all levels of income between the capacity to pay tax of families with and of families without children to support. It is possible to take two views on the question whether present child benefits should be taxable; but in what follows we treat child benefits as being exempt from tax.

With a TTSD scheme there are no personal income tax allowances. The unconditional social dividends take the place of such personal tax allowances, and all income is subject to tax. If tax started at a basic rate of 40 per cent, then it would make no difference to anyone other than the higher rate taxpayers whether benefits were paid free of tax or whether they were paid at a rate grossed up for the standard rate of tax and were then subject to tax – whether in the example of Table 13·5 tax-free child benefits of £200 or taxable child benefits of £333⅓ were paid. The higher rate taxpayers would, however, be affected. Taxable benefits would presumably be paid in the first place subject to deduction of tax at the source at the basic rate. In the example of Table 13.5 the taxpayer would receive only £200 in cash after deduction of £133⅓ tax; the basic rate taxpayer would simply retain the £200, but the higher rate taxpayer's liability to higher rate tax could be assessed on the whole benefit of £333⅓.

THE TAX UNIT

TAX UNIT WITH THE TTSD SCHEME

With the TTSD scheme the definition of the *tax unit* (discussed in more detail in Chapter 18) would make no difference if all incomes were taxed at the same basic rate. Since, in this case, all earned or investment income would be taxable at the same rate without any personal allowances, it would make no difference whether each individual were assessed to tax separately or whether the husband and wife were treated as a unit with their incomes combined into a single aggregate figure for tax purposes. With a progressive tax schedule the definition of the tax unit would still make an important difference to the higher rate taxpayers, since the joint assessment of the aggregate of husband's and wife's income might bring them into a higher range of marginal tax rates than would be applicable if each individual partner's income were taxed separately. At the lower end of the income scale where taxpayers do not pay more than the basic rate of tax it is the treatment of what may be called the *benefit unit* which corresponds to the treatment of the tax unit. If the married couple's unconditional benefit is only one and a half times that of an individual's unconditional benefit, this corresponds in principle to taxing the couple as a single unit with a married couple's tax allowance equal to one and a half times the single person's tax allowance. Since this chapter is concerned only with the treatment of those at the lower end of the income scale and since the outcome is simply determined for such persons by the determination of the scales of net-of-tax benefits (which we have already discussed at length), we do not pursue the tax arrangements further at this point.

TAX UNIT WITH AN NB SCHEME

With an NB scheme, however, the treatment of the tax unit, as well as the scale of net-of-tax benefits, can make an important difference to those at the lower end of the scale as well as to the higher rate taxpayers. There are in this case no unconditional benefits at the lower end of the income scale; there are, however, personal tax allowances. It is therefore a matter of concern at the lower end of the income scale whether, for example, husband's and wife's income are treated separately each with an individual tax allowance or whether they are jointly assessed with a single tax allowance for the married couple. In the design of an NB arrangement, therefore, the issues determining the choice and treatment of the tax unit must be taken into account.

We shall consider these issues at length in Chapter 18, where we point out the difficulty – indeed the impossibility – of finding a tax unit treatment which satisfies simultaneously all the criteria by which it might be hoped to judge the desirability of the system. We survey in Chapter 18 a large number of possible arrangements, three of which we select for further consideration and which we call: (A) A Radical Modification of the Present System, (B) Partial Income Splitting, and (C) a Partial Quotient System.

(A)   *The radical modification of the present system*

This would involve abolishing the married man's tax allowance and substituting the payment of a social benefit, namely the home responsibility payment, to those who were responsible for looking after dependants needing home care. With this system the partners of a married couple would be separately assessed on their earnings, with a single person's tax allowance to be set against each set of earnings, while the investment incomes of both partners would be aggregated and added to the earnings of the principal earner for tax purposes.

(B)   *Partial income splitting*

This would also imply the separate assessment of each partner's earnings, with a single person's tax allowance to be set against each set of earnings. The investment income of both partners would be aggregated, but instead of all being added to the income of the principal earner it would be split in two with one-half allocated to each partner for tax purposes. Moreover, unlike system A, the single person's tax allowance would in general be restricted for use only against earned income; no such allowance would be permitted against investment income.

(C)   *Partial quotient system*

This would aggregate the earnings and the investment incomes of the two partners into one single taxable income, but would allow the personal tax allowance and all the subsequent brackets for higher rates of tax to be one and a half times as generous as those applied to the income of a single individual. The partners would, however, have the option of being assessed separately on their earnings, with a single person's tax allowance against each set of earnings; but in this case they would pay the same rate of tax on any investment income as they would have paid if the option of separate assessment of earnings had not existed.

The different treatments of the tax unit can have important effects upon the tax liabilities of those who are charged to higher rates of tax; and (as explained in Chapter 18) these effects on those liable to higher rates of tax raise a number of difficult problems. But we are not concerned in this chapter with that aspect of the tax unit problem; we are considering the appropriate treatment for the lower end of the income scale where taxpayers will not find themselves paying higher rates of tax under any tax unit scheme. Our concern here is with the treatment of the personal tax allowances. Should such allowances be set only against earned incomes? Should husband's and wife's incomes be separately assessed, each with a single person's tax allowance? Or should there be a different personal tax allowance for a married couple, such as the existing married man's allowance or the personal allowance inflated by a factor of one and a half under the partial quotient system (system B above)?

With the inevitable diversity of treatment connected with the scale of benefits for married couples in different circumstances and with and without dependent children, together with the rules determining the scale and conditions of use of the personal tax allowance, the outcomes are bound to be somewhat complicated. Some of the salient features under the three different tax-unit regimes being considered are illustrated in Table 13.6 in Appendix 13.1. The outcomes illustrated in that table are based on the following assumptions:

1   The scale of benefits for married couples of £0, £12 and £24 per week is as described in Table 13.3.
2   The basic rate of income tax is 40 per cent.
3   A non-taxable child benefit of £4 per week is paid in respect of each dependent child.
4   A home responsibility payment at the grossed-up value of £6$\frac{2}{3}$ per week is paid without exception to all couples responsible for one or more dependants needing home care.
5   An adult who stays at home to look after one or more dependants needing home care is treated as not seeking paid work (N).
6   All social benefits other than child benefits are taxable and are treated as the earned income of the recipient, the home responsibility payment being treated as earnings of the partner with the otherwise lower earnings.
7   The personal tax allowance for a single adult is at the same level (in our examples £16 per week) as the supplementary benefit for a single adult.

It can be seen that, as far as basic rate taxpayers are concerned, earnings are treated similarly under tax unit systems A and B, each partner being taxed separately with a separate personal allowance of £16 per week against his or her earnings.

Some of the important results illustrated by Table 13.6 in Appendix 13.1 are as follows.

Consider first a couple without dependants needing home care. If they are receiving no benefit they must have a net income of £24 per week to keep them out of poverty. Under scheme C their tax threshold is between £24 (on single earnings or investment income) and £32 (on equal earnings). Thus any given income of £24 will be tax-free. Under schemes A and B, £24 earned equally would be tax-free; but if the £24 were earned by one party the excess over £16 would be taxable, so that £29$\frac{1}{3}$ would be needed to take the couple out of poverty. Under scheme A an investment income of £29$\frac{1}{3}$ would also suffice; but under B it would all be taxed, making £40 necessary.

If the couple received the intermediate benefit of £12 per week, this would be treated as the earnings of one of the parties. The couple would now need £12 net to keep them out of poverty, and under scheme C any income up to £12 would be tax-free. However, under schemes A and B, while £12 earned by the non-beneficiary would be tax-free the beneficiary's personal allowance would be exhausted by earning £4 on top of the benefit of £12. Thus (assuming that no earnings rule would prevent it) the beneficiary would have to earn £17$\frac{1}{3}$ to lift the couple out of poverty. In case A, if neither party worked, investment income would be attributed to the beneficiary and £17$\frac{1}{3}$ would therefore be necessary; in case B, all the investment income would be taxed and £20 would be required.

If the couple received the full benefit of £24 per week, then under all the schemes they would need nothing else to keep them out of poverty.

A family with dependent children would be eligible (provided they were not in receipt of full benefits of £24 per week) for a home responsibility payment grossed up from £4 to £6$\frac{2}{3}$ and for tax-free child benefits of £4 per child. The receipt of the home responsibility payment in all cases would reduce the amount of other income that families in receipt of benefit of £0 or £12 would have to command in order to keep themselves above the poverty level; but the extent of this reduction would depend upon the characteristics of the other income and of the tax unit regime, in the ways illustrated in Table 13.6 in Appendix 13.1.

THE COST OF A NEW BEVERIDGE SCHEME

The cost of a full NB scheme would inevitably be heavy; but it would be greatly affected by the choice of tax unit and the consequential treatment of personal tax allowances and the home responsibility payment. Estimates given in Appendix 13.2 suggest that the cost might range from £2,000 million to £3,600 million a year. To give a general indication of the implication of these costs, they would need for their finance a rise in the basic rate of income tax from 33 per cent to 37 or 40 per cent. The NB scheme consists, however, of a number of separate elements, which could be introduced at whatever speed political and economic conditions made possible.

RELATION WITH MEANS-TESTED BENEFITS

The aim of both the TTSD and NB schemes is to reduce dependence on means-tested benefits and, if possible, to abolish such schemes. In considering the extent to which this would be possible it is useful to classify such schemes into three groups:

1   Those involving regular benefits related to family characteristics which are known to those administering the social benefits (e.g. under the existing national insurance scheme).
2   Those involving regular benefits related to family circumstances which require additional information (e.g. on rent or rates).
3   Those involving once-for-all or infrequent benefits, such as legal aid.

The first category, which is typified by family income supplement, is the easiest to replace; and indeed the abolition of family income supplement is envisaged under both the TTSD and NB schemes. The combination of child benefits, home responsibility payment and new benefits for single parent families should make all families better off.[12] In the same way higher child benefits for children of school age would allow the replacement of means-tested free school meals.

The third category is the next easily replaced, in that the national insurance scheme already makes once-for-all payments such as maternity benefit and the death grant. In the case of benefits such as legal aid, prescription charges, dental and optical benefits, it is not, however, clear that the income test should be abolished.

The second category causes the most difficulty. Rent and rate rebates in particular are major factors contributing to the higher implicit marginal rates of tax, and they would not mesh easily with the schemes described above. Their abolition, however, would mean that many families with above-average rents would remain below the poverty line, despite the new TTSD or NB benefits. The resolution of this problem depends on the measures taken to reform the housing market. As we have already made clear in Chapter 11, a full solution of the tax problems relating to housing is difficult in the absence of important changes in housing policy other than tax changes, matters which we have regarded as being beyond the scope of the Committee.

ADMINISTRATION

We shall discuss in Chapter 22 the administrative aspects of the tax arrangements which would be involved in carrying out the proposals for an NB scheme. As far as the administration of benefits are concerned, in the case of the NB scheme the extension of benefits is a natural evolution of the present system. Thus the incorporation of the self-employed within the provisions for unemployment benefit could be achieved through the present test of 'availability for work'. The possible supplementation of the home responsibility payment in the case of single parent families (see p. 287 above) would mean that criteria for eligibility would have to be established and that the detailed scheme would have to cover such points as the application of an earnings rule, if this were considered desirable. Such problems do not, however, appear to be very different in magnitude from those met when the scheme has been extended on other occasions.

To the extent that the structure of benefits under a TTSD scheme was less complex than at present, there would be some simplification in their administration.

In both cases, as we have shown above, it would be possible to abolish a number of means-tested schemes, with consequential administrative simplifications and savings of cost.[13]

---

[12] The importance of single parent families in this context should be emphasised; in December 1975 they accounted for 53 per cent of family income supplement beneficiaries.

[13] See Appendix 13.3 for an analysis of the costs of administering social security benfits.

CONCLUSIONS

We have considered the principles of four different types of scheme for remedying the anomalies (described in Chapter 5) which result from the present interplay between the tax system and the system of social security. These four types of scheme are a full social dividend, a modified social dividend or minimum income guarantee, a two-tier social dividend (TTSD) and a 'new Beveridge' (NB) scheme.

We have examined the last two of these schemes in some detail, and as a result of that examination we are of the opinion that reform should proceed along the lines of an NB scheme. This implies: (i) raising tax thresholds to avoid the increasing threat of overlap between the levels of supplementary benefit and the levels of income at which tax may start to be charged; (ii) setting the regular national insurance and similar benefits at levels comparable to supplementary benefit levels; (iii) relying on child benefits for the support of children; (iv) submitting social benefits other than child benefits to tax; and (v) thus enabling a host of present means-tested benefits to be discontinued.

These reforms are found to be costly; but there is one important change in the tax system which could help to reduce their cost. At present, where both partners in a married couple are earning a full single person's tax allowance may be claimed against the wife's earnings and, in addition, the husband may claim the enlarged married man's allowance against the rest of the couple's income. We believe that in any case this duplication of allowances should be discontinued so that at the most two single person's allowances could be claimed against the couple's total income. A more radical reform would be to abolish the married man's allowance in all cases and also to permit the personal tax allowance to be set only against earned income and not against investment income. In this case it would be necessary (i) to treat taxable social benefits as earned income against which personal tax allowances could be claimed, (ii) to allow persons above, say, 40 years of age to set their personal allowance against investment income as well as against earned income, and (iii) to pay a social benefit, which we have called a home responsibility payment, to those persons who have children or other dependants needing home care.

We are in favour of this more radical tax treatment of the married couple as a contribution to the cost of an NB scheme. A full NB scheme would involve an additional cost which in present conditions could be met by an addition of four to seven percentage points to the basic rate of income tax (i.e. by a rise from 33 per cent to 37 or 40 per cent), the extent of the rise depending upon the tax treatment of the married couple. The NB reforms could, however, be carried out in a piecemeal fashion, stage by stage, at whatever speed political and economic conditions permitted.

Appendix 13.1 Three Tax-unit Treatments of the Married Couple in the New Beveridge Scheme

Table 13.6 illustrates some of the most important effects of three different tax-unit treatments of the married couple in the NB scheme of social benefits. The three treatments are what in Chapter 18 are called: (A) the radical modification of the present system; (B) partial income splitting; and (C) the partial quotient system. The natures of these three schemes are discussed in more detail in Chapter 18; those of their characteristics which are relevant for the NB arrangements for persons at the lower end of the income scale are described on page 290 of Chapter 13. The following is a summary of the relevant provisions.

In schemes A and B earnings are taxed separately; a taxable home responsibility payment of £6$\frac{2}{3}$ per week is added to the lower earnings; and all other benefits (except the child benefits) are treated as part of the taxable earnings of the recipient.

In scheme A the investment income of both partners is added to the higher earnings, but in scheme B it is aggregated and split equally between the two partners. In scheme B, but not in scheme A, the personal allowance cannot be set against any investment income.

In scheme C there is a quotient of 1·5 with optional separate assessment of the partners' earned incomes, with the taxable home responsibility payment added to the lower earnings and with benefits (other than the child benefits) included in the taxable earnings of the recipients. Aggregated investment income is top-sliced under the quotient procedure (see Chapter 18, p. 389).

In all three schemes the child benefit of £4 per child per week but not the home responsibility payment of £6$\frac{2}{3}$ per week is non-taxable, the individual tax allowance is £16 per week, the tax rate is 40 per cent, and the benefit scale of £0, £12 and £24 per married couple per week is as set out in Table 13.3.

Appendix 13.2 Alternative Tax Units, the Cost of a New Beveridge Scheme and the Yield of 1 per cent on the Basic Rate of Income Tax

In this appendix we first consider the revenue implications of alternative tax unit treatments; then we use this as a basis for estimating the cost of an NB scheme; and thirdly, on this same basis we estimate the yield of 1 per cent on the basic rate of income tax (in 1976/77), which is used to convert other items into equivalent changes in the basic rate.

ALTERNATIVE TAX UNITS

We examine the same three possible treatments of the tax unit that have been used and described in Appendix 13.1, namely:

Treatment A: The radical modification of the present system
Treatment B: Partial income splitting
Treatment C: A partial quotient system

Table 13.6 *A new Beveridge scheme for married couples (in £s per week): (a) tax unit treatments A and B*

Benefit	Tax unit Treatment	Childless couple — Income at which tax starts	Childless couple — Income needed to avoid poverty	Couple with children — Income at which tax starts	Couple with children — Income needed to avoid poverty
0	A and B	16 earned by one alone 32 earned jointly and equally by both	$29\frac{1}{3}$ earned by one alone 24 earned jointly by both (neither over 16)	16 earned by principal earner $9\frac{1}{3}$ earned by subsidiary earner	$18\frac{2}{9}$ earned by one alone $17\frac{1}{3}$ earned jointly by both (if neither pays tax)
	A	16 unearned	$29\frac{1}{3}$ unearned	16 unearned	$18\frac{2}{9}$ unearned
	B	0 unearned	40 unearned	0 unearned	$28\frac{8}{9}$ unearned
12	A and B	16 earned by non-beneficiary 4 earned by beneficiary	12 earned by non-beneficiary $17\frac{1}{3}$ earned by beneficiary	$9\frac{1}{3}$ earned by non-beneficiary 4 earned by beneficiary	$5\frac{1}{3}$ earned by non-beneficiary $6\frac{2}{3}$ earned by beneficiary
	A	0–4 unearned	$17\frac{1}{3}$ unearned	0–4 unearned	$6\frac{2}{9}$ unearned
	B	0 unearned	20 unearned	0 unearned	$8\frac{8}{9}$ unearned
24	A and B	4 earned by one alone 8 earned jointly and equally by both	0	4 earned by one alone 8 earned jointly and equally by both	0
	A	4 unearned	0	4 unearned	0
	B	0 unearned	0	0 unearned	0

Table 13.6 (cont.) *A new Beveridge scheme for married couples:* (b) *tax unit treatment C*

Benefit	Tax unit treatment	Childless couple		Couple with children	
		Income at which tax starts	Income needed to avoid poverty	Income at which tax starts	Income needed to avoid poverty
0	C	24–32 earned depending on distribution between partners 24 unearned	24 earned 24 unearned	16 principal earner 9⅓ subsidiary earner 17⅓ unearned	17⅓ earned provided that neither is paying tax 17⅓ unearned
12	C	16–24 earned by non-beneficiary 4–12 earned by beneficiary 12 unearned	12 earned by non-beneficiary 12 earned by beneficiary 12 unearned	16 earned by non-beneficiary if also principal earner 9⅓ earned by non-beneficiary if also subsidiary earner 4 earned by beneficiary if also principal earner −2⅔ earned by beneficiary if also subsidiary earner[a] 5⅓ unearned	5⅓ earned if non-beneficiary is sole earner 6⅔ earned if beneficiary is sole earner 5⅓ unearned
24	C	4 earned by either partner 0 unearned	0	4 of earnings by either partner 0 unearned	0

[a] Partner with benefit of £12 and home responsibility payments at £6⅔ would already be £2⅔ above the £16 personal allowance against earned income.

Assumptions

1　The treatment of benefits and thresholds for alternative tax units are as set out in the main text of Chapter 13.
2　(a) All people in work (I) earn at least an individual's allowance.
　　(b) All people not working (N) receive at least an individual's allowance of investment income.
　　(c) All people who are exempt have no income apart from benefits, except EE (pensionable) households in which case one member is assumed to earn $A/4$ and one to have unearned income of $A/4$, where A is the basic individual personal tax allowance.
3　A long basic-rate tax band is retained, so that as a first approximation the tax system can be treated as linear.

Basic method
Benefits and thresholds are all expressed as multiples of the basic individual personal allowance A. If everyone pays tax at the margin at the same basic rate b, then net revenue R for other expenditure is given by

$$R = b(\Sigma Y + \Sigma B - \Sigma T) - \Sigma B \tag{1}$$

where ΣT is the sum of all effective tax allowances, ΣB is the sum of all benefits (gross) while ΣY is the sum of all other personal income. Equation 1 can be rewritten as

$$R = b(\Sigma Y - \Sigma T) - (1 - b)\Sigma B$$

$$= b(\Sigma Y - \Sigma T) - \Sigma B_n \tag{2}$$

where B_n is the net benefit.

The structure of benefits and tax allowances
Table 13.7 gives in tabular form an account of the structure of benefits which have been described in the main text of Chapter 13 for the three tax unit treatments A, B and C.

From the summations in the table, $\Sigma B_n = 14\cdot85A - 9\cdot35bA$ and $\Sigma T = 33\cdot8A$, $32\cdot8A$ and $36\cdot7A$ for tax unit treatments A, B and C respectively. Substituting these values in equation 2 yields

$$R = b\Sigma Y - 14\cdot85A - \begin{Bmatrix} 24\cdot5 \\ 23\cdot4 \\ 27\cdot4 \end{Bmatrix} bA \tag{3}$$

Revenue effects of changes in the tax unit
Since we are ignoring higher rates of tax, the partial quotient system C with its couple's allowance of $3A/2$ is very similar to the present system. On the tax side it differs only in that an II couple has an allowance of $2A$ rather than the present system's $5A/2$ (including wife's earned income allowance). Since there are 4·8 million II married couples, system C raises the tax base by £2·4A million.

More precisely, in 1976 the individual allowance was £735, which if doubled would be £1,470; while a married man's allowance was £1,085, which together with wife's earned income allowance becomes £1,820. Thus system C would have cut an II household's allowance by £350, adding £4·8 × 350 million = £1,680 million to

Table 13.7   *Benefits and effective allowances*

Group	Net benefit, B_n	Effective allowance (T) with tax unit treatment: A	B	C	Number (millions)	Present basic benefit gross (£ pa) rate	(£m) value
Children	$A/4$	0	0	0	14·8	78^a	593^b
Families[a]	$A/4$	0	0	0	7·2	52^c	374
Single persons:							
I	0	A	A	A	6·8	0	0
N	0	A	0	A	0·8	0	0
E	$A(1-b)$	A	A	A	5·1	816	4,162
Couples:							
II	0	$2A$	$2A$	$2A$	4·8	0	0
EE	$3A(1-b)/2$	$7A/4$	$7A/4$	$7A/4$	2·0	1,300	2,600
NN	0	A	0	$3A/2$	0·2	0	0
IN+NI	0	A	A	$3A/2$	5·3	0	0
IE	$A(1-b)/2$	$3A/2$	$3A/2$	$3A/2$	0·9	655	590
EI	$A(1-b)$	$2A$	$2A$	$2A$	0·4	1,300 ⎫	910
EN	$5A(1-b)/4^d$	A	A	$3A/2$	0·3	1,300 ⎭	
NE	$A(1-b)/2$	A	$A/2$	$3A/2$	0·05	655	33
Σ	$A(14·85-9·35b)$	$33·8A$	$32·8A$	$36·7A$	Population 55·4	—	9,262
					Cost of administration+FIS etc.		600
					Total cost		9,862

[a] £1·50 per week for second and subsequent children.
[b] $(14·8-7·2)\times1·5\times52$.
[c] £1·00 per week for each first child.
[d] Note that under tax unit treatments A and B part of this benefit is taxable as it is all attributed to the E individual whose allowance is only A.

the tax base. With a tax rate of 33 per cent this would raise revenue by £550 million. Against this must be set the possible cost of home responsibility payment, which is estimated in the section on costs below.

Table 13.7 shows that a move from the partial quotient system C to treatment A (or B) would enlarge the tax base by a further £2·9A (or £3·9A) million. For 1976, averaging the individual allowance of £735 with $\frac{2}{3}$ times the couple's allowance of £1,085 (= £723$\frac{1}{3}$), we take A = £730, so that the increase in the base is £2,117 million (or £2,847 million), worth £700 million (or £940 million) at a tax rate of 33 per cent.

COSTS OF A NEW BEVERIDGE SCHEME

The main costs of a new Beveridge scheme are due to three ingredients:

1 Raising tax thresholds and national insurance benefits to supplementary benefit levels.
2 Child benefits on a scale considerably higher than the new 1977 scheme.
3 Home responsibility payments to households which include dependent children or others needing care.

1 *Raising tax thresholds and national insurance benefits*

In 1976/77 the individual tax allowance was £735, while long term social benefits were £81 higher at £816. A couple's benefits, at £1,295, exceeded their tax allowance of £1,085 by £206. Thus raising tax allowances to benefit levels would be similar in cost to raising by £100, from £730 to £830, the allowance A in the effective allowance columns of Table 13.7. These effective allowances total £33·8A, £32·8A, and £36·7A for tax unit treatments A, B and C respectively and £39·1A for the present tax unit treatment. A rise of £100 in the allowance A in each case would, at a tax rate of 33 per cent, mean a loss of revenue of £1,120 million, £1,080 million, £1,210 million and £1,290 million respectively.

Raising national insurance benefits to the supplementary benefit level would be a much less costly operation. In 1976/77 unemployment and sickness benefits cost some £1,300 million. The rates were about 20 per cent below the long-term supplementary benefit levels, so that the cost of the rise would be some £260 million. But these payments would be taxable, subject to the higher tax thresholds for which allowance is made above, so that the net cost would be 67 per cent of £260 million = £170 million.

2 *Raising child benefits*

The present child benefit is £1 a week for the first eligible child and £1·50 for subsequent children. From Table 13.7 it can be seen that this averages out at £65 per child a year tax-free. We have suggested that the tax-free uniform benefit should be about one-quarter of the individual personal allowance: £830/4 = £208 a year or £4 a week. With 14·8 million eligible children receiving £208 instead of £65 a year, the additional cost would be £2,120 million. At £3 a week instead of £4 a week the cost would be £1,350 million (14·8 ×[156−65]).

3 *Home responsibility payments*

Taking A again as £830, a net home responsibility payment of $A/4$ as suggested in the main text of Chapter 13 would also be £208 a year or £4 a week. We have suggested that this benefit should be taxable, so at a tax rate of 33 per cent the gross home responsibility payment would be £310 a year. As we assume for the purpose of these estimates that the benefit is always taxed, we work with the net figure of £208. If the only eligible households were the 7·2 million with dependent children, the cost would be £1,500 million.

In 1976/77 the difference between a married man's allowance and a single person's allowance was £350. At the then basic rate of tax of 35 per cent this was worth £122·5 (or £2.36 a week) to the basic rate taxpayer. If the home responsibility payment were made only at this reduced rate solely to compensate those married couples who had dependants needing home care for the loss of the dependent wife's allowance, the cost would be 7·2 million × £122·5 = £880 million.

IMPLIED RATES OF TAX

1   Equation 3 on p. 298 can be used to estimate required rates of tax *b* given values
    of ΣY, *A* and *R*. In 1976 the income tax yielded £17 *bn* while the cost of the relevant
    benefits (see the last column of Table 13.7) was £10 *bn*, so that $R = 7bn$ while
    ΣY was £70 *bn* and *A* is taken to be £816 p.a. It then follows from 3 that $b =$
    41·4 per cent, 40·6 per cent and 43·6 per cent respectively – which should be
    compared to the 35 per cent rate then ruling.
2   Yield of 1 per cent on the basic rate. The present arrangements for the married
    women's earned income relief means that the effective tax base (original income+
    taxable benefits —allowances) is $70+9-39 = £50$ *bn*, so that 1 per cent on the
    basic rate would yield £500 million. From equation 3 this yield would be £500,
    £510 or £475 million under the alternative tax treatments – the less generous
    scale of allowances being largely offset by the increase of the personal allowances
    to supplementary benefit levels. In what follows it is assumed that 1 per cent on
    the basic rate yields £500 million.

SUMMARY

The above estimates are all made on the assumption that national insurance contributions, both employer's and employee's, continue as at present. In Chapter 17 we
discuss the effect of incorporating such charges into the general income tax or
expenditure tax.

The estimates are inevitably crude. In some ways they underestimate the cost
(e.g. we have allowed for the home responsibility payment only for families with
dependent children and have assumed in all cases that it will be paid net of tax),
but in other ways they are overestimates (e.g. there would under a new Beveridge
scheme be a reduction in the cost of a number of miscellaneous means-tested benefits).
But there is no reason to believe that they do not give a true picture of the order of
magnitude of the main cost changes.

These are summarised in Table 13.8. From this table comparisons can be made
between various combinations of tax unit changes and of elements of a new Beveridge
scheme. We illustrate with the following 'packages':

Package 1.
If the present tax unit treatment were maintained but all the new Beveridge elements,
including a full home responsibility payment of £4 a week, were nevertheless introduced, the cost would be £5,066 million, which (on the assumption of the yield of
1 per cent in the basic rate of tax being about £500 million) would need an increase
of some 10 percentage points in the basic rate of tax (i.e. from 33 to 43 per cent) to
cover the cost.

Package 2.
But to maintain the dependent wife's allowance and simultaneously to make a
home responsibility payment may properly be ruled out. Package 1 without a home
responsibility payment would cost £3,570 million (7 percentage points on the basic
rate of tax).

Package 3.
Another package, which would cost much the same as package 2, would be to move
from package 1 not by eliminating the home responsibility payment but by changing
to tax unit treatment A. This would mean eliminating the married man's allowance
and concentrating the whole of the savings of cost in making home responsibility

Table 13.8 *Costs of a new Beveridge scheme and tax unit changes (in £ millions a year)*

	Present treatment	*Tax unit treatment*		
Change required		*A*	*B*	*C*
Abolition of FIS	−14	−14	−14	−14
Change of tax unit treatment	0	−1,250	−1,490	−550
Raising tax threshold to supplementary benefit level	+1,290	+1,120	+1,080	+1,210
Raising national insurance benefits to supplementary benefit level	+170	+170	+170	+170
Raising child benefits to:				
£4 a week	+2,120	+2,120	+2,120	+2,120
£3 a week	+1,350	+1,350	+1,350	+1,350
Home responsibility payment of:				
£4 a week	(+1,500)	+1,500	+1,500	+1,500
£2.36 a week	(+880)	+880	+880	+880

payments to those couples with dependants needing home care. The cost of this package would be £3,650 million (7·3 percentage points on the basic rate of tax).

Package 4.
By moving from package 2 by changing from the present tax unit to tax unit treatment C (i.e. in effect by removing the duplication of married man's allowance with wife's earned income allowance), the cost would be reduced to £2,940 million (6 percentage points on the basic rate of tax).

Package 5.
The cheapest package shown on Table 13.8 would be to combine (i) tax unit treatment B (i.e. allowing only a single person allowance and only against that individual's earned income) with (ii) a home responsibility payment that merely replaced the 1976/77 value of the loss of the dependent wife's allowance for couples with dependants needing home care, and (iii) child benefits at £3 instead of £4 a week. In this case the cost would be £1,980 million (some 4 percentage points on the basic rate of tax).

Thus if solutions that give both a married man's tax allowance and a home responsibility payment are eliminated, there remain forms of a new Beveridge scheme and tax unit treatments whose revenue effects range from costs involving a rise of 4 percentage points, to costs involving a rise of 7 percentage points, in the basic rate of tax (i.e. rises from 33 per cent to between 37 and 40 per cent).

Appendix 13.3   The Costs of Administering Social Security Benefits

This appendix is a very preliminary approach to the problem of the relative costs of administering different forms of social security benefit. Data is lacking, and no attempt has been made, for example, to ensure the precise suitability or comparability of the definitions used, so that the results must be regarded as indicative rather than definitive.

THE CLASSIFICATION OF BENEFITS

Two distinctions must be drawn between all the various benefits: (i) whether centrally or locally administered, and (ii) whether means-tested or universal. The main benefits are set out under these categories in Table 13.9.

Table 13.9   *Classification of the main social security benefits*

	Centrally administered	*Locally administered*
Universal	National insurance benefits Family allowances (now child benefit scheme)	
Means-tested	Supplementary benefits Family income supplement	Rent rebates Rent allowances Rate rebates Free school meals

In total there are at least forty-six means-tested benefits, nineteen administered by the central government and twenty-seven by local authorities. The list continues to grow, the latest addition being the electricity discount scheme.

THE MEASUREMENT OF COSTS

These distinctions provide a framework for assessing the administrative costs of all the schemes. Published data on administrative costs is meagre, so that we have used various sources in an attempt to give a reasonably comprehensive picture. For comparative purposes the unit of measurement used is the costs of administration as a percentage of total benefits paid out. This measure has distinct limitations and is especially susceptible to changes in rates of benefit; e.g. if benefit rates were doubled overnight, other conditions remaining the same, the costs of administration would be halved. But this measurement of cost is probably the best that can be managed without very substantial work, and comparisons between different benefits on this basis are likely to be less misleading than comparing the cost of the same benefit over time.

TAKE-UP

A relevant factor in assessing administrative costs is take-up. Universal benefits can be assumed to be taken up more or less 100 per cent; the only means-tested benefit of which that is true is student education grants.

Take-up is relevant to costs in two senses. In the most fundamental assessment, costs must be viewed against effectiveness. A benefit of low take-up is one of low effectiveness. The appropriate basis for comparing the administrative costs of different forms of benefits would be the same level of take-up. Thus, it could be argued that the valid cost of a means-tested benefit to use in comparison with a universal benefit would be the cost at which the benefit was wholly taken up. For most means-tested benefits this would almost certainly represent a much higher figure of administrative cost, even as a percentage of benefit paid out; the marginal cost of finding the additional claimants could be expected to rise at an increasing rate as take-up approached 100 per cent. But it is not clear what effect small changes in take-up would have on costs measured as a percentage of benefits.

Table 13.10 shows national and local estimates of take-up in 1974/75. Local

Table 13.10   *Estimated take-up of some means-tested benefits (in %)*

Benefit	Official (national) estimate	Local estimate
Free school meals	80	76
Family income supplement	75	40
Supplementary benefit	75	50
Rent rebates	70–75	65
Rent allowances (furnished)	10	5
Rent allowances (unfurnished)	30–35	20
Rate rebates	62	35

Source: Means-Tested Benefits (National Consumer Council Discussion Paper, London, January 1977).

estimates fluctuate systematically at levels *below* the national estimates, and it is suggested in the Discussion Paper that national estimates should be treated as giving an optimistic picture of the situation. It is important to appreciate the numbers involved. For example, the 25 per cent who do not claim supplementary benefits number 895,000, which represents about 1,370,000 if their respective dependants are included as well. (The Supplementary Benefits Commission recently estimated that unclaimed supplementary benefit amounted to £200 million a year.) The 38 per cent figure for non-take-up of rate rebates represents 1,300,000 claims.

UNIVERSAL BENEFITS ADMINISTERED BY CENTRAL GOVERNMENT

National insurance benefits
Table 13.11 shows how over the life of the scheme the costs of administration have nearly halved, which may reflect changes in benefit rather than increased efficiency. Currently the costs of administration are under 4 per cent, but this is rather more than double the Inland Revenue costs of tax collecting.

Table 13.11   *Administrative costs of the national insurance fund*

Year	(1) Administrative costs (£ million)	(2) Total benefits (£ million)	(1) as % of (2)
1949/50	23·9	365·8	6·5
1954/55	26·6	496·6	5·4
1959/60	39·0	916·7	4·3
1964/65	53·6	1,407·8	3·8
1969/70	85·5	2,349·2	3·6
1972/73	124·7	3,340·3	3·7
1973/74	143·4	3,775·4	3·8

Source: Social Security Statistics 1974, Table 44·02, HMSO 1975.

Family allowances
Figures given in *Hansard* (July 1974) relating to the financial year 1972/73 are as follows:

	1972/73
Administrative costs	= £11·7 million
Total benefits	= £339 million
Administrative costs as % of total benefits	= 3·5%

MEANS-TESTED BENEFITS ADMINISTERED BY CENTRAL GOVERNMENT

Supplementary benefits
In 1972/73 the scheme cost £74·4 million and required 24,500 man years to run it, the cost representing 10·8 per cent of the total benefits (*Hansard*, July 1974). The figures given in the *Supplementary Benefits Commission Annual Report* 1975 are as follows:

	1975
Administrative costs	= £190 million
Total benefits paid	= £1,420 million
Administrative costs as % of total benefits	= 13·4%

Family income supplement
The following figures for 1972/73 and 1975 are given in *Hansard* (July 1974) and *Supplementary Benefits Commission Annual Report* 1975 respectively:

	1972/73	1975
Administrative costs	= £0·9 million	£1 million
Total benefits	= £10 million	£12 million
Administrative costs as % of total benefits	= 9%	8·3%

It is clear from these figures that the (means-tested) supplementary benefits cost three to three and a half times as much to administer as the (universal) national insurance fund; while the (means-tested) family income supplement costs about two and a half times as much to administer as the (universal) family allowances.

If the costs of administering supplementary benefit, as a percentage of benefits paid out, had been equal to those of administering national insurance benefits, there would have been a saving of administrative cost of £123 million in 1975 – sufficient to have paid for the implementation of the full child benefit scheme as originally envisaged.

The latest means-tested benefit scheme is expected to incur administrative costs broadly in line with those of other centrally administered means-tested schemes. As stated by Dr John A. Cunningham (*Hansard*, 14 February 1977), the provision for payments under the electricity discount schemes is £25 million and the expected costs are £2·5 million or 10 per cent of benefits paid out. This could easily prove to be an optimistic estimate as it does not cover any staffing costs, on the grounds that, in the words of the Parliamentary Under Secretary of State for Energy, 'the effect on staffing will be negligible'.

MEANS-TESTED BENEFITS ADMINISTERED BY LOCAL AUTHORITIES

Information on administrative costs of locally administered benefits is particularly scanty, and where figures have been obtained it must be remembered that local-authority accounting practices differ markedly. Several features should perhaps be noted for a true perspective on the reliability of any figures quoted:

1 Different departments within local authorities may deal with benefits; thus, rate and rent concessions may be administered by the Housing Department or by the Treasurer's Department. Within the department itself the three benefits – rate rebate, rent rebate and rent allowance – may be dealt with entirely separately or by an integrated process. (Some people receiving rate rebates will be receiving rent allowances.)
2 The degree of computerisation involved differs between authorities, as also the amount of detailed checking.
3 The costs of administration vary according to the level of overheads.
4 The unit of measurement used, namely administrative costs as a proportion of total benefit paid out, is probably even more susceptible at the local authority than at the central government level to variation according to the amount of benefits paid out.

Figures obtained from the Department of the Environment for 1975/76 are as follows:

Rent rebates (paid to council house tenants)

Average rebate paid out per week	= £2·87
Total rebates paid out (year)	= £134·3 million
Total administrative costs (year)	= £7 million
Administrative costs as % of total benefits	= 5·2%

Rent allowances (paid to private tenants)

Average allowance paid per week	= £2·80
Total allowance paid out (year)	= £27·1 million
Total administrative costs (year)	= £3 million
Administrative costs as % of total benefits	= 11·1%

Rate rebates

Average rate rebate (year)	= £26 (£25·4 – £26·4)
Average administrative cost per recipient (year)	= £4 (£3·40 – £4·40)
Administrative cost % of benefit	= 15·4% (13·4 – 16·7%)

A further guide to administrative costs is given by a study made by Brunel University in conjunction with the Department of the Environment into the administration of national rent rebate and allowance schemes. The study estimates the cost of running the schemes in four local authorities, which were specially investigated. The findings broadly confirm the Department of the Environment's figures above, although the estimates relate to 1974/75, not 1975/76. The average cost of administering rent rebates varied between £8 and £13 a year per tenant in receipt, which would make the administrative cost as a percentage of the benefit paid out about 6 per cent, assuming that the average amount of rebate paid out was similar to the Department's figure for January 1975 at £2·42. (The figure of £2·87 given above is the amount at mid 1976.) For rent allowances, with an average amount of allowance being paid of £2·30 per week, the administrative costs were estimated at between 13 and 19 per cent for the four local authorities.

For further evidence we approached several local authorities directly, to see whether they would have information on administrative costs available or whether they would be prepared to estimate figures for the work of the Committee. Only one was able to give the information in the required form. For this local authority, the cost of administering the rate rebate scheme was given as 13 per cent of the total cost of rate rebates; for rent rebates the figure was as low as 3·7 per cent; and for rent allowances the figure was 7·2 per cent.

All the evidence gathered for the means-tested benefits administered at the local level shows the rate rebate scheme emerging as the most expensive, followed by the rent allowance scheme and then the rent rebate scheme. The high cost of the rent allowance over the rent rebate scheme may reflect its newness, its smaller size, and perhaps the fact that private tenants are less accessible to a local authority than council house tenants.

CONCLUSIONS

The high cost of administering means-tested benefits is apparent at both the central and the local government level, particularly with the supplementary benefit system and the rate rebate system. A reduction in administrative costs would obviously help in financing policies for improving the position of those with low incomes.

Various suggestions have been made[1] for reducing the cost of means-tested benefits, mainly by the use of 'passport' systems (e.g. entitlement to one benefit carries automatic entitlement to others) and by standardisation of definitions of income and expenses. But these offer only very limited opportunities for administrative savings where there is variable expenditure such as housing costs.

Another relevant consideration to the overall cost of operating social security benefit schemes is the compliance cost. The Committee are not aware of any studies of this subject, but social security benefits involve compliance costs similar to those of taxation (described in Appendix 22.1): costs of time (e.g. in making applications), money costs (e.g. bus fares in visiting social security offices), and psychic costs (e.g. anxiety about dealing with complex forms or unsympathetic officials). There can be no doubt that the compliance costs of means-tested benefits must be very high relatively to the compliance costs of universal benefits.

REFERENCE

[1] *Means-Tested Benefits* (National Consumer Council Discussion Paper, London, January 1977).

14 The Rate Structure

Up to this point in our Report we have concentrated upon the structure of the system of direct taxes, but we have said little or nothing about the pattern of tax rates within any given tax structure. The general level of tax rates must depend upon the general level of public expenditure; and in so far as this is the case we regard the matter as outside our terms of reference. But given any tax structure and the average tax rates which must be levied to meet the budgetary needs, there is a wide scope for choice of rate structures. It is not our intention in this Report to examine in detail the relative merits of different types of rate structure, i.e. of the case for and against different degrees and patterns of progressivity in the tax burden. However, there are some basic considerations which are of great importance in themselves and which also have implications for the choice of tax structure itself.

THE EXISTING PATTERN OF MARGINAL RATES OF TAX

We have given our reasons for including in our analysis of the structure of direct taxes the system of national insurance and also the various means-tested social benefits which are paid to those with low incomes; and we have treated these as negative direct taxes. We have shown that, if this comprehensive view is taken, the rate structure of the existing system of direct taxation displays: (i) very high implied marginal rates of tax on the lower incomes, rising in some cases up to or even beyond 100 per cent, since existing means tests imply that a high proportion of any additional earnings is lost through the reduction of social benefits; (ii) relatively low marginal rates of tax made up of the 33 per cent basic rate of income tax together with such national insurance contributions as are payable on a middle range of incomes; and (iii) marginal rates of tax rising to 83 per cent on earnings sufficiently high to attract the higher rates of tax.

HIGH–LOW–HIGH MARGINAL RATES OF TAX

The general shape of the pattern of pre-tax and post-tax incomes which results from this pattern of tax rates is illustrated in Figure 14.1. Pre-tax earnings are measured along the horizontal axis, and the height of the 45° line then shows what the take-home pay would be if there were no adjustment through taxes. But the actual post-tax take-home pay, which is shown by the height of the curved line, (i) starts above the 45° line for very low earnings because of the negative-tax addition to incomes from social benefits; (ii) rises very slowly at first because of the high marginal rates of tax implied by the loss of means-tested benefits; (iii) thereafter rises more rapidly as earnings move through the middle range, in which for the most part only the

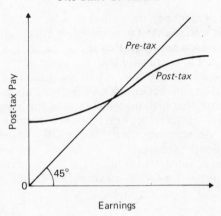

Fig 14.1   Income effect of high–low–high marginal rates of tax

33 per cent basic rate of tax together with national insurance contributions are operative; and finally (iv) changes course again and rises more and more slowly as earnings proceed through the ranges liable to higher and higher marginal rates, until at the 83 per cent marginal rate of tax the curve rises only at a gradient of 17 in 100 (i.e. £17 added to take-home pay out of every £100 additional earnings).

A FLOOR ON POVERTY AND A CEILING ON RICHES

The question arises whether this sort of pattern of tax rates is to be desired or not. As Figure 14.1 shows, this pattern tends to set a floor to excessive poverty and a ceiling to earned income (which necessarily involves high marginal rates of tax at the bottom and the top ends of the income scale); but it allows a freer play of economic forces in the middle range of earnings, with less interference from high marginal tax disincentives. Those who like the idea of a society which sets a floor to poverty and a ceiling to riches on the egalitarian grounds that extreme divergences of standards are in themselves obnoxious, and who at the same time wish to see the middle range impeded as little as possible by high marginal tax rates, will find many virtues in this type of rate structure, particularly in the distributional pattern which it implies. Let us call this the pattern of 'high–low–high marginal rates'.

But it can be argued that, when proper weight is given to the possible disincentive effects of high marginal tax rates, this pattern of high–low–high marginal rates is in fact to be avoided.

A POOR PAY-OFF BETWEEN DISTRIBUTIONAL AND EFFICIENCY EFFECTS

We seek (as argued in Chapter 2) some pay-off or compromise between the disincentive effects of taxes and their effect in achieving a less unequal distribution of economic welfare. As far as incentive effects are concerned, high marginal rates of tax are a pure loss; they simply mean that people by earning income receive a much lower reward than the value of the additional output which they produce for society's use. High marginal rates can only be desirable because of their indirect effects on the distribution of economic welfare; and it is arguable that high marginal rates at the bottom and top of the income scale in fact achieve the worst possible balance between loss of efficiency through disincentive effects and gains through a more equal distribution of economic welfare.

The argument can be illustrated by means of the numerical examples given in Table 14.1. We start with a taxpayer earning £2,000 subject to a 10 per cent

Table 14.1   *Average and marginal rates of tax*

	Pre-tax income (£)	Post-tax income (£)	Tax paid (£)	Average rate of tax (%)	Marginal rate of tax (%)
Case (i)	2,000	1,800	200	10	
	2,100	1,890	210	10	10
Case (ii)	2,000	1,800	200	10	
	2,100	1,810	290	14	90
Case (iii)	2,000	1,800	200	10	
	1,900	1,710	190	10	10
Case (iv)	2,000	1,800	200	10	
	1,900	1,790	110	6	90

average rate of tax, which raises tax of £200, leaving him with post-tax pay of £1,800. The first line in each of the four cases illustrates this same starting point. Case (i) illustrates a proportional tax. If income rises from £2,000 to £2,100 and the average rate of tax remains at 10 per cent, then post-tax income rises from £1,800 to £1,890; the marginal rate of tax on an additional earnings of £100 is 10 per cent, and post-tax earnings can go up by £90 or 90 per cent of the additional earnings of £100. Case (ii) illustrates the same change of earnings from £2,000 to £2,100, but with a highly progressive tax structure under which the marginal rate of tax is 90 per cent, so that of the additional earnings of £100 only £10 can be retained; the amount of tax rises from £200 to £290, which implies a rise in the average rate of tax from 10 per cent to 14 per cent.

On what considerations should the choice between these two structures of tax rates be made? There are at least three relevant factors:

1 *Marginal incentives*

Case (i) clearly gives people at the £2,000 level a better incentive to earn more than does case (ii). The marginal rate of tax on additional earnings will be only 10 per cent instead of 90 per cent. This consideration will be of great importance if persons at this point are specially sensitive to such incentives; it will be relatively unimportant if such persons are not much affected in their work decisions by the marginal rates of tax to which they are subjected.

There is in fact relatively little reliable empirical evidence about the sensitivity of economic decisions to changes in marginal rewards, except for some evidence which suggests a relatively high sensitivity to marginal rates of post-tax reward in the case of decisions to work by married women; and it is for this reason that in the discussion of arrangements for the taxation of families (see Chapters 5, 13 and 18) we have emphasised the importance of keeping down the marginal rates of tax on the earnings of married women.

2 *Egalitarian principles*

To return to the numerical examples of Table 14.1, from the point of view of incentives at the £2,000 level, case (i) is clearly preferable to case (ii) since in case (i) the marginal rate of tax is lower than in case (ii). The only question with which we were concerned in the previous paragraphs was the relative importance of this incentive advantage of case (i). The possible advantage of case (ii) relies solely on the fact that with case (ii) the £2,100 taxpayer will pay a higher average rate of tax than he would with case (i). A high marginal rate of tax between £2,000 and £2,100 is necessary if on distributional grounds it is desired to levy a relatively high average rate of tax on the £2,100 taxpayer.

Individual opinions on this distributional issue will depend basically on social and moral judgements which form a fundamental feature of the different social philosophies of different political parties. Persons with an egalitarian philosophy will put great stress on obtaining the necessary tax revenue by raising the rate of tax on the £2,100 citizen in order to be able to lower it on the £2,000 citizen. But the more the tax structure moves in this egalitarian direction, the higher the marginal rate of tax between the £2,100 and £2,000 levels and the worse, therefore, the incentive effects.

3 *The numbers of taxpayers involved*

Up to this point it would seem that the choice between cases (i) and (ii) depends upon a balancing of two factors: how sensitive people at the £2,000 level are considered to be to marginal incentives, and how great an egalitarian stress is put upon raising revenue by a high average rate of tax at the £2,100 level as compared with the average rate of tax at the £2,000 level. But there is a third very important factor to be taken into account, namely the relative number of persons at the two levels. If there are a very large number of taxpayers at the £2,000 level but very few at the £2,100 level, the arguments for preferring case (i) to case (ii) will be greatly strengthened. Since there are many persons at the £2,000 level it is important to maintain incentives for them to earn more. Since there are very few persons at the £2,100 level, raising the average rate of tax at that level will raise very little revenue and will therefore give very little opportunity to cut rates at the £2,000 level, where every reduction in the tax rate will lose much revenue. There will thus be little advantage in having a high marginal rate of tax between the £2,000 and £2,100 levels.

THE CASE FOR LOW MARGINAL RATES OF TAX AT THE TOP END OF THE INCOME SCALE

It can be argued that for this last reason marginal rates of tax (although not, of course, the average rates of tax) should be kept low at the top end of the income scale. At this top end the number of taxpayers is rapidly thinning out, as one goes up the scale. There is very little to be gained distributionally from raising the average rate of tax at the very top end because there are so few taxpayers there that the gain in revenue would be insignificant; but the very high marginal rate that this would involve on those at somewhat lower rates of earnings might have significant disincentive effects of the various kinds described in Chapter 2 (pp. 7–11).

At present in the United Kingdom it is reckoned that, if the top marginal rate of tax (excluding investment income surcharge) were set at 70 per cent instead of 83 per cent, the loss of revenue would be £85 million, the replacement of which would require the basic rate of tax to be raised only from 33·0 per cent to rather less than 33·2 per cent. This calculation rests on the assumption that the change would have no desirable incentive effects; but if the reduction of the marginal tax rate from 83 to 70 per cent[1] increased the incentives to earn of persons at the top end of the scale, there would *pro tanto* be an increase in tax revenue. There might well be no need for any increase in the basic rate of tax; indeed it might well make possible a reduction rather than an increase, although in either case the change would be insignificant. Moreover, in so far as the greater incentive to work at the margin at the top end caused an increase in the amount of work and effort offered at that level, such work would become less scarce and the pre-tax rate of pay for such work would tend to fall. This consideration reinforces the view that there is little or nothing to be said on distributional grounds against reducing the very high top-end marginal rates – unless the view is held that high post-tax incomes are in themselves distributionally offensive and should be cut down to a limited ceiling, even though there is no direct advantage to be gained thereby for persons lower down the income scale.

THE CASE FOR LOW MARGINAL RATES OF TAX AT THE BOTTOM END OF THE INCOME SCALE

A somewhat similar analysis leads to the view that marginal rates of tax should also be kept exceptionally low at the bottom end of the income scale.

---

[1] It is important to note that this would represent an important increase in the incentive to effort, since anyone in this range who earned an additional £100 would keep £30 instead of only £17; i.e. he or she would receive a 76 per cent increase in his or her marginal reward.

The reasoning can be illustrated from cases (iii) and (iv) of Table 14.1. Case (iii) illustrates what happens to the taxpayer at the £2,000 level if he decides to earn £100 less in a proportional tax regime with an average and a marginal rate of tax of 10 per cent. He saves tax of £10, and his post-tax income falls by £90 from £1,800 to £1,710. We compare this with case (iv), in which he starts in the same position but with a marginal tax rate of 90 per cent instead of 10 per cent, so that when his earnings fall by £100 he loses only £10 of post-tax income, which falls from £1,800 to £1,790.

Clearly, case (iii) is better than case (iv) in so far as incentives are concerned. The earner of £2,000 will have less incentive with case (iii) than with case (iv) to cut down his work and effort. The disadvantage of case (iii) is the distributional effect which leaves any person who can earn only £1,900 with only £1,710 instead of the £1,790 of case (iv). But, to take the extreme example, if there were no persons who could not earn at least £2,000, then the distributional argument for case (iv) would disappear, while the incentive argument for case (iii) for the earner of £2,000 would still be valid.

LOW–HIGH–LOW MARGINAL RATES OF TAX

This argument for exceptionally low marginal rates of tax or of implied tax at the bottom and the top ends of the income scale would lead to the pattern of low–high–low marginal rates illustrated in Figure 14.2, which is the exact opposite of the existing pattern of high–low–high marginal rates illustrated in Figure 14.1.

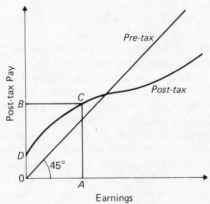

Fig 14.2   Income effect of low–high–low marginal rates of tax

The argument for low implied marginal rates of tax at the lower end of the income scale rests upon the assumption that there are no, or virtually no, income earners unable to rise at least up to some minimum acceptable level of earnings. This is illustrated in Figure 14.2. If OB represents a minimum poverty level of post-tax pay below which it is desired that no one should be allowed to sink, then the curved pattern of post-tax pay illustrated in Figure 14.2 will be acceptable only if there are virtually no persons whose opportunity to earn is less than OA. In this case the earner at the minimum level of OA will have the least possible incentive to reduce his earnings, since his post-tax pay would fall rapidly down the curve from point C towards point D. At the same time, if there are virtually no persons with earnings below OA, the shape of this part of the curve of post-tax pay will not cause hardship.

THE NEED FOR SOCIAL BENEFITS

But there are, of course, persons with incomes below OA. In particular there are those who through unemployment, sickness, disability or other such causes are without income. For this reason the sort of pattern of tax rates illustrated in Figure 14.2 must be combined with a system of social benefits (e.g. unemployment, sickness and child benefits) of the kind described in Chapter 13. Those with zero or very low incomes are supported with social incomes which are conditional upon their accepting earned work when it is offered to them. They are not left free to choose simply to reduce their earnings below OA by not working and yet to maintain their post-tax income at the adequate level of OB.

ARGUMENTS AGAINST LOW–HIGH–LOW MARGINAL RATES OF TAX

There would, however, be very real difficulty in moving to the low–high–low pattern of marginal rates of Figure 14.2.

In the first place, the fact that at the top end of the income scale marginal rates of tax (although not, of course, average rates) would be reduced as income increased would involve some real administrative problems. In such a situation taxpayers at the top end of the scale could reduce their tax burdens by arranging that their income should be received at an uneven rate over the years. Thus by receiving £1,000 less this year and £1,000 more next year, a taxpayer might avoid tax this year on £1,000 at, say, a marginal rate of 60 per cent and incur tax next year on £1,000 at, say, a marginal rate of 55 per cent, when his income would be greater. Thus he would save £50 in tax. If marginal tax rates rise as income rises (the pattern of the normal progressive tax), the taxpayer whose income varies from year to year is treated more harshly than the taxpayer whose income is steady from year to year; and the taxpayer with the uneven income must seek the privilege of some form of averaging in order to avoid excessive tax. With a pattern of tax rates which reduced the marginal rate of tax as income increased, uneven incomes would gain at the expense of even incomes; and it would be the tax authorities who would have to insist on some form of averaging in order to prevent tax avoidance.

But quite apart from any administrative problems in the application of the low–high–low pattern of marginal tax rates, it is doubtful whether such a pattern could ever command political acceptance. It would involve relatively high marginal rates of tax over the middle range of incomes, with lower marginal rates at the top as well as the bottom ends. This is so far removed from the idea of a floor on poverty and ceiling on riches, illustrated by the high–low–high pattern of Figure 14.1, that it would almost certainly be unacceptable.

CONSTANT MARGINAL RATES OF TAX

There remains, however, force in the argument that steps should be taken to avoid the exceptionally high marginal tax rates of the 'poverty trap' at the lower end and of the existing 83 per cent charge at the top end, in both of which cases, for the reasons discussed above, the resulting disincentives may be counterbalanced with little distributional advantage. This suggests the compromise of a pattern of 'constant marginal rates', which is illustrated in Figure 14.3. With this pattern the taxpayer receives a tax credit or uncondi-

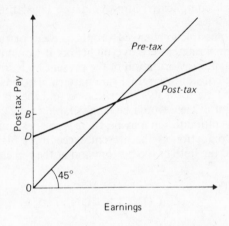

Fig 14.3   Income effect of a constant marginal rate of tax

tional social benefit of OD, and all the other income of all taxpayers at all levels is subject to a single constant tax rate. The higher is the tax credit OD, the higher will be the marginal rate of tax required to finance the tax credit as well as the rest of the budgetary expenditure; the less steeply, therefore, the post-tax line will slope upwards; and the more egalitarian and the less incentive-orientated will the tax pattern become. The tax credit OD can be varied according to family circumstances and need not be set as high as the level OB which is needed to avoid poverty. The constant marginal tax pattern would in this case have to be associated with conditional benefits of the new Beveridge type, which were required to maintain incomes for those in special categories of need.

ADMINISTRATIVE SIMPLIFICATION

The great attraction of the constant marginal rate pattern is not merely that it is a compromise between the high–low–high and the low–high–low patterns of marginal rates, but that it brings with it the bonus of great simplification of the tax system. If all income (under an income tax regime) or all expenditure (under an expenditure tax regime) were subject to one single rate of tax, the administrative problems of the direct tax system could be simplified out of all recognition. Averaging would be unnecessary; a cumulative pay-as-you-earn (PAYE) scheme would have no point; the problem of the taxation of social benefits would disappear; the deduction of tax at source could remove most end-year adjustments of tax; close company problems would not arise; the treatment of trusts would be greatly eased; the treatment of married couples for tax purposes (discussed in Chapter 18 on the tax unit) would be greatly simplified since, apart from the question of the proper levels for personal tax allowances, it would make no difference to tax rates whether the couple's incomes were treated individually or aggregated in one way or another; and much complicated anti-avoidance legislation would become unnecessary.

It would not be possible to change from the present pattern of tax rates to the constant marginal rate pattern overnight; but it would not be impossible to aim at the gradual transformation of the present high–low–high marginal rate pattern into a constant marginal rate pattern. There is much to be said for the latter on the merits of its rate structure, and the advantages from an administrative point of view would be incalculable.[2]

But whatever the ultimate aim may be, there is a very strong case indeed for some appreciable reduction of the present exceedingly high marginal rates of tax or of implied tax both at the bottom and at the top ends of the income scale.

CONCLUSION

High marginal rates of tax are needed only on distributional grounds; on incentive grounds they are to be avoided. The choice of detailed figures for the rate structure for any system of direct taxation must therefore balance distributional against efficiency considerations, which is a matter for political decision. There are, however, good reasons for believing that as a general principle (i) *average* rates of tax should be high on high incomes and low on low incomes, but at the same time (ii) *marginal* rates of tax should be exceptionally low at both the bottom and the top ends of the income scale. At present in the United Kingdom they are exceptionally high at both these extreme ends of the scale, if the implied tax rates due to means-tested benefits are taken into account, as they should be. We are of the opinion that tax schedules should never be set so as to cause such marginal rates of tax to exceed, say, 70 per cent.

[2] The ITVAT outlined in Appendix 8.3 illustrates one way of operating an expenditure tax with a constant marginal rate of tax.

15 Capital Taxes I: Taxes on the Transfer of Wealth

In the preceding chapters of our Report we have been concerned with taxes which are levied on current flows such as income, expenditure, profits, dividends, etc. We turn in this chapter to a consideration of taxes which are based upon capital funds, the clearest example of which is an annual tax levied on the amount of wealth held by the taxpayer. The distinction between the two types of tax is not, however, as clear-cut as may at first sight appear. The one type of tax often shades into the other.

Thus a tax on the transfer of inherited wealth as it passes down from parent to child is in effect a periodic charge, levied once a generation, on the holding of such wealth. In so far as this is the case it may be regarded as a capital tax, like an annual wealth tax, but one which is levied once a generation instead of once a year on the holding of wealth. But (as argued in Chapters 7 and 9) the receipt of a gift or of an inheritance can be treated for tax purposes as part of the recipient's current income under a comprehensive income tax, and the making of such a gift or bequest can be treated as part of the donor's current expenditure under a universal expenditure tax.

In Chapters 7 and 9 we have discussed the possibilities of taxing transfers of wealth by gift or bequest in this way as part of the income of the donee or as part of the expenditure of the donor. We have noted that an alternative treatment is to exclude such transfers of wealth from the taxable income of the donee or from the taxable expenditure of the donor and to subject them to a separate regime of taxation of capital transfers. In this chapter we discuss such separate regimes for the taxation of transfers of wealth by gift or bequest.

THREE OBJECTIVES OF CAPITAL TAXES

To what extent do taxes on the transfer of wealth meet the objectives which it is desired to achieve through the taxation of capital? There are three major sets of objectives which people have in mind when they consider this range of capital taxes.

BENEFITS CONFERRED BY WEALTH

The first of these is to recognise that the ownership of wealth confers benefits upon the owner and is therefore a proper subject for tax. We have already discussed these issues in Chapter 3; we need only briefly to summarise the argument at this point. Capital produces an income which, unlike earning capacity, does not decline with age and is not gained at the expense of leisure. It is true that a shift from the taxation of income to the taxation of expenditure reduces, although it does not entirely remove, this case for an additional tax on income from capital or, as an alternative, on the capital itself; but in any case wealth itself, quite apart from any income which it produces, confers independence, security and influence. Moreover, a tax on wealth, as contrasted with a tax on income from wealth, will (in so far as it is possible to apply it to all forms of wealth without any distorting distinctions) increase the incentives of the owners of wealth to seek the most productive uses of their capital so as to yield the highest possible rate of return.

THE DISTRIBUTION OF WEALTH

A second set of objectives is to promote a more equal distribution of the ownership of wealth. High rates of taxation on the holding of wealth will impede the accumulation of large fortunes; high rates of taxation on the transfer of wealth will impede the inheritance of large fortunes. But capital taxes may have the effect not merely of impeding the accumulation or inheritance of large fortunes by surrender of part of them to the state in the form of capital taxes; they may also have the effect – indeed (as we argue below) they may be imposed in a form expressly designed to have the effect – of giving an incentive to owners of wealth to disperse their fortunes more widely by gift or bequest to those with smaller fortunes.

THE DISTINCTION BETWEEN INHERITED AND SAVED WEALTH

Closely connected with this is a third set of objectives, which is very generally in mind when capital taxes are considered, namely a differentiation of the treatment of inherited wealth as contrasted with wealth accumulated out of the owner's own earnings and savings. Inherited wealth is widely considered – and we share the view – to be a proper subject for heavier taxation on grounds both of fairness and of economic incentives. The citizen who by his own effort and enterprise has built up a fortune is considered to deserve better tax treatment than the citizen who, merely as a result of the fortune of birth, owns an equal property; and to tax the former more lightly than the latter will put a smaller obstacle in the way of effort and enterprise. Whereas an annual wealth tax will fall on wealth which results from a man's own effort, enterprise and saving just as much as on inherited wealth, taxes on capital transfers may be chosen so as to fall on the inheritance of wealth without falling on the accumulation of wealth.

DONEE-BASED VERSUS DONOR-BASED TRANSFER TAXES

At first sight it might appear that this last objective simply means that a capital transfer tax (CTT) should be levied on the donee (who will in any case be inheriting) rather than on the donor (who may be handing on wealth due to his own effort, enterprise and saving). But this is, of course, a misleading distinction. Consider a flat rate tax on all capital transfers from donor to donee. If the donor does not change his behaviour as the result of the tax and passes on gross of tax the same amount as before, then the tax falls on the donee whether it be collected from the donor or the donee. If, however, the donor decides that he wants to leave the same sum free of tax to the donee, then he will have to save more during his lifetime to meet the tax; the tax will fall on the donor and this will be the case whether it be collected from the donor or from the donee.

The situation is, however, changed in a material way if the tax on the transfer of capital is made progressive. Under the present CTT in the United Kingdom (as described in Appendix 15.1), the rate of tax rises progressively according to the total cumulative amount of gifts which the donor has made up to date. The rate of tax depends in no way upon the circumstances of the donee but upon what the donor has given to any donees, whether rich or poor, in the past. The corresponding tax on the donee is an accessions tax, under which the rate of tax does not depend at all upon the donor's circumstances but upon the cumulative amount of gifts or inheritances which the donee has received up to date from any number of donors, rich or poor.

THE CASE FOR A CUMULATIVE TAX ON ACCESSIONS

It is often argued that if one wants to tax inherited wealth progressively and to do so in a way which gives the maximum incentive for a wider dispersion of the ownership of wealth, then the principle of the accessions tax is to be preferred to that of the CTT.

We agree with this, although the force of the argument can be overstated.

Suppose that wealthy Mr Smith is considering whether to leave his wealth to his favourite nephew Dick, who has already inherited a handsome fortune, or to his other nephew Harry, who has so far inherited nothing, and that his choice may be affected by tax considerations. Under an accessions tax, more tax will be payable if he leaves his wealth to Dick rather than to Harry. Under the CTT the same tax will be payable whether he leaves his wealth to Dick or to Harry; but Mr Smith may pause to consider the fact that when Dick and Harry come in turn to pass the wealth on to their heirs more tax will be payable on the wealth under a CTT if it has been added to Dick's existing wealth than if it is to be handed on unaugmented by Harry. The progressive CTT thus at second remove also gives a tax incentive to leave property to those who have already inherited little rather than to those who have inherited much.

Nevertheless, there are three good reasons for preferring the principle of the accessions tax to that of the CTT:

1 There is what may be termed 'fiscal myopia'. Mr Smith may very well be more affected by the immediate saving of tax (under the accessions tax) than by the remoter saving of tax (under the CTT) which would result from his leaving his wealth to Harry rather than to Dick.
2 The future is uncertain, and Dick or Harry or both might, when their turn came, have little wealth left to hand on to their heirs. In so far as they did in fact lose or live on their wealth, there would be no second-

generation tax effects to take into account. The immediate saving of tax (under the accessions tax) from leaving the wealth to Harry rather than to Dick would turn out to be the only relevant tax consideration.

3 While Harry has received no previous inheritance, he may nevertheless be an able, enterprising and abstinent man who has built up a valuable business of his own. Under an accessions tax there would still be an immediate tax advantage if Mr Smith left his money to Harry; but with a CTT there would be no second-generation advantage in leaving it to Harry rather than to Dick. Thus as between two heirs with the same property, one of whom is likely to use wealth in an enterprising manner and the other of whom is likely simply to live on the inherited wealth, the accessions tax unlike the CTT will differentiate in favour of the former.

For these reasons we would favour the substitution of the principle of the accessions tax for that of the CTT.

THE DEFECTS OF AN UNMODIFIED ACCESSIONS TAX

But there remains one feature of an accessions tax which may be considered undesirable: it levies the same tax whether the wealth is held for a long or for a short period. Inherited wealth which changes hands frequently is taxed more heavily than inherited wealth which stays in the same ownership for long periods. In so far as the tax objective is progressively to tax the possession of inherited wealth, an annual wealth tax is deficient in that it does not distinguish between the holding of inherited wealth and the holding of wealth accumulated out of the owner's own savings, and an accessions tax is deficient in that it taxes only the occasion of transfer and does not distinguish between inherited wealth which is held for five years and inherited wealth which is held for fifty years.

The fact that no distinction is drawn between short and long periods of ownership of the wealth is true not only of an accessions tax but also of other transfer taxes such as the CTT; and this fact has two serious drawbacks:

1 It is inappropriate that someone who owns £100,000 for five years should pay the same tax as someone who owns it for fifty years.
2 It leads to various devices whereby the frequency of formal transfers of family wealth are reduced; and thus it is a major cause of the use of trusts to hold wealth for long periods for many beneficiaries and of generation skipping whereby a grandfather leaves his property to his grandson or great-grandson rather than to his son.

PAWAT: A COMBINED PROGRESSIVE ANNUAL WEALTH AND ACCESSIONS TAX

It would be possible to modify the operation of an accessions tax in such a way as to remove this deficiency. The procedure would be as follows.

As with an ordinary accessions tax, for every taxpayer there would be recorded a cumulative total of all the gifts and inheritances (subject to exemption of small gifts) received up to date. As with an ordinary accessions tax, a donee would pay tax on any fresh gift received at a progressive rate which depended upon the total cumulative amount of gifts already received. But the rate of tax would now depend not only upon the cumulative amount of gifts already received but also upon his age, the tax rate being higher the younger the donee.

The tax payable would be determined on the following principle. The donee on receipt of a gift pays in transfer tax an amount which corresponds to a lump-sum advance payment to cover an annual wealth tax for a given future period, say to his 85th birthday;[1] and it is thus related to the prospective period for which the donee might hold the wealth. The rate of the corresponding annual wealth tax which is thus, as it were, covered in advance is itself progressively related to the donee's cumulative total of gifts received up to date.

The tax differs from an annual wealth tax in that it is charged only on inherited wealth and it assumes that the donee will continue to hold wealth of the same value. Spending the capital has no effect on the liability as it would with an annual wealth tax.

Thus the donee on receipt of a gift pays a lump sum tax which, as it were, franks that inherited wealth for annual tax up to some future date. But if and when, on his death or on the occasion of a gift *inter vivos*, the donee becomes a donor and hands on the wealth to someone else, the process is put into reverse. The donor now subtracts the gift from his cumulative total of gifts received up to date, this total being in effect a net cumulative total of gifts received less gifts made.

But he is handing on a gift of property which he has already in the past franked for annual wealth tax up to some future date. The new donee will be liable on the receipt of the gift to take over the liability to frank the wealth for future wealth tax. Therefore on the occasion of handing on the gift the donor, or on death the donor's estate, receives a repayment of tax to cover the remainder of the period for which he has already franked the property by the transfer tax which he paid when he received the gift.

By this process the person who inherits wealth and then in turn hands the wealth on to a new donee will have paid a net tax which corresponds to a progressive annual wealth tax levied precisely over that period during which he did in fact hold the wealth.[2, 3]

For this very reason this type of transfer tax will give very little incentive for tax avoidance either by reducing the number of transfers of wealth by

---

[1] The 85th birthday is used for illustrative purposes. Factors affecting the choice of terminal age are discussed in Appendix 15.2.

[2] Except for the fact that persons over 85 years of age will, as it were, get a free run until their death.

[3] See Appendix 15.2 for a discussion of alternative formulae which would satisfy this general principle.

the use of trusts or by routing a transfer of wealth indirectly from donor to ultimate donee through intermediary donees and donors. Every holder of the wealth in effect pays tax at his own appropriate rate of tax to cover his own period of ownership, and, like a wealth tax, the rate is low if the wealth is dispersed. Because of this a family which disperses its wealth over two or more generations will pay less tax than one where the bulk of the wealth is held by one generation.

Since this tax levies by the mechanism of an accessions tax what amounts to a progressive annual wealth tax on inherited wealth, we shall call it a *progressive annual wealth accessions tax* or PAWAT for short.

THE OPERATION OF A PAWAT

It will be useful to take an example in order to illustrate the way in which the tax would operate. For this purpose let us suppose (i) that in 1977 when he is 45 Mr Smith inherits £500,000, and (ii) that 15 years later when he is 60 he makes a gift of £100,000 to his son, who has hitherto received nothing by way of gift or inheritance and who is then 25 years of age. Mr Smith is assumed neither to have received nor to have made any other gifts.

To calculate the PAWAT implications for the Smith family of these inheritances and gifts, it is necessary to have (i) a schedule showing the scale of progressive rates of equivalent annual wealth tax for which PAWAT represents a lump-sum advance payment, and (ii) a table of annuity multipliers which shows for a donor of any given age what is the present value at that age of £1 of annual wealth tax payable up to, say, the taxpayer's 85th birthday. An illustrative schedule of rates of equivalent annual wealth tax and an illustrative table of annuity multipliers are shown in Table 15.1.

When in 1977 Mr Smith, aged 45, inherits £500,000 he will, according to the progressive tax schedule shown in Table 15.1, be liable for an underlying annual wealth tax of £4,250 a year, as is shown by the following calculation:

Slices of the £500,000 inheritance (£)	Rate of equivalent annual wealth tax (%)	Amount of annual wealth tax (£)
50,000	0	0
50,000	$\frac{1}{2}$	250
400,000	1	4,000
TOTAL 500,000		4,250

From the table of annuity multipliers it can then be calculated that the value in 1977 of an annuity of £4,250 for the next forty years, until Mr Smith's 85th birthday, is £4,250 × 23·11 = £98,217; and this is therefore the PAWAT payable by Mr Smith on receipt of the inheritance.

When in 1992 at the age of 60 Mr Smith makes the gift of £100,000 to his son, he will be passing on £100,000 which has been franked for annual wealth

Table 15.1   *Illustrative rate schedule for PAWAT*

(A)   *Illustrative schedule of progressive rates of annual wealth tax*

Value of net cumulative PAWAT (£)	Rate of annual wealth tax (%)
0– 50,000	0
50,001– 100,000	$\frac{1}{2}$
100,001– 500,000	1
500,001–1,000,000	$1\frac{1}{2}$
1,000,001–2,000,000	2
2,000,001–5,000,000	$2\frac{1}{2}$
5,000,001 plus	3

(B)   *Table of annuity multipliers[a]* (i.e. the present value of an annuity of £1 for a number of years up to the taxpayer's 85th birthday)

Age of taxpayer[b] (years)	Annuity multiplier
0	30·63
5	30·20
15	29·12
25	27·68
35	25·73
40	24·52
45	23·11
50	21·49
55	19·60
60	17·41
65	14·88
70	11·94
75	8·53
80	4·58
$82\frac{1}{2}$	2·37
85	0

[a] Based on a discount rate of 3 per cent a year.
[b] Age of donee (for tax paid on gifts received). Age of donor (for tax refund on gifts made).

tax for the remaining twenty-five years up to his 85th birthday. Mr Smith has a claim to a repayment of PAWAT, which 'defranks' the £100,000 from his annual wealth tax liability for the coming twenty-five years; but his son is now liable to PAWAT, which will frank this £100,000 for the son's underlying liability to annual wealth tax for the next sixty years, i.e. until the 85th birthday of the son who is now aged 25.

On what principle should the refund of PAWAT due to Mr Smith be calculated? He is to have £100,000 'defranked' for equivalent annual wealth tax. But from the calculation given above it can be seen that the first £100,000 of his inheritance of £500,000 has been franked for only £250 of equivalent annual wealth tax, whereas the last £100,000 slice of the inheritance has been franked for £1,000 of equivalent annual wealth tax. If it is assumed that Mr Smith is making his gift out of this top slice, then he needs a repayment which 'defranks' the £100,000 which he is passing on from equivalent annual wealth tax of £1,000 a year for the next twenty-five years till his 85th birthday. From the table of annuity multipliers it can be seen that the present value of £1,000 for twenty-five years is £1,000 ×17·41 = £17,410. On the other hand, if Mr Smith is treated as passing on the less highly taxed first slices of his inheritance of £500,000, the refund due to him will be only £250 ×17·41 = £4,353.

An alternative procedure would be to use an average for the amount of equivalent annual wealth tax in respect of which the gift of £100,000 should be 'defranked'. Mr Smith has franked his whole inheritance of £500,000 for a total annual wealth tax liability of £4,250 a year; and this represents an average rate of annual wealth tax of 0·85 per cent on his whole inheritance. A simple and fair way to proceed may be to 'defrank' each of Mr Smith's subsequent gifts and bequests as he makes them at this average rate of 0·85 per cent. This is to proceed as if each gift is made up of the same *pro rata* share of each slice of Mr Smith's inheritance which has been subject to a different marginal rate of tax. On this basis Mr Smith needs a repayment which 'defranks' the £100,000 which he is handing on from annual wealth tax of £850 a year for the next twenty-five years. From the table of annuity multipliers it can be seen that the present value of £850 for the twenty-five years is £850 ×17·41 = £14,799.

There is much to be said for the assumption that Mr Smith is handing on the slice of his existing inheritance which has been subject to the highest rate of marginal tax. It is this procedure which will give anyone who has received a large amount of inherited property the maximum incentive to pass it on quickly to someone who has received only a small inheritance. The recipient will be taxed at his top rate, and it is therefore important that the donor should be relieved at his top rate to give an appropriate incentive to pass the property on. If the donor were relieved at his bottom marginal rate (which could be zero), while the donee was taxed at his top marginal rate, a net *increase* in tax burden could result from a gift by a donor who had received a large inheritance to a donee who had in fact received comparatively little.

Nevertheless, there are powerful arguments for adopting the procedure of assessing tax refunds at an average rate. These arguments rest upon avoiding the complications of calculation which arise when allowance is made for the facts (i) that the schedule of tax rates may be changed between the receipt of a gift and the time when it is passed on, and (ii) that adjustments have to be made to index the tax against inflation. We consider these complications in Appendix 15.3. Meanwhile, in order to avoid them, we proceed on the basis of paying to Mr Smith the refund of £14,799 which results from the averaging process. Mr Smith's son must now frank this £100,000 for sixty years. His liability to annual wealth tax can be calculated as follows:

Slices of £100,000 inheritance (£)	Rate of annual wealth tax (%)	Amount of annual wealth tax (£)
50,000	0	0
50,000	$\frac{1}{2}$	250
TOTAL 100,000		250

The present value of £250 for sixty years can be calculated from the table of annuity multipliers as £250 × 27·65 = £6,913; and this is the PAWAT payable by the son.

The above example is a very simple one and neglects at least three important complications.

(1) It does not illustrate the procedure when a donee receives a series of gifts and bequests of different amounts at different dates.

(2) It is based on the assumption that both the schedule of progressive rates of annual wealth tax and the table of annuity multipliers remain unchanged from year to year. It is to be hoped that the annuity multipliers would be continued unchanged from year to year. Their values depend solely upon the rate of interest at which it is chosen to discount the future value of an annuity payment. This rate should represent a typical real rate of return on capital. If expenditure rather than income is the base for personal direct taxation, then the real rate of return to all owners of wealth is measured by the same real rate of return on invested capital; and some reasonable rate such as 3 per cent a year may be chosen and maintained over the years as adequately representing this real rate of return. But it cannot be assumed that the schedule of progressive rates of annual wealth tax will remain unchanged, since different governments with different social philosophies and operating in different economic conditions may certainly wish to change the schedule from time to time.

(3) The example given makes no allowance for inflation and for the need to index the PAWAT calculations against price inflation. If PAWAT were to be indexed for inflation, it would be necessary to adjust for price changes the brackets in the schedule of progressive rates of annual wealth tax. It would also be necessary, when a gift was received or made, (i) that the existing net cumulative total of gifts received less gifts made should first be multiplied up by the rise in the general price index since the date when the last previous gift was received or made (i.e. since the last revision of the total for inflation), and (ii) that the new gift received or made should then be added to, or subtracted from, this revised total.[4] Even if the tax brackets in the schedule

---

[4] This would not be a new set of problems introduced by the adoption of a PAWAT. This process of revising the cumulative totals as well as the brackets for the tax rates in order to adjust for inflation is as necessary for the existing CTT as it would be for a PAWAT.

of progressive rates of annual wealth tax were not automatically indexed each year, there would still be a strong case for indexing the PAWAT cumulative totals for the possibly long intervals between one gift and another. The totals would be in real terms; unchanged tax brackets would represent a revised schedule of rates on a real basis.

In Appendix 15.3 we give a more detailed and elaborate numerical example, which covers these three points and thus shows in a more realistic way how a PAWAT could in fact be operated.

INCENTIVES FOR THE WIDER DISPERSION OF OWNERSHIP

A marked feature of a PAWAT would be the incentive which it gave to persons who had inherited much property to pass it on at an early date to persons who had inherited little property. In such a case the immediate tax rebate would be high and the new tax liability would be low.[5]

INCENTIVES FOR THE EARLY GIVING OF SAVED WEALTH

But there would not be the same incentive to pass on at an early date the ownership of wealth which a person had accumulated out of his own savings. Indeed, such wealth would not be subject to tax so long as the saver himself held the wealth. But as soon as it was passed on it would be subject to transfer tax in the hands of the donee. The donor, if he had no inherited wealth to pass on, would receive no tax rebate when he gave his own saved wealth away; his net cumulative total of gifts received would be zero, and he would therefore be entitled to no tax refund. There would be no need to identify the source of wealth given away; inherited wealth would be treated as given away first.

There would, of course, remain a tax incentive to select as donees persons whose cumulative totals were low, because they had not hitherto received much wealth by way of gift or inheritance; but there would be a tax incentive to postpone such gifts as long as possible, since saved wealth would escape the tax net altogether until it was passed on and became inherited wealth.

This is an inevitable feature of any unmodified system of taxation of inherited, as contrasted with saved, wealth. But a PAWAT could be modified in such a way as to give donors of saved wealth (i.e. donors who had zero net cumulative totals of gifts received up to date) some special incentive to make early gifts.

One way would be to treat the saved wealth as franked at an assumed arbitrary rate of wealth tax, say 1 per cent up to the donor's 85th birthday.

---

[5] As already noted, the tax would give the maximum incentive for a wider dispersion of the ownership of inherited wealth, if PAWAT refunds were based on the assumption that the donor was passing on the slice of his existing inheritance which had been subject to the highest marginal rate of equivalent annual wealth tax. If for reasons of administrative simplification the procedure of assessing refunds at an average rate were adopted, there would be a saving of tax only so long as the donor's *average* rate of tax exceeded the donee's *marginal* rate of tax.

To prevent the donor from receiving a refund of tax which had never been paid, it could be provided that any payment to the donor should not exceed the tax payable by the donee. This restriction would be easy in cases where the repayment to the donor was treated as part of the gift (see Appendix 15.3). In this way the incentive to late giving would be fully neutralised in cases where the donee's implied tax rate was less than or equal to the arbitrary rate chosen; where the donee's implied tax rate was greater than the arbitrary rate chosen, the incentive to late giving would still be partially, but not wholly, offset.

Another method would be to give a discount on the tax payable by the donee which depended upon the age of the donor, the tax payable by the donee being more reduced the younger the age of the donor. A disadvantage of this arrangement would be that, if the discount depended upon the tax payable by the donee, it could lead to tax avoidance by the indirect routing of gifts through wealthy intermediaries. Thus if Father Smith gave at an early age his saved wealth to Lord Jones who had already inherited much wealth, the reduction in Lord Jones's tax liability would be a large absolute sum simply because Lord Jones's tax rate was high. If Lord Jones then handed the wealth on to Son Smith, Lord Jones would obtain a large tax rebate, again because his tax rate was high. He would have paid a *discounted* tax and would have received an *undiscounted* tax repayment on a large amount of tax. He could for that reason afford to be generous in the amount which he passed on to Son Smith. It might be possible to avoid this effect by introducing some tax discount on the handing on of saved wealth which depended solely on the amount of wealth so transferred and on the age of the donor but not at all on the tax situation of the donee.

THE TAX UNIT

A problem arises concerning the treatment of gifts made between husband and wife. It is difficult and probably undesirable to monitor and to tax transfers between husband and wife. Such transfers are not taxed under the present CTT. But the introduction of the age element into the PAWAT tax schedules raises a new consideration. If the two partners in a marriage each maintained their own individual net cumulative total of gifts received and if, at the same time, gifts from one partner to the other were untaxed and unrecorded, arrangements could always be made for gifts to the partners from third parties to go to that partner whose age and PAWAT total would cause the smaller tax payment and for gifts from the partners to third parties to be made by that partner whose age and PAWAT total would cause the larger tax refund. Any transfers between partners which were desired to match such arrangements would be untaxed and unrecorded.

For these reasons, if it were decided to disregard transfers of wealth between spouses, it would be necessary to treat the couple as a single unit for a PAWAT. This might be achieved on the following lines:

1   Upon marriage the two partners would combine their two cumulative

totals of net gifts received before marriage into an aggregate cumulative total, one half of which would be taken as the operative total for determining rates of tax on subsequent gifts received or of tax repayments on subsequent gifts made.

2   The new tax unit would be treated as having an age which was an average – either weighted or arithmetic – of the age of the two partners.

3   Gifts between spouses would be exempt from tax and from tax rebate, and no record would be kept of them in the partners' joint net cumulative total of gifts received.

4   Any gift coming into the tax unit would be added to the unit's joint cumulative total and would be taxed at the rate appropriate (i) to an individual cumulative total equal to one-half of the existing joint cumulative total, and (ii) to the average age of the partners. A similar treatment would be given to the tax rebate for the tax unit in respect of any gift made by a partner to an outside donee.

5   Upon the death of either of the partners, bequests to persons other than the surviving spouse would be treated as gifts made by the married tax unit, i.e. as gifts to outsiders would have been treated before the death occurred.

6   The surviving partner would take on the whole of the remaining sum of the two partners' cumulative totals of net gifts received.

7   On dissolution of a marriage other than through the death of one of the spouses, each party would take with them a proportion of the joint cumulative total of net gifts received which was equal to the proportion of the total property of the couple which each took with him or her out of the marriage.

The proposals set out above introduce serious administrative complications. Although the Inland Revenue must maintain records of marriages and divorces for income tax purposes, this is much easier when periodic communication is required in any case. With a transfer tax, when dealings with the taxpayer were infrequent there would be a serious danger that the register of tax units was not up to date. Marriages and divorces taking place abroad would introduce difficult questions of their recognition in the United Kingdom.

Other problems include the method of calculating the average age of the parties. If it were a simple arithmetic average, a rich man could reduce his rate of tax by marrying a young poor wife. But if the average were weighted by the amounts of wealth which each partner brought into the marriage, it would be subject to considerable variation according to small gifts received by either party before marriage. Even if a satisfactory solution to the problem could be found, there would remain the further one of what would happen to the average age when one party died or there was a divorce. The division of the cumulative total on divorce could also raise serious practical difficulties.

If the taxation of gifts and bequests is to depend upon the ages of donor and donee, it is in fact very difficult to devise any satisfactory procedure other than to treat the individual as the tax unit. The principal disadvantage of doing this is that gifts between spouses must be monitored; this is difficult, although the fact that it is the practice in many other countries, and that it was in any case necessary to a limited extent under estate duty, suggest that it is not impossible. It would, however, seem absurd to treat as a gift a transfer from, say, husband to wife to meet their expenditures on housekeeping or other personal consumption; if the husband paid the bills directly it would not be a gift, whereas it would be a gift if he transferred the funds to the wife who paid the bills. It is our view that only substantial transfers from one spouse to another which were in excess of that necessary to finance the couple's consumption expenditures should be counted as a gift.[6]

This treatment of interspousal gifts under a PAWAT could, however, be open to abuse in some circumstances. Thus a husband who had inherited a large fortune and who was married to a wife who had inherited little or nothing could under a PAWAT obtain a net refund of tax if in any one year he took over the whole of their joint personal consumption and in addition made a substantial transfer of capital to his wife. The wife could then over the subsequent years in effect return the capital free of tax to her husband by using it for the finance by herself of their joint personal consumption. It might be necessary to contemplate some form of anti-avoidance legislation to cope with blatant cases of this kind.

THE TREATMENT OF TRUSTS

The principles underlying PAWAT could be applied to trusts in the following manner.

When a settlor made a trust he could be treated as a donor of a gift of that amount at that time and would be entitled to a tax repayment depending upon his cumulative net total of gifts received and his age at the time of setting up the trust. When subsequently any beneficiary received a payment out of the trust, whether of income or capital, he would treat that as a gift and add it to his net cumulative total of gifts received; the tax which he would pay on the gift would be reckoned in the normal manner, except that the beneficiary's age would be reckoned as if he were receiving the benefit at the date when the settlor paid the funds into the trust.

As explained in Appendix 15.5, this treatment approximates closely to a system which applies the principles of PAWAT as between donor (or settlor) and donee (or beneficiary) at the time when the trust is set up. It would, however, unless it were modified, mean that the Revenue authorities paid out any tax repayment which was due to the settlor at the time of the settlement of the trust but only received any tax due from the beneficiary later when payment was made out of the trust. The system would imply that the Revenue authorities had obtained interest on the tax which was thus delayed, because the tax is assessed on the value of what is drawn out, which is assumed to have earned interest since it was paid in by the settlor. But even so the delay

---

[6] The implications of this definition of interspousal gifts are considered in more detail in Appendix 15.4.

might well be unacceptable. In Appendix 15.5 methods are explained whereby this time gap between tax repayment and tax payment could be closed either by delaying the tax repayment or by anticipating the tax payment.

THE TRANSITION TO A PAWAT

If it were decided to move from the present CTT to a PAWAT, how could the transition be managed? The basic problem is that taxpayers start with no record of their net cumulative totals of gifts received over gifts made and that it would be impossible to require them to job backwards and make up such a total covering the whole of their lives to date. It should, however, be possible to require anyone who received a gift after the change to state the net amount of gifts he had received over, say, the last seven or ten years and to use this as his starting net cumulative total.

At the end of the seven- or ten-year period this requirement would automatically lapse. The reconstitution of such initial starting net cumulative totals of gifts received should be much assisted by the fact that the Revenue authorities in the administration of CTT already require the names and addresses of the donees as well as of the donors to be recorded. As time passes, particulars of donees and of donors will thus be available for a longer span of past years.[7]

So much for the building-up of net cumulative totals of gifts received for the purpose of assessing the donee's liability to PAWAT.

The question arises of appropriate rates for the repayment of the tax rebates during the transition to a PAWAT. If the averaging procedure discussed above for the calculation of refunds of PAWAT on the occasion of making a gift is adopted, no transitional safeguards will be necessary. PAWAT cumulative totals will be credited as franked for equivalent annual wealth tax only to the extent that post-D-day PAWAT has actually been paid. To give post-D-day refunds will thus imply refunds only in respect of post-D-day actual payments of PAWAT. The averaging procedure will, however, mean that the average rate of equivalent annual wealth tax paid on PAWAT totals will be diluted in so far as PAWAT totals include gifts received before D-day on which no PAWAT has been paid; and in so far as this is the case the incentive to pass on inherited property to those who have inherited little will be somewhat weakened during the transitional period.

There could, at the same time, be a quick succession relief on death after the introduction of a PAWAT where CTT or estate duty had been paid before.

LAWAT: A NON-PROGRESSIVE FORM OF PAWAT

One important feature of PAWAT is that on each transfer it involves two separate tax calculations: one of the donor who receives a tax rebate, and

---

[7] Incidentally, the date of birth of donors is recorded for identification purposes. Age of donor is thus already used as a helpful administrative device.

one of the donee who incurs a tax liability. This is the case even where the tax repayment is treated as part of the gift. This feature is due to the progressive nature of the tax. If the progressivity of the tax according to the cumulative totals of net gifts received of the donor and donee were removed, the tax could be much simplified in its administration and only one single tax calculation, of the net liability of the donor, would be necessary.

The removal of the progressivity of the tax would mean that on receiving a gift the donee would pay a transfer tax which franked the gift for a fixed proportionate rate of annual wealth tax for a given future period (e.g. up to the time of the donee's 85th birthday). But it would be assumed that the donor had already franked the gift at the same fixed proportionate rate of wealth tax up to his, the donor's, 85th birthday. A corresponding tax rebate could be deducted from the donee's liability.

In effect, the donee would be required to pay a net transfer tax which extended the franking of the gift for the same constant rate of annual wealth tax from the 85th birthday of the donor until the 85th birthday of the donee. The net tax liability would thus, given the single proportionate rate of underlying annual wealth tax, depend solely upon the age of the donor and the age of the donee.

Such a tax may be called a *linear annual wealth accessions tax* or LAWAT for short.

The logic of this tax would require that in the exceptional case in which the donee was older than the donor there should be a net repayment of tax to the donee. The wealth would have been franked for annual wealth tax up to a date (the 85th birthday of the donor) which was more remote than the date (the 85th birthday of the donee) up to which it should now be franked into the hands of the new owner. But it might be preferable to rule that in such cases no refund would be paid; gifts from younger donors to older donees would simply be free of tax, but gifts from older donors to younger donees would be subject to tax. A rule of this kind would effectively prevent under a LAWAT any abuse of the kind discussed above on page 329 – in the case of interspousal gifts under a PAWAT.

For the administration of a LAWAT it would be unnecessary to maintain any records of cumulative totals of net gifts received. But upon the receipt of any gift it would be necessary for the donee to notify the Revenue authorities of his own age and the donor's age. The relevant tax rate would then be obtained from a schedule of rates of the kind illustrated in Table 15.2. The possible formulae for the construction of such a schedule are described in Appendix 15.2.

In order to operate a LAWAT in this simple fashion it would be necessary to avoid any cumulative exemption of the first tranche of gifts received over a donee's lifetime. All gifts received would have to be subject to the same rate of tax. There could, and no doubt would, be some system of annual exemption of gifts up to a certain figure. These exemptions would probably have to relate to the maximum amount which any donee could receive in any one year directly or indirectly from any one donor. There would be tiresome problems involved in linking donor and donee in any such system of exemption of moderate gifts, but these would not be unmangeable.

With trusts, the donor's age when he made the trust could be calculated, as suggested in relation to a PAWAT.

Table 15.2   *Illustrative rate schedule for a LAWAT*

						Age of donor (years)										
	0	5	15	25	35	40	45	50	55	60	65	70	75	80	82½	85
						Rate of LAWAT (%)										
0	—	—	2	3	5	6	8	9	11	13	16	19	22	26	28	31
5	—	—	1	3	5	6	7	9	11	13	15	18	22	26	28	30
15	2	1	—	1	3	5	6	8	10	12	14	17	21	25	27	29
25	3	3	1	—	2	3	5	6	9	10	13	16	19	23	25	28
35	5	5	3	2	—	1	3	4	6	8	11	14	17	21	23	26
40	6	6	5	3	1	—	1	3	5	7	10	13	16	20	22	25
45	8	7	6	5	3	1	—	2	4	6	8	11	15	19	21	23
50	9	9	8	6	4	3	2	—	2	4	7	10	13	17	19	21
55	11	11	10	9	6	5	4	2	—	2	5	8	11	15	17	20
60	13	13	12	10	8	7	6	4	2	—	3	5	9	13	15	17
65	16	15	14	13	11	10	8	7	5	3	—	3	6	10	13	15
70	19	18	17	16	14	13	11	10	8	5	3	—	3	7	10	12
75	22	22	21	19	17	16	15	13	11	9	6	3	—	4	6	9
80	26	26	25	23	21	20	19	17	15	13	10	7	4	—	2	5
82½	28	28	27	25	23	22	21	19	17	15	13	10	6	2	—	2
85	31	30	29	28	26	25	23	21	20	17	15	12	9	5	2	—

Age of donee (years) is the label for the rows.

Note: This table is calculated in accordance with formula A in Appendix 15.1 (the difference between the present values of an annuity to the 85th birthday of the donor and donee), discounted at 3 per cent and rounded to the nearest whole number. The equivalent rate of wealth tax is 1 per cent. The figures to the right of the diagonal represent rates of tax payment and those to the left represent rates of tax refund. If no refunds were payable on gifts from younger donors to older donees, the figures to the left of the diagonal would all be reduced to zero.

There is one interesting and significant difference between a PAWAT and a LAWAT in addition to the lack of progressivity in the rate structure of the LAWAT. Both taxes exempt wealth from tax so long as it is held by the original saver. Wealth becomes subject to tax only when it is handed on and received by a donee who pays in advance a charge which franks it for tax for some years in advance. But whereas under a PAWAT saved wealth becomes subject to tax just as soon as it is passed on, under a LAWAT, however soon it is passed on, it does not become subject to tax until the saver's 85th birthday. Under an unmodified PAWAT the donor receives no tax rebate when he hands on saved wealth (i.e. when his cumulative total of net gifts received is zero). Under a LAWAT the donee pays a tax which does no more than extend the franking period from the donor's 85th birthday to the donee's 85th birthday. This is the rule whether the gift received is paid by the donor out of inherited or out of saved wealth. The saved wealth of the donor thus remains untaxed up to the donor's 85th birthday. While an unmodified PAWAT gives an incentive to postpone the handing-on of saved wealth, this is not the case with a LAWAT.

The main attraction of a LAWAT is the fact that unlike a PAWAT it does not involve two separate calculations: one for donor and another for donee. This presents no difficulty so long as the proportionate rate of tax for the LAWAT remains unchanged. But if this is not the case, either separate calculations must be made for donor and donee (since the refund to the donor and the payment by the donee may properly have to be related to different rates of equivalent annual wealth tax) or else the donor's refund must be related to the rate of the tax which is operative at the time when he passes his wealth on and not at the time when he received it. In this case, if, for example, the donor has in effect franked his wealth up to his 85th birthday at an equivalent rate of annual wealth tax of 1 per cent and if this rate has been raised to $1\frac{1}{2}$ per cent when he hands his wealth on, he will obtain an inappropriately large refund. Conversely, he will obtain a deficient refund if the rate of tax has been reduced. But if it is desired to obtain the advantages of a LAWAT in necessitating only one tax calculation on the occasion of a gift, this element of rough justice must be accepted.

AGAWAT: AN AGE GAP FORM OF PAWAT

The disadvantages of the LAWAT are that it cannot properly cope with changes in the rate of tax and that the implied annual wealth tax which it reflects can have no element of progressivity in it. All gifts (subject only to moderate annual exemptions) will be taxed at the same implied rate of annual wealth tax. It is, however, possible to construct a tax which is based on an underlying implied progressive annual wealth tax, which takes account of the age gap between the donor and the donee, which is not disturbed by changes in rates of tax, but which nevertheless is levied only as a net charge on the donee. Such a tax we shall call an *age gap annual wealth accessions tax* or AGAWAT for short.

An AGAWAT would be constructed on the following lines. For all taxpayers a record would be kept, as with an ordinary accessions tax, of all gifts received up to date. This would not be a net total after deduction of gifts made, as with the PAWAT; it would be a gross cumulation of all gifts received. The donee would on receipt of the gift be liable for a transfer tax which would cover an implied annual wealth tax for a number of future years. The implied annual wealth tax would, as with the PAWAT, be progressive according to the taxpayer's total cumulative sum of gifts already received. But the future period for which he franked the wealth would not, as with the PAWAT, be up to some fixed date such as his 85th birthday, but would be up to the date at which he, the donee, would reach the present age of the donor. In other words, the arbitrary assumption would be made that the donee would pass the wealth on at the same age at which the present donor had given the wealth to him.

For the administration of an AGAWAT a schedule of rates of tax to be levied on receipt of a gift can be constructed, which depends upon the cumulative amount of gifts received by the donee and upon the gap between his age and the age of the donor. Such a schedule is illustrated in Table 15.3.

Table 15.3 *Illustrative rate schedule for an AGAWAT*

	Brackets of cumulative total of gifts received (£)					
Age gap between donor and donee (years)	50,000–100,000	100,000–500,000	500,000–1 m	1 m – 2 m	2 m – 5 m	5 m+
	Rate of equivalent wealth tax (%)					
	$\frac{1}{2}$	1	$1\frac{1}{2}$	2	$2\frac{1}{2}$	3
	Rate of AGAWAT (%)					
85	15	31	46	61	77	92
80	15	30	45	60	75	90
70	15	29	44	58	73	87
60	14	28	42	55	69	83
50	13	26	39	51	64	77
45	12	25	37	49	61	73
40	12	23	35	46	58	69
35	11	21	32	43	54	64
30	10	20	29	39	49	59
25	9	17	26	35	44	52
20	7	15	22	30	37	45
15	6	12	18	24	30	36
10	4	9	13	17	21	26
5	2	5	7	9	11	14
$2\frac{1}{2}$	1	2	4	5	6	7

Note: The AGAWAT figures represent the rate of tax payable by a donee whose age exceeds that of the donor, or the rate of tax refund received by a donee in the exceptional case in which the donee is older than the donor.

Each column of this table is obtained by multiplying the rate of equivalent wealth tax at the head of each column by the annuity multipliers given in section B of Table 15.1. It is in effect simply an application of the use of Table 15.1 to calculate the tax payable by a donee, with the age gap between donee and donor replacing the number of years which must elapse until the donee reaches his 85th birthday.

As compared with a PAWAT this tax would have the advantage that there was only one tax computation of a net liability to tax of the donee; the donor would receive no tax rebate.[8] But as compared with a PAWAT it suffers from three important disadvantages:

1 The combination of age gap and total previous accessions as elements in determining the rate of tax means that tax may be avoided in some cases through an indirect routing of a gift or bequest. Thus suppose that A wishes to transfer a gift to B who is both considerably younger than A and has already received considerable previous gifts; the rate of tax under an AGAWAT would be high on both counts. If A can find someone else C, who is of B's age but has so far received no gifts, a transfer from A to C will attract relatively little tax because C has received no previous gifts, and a transfer from C to B will attract no tax because they are of the same age.

2 AGAWAT could work rather arbitrarily in some cases. A young donee who receives a gift from an aged donor may have no intention of himself keeping the wealth for anything like as long as it will take him to reach the donor's age. The donee will in fact be paying a tax which exaggerates the period for which the holding of the wealth should be franked. This will be particularly anomalous if the donee has already received much inherited wealth and intends to pass on his new inheritance quickly. He will overpay at an exceptionally high rate for an exceptionally long period.

3 We have shown that an unmodified PAWAT, unlike a LAWAT, gives a tax incentive for someone who has accumulated wealth to hold on to that wealth as long as possible, since saved wealth does not become liable to tax until it is passed on and becomes inherited wealth. AGAWAT also gives a tax incentive to delay the passing on of saved wealth since, as with an unmodified PAWAT, such wealth does not become taxed until it is passed on and becomes inherited wealth. But AGAWAT goes further. Unlike PAWAT it gives the same tax incentive to delay the handing on of inherited wealth as it does to delay the handing on of saved wealth. Once AGAWAT has been paid there will, unlike the case with PAWAT, be no return of tax however quickly the wealth is handed on. We have suggested above (pp. 326–327) that with a PAWAT it might be desirable to give some repayment or discount or other tax advantage to promote the early giving of gifts of wealth saved out of the donor's own resources. With an AGAWAT it would be necessary to extend such an incentive for early giving to cover all gifts whether of saved or of inherited wealth.

For these reasons the Committee would prefer the use of PAWAT to the use of AGAWAT, if it were desired to introduce a progressive accessions tax which also took account of the length of time which the inherited wealth was held by the donee. If, however, the complication of dealing with separate calculations for the donor and donee and making refunds to the donor, unless the refund were treated as part of the gift, made the administration of a PAWAT too difficult, an AGAWAT would be a feasible alternative.

[8] A net tax repayment to the donee would arise in the exceptional case in which the donee was older than the donor.

CONCLUSIONS

Taxes on the transfer of wealth by gift or inheritance have the effect of taxing more heavily the ownership of inherited wealth than that of wealth accumulated out of the owner's own savings, and they can be designed to give incentives for a wider dispersion of the ownership of such wealth. For this purpose a form of tax which is progressively related to the cumulative amount which the donee has received to date by way of gift or inheritance (an accessions tax) is more suitable than a tax which is progressively related to the cumulative amount which the donor has given away to date in the form of gifts and bequests (the present capital transfer tax or CTT).

The accessions tax would be much improved if it were so designed as to relate the tax also to the ages of donor and donee and so to the period for which the donee was going to enjoy his inheritance before he passed it on. Such a tax, which takes the form of an advance payment of an annual wealth tax on inherited wealth and which we call a progressive annual wealth accessions tax or PAWAT, can be devised and has great merit as a progressive tax on inherited wealth combined with maximum incentive for persons who have inherited much to pass the wealth on quickly to those who have inherited little. It suffers from some administrative problems, the solution of which might blunt the effects of the tax; and there would be difficulty in avoiding its application to gifts between husband and wife.

A non-progressive form of PAWAT, which we call LAWAT, would be much simpler to apply; and we shall consider in the next chapter the possible use of a LAWAT in connection with a progressive annual wealth tax.

An accessions tax can be devised which falls progressively on the cumulative total received by the donee but also takes into account the age gap between donor and donee; this we call an AGAWAT. This has some merits; but it would be much less closely related to the period during which any particular donee in fact enjoyed his inheritance and in some cases could be open to serious avoidance by the indirect routing of gifts.

Appendix 15.1   The Capital Transfer Tax

The CTT is levied on transfers of wealth by gift or by bequest at death. The rate of tax is cumulative over the life of the donor, depending, when any transfer is made, upon the total amount which the donor has already given away on previous occasions. The amount of wealth transferred is reckoned inclusive of the CTT payable upon it. The rate of tax is, however, lower on the first £300,000 in the case of gifts *inter vivos* than in the case of wealth transferred on, or within three years of, death. There are, moreover, certain exemptions. A donor may give £100 in any one year to any donee without incurring tax, and in addition habitual expenditure out of income and the first £2,000 worth of transfers in any one year are exempt from tax and excluded from his cumulative liability. In addition, the first £15,000 of further transfers cumulated over the donor's life are taxed at a nil rate. Table 15.4 shows the current scale of tax rates.

The tax unit is the individual, but transfers between spouses are exempt from tax and do not cumulate.

Table 15.4   *Rates of capital transfer tax, 1976/77.*

Slice of cumulative transfers		Transfers during life (but not within 3 years of death)		Transfers on or within 3 years before death	
Over (£)	Not over (£)	Marginal rate of tax (%)	Average rate of tax at top of slice (%)	Marginal rate of tax (%)	Average rate of tax at top of slice (%)
—	15,000	nil	nil	nil	nil
15,000	20,000	5	1·25	10	2·50
20,000	25,000	7·5	2·50	15	5·00
25,000	30,000	10	3·75	20	7·50
30,000	40,000	12·5	5·94	25	11·88
40,000	50,000	15	7·75	30	15·50
50,000	60,000	17·5	9·38	35	18·75
60,000	80,000	20	12·03	40	24·06
80,000	100,000	22·5	14·13	45	28·25
100,000	120,000	27·5	16·35	50	31·88
120,000	150,000	35	20·08	55	36·50
150,000	200,000	42·5	25·64		42·38
200,000	250,000	50	30·51	60	45·90
250,000	300,000	55	34·59		48·25
300,000	500,000	60	44·75		52·95
500,000	1,000,000	65	54·88	65	58·98
1,000,000	2,000,000	70	62·24	70	64·49
2,000,000	—	75		75	

In the case of a trust, the capital is regarded as belonging to any beneficiary who has a beneficial interest in possession, i.e. a right to receive income, such as a life interest. Such capital is regarded as being transferred when the individual's interest changes, and tax is calculated with reference to the cumulative transfers of that person.

Where there is no such interest in possession in settled property, typically in the case of a discretionary trust, a charge to tax arises when there is an actual or deemed capital distribution, the tax on existing trusts being calculated as if the trust were an individual but on new trusts being calculated with reference to the tax rate of the original settlor. In particular there is a periodic charge every ten years when the whole of the property is deemed to be distributed, but in this case the rate is 30 per cent of that which would normally apply to capital distributions and the charge does not enter into the cumulative total of transfers of the settlement. These charges do not, however, apply to settlements made for the maintenance of persons aged under 25.

Broadly, all property situated in the United Kingdom is subject to the charge.

Property situated outside the country is also chargeable, unless (i) the beneficial owner is domiciled outside the United Kingdom, or (ii) if it is settled property, the settlor was domiciled outside the United Kingdom when he made the settlement.

For CTT purposes domicile is artificially extended (i) for three years after ceasing to be domiciled, (ii) to include a person who has been resident for income tax purposes for seventeen out of twenty consecutive years, or (iii) to include persons who emigrate to the Channel Isles or Isle of Man.

Detailed reliefs are given in respect to (i) gifts to charities and political parties, (ii) works of art and historic buildings, (iii) businesses,[1] and (iv) agriculture and forestry.[1]

NOTE

1 These are described in Appendix 16.1.

Appendix 15.2　Tax Formulae for PAWAT, LAWAT and AGAWAT

The basic principle is to levy, in an advance lump sum payment, an amount which represents a future annual charge on the wealth. In the main text we have considered three possible forms which such a payment might take: PAWAT, LAWAT and AGAWAT. In the case of PAWAT these forms can be expressed by three formulae, which we call formula A, formula B and formula C.

FORMULA A

A straightforward principle would be to levy a transfer tax on the donee which was equal to the present value of a rate of annual wealth tax (w) payable on the holding of the inherited property (P) for a number of future years (n) equal to the difference between, say, age 85 and the donee's present age, the rate of tax w being progressively related to the net cumulative total of gifts received less gifts made up to date by the taxpayer. When the donee became a donor he would receive in tax rebate an amount equal to the then present value of this underlying annual wealth tax for the remainder of the period up to his 85th birthday. He would in fact have paid what corresponded to the annual wealth tax w on the property P for the precise number of years which had elapsed before he handed the wealth on.

Formula A for the transfer tax payable or transfer tax repayment would then be

$$T_A = P \frac{w}{r} \left(1 - \frac{1}{(1+r)^n} \right)$$

where r is the rate of interest at which the annual payment of tax of Pw for n years is discounted to give its present value.

It would be possible to use an actuarial expectation-of-life figure instead of the time until reaching an arbitrary age such as 85. This has the advantage that the refund is always a positive amount whatever the donor's age, whereas over 85 there would be no refund under formula A. It is doubtful whether it would be worth strictly applying actuarial tables, because there would still be differences between expectations of life between environments and occupations and because the differing expectations of males and females would need to be covered.

Another reason against using the expectation of life to calculate formula A is that it would be illogical to make refunds on death, and this in turn would mean introducing anti-avoidance legislation to prevent death bed gifts.

The simplest solution seems to be to calculate formula A to a fixed age, which we have taken to be 85, and to ignore the possibility of people living beyond this age. Taxpayers who did so would get a period free of PAWAT.

Although we have taken 85 as the terminal age for PAWAT in our illustrations, the lifetime rate pattern which emerges (see the annuity multipliers of Table 15.1, p. 323) may not give a sufficiently clear incentive for giving in early middle age. An earlier terminal age, such as 70, would give such an incentive, since the period when PAWAT credits declined rapidly with age would now start earlier. However, against this advantage of an earlier terminal age must be set the disadvantage that there would be no incentive for those beyond the terminal age to give to younger persons: on the contrary, the reverse would apply, since the potential donor aged 70 or more would experience no further loss of refund with increasing age, whereas the prospective liability of any potential donee would decline as he grew older.

The use of a formula of this kind, in the form of a table, is not unknown in the existing tax system; the curved line depreciation of short leases for capital gains tax is the present value of an annuity discounted at 6 per cent.

The question arises, however, whether or not the corresponding future annual wealth tax, whose present value is being calculated for lump-sum transfer tax, should be based on the assumption that the capital fund of the wealth is maintained intact over the future period during which the donee is assumed to be going to hold it, or whether allowance should be made for the fact that the capital sum may be eroded by payment of the tax, so that the corresponding annual tax would itself decline from year to year.

Formula A is based on the assumption that the property should be maintained intact – each generation of owners saving enough to make up for the transfer tax.

FORMULA B

This second formula is based on the assumption that the property will be diminished each generation by the transfer tax levied on it.

The logic of the distinction between the two assumptions lying behind formulae A and B can be seen clearly if it is thought of in terms of the implied annual wealth tax which the lump-sum advance payment of inheritance tax is replacing. Suppose that the rate of annual wealth tax is 2 per cent a year. Suppose that the wealth itself yields more than this to the owner, e.g. 5 per cent a year. The owner may very well decide to consume only the difference, i.e. 3 per cent a year, and to pay the wealth tax out of the yield. The alternative assumption would be that the owner pays the wealth tax out of the capital fund, so that the capital fund is reduced to 0·98 by the end of the first year, to $0·98 \times 0·98$ by the end of the second year, and so on. If the annual wealth tax payable each year were at a rate w, then the tax payable each year would be as follows:

Year	Assumption A	Assumption B
1	Pw	Pw
2	Pw	$Pw(1-w)$
3	Pw	$Pw(1-w)^2$
.	.	.
.	.	.
.	.	.
n	Pw	$Pw(1-w)^{n-1}$

The corresponding transfer tax payable on receipt of the inheritance to be held for n years would be the present value of the first column on the assumption that the wealth was maintained and of the second column if the wealth was eroded by the wealth tax. The present value of the first column is the expression given above for T_A, and the present value of the second column is

$$T_B = P \frac{w}{r+w} \left[1 - \left(\frac{1-w}{1+r} \right)^n \right]$$

which gives formula B for the lump sum transfer tax.[1]

Which of the two assumptions lying behind formula A and formula B is to be preferred is clearly in part dependent upon the severity of the tax rates. If top rates of tax were planned to be so high that property could not be maintained intact, it would be inappropriate to structure the whole schedule of rates on the assumption that it would be so maintained. On the other hand, if the tax rates were so moderate that maintenance of the value of the property could readily be achieved through saving a fraction of the annual yield on the property, the construction of tax scales on the assumption of the maintenance of the property would not be unreasonable.

One factor which should clearly influence the choice of assumption is whether there is an income tax or an expenditure tax regime for current direct taxation. If the market yield on capital is eroded by capital gains tax and income tax (particularly if there is an investment income surcharge and the marginal rates of tax on investment income rise to the present extremely high levels), the ability to maintain large inherited properties out of the post-tax yield on the property is reduced or eliminated.

If there is an expenditure tax regime which exempts from tax any yield on property which is itself saved, then, provided that the rate of annual wealth tax is itself not higher than the yield on wealth, it will always be possible to maintain the property intact and to have something left over – however small – to spend on current consumption.

FORMULA C

Formulae A and B both use some market rate of discount r in order to calculate the present value of a stream of imaginary annual liabilities to wealth tax, the difference between them depending upon whether this stream of annual tax payments is assumed to remain constant or to fall through time. Formula C is based upon a rather different principle.

As with formulae A and B, when a donee receives a gift the transfer tax is related to an imaginary rate of annual wealth tax w, which is progressively dependent upon the cumulative net total of gifts received less gifts made by the donee up to date. But the rate of corresponding lump-sum transfer tax T_C is derived from this imaginary rate of annual wealth tax w in a rather different manner. Transfer tax is deducted from the gift at a rate such that, if the remaining gift net of tax were set aside and accumulated at a compound rate of interest equal to the rate of annual wealth tax w, then, after a specified number of years (equal, for example, to the years which must elapse before the donee's 85th birthday) the capital sum would have grown once more back to its original pre-transfer-tax gross value. Moreover, since any tax rebate on the making of a gift would be calculated on the same basis, any donee who received a gift and did in fact accumulate the post-transfer-tax net amount at a compound rate of interest equal to w could at any time hand on the gift intact, since the accumulated sum plus tax repayment would be equal to the gross pre-transfer-tax value of the original gift.

Formula C[2] for the transfer tax is

$$T_C = P \left(1 - \frac{1}{(1+w)^n}\right)$$

Another way of describing the situation is to say that the transfer tax is such that, if the donee can obtain a rate of yield w on the gift after the payment of transfer tax, then by saving up the whole of the yield w he can just manage to maintain intact the value of his inherited property (inclusive of any tax rebate if he gives it away). If he can obtain a yield greater than w, then he can maintain his capital intact and add to his consumption. If he can only obtain a yield less than w, then he cannot maintain the inherited wealth intact without boosting it from some other source of income. Since w is set at a progressive rate depending upon the net amount of wealth which has been inherited, those who have inherited much are set a harder yield target than those who have inherited little. Indeed, as a matter of deliberate policy, w may be set so high for the very large inheritances that it is virtually impossible to achieve such a rate of yield and to maintain the property intact.

THE CHOICE OF FORMULA FOR A PAWAT

In the main text of Chapter 15 we have adopted formula A; and section A in Table 15.1 gives a schedule for the values of w on different slices of inherited wealth, while the annuity multipliers in section B of the table are obtained from the expression

$$\frac{1}{r} \left(1 - \frac{1}{(1+r)^{85-a}}\right)$$

where the discount rate r is assumed to be 3 per cent a year and a represents the age of the taxpayer when the gift is made.

With formula A, unlike formulae B and C, it is possible to separate the expression into the two elements of w (the marginal rate of equivalent annual wealth tax) and the r expression displayed above (the annuity multiplier). This fact makes it much easier to cope with situations in which the rates of equivalent annual wealth tax change between the date when a taxpayer receives a gift and the later date when he hands the wealth on to someone else. The problems associated with such changes in tax rates and the way in which they may be handled with formula A are described in Appendix 15.3.

From formula A, namely

$$T_A = P\frac{w}{r}\left(1 - \frac{1}{(1+r)^n}\right)$$

it can be seen that, if n is large (i.e. if the donee is very young) and w is greater than r, the tax liability on a donee can amount to more than 100 per cent of the gift. In order to avoid this absurd result it is necessary to choose a rate of discount r which is at least as great as the highest marginal rate of equivalent annual wealth tax w.

This does not, however, rule out the possibility of choosing rates of tax which are so high that it is impossible for the owner of inherited wealth to maintain the capital value of that wealth intact. Suppose that the rate of yield which the owner of such property can obtain on the property (after payment of any income tax on the yield) is y. Then if $w > y$, he cannot meet the equivalent annual wealth tax w out of the yield on the wealth y. He must either run down the capital sum or maintain it from some other source of savings. Thus by choosing values for r and w such that $r > w > y$, the absurdity of the rate of transfer tax exceeding 100 per cent can be avoided while rates of tax that are bound to erode inherited wealth can yet be imposed.

It is of interest to consider some other aspects of the relationship between the three rates of tax w, of yield y and of discount r in the case of our formula A. For this purpose it can be asked what level of consumption the recipient of a gift could maintain out of the yield on that gift if he intended to keep the capital value of the gift intact. For this purpose let P be the value (gross of tax) of a gift received, so that

$$T_n = P\frac{w}{r}\left(1 - \frac{1}{(1+r)^n}\right)$$

is the refund of PAWAT which he could receive if he passed on the gift P intact when he was aged $(85-n)$. Let K_n be the value of the gift net of transfer tax at the beginning of the year in which the owner is $(85-n)$ years of age. If the value of the gift is to be passed on intact, then

$$K_n = P - T_n = P\left[1 - \frac{w}{r}\left(1 - \frac{1}{(1+r)^n}\right)\right]$$

and

$$K_{n-1} = P - T_{n-1} = P\left[1 - \frac{w}{r}\left(1 - \frac{1}{(1+r)^{n-1}}\right)\right]$$

But

$$C_n = K_n(1+y) - K_{n-1}$$

where C_n is the level of consumption when the owner is aged $(85-n)$. From the expressions for C_n, K_n and K_{n-1},

$$C_n = P\left[y - w - \frac{w}{r}(y-r)\left(1 - \frac{1}{(1+r)^n}\right)\right]$$

From this expression it can be seen that if $y = r$, $C_n = P(y-w)$, which is the steady level at which consumption would be maintained with an actual annual wealth tax, if only the excess of yield y over annual tax w were consumed. If $r > y$, then C can start at a value higher than $P(y-w)$ at age $(85-n)$ and falls gradually to $P(y-w)$ at age 85; a high r is favourable to the taxpayer because it reduces the lump-sum transfer tax by reducing the calculation of the present value of the future equivalent annual tax payments. Conversely, if $r < y$, C must start below $P(y-w)$ but can rise to $P(y-w)$ by age 85.

THE CHOICE OF FORMULA FOR A LAWAT

For the reasons given in the main text of Chapter 15, LAWAT is useful only if there is a willingness to disregard the fact that the rate of tax w at the time when a gift is received may be different from that ruling when the gift is passed on. A main reason for restricting the choice of formulae to formula A is thus removed. Thus for a LAWAT the formulae for the net tax liability of the donee can be derived from the expressions already given for T_A, T_B and T_C in the case of a PAWAT by taking the difference between the tax payable by the donee and the tax repayment due to the donor at a common value of w. The results are:

Formula A: $\quad P\dfrac{w}{r(1+r)^{85}}[(1+r)^{a_g} - (1+r)^{a_r}]$

Formula B: $\quad P\dfrac{w}{r+w}\left(\dfrac{1-w}{1+r}\right)^{85}\left[\left(\dfrac{1+r}{1-w}\right)^{a_g} - \left(\dfrac{1+r}{1-w}\right)^{a_r}\right]$

Formula C: $\quad \dfrac{P}{(1+w)^{85}}\ [(1+w)^{a_g} - (1+w)^{a_r}]$

where a_g is the age of the donor (or giver) and a_r is the age of the donee (or recipient). The illustrative Table 15.2 given in the main text on p. 332 is derived from formula A with $w = 1$ per cent and $r = 3$ per cent.

THE CHOICE OF FORMULA FOR AN AGAWAT

For an AGAWAT also there is no restriction to the use of formula A; and the three formulae T_A, T_B and T_C as expressed for PAWAT can be used for AGAWAT if n is interpreted as the age gap between donor and donee instead of the number of years before the taxpayer reaches the age of 85. Table 15.3 (given in the main text on p. 334) is derived from formula A, with the same values for w and r as those given for PAWAT in Table 15.1 (on p. 323 of the main text).

NOTES

1 The expression for T_B can never rise above unity however great n may be. The transfer tax will always be less than 100 per cent however young the donee and however high the implied rate of annual wealth tax (i.e. however great n and w may be). On the other hand, the expression for T_A could rise above unity if the donee were sufficiently young (n sufficiently great) and the rate of implied annual wealth tax were sufficiently raised above the rate of interest (w/r greater than unity). For rates of wealth tax sufficiently high relatively to possible rates of yield, i.e. for rates of wealth tax which are expressly designed to make impossible the maintenance of large inherited properties, formula B is for this reason more appropriate than formula A.

2 $(P - T_C)$ is the post-transfer-tax value of the inherited wealth. This sum accumulated for n years at a compound rate of interest w is equal to $(P - T_C)(1+w)^n$. If this is equated to the original pre-transfer-tax value of the wealth, $(P - T_C)(1+w)^n = P$ or $T_C = P[1 - 1/(1+w)^n]$. If after m years the donee hands on wealth equal to P, he has accumulated $(P - T_C)(1+w)^m = P/(1+w)^{n-m}$ and he receives in tax rebate $P[1 - 1/(1+w)^{n-m}]$, a total of P.

Appendix 15.3 The Working of PAWAT with a Succession of Gifts, with Changes in the Tax Schedule and with Indexation for Inflation

Example A.

In 1977 a donee aged 60 receives an inheritance of £1 million, having received no previous gifts or inheritances. The current schedule of progressive rates of equivalent annual wealth tax and the table of annuity multipliers is as shown in Table 15.1 in the main text. The donee's liability to PAWAT can then be calculated as follows:

	PAWAT total (£)	Rate of equivalent annual wealth tax (%)	Amount of equivalent annual wealth tax (£)
	50,000	0	0
Slices	50,000	$\frac{1}{2}$	250
of	400,000	1	4,000
inheritance	500,000	$1\frac{1}{2}$	7,500
TOTAL	1,000,000		11,750

PAWAT payable = present value of annual payment of £11,750 for twenty-five years till donee's 85th birthday = £11,750 × 17·41 = £204,568.

In the donee's tax records two figures are carried forwards:

1 PAWAT total   = £1,000,000
2 Amount of equivalent annual wealth tax for which this is franked   =   £11,750

Example B.

In 1982 the same donee, now aged 65, receives a second inheritance of £1 million. The price index used for indexation against inflation has risen by 25 per cent since 1977; and the two figures carried forwards in the donee's tax record are accordingly adjusted:

1 PAWAT total indexed   = £1,000,000 × 1·25 = £1,250,000
2 Amount of equivalent annual wealth tax for which this is franked, indexed   =   £11,750 × 1·25 =   £14,688

The annuity multipliers remain unchanged as in Table 15.1, but the schedule of progressive rates of equivalent annual wealth tax has been revised as follows:

Slices of PAWAT total (£)	Rate of equivalent annual wealth tax (%)
0– 60,000	0
60,001– 120,000	$\frac{1}{2}$
120,001– 550,000	1
550,001–1,100,000	$1\frac{1}{2}$
1,100,001–2,000,000	2
2,000,001–5,000,000	$2\frac{1}{2}$

The donee's PAWAT liability on his new inheritance of £1 million can then be calculated as follows:

	PAWAT total (£)	Rate of equivalent annual wealth tax (%)	Amount of equivalent annual wealth tax (£)
Brought forward	1,250,000	—	—
Slices of new inheritance	750,000	2	15,000
	250,000	$2\frac{1}{2}$	6,250
TOTAL	2,250,000		21,250

PAWAT payable on new inheritance = present value of annual payment of £21,250 for twenty years till donee's 85th birthday = £21,250 ×14·88 = £316,200. In the donee's tax record the two figures are carried forwards:

1 PAWAT total   = £2,250,000
2 Amount of equivalent annual wealth tax
   for which this is franked   = £14,688 + £21,250 =   £35,938

Example C.
In 1992 when he is now aged 75 the donee becomes a donor and makes a gift of £1 million. The price index has gone up by 12 per cent since 1982, and the two relevant figures in the donor's tax record are adjusted accordingly:

1 PAWAT total indexed   = £2,250,000 ×1·12   = £2,520,000
2 Amount of equivalent annual wealth tax
   for which this is franked, indexed   =   £35,938 ×1·12   =   £40,249

The donor is giving away £1,000,000 ÷ £2,520,000 = 40 per cent of his PAWAT total. His PAWAT total should therefore be 'defranked' in respect of 40 per cent of the equivalent annual wealth tax of £40,249, i.e. in respect of £16,100 of equivalent annual wealth tax payable for the next ten years until the donor's 85th birthday. The present value of this is £16,100 ×8·53 = £137,330; and this is the refund of PAWAT that is due to the donor. The new donee will, of course, be liable to PAWAT on the receipt of the £1 million at a rate which will depend both upon his age and upon his existing PAWAT total.

The two relevant figures to be carried forwards in the new donor's tax record are now:

1 PAWAT   = £2,520,000 − £1,000,000 = £1,520,000
2 Amount of equivalent annual wealth
   tax for which this is franked   =   £40,249 − £16,100 =   £24,149

Example D.
In the same year 1992, almost immediately after making the gift discussed in example C, the new donor dies, still aged 75. There is no change in the price index, and his PAWAT total remains unchanged at £1,520,000. There is, of course, no reason to believe that the amount of wealth to be inherited by his heirs will be equal to the

donor's PAWAT total of £1,520,000. The donor may have dissipated his inheritance or failed to invest it so as to keep up with inflation; or, on the other hand, he may have accumulated a big additional fortune from his own enterprise and savings.

Let us first illustrate the position with the supposition that the donor dies owning property worth only £500,000. His heirs will, however, be able to inherit more than £500,000 because a PAWAT refund will be due to the donor's estate when the property is handed on. In other words, the £500,000 must be grossed up by the rate of PAWAT refund due on the passing on of the property. This rate of PAWAT refund is in fact 13·733 per cent, as is shown in the calculations for the gift of £1 million made in example C. The relevant figures have remained unchanged; and (as shown) in these conditions the refund averages at £137,330 on £1 million or 13·733 per cent. The £500,000 grossed up at 13·733 per cent gives £579,596. This is the value of the inheritance received by the heirs, of which £500,000 represents the property actually received from the donor's estate and £79,596 represents the PAWAT refund due from the Inland Revenue. The heirs would have to pay their own PAWAT liability on their inheritance of £579,596; but the net amount payable by them to the Inland Revenue would be this liability less £79,596.

If the donor in fact dies worth a great deal more than his existing PAWAT total of £1,520,000, not the whole of his net property at death can be grossed up in this way. He is owed a PAWAT refund only on his PAWAT total; and it is therefore only on the part of his property which, when grossed up at 13·733 per cent, amounts to £1,520,000 that a PAWAT refund can be obtained. Any property which he leaves over and above £1,311,258 (which grossed up at 13·733 per cent equals £1,520,000) will be treated as property which has resulted from his own accumulated savings.

In example C the gift of £1 million was not a grossed-up figure. In fact the donor was out of pocket by only £862,670, i.e. the gift of £1 million less the £137,330 PAWAT refund. On death the method of grossing up must be employed in order to clear the books. In fact it would be possible, if desired, to treat all gifts on the grossing-up method. Thus, in example C the gift could be treated as one of £862,670 by the donor made on the arrangement that the recipient of the gift would be entitled to the PAWAT refund on the grossed-up figure of £1 million. In this case the donor's gift would express just the amount by which the donor intended to be out of pocket, and the donee would be liable to pay to the Revenue his PAWAT liability on the grossed-up value of the gift less the refund due to the donor. This arrangement could be required as obligatory in all cases if, on administrative grounds, it were desired to avoid two independent tax transactions (a refund to donor and tax on donee) and to rely on a single tax transaction instead (a net payment by donee). The method might, however, raise problems of confidentiality in respect of information which the donor did not wish to reveal to the donee. If such considerations were held to outweigh any administrative gains due to the avoidance of two separate transactions, the grossing-up system could operate by election, in a similar way to the donee being able, under existing arrangements, to pay CTT instead of the donor.

Appendix 15.4   The Definition of Gifts between Members of the Same Family

For certain tax purposes it may be necessary to assess the value of gifts between members of the same family. We assume that a transfer of funds from husband to wife for the finance of their joint housekeeping and consumption expenses cannot be treated as a taxable gift, and indeed that in general it is impossible to allocate personal consumption between members of a family. If this is so, a member of a family can be treated as having received a gift from another member of the family only if the increase in his ownership of assets (registered and unregistered) plus gifts made by him to outsiders is greater than his income (net of direct taxes paid) plus gifts received by him from outsiders. An individual's flow-of-funds table shows this to be equal to the individual's receipt of transfers of funds from other members of the family less his transfers of funds to other members of the family less his own financing of personal consumption on behalf of the family:

$$
\left.\begin{array}{l}
\text{Income} \\
+\text{Gifts from outside} \\
+\text{Transfers from other} \\
\quad \text{members of the family}
\end{array}\right\}
=
\left\{\begin{array}{l}
\text{Consumption} \\
+\text{Increase in assets owned} \\
+\text{Direct taxes paid} \\
+\text{Gifts to outsiders} \\
+\text{Transfers to other members} \\
\quad \text{of the family}
\end{array}\right.
$$

In the case of a married couple without children, this is in principle fairly straightforward. The husband is treated as having made a gift to the wife if the wife's assets (which must include unregistered assets in case the husband gives the wife a Rembrandt or the money with which she purchases a Rembrandt) go up by more than her own resources of income (net of tax) plus net gifts received from outsiders. That is how it should be assessed. In fact it is equal to all transfers from the husband (including any housekeeping money which he transfers to the wife) less the wife's expenditure on consumption, provided that this sum is positive.

The same principle could be adopted for the definition of gifts between parents and children. Any individual member of a family can be treated as having received a gift from other members of the family if the increase in his ownership of assets plus any gifts which he makes to outsiders is greater than his own income (net of tax) plus gifts received from outsiders.

But there is now an added complication. It may be arbitrary as to which of the other members of the family is deemed to have made the gift to him. If, for example, both parents make transfers of money to a child, some of which the child spends on consumption, which parent is to be treated as having merely financed part of the family consumption and which as having made the net gift to the child? This must be decided either by agreement within the family or by the application of some rather arbitrary *pro rata* formula.

It is not suggested that these formulae should be meticulously calculated every year for every family member. It is merely suggested that, if and when there is a dispute between the taxpayer and the Revenue authorities as to the existence or the magnitude of a gift between members of the same family, the decision should be based upon the principles outlined above. Many countries do in fact find it possible to cope with the taxation of gifts between spouses; but it is desirable to have a more-or-less precise definition of what is the tax base. The formulae outlined in this appendix would appear to us to provide the best definition of such gifts.

Appendix 15.5   The Treatment of Trusts under a PAWAT

Suppose that a beneficiary with n years to elapse before his 85th birthday receives a payment P out of a trust set up m years ago. The amount of money needed m years ago to produce the funds for P would be $P/(1+y)^m$, where y represents the rate of yield on the trust funds. The tax payable on this sum under formula A would have been

$$\frac{P}{(1+y)^m} \cdot \frac{w}{r} \left(1 - \frac{1}{(1+r)^{n+m}}\right)$$

if this sum had been paid to this beneficiary m years ago and if the beneficiary's net cumulative total of gifts received had been m years ago what it is now. But the Revenue authorities have had to wait m years for this tax, so that its present value may be reckoned at

$$P\frac{w}{r} \left(1 - \frac{1}{(1+r)^{n+m}}\right) \left(\frac{1+i}{1+y}\right)^m$$

where i is the rate of interest charged on loans by the Revenue to the taxpayer. With $i = y$ (which implies that the Revenue charges a rate of interest equal to the rate of yield on the trust funds), this means that the beneficiary at the time of the actual receipt of P should pay transfer tax on it at the rates appropriate (i) to his net cumulative total of gifts received up to date, and (ii) to what his age would have been at the date at which the trust was set up.

Three queries can be raised:

1   Should not the beneficiary add $P/(1+y)^m$ rather than P to his net cumulative total of gifts received?

2   Should not the rate of tax be related to what his cumulative net total was m years ago when the trust was set up rather than to what that total is when the payment P is actually received by him?

3   Should not the tax on all gifts made or received by him in the years since the date of the settlement of the trust be consequentially adjusted with appropriate compound interest?

It would, however, be administratively impossible to job backwards in this way. It seems inevitable that the current values both of the gift itself for addition to the net cumulative total and of the net cumulative total itself should be used in the tax computation. Only the age of the beneficiary can be jobbed backwards. The first two items above increase the tax, but this may be to some extent offset by lower tax charges on other gifts received since the settlement. The net effect would probably be a net loss to the taxpayer, which would perhaps be a not unreasonable discouragement against the unnecessary use of trusts.

It may well be that a system as described above, which involves the repayment of tax to the settlor of a trust at the time of its institution and the gathering of the tax from the beneficiary only m years later, would be unacceptable – even though the system implies a rate of interest on the loan from the Revenue authorities to the trust. There are two possible ways in which this feature of the scheme might be suitably modified:

1   It could be ruled that the tax repayment due to the settlor at the time when the

trust was set up should not be paid to the settlor but should be added to the capital of the trust in the form of a tax credit due from the government, which would accumulate over time at some given rate of interest. When payments were made to beneficiaries out of the trust, this accumulated tax credit could be used to meet the tax liabilities of the beneficiaries.

2   The problem could also be dealt with by making the tax repayment in the normal way to the settlor when the trust was set up, but at the same time levying an advance accessions tax at some more or less arbitrary rate (e.g. 40 per cent) on the trust capital.[1] When any payment was made out of the trust, the amount would be grossed up by the 40 per cent rate of tax and the grossed-up figure would be added to the beneficiary's net cumulative total and would be employed to calculate his tax liability. But against this tax liability would be set the 40 per cent grossing-up of the amount of benefit which he actually received from the trust. If his calculated tax rate were 40 per cent, he would pay no net tax; if it were more than 40 per cent, he would pay the difference; and if it were less than 40 per cent, he would receive a tax repayment of the difference.

In effect, all the current values in the trust would be treated as if they had been reduced by 40 per cent through the 40 per cent reduction in the original capital of the fund as a result of the initial advance accessions tax. Subsequently, all payments would be treated as if this tax had not been levied; i.e. they would be grossed up by 40 per cent with a 40 per cent tax credit attached.

NOTE

1 One possibility would be to levy this advanced accessions tax at the same rate as the rate of tax repayment to the settlor. In this case, on the setting-up of a trust there would be no net tax paid or received by the Revenue authorities. But each trust would then have to be conducted (for grossing-up of benefits and for tax credits) on its own individual rate of advance accessions tax.

16 Capital Taxes II: An Annual Wealth Tax

DIFFERENCES BETWEEN A TRANSFER TAX AND AN ANNUAL WEALTH TAX [1]

We have so far examined taxes which are levied on the occasion of a *transfer* of wealth. We turn now to a consideration of an annual tax levied on the *holding* of wealth. In our examination of transfer taxes we pointed out that such taxes could be so devised as to represent a lump sum prepayment of an annual wealth tax (AWT). But even if transfer taxes are devised in this way, there remain some important differences between taxes levied on the occasion of a transfer of wealth and taxes levied annually on the holding of wealth. The two types of capital tax cannot be complete substitutes for each other, and it is important to appreciate what are the significant differences between them.

1 THE DISTINCTION BETWEEN INHERITED AND SAVED WEALTH

The first outstanding difference is that taxes on the transfer of wealth are not levied on wealth which is accumulated out of an individual's own savings until that wealth is transferred to some other owner. An AWT, on the other hand, which is levied on the holding of all wealth, will levy a charge on the wealth which an owner has himself accumulated by his own effort and out of his own savings.

We have already (p. 318 above) expressed our agreement with the view that both on grounds of fairness and on grounds of economic incentives it is a virtue of such transfer taxes that they do thus discriminate against inherited wealth. But this does not necessarily imply that there should be no taxation of saved wealth.

Investment income is more valuable to the recipient than an equal earned income for two main reasons: (i) unlike earning capacity it does not decline with age, so that there is less need to save from it for old age or for one's heirs; and (ii) it is obtained without the sacrifice of leisure. Under an income tax regime there is therefore a powerful case for taxing investment income more heavily than earned income. This can be done by a supplementary tax on investment income or by a special relief of earned income. Alternatively it can be done by means of an AWT on the source of the investment income.

---

[1] The problems connected with AWT have been recently exhaustively reviewed in the reports of the Select Committee on a Wealth Tax (H.C. 696 I–IV, January 1977) and in an earlier volume prepared for the Institute for Fiscal Studies by three of the members of the present Committee (C. T. Sandford, J. R. M. Willis and D. J. Ironside, *An Annual Wealth Tax*, London: Heinemann Educational Books, 1975). Accordingly, in this part of our Report we shall express our attitude to the main issues without discussing many of the detailed problems involved.

There may be other reasons (described later) for preferring an annual tax levied on the wealth from which investment income is derived to a tax levied on the annual income derived from such wealth; and in this case it would be appropriate to replace the investment income surcharge by an AWT with a relatively low threshold and a relatively mild schedule of rates of tax.

This argument is weakened if the income tax regime is replaced by an expenditure tax regime. Someone with an investment income can live at a higher standard than someone with an equal earned income because he does not have to save for his old age or for his heirs; but he will automatically pay a higher expenditure tax on his higher consumption, whereas he would have paid the same income tax on his equal income. But even with an expenditure tax regime the case for some special tax on investment income or on the wealth from which it proceeds is not completely met, for two reasons:

1   A given level of expenditure will be achieved at the expense of leisure if it is financed out of earned income, but without such expense if it is financed out of capital or investment income.
2   The holding of wealth itself, whether it arises from inheritance or from the owner's own effort and savings, can confer on the owner benefits of security, independence, influence and power, quite apart from any expenditure which the income from it may finance.

This last consideration, namely that the ownership of wealth itself may confer benefits quite apart from any income which it may produce, is an argument for preferring an AWT to an investment income surcharge. The former is levied on the wealth even if it is held in a form which produces little or no income. And this suggests a further reason why the AWT may be preferred. The AWT remains the same on any wealth, regardless of the income it yields, whereas the investment income surcharge rises with the income. The AWT is thus more likely than an investment income surcharge to give an incentive to seek out higher yielding assets, and may thus lead to a more efficient and productive use of capital resources.

These arguments speak for a tax on all wealth, whether it be inherited or accumulated out of the owner's own savings, and therefore apply to an AWT rather than to any system of taxation on the transfer of wealth. While they are the basic arguments for the imposition of some tax on all forms of wealth, whatever the source of the wealth may be, they are not the only reasons for wishing to tax saved wealth as well as inherited wealth.

As we have shown in the preceding chapter, accessions taxes, just because they exempt saved wealth from taxation until it is handed on, give an incentive for owners of saved wealth to postpone any gifts of such wealth as long as possible. A progressive AWT, on the other hand, gives an owner of large wealth (on which a high rate of AWT will be payable) a tax incentive to transfer such wealth as soon as possible to persons who own little wealth (on which only a low rate of AWT will be payable); and this tax incentive for rich owners to transfer their wealth at an early date to poor owners will apply to all wealth, whether it be in origin inherited wealth or saved wealth.

This aspect of a progressive AWT is particularly relevant if it is combined with a progressive expenditure tax regime rather than with a progressive income tax regime. In the latter case a man of wealth can escape AWT either by giving his wealth away to persons who own little wealth or by spending it lavishly on his own consumption; in the former case he can escape tax only by giving his wealth away.

Moreover, while it is true that a progressive AWT and a progressive accessions tax (e.g. the PAWAT and AGAWAT described in Chapter 15) both provide incentives to disperse the ownership of wealth more widely, the effect on inequalities in the ownership of property is likely to be more quickly realised with a progressive AWT than with a progressive accessions tax. This is clearly true if it is a question of introducing *ab initio* either an AWT or a PAWAT; the former will bite on all wealth at once, but the latter will bite only as wealth comes to be transferred. But the difference will remain also in the long run; the AWT will give an incentive to disperse large holdings of saved wealth as soon as they are accumulated, whereas the PAWAT will do so only when they come to be transferred.

So much for the distinctions between an AWT and an accessions tax that are due to the fact that the former covers all wealth whereas the latter covers only inherited wealth. There are a number of other relevant differences.

2   THE FLEXIBILITY OF TAX RATES

Different governments are likely to put different emphases on conflicting social and economic objectives. Some will put more emphasis on egalitarian objectives and will for that reason wish, *inter alia,* to tax wealthy persons at exceptionally high rates; others will put more weight upon the avoidance of tax disincentives to work and saving and will for that reason wish, *inter alia,* to avoid exceptionally high rates of tax. Variations in the rates of AWT are a fairer way of expressing such changes in political emphases than are variations in the rates of any form of transfer tax. The latter are unfair in so far as the effect on individuals depends in an arbitrary manner upon whether an owner happens to die under an egalitarian or under an incentive-loving government; the former affects all wealth holders equally just so long as the particular political regime lasts. If the objective sought for is a structure of taxes which (within limits) can be used by different political parties for rather different ends by altering tax *rates* rather than tax *structures,* a wealth tax which is levied annually has an important advantage over a once-for-all wealth tax levied in a lump sum on the occasion of a transfer.

3   INDEXING AGAINST INFLATION

Another distinction between the two types of capital taxes arises if there is a need to index them against the effects of inflation. Both an AWT and a transfer tax will require bracket indexation, in the sense that the slices of wealth which will be exempt or subject to different rates of tax must be increased in money terms each year to keep in step with the general inflation of money prices. With an AWT that is the end of the problem. But with any form of cumulative transfer tax (whether it be the existing capital transfer tax, which cumulates total gifts made over time, or an accessions tax, which cumulates total gifts received over time) it will in addition be necessary on the occasion of any gift to mark up the cumulative totals of gifts made or gifts received in the past by the movements in the price index since the last previous gift, when the total will have received its most recent adjustment for price changes.

4   AN AWT AS AN INSTRUMENT OF CONTROL

One further advantage of an AWT over any form of transfer tax is that it might serve as a more useful instrument of control and monitoring of other taxes. With an income tax regime a capital gains tax is necessary, which involves monitoring acquisitions and disposals of the relevant assets; and, even more important, with an expenditure tax regime an annual statement of the amount of acquisitions and disposals of all registered assets is required. In so far as an AWT involves the maintenance of an up-to-date inventory of assets, the monitoring of an AWT should be usefully integrated with the monitoring of a capital gains tax or of an expenditure tax; and if there were to be a transfer tax as well, that tax also might be usefully integrated into the same system of control. The usefulness of an AWT as an instrument of control would be the greater, the lower the threshold at which AWT became payable and the greater, therefore, the coverage of owners of wealth. The importance of an AWT from this point of view of control should not be exaggerated; but at least, if there are to be a body of taxes (capital gains tax, expenditure tax, AWT and/or transfer tax) that rely upon the assessment of holdings, or of changes in holdings of assets, then it would seem sensible that in the long run they should be co-ordinated into a single instrument of control.

5   PROBLEMS OF ADMINISTRATION

We come finally to a distinction between an AWT and a transfer tax which tells very heavily in favour of the latter, namely the problems of administrative and compliance costs and of feasibility. The basic point is a simple one. If properties change hands on the average once a generation – say once every twenty-five years – there will be only one-twenty-fifth as many cases each year for disclosure, valuation and assessment to tax under a transfer tax as there will be under an AWT. Moreover, on the occasion of transfer at death, valuations of property will normally be needed for purposes other than assessment to tax so as to carry out a proper distribution of the property between the beneficiaries. Thus with a transfer tax there will be many fewer assessments to be made each year, and these will be made at a time when properties are to a large extent being valued in any case.

THE ADMINISTRATION OF AN AWT

It is a matter of crucial importance whether or not an AWT can be applied without intolerable levels of administrative and compliance costs so as to attain as satisfactory a degree of precision and fairness as is possible with a transfer tax. If this were possible, then a case could be argued for relying wholly on an AWT and for imposing no transfer tax. But for this to be acceptable it would be necessary to have an AWT which had a low enough threshold to cover the whole range of properties which would otherwise have been covered by a transfer tax together with a progressive scale of tax rates which rose at the top end to levels sufficient to perform the whole function of redistributing the ownership of property. However, for such a severe and basic instrument of taxation to be acceptable it would have to be reliable, fair and immune against extensive evasion and avoidance. Rough-and-ready justice might be acceptable for a subsidiary levy with low rates of tax and a high threshold; but the possibility of using an AWT as a principal tax instrument depends crucially upon the possibility of administering such a tax effectively, fairly and without excessive cost.

The problems which arise in this connection may be considered under the following six headings: coverage of the tax, problems of valuation, methods of administration, the tax unit, the treatment of trusts, and overseas property.

1 COVERAGE

The tax should in general cover all types of valuable asset, although there would inevitably be some exemptions. On administrative grounds, if for no other reasons, it would be necessary to give some exemption for personal chattels (e.g. for all objects or collections worth less than £1,000) and it would be impossible to include the value of human capital (e.g. the value of a taxpayer's enhanced earning power due to the resources previously invested in his education and training).

But on grounds of equity it would be essential in our view to include both the value of owner-occupied houses and also the value of future pension rights.[2] The exemption of owner-occupied houses would introduce an intolerable inequity between such owners and those who had chosen to invest their property in other directions. The exemption of pension rights would introduce an intolerable inequity between, on the one hand, persons employed in occupations with favourable pension arrangements and, on the other hand, persons employed in occupations with inadequate pension arrangements and the self-employed who had inadequate tax relief for saving for their own retirement. We have already described some of the tax anomalies which already exist in this field. The value of a future pension, indexed against inflation and related to the employee's closing salary, can amount for a senior public servant to £100,000 or more.

---

[2] It should, however, be noted that in none of the dozen OECD countries with an AWT are pension rights included. This is the only asset which none includes.

The problem which is raised for an AWT by the need to include the value of pension rights does not arise in the case of a transfer tax, since both pension rights and also private savings consumed in retirement disappear upon death and are not subject to the tax. It therefore presents no obstacle to the use of a transfer tax; but it does present one of the most formidable obstacles to the use of an AWT as a principal tax instrument. The difficulty might not be insurmountable if the tax had a sufficiently high threshold, e.g. £100,000, so that even with the inclusion of the value of owner-occupied houses and of future pension rights there would be only a limited number of persons who were liable to the tax and whose future pension rights would therefore need to be properly assessed annually. But the problem does present a very serious difficulty for an AWT with a low threshold.

2 VALUATION

While theoretically an open market valuation might be preferable, it is a characteristic of the AWT that all assets must be assigned a tax value every year and at a time when they are not changing hands and being valued for other reasons. A specific valuation has to be made for wealth tax purposes. In determining the choice of valuation methods, two major considerations should be borne in mind: (i) the need to keep down administrative and compliance costs; and (ii) the need to have methods which reduce as much as possible uncertainty about, and delay in, arriving at valuations. It is proper that these considerations should on occasion take precedence over the desire to obtain a genuine open-market valuation.

It is for these reasons that standardised valuation methods may well be preferable for certain kinds of assets. Particular problem areas for valuations are the value of pension rights, valuable personal chattels, business assets and real property.

The possibility of valuing pension rights was considered by the Select Committee on Wealth Tax, and the Government Actuary submitted a memorandum suggesting how tables might be prepared for normal circumstances. The evidence showed that a table of eighty-eight columns would cover the majority of cases. For the remainder the Revenue would need to fix each year the rate of interest to be used for discounting, the mortality tables to be used, and perhaps other factors such as the future rate of inflation; individual calculations would then have to be made. Although this approach would result in a figure for use for wealth tax purposes, the evidence showed that it would be extremely sensitive to the assumptions made in calculating it, particularly the rate of interest. The result would inevitably be somewhat arbitrary. There might also be conflicting views about the theoretical basis of the methods proposed by the Government Actuary.

There would also be avoidance problems; e.g. a director of a profitable close company might have no formal pension rights but in the event would be likely to receive one.

The proposal to exempt individual assets of a value less than £1,000 would help to ease the problem of dealing with personal chattels. For others use of the cost price, if fairly recent, indexed for inflation might be appropriate.

In other countries the use of standardised formulae for valuing the assets of business property in closely owned companies (such as the Stuttgart formula in Germany) seems to have worked fairly well.

A recent development of significance for valuation is the recommendation of the Layfield Committee, which the government has accepted, that henceforth ratable values of domestic property should be based upon capital values and not rental values. If this were applied and the same valuation were used for wealth tax purposes, then the difficulties of lowering the wealth tax threshold in the United Kingdom would be much reduced. Estimates by the Royal Commission on the Distribution of Income and Wealth suggest that around 40 per cent of personal wealth would be in the form of housing accommodation for those whose wealth would be brought into the tax base in the United Kingdom by a reduction in the threshold from £100,000 to £30,000. The Layfield Committee recommendation and the possibility of using capital values for housing both for local tax and wealth tax purposes emphasise the point, which is borne out by the experience of other countries, that the administrative costs of a wealth tax can be substantially reduced if the same valuations are used for a number of different taxes. There seems no reason, for example, why in this country valuations for wealth tax, if such a tax were introduced, should not be used also for any transfer tax; and if an imputed rent were to be reintroduced for owner-occupied houses, then the simplest way would be to do so on the basis of a percentage of the capital value for rating and wealth tax purposes.

3 SELF-ASSESSMENT

The Inland Revenue has proposed that in the case of an AWT the method of administration should be through a system of self-assessment. This involves three steps:

1 Self-revelation: the taxpayer lists his own taxable assets.
2 Self-valuation: the taxpayer attributes a valuation to those assets.
3 Self-assessment: the taxpayer calculates the wealth tax payable and sends a cheque to the Revenue.

Self-revelation must necessarily play a larger part in a wealth tax than in an income tax where income flows from A to B, giving the chance of checking B's return by information from A and also requiring A to deduct tax before passing income to B.

Self-valuation is the difficult part. If taxpayers are required to value all their own assets with very little guidance other than that the valuation should be 'open-market', a considerable burden of compliance costs is placed on the conscientious taxpayer and the way is open for much horizontal inequity between taxpayers of various degrees of integrity and for a decline in tax morality. Self-valuation is a component in self-assessment to wealth tax which does not apply to income tax; and it is a difficult component, since valuation is a matter of judgement rather than fact. The difficulties of self-valuation can be reduced by appropriate details and more guidelines, such as (i) exemption of individual chattels of less than £1,000, (ii) house values given by the local property tax, and (iii) valuation formulae for businesses etc. If these methods were not to be adopted, then self-assessment would be very difficult; and it is not surprising that in the absence of these alleviations the Inland Revenue wanted a high threshold, which would mean few payers of wealth tax, almost all with professional advisers. But in other countries these simplifying methods are used much more and low thresholds are the rule.

Self-assessment – the actual process of doing the calculations of tax liability – is not likely to be unduly complicated with a wealth tax; indeed the calculations are likely to be easier with a wealth tax than with an income tax, which is liable to be a good deal more complicated.

We conclude that self-assessment without detailed guidelines would mean high compliance costs and great inequity. Given detailed guidelines etc. a self-assessment to wealth tax should not be too difficult. But the simplifications necessary to make the operation feasible might introduce an element of approximation to true market values which would be tolerable for an AWT with relatively low rates of tax, which was designed to serve as a subsidiary element in the tax structure, but unacceptable for an AWT with a low threshold and very high marginal rates of tax at the top end, which was designed to be the principal or the only instrument of capital taxation.

4 TAX UNIT

We shall discuss the problem of the tax unit at length in Chapter 18, and there is nothing in the nature of a wealth tax which dictates any particular treatment. If the spouses were taxed as two separate single persons, there could be difficulties over the ownership of household assets and over the allocation of minor children's wealth (if it were to be aggregated with the parents') to one or the other parent; but these difficulties would not be insuperable if separate treatment were considered desirable on other grounds. The most notable effect of separate treatment would be that the total liability on a given aggregate wealth would vary according to the distribution of the wealth between the spouses. Moreover, it would be necessary to monitor and record transfers of wealth between the spouses. To avoid these problems, aggregation would have to be the rule. In that event there would have to be a higher threshold than for a single person; the bands chargeable at each rate of a progressive tax could be wider; or – the most favourable treatment in comparison with single persons – a quotient system could be adopted, under which the tax would be twice the amount which would be payable by a single person on half the aggregate wealth.

5 AND 6 TRUSTS, AND OVERSEAS PROPERTY

We shall consider the treatment of trusts in Chapter 19 and of overseas property in Chapter 21.

THE PROBLEM OF PRIVATE BUSINESSES AND FARMS

There is one problem which is common to all forms of capital taxes, whether on transfers or on the holding of wealth, namely the difficulty that may be encountered by the owners of private businesses or of farms in raising the necessary funds to meet their tax liabilities. The problem is basically due to imperfections in the capital market, which make it difficult for a small company whose shares are not quoted or for the owner of a farm or of some other unincorporated business to raise money by sharing the equity in the business with outside persons or institutions. We are of the opinion that the problem should be tackled by increasing the possibilities for raising outside funds rather than by special tax concessions.

THE EFFECT OF OTHER TAX CHANGES

Certain tax changes which may be advocated on their own merits on other grounds would, however, significantly ease these problems for private businesses. In particular the replacement of an income tax regime by an expenditure tax regime would be of great assistance. It would be possible to build up and maintain private business by ploughing back the profits without incurring income tax on the sums so saved. The payment of a given level of AWT would thus put much less strain on private businesses if it were combined with an expenditure tax rather than with an income tax.

Moreover, if the amount paid in AWT by owners of a business were itself exempt from expenditure tax,[3] one very important difficulty would be removed. With a progressive income tax it would with present arrangements be very expensive for the owners of a close company to take out of the business, either in the form of directors' salaries or in the form of dividends, sufficient extra funds to pay a given rate of AWT on the value of the business. Such liabilities to AWT would have to be paid out of these additional salaries or dividends after payment of the high marginal rates of income tax which might be payable by them on the necessary additions to their personal incomes. For example, a taxpayer with a marginal rate of income tax of 83 per cent would have to receive an addition of £5,882 to his salary in order to meet an AWT liability of £1,000. With an expenditure tax regime the owner would have to take out of the company only sufficient to meet the AWT liability without any payment of expenditure tax on the amounts involved.

The substitution of a PAWAT, or any one of the other variants of an accessions tax discussed in Chapter 15, for the existing capital transfer tax would also help to ease the problem. By dispersing ownership on transfer among many members of the family or indeed among the employees of the business itself, the previous owner could avoid a heavy burden of transfer tax and maintain the business as a going concern.

---

[3] That is, if the annual payments of the tax were included in item 4 of Table 8.1 (p. 151) for the calculation of the 'expenditure tax adjustment'.

TAX RELIEFS

But these changes, while they would be helpful, would probably not wholly solve the problem, especially in the short run. In Appendix 16.1 we enumerate some of the special tax privileges which have already been conferred on private businesses and farms. If some special tax privilege is considered necessary in the case of an AWT, a suitable form might be found in the relief suggested in the draft reports of the Chairman of the Select Committee on Wealth Tax for cases in which business assets exceeded 50 per cent of the owner's total assets. There would be a reduction in the wealth tax on the business assets by the percentage that business assets exceeded 50 per cent of total assets, so that if the business assets amounted to 60 per cent of the total, the wealth tax on those assets would be reduced by 10 per cent. A relief on these lines would be possible but perhaps less necessary under an expenditure tax regime than under an income tax regime.

But we consider the granting of such tax privileges as a much less desirable way of dealing with the problem than measures which make it easier for owners of private businesses and farms where necessary to raise outside capital funds to meet tax liabilities without breaking up their businesses. The granting of tax privileges helps those who need no such help as well as those who do; it reduces the tax base and thus makes higher tax rates necessary in general; it relieves a special class of wealthy persons from taxation which is designed to fall progressively on all owners of wealth; and it attracts funds simply for tax avoidance purposes into the specially privileged forms of activity.

In the case of agriculture, for example, the excessively high cost of land and the exceptionally low rate of yield on it are in part due to the special tax privileges which it attracts; and this high price of land in turn makes it exceptionally difficult for outside persons with new talents and enterprise to purchase farms so as to enter the agricultural industry. The low yield on farming which results from the excessively high price of land may well be an important obstacle to the development of agriculture through the formation of companies which would enable their shareholders to achieve the joint ownership of farms of sufficient size to be economic, managed either by tenant farmers or by the companies themselves.

ACCESS TO ALTERNATIVE SOURCES OF CAPITAL

In our opinion great emphasis should be placed upon measures which would extend the market for loans to, and for minority equity investment in, private businesses. There are a number of possible developments, which we can do no more than list but which merit further careful examination.

In order to extend the market for minority equity holdings in relatively small concerns it is important that the rights of minority shareholders should be better safeguarded than they are at present under the existing law.

With the existing corporation tax, the issue of preference shares is at a disadvantage in that the dividend on it, unlike the interest on debentures, is not deductible from the tax base. With a corporation tax reformed on the lines discussed in Chapter 12, this disadvantage would disappear. Rehabilitation of the preference share, particularly in its participating forms, would assist the widening of the market for outside investment in private businesses, since it can do much to protect the interests of such shareholders.

There are already a number of institutions which can provide equity funds for private businesses without threatening their managerial independence. Such aid is already provided by Finance for Industry (which now incorporates the Industrial and Commercial Finance Corporation (ICFC) and its subsidiary the Estates Duty Investment Trust Ltd (EDITH), which was specifically set up to assist companies adversely affected by estate duty). The Agricultural Mortgage Corporation might perform a similar function in the case of farming.

It is through further development and extension of such bodies that, in our opinion, a solution should be sought. If the rights of minority shareholders were properly safeguarded, unit trusts might be developed for this purpose.

If necessary it would be possible to institute special public bodies. The state might create a National Agricultural Trust, which would accept farms in lieu of tax but allow the owner's successors to become tenants of the farm. Or owners who had outside their businesses assets which were inadequate to meet their capital tax liabilities might be entitled to pay in kind, as it were, by transferring part ownership of the concern at its valuation for tax to a specially instituted public body, which would then be free, if it thought fit, to dispose of its holdings to the public on the best terms which it could command in the market.

VARIETIES OF WEALTH TAX

There are in fact many main varieties of AWT, which would have very different effects and raise very different sets of problems.

(1) One extreme possibility would be to have an AWT with a low threshold and with a highly progressive rate structure which imposed such high rates on the largest fortunes that it was impossible to maintain such properties intact. Such a tax might be used as the principal, and possibly the only, form of capital tax, with little or no reliance placed upon any form of transfer tax. One disadvantage of such a tax is that it would do nothing to discriminate in favour of saved as contrasted with inherited wealth. An advantage is that it would give an incentive to disperse saved wealth as well as inherited wealth by early giving to less wealthy beneficiaries. But quite apart from its general merits or demerits, we doubt whether an AWT could be administered without excessive cost with a sufficient degree of certainty and fairness to enable it to be used in this comprehensive way as the principal or sole form of capital tax.

(2) If an AWT were to be applied with a high threshold so that it was levied only on a restricted number of the wealthiest owners, the problems of applying it in a sufficiently certain and fair manner might be manageable, even if the rates of tax at the top of the scale were so severe as to make it difficult or impossible to maintain such properties intact. Such a tax would

levy a charge on the benefits derived from the ownership of really large properties, and it would give an incentive for the early transfer of such wealth to less wealthy beneficiaries. It could appropriately be combined with a transfer tax which made a moderate charge, perhaps at a single proportionate rate on all inherited wealth, subject to moderate exemption levels. The LAWAT which we described in Chapter 15 would constitute just such an appropriate tax. Everyone (subject to moderate exemptions) would be charged on the possession of inherited wealth at a moderate rate for just so long as he held it; and in addition the very wealthy would be charged at high rates on all wealth, whether saved or inherited, so long as they held it.

(3) Another form of AWT is a tax with a low threshold but with a low rate of tax with little or no progression in the rates. Such a tax would be the appropriate form if an income tax regime were maintained and it were desired for the reasons given above (p. 351) to replace an investment income surcharge with a charge on the capital from which the investment income was derived. It would need to be combined with some progressive form of transfer tax.

(4) Another form of AWT would be to combine a relatively low rate of tax with a high threshold, so that only the wealthiest owners were liable to tax and that only at a relatively low rate. Such a tax might be appropriate if the main emphasis in capital taxation were placed on a transfer tax with a wide scope and with a progressive schedule of rates which rose to high levels on the biggest fortunes. The PAWAT which we described in Chapter 15 would constitute such a tax. This combination of capital taxes would rely principally on the resulting heavy taxation of inherited wealth; but by means of the moderate AWT it would also provide a supplementary charge at the top end, which would cover saved as well as inherited wealth.

(5) A final and extreme possibility would be to have no AWT at all but to rely exclusively on transfer taxation.

There is thus a very wide range of choice, since all the above varieties of AWT could be combined with a wide range of varieties of transfer tax – capital transfer tax, accessions tax, PAWAT, LAWAT, AGAWAT – each with a wide range of different patterns of tax rates.

THE COMBINATION OF WEALTH TAX AND EXPENDITURE TAX

In considering the merits of the various possible structures, one important consideration is whether the capital taxes are accompanied by a progressive income tax regime or a progressive expenditure tax regime. We have already referred to a number of the relevant points; but it may be useful to summarise them at this point.

(1) The institution of an expenditure tax regime reduces the case for discriminating against investment income through an investment income surcharge or an AWT, in so far as an expenditure tax automatically taxes more heavily the higher standard of living which can be financed out of capital or investment income (p. 351 above).

(2)   Moreover, the transition to an expenditure tax regime which initially treats all assets as if they were registered assets itself levies a charge on all existing assets, in the sense that their realisation and use to finance consumption will be subject to expenditure tax from which they were previously immune. The value of all existing assets in terms of consumption goods is automatically reduced (p. 191 above).

(3)   On the other hand, an expenditure tax regime makes it easier to accumulate new properties through future saving; and since the ownership of saved wealth as well as inherited wealth confers benefits of security, independence, influence and power, the case for a wealth tax is to this extent increased. A progressive expenditure tax combined with an AWT with a high threshold would levy a charge on the largest fortunes, but would make it easier than with an income tax regime to accumulate saved wealth up to this wealth tax threshold.

(4)   A progressive AWT in the absence of an expenditure tax may induce owners to dissipate their existing wealth through high personal consumption. The simultaneous existence of a progressive expenditure tax will restrict this possibility, and will thus serve either to increase the tax yield or else to induce wealthy owners to hand on their wealth at an early date to less wealthy beneficiaries (p. 352 above).

(5)   The difficulties which private businesses and farms would encounter as a result of a progressive AWT would be greatly mitigated if it were accompanied by a shift from an income tax regime to an expenditure tax regime. The effect may be illustrated numerically by the following example. If the rate of profit yielded on an investment were 5 per cent, then an AWT of 1 per cent would account for one-fifth or 20 per cent of the profits, an AWT of 2 per cent would account for 40 per cent of the profits, and so on. Both income tax and AWT must be paid out of the profits before any amount can be distributed to the owners or ploughed back into the business. Then the following combinations of rates of income tax and of wealth tax would account for the whole of the 5 per cent a year profit yield:

Income tax (%)	Wealth tax (%)
80	1
70	$1\frac{1}{2}$
60	2
50	$2\frac{1}{2}$

With an expenditure tax regime a rate of AWT up to 5 per cent a year would be possible without making it impossible to maintain the capital investment intact.

(6)   One possible way of mitigating the problems which private businesses and farms might encounter as a result of the imposition of an AWT is to allow such businesses to defer the payment of the tax, to accumulate the liability to tax at a commercial rate of interest, and to pay the resulting liability on the occasion of the transfer of the business to another owner.

Such an arrangement amounts to the borrowing from the government of the funds necessary to meet the AWT. This arrangement would make much better sense under an expenditure tax regime than under an income tax regime, since in the former case the funds necessary to meet the ultimate liability could be accumulated without any payment of tax on the profit or other income put aside for that purpose.

THE CHOICE BETWEEN ALTERNATIVE FORMS

We feel that the following are the combinations of capital taxes which, in conjunction with an expenditure tax, most merit consideration:

1 A PAWAT with a low threshold and a progressive tax schedule, with rates at the top end which are sufficiently high to disperse the ownership of large inherited properties, unaccompanied by any AWT.
2 A PAWAT with a low threshold accompanied by an AWT with a high threshold and moderate rates of tax to bring saved wealth into the tax net for the wealthiest owners.
3 A PAWAT with a low threshold accompanied by an AWT with a low threshold and a single low proportionate tax rate to bring a larger range of saved wealth into the tax net and to act as a control for a two-tier expenditure tax.
4 A LAWAT with a low threshold accompanied by an AWT with a high threshold and a rate structure which rises progressively to high rates on the largest fortunes.

CONCLUSIONS

The transfer taxes discussed in Chapter 15 do not levy any charge on the holding of wealth accumulated from the owner's own savings. There are, however, good reasons for such a tax, since the ownership of wealth itself confers benefits and since a progressive tax on the ownership of wealth, particularly if it is combined with a progressive tax on expenditure, gives the maximum tax incentive to distribute ownership widely and at an early date. Moreover, changes in the tax rates of an AWT are fairer and less arbitrary in their incidence than changes in the rates of tax on transfers of capital. On the other hand, the administrative problems of an AWT are more formidable than those of taxes on capital transfers. In particular, the problems of valuation and of the equitable treatment of pension rights present considerable difficulty.

Private businesses and farms might be faced with difficulties in the payment of an AWT, but these difficulties would be much reduced if the wealth tax were combined with an expenditure tax in place of an income tax. Some tax privileges for such concerns might be necessary; but measures to give such concerns access to outside capital resources are much to be preferred to tax privileges.

Various combinations of transfer taxes and forms of AWT are possible. We shall return in our final Chapter 23 to two possibilities:

1   A PAWAT of the kind discussed in Chapter 15 with a low threshold and with a progressive tax schedule with rates at the top end which are sufficiently high to disperse the ownership of large inherited properties, unaccompanied by any annual wealth tax, as the sole weapon for the taxation of large fortunes.
2   A LAWAT of the kind discussed in Chapter 15 to provide a general tax on, and discrimination against, inherited property, combined with an AWT with a high threshold and with a rate structure which rises progressively to high rates on the largest fortunes as a main weapon to encourage the wide dispersion of wealth and to levy a charge on large holdings of wealth, whether inherited or accumulated by the owner.

Appendix 16.1 The Existing Tax Privileges of Small Businesses, Agriculture and Forestry

As noted in Appendix 15.1, under the capital transfer tax the rates of tax on gifts *inter vivos* are lower than in the case of properties left at death. One reason for this provision was to reduce the threat of the break-up of small family businesses or farms which might occur as a result of heavy charges on the death of the owner; the lower rates on earlier gifts would, it was hoped, ease the transfer of such properties from father to son at a suitable earlier period.

In addition the following special provisions may be noted.

In the case of businesses and small companies:

1   The rate of corporation tax is lower for small companies than for large companies (see section 5(1) of Appendix 4.1).
2   Gains up to £20,000 are exempt from capital gains tax if the disposal is by the owner of a business or a full-time working director, who has been owner or director for ten years and who is aged over 60. The full exemption is not available until age 65, and is given in respect only of business assets including goodwill but not of shares or securities held as investments.
3   Transfers of value of relevant business property may be reduced by 30 per cent for the purposes of capital transfer tax. Such property consists of an interest in a business, unquoted shares which gave the transferor control, and land, buildings, machinery and plant used by a company controlled by the transferor or a partnership of which he was a member. The relief is not available where the business carried on is mainly dealing or investing in securities, land and buildings, and to obtain relief the property must generally have been owned by the transferor for the preceding two years.
4   Postponement of capital gains tax on disposal by gift and of capital transfer tax is available in respect of businesses or companies controlled by the taxpayer.

In the case of agriculture:

1   Under the income tax and corporation tax the cost of construction of buildings, including one-third of the expenditure incurred in constructing a farmhouse, is written off over ten years regardless of actual depreciation (see section 2(3) of Appendix 4.1).
2   For capital transfer tax purposes, the agricultural value of agricultural property is reduced by half, subject to a ceiling limit on the value and size of property relieved. To obtain relief, the transferor is required to have been engaged in farming for at least five out of the previous seven years, and to have farmed the property transferred for two years.
3   Where agricultural property is disposed of by way of a bargain not at arm's length, in particular a gift, then for capital gains tax purposes the value of the property may be reduced either by the proportion that the relief under (2) bears to the full agricultural value or by the excess over allowable cost, whichever is the smaller.
4   Agricultural land and buildings are exempt from rates.

5   Most farm produce, unless supplied in the course of catering, is zero-rated for VAT purposes.

In the case of forestry:

1   Income from woodlands managed on a commercial basis may be taxed for income tax purposes on the basis of either (i) one-third of the annual value of the land on the basis that it is undeveloped land, or (ii) the full income on the basis that a trade is being carried on. The taxpayer may elect to be taxed under (ii), but that election is binding on him so long as he occupies the woodlands. If the woodlands are divided into plantations, elections may be made in respect of each plantation.

It is usually possible to ensure that plantations on which trees are felled and sold are taxed under (i) and that those on which replanting is taking place, and as such returning trading losses, are taxed under (ii).

2   Where the basis of taxation is 1(i), the sale of trees is exempted from any charge to capital gains tax.
3   The writing-down allowances available to agriculture are also given to forestry when taxed under 1(ii).
4   The value of trees on woodland is excluded from any ratable value.
5   Relief from capital transfer tax is given in respect of growing timber transferred on death, provided the deceased had not purchased it within the previous five years. Tax is only payable if the timber is sold before the next death, and is charged on the sale proceeds less any expense of replanting.

17 National Insurance Contributions, Payroll Taxes, Investment Income Surcharge, Earned Income Relief and Capital Taxes

In the preceding chapters of our Report we have not expressed any definite view about the future of the existing national insurance contributions or of the existing investment income surcharge. In our opinion the proper roles to be performed by these charges are so closely bound up with possible future developments of a payroll tax and of capital taxes that the whole system must be considered as a complete structure. We attempt in this chapter to outline some of the most important relationships between these various charges.

INVESTMENT INCOME SURCHARGE AND EARNED INCOME RELIEF

Historically the investment income surcharge is the successor to the distinction between earned and unearned income that was introduced early this century, at a time when several other countries introduced annual wealth taxes and shortly after estate duty was introduced in the United Kingdom. All these measures were designed to give fiscal recognition to differences between earned income and investment income – especially income from inherited wealth. Such discrimination was justified by reference to the facts that earned income, unlike investment income, involves the sacrifice of leisure and that a man's income from earnings is essentially a forty- to fifty-year annuity while the taxable return on many investments is essentially in perpetuity. Further discrimination against inheritance, or the return on inherited wealth, is related to a judgement that differences in income or consumption due to differential skills, abilities or effort are more acceptable than those due to the luck of inheritance.

THE EFFECT OF NATIONAL INSURANCE CONTRIBUTIONS

However, the role of the earned income relief and investment income surcharge as providing such discrimination has been undermined progressively over the last half-century or so as a result of the development of a national insurance system financed by compulsory contributions imposed on earnings. Since employee plus employer national insurance contributions (and the new 2 per cent payroll tax) currently amount to about 15 per cent of a worker's earnings (inclusive of the employer's contribution and tax, and subject to the earnings limit),[1] while the investment income surcharge is also 15 per cent there is not really very much discrimination against investment income in the combined system. The two lots of 15 per cent do not offset one another completely, as the 15 per cent investment income surcharge is levied over and above the ordinary income tax, while the employer's part of the 15 per cent borne by earned income reduces the wage which is subject to income tax.

Consider a man whose services are worth £110·75 to his employer, who pays him a gross wage of £100 on which the employee pays basic tax (ignoring personal allowances) of £33. Thus the total tax burden is £33+£16·50 = £49·50 or 44·7 per cent of £110·75, while investment income of £100 is taxed at £33+£15 = £48; i.e. there is 3·3 per cent discrimination against investment income.

Discrimination on this scale is quite important if the underlying income tax rate is 83 per cent when, if the earnings were subject to contributions etc., the total rate on earnings would be 90 per cent as against 98 per cent on investment income; there is a spread of 8 per cent, and the net earned income is five times the net investment income. Except at these high rates there is on this argument not very much discrimination; indeed small investment incomes exempt from investment income surcharge are much less heavily taxed than earnings.

NATIONAL INSURANCE CONTRIBUTIONS AS A FORM OF TAX

One might, however, question the legitimacy of treating national insurance contributions as a tax without reference to the relationship between contributions and benefits. If the national insurance system were actuarially based on an individual basis, the compulsory contributions would be no more appropriately regarded as a tax than, say, the cost of compulsory third-party motor insurance. However, the system is not actuarially based in this sense, as the following features attest:

1　Pension benefits are not paid from a fund accumulated out of contributions; they are not 'funded' but financed on a 'pay-as-you-go' basis.
2　Even on the pay-as-you-go basis the system is not self-financing, the Treasury making regular subventions.
3　Benefits, especially basic state pensions but also unemployment benefit and sickness benefit, rise less than proportionately with earnings, although over a certain range of income contributions are strictly proportional.
4　Contribution rates in different income classes, regions and industries are not related to a knowledge of the differences in the incidence of unemployment, accidents or sickness.

---

[1] On a wage of £100 the employer pays £10·75 (i.e. £8·75 national insurance contribution plus £2 payroll tax) and the employee pays £5·75 national insurance contribution. The total 'tax' (£10·75+£5·75 = £16·50) is therefore 14·9 per cent of the cost to the employer (£100+£10·75 = £110·75).

5 The National Health Service may be used by all sick persons without reference to any record of contributions, although some part of the compulsory contribution is nominally regarded as being levied to finance the health service.

Thus from the point of view of the individual the relationship between his national insurance contributions and benefits is not very much looser than that between his income tax and the benefits to him of other public expenditures, although the *number* of contributions he makes does affect his eligibility for benefits. The compulsory national insurance contributions are more nearly akin to a tax than to an actuarially balanced insurance premium.

THE INTEGRATION OF INVESTMENT INCOME SURCHARGE AND NATIONAL INSURANCE CONTRIBUTIONS INTO THE INCOME TAX OR EXPENDITURE TAX

If national insurance contributions are in this light regarded simply as one form of tax, and if the present situation in which the surcharge on investment income is largely offset by the compulsory contributions assessed on earnings is accounted as satisfactory, then there is a case for a cleaning-up operation in order to simplify the tax system. The two sets of charges, being of the same order of magnitude, could be abolished and replaced by a corresponding increase in the rate of tax under an income tax or a general expenditure tax without any substantial change in the tax burden on either category of income. This would necessitate relying on the existing capital transfer tax or on any alternative system of taxation of inherited wealth (such as the PAWAT discussed in Chapter 15) to provide the discrimination against income, expenditure and the ownership of property which was inherited and not obtained as the result of the taxpayer's own work and effort.

Although the present investment income surcharge and national insurance contributions impose more or less similar charges on unearned and on earned incomes, they are not, of course, precisely similar. To replace both of them by a general addition to the rates of income tax or of expenditure tax would raise a number of tiresome particular problems, especially for the transition from one system to the other. We discuss some of these in Appendix 17.1.

The radical aim might be ultimately, with an income tax regime, to replace both the national insurance contributions and the investment income surcharge with an appropriate rise in the schedule of rates under the income tax or, with an expenditure tax regime, to replace these charges with an additional charge on value added, either through the machinery of the existing VAT or by means of the ITVAT described in Appendix 8.3.

A half-way house under the present income tax regime would be (i) to replace the existing employee's national insurance contributions and a corresponding part of the investment income surcharge with a rise in the basic rate of income tax of 5 per cent, and (ii) to impose a 10 per cent payroll tax and a 10 per cent investment income surcharge to account for the existing employer's national insurance contributions and the remaining part of the investment income surcharge. With an expenditure tax regime the same sort of half-way house would be possible, with the exception that the investment income surcharge would have to be imposed on investment income plus net sales of registered assets, i.e. upon the taxpayer's resources other than earnings which were available to finance expenditure upon consumption.[2]

The elimination of both the compulsory national insurance contributions and the investment income surcharge and their replacement with an appropriate rise in the tax schedule of the income tax or of some form of expenditure tax might perhaps be regarded as an ultimate goal. But before any such action was taken there would be need for a further detailed examination of some of the implications.

PROBLEMS ARISING FROM THE ELIMINATION OF NATIONAL INSURANCE CONTRIBUTIONS

1 At present the payment of some of the existing social benefits depends upon a past record of national insurance contributions. We have not been able to consider adequately the full implications of removing all contribution conditions for the receipt of benefits, and in our discussion of these problems in Chapter 13 we have not assumed that all contribution conditions should be removed.

2 All the political parties are agreed upon the desirability of some form of earnings-related pensions dependent upon some record of earnings-related contributions, the acceptance of which involves the maintenance of some form of compulsory contributions in respect of earnings, for the finance of pensions if for no other purpose.

3 Some form of payroll tax is a convenient instrument for discriminating between employment in regions with high unemployment and regions with low unemployment.

4 There are EEC regulations which govern the eligibility of a UK national for the receipt of benefits in other member countries of the European Economic Community. Such eligibility under the present rules depends in many cases upon the contribution record of the UK national.

5 In the other EEC countries, compulsory national insurance contributions are much heavier than they are in the United Kingdom and also make up a much larger proportion of the total tax revenue. Their elimination in the United Kingdom would appear to make the UK tax system even more out of harmony with the EEC tax systems than at present, even though the replacement of the UK compulsory national insurance contributions with a rise in the income tax on earned income would have little signifi-

---

[2] If it were then decided, in memory of 'the good old days', to return to an earned income relief in preference to an investment income surcharge as the means for discriminating against investment income, the basic rate of tax could be raised and in addition a payroll tax (or earned income surcharge) of 10 per cent could be combined with an Earned Income Relief of 10 per cent, an arrangement which would, at the expense of a few extra bureaucrats, at least highlight the basic logic of the situation.

cance in its real effects beyond constituting a simplifying cleaning-up operation.

HARMONISATION WITH EUROPE THROUGH SOCIAL INSURANCE CONTRIBUTIONS

The question of effective harmonisation with the other EEC countries does, however, raise a very real issue. If the UK tax burden is compared with the tax burdens in the other countries of Europe, it can be seen that the proportion of the national income taken in all forms of direct tax (including national insurance contributions) is not in general higher in the United Kingdom than in the other countries. A striking difference, however, is that in the other countries of Europe the proportion of the total direct tax burden which takes the form of compulsory contributions for social insurance is higher and the proportion which is represented by a formal income tax is lower.[3]

A PAYROLL TAX OR EARNED INCOME SURCHARGE

If a reduction were made in the rates of income tax in the United Kingdom and if the lost revenue were replaced by a payroll tax or an increase in employers' national insurance contributions, the resulting system would be more in harmony with those of the other European countries. But this change would introduce a heavy discrimination against earned incomes. A payroll tax might sound less attractive if it were called an earned income surcharge. Of course, it would be possible (i) to reduce the basic rate of income tax, (ii) to introduce a payroll tax, and then (iii) to raise the existing investment income surcharge to offset the discrimination against earned incomes. In the end everyone would be subject to the same tax burdens as before, and it might well have been more sensible not to have complicated the tax system unnecessarily by a combination of offsetting changes. Such a manoeuvre might have an immediate effect on money costs and prices. If nominal money wage rates remained unchanged, the money cost of labour to the employer would be raised by the payroll tax, and the net-of-tax wage of the worker would be increased by the reduction of the income tax. An impact effect might be to reduce profitability in industry and to increase the real spendable incomes of wage earners. But if sooner or later the prices charged by industry for its products were raised to cover industry's increased costs, the real disposable wage rate would be unaffected, since the rise in prices would offset the reduction in the income tax. If it were desired to inflate money demand and money costs, the manoeuvre might make sense.

As a long-term structural change a shift from income tax to a payroll tax makes sense only if it is wished to discriminate against earned incomes or to remove a discrimination against investment incomes.

---

[3] See Appendix 5.2.

FOUR REASONS FOR DISCRIMINATING IN FAVOUR OF EARNED INCOME

The tax structure as a whole must be considered. There are in principle four possible types of reason for wanting to discriminate in favour of earned income:

1   There is the possibility that earned incomes are less permanent than investment incomes; and we have discussed the validity of this distinction between earned and unearned incomes in Chapter 3 (pp. 39–40).

2   A relevant distinction is that consumption financed out of earned income is at the expense of leisure and of the alternative opportunities which have to be sacrificed in order to spend time and effort at work. This sacrifice of leisure is involved whether the earned income is spent on immediate consumption or is put aside to finance consumption in old age. Consumption out of earned income or out of capital accumulated from earned income involves a sacrifice of leisure which is not involved by consumption out of inherited property or out of the income on inherited property.

3   Quite apart from any sacrifice of leisure, it may be thought appropriate that a heavier tax should fall on the enjoyment and use of income and wealth which has accrued through the luck of inheritance than on the enjoyment and use of income and property which is the creation of a taxpayer's own skill, ability and effort.

4   It may be argued that, quite apart from origin (whether through the taxpayer's own efforts or through inheritance) and from its use (whether for immediate or postponed consumption or for making gifts to others), the mere ownership of wealth confers prestige, security, independence and influence.

It is important to recognise what sorts of tax discriminations are justified by each of these four considerations.

The first consideration – namely the difference between temporary and permanent income – will justify some differentiation between the taxation of temporary and of permanent incomes under an income tax regime, although for the reasons discussed on pp. 39–40 of Chapter 3 it is not always easy to make the relevant distinction. But with an expenditure tax regime this reason for a tax discrimination is no longer relevant. A permanent income will finance a higher level of consumption than will a temporary income from which savings must be made to prepare for the disappearance of the income. Since more expenditure can be financed out of a permanent income than out of a temporary income, the expenditure tax itself discriminates appropriately in favour of temporary income.

The second and third considerations – namely those which militate in favour of the use and enjoyment of income and property originating from the taxpayer's own efforts rather than from the luck of inheritance – justify a system of inheritance taxes, since this will reduce the amount of immediate or postponed consumption which an heir can finance out of his inheritance.[4]

A tax on inherited wealth does not, however, levy any tax on the holding of wealth which the taxpayer has accumulated for himself. If the fourth consideration – namely the social benefits derived from owning wealth, whatever its origin – leads to the conclusion that there should be some tax on large holdings of such wealth as well as on inherited wealth, there is then a justification for an annual wealth tax or, in its default, for an investment income surcharge as a proxy for an annual wealth tax (see p. 40 of Chapter 3).[5]

A SUITABLE COMBINATION OF TAXES

We conclude that a combination of taxes which would accommodate these four considerations would be an expenditure tax together with an adequate system of taxation of capital transfers by way of gift or inheritance, combined also, if it were thought essential to tax the holding of large properties whether they be inherited or accumulated by the taxpayer himself, with an annual wealth tax with a high threshold.

CONCLUSIONS

While the investment income surcharge discriminates against investment incomes, the national insurance contributions discriminate against earned incomes. To a large extent, although not exactly, these two charges offset each other. National insurance contributions are essentially a form of tax; and there is thus some case for a cleaning-up operation which would integrate these two charges into a single scale of income tax or expenditure tax. However, the elimination of national insurance contributions would raise a number of problems which would need further detailed consideration before any such step was taken.

In general, the other countries of Europe put much more stress on social insurance contributions and much less stress on income tax than does the United Kingdom. But to lower the income tax and to raise a payroll tax is a form of discrimination against earned incomes which, in our opinion, should be avoided. A tax on expenditure combined with the taxation of the receipt of gifts and inheritances and/or of the ownership of wealth would give a better balance.

---

[4] These considerations are not met by a simple discrimination in favour of earned income. An earned income relief will enable the taxpayer to accumulate more wealth out of his own earnings, which, in the absence of any tax on gifts and bequests, will enable him to leave more to his heirs. The heir will in this case gain as much as the benefactor from the benefactor's work and effort. An effective discrimination against the use and enjoyment of inherited wealth requires a tax on inheritances.

[5] Since the objective in this case is to levy a tax that is related to the actual holding of wealth and not to its use as a means of financing consumption, the proxy surcharge must be simply on investment income and not on investment income plus the sale of registered assets; and since one of the attractions of an expenditure tax is that it is not necessary to distinguish between the use of investment income and of the investment capital itself, the case for using a proxy investment income surcharge rather than an annual wealth tax is weaker under an expenditure tax regime than under an income tax regime.

Appendix 17.1 The Consolidation of the Investment Income Surcharge and National Insurance Contributions

Section 1

If national insurance contributions were treated as taxes on earned income and if it were accepted that discrimination between earned and investment income could be left to transfer taxes, it would be appropriate to treat both types of income in the same way. If the tax structure were being designed from scratch, the decision not to have national insurance contributions or an investment income surcharge would simply imply a higher level of tax rates for income tax, expenditure tax or tax on value added.

Section 2

Under an income tax of the present type (*not* a comprehensive income tax) the following evolutionary reforms would clarify the situation while leaving the present level of discrimination against investment income virtually unchanged:

1 The employee's contribution would be consolidated into the basic rate of income tax with no separate maximum on liable earnings. This would involve about a 5 per cent rise in the basic rate and the substitution of the basic rate band of income for the present range of earnings subject to national insurance contributions.[1]

2 The employer's contribution would be converted into a payroll tax on all wages and salaries; a rate of 10 per cent (tax-exclusive) would be the right order of magnitude. The self-employed would pay 9 per cent (tax-inclusive) on their earned income; the payroll tax would be deductible from the income of the self-employed for the purposes of the income tax, to ensure equivalence with the employed. The 10 per cent across-the-board payroll tax would increase the progressivity of the taxation of earned income, but not by very much; it would raise the effective top earned income rate from 83 to 84·5 per cent.[2] But in Chapter 14 we have argued that the top rates should in any case be reduced.

3 Given the 5 per cent increase in the basic rate of income tax, the investment income surcharge should be reduced from 15 to 10 per cent. The net effect of this change would be two-fold. Small investment incomes, which are at present treated more generously than earned income, would be treated slightly less generously as a result of the increase in the basic rate. For non-exempt investment incomes the basic rate inclusive of investment income surcharge would be unchanged but the higher rates inclusive of the surcharge would fall, e.g. from 98 to 93 per cent. Thus the top effective rates would be 84·5 per cent on earned income and 93 per cent on investment income. This would substantially narrow the differential from 13·5 to 8·5 per cent, but the net earned income (15·5 per cent) would still be more than twice the net investment income (7 per cent).

Section 3

If it were wished to leave all discrimination to transfer taxes, then the investment income surcharge should be reduced to 5·6 per cent and applied to *all* investment income to make it neutral for the basic rate taxpayer.[3]

At the top of the tax schedule the effective rate would be 84·5 per cent on earned income (as above) and 88·6 per cent on investment income – a discrimination of 4·1 per cent. Net earned income would be 15·5 per cent, compared with an 11·4 per cent net investment income – a ratio 1·4:1.

Given the tax-exclusive nature of the payroll tax and the tax-inclusive nature of the investment income surcharge, it would not be possible to make them equivalent at all income tax levels.

Section 4
The scheme sketched in section 3 is a devious way of approximating a consistent treatment of all income. Instead of a simple income tax it involves both an additional payroll tax and an investment income surcharge at different but broadly equivalent rates (say 10 and 5 per cent respectively). Administratively these excrescences are probably not very costly, despite their inelegance. More elegant solutions would involve consolidating the payroll tax and investment income surcharge either into the income tax itself or into a tax on value added, which might be collected on an accounts basis as outlined in the description of ITVAT in Appendix 8.3.

Section 5
Consolidation into the income tax would present three problems:

1   It would exempt earnings below the tax threshold from the payroll tax, which, as proposed in section 2(2), would fall on *all* earnings.
2   The substitution of income tax for the payroll tax would require legislation for the reinterpretation of 'income' to include the payroll tax previously paid by the employer. This 10 per cent increase in the income tax base would raise revenue so that the actual increase in the tax rate might be relatively modest. Thus if all earnings were subject to tax at the basic rate of 33 per cent, income tax revenue would rise by 3·3 per cent as a result of the increased base, and the rate would have to be increased by a further 6·1 per cent to 39·1 per cent ($43/110 = 39·1$ per cent).
    However, this effect is partly offset by the exemption of the lowest band of earnings mentioned at (1). If a man earning £100 paid income tax at 33 per cent on £50 while his employer paid £10, the total tax would be £26·5. If the threshold were kept at £50, the new tax base would be £60, and to raise the same revenue the rate would have to be 44·2 per cent. Thus the basic rate of income tax would rise to 40–45 per cent, with possible adjustment in the progression of higher rates. The reinterpretation of the gross wage to include the payroll tax would probably cause temporary confusion.
3   The increase of the basic rate of income tax from 33 to 40–45 per cent might strengthen demands for the reintroduction of reduced rates.[4]

Section 6
Consolidation into the present (invoice-based) VAT might also present problems:

1   It would involve a switch from the income base to the expenditure base; and although this is not in fact a point of great substance there might be misinterpretation, especially in the case of the investment income surcharge, which might not be recognised as corresponding to the tax on the profit element in value added.
2   This problem is aggravated by the fact that the invoice-based VAT is not always seen as a tax on wages plus salaries plus profits, e.g. when exporters receive large rebates. The payroll tax and investment income surcharge are (roughly) origin-based taxes (taxes on producers), whereas the invoice-based VAT with its export rebates and charges on imports is a destination-based tax. The switch from payroll tax and investment income surcharge to VAT would therefore call for an adjustment in the exchange rate of the pound – which should rise (the consequent

fall in import prices being offset by the VAT charge, and vice versa for exports).
3 If firms did not realise that the abolition of the investment income surcharge meant that they could pay lower dividends, there might be a tendency for them to try to raise profit margins and prices, with transitional consequences for output and employment. Misunderstanding of the role of the exchange rate adjustment might also cause temporary confusion.
4 In the case of foodstuffs, and in general under a multirate VAT, the fall in import prices due to the adjustment of the exchange rate would not be offset by an equivalent VAT change. Thus the consolidation would increase the fiscal discrimination in favour of consumption of exempt items and would change relative prices.

Section 7
The problems mentioned in section 6 above would be lessened if the VAT were collected on an accounts basis, as described in Appendix 8.3 on ITVAT, without an export rebate or a charge on imports.

Section 8
Under an expenditure tax the evolutionary 'reforms' suggested in section 2 are less natural because the base is being changed. While the income tax base is the sum of the bases for payroll tax and investment income surcharge, this is not true of the expenditure tax. More importantly, even if the requirement in section 2(1) were changed to being a 5 per cent increase in the basic rate of expenditure tax and the 10 per cent payroll tax in section 2(2) were retained, the 10 per cent investment income surcharge in section 2(3) would involve the *definition* of investment income – an issue the avoidance of which is a major virtue of the expenditure tax.

In principle, a 10 per cent investment income surcharge is equivalent to a higher set of income tax or expenditure tax rates and a 10 per cent earned income relief; but to raise the expenditure tax rates by 15 per cent in all and to combine this with a 10 per cent payroll tax *and* a 10 per cent earned income relief is patently absurd.

Thus under the expenditure tax the payroll tax and investment income surcharge should be consolidated either into the expenditure tax rate structure or into VAT (invoice system) or ITVAT (accounts system), possibly with VAT on a destination, and ITVAT on an origin, basis for international trade.

NOTES

1 For the single earner the basic rate of rate is levied on earnings between £805 and £6,805 a year, i.e. between £15·5 and £130·9 a week. National insurance contributions are charged on total earnings up to £105 a week in respect of all employed persons earning more than £15 a week.
2 Consider the self-employed man with earnings of £100 liable now to income tax at 83 per cent. If he paid 9 per cent payroll tax and 83 per cent income tax on the balance of £91 (£75·5), the total would be 84·5 per cent of his earnings.
3 With payroll tax of £10 and income tax of £38 on a wage of £100, the tax (£10+£38 = £48) is 43·64 per cent of the cost to the employer (£100+£10 = £110). The investment income surcharge required for neutrality is therefore £43·64−£38 = £5·64.
4 With a basic rate of 40 per cent a man at the (unindexed) tax threshold would need a 10 per cent wage increase to compensate him for a 6 per cent increase in the price level.

18   The Tax Unit

Whether the individual, the married couple, the family including children, or some other group of persons should constitute the unit to be assessed for the levying of direct taxes raises a number of conflicting considerations, which become especially marked in a period such as the present during which social attitudes are rapidly changing. The idea that a woman on marriage becomes a dependant of her husband, who is then responsible for her welfare and for that of the family, accounts for much of the present treatment of the tax unit. This notion of the dependency of the woman on the man does in fact correspond with reality in many of the older married couples, where the wife, having from the start of the marriage stayed at home to care for the family and to bring up the children, has only a limited possibility of supporting herself at a later date by her own earnings. On the other hand, the notion is becoming less and less compatible with modern attitudes to the relationship between men and women, and in fact it corresponds less and less closely with reality when an increasing number of married women work in paid occupations.

CONFLICTING CRITERIA FOR THE CHOICE OF TAX UNIT

There are a number of different criteria concerning the tax treatment of married couples, each of which would find its enthusiastic supporters but many of which are not in fact compatible with each other. As a result the treatment of the tax unit must inevitably be a matter of compromise between a number of conflicting considerations. The following is a list of some of the most important of these criteria:

1   The decision to marry or not to marry should not be affected by tax considerations.
2   Families with the same joint resources should be taxed equally.
3   The incentive for a member of the family to earn should not be blunted by tax considerations which depend upon the economic position of other members of the family.
4   Economic and financial arrangements within the family (e.g. as regards the ownership of property) should not be dominated by sophisticated tax considerations.
5   The tax system should be fair between families which rely upon earnings and families which enjoy investment income.
6   Two persons living together and sharing household expenditures can live more cheaply and therefore have a greater taxable capacity than two single persons living separately.
7   The choice of tax unit should not be excessively costly in loss of tax revenue.

8   The arrangements involved should be reasonably simple for the taxpayer to understand and for the tax authorities to administer.

It is not necessary to go further than the first two items in the above list to realise that compromise may be necessary. Item 1 would suggest that an individual basis of tax should be maintained; but item 2 would suggest that a family in which one partner had an investment income of £10,000 and the other partner no investment income should not be taxed more heavily than a family in which the partners had investment incomes of £5,000 each. With a progressive tax, however, the individual basis of tax would tax more heavily the family in which the ownership of the income-yielding property was concentrated in the hands of one of the partners. An examination of the other items in the list will quickly reveal other potential conflicts.

Accordingly it is necessary to search for definitions of the tax unit which will provide reasonable compromises between these different desiderata. The most intractable part of the problem is to find an acceptable treatment for the married couple, and we accordingly start with an examination of this problem.

THE MARRIED COUPLE UNDER AN INCOME TAX AND UNDER AN EXPENDITURE TAX

In discussing the treatment of the married couple it is necessary to bear in mind whether the tax regime is that of an income tax or that of an expenditure tax. Under an income tax regime it is possible to distinguish between a couple's earned income and their investment income. For example, at present in the United Kingdom each partner may opt to be assessed separately on his or her earned income, but the wife's investment income must be aggregated with the husband's income for tax purposes; and the question may be raised whether each partner should not be allowed to be assessed separately as an individual on his or her total income whether earned or unearned.

This question would have different implications under an expenditure tax regime. In this case what we have called the expenditure tax adjustment must be added to (or subtracted from) investment income. Wherever investment income is considered under an income tax regime, under an expenditure tax regime the item considered must be investment income plus the net sales of, or minus the net purchases of, registered assets. No distinction is to be drawn between expenditure out of investment income or out of the realisation of the capital asset itself.

It is one thing under an income tax regime to ask whether each partner's investment income should be assessed on an individual basis or should be treated as a joint aggregate for tax purposes. Under an expenditure tax regime the corresponding question is whether each partner's investment income plus his or her dissavings or minus his or her savings should be taxed on an individual basis or should be combined with the other partner's as a joint aggregate for tax purposes. In other words, under an income tax the issue is whether investment income should be treated individually or jointly; under an expenditure tax it is whether in addition the husband's and wife's savings or dissavings should be treated individually or jointly.

The matter is closely connected with the treatment of gifts. We have argued in Chapter 15 (p. 329) and Appendix 15.4 that transfers of funds between spouses which are not sufficient to do more than cover their joint expenditures on housekeeping and personal consumption should not in any case be treated as gifts for tax purposes. We shall return later to a discussion of the cases in which transfers between spouses might be liable to tax as gifts; for the moment we assume that any transfers between spouses are not on a sufficient scale to be treated as gifts.

Suppose, then, that a husband transfers some registered assets to his wife. This transfer can take place indirectly if the husband meets more of the household bills and saves less while the wife meets less of the household bills and saves more. But whether the transfer takes place by a direct transfer of a registered asset or in this indirect way, it will increase the husband's and reduce the wife's liability to expenditure tax if husband and wife are being taxed on an individual basis.

If the expenditure tax schedule is a progressive one, the married couple will minimise their liability to tax by equalising their taxable expenditures. This could have an undesirable effect upon the influences affecting transfers of assets between spouses. Consider a couple in which the husband has a high income and the wife a low income. Suppose that each is saving the same proportion of their incomes. The husband's expenditure tax base will be higher than the wife's. Expenditure tax liability could be reduced by increasing the wife's expenditure (which is liable to a low marginal rate of tax) and decreasing the husband's expenditure (which is liable to a high marginal rate of tax). In other words, the husband with the high income should increase his savings and the wife with the low income should decrease her savings or actually dissave. In the normal case this would accentuate the inequalities of income and property between husband and wife.[1] It may be a difficult choice for the couple to take between reducing their current expenditure tax liability and transferring some property from the richer to the poorer partner.

The choice could be made even more difficult under certain regimes for the taxation of gifts. Suppose that under an expenditure tax gifts were not included in the expenditure tax base but were subjected to a separate tax on capital transfers (as discussed in Appendix 9.1). Suppose further that the separate transfer tax took the form of a PAWAT (described in Chapter 15) and that it was applied to gifts between spouses. If the husband with the high income had inherited much property while the wife with the low income had inherited little property, under a PAWAT tax could be saved by transferring property from husband to wife. But with a definition of interspousal gifts

---

[1] In the special case in which the husband owned no property and obtained his high income entirely from earnings, whereas the lower income of the wife was entirely from the yield on property, saving by the husband rather than by the wife would help to equalise the ownership of property.

which treated as gifts between husband and wife only such transfers as exceeded what was necessary to absorb all the joint personal consumption of the couple, the husband would in effect have to take over the whole of the couple's joint personal consumption (and thus under a progressive tax maximise the couple's liability to expenditure tax) before they could enjoy any tax relief under a PAWAT from the transfer of inherited property from husband to wife.

To some extent, in some circumstances the disadvantages due to the increase of expenditure tax liability resulting from a transfer of funds from the husband with a high income to the wife with a low income may be illusory. It may be asked what the partners intended to do ultimately with whatever wealth they did accumulate or maintain. If both wish to use it to finance their old age and if the marginal rates of expenditure tax for each partner remain unchanged over the years, then it is in reality a matter of indifference which partner spends and which saves. A simple numerical example may serve to illustrate the point. Suppose that the husband has a marginal rate of expenditure tax of 100 per cent (tax-exclusive) and that the wife has a marginal tax rate of 50 per cent. Suppose that the husband spends £100 less on consumption. He can purchase £200 of registered assets. Suppose that he accumulates this sum for ten years at 5 per cent a year and then spends it in retirement. He will have accumulated £200 $\times 1 \cdot 05^{10}$ pre-tax, which after expenditure tax at 100 per cent (tax-exclusive) will leave £100 $\times 1 \cdot 05^{10}$ to be spent. If instead the wife cuts down her expenditure by £100, she can buy only £150 of registered assets; this after ten years will be worth £150 $\times 1 \cdot 05^{10}$ pre-tax but only £100 $\times 1 \cdot 05^{10}$ post-tax. The result will be the same whichever of them does the saving, so that in the interests of the equalisation of property the wife should do the saving.

However, the ultimate intentions of the two partners may not be to use the capital for the finance of their old age. If, for example, they are accumulating in order to leave the property to their children and if gifts are taxed under a transfer tax the rate of which depends upon the circumstances of the donor, the relation between the husband's and the wife's rates of transfer tax may differ from that between their marginal rates of expenditure tax. Moreover, they may not be saving for the same purpose. If the husband is doing so with the intention of leaving the property to the children, while the wife is saving for expenditure in old age, there is no reason to believe that the outcomes after tax will be the same. Nor is there any reason to believe that their marginal rates of tax will remain unchanged. Moreover, they may well (either through fiscal myopia or because of uncertainties about the future) be attracted by the immediate saving of expenditure tax which results from concentrating the saving on the richer partner.

These problems disappear if, under an expenditure tax regime, the investment incomes plus expenditure tax adjustments of the two partners are aggregated and treated jointly for tax purposes. In that case it makes no difference to liability to expenditure tax which partner saves or dissaves. Transfers between spouses can take place without any tax implications in so far as they are not on a sufficient scale to qualify as interspousal gifts and will be subject simply to treatment as gifts if they exceed that level. We postpone until later the tax implications of such interspousal gifts. We now proceed to consider the tax treatment of married couples on the assumption that, while transfers of funds between them may be taking place, they do not raise issues concerning the taxation of interspousal gifts.

THE PRESENT TAX TREATMENT OF MARRIED COUPLES IN THE UNITED KINGDOM

At present in the United Kingdom the married couple are treated as a single unit for the income tax. The wife's income is in general aggregated with that of the husband, who enjoys a married allowance which is about one and a half times his tax allowance as a single person. If the wife goes out to earn, the couple enjoy a personal allowance against the wife's earnings in addition to the married allowance, so that the couple enjoy a tax allowance which is about two and a half times the single personal allowance. Alternatively, the wife can choose to be assessed as a separate individual on her earned income, in which case the husband's married allowance is reduced to a single personal allowance. This option will be selected only if the wife's earnings and the marginal rate of tax on the couple's joint income are sufficiently high to compensate for the loss of the married allowance.

The fact that with this system the great majority of married couples in which both partners are working enjoy a married allowance plus a single personal allowance instead of two single personal allowances is open to a number of objections. It means that by marriage two wage earners can reduce their total tax liability, although they can in fact probably live somewhat more cheaply if they set up house as a married couple. It is also costly in revenue.

MODIFICATIONS OF AND ALTERNATIVES TO THE PRESENT SYSTEM

A FIRST MODIFICATION OF THE PRESENT SYSTEM

For the reasons given in the preceding section we believe that it would in any case be desirable to modify the present system by removing the duplication of both a single person's allowance against the wife's earnings and also a married man's allowance against the rest of the couple's income. Where the single person's allowance is claimed against the wife's earnings the husband should cease to receive more than a single person's allowance.

Against this view it may be argued that the retention of the married man's allowance may have some incentive effects in encouraging married women to take paid work, since it means that a larger first slice of such earnings will be free of tax than would be the case if the advantage of the married allowance were lost when the wife went out to work. But this effect depends upon the married allowance being available in the first place in respect of a dependent wife who does not seek paid work. It can be argued that it is the very existence of a married allowance for dependent wives that should be blamed for causing any disincentive to seek paid work.

A RADICAL MODIFICATION OF THE PRESENT SYSTEM

This suggests a more radical modification of the present system, involving the abolition of the married man's allowance in all cases. If this were done, it would be necessary to recognise circumstances in which one partner (usually the wife) must stay at home or make other special and costly arrangements to look after children or other dependants needing home care. The suggestion which we have outlined in Chapter 13 is that this should be done by means, not of a tax allowance, but of a social benefit or home responsibility payment.

With this arrangement the married couple would in all cases enjoy a single personal allowance, and if both partners were earning there would be a second personal allowance against the second set of earnings. Thus, between two families with the same total of earned income, the family in which the income was due to the earnings of both partners would be more leniently treated than the family in which the same total income was earned by only one of the partners. But this might be regarded as a suitable recognition of the fact that there would be more expenses and more sacrifice of leisure, of home care and of do-it-yourself activity in the case of the former family. In this set-up the costs and needs of children and of other dependants needing home care would be met, not by additional tax allowances, but by social benefits such as the child benefits which are already being introduced into the UK system and the proposed home responsibility payment.

But it would seem essential, certainly for a transitional period and perhaps permanently, to recognise the fact that a married partner (normally the wife and mother) who has stayed at home to bring up a family may very well as a result have lost or much impaired her independence as an earner, so that some form of married allowance or other relief is in fact appropriate. Such a relief might be made dependent upon the ages of the married partners and/or upon there having in the past been dependants needing home care in the family.

With the removal of the married man's allowance, it would always pay the husband and wife to be assessed separately on their earned income. This would have the incidental advantage of removing the need for the option between joint and separate assessment of the wife's earned income; such options are a nuisance both for the administration of the tax and also for the clear understanding of the tax by the taxpayer. Moreover, in order to rid the tax system of its present sex discrimination, it might be ruled that the couple's investment income (or in the case of an expenditure tax their investment income plus their expenditure tax adjustment) should be aggregated and added, not to the husband's earnings, but rather to the higher of the two sets of earnings. Under the resultant system each partner would have a single personal allowance, their earnings would be assessed separately, and their combined investment incomes (or investment incomes plus expenditure tax adjustments) would be added to the higher of the two earnings. We shall call this system the *radical modification of the present system*.

There are two disadvantages to this system:

1   The marginal rate of tax on the earnings of the principal earner could be raised with possible disincentive effects by the aggregation of those earnings with the couple's joint investment income.
2   The fact that the partners' investment incomes were aggregated with the higher of the two earnings would lead in some cases to a serious tax on marriage. It would mean, for example, that if a woman had only an investment income and a man had a substantial income, whether from earnings or investment, tax would be avoided by avoiding marriage. The woman would keep a personal tax allowance; and, in addition, with a progressive tax schedule the woman's investment income and the man's income would be taxed separately at lower marginal rates of tax. In such circumstances there could be a heavy tax on marriage and a subsidy to divorce.

These two disadvantages might themselves be mitigated by other changes in the tax system. A reduction in the highest marginal rates of tax, which we have advocated in Chapter 14, would in the most extreme cases mitigate the effect of aggregating the investment income of the wife with the income of the husband. Moreover, we have argued in the previous paragraph as if a woman would enjoy a personal allowance against investment income so long as she remained single but would lose it if she married. This particular discrimination against married women, which many persons would regard as inequitable, would be removed if (as discussed later in this chapter) the rule were adopted that in general the personal tax allowance could be set only against earned income and not against investment income.

THE INDIVIDUAL BASIS

However, it may well be asked whether, in order to meet the objections to the radical modification of the present system described above, it would not be preferable to take the individual as such and not any family group as the unit for tax purposes, for investment income as well as for earned income. We shall consider the implications of this arrangement in the first instance in the case of an income tax. In this case each individual would be taxed on his or her total income, whether earned or unearned, after deduction of a single personal allowance and on the progressive scale for a single individual. The system of social security benefits such as child benefits and home responsibility payments could be maintained with appropriate rules as to which partner in a marriage should receive them. There would, however, be nothing corresponding to the married allowance for dependent wives, and the question would remain whether some special relief should be given in the case of older married partners in families in which children had been reared.

But the adoption of the *individual basis* would mean that the tax burden for two families with the same total income would not be the same if the income were concentrated in the hands of one partner in the one family but divided between the two partners in the other. The latter family would enjoy two personal tax allowances instead of one and would avoid the high marginal rates of tax which, on a progressive scale of tax, might result from replacing the two smaller incomes with one larger one. We have argued that for earned incomes there is a strong case for taxing the concentrated income more heavily than the divided income which depends upon both partners going out to work; but in the case of investment income it may seem anomalous that the tax burden of a family which does in fact share the use of the joint income should depend upon the accident of the division of its ownership within the family.

Of course, it would always be possible for a couple who owned property to seek to equalise their taxable incomes by a suitable transfer of the ownership of income-yielding property from one partner to the other. The tax advantage from such transfers of property ownership within the marriage partnership would depend among other things on the tax treatment of gifts. We have suggested above that transfers between spouses which do no more than cover the joint expenditure of the couple should not be treated for tax purposes as gifts. But if the transfer of property needed to equalise incomes went further than this, there might be a further set of tax considerations to be taken into account.[2] Some would regard it as a positive virtue of a tax arrangement that it would encourage a more equal division of income between married partners. But to treat the individual as the tax unit would lead either to different tax treatments of families with similar total investment income or else to property arrangements between spouses planned in such a way as to avoid taxation.

Another possible disadvantage of this arrangement is that it could easily lead to a substantial loss of tax revenue. A married couple in which only one partner had a taxable income would, under the present rules, enjoy a personal allowance equal to one and a half times the single adult's personal allowance; and we have already suggested a modification of present arrangements which would remove the married allowance and permit in these circumstances only one single personal allowance. If the individual basis were adopted for the tax unit, the transfer of unearned income from the partner with income to the partner without income would, up to the limit of a second full personal allowance, attract complete relief from tax.

This danger could be avoided by permitting personal tax allowances to be set only against earned income. If this were done, in order to prevent hardship it would be necessary to treat all social benefits as earned income, so that they would be tax-free up to the taxpayer's personal allowance. If (as

---

[2] These considerations would not necessarily reduce, and might even increase, the incentive to equalise the ownership of property. For example, with the PAWAT proposals made in Chapter 15 there would be a saving of PAWAT through the transfer of property from a husband who had inherited much to a wife of the same age who had inherited little. We return to this problem later in this chapter.

argued in Chapter 13) the level of personal tax allowances were eventually raised to match the level of social benefits, this would mean that all persons in receipt of social benefits would enjoy the full personal allowance.

However, even if this were done, objection might be taken to an arrangement which permitted a personal allowance against earned incomes, however large, but not against investment incomes, however small they might be. The widow who was left with a small investment income by her husband and the man or woman who maintained an independent but not necessarily inactive existence (as scholar, artist, inventor or voluntary social worker) on a small investment income would be among the losers. Some of these cases could be met by permitting the personal allowances to be set against all income, whether earned or unearned, by any taxpayer who was more than, say, 45 years of age.[3]

So much for the consideration of the individual basis for the tax unit under an income tax regime. We have already considered at length (pp. 378–381) the additional tax implications which would in any case arise if the individual basis were adopted under an expenditure tax regime.

But in the case of an expenditure tax there would be one further problem if the personal allowance were permitted only against earned income. Consider a sole trader whose only earned income is from the conduct of his trade. Suppose that he is ploughing back the whole of the profit from his business in the purchase of additional assets to expand his operations, is taking nothing out of the business, and is living, for the time being, on the realisation of some securities which he owns outside his business. He apparently has no earned income, and he would therefore be denied any personal tax allowance. With an expenditure tax the distinction between earned and unearned income becomes even more blurred than with an income tax, and the restriction of the use of the personal allowance as an offset against earned income becomes more difficult to maintain. One way of dealing with this problem would be to give such people the option of presenting a statement of their profits and retentions rather than of the net amount which they had taken out of the business. This option would be taken up only when they took out of the business less than the personal allowance.

PARTIAL INCOME SPLITTING

A possible arrangement which would avoid some of the disadvantages of the individual basis would be to keep the individual as the tax unit with the modification that the joint investment income of a married couple should for tax purposes be treated as if it accrued in equal halves to each partner. This

[3] As explained in Chapter 13, we have chosen to consider the tax unit problem on the basis of a tax system which relies on personal allowances against a first slice of income rather than on a system of tax credits or of unconditional social benefits. If it were desired at a later date to shift from the former to the latter type of system, it is difficult to see how personal allowances which were permitted against certain forms of income but not against other forms could be translated into tax credits or unconditional benefits.

may be called the system of *partial income splitting*. With this system each partner in a marriage would be taxed on a single-person progressive scale on his or her earnings plus one-half of their joint investment income, against which each partner could set a single personal allowance. It is in effect what would result from the individual basis if investment income were in fact owned equally by each partner. Equalisation of investment income for tax purposes would be brought about automatically without the need for any equalisation of the legal ownership of the income-yielding property.[4]

The danger to the revenue which we have discussed in the case of the individual basis, from permitting personal allowances to be set against investment income as well as earned income, would still exist under a system of partial income splitting, since, while it would be impossible for one partner to transfer the whole of his or her investment income to the other partner, one-half of such investment income would now be automatically so transferred. It would be possible to operate the system of partial income splitting with the limitation that personal allowances could be set only against earned incomes but with the safeguards discussed in the case of the individual basis, namely (i) that social benefits should be treated as earned income, and (ii) that personal allowances could be set against total income (or total expenditure) in the case of persons over, say, 45 years of age.

The application of this system under an expenditure tax regime would not raise tax considerations to affect the decision as to which partner should save and which should spend. The expenditure tax adjustment (i.e. their net savings or dissavings) would, together with their investment income, be split equally between the couple, and it would make no difference to their expenditure tax liability which partner did the saving. There would, however, arise one tiresome problem. Consider a couple in which one partner has a considerable earned income and very little investment income, while the other partner has little or no income. Suppose that this couple saves a high proportion of income. The couple's investment income minus their savings will be a negative figure; and if this were split evenly between the two partners, the partner with little or no income would end up with a negative tax base. The problem would arise regarding what scale of negative tax he or she should receive as a subsidy on his or her share of the savings. A possible rule would be to refund tax in these cases always at the basic rate.

A main disadvantage of this system would arise from the different treatments of earned income and investment income. In particular, in those cases in which the family income was concentrated in the hands of one partner,

---

[4] The compulsory equalisation of investment income for tax purposes might in some cases work to the disadvantage of the married couple. Thus if a husband had a high earned income and his wife a high investment income, the shifting of half the investment income from wife to husband (which would be optional under an individual tax base but compulsory under a partial income-splitting system) might involve a higher tax burden under a progressive tax scale. Partial income splitting in the case of such a couple would thus impose some tax penalty on marriage, although the penalty would be much less than with the existing system, under which the whole of the wife's investment income is aggregated with the husband's income for charge at the progressive scale of tax.

partial income splitting would give an advantage to investment income as contrasted with earned income. Consider two families in both of which the wife has no income and the husband has an income of £10,000 a year, this income being earned income in family A and investment income in family B. Family A would enjoy only one personal tax allowance and would be subject to marginal tax rates on personal incomes up to £10,000. Family B would enjoy two personal tax allowances and would be subject to marginal tax rates on personal incomes up to £5,000. The advantage to family B would, of course, be reduced if no personal allowances could be set against investment income or if there were an additional investment income surcharge on such income. But such additional charges would presumably be intended to be levied on investment incomes as contrasted with earned incomes, whatever the distribution of such incomes was between the partners in a married couple. They would not be devised as offsets to the advantages which unequally distributed investment incomes had over unequally distributed earned incomes.

THE UNRESTRICTED QUOTIENT SYSTEM

Two disadvantages of partial income splitting – namely (i) the differential treatments of earned income and investment income, and (ii) the possibility of negative tax bases under an expenditure tax – would be avoided by splitting earned income in the same way as investment income between the two partners in a marriage. With this system, which we shall call the *unrestricted quotient system*,[5] one-half of the total joint income (whether earned income or investment income) of the two partners is allotted to each partner, who enjoys a single person's tax allowance and is subject to a single person's progressive tax schedule.

Such a system is, however, open to very serious objections. It gives to every married couple, whether both partners are working or not, the equivalent of two personal allowances. Thus, far from eliminating the married man's allowance for a dependent wife, in effect it raises it from one and a half times to twice the single person's allowance. It is for this reason exceedingly expensive in revenue. It makes no allowance at all for the fact that by sharing household expenses a married couple can probably live more cheaply than can two single adults. Moreover, it can seriously blunt the incentives for married women to seek paid work. For example, if a man is earning more than enough to account for two personal tax allowances, the splitting of his earnings between himself and his wife will exhaust the wife's personal allowance so that, if she goes out to work, she will be taxed on the whole of her earnings.

THE RESTRICTED QUOTIENT SYSTEM

However, some of these objections could be removed and the force of others

---

[5] See Appendix 18.1 for a more formal description of what is implied by a quotient system.

reduced by limiting the operation of the quotient system. Such a *restricted quotient system* could be constructed on the following lines. The earnings and the investment incomes of the partners in a marriage would be aggregated. As far as the tax-free personal allowances were concerned, the married couple would unconditionally enjoy only one single person allowance, with an additional single person allowance that could be set only against the second set of earnings if both partners were earning. After deduction of these personal allowances, the combined income of the married couple would be subject to tax on a married couple progressive scale, the brackets in this scale being, say, one and a half times as broad as those applying to a single person.

In this system there are two basic restrictions of the unrestricted quotient system. In the first place, the married couple instead of enjoying in all cases two single-person tax allowances enjoys only one unconditionally plus a second which can only be set against the wife's earnings. In the second place, whereas with the unrestricted quotient system the married couple are taxed on their taxable income at the single person's rate of progression but with the bands of the tax brackets twice as broad as those for the single person, with the restricted quotient system the couple enjoy bands for the tax brackets which are less than twice as broad as those for a single person. We have chosen to illustrate the system with a quotient of 1·5, because this corresponds approximately to the present difference between the single person's and the married man's tax allowances.

This system avoids the discrimination in favour of investment income which (as we have shown) could occur with partial income splitting, without incurring the excessive cost in revenue involved in the unrestricted quotient system. Moreover, it avoids much of the blunting of incentives for married women to seek paid work, since such earnings will still attract an additional personal allowance. But at the higher levels of earnings and rates of tax it may well blunt incentives as compared with partial income splitting. Thus consider the case of a married couple with little or no investment income but with one partner earning a very high salary. With partial income splitting, if the second partner goes out to work, the taxation of his or her earnings will in no way be increased because of the high earnings of the first partner. But with a restricted quotient system the splitting of the existing high salary between the two partners may mean that the marginal rate of tax on additional earnings by the other partner will already be high, in spite of the restricted broadening of the bands for the brackets of the progressive scale of tax. With partial income splitting the incentive for the wife to work may be blunted by tax on her earnings due to the fact that she is already taxed on one-half of her husband's investment income. With the restricted quotient system her incentive to work may be blunted by tax on her earnings due to the fact that she is already taxed on one-half of her husband's earnings as well as his investment income.

There remains, however, one more serious disadvantage to this arrangement, namely the effect which it can have on the tax liabilities of two unmarried persons who decide to get married. At the lower end of the income scale the effect of marriage could not be to reduce tax liability, and, if the personal allowance could be used against investment income, it could in some cases increase tax liability; this would occur if one partner had investment income but no earned income, in which case marriage would mean the loss of one personal allowance. At the upper end of the income scale marriage could greatly reduce tax liability if the partners' incomes were very unequal (in which case the expansion of the bands of the tax brackets through the quotient system would reduce the marginal rates of tax on the high income), but it could greatly increase tax liability if the partners' incomes were more or less equal (through the aggregation of their earnings for higher rates of tax, which would more than outweigh any advantage from the partial expansion of the bands of the tax brackets which would result from a quotient of 1·5). If investment income is aggregated on marriage (a procedure which, as we have shown, is necessary to avoid certain tax complications under an expenditure tax), there are bound to be certain tax implications from a decision of two individuals to be married. But in any system in which earned incomes are separately assessed, one main cause of these arbitrary effects of marriage on tax liabilities can be avoided in so far as earnings are concerned.

THE PARTIAL QUOTIENT SYSTEM

It would be possible to devise a treatment which permitted separate assessment for earned incomes but maintained joint assessment with a quotient of, say, 1·5 for investment income; this we shall call a *partial quotient system*. A single individual would have a personal allowance which could be set against all income whether earned or unearned, and income above that would be liable to a progressive rate of tax.

For a married couple, one option would be to aggregate the whole of their incomes whether earned or unearned and to be taxed on it with a quotient of 1·5. This would mean that they would be taxed as a single individual but with the personal allowance and the bands of the following tax brackets all one and a half times as great as for the single individual.

A second option would be open to them, under which each could choose to be taxed separately on the single individual's scale on his or her earned income. In this case their investment incomes would continue to be aggregated and to be taxed as the top slice of what their tax liability would have been if they had not chosen to be taxed separately on their earned incomes. This liability to tax on their joint investment income would thus be calculated as the difference between what their tax liability would have been with the quotient of 1·5 if all their income (earned and unearned) had been aggregated for tax and what their tax liability would be with the quotient of 1·5 on their earned incomes alone if these had been aggregated for tax.

In the case of an expenditure tax the couple's joint investment income plus joint expenditure tax adjustment would be treated in this fashion as the top slice of what would have been their tax liability if there had been complete aggregation of all income plus the expenditure tax adjustment with the quotient of 1·5.

If the couple were saving less than their investment income, there would be some tax payable on this top slice; but if they were saving more than their investment income, there would be some tax refund on this top slice. The resulting joint tax liability or refund would presumably be levied from, or repaid to, each of the partners *pro rata* to their individual contributions to the joint investment income plus expenditure tax adjustment of the couple.

This system has many attractive features. By allowing a quotient of 1·5 on the aggregation of investment income it avoids the severe tax consequences of marriage which may result under the radical modification of the present system with its simple aggregation of investment income with the higher of the earned incomes. It avoids also the other extreme, which may result from partial income splitting, namely of giving an advantage to investment income by allowing, as it were, complete disaggregation of such income through its equal splitting between the two partners.[6] But at the same time, unlike the restricted quotient system it permits the complete disaggregation of earned incomes for tax purposes, and thus it avoids some of the anomalies and disincentives which may result from the restricted quotient system.

But the partial quotient system, like all the others, has its own disadvantages. It is necessary to give the married partners the option between being assessed separately or being taxed on the aggregation of their earned income with the rest of their income with the quotient of 1·5.[7] Even in the absence of this option the partial quotient system would suffer from being a rather complicated system, since it would involve three separate assessments: one on each of the earnings, and one on the difference between the aggregation of the couple's total income and the aggregation of their combined earned incomes. With the necessary retention of the freedom for the couple to opt out of separate assessment of their earned incomes, the complications would be compounded.

The application of the quotient of 1·5 would also amount to the maintenance of what was in fact equivalent to the married man's allowance in the cases in which one partner was not earning. One feature of the radical modi-

---

[6] The radical modification of the present system is equivalent to the aggregation of investment income with a quotient of 1, whereas partial income splitting is equivalent to aggregation with a quotient of 2. The partial quotient system steers a middle course with a quotient of 1·5.

[7] In the absence of this option some taxpayers might be taxed twice on an addition to their earnings. Consider the case in which the single person's allowance is £1,000. With a quotient of 1·5 this would mean that on the aggregated income of a married couple there would be a joint personal allowance of £1,500. Consider in these circumstances a couple with an investment income of £1,000 and with the husband alone earning £1,000. Tax will be being paid on £500, since total income is £2,000 and the investment income tax must be paid on any investment income which brings the aggregate income above £1,500. Suppose now that the husband increases his earnings to £1,100. If he cannot aggregate them with the investment income to be taxed with the quotient of 1·5, he will pay tax on the additional £100 twice over. His earnings are now £100 above the earned income allowance of £1,000, and in addition the total income is now £2,100 instead of £2,000, so that £600 instead of £500 of investment income are now taxable. This double taxation will go on until the husband is earning £1,500. From that point onwards, the full, but constant, amount of investment income of £1,000 will be taxed and additional tax will fall only on additional earnings.

fication of the present system and of partial income splitting is the abolition of this allowance, in order both to save revenue and to encourage labour force participation; this feature is lost in the partial quotient system.

THE PROBLEM OF THE AGGREGATION OF INVESTMENT INCOME

The radical modification of the present system suffers from the disadvantage of the tax burden and disincentives which it may impose on marriage through the aggregation of investment income. We have considered a number of ways of mitigating this effect. No one of them is perfect; as we indicated at the beginning of this chapter, there are unresolvable clashes between the different criteria which one would like to see met by the choice of tax unit. The three systems for which (as indicated in Chapter 13) we have chosen to illustrate the different possibilities are the radical modification of the present system, partial income splitting, and the partial quotient system. In what follows we confine our attention to these three possibilities.[8]

THE TREATMENT OF CHILDREN AND OF SOCIAL BENEFITS

SOCIAL BENEFITS

Child tax allowances are in the process of being replaced in the United Kingdom by child benefits, a substitution which (as indicated in Chapter 13) we regard as an essential feature of the new Beveridge scheme. Such benefits are at present not subject to tax. For the reasons given on p. 288 of Chapter 13, we believe that they should continue to be exempt from tax.

Other social benefits, however, should in our view be subject to tax (see p. 288 of Chapter 13). If, as suggested earlier in this chapter in discussing the radical modification of the present system and partial income splitting, the personal tax allowance were restricted to earned income, social benefits would have to be treated as earned income in order to ensure that persons without other income receive the full benefit. Suitable detailed rules would have to be made to decide in the case of a married couple which partner was to count as the earner of the social benefit. In some cases the attribution is clear (e.g. unemployment or sickness benefit to the individual who is unemployed or sick); in other cases (e.g. the pension received by a married couple) an equal division may be more appropriate.

THE INCOME (OR EXPENDITURE) OF CHILDREN

It remains to be decided how any income (or expenditure) of the children in a family should be treated. Under all three of the tax unit arrangements for married couples which we are considering, earned income may be separately

---

[8] In Appendix 18.2 some numerical illustrations are given of the effects of the various treatments of the married couple which have been described in the main text of this chapter.

assessed but investment income (or investment income plus the expenditure tax adjustment) will be aggregated in one way or another.

A natural arrangement would therefore be to assess the earnings of any child in the family separately, against which earnings the child would enjoy a separate personal allowance. In principle, to avoid duplication in the relief of tax, the child's personal allowance to be set against his or her income should be reduced by the amount of the child benefit which the family receives on his behalf. But it may be open to question whether this refinement of the system would be worthwhile. On the other hand, the child's investment income (or investment income plus expenditure tax adjustment) would appropriately be aggregated with that of the parents to be added to the father's income (in the case of the radical modification of the present system) or split between the parents (in the case of partial income splitting) or subjected to the quotient of 1·5 (in the manner proposed for the partial quotient system).[9]

GIFTS BETWEEN MEMBERS OF THE FAMILY

There remains for consideration some problems relating to gifts and in particular to gifts between members of the family. This includes gifts between parents and children as well as gifts between husband and wife. We are of the opinion that, in so far as gifts between members of a family are to be taxed, only transfers of wealth within the family which go beyond what is sufficient to cover the joint expenditures of the family on personal consumption should be regarded as gifts for tax purposes; and in Appendix 15.4 we have considered in more detail what this implies for the measurement of gifts between members of the family.

The tax treatment of such intrafamily gifts must depend upon the system of tax which is adopted for the treatment of gifts between a donor and donee who are not members of the same family. We shall consider four such possible cases, namely:

1   A comprehensive income tax (CIT).
2   A gifts-inclusive expenditure tax (GIET).
3   An income tax with a separate tax on transfers of capital, such as the PAWAT or LAWAT discussed in Chapter 15.
4   An expenditure tax with a separate tax on transfers of capital, such as the PAWAT or LAWAT.

1   COMPREHENSIVE INCOME TAX (CIT)

With a CIT gifts will normally be included as a taxable element in the donee's income base. Receipts of gifts by members of the family from outside would presumably be treated as investment income; since we are confining our attention to treatments of the tax unit which involve aggregation of investment incomes receipts of gifts would also be aggregated.

---

[9] Special treatment for the single parent family is discussed in Chapter 13 (p. 285).

In this case gifts between members of the family could be completely disregarded; but it is by no means clear that they ought to be disregarded. CIT is based on the belief that a gift should be taxed twice, i.e. in the hands of the donor when he received the resources from which he finances the gift, and in the hands of the donee when he receives it. A net gift from one member of the family to another should logically be treated on this principle, which implies adding to gifts received from outsiders all intrafamily gifts, to obtain the aggregate of gifts to be added to the aggregate of the family's investment income. This is the logical treatment, although it may sound odd to some people to add the gifts between husband and wife to the joint sum of gifts received by husband and wife.

If, however, intrafamily gifts were disregarded, two problems would arise. The first is due to the possibility of marriages of convenience, whereby A marries B simply to enable B to receive a gift from A without incurring tax. This possibility might be met by ruling that gifts between husband and wife in a short-lived childless marriage would not be exempt from tax.

The second problem arises in the case of gifts from parents to dependent children, which would remain free of tax indefinitely unless special measures were taken to prevent this from happening. A solution would be to treat as the child's income under the CIT all the wealth which he took with him from the family when he grew up, left home and first set up his independent tax unit; such wealth would in fact be the initial income of the new tax unit. In this case some averaging arrangement would be necessary in order to avoid such lump-sum initial incomes from being taxed at unduly high marginal rates of tax. But unless this rule were further modified, gifts received by dependent children from persons other than their parents would be taxed twice: once when they were received by the family, and again when they were taken out of the family and 'received' by the new tax unit. It would appear fair to exempt such gifts from one of these two taxes, either by excluding from the family's taxable income gifts received by dependent children from donors outside the family tax unit, or else by taxing the child when he or she left the family only on such wealth as he or she had acquired from the parents.

2 A GIFTS-INCLUSIVE EXPENDITURE TAX (GIET)

The problems with a GIET are very similar to those with a CIT. In this case also gifts from outside the family should be added to the family's investment income (subject, of course, to an offset in the expenditure tax adjustment if the gifts were used for the purchase of registered assets). Intrafamily gifts could be disregarded, although a more logical procedure would be to add them to the family's investment income, since, as in the case of a CIT, gifts are not subject to any independent transfer tax but are normally subject to tax as an element of the donor's expenditure.

If, however, intrafamily gifts were disregarded for tax purposes, the two problems of marriages of convenience and of gifts between parents and children would arise as in the case of the CIT. These problems could be handled on the same lines as those suggested for a CIT. In this case, when a child leaves the family and sets up his own new tax unit the wealth which he takes with him may be treated as a gift from the old family to the new tax unit, subject to the old family's rate of expenditure tax, in order to avoid gifts from parents to dependent children escaping tax indefinitely. But to avoid the double taxation of gifts, one of two modifications of the rules is necessary: either (i) gifts from outside donors to dependent children must be exempt from the donor's expenditure tax, or else (ii) only that part of the wealth taken by a child out of the family tax unit that is due to gifts from the parents must be subject to the family's expenditure tax.

3 AN INCOME TAX WITH A SEPARATE TAX ON TRANSFERS OF CAPITAL

In the case of an income tax combined with some independent tax on transfers of capital (such as the PAWAT or LAWAT discussed in Chapter 15) no special problem arises. Gifts do not affect liability to income tax. We have suggested in Chapter 15 that in the case of PAWAT it would be difficult to avoid charging gifts between husband and wife on an individual basis, in which case an intrafamily gift would be treated for tax purposes simply as an ordinary gift from one individual to another. In the case of LAWAT also it would be logical to treat gifts between spouses on an individual basis; but it would be possible, as with the present capital transfer tax, to ignore inter-spousal gifts for tax purposes, provided that (as suggested in Chapter 15, p. 331) no refunds were made on the occasion of a gift from a younger donor to an older donee. This provision would be necessary in order to prevent avoidance on the following lines. If refunds were allowed while interspousal gifts were disregarded, an elderly husband could make a gift to his young wife (with no tax on the interspousal gift), who would give it to a friend of the same age as her husband (receiving a refund in respect of a gift from a young donor to an older donee), who would give it back to the husband (paying no tax on a gift between persons of the same age).

4 AN EXPENDITURE TAX WITH A SEPARATE TAX ON TRANSFERS OF CAPITAL

The same conclusion can be reached in the case of an expenditure tax with an independent tax on transfers of capital (such as the PAWAT or LAWAT discussed in Chapter 15). Intrafamily gifts would be disregarded for the purpose of assessing liability to expenditure tax;[10] they would be treated for

---

[10] In Appendix 9.1 we have considered two different ways in which gifts might be treated for the purposes of a universal expenditure tax if it were desired not to operate a GIET but to subject them to an independent tax on transfers of capital. In Appendix 18.3 we give reasons for believing that, whichever of these two treatments of gifts under the universal expenditure tax was adopted, the proper treatment of intrafamily gifts would be to disregard them for expenditure tax purposes.

PAWAT in the ordinary way as a gift from one individual to another; and in the case of LAWAT they could also be treated on the individual basis or ignored.

CONCLUSIONS

The treatment of a married couple for income tax or expenditure tax purposes raises problems of peculiar difficulty. There are a number of very reasonable criteria – we have listed eight such items on pp. 377–378 – all of which it would be desirable to achieve but which inevitably clash. The choice of tax unit treatment thus depends to an exceptionally high degree on the relative weights which are set on the different conflicting objectives.

We all agree that the present arrangement by which, when both husband and wife are earning, the couple can enjoy both the married man's allowance and a single person's allowance against the wife's earnings is unsatisfactory, and that where a personal allowance is claimed against the wife's earnings the husband should enjoy only a single person's allowance. We all agree also that it is desirable to have a tax treatment for married couples which allows separate assessment of the earned incomes of the two partners.

A major problem arises with the treatment of investment income (in the case of an income tax) or of investment income plus the expenditure tax adjustment (in the case of an expenditure tax). The majority of us believe that in the case of an expenditure tax there should be some form of aggregation of the investment income and expenditure tax adjustments of husband and wife. Accordingly we have illustrated our analysis with three treatments, which we call a radical modification of the present system, partial income splitting, and a partial quotient system. All three of these (i) permit separate assessment of earned incomes, and (ii) require some form of aggregation of investment incomes plus expenditure tax adjustments. We have considered in some detail the relative merits and demerits of these three systems.

With all of these three systems it would be appropriate to assess any child's earnings separately on an individual basis, but to aggregate a child's investment income (or investment income plus expenditure tax adjustment) with that of the parents.

Appendix 18.1   The Implications of a Quotient System

With a quotient system, the starting point is a progressive scale of taxation for a single person. Then the combined income (or expenditure or whatever is the base for the tax system) of a group of persons is taken and taxed as if it were spread evenly over q persons, each of whom was liable at the single-person progressive scale of tax on his share (one-qth) of the total income. Thus in the case of a married couple a quotient of 2 (the unrestricted quotient system) would mean that the married couple were taxed as if they constituted two separate individuals, each with one-half of the joint income, while a quotient of 1 (full aggregation) would mean that the married couple were taxed simply as if they constituted one single individual. A quotient of, say, 1·5 (a restricted quotient) would treat the married couple as if their taxable capacity were intermediate between that of two separate individuals, each owning one-half of the joint income, and that of a single individual owning the whole of the joint income. It could be interpreted as recognising the fact that two persons can live more cheaply together in a single household than they can in two separate households, but not as cheaply as a single person in a single household. In this appendix we take the figure of 1·5 merely for purposes of illustration. A quotient system could be operated on any figure between 1 and 2.

The quotient system can be applied in practice by taking the personal allowance and the bands of the successive tax brackets in the progressive scale for a single individual, multiplying each of these bands (including the personal allowance) by the quotient q, and calculating the tax due by applying this new scale of tax to the total aggregated income of the tax unit. Thus with a quotient of 1·5 for a married couple, the single person's bands of tax-free personal allowance and of subsequent tax brackets would all be enlarged by 50 per cent and the new scale would be applied to the joint income of the married couple.

The restricted quotient system described in the main text can be regarded as a quotient system in which (i) for the personal tax allowance there is a quotient of 1 if only one partner is earning and a quotient of 2 if both partners are earning, and (ii) for all subsequent bands in the progressive tax brackets there is a quotient of 1·5.

The quotient system can be applied to groups larger than a married couple. For example, children could be included in the tax unit with a quotient of, say, 0·5 for each child. Thus a family consisting of married couple (quotient 1·5) and two children (quotient $2 \times 0·5 = 1$) could have their total joint income taxed with a combined quotient of 2·5. This in an unmodified form would mean that their combined income was subject to a single progressive scale of tax in which the personal allowance and each of the subsequent bands for the tax brackets in the progressive scale were two and a half times as great as for a single person.

Appendix 18.2   Some Numerical Illustrations of Different Tax Treatments of Married Couples

Table 18.1 shows the total personal allowances which could be set against the couple's total income under the various tax unit treatments discussed in the main text.

Table 18.2 is designed to illustrate the effect of the different tax unit treatments on

Table 18.1 *Total personal allowances of a married couple (in £s)* [a,b]

Wife's income	Present system	First modification of present system [c]	Radical modification of present system [d]	Individual basis with personal allowance against		Partial income splitting with personal allowance against		Unrestricted quotient system	Restricted quotient system	Partial quotient system
				All income	Earned income only	All income	Earned income only			
Earned income										
0	1,225	1,225	805	805	805	805	805	1,610	805	1,207
400	1,625	1,225	1,205	1,205	1,205	1,205	1,205	1,610	1,205	1,207
2,000	2,030	1,610	1,610	1,610	1,610	1,610	1,610	1,610	1,610	1,610
Investment income										
0	1,225	1,225	805	805	805	805	805	1,610	805	1,207
400	1,225	1,225	805	1,205	805	1,005	805	1,610	805	1,207
2,000	1,225	1,225	805	1,610	805	1,610	805	1,610	805	1,207

[a] Figures based on 1977/78 tax rates.

[b] It is assumed throughout that the husband's earnings are sufficient to cover all available allowances and that in none of the relevant cases is anything done to compensate for the loss of the married allowance for a dependent wife.

[c] The present system with the removal of the husband's extra married allowance when the wife has a personal allowance against her earnings which it would be advantageous to claim.

[d] The present system with the elimination of the married man's allowance.

Table 18.2   *Percentage of income levied in tax: married couples each with an earning capacity of £5,000 or £8,000*[a]

	Married couple both with earning capacity of £5,000			Married couple both with earning capacity of £8,000		
	Unrestricted quotient system	*Restricted quotient system*	*All other systems*	*Unrestricted quotient system*	*Restricted quotient system*	*All other systems*
Average rate of tax on total income if both are earning	28	28	28	31	34	31
Percentage of wife's income paid in tax as a result of decision to add her earnings to her husband	33	28	28	35	39	31
Marginal rate of tax on additional earnings by either partner when both are earning	33	33	33	45	55	45

[a] Figures based on 1977/78 tax rates.

Table 18.3 Percentages of income levied in tax (exclusive of investment income surcharge): married couples with joint incomes of £3,000 and £20,000[a]

	Present system	First modification of present system	Radical modification of present system	Individual basis with personal allowance against		Partial income splitting with personal allowance against		Unrestricted quotient system	Restricted quotient system	Partial quotient system
				All income	Earned income only	All income	Earned income only			
Joint income of couple £3,000										
Income divided equally:										
earned	11	15	15	15	15	15	15	15	15	15
unearned	20	20	24	15	33	15	33	15	24	20
Income owned by one partner:										
earned	20	20	24	24	24	24	24	15	24	20
unearned	20	20	24	24	33	15	33	15	24	20
Joint income of couple £20,000										
Income divided equally:										
earned	34	34	34	34	34	34	34	34	39	34
unearned	49	49	51	34	39	34	39	34	42	41
Income owned by one partner:										
earned	49	49	51	51	51	51	51	34	42	41
unearned	49	49	51	51	54	34	39	34	42	41

[a] Figures based on 1977/78 tax rates.

the tax rates of married couples both of whom have considerable earning capacity. All the systems except the unrestricted quotient system and the restricted quotient system permit separate assessment for the husband's and wife's earnings; and for that reason they all have the same effect on the earnings of married couples at the higher end of the income scale. The first line of the table shows how aggregation with the restricted quotient system (a quotient of 1·5) can add to the tax liability of the couple. The second line shows the proportion of the couple's additional income which will be taken in additional tax when the wife decides to take paid employment, and illustrates how the aggregation of incomes under the two quotient systems can raise this rate of tax. The third line shows the possible effect of aggregation with the restricted quotient system, in raising the marginal rate of tax on the earnings of both husband and wife when both are earning.

Table 18.3 illustrates the different effects of the tax unit systems discussed in the main text on the married couple's joint incomes according to (i) the level of the joint income, (ii) whether it is earned income or investment income, and (iii) whether it is divided equally between the two partners or is concentrated on one of them.

Appendix 18.3   The Treatment of Intrafamily Gifts for Universal Expenditure Tax

In Appendix 9.1 we have outlined two possible treatments of gifts for the purposes of a universal expenditure tax if it were desired to submit gifts to an independent tax on transfers of capital. We shall call the first treatment, given on p. 195 of Appendix 9.1, 'treatment 1' and the second treatment, given on p. 196, 'treatment 2'.

With treatment 1 the transfer of a registered asset from donor to donee has no effect on the tax base of either party, while a transfer of an unregistered asset reduces the expenditure tax adjustment for the donor and raises it for the donee by the same amount. If this is an intrafamily gift and if, as is the case with the tax unit treatments which we are considering, the donor's and donee's expenditure tax adjustments are being aggregated for expenditure tax purposes, there is no change in the aggregated family base for the universal expenditure tax.

With treatment 2 the transfer of both registered and unregistered assets leaves both the donor's and donee's expenditure tax adjustments unchanged. There is therefore no change in the family's tax base resulting from intrafamily gifts.

19 Trusts

In this chapter we shall depart from our usual pattern of not setting out how existing taxes treat the subject, partly by way of background because the treatment of trusts is probably less familiar to readers, and partly to help demonstrate that considerable simplification would be possible under an expenditure tax. We shall also deal with the other taxes considered in this Part of our Report, except for PAWAT, which has been more conveniently dealt with in Chapter 15.

As each new tax has been introduced, a system of taxing trusts has been invented without, it seems, very much thought about how the new tax would fit in with other taxes. The following is a brief outline of the main points concerning the taxation of trusts at present.

Capital transfer tax contains the most recent legislation dealing with trusts and categorises them into three types, which for ease of reference we shall call A, B and C.

1   With *type A* trusts there is a beneficiary entitled to income (an 'interest in possession'), e.g. a trust to pay the income to Mr Smith for life and then to pay the capital to his children equally.
2   With *type B* trusts there is no such beneficiary, e.g. an accumulation or discretionary trust, such as a trust to pay income or capital to such of Mr Smith and his children as the trustees in their discretion decide.
3   *Type C* trusts are children's trusts, e.g. a trust for Mr Smith's children at age 21 equally. These are really a branch of type B, because the law implies a power to use income for the maintenance of the child under age in the trustees' discretion, the balance being accumulated.

It will be seen that this categorisation is in terms of entitlement to income. It fits most of the trusts commonly met in practice, and we shall accordingly use it to describe how trusts are dealt with under other taxes.

In taxing trusts there are only two possibilities: (i) taxing the trust itself as a separate entity (which we shall call *personification*); and (ii) taxing by reference to the circumstances of the beneficiary as if the trust did not exist (which we shall call *transparency*), although obviously the tax will have to be paid out of the trust if it is a tax which is normally paid out of capital, but nevertheless the beneficiary's circumstances determine the rate.

CAPITAL TRANSFER TAX

Type A trusts are transparent. The person entitled to the income is treated as owning the capital for all purposes (the trustees, of course, pay the tax because he does not actually own the capital). Receipt of capital by the income beneficiary is therefore not an occasion of charge as he is receiving what he is already deemed to own. Conversely, if some other person receives the capital, this is treated as a gift made by the life tenant. Since the life tenant has the whole capital attributed to him there is normally no charge to tax on reversionary interests. An exception to the principle of transparency arises if the settlor has a different domicile from the beneficiary, when the settlor's domicile over-rides the domicile of the beneficiary, giving rise to a charge to capital transfer tax on a non-domiciled beneficiary (if the settlor was domiciled) or no tax on a domiciled beneficiary (if the settlor was non-domiciled).

Type B trusts are in contrast personified, so far as trusts created before 27 March 1974 are concerned. This is interesting because it is not what happened under estate duty and not what might be expected with a progressive tax. Each existing trust is treated in exactly the same way as an individual and has the lower rates of tax given to an individual during his lifetime. A number of small trusts is therefore more favourably treated than one large one. The occasions of charge are:

1   Capital leaving the trust.
2   Conversion into a type A or C trust.
3   A ten-yearly periodic charge.

Until 1980 the charges under (1) and (2) are at reduced rates if the beneficiary is domiciled in the United Kingdom, and the charge under (3) cannot arise before 1980. The receipt of income by, and the personal circumstances of, the beneficiary are irrelevant, giving complete personification.

On the usual cumulation principle of capital transfer tax, the rate of tax depends on previous events. However, with type B trusts the system is modified in that only occasions of capital leaving the trust lead to cumulation (without indexation). It follows that the periodic charge, which is at 30 per cent of the rate applicable on a distribution of the whole fund, does not affect the rate of tax on subsequent events, because no capital leaves the trust. Similarly, capital leaving the trust via a type A or C trust in another part of the fund still cumulates and therefore affects the rate of tax on subsequent events occurring in the type B trust, even though those events are not themselves chargeable, such as the income beneficiary receiving the capital. Where there has been a charge on the conversion to a type A or C trust and later capital leaves the trust, only the excess value cumulates for this purpose. There is an exception to the charge if the settlor or his spouse or widow or a charity is the recipient. The payment still cumulates except in the case of charity.

Post-26 March 1974 type B trusts take the settlor's circumstances into account in determining the rate of tax. The rate is the rate at which the settlor would have to pay tax if he had made a transfer of the after-tax amount going into the trust, rather than the gross amount which he in fact transferred. This rate applies until capital equal to this amount has left the trust, after which the tax payable climbs up the normal rate scale from that point. The circumstances of the settlor after he has made the trust are irrelevant. This might be regarded as partial personification.

Both the domicile of the donor and the situs of the assets normally determine taxability to capital transfer tax. This is followed for trusts by taxing trusts set up by someone domiciled in the United Kingdom at the time, and by taxing the assets in the United Kingdom of other trusts. If the settlor is not domiciled at the time the trust was set up, there is no charge under a type A trust holding foreign assets, regardless of the circumstances of the beneficiary, which is an exception to the principle of transparency. If a type B trust has non-resident trustees but the settlor was domiciled when it was made, there is an annual periodic charge at 3 per cent of the rate which would apply on full distribution. In effect, the ten-yearly charge is being collected by annual instalments. The settlor is normally accountable for the charges in these circumstances.

Type C trusts are transparent. There are no ten-yearly charges nor any charges when the child becomes entitled to income (when the trust becomes a type A trust) or to capital. The result is the same as if the beneficiary were the owner of the capital, which he cannot be because he is a minor. In one way it is more favourable as there is no tax if the beneficiary dies under age.

CAPITAL GAINS TAX

Apart from normal disposals by trustees, e.g. when changing investments, capital gains tax is charged:

1 When a beneficiary becomes absolutely entitled to capital (but if this occurs on death there is no tax payable and the trust is treated as acquiring the assets at their new value).
2 When a life interest ceases (but if this occurs on death there is no tax payable and the trust achieves a new base value).

Officially there is no recognition of different types of trusts. However, a type A trust is in effect recognised by giving the tax-free uplift on death, whereas with a type B trust there will eventually be a charge to tax on the whole of the gain, because of the charge at (1) above. Before 1971 there was also a fifteen-yearly periodic charge on type B trusts. There is a very limited recognition of type C trusts in the case where the child has an absolute interest but, being a minor, cannot give a receipt. Here the trust is treated as transparent; the rate of tax is the child's and there is no charge at (1) above on his attaining his majority. However, in the more normal case of the child's interest being contingent there is complete personification; the rate is the flat rate of 30 per cent and there will be a charge under (1) above on the child attaining the specified age and becoming entitled to capital.

The normal rule for capital gains tax is therefore personification, to which there exist three exceptions:

1 Events occurring on death, when the type A trust is treated as transparent because the same treatment is applied as if the life tenant owned the assets himself, namely a tax-free uplift.

2   The possibility that losses made by the trustees can be carried forwards by the beneficiary when he becomes entitled to capital.
3   The owner-occupied house exemption can be obtained under all types of trust.

This lack of recognition of different types of trusts means complete freedom of interchange. A type B trust which has existed for many years without any charge can convert into a type A trust and obtain the tax-free uplift on the beneficiary's death, without provoking a charge to capital gains tax on conversion, although there will be a capital transfer tax charge both on conversion and on death.

Capital gains tax is payable by UK residents only; non-residents are not even charged on UK assets (except business assets). To fit in with this test of taxability the deciding factor is the residence of the trustees. A trust which was entirely foreign, having a foreign settlor and beneficiaries, would still pay capital gains tax if the trustees were in the United Kingdom, although there are exceptions for professional trustees. To appoint non-resident trustees would therefore be an easy method of avoiding capital gains tax by UK trusts. This is countered by an anti-avoidance provision, which charges UK-resident and domiciled beneficiaries on their proportion of the trustees' gains, if the settlor was resident and domiciled either when the settlement was made or at the time of the gain. With a type B trust the measure of the beneficiary's interest is the value of an annuity producing the average income over the previous three years. If a beneficiary has received capital representing a gain, he is also taxed.

INCOME TAX

Type A trusts are transparent. The source of the income is the underlying investments, not the trust itself. If the trustees permit the income to be paid direct to the beneficiary, they cannot be assessed to income tax. If the trustees receive the income, they are assessed at the basic rate of tax only, the beneficiary being liable for the higher rates and the investment income surcharge.

Type B trusts are personified. The source of the income is the trust itself, and the applicable year is the year of payment rather than the year in which the income arose. The trustees pay the basic rate as mentioned above and are also liable to the investment income surcharge at 15 per cent without any minimum limit. The treatment shows two signs of transparency. First, if income is paid to the beneficiary it is treated as having suffered the basic rate and the surcharge, and therefore the beneficiary can recover the surcharge if he is not liable to it; but this applies only to a payment made as income, and once income has been accumulated this is no longer possible. Secondly, if the income so distributed includes foreign income, the trustees are still taxed in the same way but the beneficiary is entitled to claim double taxation relief as if the income had been his.

Type C trusts are not recognised, except negatively where the parent is the settlor, when all distributions up to the amount of available income are treated as income of the parent. Apart from this, type C trusts are regarded as type B trusts.

Anti-avoidance provisions deeming the trust's income to be the income of the settlor during his lifetime exist in cases where: the settlor or his spouse may benefit; income is paid to the settlor's minor children; the settlement is revocable; income is accumulated and the settlor has an interest under the trust; the settlor is a beneficiary of a discretionary trust; and, while there is accumulated income, a capital payment (even a loan) is made to the settlor.

If the trustees are non-resident and a UK-resident beneficiary has power to enjoy the income (widely defined so as to include a discretionary beneficiary), the beneficiary can be taxed on the trustees' income. Similarly, if a capital payment is received by such a beneficiary, he can be assessed to tax on the income of the trustees.

SUMMARY OF TREATMENT UNDER EXISTING TAXES

Type A trusts are therefore transparent for all taxes except capital gains tax, when they are only partly transparent; in particular, the life tenant's rate of tax is not material. Type B trusts are personified for all three taxes, although the rate of capital transfer tax on new trusts takes the settlor's circumstances into account. Type C trusts are transparent for capital transfer tax but not recognised, and therefore treated in the same way as type B trusts, for income tax and for capital gains tax.

It will be seen that capital gains tax and capital transfer tax particularly do not fit well together. There would be a considerable benefit if the same categorisation were used for all trusts, so that a type C trust would be recognised for capital gains tax and income tax. The income of a child, whether or not it was paid to him, would be charged to income tax as income of the child instead of being charged to the higher investment income surcharge, which applies only to individuals with an investment income of more than £2,000 a year. Capital gains would also be charged at the child's rate of tax, and there would be no charge to capital gains tax when the child became entitled to capital. The conversion of a type B trust into a type C trust would be treated as an occasion of charge. This would bring the occasions of charge to capital transfer tax and capital gains tax into line, and at the same time it would avoid the difficulty of charging capital transfer tax on accrued capital gains merely because the charges occurred at different times.

Type A trusts could be made completely transparent, so that the beneficiary's rate of tax would be used to determine the rate of capital gains tax payable by the trustees and there would be no charge to that tax on the life tenant becoming entitled to capital, in the same way as there is no capital transfer tax charge on this occasion. Transparency could be extended to capital transfer tax in one respect by ignoring the domicile of the settlor, so that a non-domiciled life tenant of a trust made by a UK-domiciled settlor would not be charged to capital transfer tax in respect of non-UK assets. There would be a difficulty of collection in taxing in the converse case, i.e. that of a UK-domiciled life tenant of a foreign trust, but the rate of tax on his free estate could take the value of the trust into account.

The fact that type B trusts take the settlor's circumstances into account for capital transfer tax could be extended to income tax, so that undistributed income could be charged as if it were the highest part of the settlor's income. While it is true that the settlor has ceased to own the capital from which the income arises, he has not transferred it to any other person who can be charged to tax at higher rates or the investment income surcharge, and therefore it is not unreasonable to regard the income as still being the settlor's. If the income were subsequently to be distributed as income, there would have to be a credit. The administration could perhaps be simplified by providing that, if the income had not been distributed by the end of the tax year following that in which it arose, it should be regarded as having been accumulated and therefore charged at the settlor's rate of tax.

If capital gains tax were reintroduced on death, the periodic charge to capital gains tax on a type B trust could be made at the same time as the periodic charge to capital transfer tax, thus preventing a charge to one tax on the amount of the other.

With type B trusts there is a difference about whose domicile or residence the trust should take. For capital transfer tax it is the settlor's domicile at the date of making the trust, whereas for capital gains tax the settlor's status is normally irrelevant and it is the residence of the trustees from time to time which counts. If for capital gains tax the trust were to take the settlor's residence, avoidance by appointing non-resident trustees would be prevented, although it is appreciated that this would necessitate collecting the tax from the settlor, which occurs under capital transfer tax. There would be an advantage in the opposite case of not inhibiting non-resident settlors from making trusts in the United Kingdom unless they had professional trustees, who are deemed to have the settlor's domicile and residence. The charge to capital transfer tax on UK assets, which can give rise to the annual periodic charge under a foreign trust investing in the United Kingdom, might also be eliminated, perhaps by having an additional test of the proper law as was the case under estate duty, although under that tax a trust governed by foreign law would not have been exempt on assets in the United Kingdom.

EXPENDITURE TAX

The treatment of trusts would be greatly simplified under an expenditure tax. Many of the rules for taxing trusts now are designed to prevent avoidance by making use of a trust in which the income does not belong to anybody. Thus the investment income surcharge is applied to type B trusts because otherwise the only income tax payable would be at the basic rate, which was no doubt thought to be too generous when the standard rate (which was a rate for investment income) became the basic rate (which is a rate for earned income) in 1973. The rules for taxing the income of the trust as that of the settlor were also designed to prevent a settlor liable to income tax at a high rate from using the trust as a vehicle to avoid charges to higher rate tax when he could later obtain the use of the funds. None of these rules is of advantage under an expenditure tax. Tax can always be avoided, or rather postponed, by investing in registered assets. Because trusts would no longer have these advantages the rules for taxing them could be greatly simplified.

The ways of taxing gifts, to which the treatment of making trusts must be equated, described in this Report are as follows:

1 Treating the gift as expenditure (see p. 184), in which case the donor pays tax on a gift of a registered asset and the donee on a gift of an unregistered asset (unless he reinvests it in a registered asset).
2 Treating the gift as the equivalent of saving (Appendix 9.1, first method), in which case the donor pays no tax on a gift of a registered asset and receives a tax repayment on a gift of an unregistered asset, while the donee pays tax on the acquisition of an unregistered asset (unless he reinvests it in a registered asset).
3 Ignoring the gift (Appendix 9.1, second method), in which case neither the donor nor the donee pays any tax, whatever the nature of the gift.

Where the donor is charged there is no problem; it makes no difference that the donee is a trust rather than an individual. The problem arises where the donee is charged, which occurs with a gift of unregistered assets in methods 1 and 2 above. With a trust there is no donee with a tax rate to use. This points to method 3 being preferable.

If it were desired to use method 1 or 2, a possible alternative would be to treat the unregistered assets as if they were registered and to charge tax on the settlor under method 1 and not give him the tax repayment under method 2.

During the life of a trust the following events have to be catered for:

(a) a registered asset remaining as such;
(b) an unregistered asset remaining as such;
(c) a registered asset being turned into an unregistered one, e.g. by the sale of it or by the receipt of income from it;
(d) an unregistered asset being turned into a registered one, e.g. by investing the cash in a registered asset; and
(e) making payments to the beneficiaries or allowing them the use of assets.

We can ignore cases (a) and (b) because they are no different from the case of the individual donee doing the same thing. Case (d) need not concern us either, because an individual would obtain a deduction in computing his expenditure, and there is therefore a positive disadvantage in having a trust which cannot obtain any deduction (except possibly at the basic rate) until

the registered asset is distributed to a beneficiary. At this stage the beneficiary records the receipt of the registered asset and claims the deduction.
This leaves case (c), which would be an occasion of charge, or rather would be
an addition in computing expenditure, in the case of an individual donee,
but which cannot be charged because the trust has no rate of tax at which to
charge it. So long as no beneficiary has the immediate use of the unregistered
asset there is no loss of tax, because the asset is not spent. Recording disposals of registered assets is an indirect method of measuring expenditure,
and if the asset is still in trust it has not been spent. In effect, therefore, something which would normally be treated as an unregistered asset will be
treated as a registered one so long as it remains in trust. A charge will be
made when the asset leaves the trust.

The only time in which it matters that the trust asset is in unregistered form
is where the beneficiary has the use of the asset without its producing any
income which is paid to him. An example would be the beneficiary being
allowed the custody of a valuable chattel. In this case the beneficiary can be
charged to tax on its annual value. In the same way, when the beneficiary is
allowed the use of a house the charge on the annual value can be attributed
to the beneficiary.

On assets being distributed from the trust either during its life (case (e)
above) or on its termination, the receipt from the trust would be treated as an
addition to the beneficiary's income, with a corresponding deduction if it is
a registered asset. The treatment of trusts under a PAWAT which would be
linked with methods 2 and 3 above is considered in Appendix 15.5.

TWO-TIER EXPENDITURE TAX

The treatment of trusts under a two-tier expenditure tax would be similar.
As we have shown (p. 205), the taxation of gifts generally would be under
methods 2 or 3, although method 1 would be possible if gifts were also liable
to basic rate tax. Again method 3 would be preferable; but if it were desired
to use method 2 the settlement of an unregistered asset could be treated as a
registered one, so that the settlor did not obtain any refund and the trust
would not be taxed.

If the basic rate tier were an income tax with 100 per cent capital allowances, the income of the trust would be liable to the basic rate of income tax
as at present, which would mean that the distinction between income and
capital would have to be maintained. Where distributions were made they
would be an addition to other income in calculating expenditure for the
upper tier of the tax and there would be a deduction for the basic rate tax
already suffered on income. Otherwise the treatment would be the same as
that outlined above for a universal expenditure tax.

If the basic rate tier were a tax on value added (as suggested in Chapter 10
and Appendix 8.3), there would be no need to maintain a capital–income
distinction and the problems would be the same as for a universal expenditure tax.

ANNUAL WEALTH TAX

Trusts could be treated on the following lines. Where income was distributed the trust capital would be attributed to the beneficiaries in the same proportions as the share of income which each had received, and the wealth tax payable (if any) would be calculated by treating the attributed amount as the top slice of the beneficiary's wealth. The tax would, however, be payable by the trust, not by the beneficiary. This arrangement would apply both where the beneficiary had an interest in possession in the trust and where the income he received was paid at the discretion of the trustees.

It is arguable that the liability should be charged, not on the slice of trust capital attributed to the beneficiary, but on the value of his interest, since that is all he could realise on selling it. The effect, however, would be to give trust capital an advantage compared with capital owned absolutely by an individual, since the value of the interest would be less than that of the proportionate share of the capital. Moreover, the valuation of reversionary interests as well as of interests in possession would be involved, and special provisions would be needed in the case of discretionary payments of income.

Where income or some part of the income was accumulated, some relatively arbitrary charge on the slice of trust capital corresponding to the fraction of income accumulated would be inevitable.

It has been proposed that that slice of trust capital should be attributed to the settlor (the resulting tax being paid by the trust, as in the case of capital attributed to beneficiaries). In the case of accumulation for identified minor children, however, the capital could be attributed to the children *ab initio*.

It would seem that these arrangements would be as appropriate in conjunction with an expenditure tax as with an income tax, although it would be necessary to maintain for trusts a distinction between income and capital payments, whereas this distinction need not be maintained by trustees for expenditure tax purposes.

COMPREHENSIVE INCOME TAX

The general principles which we would advocate for trusts under a comprehensive income tax would be to levy a withholding tax on all income of the trust, including the initial capital paid in and all subsequent receipts, whether conventional income or realised capital gains. The tax credit associated with dividends would be set against the withholding tax payable by the trustees. In this way the trust would be treated as an individual with a personal tax rate equal to the rate of withholding tax. A withholding tax rate of about 50 per cent would seem to be in the right sort of region. All distributions out of the fund would be grossed up by the rate of withholding tax, and the grossed-up amount would be taxable income in the hands of the beneficiary, who would, however, receive a tax credit equal to the rate of withholding tax multiplied by the grossed-up distribution. The problem would be more complicated if withholding rates changed over time.

CONCLUSIONS

The taxation of trusts is an area which would be greatly simplified under an expenditure tax. The present rules for income tax are designed to prevent avoidance of high rates of tax by the use of trusts, so that the higher rate of investment income surcharge is imposed on discretionary trusts and in some cases the income is treated as that of the settlor. None of these would be necessary under an expenditure tax, because a trust would have no advantage over any registered asset. The consequent abolition of capital gains tax would be a simplification.

The method of taxing trusts under an annual wealth tax and a comprehensive income tax has also been considered. The treatment under a PAWAT is dealt with in Chapter 15.

20 The Effects of Tax Structure on International Migration and Capital Movements

STRUCTURAL DIFFERENCES BETWEEN AN ET COUNTRY AND AN IT COUNTRY

When the tax relations with other countries which would rule under an expenditure tax regime are considered, allowance must be made for the fact that this is likely to involve relations between a country with an expenditure tax (which we shall call an 'ET country') and a country with an income tax (which we shall represent as an 'IT country'). There are some special problems which arise simply because of the difference in tax regimes. In order to isolate these problems we confine our examination in this chapter to cases in which both the ET and the IT countries are similar in their other economic characteristics (e.g. have the same general levels of economic productivity), so that in the absence of tax differences there would be no great incentive for capital or labour to move from the one country to the other; and we assume further that both countries have the same general level of tax rates (e.g. a rate of 50 per cent, tax-inclusive, or 100 per cent, tax-exclusive), so that there is no incentive for movements of labour or capital between them simply in order to enjoy a lower rate of tax. We are then confined to the question whether the mere difference in the tax structure – tax being on consumption expenditure in the ET country and on income in the IT country – will itself have some special tax influence on movements of capital funds or of people between the two countries.

In order to answer this question certain distinctions must be drawn between the types of expenditure tax applied in the ET country. In this connection there are two relevant distinctions: one relating to the rate of interest in the ET country, and one relating to the cost of living in the ET country.

1 EXPENDITURE TAX AND THE RATE OF INTEREST

In Chapter 8 we have explained four methods of applying the expenditure tax principles. Of these the method of income tax with 100 per cent capital allowances tended to cause the market rate of interest on savings to exceed by the rate of tax the yield on the real investment which the savings served to finance; in this case it is the post-tax rate of interest which is linked to the yield on the underlying real investment (see pp. 155–156 above). The other methods which we have considered – namely the expenditure-tax adjustment method which would be employed for a universal expenditure tax and for the upper tier of a two-tier expenditure tax, and a tax on value added which might be used for the lower tier of a two-tier expenditure tax – would not have this effect; in so far as they were used, it would be the market rate of interest itself which was linked to the return on the underlying physical investment.

2   EXPENDITURE TAX AND THE MONEY COST OF LIVING

There is a second relevant distinction between the forms of expenditure tax. Suppose that the ET country is employing a destination-based tax on value added, such as the present VAT. Then with VAT at a 100 per cent (tax-exclusive) rate the cost of living in the ET country will tend to be twice as high in money terms at the current rate of foreign exchange as it will be in the IT country. Imports from the IT country will have a 100 per cent VAT levied on them when they are consumed in the ET country, while goods exported from the ET country will not be charged to VAT when they are exported, although they would be charged to VAT if consumed in the ET country. If, however, the ET country were using an origin-based tax on value added, or an income tax with a remission of tax either on investment (i.e. an income tax with 100 per cent capital allowances) or on savings (i.e. an income tax with an expenditure tax adjustment), no tax would be charged on imports as such and tax would not be rebated on exports; at the current rate of foreign exchange there would be no tax effect to raise the cost of living in the ET country relatively to that in the IT country.

Having made these distinctions, we can turn to the main question whether the difference of tax structure between the two countries will itself influence the movement of capital funds or of persons between the two countries.

EFFECTS OF TAX STRUCTURE ON THE INTERNATIONAL FLOW OF CAPITAL FUNDS

THE PROBLEM OF DOUBLE TAXATION RELIEF ON FOREIGN INVESTMENT INCOME

We start, then, with possible effects upon the movement of capital funds. Of course, these effects cannot be considered without first considering what regime of double taxation relief on investment income is adopted in the ET country. Should the ET country give relief against its expenditure tax in respect of income tax levied on investment income arising in the IT country?

An expenditure tax regime under which savings (or investment) are exempt from tax is in one essential feature equivalent to a tax regime under which savings (or investment) are not exempt from tax, but the yield on the savings (or investment) is exempt from tax. We have shown this equivalence in

Chapter 8.[1] For ease of reference we repeat the basic features of this equivalence in Table 20.1.

Thus the problem of double taxation relief on foreign investment income by the ET country can be approached on the basis of column B of Table 20.1 by asking what would be the appropriate policy if the only difference between the ET country and the IT country were that the former did not tax the yield on savings-investment while the latter did levy such a tax. An obvious first answer is that the ET country would give no double taxation relief on foreign investment income for the simple reason that there was no equivalent domestic tax against which the relief could be given. The common principle that the income bears the higher of the foreign or the domestic tax would rule; the income would bear the foreign tax because the domestic tax was zero.

Table 20.1 *Remission of tax on savings or on the yield of savings*

	A *Remission of tax on savings* (£)	B *Remission of tax on yield on savings* (£)
Amount saved (pre-tax)	150	150
Less tax	nil	(50)
Amount saved (post-tax)	150	100
10% yield	15	10
Less tax	(5)	nil
Post-tax yield	10	10

This principle is essentially unchanged if, on the basis of column A of Table 20.1, the ET country remits the tax when the funds are saved and invested instead of remitting the tax on the subsequent yield on such funds. As the table shows, by remitting the tax on the occasion of savings (column A) the ET country has had the same effect on the yield as remitting the tax on the yield itself (column B). Thus, if the ET country extends its remission of tax to savings that are invested overseas, it does the equivalent of remitting from tax the yield on that overseas investment. The obvious first answer in this case is that the ET country should either refuse the tax relief on savings which are invested overseas or else refuse double taxation relief on the yield

[1] See columns B and D of Table 8.2 on p. 153. In the main text of this chapter we discuss the principles involved in terms of an income tax with 100 per cent capital allowances (i.e. tax relief on investment) or of an income tax with an expenditure tax adjustment (i.e. tax relief on savings). In the second part of Appendix 20.1 we show how the same principles could be applied with a tax on value added.

on overseas investment. If it gives both reliefs, it is in effect giving a tax subsidy on foreign investment.[2]

However, if one or other of the two reliefs is denied to foreign investment, the result will be that the person who saves in the ET country (i) will obtain a rate of yield on his savings equal to the *pre-tax* rate of return on the physical investment which his savings serve to finance, if he invests the funds in the ET country; but (ii) will obtain a rate of yield on his savings equal to the *post-foreign-tax* rate of return on the physical investment which his savings serve to finance, if he invests his funds in the IT country. This is the inevitable outcome of a state of affairs in which one country does not, and the other does, levy a tax on the rate of yield on invested funds. To take the simplest possible example, if country A had no income tax and country B had an income tax at a 50 per cent (tax-inclusive) rate, then a physical investment which yielded 10 per cent in both countries would give a 10 per cent return on savings in country A but only a 5 per cent return on savings in country B.

Thus, for the ET country to deny either tax relief on overseas investment or double tax relief on the yield on overseas investment will give an incentive for the ET country's savings to be invested at home rather than abroad – an incentive which springs, not from any tax discrimination by the ET country,

---

[2] With a tax on value added or an expenditure tax on the expenditure adjustment method, the obvious choice is to refuse double taxation relief for foreign income tax against domestic expenditure tax or VAT. With an income tax with 100 per cent capital allowances, the natural choice would be to refuse the capital allowance but to allow double taxation relief for foreign income tax against the domestic income tax. The two alternatives, however, in fact lead to the same result, although the maintenance of the double taxation of income may at first sight appear incongruous. The following table illustrates the two situations for income tax with 100 per cent capital allowances:

	Double taxation relief on foreign investment income together with refusal of capital allowances on foreign investment	*100% capital allowances on foreign investment together with refusal of double taxation relief on foreign investment income*
	(£)	(£)
Savings	100	100
Tax remission equal to 100% of investment	nil	100
Foreign investment	100	200
Yield	10	20
Less Foreign IT	(5)	(10)
Yield net of foreign tax	5	10
Less Domestic IT	nil	(5)
Yield net of domestic IT	5	5

but from the simple fact that the ET country has devised a tax regime to stimulate savings-investment (as explained in Chapter 3, this is an essential purpose of the expenditure tax regime), while the IT country has not chosen to do so. Should the ET country be concerned at this result? This question can be considered both from the point of view of the national interests of the ET country and also from a wider international point of view.

DOUBLE TAXATION RELIEF ON INVESTMENT INCOME AND THE NATIONAL INTEREST

As far as the national interests of the ET country are concerned, there is on the face of it no cause for concern. With the numerical example already taken, the ET country will get a 10 per cent return on an investment in the ET country but only a post-tax 5 per cent return on an investment with the same 10 per cent physical yield in the IT country. From the national point of view it should on the face of it prefer the former. There may, however, be some indirect advantages from overseas investment which accrue to the nation as a whole without entering directly into the profit-and-loss account of the persons or enterprises which are financing the overseas investment, e.g. the opening up of foreign markets for the ET country's exports or of foreign sources of supply for the ET country's imports. On the other hand, there may be indirect advantages of a similar kind from domestic investment, e.g. the general promotion of productivity through industrial experience. The ET country would be justified on national grounds in subsidising overseas investment (which is what in effect it would be doing at the expense of its own tax revenue if it gave both remission of tax on overseas investment and double taxation relief on the yield on that investment) only if it considered the *indirect* national benefits from increasing overseas investment to exceed those accruing from domestic investment by more than the subsidy.

INTERNATIONAL EFFECTS OF DOUBLE TAXATION RELIEF ON INVESTMENT INCOME

From the international point of view there is some loss in a state of affairs whose outcome may be a tendency for investment in the ET country to continue until the pre-tax rate of return is as low as the post-tax rate of return in the IT country. The real rate of return in the former country might be as low as 5 per cent, while its real yield in the latter country was still 10 per cent. In this case capital invested in the IT country would be more productive than capital invested in the ET country. But should the ET country bear the strain on its budget to remit the tax which the IT country levies on investment in the IT country? If the problem is to be regarded from an international point of view, is it not up to the IT country to remit the IT country's tax on the investment of the ET country's funds in the IT country? But, if it does so, what will the IT country's own savers and investors think if their government taxes their own investments in their own country but remits the tax on investments in their own country by tiresome competing foreigners from the ET country?

The obvious solution is for the IT country to adopt an expenditure tax regime. But until that happy day arrives it is inevitable that there should be either (i) some discrimination in favour of investment in the ET country over investment in the IT country, or else (ii) some discrimination in favour of the ET country's finance of investment over the IT country's finance of investment in the IT country as well as in the ET country.

THE APPLICATION OF THE ANALYSIS TO CORPORATION TAX

We have conducted the above analysis in terms of a simple basic rate of income tax. But, as will be clear from a reading of Chapter 12, exactly the same arguments apply to a flow-of-funds corporation tax on an R basis, an $(R+F)$ basis or an S basis. In all three cases the effect on the relevant investments is to give tax relief on the investment but to tax the yield on the investment. The net effect is (as shown in Chapter 12) to give on the funds used to finance new investment a yield equal to the underlying real yield on the investment itself. The basic argument for denying either tax relief on overseas investment or double taxation relief on the yield thus applies with equal force to corporation tax, as do the possible national and international counterarguments in favour of some relaxation of this rule.

TRANSITIONAL PROBLEMS AFFECTING DOUBLE TAXATION RELIEF ON INVESTMENT INCOME

Finally, it should be noted that, in the case of a country which changes over from an income tax to an expenditure tax regime, the above analysis applies only to new overseas investment made after the change. If investments made before the change did not receive remission of tax when the funds were saved and invested,[3] the basic case for denying double taxation relief on the yield would not exist.

The question of the choice of policy is then comparable to the choice of policy (discussed in Chapter 9) for the transitional treatment under a universal expenditure tax of pre-D-day personal savings previously accumulated out of taxed income. In Chapter 9 we have raised the question to what extent a 'radical transition' should be adopted, with the submission to expenditure tax after D-day of dissavings of wealth previously accumulated out of taxed income, or to what extent a 'conservative transition' should be adopted, with the application of the post-D-day expenditure tax levy on dissavings only to wealth accumulated out of post-D-day net savings or (as in the case of occu-

---

[3] In fact much past overseas investment by the United Kingdom did in effect receive remission of tax when it was made through the enjoyment of 100 per cent capital allowances.

pational pensions) to pre-D-day savings that had been specifically exempt from tax under the previous tax regime.[4]

There is a comparable problem in the treatment of double taxation relief. If the preferred policy is to refuse tax relief in the future on the occasion of new overseas investment, no further transitional arrangement is needed; the arrangement itself implies a 'conservative transition'. If, however, the preferred policy is to deny double taxation relief, then, just as in the case of the treatment of personal dissavings under a universal expenditure tax, thought must be given to the treatment of the yield on pre-D-day foreign investments.

IS IT NET OR GROSS FOREIGN INVESTMENT THAT IS RELEVANT?

However, whichever of these two policies is preferred, there remains one further basic issue. Is overseas investment to be measured net or gross? Consider a company which before D-day invests in equipment overseas which is to last for, say, ten years. The depreciation allowances on this machine can be used to replace the equipment overseas or to replace it at home. The pre-D-day overseas investment in the equipment is made in the expectation of post-D-day double taxation relief on its yield. But does this, or does it not, imply that there is an expectation of, and a case for a claim for, double taxation relief on the new replacement machinery when the old asset needs to be renewed?

In so far as the occasion of the replacement is treated as an occasion for a new decision as to whether investment should be made overseas or at home, there is no case for a continuation of double taxation relief on the yield on the new assets. If this is the correct interpretation of the situation, it follows that, if the preferred policy is the submission to tax of new overseas investment, then it should be gross post-D-day overseas investment (inclusive of replacement investment) which is so submitted to tax;[5] or if the preferred policy is to allow double taxation relief only on past overseas investment, then such relief should be phased out as old overseas assets depreciate and are replaced by new. If, however, a claim to relief on pre-D-day overseas investment were interpreted as implying that, because of expectation, relief should be given in perpetuity on a net amount of equivalent assets, a case would exist for denying tax remission only on post-D-day *net* foreign investment or, alternatively, for allowing double taxation relief to continue inde-

---

[4] Personal savings which had been accumulated out of untaxed income under the previous income tax regime (e.g. contributions to occupational pension funds) would be analogous to pre-D-day overseas investment which had in fact enjoyed tax remission under the previous tax regime (e.g. overseas investment which had benefited from 100 per cent capital allowances). There is, however, this important difference between the two cases. Whereas tax-free contributions to pension funds under the previous tax regime would have been made in the expectation that the pension would be taxed when it was taken out of the fund, overseas investments which had enjoyed 100 per cent capital allowances under the previous tax regime would have been undertaken in the expectation that the yield on them would also enjoy double taxation relief.

[5] Of course, those new investments to which 100 per cent capital allowances have been denied – or on which tax relief has in some other way been denied – should be permitted to set true depreciation allowances against their tax base.

finitely on the yield on a total of overseas investment equal to the pre-D-day amount.

We turn then to the question of the effect which the difference of tax structure between the two countries will have on the international flow of foreign funds, on the assumption that the ET country does not give both tax relief on foreign investment and also double taxation relief on foreign investment income.

Consider what would happen if initially the underlying rate of yield on real capital assets is the same, say 10 per cent in both the ET and the IT countries. In the IT country the market rate of interest will be linked to this 10 per cent yield. This will also be the case in the ET country if it applies its expenditure tax either through a tax on value added or else through an income tax with remission on savings (i.e. an income tax with an expenditure tax adjustment). In this case there will be no tax incentive for capital funds to move in either direction between the two countries. Savers in the IT country cannot get a higher yield by investing their savings in the ET country, because the interest will be liable to the IT country's income tax. Savers in the ET country cannot get a higher return by investing their savings in the IT country even if they enjoy relief from income tax on their foreign investment income, because in any case under the expenditure tax regime at home they will enjoy the full pre-tax rate of return on their savings at home. The basic difference will be simply that savers in the IT country will get a post-tax rate of return of 5 per cent on their savings whether they invest them in the ET country or in the IT country; whereas savers in the ET country will enjoy the pre-tax rate of return of 10 per cent on their savings if they invest them at home in the ET country and of 10 or 5 per cent if they invest them in the IT country, according to whether they do or do not enjoy in the ET country double taxation relief from income tax on their foreign investment income.

The situation will be quite different if the ET country applies its expenditure tax regime through an income tax combined with 100 per cent capital allowances. In that case (as explained in Chapter 8, pp. 155–156), it will be the post-tax rate of interest which will be linked to the rate of return on the underlying investment in real assets. This means that, with an initial real yield of 10 per cent in both countries, the market rate of interest would tend to be 20 per cent in the ET country and only 10 per cent in the IT country. With double taxation relief on foreign investment income in the IT country, capital funds would be attracted from the IT country to the ET country for investment in the ET country. If the international capital market and both national capital markets were perfect, this attraction of capital funds from the IT country into the ET country would go on until physical investment in the ET country was so expanded that the underlying rate of yield on investment in real assets had fallen to 5 per cent. The post-tax rate of interest in the ET country would tend to be 5 per cent, and the pre-tax market rate of interest would tend to be 10 per cent. At this point the attraction of capital funds from the IT country would cease.[6]

EFFECTS OF TAX STRUCTURE ON THE INTERNATIONAL MOVEMENTS OF PEOPLE

IMMIGRATION TO ENJOY TAX RELIEF ON SAVINGS

We are disregarding differences in net earnings due to differences in labour productivity or to differences in the rate of tax as influences on the international movement of people. But the migration of persons between the ET and the IT countries may be influenced by the differences in the tax structures. One such possible influence is illustrated by the effects of the distinction between different forms of expenditure tax which has been examined in the preceding section, namely the difference between the case in which the ET country applies its expenditure tax by means of an income tax with 100 per cent capital allowances and the case in which it uses a tax on value added or an income tax with remission of tax on savings for that purpose. In the former case, savers in the IT country can enjoy the enhanced yield on savings invested in the ET country without being obliged for that purpose to migrate to the ET country and to make their savings under the expenditure tax regime; the 100 per cent allowances on capital invested in the ET country are enjoyed on all investments in that country whether these are financed by savers in the ET country or by savers in the IT country. With a tax on value added or an income tax with remission of tax on savings as the means of applying the expenditure tax, the savings have to be made by persons who are subject to the expenditure tax regime (e.g. resident in the ET country) in order to enjoy the tax-free yield on the capital invested in the ET country. In this case, therefore, unlike the former case, there will be some tax incentive for people to migrate from the IT country to the ET country in order to earn their incomes under the expenditure tax regime so long as they wish to accumulate savings out of such incomes.

EMIGRATION TO AVOID TAX ON DISSAVINGS

The question then arises whether people will have a tax incentive to emigrate from the ET country to the IT country (or to refrain from immigrating into the ET country from the IT country) if instead of saving they wish to dissave and to live on any capital which they have inherited or saved out of their earlier earnings. The answer to this question also depends upon the form in

---

[6] Of course, neither the national nor the international capital markets would operate with this smooth perfection. Our intention is merely to highlight the very real tendency for the difference in tax structures to attract capital funds into the ET country, causing the rate of yield on investment in real assets in that country to be lower than would otherwise be the case relatively to the yield on such assets in the IT country.

which the ET country applies its expenditure tax. If it is applied through a remission of tax on savings, together with the submission of dissavings to tax (the method of the expenditure tax adjustment), there will be a tax incentive for those who wish to dissave to emigrate and to spend their existing capital under an income tax regime which does not levy tax on dissavings. There will also be a tax incentive to emigrate in order to spend in the IT country, if the ET country operates its expenditure tax by means of a destination-based tax on value added; in this case the VAT charged on imports and the VAT rebated on exports will cause the money cost of living to be *pro tanto* higher in the ET country than in the IT country, and there will be an advantage to emigrate to spend in the country with the lower cost of living.

On the other hand, if the ET country operates its expenditure tax by means of an income tax with 100 per cent capital allowances or by means of an origin-based tax on value added, the cost of living will not be higher in the ET country than in the IT country, and in neither country will there be any other tax on dissavings of money capital funds. There will be no tax advantage in spending capital funds in one country rather than in the other.[7]

DOUBLE TAXATION RELIEF ON FOREIGN EARNINGS

A closely related question is whether in the ET country double taxation relief from expenditure tax should be given in respect of income tax on earned income in the IT country. From an examination of the numerical examples given in Appendix 20.1 a good case can be made, in respect of income earned and subject to income tax in the IT country, for granting relief in the ET country (i) from income tax levied in the ET country if that country is operating an income tax with 100 per cent capital allowances, or (ii) from any withholding tax on income in the ET country if that country is operating an income tax with remission of tax on savings (i.e. an income tax with an expenditure tax adjustment), or even (iii) from any VAT levied in the ET country on a destination basis, since this tax has the effect of raising the money cost of living in the ET country relatively to the cost of living in the IT country. But there seems to be no case for granting relief from tax in the ET country if the expenditure tax is being operated by means of an origin-based tax on value added, since this tax does nothing to raise the cost of living in the ET country above its level in the IT country.

[7] The conclusions of this and the preceding paragraph are illustrated by means of numerical examples in Appendix 20.1.

Appendix 20.1   Some Relations between Incomes in ET and in IT countries

EARNED INCOME

If one country (which we shall call the ET country) has an expenditure tax regime while the rest of the world (which we shall call the IT country) has an income tax regime, there are some important tax relationships between money earnings and the cost of living in the two countries which depend in an important way upon the form taken by the expenditure tax in the ET country. These tax relationships raise two important questions:

1   Is there a case for giving double taxation relief against expenditure tax to a resident in the ET country in respect of income tax which he has paid in the IT country on earnings in that country?
2   Will there be a tax incentive for persons to earn and save in the ET country under the expenditure tax regime and then to emigrate to the IT country in order to spend their savings under the income tax regime?

There are, of course, many factors other than the structure of the tax system which will affect the answers to these questions. Thus the amount net of tax which a taxpayer can earn in the two countries will depend not merely upon whether the tax structure is built on the expenditure tax or the income tax principle, but also upon such matters as the productivity of labour in the two countries (since the higher the real output per head, the higher the pre-tax wage) and the rate of tax (since the higher the tax rate, the lower the post-tax wage).

Since in this appendix we wish to concentrate attention upon the effects of the tax structure, we shall isolate the effects of the expenditure tax and income tax structures by making a number of simplifying assumptions, which in effect get rid of the effects of differences both in the rate of tax and also in the productivities of labour in the two countries. For this purpose we assume that the rate of tax is the same in both countries, namely 100 per cent (tax-exclusive) or 50 per cent (tax-inclusive). Furthermore, we assume that one hour's work in both countries will produce the same amount of physical output, namely either one unit of goods for consumption or one unit of goods for use as physical capital equipment. We call both of these goods a 'product'. Thus in both countries one hour's work produces one 'product', which can either be consumed (e.g. in the form of a loaf of bread) or invested in industry for further productive purposes (e.g. in the form of a component of a machine). We assume (i) that the ET country has a currency unit called a pound (£) and that the money pre-tax wage of one hour's work is in all our examples fixed at £2, and (ii) that the IT country has a currency unit called a dollar ($) and that the money pre-tax wage of one hour's work is in all our examples fixed at $4. Since consumers live on 'products', the cost of living in both countries is measured by the price which a consumer must pay to purchase a 'product'.

On these assumptions we examine in Tables 20.2 to 20.5 four cases in all of which the IT country sticks to its income tax regime, while the ET country operates: an income tax with 100 per cent capital allowances in case 1 (Table 20.2); a tax on value added on an origin basis in case 2 (Table 20.3); a tax on value added on a destination basis in case 3 (Table 20.4); and an income tax with remission of tax on savings (i.e. an expenditure tax by means of an expenditure tax adjustment) in case 4 (Table 20.5).

Table 20.2   *Case 1: an income tax with 100 per cent capital allowances*

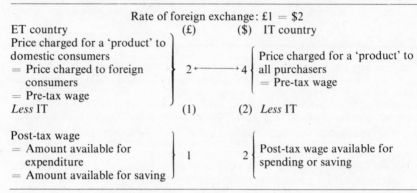

	Rate of foreign exchange: £1 = $2		
ET country	(£)	($)	IT country
Price charged for a 'product' to domestic consumers = Price charged to foreign consumers = Pre-tax wage	2 ←——→ 4		Price charged for a 'product' to all purchasers = Pre-tax wage
Less IT	(1)	(2)	*Less* IT
Post-tax wage = Amount available for expenditure = Amount available for saving	1	2	Post-tax wage available for spending or saving

1   At the current exchange rate of £1 = $2 the money cost of a 'product' and hence the cost of living is the same in both countries.

2   To enable the money earned from making a 'product' selling for $4 in the IT country to lead to the same spending power in the ET country as does the money earned from making a 'product' selling for £2 in the ET country, double taxation relief against the ET country's income tax must be given for the IT country's income tax; i.e. the $2 post-tax wage earned in the IT country must not be taxed again before it is spent in the ET country. On that basis the money earned in either country if spent in either country would buy half a 'product'.

3   There is no advantage, having earned and saved net of tax £1 in the ET country, in converting it into $2 and emigrating to spend it in the IT country, since the cost of living at the current exchange rate is the same in both countries.

Table 20.3   *Case 2: an origin-based tax on value added*

	Rate of foreign exchange: £1 = $1		
ET country	(£)	($)	IT country
Price charged for a 'product' to domestic consumers = Price charged to foreign consumers	4 ←——→ 4		Price charged for a 'product' to all purchasers = Pre-tax wage
Less Tax on value added	(2)	(2)	*Less* IT
Pre-tax wage = Amount available for expenditure = Amount available for saving	2	2	Post-tax wage available for spending or saving

1   As compared with case 1, the £ has depreciated in terms of the $ because the pre-tax wage has remained at £2 but is now free of income tax in the ET country. The tax on value added is now added to the labour cost of £2 to raise the selling price of a 'product' to £4. In effect all money prices and costs have doubled in the ET country, the foreign exchange value of the £ has halved, and as a result the money cost of a 'product' and hence the cost of living in the ET country remain the same as in the IT country after allowing for the change in the foreign exchange rate.

2   To enable the money earned from making a 'product' selling for $4 in the IT country to lead to the same spending power in the ET country as does money earned from making a 'product' selling for £4 in the ET country, no double taxation relief is necessary, since the post-tax wage of $2 earned in the IT country will not be taxed again before it is spent in the ET country.

3   There is no incentive, having earned and saved £2 in the ET country, to convert it into $2 and to emigrate to spend it in the IT country, since the cost of living at the current exchange rate is the same in both countries.

Table 20.4   *Case 3: a destination-based tax on value added*

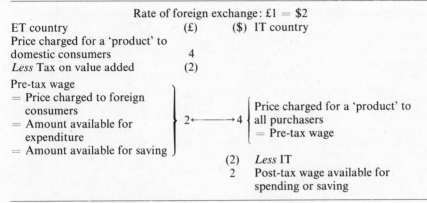

	Rate of foreign exchange: £1 = $2		
ET country	(£)	($)	IT country
Price charged for a 'product' to domestic consumers	4		
Less Tax on value added	(2)		
Pre-tax wage = Price charged to foreign consumers = Amount available for expenditure = Amount available for saving	2 ⟷ 4		Price charged for a 'product' to all purchasers = Pre-tax wage
		(2)	*Less* IT
		2	Post-tax wage available for spending or saving

1   The tax on value added being charged on imports into the ET country and being rebated on exports from the ET country results in an exchange rate of £1 = $2, since the relative price of 'products' is £2 to $4. As a result of the tax on value added, the domestic money cost of a 'product' and hence of the cost of living at the current exchange rate is now twice as high in the ET country as in the IT country, although real incomes are the same in both countries.

2   To enable the money earned from making a 'product' selling for $4 in the IT country to lead to the same spending power in the ET country as does the money earned from making a 'product' selling for £4 in the ET country, double taxation relief against the tax on value added in the ET country is needed for income tax paid in the IT country, so that the $2 of post-tax wage earned in the IT country that exchange for £1 will purchase as much as the £2 of earnings in the ET country.

3   Since the cost of living is twice as high at the current exchange rate in the ET country as in the IT country, there is an incentive, having earned and saved in the ET country, to emigrate and spend in the IT country.

Table 20.5   *Case 4: remission of tax on savings*

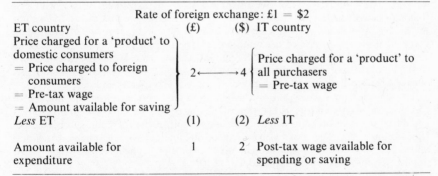

	Rate of foreign exchange: £1 = $2		
ET country	(£)	($)	IT country
Price charged for a 'product' to domestic consumers = Price charged to foreign consumers = Pre-tax wage = Amount available for saving	2 ⟷ 4		Price charged for a 'product' to all purchasers = Pre-tax wage
Less ET	(1)	(2)	*Less* IT
Amount available for expenditure	1	2	Post-tax wage available for spending or saving

1   The rate of foreign exchange and the relationship between the money costs of living in the two countries is the same as in case 1.

2   To enable the money earned from making a 'product' selling for $4 in the IT country to lead to the same spending power in the ET country as does the money earned from making a 'product' selling for £2 in the ET country, the post-tax wage of $2 in the IT country must not be taxed again before being spent in the ET country. Double taxation relief against the ET country's expenditure tax must be allowed for the IT country's income tax.

3   Although at the current rate of exchange the money cost of living is the same in both countries, there is an incentive, having earned and saved £2 in the ET country, to exchange it into $4 and to emigrate to spend it tax-free in the IT country.

INVESTMENT INCOME

These numerical examples can be used to examine another question connected with double taxation relief in respect of foreign investment income. In the main text of Chapter 20 (pp. 412–419) we have considered the case for and against denying, under an expenditure tax regime, either tax relief on savings invested abroad or else double taxation relief on the foreign income earned on such investment. It has been made clear that, for an ET country to deny one or other of these reliefs in respect of foreign investment, would mean that the ET country earned the *post-tax* rate of return on foreign investment but the *pre-tax* rate of return on home investment. Thus, if the rate of return were 10 per cent in both the ET and the IT countries, and the rate of tax were 100 per cent (tax-exclusive) or 50 per cent (tax-inclusive), the saver in the ET country would receive a yield of 10 per cent on home investment but only 5 per cent on foreign investment.

The arrangements necessary to deny one or other of the forms of tax relief on foreign investment, and thus to lead to a yield of 10 per cent on home investment and of 5 per cent on foreign investment, are straightforward if the ET country is operating its expenditure tax by granting 100 per cent capital allowances on investment (case 1 above) or an expenditure tax adjustment on savings (case 4). With the numerical assumptions made for Tables 20.2 to 20.5, these two cases are illustrated in Tables 20.6 and 20.8 respectively. In Tables 20.6 to 20.8, numbers in the columns headed 'P' represent the amount of 'products' bought or sold for consumption or investment purposes; the numbers in the columns headed £ and $ represent the amounts of the ET country's currency and the IT country's currency respectively received or paid for various transactions; and the arrows signify the exchange at the current rate of exchange of the one currency for the other.

Cases 1 and 4 of Tables 20.6 and 20.8 need little explanation. They illustrate in the first two columns the series of transactions by which (in a way which we hope is by now familiar to the readers of our Report) 100 per cent capital allowances (case 1) or the remission of tax on savings (case 4) cause the rate of return to the savers to be 10 per cent (e.g. the once-for-all sacrifice of consumption of 50 'products' in line 4 of case 1 leads to an annual consumption of 5 'products' in line 13), which is the same as the rate of yield on the physical investment (e.g. a capital investment of 100 'products' in line 7 of case 1 has a real annual yield of 10 'products' in line 8). Cases 1 and 4 show in the last six columns how the denial *either* of double taxation relief on foreign investment income *or else* of tax remission on the foreign investment itself (case 1) or on the savings used to finance the foreign investment (case 4) cuts the rate of return to the saver to 5 per cent (e.g. the sacrifice of 50 'products' of consumption in line 4 of case 1 leads to an annual consumption of only 2·5 'products' in line 13).

The question may, however, be asked what arrangements for the finance of foreign investment and for the taxation of income earned on such foreign investment should be made in order to achieve the same result, if the ET country operates its expenditure tax regime, not by means of an income tax with 100 per cent capital allowances or with an expenditure tax adjustment, but by means of an origin-based or destination-based tax on value added.

Table 20.7, which covers cases 2 and 3, is designed to answer this question; it shows that the desired result will be achieved if no action is taken to tax or to subsidise foreign investment and no double taxation relief against the tax on value added in the ET country is given for income tax paid in the IT country, whether the tax on value added be origin-based or destination-based. The only relevant difference between the origin-based VAT (case 2) and the destination-based the tax on value added (case 3) is that, since the rate of exchange will be £1 = $1 in the former case and £1 = \$2 in the latter case, savings invested abroad will purchase twice as many 'products' for investment abroad in the destination-based case as they will in the origin-based case; but against this must be set the fact that, when the foreign money proceeds from the foreign investment are brought home for expenditure on consumption, twice as large a foreign yield will be needed in the destination-based case as in the origin-based case in order to purchase a given amount of 'products' for consumption in the ET country.

Table 20.6 *Case 1: income tax with 100 per cent capital allowances*

| | | | | Investment abroad without: | | | | | |
| | | Investment at home | | Double taxation relief | | | Capital allowances | | |
		(P)	(£)	(P)	(£)	($)	(P)	(£)	($)
1	Sale of output of 'products' = Pre-tax wage	100	200	100	200		100	200	
2	*Less* IT		(100)		(100)			(100)	
3	Post-tax wage		100		100			100	
4	Purchasing power over consumption	50	100	50	100		50	100	
5	Savings		100		100 → 200			100 → 200	
6	Value of capital allowance		100		100 → 200			nil → nil	
7	Investment	100	200	100		400	50		200
8	Pre-tax yield	10	20	10		40	5		20
9	*Less* Foreign IT		—			(20)			(10)
10	Foreign yield net of foreign tax		—		10 ← 20			5 ← 10	
11	*Less* Domestic IT		(10)		(5)			nil	
12	Yield net of all tax		10		5			5	
13	Purchasing power over consumption	5	10	2·5	5		2·5	5	

Table 20.7   *Cases 2 and 3: tax on value added*

| | | Investment at home | | Investment abroad without double taxation relief | | | | | |
| | | | | Origin-based tax on value added | | | Destination-based tax on value added | | |
		(P)	(£)	(P)	(£)	($)	(P)	(£)	($)
1	Sale of output of 'products'	100	400[i]	100	400[i]		100	400[i]	
2	*Less* Tax on value added		(200)		(200)			(200)	
3	Wage		200		200			200	
4	Purchasing power over consumption	50	200[i]	50	200[i]		50	200[i]	
5	Savings		200		200 →	200		200 →	400
6	Investment	100	200[e]	50		200	100		400
7	Pre-tax yield	10	40[i]	5		20	10		40
8	*Less* Foreign IT		—			(10)			(20)
9	Foreign yield net of foreign tax		—		10 ←	10		10 ←	20
10	*Less* Tax on value added		(20)		—			—	
11	Yield free of tax		20		10			10	
12	Purchasing power over consumption	5	20[i]	2·5	10[i]		2·5	10[i]	

Notes:

i Represents payments inclusive of tax on value added.

e Represents payments exclusive of tax on value added.

Table 20.8   *Case 4: income tax with expenditure tax adjustment*

| | | Investment at home | | Investment abroad without: | | | | | |
| | | | | Double taxation relief | | | Tax remission on savings | | |
		(P)	(£)	(P)	(£)	($)	(P)	(£)	($)
1	Sale of output of 'products' = Pre-tax wage	100	200	100	200		100	200	
2	*Less* ET		(100)		(100)			(100)	
3	Purchasing power over consumption	50	100	50	100		50	100	
4	Remission of expenditure tax		100		100			nil	
5	Savings		200		200 →	400		100 →	200
6	Investment	100	200	100		400	50		200
7	Pre-tax yield	10	20	10		40	5		20
8	*Less* Foreign IT		—			(20)			(10)
9	Foreign yield net of foreign tax		—		10 ←	20		5 ←	10
10	*Less* Domestic ET		(10)		(5)			nil	
11	Purchasing power over consumption	5	10	2·5	5		2·5	5	

21 Tax Relations with Other Countries

In discussing in Chapter 11 the characteristics of a good tax structure, we have stressed (pp. 16–18) the importance of international aspects. We now consider how the various reforms suggested in this Report might be applied to the circumstances of taxpayers who:

1 Are based in the United Kingdom but have income or resources abroad.
2 Are based overseas but have income or resources in the United Kingdom.
3 Change their base from the United Kingdom to overseas (emigrants) or from overseas to the United Kingdom (immigrants).
4 Are liable to UK tax on income which has borne foreign tax.

Since the tax codes of other countries vary enormously we can only speak in general terms. If there is a working principle which can be discerned, it is that international tax arrangements presuppose an income tax rather than an expenditure tax and assume that a country may, if it so wishes, apply its tax to: (i) all income accruing to residents of that country, no matter where it arises; and (ii) all income arising in that country, no matter where its recipient resides. Clearly that rule means that income which crosses national boundaries may be taxed twice, once in the country where it arises and again in the country where it is received. Because such double taxation would discourage international investment, trade or employment, governments have sought to avoid double taxation by making bilateral or unilateral arrangements which either exempt the income in one or other country or provide that the tax payable in the country where the income is received is reduced by the tax payable in the country where it arose. The effect on the taxpayer is usually that, on doubly taxed income, he bears tax equal to the higher of the rates imposed by the two countries. Such arrangements often limit the rate of tax levied in the country where the income arises. They also contain rules which seek to clarify, in cases of doubt, in which of the two countries a particular taxpayer resides.

The Organisation for Economic Co-operation and Development (OECD) has published a model agreement on which many double taxation treaties have been based. The model provides that in cases of dual residence and for the purposes of a treaty the fiscal domicile of individuals should be decided as follows:

'(a) He shall be deemed to be a resident of the Contracting State in which he has a permanent home available to him. If he has a permanent home available to him in both Contracting States, he shall be deemed to be a resident of the Contracting State with which his personal and economic relations are closest (centre of vital interests);
(b) If the Contracting State in which he has his centre of vital interests can-

not be determined, or if he has not a permanent home available to him in either Contracting State, he shall be deemed to be a resident of the Contracting State in which he has an habitual abode;

(c) If he has an habitual abode in both Contracting States or in neither of them, he shall be deemed to be a resident of the Contracting State of which he is a national;

(d) If he is a national of both Contracting States or of neither of them, the competent authorities of the Contracting States shall settle the question by mutual agreement.'

The model also provides that a company is deemed to reside in the country in which its place of effective management is situated. The model is, of course, persuasive and not mandatory.

The rules which determine liability to UK tax on foreign income are particularly complex. They are summarised in Appendix 21.1, together with the rules about liability to capital gains tax. Liability depends on whether the taxpayer is or is not: resident in the United Kingdom, ordinarily resident in the United Kingdom, or domiciled in the United Kingdom.[1] Some explanation of these phrases, together with an indication of typical cases falling within various categories, is given in Appendix 21.1.

Historically the development of these rules has been influenced by the worldwide interests of the United Kingdom during the nineteenth century and first half of the twentieth century and, more recently, by the wish that overseas nationals should not be deterred from coming to the United Kingdom, particularly for business reasons, by the high UK rates of personal tax. It has been held that the United Kingdom has gained in other ways much more than it has lost in tax revenue by reason of these concessions.

At present an ordinarily resident, UK-domiciled taxpayer who is absent from the country for the whole of a tax year from 6 April to 5 April is treated as not resident and thus is not liable to UK tax on any income (whether from earnings or investments) which arises abroad in that year. If a similar taxpayer is absent from the country for any continuous period of employment of 365 or more days, he is not liable to UK tax on remuneration for services performed wholly abroad. There is a special definition of 'continuous', so that short visits to the United Kingdom do not break continuity. For someone who has his ordinary residence in the United Kingdom the treatment of these two cases seems unduly favourable. It may be a better rule that the taxpayer should be liable to UK tax on worldwide income in any year in which he has his ordinary residence in the United Kingdom whether physically present here or not.[2] But undoubtedly there is a case for giving relief because

---

[1] In addition, in the case of employment income, liability is influenced by whether the employer is a UK employer or foreign employer and by where the services are performed. The liability on income from foreign investments, trades or pensions can in some cases depend on whether the taxpayer is a British subject or Irish citizen or not.

[2] Domicile in the sense given in Appendix 21.1 is an additional factor which could be taken into account, but overseas administrations tend to give it less weight than does that of the United Kingdom.

of extra expenses falling on the taxpayer by reason of absence abroad in the course of employment or profession. The Finance Act 1977 has somewhat relaxed the rules with regard to such expenses.

COMPREHENSIVE INCOME TAX (CIT)

We have described in Chapter 7 the ways in which a CIT would broaden the tax base and thereby enable either (i) the same revenue to be raised with lower rates of tax, or (ii) increased revenue to be raised from the same rates as those previously prevailing or from rates which were intermediate. If rates were lower, it might enable the present preferential treatment of taxpayers who are not domiciled or not ordinarily resident in the United Kingdom (see Appendix 21.1) to be withdrawn without causing an exodus of such persons from the country.

But even so there would be problems. Gifts and bequests received are included in the CIT tax base. If derived from overseas sources they may have borne transfer tax in another country (as either a donor or donee tax). This would necessitate an extension of double tax arrangements, since present treaties do not provide for setting transfer tax against income tax. And if the donee, if resident elsewhere, would not have been taxed at all on gifts received, or taxed only at much lower rates, it would be likely that some taxpayers would leave the country. Similar considerations apply to other extensions of the tax base implicit in a CIT: taxing real capital gains at full personal rates, withdrawal of 100 per cent capital allowances and substitution of economic depreciation (as compared with countries that give accelerated depreciation allowances), the taxation of retained company profits at full rates, and possibly less favourable treatment of retirement benefits. These considerations might well lead to the continuation under a CIT of similar concessions to those given at present to non-domiciled taxpayers. But in that case it might be reasonable to apply to CIT the concept of 'deemed' domicile in the United Kingdom, which is applied to capital transfer tax when a taxpayer has been resident in the country in not less than seventeen out of the twenty consecutive years ending with the relevant year of assessment.

GIFTS AND BEQUESTS

Since a CIT includes gifts and bequests received, it is unlikely that it would be coupled with a transfer tax. All gifts received by taxpayers who were ordinarily resident in the United Kingdom, even if abroad for the whole of a particular tax year, would be liable to CIT. Persons not ordinarily resident in the United Kingdom should, we think, be liable to CIT on their receipt of: (i) gifts of UK property by whomsoever made; and (ii) gifts of foreign property if made by a person ordinarily resident in the United Kingdom. The charge on non-residents at (ii) is necessary in order to close an avoidance route; in its absence UK taxpayers wishing to make a gift of UK property to an overseas resident would transmute it into foreign property before making the gift.

The UK Revenue cannot compel non-residents to render returns or to pay tax, so that it would be necessary to make UK executors and donors primarily accountable for tax on gifts or bequests to non-residents. The progressive CIT scale applied to the comprehensive income of ordinarily resident taxpayers, even with averaging, is probably not suitable for non-resident taxpayers; it is likely that a proportional tax with or without an annual threshold would be the preferred alternative.

COMPANY PROFITS

A full CIT involves the integration of individual and corporate tax systems, so that retained profits are taxed as if they had been distributed. Taxpayers resident in the United Kingdom would be entitled to a tax credit which imputed to dividends and retained profits the full rate of corporation tax paid by a company; but overseas taxpayers would not be entitled to the tax credit associated with retained profits, and would receive the tax credit associated with dividends only if they were entitled to it under a double taxation treaty. An integrated corporation tax of this kind could be applied to domestic corporations and to overseas corporations controlled by UK individuals or companies but not to other overseas companies. It might then be advantageous for a UK taxpayer to invest in overseas companies with high retentions, unless the benefit of deferral of tax on capital gains were counteracted as suggested in Chapter 7. That benefit might also be eroded by the loss of double taxation relief.

In theory, overseas taxpayers receiving income from UK sources are liable to higher rate tax and investment income surcharge if the amounts received from the United Kingdom are high enough for those taxes to be payable. In practice, it is often difficult for such taxes to be levied, and most double taxation treaties have the effect of restricting the liability of overseas taxpayers on UK investment income to stipulated rates which are below the current basic rate. Treaty negotiations start on the basis that overseas taxpayers are not entitled, as of right, to the tax credit which is imputed to dividends paid by UK companies. But many recent treaties provide, in relation to dividends from UK companies, that the overseas taxpayer shall be entitled to the same tax credit as a UK taxpayer and be liable to UK tax at 15 per cent on the aggregate of the dividend plus the tax credit. The effect is as follows:

	£
Company profit	100
Less UK CT	(52)
Profit	48
Dividend paid to overseas resident	48
Tax credit (£48 × 33 ÷ 67)	23·6
Dividend + Tax credit	71·6
Less 15% UK tax	(10·7)
Net dividend after UK tax but before overseas tax	60·9
∴ Effective rate of tax (100 − 60·9)%	39·1%

This is more than the present basic rate of 33 per cent, so that if the basic rate were the rate used for the integrated corporation tax suggested in Chapter 7 (p. 144), it would have the effect of submitting both retained and distributed profits accruing to overseas taxpayers to a tax rather less than that now levied under most double taxation treaties. However, this would mean that when negotiating double taxation treaties the UK authorities would, in relation to dividends, have nothing to concede, since overseas taxpayers would already be entitled to treatment more favourable than they could expect under a treaty.

For this reason it would be desirable that the rate of corporation tax referred to in Chapter 7 (p. 144) should be of the order of 50 per cent, in the expectation that double taxation treaties would either (i) give the full credit of 50 per cent subject to tax at, say, 33 per cent on the dividend plus the credit, or (ii) limit the credit to say 36·6 per cent in order that the apparent rate of tax on the dividend plus credit could be the 15 per cent which is often used.[3] The disadvantage of a 50 per cent rate is that, because full imputation would be given to UK taxpayers, it would have the result that taxpayers assessable at a lower rate and resident in the United Kingdom would be entitled to repayment of the difference between their rate and the corporation tax rate. But a large number of year-end adjustments of that kind is in any case probably inherent in a CIT system.

If there were a 50 per cent corporation tax rate, reduced for many overseas taxpayers by virtue of treaty relief to an effective 33 per cent or thereabouts, they would, as now, bear a higher rate of tax on retained profit, since it would not be normal practice to repay to overseas taxpayers any part of the tax credit relating to retained profits. In effect, capital gains which in the absence of tax would have accrued to overseas taxpayers as a result of retained profits would be reduced by 50 per cent; but capital gains or losses due to changes in profit expectations or interest rates would escape UK tax.

EMIGRANTS AND IMMIGRANTS

Both under the present system and under a CIT, a taxpayer who leaves the UK tax net ('emigrates') ought to be treated for capital gains purposes as if all his assets are realised at the time when he emigrates.

The difficulty is to decide whether and when a taxpayer has ceased to be ordinarily resident; that may not become clear until some time after a taxpayer has physically left the country. Having established that ordinary residence has ceased, what date is to be used for the valuation of his assets for capital gains tax purposes?

Sometimes the date of emigration may be very clear; but in other cases it may be difficult to do other than choose an arbitrary date, such as the commencement of a particular fiscal year. That may be thought to give rise to a very arbitrary capital gain. Another difficulty is to find an effective means

---

[3] A dividend of £50 grossed at 36·6 per cent = £78·8, less 15 per cent = £67; which is the same as £50 grossed up at 50 per cent, less 33 per cent.

of recovering tax from someone who may already have severed all links with the United Kingdom. These problems arise in even more acute form under an expenditure tax and are further discussed in that context on pp. 441–442.

The base for computing the capital gains accruing to immigrants ought to be market value at the time when they first become ordinarily resident and so liable to UK tax.

DOUBLE TAXATION RELIEF

Because a CIT is based on income, it does not raise many new issues with regard to double taxation relief; but the integrated CIT/corporation tax does revive a problem which is inherent in imputation systems, namely what should be the link, if any, between double taxation relief given to companies and the tax credit given to its shareholders. We discuss this in Appendix 21.3.

EXPENDITURE TAXES IN GENERAL

We have discussed in Chapter 20 some of the basic issues which arise if a country (called an ET country) adopts an expenditure tax regime in a world in which most countries (called IT countries) are operating income tax regimes. In particular we have considered:

1 Whether it would be appropriate for the ET country to give both tax relief on funds invested abroad in an IT country by its own residents and also double taxation relief in respect of the foreign tax levied by the IT country on the yield from that investment.
2 In which cases, if any, it would be appropriate for the ET country to deny to its own residents double taxation relief in respect of income tax levied in an IT country on earned income accruing to a resident of the ET country.
3 In what circumstances the adoption of an expenditure tax regime would encourage the emigration out of the ET country and discourage immigration into the ET country of wealthy persons who wished to spend their capital wealth on consumption.

In the light of the general conclusions reached in Chapter 20 we turn now to a more detailed discussion of the problems concerning tax relations with other countries which would arise if the United Kingdom were to adopt a universal expenditure tax or a two-tier expenditure tax together with a flow-of-funds corporation tax of the R or S type for its structure of direct taxation.[4]

---

[4] For ease of exposition we have confined our analysis of this issue to taxes on individuals. The R, $(R+F)$ and S-based corporation taxes (discussed in Chapter 12) are similar to a universal expenditure tax in two relevant respects, in that (i) they do not break the link between the market rate of interest and the rate of yield on the company's assets, but (ii) they raise the issue whether it is desirable to give tax relief both on foreign investment and also on the subsequent income earned on that investment.

UNIVERSAL EXPENDITURE TAX (UET)

In principle we believe that it would be neither desirable nor feasible to treat overseas investments as unregistered assets when corresponding UK investments were registered. There should, in fact, be no general attempt to restrict the privileges of registration to the investment of savings within the United Kingdom. But the overlap between relief for savings and relief for double taxation might in some circumstances make it desirable to treat some kinds of overseas investment as unregistered. We deal with this problem in Appendix 21.2.

After the introduction of a UET some persons – e.g. persons who fulfilled all three conditions of being not resident, not ordinarily resident, and not domiciled in the United Kingdom – would presumably have to remain on an income tax basis, since there would be no effective way of monitoring the savings and dissavings of such persons and thus of making the necessary expenditure tax adjustment to their taxable income. The dividing line between those who were liable to the expenditure tax regime and those who continued under the income tax regime might well be based on ordinary residence and not depend on whether or not the taxpayer was physically present in the United Kingdom in any particular year.

Under an expenditure tax, as under an income tax, relief should be given to UK taxpayers who incur extra expense because they spend considerable periods abroad in the course of their employment or profession. But we do not think that a taxpayer who is ordinarily resident in the United Kingdom should be permitted to omit 100 per cent of his foreign earnings (and hence to escape tax on his expenditure from those earnings) simply because he is overseas for a continuous period of 365 or more days.

Apart from the question of double taxation relief, to which we refer in Appendix 21.3, the treatment of overseas income accruing to persons ordinarily resident in the United Kingdom does not appear to be particularly troublesome under a UET. This is because the emphasis is on the taxpayer's expenditure. The question arises, however, of foreign income accruing to persons who are not ordinarily resident but are resident in a particular year. Appendix 21.1 shows that at present they are liable on their overseas income, in most cases on the basis of remittances out of income. We question if it is worth retaining this charge.

Persons who are not ordinarily resident in the United Kingdom, whether resident in a particular year or not, would not pay expenditure tax but instead would pay income tax on investment income from the United Kingdom and on earned income relating to services performed in the United Kingdom. In the case of earned income accruing to persons not domiciled in the United Kingdom, whether ordinarily resident or not, there might, because of the considerations mentioned on p. 429, be pressure to continue to give some relief against such income.

How should dividends received by overseas taxpayers from companies liable to an *R* or *S* type of UK corporation tax be treated? It will be apparent from the discussion in Chapter 12 that, when tax rates are stable, an equity shareholder in such a company gets, in the form either of dividend or of potential capital gain, a rate of return on his investment equal to the rate of return on the underlying investment. The tax relief on investment made by the company (*R* type) or on subscription of new share capital (*S* type) is balanced by the tax levied on cash flow (*R* type) or dividends paid (*S* type). That being so, there is a clear case for a tax on such dividends. This would be feasible since there would be a withholding tax, probably at basic rate, applied to all shareholders. There might be difficulty in applying higher rates of tax; and, if overseas shareholders were entitled under double taxation treaties to lower rates of tax than basic rate, there would, as now, be repayment claims or a procedure whereby the Revenue notified companies of lower rates of tax applicable to specified overseas shareholdings. Similar arguments apply to interest, but here it is quite common for interest paid to overseas investors to be exempt from UK tax because of treaty provisions. Persons who are neither resident nor ordinarily resident in the United Kingdom would probably, as now, be exempt from UK capital gains tax on UK assets, including shares. But the market value of shares of companies with a high retention of profits would be affected by the considerations referred to in Chapter 12 (pp. 236–238).

We have already pointed out (p. 431) that the effective rate of tax on dividends paid to overseas shareholders is at present 39·1 per cent in cases where their income tax liability is limited by double tax treaties to 15 per cent of the dividend plus tax credit. Under an *R* or *S*-based tax with corporation tax at 50 per cent (tax-exclusive) (*R* basis) or 100 per cent (tax-inclusive) (*S* basis) and a $33\frac{1}{3}$ per cent withholding tax, their effective rate of tax on dividends would be $33\frac{1}{3}$ per cent only:

	£
Capital subscribed	1,000
S or *R*-type relief (50% of capital expenditure or 100% of capital subscribed)	1,000
Invested by the company	2,000
Yield 10%	200
Less CT (50% of yield or 100% of dividend)	(100)
Dividend	100
Less Withholding tax	$(33\frac{1}{3})$
Net dividend	$66\frac{2}{3}$
∴ Yield ($£66\frac{2}{3} \div £1,000 \times 100$)	$6\frac{2}{3}\%$

This is, of course, the classical system but the *S*-type imputation system (described in Chapter 12, pp. 250–251) puts an overseas investor in a similar position:

	£
Share capital subscribed by overseas investor	1,000
S-type relief (at 100% of one-third of foregoing)	$333\frac{1}{3}$
Invested by the company	$1,333\frac{1}{3}$
Yield 10%	$133\frac{1}{3}$
Less CT (100% of dividend)	$(66\frac{2}{3})$
Dividend	$66\frac{2}{3}$
∴ Yield ignoring tax credit (£$66\frac{2}{3}$ ÷ £1,000)	$6\frac{2}{3}$%
Tax credit (for UK residents)	£$33\frac{1}{3}$

Provided the overseas investor is not given the tax credit, he gets the same yield as under the classical method. This is in contrast to the imputation system which would be necessary with a two-tier expenditure tax, if the lower tier tax were operated by means of an income tax with 100 per cent capital allowances and not by a tax on value added; in this case, even without the tax credit, the foreign investor would get a yield of 10 per cent (see p. 255).

UNINCORPORATED BUSINESSES

The need to retain an income tax code to deal with overseas taxpayers is not particularly troublesome in relation to remuneration and the common investment sources such as dividends, interest, royalties, etc. But there is a problem with regard to unincorporated businesses carried on by such taxpayers, typically overseas partners in UK partnerships. How should they get relief for capital expenditure which they incur? For UK taxpayers the concept of capital allowances as it is now known would disappear, since the UK resident carrying on such a business would get tax relief on what he put into it and be taxed on what he draws out – or alternatively on what it cost him to acquire the business and what he receives when he sells it, if that course is followed. In a straightforward case a similar rule could be applied to overseas taxpayers, except that relief would only be given against future drawings from the business and not, as in the case of the UK taxpayer, against other tax payable in the year when the investment was made. Unrelieved amounts carried forward could be increased by an interest factor. But that method would break down if an overseas taxpayer, having had relief for his investment against subsequent drawings, then sold out to another overseas resident. It would be difficult for the UK Revenue to enforce a tax on the sale proceeds since the purchaser might have acquired the business without knowledge of any tax unpaid by the vendor. However, such a purchaser could be denied any relief on his acquisition cost, so that anything he drew from the business would be taxed without relief for that cost. But if he drew nothing from the business, he could later sell it free of UK tax to another overseas resident.

An adjustment would also have to be made if such a business acquired UK equities or similar investments, since an overseas resident investing directly in such assets would get no relief for the cost of acquiring those investments against subsequent income.

These difficulties might make it necessary to have a full income tax system, with economic depreciation and a method of taxing capital gains for overseas investors in UK unincorporated businesses – an unattractive prospect. Perhaps the methods described in the two preceding paragraphs could be extended to such businesses where the overseas taxpayer was able to give security to the UK Revenue for any tax which might become due when he disposed of his interest in it. To the extent that that was done, the overseas taxpayer would, of course, be on an expenditure tax rather than an income tax basis.

Similar problems would arise in relation to overseas residents who invest in houses, offices, factories, agricultural land and buildings in the United Kingdom, but here the problems of retaining a capital allowance system are probably not as formidable as in the case of unincorporated businesses.

CHANGE OF STATUS

A difficult set of issues arises over the proper treatment of persons who change their status between being ordinarily resident in the United Kingdom and ordinarily resident elsewhere. The taxpayer who from being ordinarily resident elsewhere becomes ordinarily resident in the United Kingdom we shall call an *immigrant*; the taxpayer who changes in the reverse direction we shall call an *emigrant*. Unless special provisions are made, an immigrant would shift from an income tax regime to an expenditure tax regime in so far as his liability to UK tax was concerned; and this would discourage people from coming to the United Kingdom who intended, while here, to dissave from resources which they possessed before they came into this country. On the other hand, an emigrant would shift from an expenditure tax to an income tax regime; and this would encourage persons who had saved tax-free in the United Kingdom under the expenditure tax regime to emigrate later in order to spend their capital tax-free under an income tax regime.

THE TREATMENT OF IMMIGRANTS

The problem of the immigrant is less serious than that of the emigrant. If it were desired to remove the discouragement to the immigration of wealthy persons who might want to spend their capital in the United Kingdom, it would be possible to make the following provisions. On immigration the taxpayer would record and value all his existing registered assets and would be given a credit to that amount against his future tax base for liability to expenditure tax. Because of inflation, the initial credit would have to be indexed. As he dissaved and ran down his recorded registered assets, he would use up this credit and thus avoid expenditure tax. If there were difficult valuation problems, they could be deferred until the assets in question were realised, but the valuation when made would be as at the date of immigration.

If he subsequently built up his holding of registered assets, he would not receive any tax relief but could restore his initial credit. He would receive tax relief only on any acquisition of registered assets after the full restoration of his initial credit. By this means he would, as it were, be under an income tax regime for his wealth at the time when he came into the United Kingdom, but under an expenditure tax regime for any net addition to this wealth which, on a cumulative basis, was due to net savings while in this country. If under these proposals an immigrant held assets which gained in value after he arrived in the United Kingdom, he would, once he had dissaved an amount equal to his wealth on arrival (as indexed), be liable to expenditure tax on any further dissaving out of the real gain accruing after his arrival. This seems not unreasonable, although it would be possible to modify the proposals so as to exclude dissaving out of such gain from any charge to expenditure tax.

It should be noted that if an immigrant is dissaving he is, in effect, on an income tax basis. So long as he was in no danger of using up his initial credit, it would pay him to invest in low yielding assets.

Since it is not always immediately clear that someone arriving in the United Kingdom is going to become ordinarily resident, the income tax basis would no doubt be applied until his status was clarified. Uncertainties of this kind would, however, have an impact on the value of the initial credit, since that would depend on the date at which the valuation was made.

This is an area where, as under the existing income tax regime, there would be pressure to give concessions to taxpayers who might be ordinarily resident in the United Kingdom but not domiciled here under the present law, or not British subjects, or have been sent here by overseas employers. These pressures might be reduced because of the relief for savings under a universal expenditure tax; but, on the other hand, such taxpayers might have considerable expenditure overseas on education or second houses.

EMIGRANTS

The problem of the emigrant would be more serious. Taxpayers who during their working lives in the United Kingdom had saved tax-free for their retirement might be greatly tempted to emigrate, so as to spend these savings tax-free on their retirement. This would be particularly true of persons who had inherited large amounts or of high earners whose expenditure on retirement might be at a high level and therefore subject in the United Kingdom to high rates of expenditure tax. The existence of an annual wealth tax or a transfer tax might be added incentives. It is a matter for conjecture how many wealthy persons would be moved to emigrate for such tax advantages. Undoubtedly some persons would do so; and the possibilities of such emigration occurring would almost certainly make it necessary to devise some special provisions to offset the tax incentive for such movements. There are two problems: (i) how to compute the charge on an equitable basis; and (ii) how to ensure that it is paid, bearing in mind that the courts of one country will not enforce the taxes of another country (although in the course of time this may change within the EEC).

There are, however, some counterarguments. Under the present UK regime, an emigrant with high income (earned or investment) can leave the country without any tax charge – whether income tax, capital gains tax (if realisations are deferred until he is not ordinarily resident) or capital transfer tax (if his assets are outside the United Kingdom and he has or has acquired a foreign domicile). The difference is that under the present regime that emigrant will have had only limited savings relief, whereas under a UET there would be no formal limit on relief for savings. Even so, a UK resident, having had exemption from income tax and capital gains tax on amounts set aside to provide a pension, can under the terms of many double taxation treaties go abroad to reside and cease to be liable to UK tax on his pension (unless it is paid by the UK government or other UK public authority). And by emigrating a taxpayer also avoids the VAT and other indirect taxes which he would pay if he were to remain in the country, and incurs instead those of the territory to which he emigrates. Nor can the issue be considered in isolation from the scope of any annual wealth tax or transfer tax which may be in force (see pp. 447–452).

For example, if a PAWAT (a form of transfer tax, described in Chapter 15) had been in operation for many years, it could be argued that, by paying through that tax the equivalent of an annual wealth tax up to the taxpayer's 85th birthday on all gifts and bequests received, sufficient tax had been levied on inherited wealth.

It is by no means easy to devise an equitable basis for a charge on a taxpayer who emigrates; and yet it is essential to have a generally acceptable method if frequent changes in the basis of an exit tax are to be avoided. The comparison with the existing regime made in a previous paragraph suggests that the aim should be to withdraw the savings relief given to the taxpayer. Even that is not easy to compute; it is not simply the overt relief shown in the taxpayer's past returns, since that omits the growth in the value of assets still retained. The best measure of past relief would be to value the taxpayer's registered assets at the date of emigration and to deduct:

1   The indexed value of his registered assets at the introduction of expenditure tax (this should be capable of ascertainment, as his registered assets would have been listed although not valued at that date);
2   The indexed value of gifts or bequests received since the appointed day which were subject to transfer tax and were in the form of registered assets; and
3   If he was previously an immigrant, the indexed value of his registered assets at the date of immigration.

This calculation would bring into account at the date of emigration the capital gain on assets still held at that date (which escapes tax under the present regime if realisation is deferred until the taxpayer is not ordinarily resident). As with immigration, there would be a problem about the choice of date, since when a taxpayer leaves the country it is not always clear that he is going to cease to be ordinarily resident.

An alternative view is not to make the deductions at (1) and (2) above but instead to deduct the value of any unused transitional age credit of the type described in Chapter 9 (pp. 189–191).

But a yet more radical view is that account should also be taken of the fact that, if the taxpayer remained in the country, the *whole* of his assets (registered and unregistered) would be liable to either expenditure tax or transfer tax (subject to thresholds and annual exemptions). If this argument prevailed, the only deduction would be that applicable to an immigrant (3 above), and significant unregistered assets would have to be valued.

Whichever view were taken, some form of averaging relief would be needed, e.g. twenty times the tax which would be payable on annual expenditure equal to one-twentieth of the computed figure. The question would then arise of whether the tax payable should be computed on a top slice or a bottom slice basis. If on a top slice basis, the choice of the figure above which the average calculations should be done is far from simple. The indexed average of recent years' expenditure might ignore the fact that the taxpayer was on the point of retiring and was expecting to spend less; or that one spouse had died. And if there were a special exemption for elderly taxpayers (see Chapter 9, pp. 189–191), this also would need to be taken into account. The simplest course, and one for which there is some justification, would be to calculate expenditure tax on one-twentieth of the computed figure, on the basis that there was no other expenditure – perhaps without deducting any personal allowance. The resulting figure would then be multiplied by twenty (a bottom slice calculation).

A less radical approach might be to charge transfer tax on the value of the taxpayer's assets at the date of emigration to the extent that they exceeded his indexed PAWAT total (assuming that this form of transfer tax was in operation). (A taxpayer's PAWAT total is the total of chargeable gifts and bequests received by him less chargeable gifts made.) The tax would be computed as on the value of a gift of that amount to himself; it would in effect impose on his lifetime savings an annual wealth tax up to his age 85. Again there are radical alternatives; e.g. PAWAT could be charged on the value of all the taxpayer's assets at the date of emigration. But this could only be done on an arbitrary basis since there would be no donees whose PAWAT total and age could be used to compute the tax. If instead of a transfer tax there were a gifts-inclusive expenditure tax (see Chapter 9, pp. 183–185), it would be possible to tax an emigrant on a top or bottom-slicing averaging basis as if he had made a gift of the whole of his wealth at the date of emigration.

But there is a case to be made (on exchange control rather than fiscal grounds) for saying that there should be no exit tax on UK assets which were in registered form and which were retained by the taxpayer after he had emigrated, particularly if there were an annual wealth tax. Continued ownership by the emigrant might avoid some loss of foreign exchange. Exit tax would have to be charged if the emigrant borrowed in the United Kingdom against those assets to the extent that the proceeds of the borrowing were remitted abroad.

What would happen when an emigrant decided to return to the United

Kingdom and again had his ordinary residence in this country? The absence abroad might be a short or a long one. Some method would have to be found of reversing the exit tax (and allowing for inflation). Perhaps this would be easiest if the exit tax took the PAWAT form suggested in a previous paragraph. There would be a PAWAT refund based on the lesser of: (i) the amount on which the exit charge was made (duly indexed); or (ii) the value of the taxpayer's assets at the re-entry date plus the exit tax less his PAWAT total immediately before the exit tax was charged (the exit tax plus PAWAT total being duly indexed). The refund would be based on the tax-payer's age at the re-entry date. If (ii) exceeded (i), some procedure would be required to permit the tax-free consumption of the excess along the lines already proposed (pp. 437–438) for other immigrants. If the exit tax were not based on PAWAT, or as an alternative to a PAWAT refund, the exit tax could be repaid with interest, particularly if the absence abroad had been fairly short. If it were very short, the taxpayer might be required to pay expenditure tax for the period of absence, on the basis that he had never in fact abandoned his ordinary residence in the United Kingdom.

The second limb of the problem is how to secure payment of any exit tax. While exchange control continued, its procedures could be modified to en-force payment in most cases. But whether or not restrictions on foreign in-vestment should be continued on exchange control grounds is a separate matter which is not relevant for our present purpose. We shall therefore dis-cuss the operation of 'tax control' on the assumption that there would no longer be any limitation on the movement of capital funds abroad. Foreign assets could, we assume, be bought freely without limitation at the current rate of exchange. But all foreign assets would have to be held, as now, through UK authorised depositaries, a rule which would be applied to assets in all territories not subject to the UK tax regime. In addition, all remittances sent abroad would have to continue to be transmitted through authorised de-positaries, who would be required to obtain a tax clearance before making substantial remittances or releasing their control over foreign assets de-posited with them. The tax clearance would only be given when all outstand-ing tax, including exit tax, had been paid or when arrangements had been made for the authorised depositary to retain adequate security pending ascertainment of the tax due. These arrangements would have to apply to the Channel Islands, the Isle of Man and the Republic of Ireland as they applied to other territories.

There must be some doubt whether it would be worth retaining such elaborate mechanism solely in order to collect tax from those emigrants who wished to evade payment of tax. An alternative might be to require selected taxpayers to provide security for stipulated amounts. That could be done by giving the taxpayer the option of either: (i) lodging securities to the stipulated value with an authorised depositary, who would not release them without Revenue clearance; or (ii) furnishing to the Revenue a standard form of letter of credit for the stipulated amount, issued by one of a number of institutions approved for the purpose (banks, insurance companies, etc.). In the latter case the taxpayer would have to make his own arrangements to provide security to the institution and to meet their charges for the letter of credit. The establishment of the criteria by which taxpayers were selected and by which the required amounts of security were determined would be a very sensitive issue. The selection of those required to give security would be easier if there were an annual wealth tax, since the main criteria could then be the amount of the taxpayer's wealth. It must be recognised that the giving of security in this way would limit the taxpayer's ability to borrow for other purposes.

However, it may well be asked whether control arrangements of this kind would be justified by the extent of the risk. Evasion of the exit tax would be a criminal offence, so that an evader might face non-renewal of his passport and, if he returned to the United Kingdom, risk being caught.

DOUBLE TAXATION RELIEF

We discuss in Appendix 21.2 the methods by which a double allowance for investment subsidy and double taxation relief might be avoided. Since double taxation relief would continue to be given on expenditure out of earned income which had borne overseas tax or might be needed, at least for transitional reasons, on overseas investment income, we examine in Appendix 21.3 the methods by which double taxation relief might be calculated under a UET.

TWO-TIER EXPENDITURE TAX (TTET)

This consists of two elements:

1 A lower tier proportionate tax on expenditure, operated by either (i) a basic rate of income tax with 100 per cent capital allowances on all forms of investment, or (ii) a tax on value added, which in turn may be origin-based or destination-based (to correspond with the present basic rate income tax).

2 An upper tier progressive surcharge on expenditure above a certain level, operated by means of an expenditure tax adjustment (to correspond with the present higher rate tax) (see Chapter 10).

The expenditure tax surcharge raises problems concerning tax relations with other countries similar to those discussed in connection with the UET, except that the number of taxpayers involved is much smaller and the rates of tax involved are lower, since it is only the excess of present higher rates over basic rate which is levied by means of the surcharge.

The new issues which arise concern the effects of the lower tier basic rate. This may be operated by any one of three means, namely (i) an income tax with 100 per cent capital allowances; (ii) an origin-based tax on value added; or (iii) a destination-based tax on value added. These different methods give rise to different problems in connection with the tax relations with other countries. There are four important issues which might be affected by the choice of method for operating the lower tier tax for a TTET if such a tax system were adopted in the United Kingdom, namely:

1   The tax treatment of investment income arising in the United Kingdom but paid to persons not ordinarily resident in the United Kingdom.
2   The treatment for double taxation relief of investment incomes drawn from overseas by residents in the United Kingdom.
3   The treatment for double taxation relief of earned income drawn from overseas by residents in the United Kingdom.
4   The tax treatment of immigrants into and emigrants out of the United Kingdom.

(1)   We start, then, by considering the implications for the tax treatment of UK investment income which is paid to persons not ordinarily resident in the United Kingdom. Since investment in companies is quantitatively important, we illustrate the position by reference to investment in companies, but the same principle holds with regard to investment by overseas taxpayers in unincorporated businesses, offices, factories, farms, etc.

On the assumption of a basic rate of income tax or value added tax of $33\frac{1}{3}$ per cent (tax-inclusive) and of an S or R-based corporation tax of 50 per cent (tax-inclusive), Table 21.1 gives the picture for a UK taxpayer investing in the United Kingdom, with income tax with 100 per cent capital allowances in column A and a tax on value added (whether origin or destination-based makes no difference in this case) in column B. Column A is based on Table 12.5, in which we showed the need for the imputation of a tax credit to the domestic investor at the basic rate of income tax in order to achieve the same rate of return to the saver as the 10 per cent yield on the underlying physical investment. Column B shows how the same rate of return is achieved by means of a tax on value added.

The overseas investor would come into the picture at line 5, with savings of £100 to invest in column A and with savings of £150 to invest in column B. At line 10 he would receive a dividend which in each case would represent 10 per cent on his savings. If, as would be the intention, he were to be subject to a continued income tax regime, he ought to be taxed on this dividend, subject to any double taxation agreements. But, far from being subject to any income tax, in column A the foreign investor would get the full dividend of £10 and, under normal double taxation conventions, would also expect to be repaid part of the tax credit – clearly inappropriate under this system. The tax on value added of column B has the advantage over the method of column A that it would not involve any payment of a tax credit on the dividend and would not therefore lead to any expectation of such a credit on the part of the foreign investor. In fact, what is really required in the case of both columns A and B is a withholding tax deducted from all dividends paid to non-resident shareholders but not from dividends paid to UK residents. It would be troublesome, or indeed impossible in many cases, to have to make this distinction. The same argument applies to interest, but here

Table 21.1 *A UK taxpayer investing in the United Kingdom (in £s)*

		A IT with 100% capital allowances	B Tax on value added
1	Earnings	150	150
2	*Less* IT	(50)	—
3	*Less* Tax on value added	—	(50)
4	Consumption	100	100
5	Savings	100	150
6	*S* or *R* relief against CT	100	150
7	Investment	200	300
8	Yield 10%	20	30
9	*Less* CT	(10)	(15)
10	Dividend	10	15
11	Tax credit	5	—
12	Dividend + Tax credit	15	15
13	*Less* IT	(5)	—
14	*Less* Tax on value added	—	(5)
15	Consumption	10	10

double taxation treaties frequently exempt interest from tax in the country of origin.

In so far as the United Kingdom already has a partial system of 100 per cent capital allowances and an imputation system, these forces are already operative. If yields are 10 per cent, the amount needed to be provided by an overseas shareholder to produce the income of £100 shown in the example on p. 431 is only £480 if investment of £1,000 is made in assets in the United Kingdom attracting 100 per cent capital allowances; the balance of £520 comes from tax relief. Since the overseas investor in that example gets a return of £60·9 on his investment of £480, it is evident that he is getting a greater return (12·7 per cent) than that on the underlying investment (10 per cent).

(2) In Chapter 20 we have discussed the case for denying on foreign investment either any tax relief given on the investment itself or double taxation relief on the income earned on such foreign investment. The arrangements necessary to achieve this result are in principle straightforward if the United Kingdom is operating an income tax with 100 per cent capital allowances, although there are a number of important problems in practice which will affect the choice between the denial of capital allowances and the

denial of double taxation relief on the foreign investment income, which are discussed in Appendixes 21.2 and 21.3. The question arises, however, as to the arrangements which would be necessary to achieve a similar result if the United Kingdom were operating the lower tier of a TTET, not by means of an income tax with 100 per cent capital allowances, but by means of an origin-based or destination-based tax on value added. We examine this question in Tables 20.6 to 20.8 of Appendix 20.1, from which it is clear that it would be necessary to deny double taxation relief against UK tax on value added for any foreign income tax paid on the foreign investment income.

There is, however, one possible exception to this conclusion. If a high tax on value added were introduced abruptly on a destination base, this would (as shown in Appendix 20.1) raise the money cost of living in the United Kingdom relatively to the level of money prices abroad. Past foreign investment would have been made in the expectation of the possibility of spending the yield in the United Kingdom at the previous cost of living uninflated by the heavy tax on value added. The question would then arise whether on these grounds any tax relief should be given on income earned on foreign investments made before the tax change. This issue would not arise with a tax on value added on an origin base, since in this case the cost of living in the United Kingdom would not be raised relatively to the level of money prices in the outside world.

(3)   We also examine in Appendix 20.1 the case for giving double taxation relief against UK tax for foreign tax on foreign earned income accruing to UK taxpayers. We there give reasons for the views (i) that such relief should be given against UK income tax if the lower tier of the TTET is operated by means of an income tax with 100 per cent capital allowances, and (ii) that there is a strong case for giving such relief against UK tax on value added if this tax is operated on a destination basis but not if it is operated on an origin basis. The difference in (ii) is due to the fact that the destination-based tax will raise the UK cost of living at which the foreign earnings can be spent, whereas the origin-based tax will not.

(4)   Finally, there is a significant difference between a destination-based tax on value added, on the one hand, and a tax on value added on an origin basis or an income tax with 100 per cent capital allowances on the other hand, in their effects on the incentives for wealthy persons who wish to live on their savings to emigrate from the United Kingdom or to refrain from immigrating into the United Kingdom. The destination-based tax on value added, by raising the cost of living in the United Kingdom relatively to that in other countries, will give such an incentive, whereas the other methods will not do so.

In the light of these considerations, there would appear to be a clear advantage from the point of view of tax relations with other countries to operate the lower tier of a TTET by means of an origin-based tax on value added:

1   Unlike the income tax method it does not involve the problem of offering a tax credit to UK taxpayers which must be disregarded in the case of overseas taxpayers.

2   No double taxation relief against UK tax on value added need be given for any foreign income tax on foreign investment income, whereas with a destination-based tax on value added the awkward question arises whether such relief should not be given in respect of foreign investments made before the UK tax change.

3   No double taxation relief against UK tax on value added need be given for any foreign income tax on earnings made abroad by UK taxpayers, whereas such relief should be granted under an income tax with 100 per cent capital allowances or under a destination-based tax on value added.

4   Unlike a destination-based tax on value added, such a tax on an origin basis will have no effect in causing wealthy persons who wish to live on their capital to take up their ordinary residence abroad.

CORPORATION TAX

The OECD model treaty referred to on pp. 428–429, and most recent treaties, provide that when a company is resident in two countries it shall for treaty purposes be deemed to be resident in the country in which 'effective management' is situated. In UK terms this is where the directing and controlling power is exercised or 'where the central management and control actually abides'. This concept is not always understood by overseas countries, still less accepted by them as being the equivalent of the place of effective management. For this reason, and because in some treaties different definitions are used, the elimination of double residence has not been fully achieved.

The UK concept of 'central management and control' has the effect that some foreign companies (perhaps the subsidiaries of UK companies) are resident in the United Kingdom for tax purposes because, for example, meetings of directors are held here. This may or may not be advantageous or disadvantageous to the company concerned, depending on the foreign and UK rates of tax, treaty provisions, the rates at which capital allowances are given, the possibilities for setting off losses against UK income, and so on.

The general effect of treaties is that a company's profits are taxed where it is deemed to reside and also, in overseas territories where it has a branch, on profits which it makes from that branch. It may also bear foreign tax on income which it receives from subsidiary and associated companies or from portfolio investment. The country where it resides gives double taxation relief for tax on overseas income, which includes, in cases where dividends are received from associated companies (usually defined as requiring 10 per cent or more of voting control), underlying tax on the profits from which dividends are paid.

For exchange control and tax reasons it is unlawful for a company resident in the United Kingdom, without Treasury consent, to transfer its residence overseas or to transfer its trade or business to a non-resident person (section 482, Taxes Act 1970). This was criticised by the 1955 Royal Commission on Taxation, which regarded it as a temporary regulation to deal with an emergency. The introduction of an *R* or *S*-type corporation tax renders it more rather than less likely that a control of this kind will be maintained. This is because of the subsidy to investment which is given under both of those methods. There is an obvious parallel with emigration of individuals (discussed earlier in this chapter). In the absence of control, companies would remain in the United Kingdom long enough to benefit from investment subsidy and would then emigrate to a country where corporation tax was at a low rate on profit after economic depreciation. The influence of these taxes on the immigration of companies or the establishment in the United Kingdom of companies which might equally well be established elsewhere is less clear. For some the investment subsidy might be attractive, but for companies with a very high expected rate of profit it might be unattractive, since they might prefer to forego the subsidy and instead be based in a country with a lower rate of tax on profit after economic depreciation.

It should be noted that the withholding tax of the classical type, R and S corporation taxes, and the structure of the S-type imputation system (described in Chapter 12, pp. 250–251) all result in a yield to a foreign investor in UK companies less than the return on the physical investment; whereas the imputation system which would be necessary with a TTET if the lower tier tax were operated by means of an income tax with 100 per cent capital allowances, and not by a tax on value added, would give a yield equal to that return unless a special tax could be imposed on dividends paid to non-residents (an imposition that would be difficult to achieve in practice).[5]

The question of double taxation relief for companies is of great importance, as the sums of money involved are very large indeed. We have referred in Chapter 20 and in Appendix 21.2 shall refer to the problem of double relief for investment subsidy and for double taxation; and in Appendix 21.2 we also discuss the question of reliefs, one or other of which are or may appear to be ineffective. In Appendix 21.3 we deal with some detailed points relating to double taxation relief. If only one of the two reliefs is to be given, then the difficulties referred to in Appendix 21.2 would need consideration; and (as shown in that appendix) the issues are not identical for the R and S-type taxes.

ANNUAL WEALTH TAX

The draft reports considered by the Select Committee on a Wealth Tax,[6] other than that of Dr Bray, agreed in recommending the following:

1 Residence for wealth tax purposes should be determined purely by reference to the length and frequency of the taxpayer's visits and should not take account of whether he has accommodation in the United Kingdom available for his use.

[5] In the case of the two imputation systems it is assumed that the foreign investor does not receive the associated tax credit.

[6] Session 1974/75, Vol. I, Report and Proceedings of the Committee, HC 696–1, HMSO, November 1975.

2   A charge on worldwide assets should arise only if the taxpayer fulfilled all three conditions of being resident, ordinarily resident and domiciled in the United Kingdom.

3   If the taxpayer is resident and ordinarily resident but not domiciled in the United Kingdom, the charge should be on all UK assets.

4   If the taxpayer is (i) not resident in the United Kingdom, whether or not ordinarily resident or domiciled, or (ii) resident but not ordinarily resident nor domiciled, the charge should be on UK land and permanent establishments.

We agree with these proposals, but think that the concept of 'deemed domicile' now used for capital transfer tax (and described under the next heading) may also need to be used for annual wealth tax.

A charge on all UK assets would be justifiable in the case of persons in class 4; but, since a wealth tax does not lend itself to a system of deduction at source, difficult problems of enforcement against non-residents would arise if the charge extended beyond fixed and visible assets. The charge for class 4 accords broadly with the practice of other countries.

A person who was resident and domiciled, but not ordinarily resident, in the United Kingdom might be included in class 2 because his domicile indicated a continuing connection with the United Kingdom. Or he might be included in class 3 because his residence was an exception to his ordinary course of life; if it were not, he would be ordinarily resident. On the whole, inclusion in class 3 seems preferable.

The above arrangements have been proposed in the context of the existing income tax. If the income tax charge on foreign income were to be enlarged in the case of long term residents not domiciled in the United Kingdom by the introduction of 'deemed domicile', the same enlargement would be appropriate for wealth tax.

An expenditure tax, if it were to be introduced, might be made applicable to persons ordinarily resident and domiciled in the United Kingdom, with liability to the tax continuing even if the individual, although remaining ordinarily resident, was not resident for a particular year. In this way the problems associated with a change from expenditure tax liability to income tax liability and vice versa would be avoided in this area. There would then be a case, if only on grounds of simplicity, for adopting the same rule for wealth tax, so that a person who was ordinarily resident and domiciled in the United Kingdom would remain chargeable to wealth tax on worldwide assets for an exceptional year of non-residence. Apart from this case, it seems that the scope of the wealth tax charge should be the same under the expenditure tax as under the income tax.

PAWAT AND LAWAT

The existing capital transfer tax, which is of course a donor-based tax, applies to: (i) all transfers of assets (wherever situated) by a person domiciled or deemed to be domiciled in the United Kingdom; and (ii) all transfers of assets in the United Kingdom regardless of the domicile of the transferor, the situs of the assets following the same rules as were used for estate duty.

For the purpose of this tax a person is treated as having a 'deemed domicile' in the United Kingdom at a given point in time if he satisfies any of the following conditions:

1 He was domiciled in the United Kingdom on or after 10 December 1974 and at any time within the three years prior to the time in question.
2 He was resident in the United Kingdom in at least seventeen of the twenty years of assessment ending with the year in which that time falls. (Residence will be determined using income tax principles but ignoring any house available for use in the United Kingdom.)
3 He has, since December 1974, become and has remained domiciled in the Channel Islands or the Isle of Man and, immediately before becoming domiciled there, he was domiciled in the United Kingdom.

This does not, however, apply to a person who had his domicile of origin in the islands, or who, when he became domiciled there, was incapable of having an independent domicile (e.g. minors).

It will be observed that the rules for capital transfer tax place great emphasis on domicile or deemed domicile and in this respect differ from those proposed by the Select Committee for annual wealth tax. The PAWAT and LAWAT (described in Chapter 15) share some of the characteristics of an annual wealth tax and some of those of a donee-based transfer tax. The question of the scope of a donee-based transfer tax was considered in *An Accessions Tax* by Sandford, Willis and Ironside,[7] who proposed that accessions tax should apply to the following:

1 All accessions of property situated in Great Britain, regardless of the residence of the donor or testator or beneficiary.
2 All accessions of property situated abroad which are received by a person ordinarily resident in Britain, regardless of the residence of the donor or testator.
3 All accessions of property situated abroad which are received by a person not ordinarily resident in Britain from a person ordinarily resident here.

These proposals seem to us to be suitable for application to a PAWAT and a LAWAT, particularly as these authors contemplated some modification of them to deal, for example, with people who were posted to the United Kingdom in the course of a business career, on terms that in due course they would move elsewhere.

Furthermore, it was suggested that, just as deemed domicile persists for a period after actual domicile has ceased, so ordinary residence, for the purpose

---

[7] C. T. Sandford, J. R. M. Willis and D. J. Ironside, *An Accessions Tax* (London: Institute for Fiscal Studies, 1973), ch. 4.

of these provisions, should persist for a period after ordinary residence has ceased. Deemed domicile for capital transfer tax persists for three years, although this is short by comparison with the corresponding ten years for Dutch citizens, five years for German citizens, or ten years suggested by the authors of *An Accessions Tax*.

Under the Select Committee proposals, liability to wealth tax would cease if ordinary residence came to an end and a taxpayer ceased to hold UK assets. It may be asked whether, since PAWAT and LAWAT are in some respects equivalent to a wealth tax, those taxes should be refunded for the unexpired period up to age 85 when a taxpayer ceases to be ordinarily resident and ceases to hold UK assets. If regarded as transfer taxes, it would certainly seem strange to make a refund, particularly in view of the rules for the present capital transfer tax and those suggested in *An Accessions Tax*, which we have just endorsed. This issue needs to be considered in conjunction with the proposal for an exit tax under a UET (discussed on pp. 438–442).

The treatment of emigrants also needs to be symmetrical with the treatment of immigrants who become ordinarily resident or domiciled in the United Kingdom. For example, immigrants would not expect, when they came to the country, to be charged PAWAT or LAWAT on the value of previous gifts, although to take the value of recent gifts into account in establishing the rate applicable to gifts received after they arrive here may be another issue. Yet, under the Select Committee's proposals, once an immigrant was resident, ordinarily resident and domiciled in the United Kingdom, he would be liable to annual wealth tax on worldwide assets.

THE EFFECT ON TREATY NEGOTIATIONS

On p. 432 it has been pointed out that, under the integrated CIT/corporation tax proposals of Chapter 7, the rate of corporation tax (which would be imputed in full to dividends) would have to be of the order of 50 per cent if negotiators acting on behalf of the United Kingdom were to have anything to concede in return for concessions from other countries. We have also there explained the form which the concessions would probably take.

Overseas governments and investors might well be slow to recognise (i) that, for example, a 33 per cent withholding tax under a classical R or S-type corporation tax is substantially less than a 15 per cent withholding tax imposed by an overseas government after a 40 per cent corporation tax based on economic depreciation; or (ii) that, under the imputation system which would be necessary with a TTET if the lower tier tax were operated by means of an income tax with 100 per cent capital allowances, an overseas investor should receive no tax credit and even then would, in a sense, have paid no UK tax because of investment subsidy. Even so, a UK government might be willing to make some concession on a 33 per cent R or S-type withholding tax, but should not be willing to give tax credits to non-residents under the imputation system necessary with a TTET of the kind described above.

If (as suggested on pp. 436–437) relief for investment in the United

Kingdom were given to overseas investors who carried on unincorporated businesses in the United Kingdom, and if overseas shareholders received *R* or *S*-type relief against corporation tax, there would be times when the return to those investors was free of UK tax except for such withholding tax as was provided for in treaties between the two countries. So far as an individual carrying on an unincorporated business is concerned, it is likely that the effect would be that more tax would be payable in the country where he had his fiscal domicile (since there would be less UK tax to set against it). Individuals receiving dividends from UK companies would regard the position as normal, since they would not expect to do more than set any withholding tax or any tax credit not repaid against domestic tax. But an overseas company controlling more than 10 per cent of the votes of a UK company might find that there was, for a time, no underlying UK corporation tax which could be set against domestic tax, thus increasing the latter. In these ways reliefs given by the United Kingdom might be frustrated; they should therefore only be given in treaty negotiations in return for some equivalent concession to UK investors, or for concessions in the territories concerned which enabled taxpayers of those territories to retain the benefit of reduced UK tax.

Foreign governments might be concerned if UK residents were denied double taxation relief because they received investment subsidy (see Appendix 21.2), since the effect would be that, after the appointed day, investment in the United Kingdom would be preferred to overseas investment unless the post-foreign-tax return on the foreign investment (including any indirect effect on the return on domestic investment) exceeded the pre-tax domestic return. If, instead, relief on the overseas investment were denied but double taxation relief were allowed, the cost of financing investment in the overseas territory would be greater, so that the comparison would be much the same.

HARMONISATION

We have referred in Chapter 12 (pp. 249–250) to the draft directive of the Commission of the European Community suggesting that harmonisation of corporation taxes should be on the basis of an imputation system with tax credits extending to shareholders and all member countries. We have there discussed how the *R* and *S*-based corporation taxes could be made compatible with those proposals; and in Chapter 12 (pp. 254–256) we have discussed an imputation system in conjunction with a TTET in the case in which the lower tier tax is operated by an income tax with 100 per cent capital allowances.

With the exception of the draft directive, the cause of harmonisation has made little progress, and there are few signs that progress is likely to become more rapid. Clearly there are bound to be some anomalies and difficulties in relationships between (i) a country with expenditure-based personal taxes, an *R* or *S*-based corporation tax and a transfer tax of PAWAT or LAWAT type on the one hand, and (ii) a country with an income tax (particularly of the comprehensive type), a corporation tax based on profit after economic depreciation, a gift tax and an inheritance tax on the other. We have tried in this chapter, the preceding chapter and their appendixes to show what the more important anomalies and difficulties might be and to discuss ways of dealing with them; but we do not claim, in view of the range of the subject and the limited time available to us, to have made as full a survey as the importance of the subject justifies. Many of the problems discussed would disappear or be greatly eased if other countries adopted expenditure-based taxes; and although that may appear improbable we note with interest that an expenditure-based personal tax system is one of the options discussed in the US Department of the Treasury's publication *Blueprints for Basic Tax Reform* and that the Swedish Royal Commission has had a survey made of the possibility of introducing such a tax in Sweden.

[8] US Government Printing Office, 17 January 1977.
[9] *Progressiv utgiftskatt—ett alternative:* Rapport av 1972 års. Skatteutredning (Stockholm, 1976).

Appendix 21.1 Taxpayers with Overseas Connections

The extent to which a person is liable to UK income tax on foreign income depends on whether or not he is (i) resident in the United Kingdom, (ii) ordinarily resident in the United Kingdom, or (iii) domiciled in the United Kingdom.

There are five main factors that influence whether a particular individual is *resident* or *non-resident*:

1 Physical presence in the United Kingdom for a particular year. For example, someone who is in the country for a temporary purpose and not with a view to establishing residence here is treated as resident if he spends at least six months in the country in a particular assessment year. But someone who is ordinarily resident in the United Kingdom but is absent from the country for a whole assessment year is not treated as resident for that year.

2 Residence in a previous year. A British subject (which in this appendix will usually include a citizen of the Republic of Ireland), whose ordinary residence has been in the United Kingdom and who leaves the country for the purpose only of occasional residence abroad, and does not cease to be ordinarily resident, will usually be treated as resident in any assessment year in which he enters the United Kingdom, even if for quite a short period.

3 Regularity of visits to the United Kingdom. A person who pays regular visits to the country, even though he has no place of abode here, may still be treated as resident if those visits are sufficiently frequent and substantial to form part of his normal way of life. The working rule is that an average annual period or periods amounting to three months is substantial and that visits become habitual after four years. But if it is apparent from the start that regular visits for substantial periods are to be made, the visitor will be regarded as resident in and from the first year.

4 The purpose of the visits. Visits merely in the course of travel are probably not sufficient to make a taxpayer resident in the United Kingdom.

5 Place of abode within the United Kingdom. If a taxpayer maintains a place of abode in the country and visits it, even for a short period, during a particular assessment year, this establishes residence for that year (but not if he works full time abroad).

Ordinarily resident implies a measure of continuity, so that someone who is resident because he spends more than six months of a particular assessment year in the United Kingdom will not be ordinarily resident if that is the only year in which he is resident. But a person who is not resident for a particular assessment year because he is physically absent for the whole year may be ordinarily resident in that year if he was ordinarily resident in the year before and in the year following.

An individual is normally regarded as resident or ordinarily resident for a whole tax year; by concession, however, the Inland Revenue splits the year when the individual arrives or leaves permanently.

An individual is born with a domicile known as his *domicile of origin*, which can be changed to a *domicile of choice* by residence in another jurisdiction plus an intention to reside there indefinitely. A domicile of choice can be abandoned by acquiring another domicile of choice or by reviving the domicile of origin. The concept of domicile is not usually given as much weight by foreign tax jurisdictions as it is by

Table 21.2 *The extent of liability on foreign income with particular reference to status as to residence, ordinary residence and domicile (up to 5 April 1977)*

Status:
R = Resident
OR = Ordinarily resident
D = Domiciled
UKE = UK employer
FE = Foreign employer
B = British subject or Irish citizen
N = Not

Status (1)	Foreign investment income (2)	Foreign trade, profession or vocation (3)	Foreign pensions (4)	Employment (on that part of remuneration for services performed)			
				Wholly in UK (5)	Partly in the UK and partly abroad		Wholly abroad (8)
					The part in the UK (6)	The part abroad (7)	
1A R OR D UKE	Arising	75%	90%	All	All	All[1,2]	All[1,2]
1B R OR D FE	Arising	75%	90%	All	All	All[1,2]	75%[1,2]
2A R OR ND UKE	Remittances	Remittances	Remittances	50%/75%[3]	50%/75%[3]	All[1,2]	All[1,2]
2B R OR ND FE	Remittances	Remittances	Remittances	50%/75%[3]	50%/75%[3]	50%/75%[3]	Remittances
3 NR OR D	Exempt	Exempt	Exempt	All	All	Exempt	Exempt
4A NR OR ND UKE	Exempt	Exempt	Exempt	All	All	Exempt	Exempt
4B NR OR ND FE	Exempt	Exempt	Exempt	50%	50%	Exempt	Exempt
5A R NOR D NB	Arising	75%	90%	All	All	Remittances	Remittances
5B R NOR D B	Remittances	Remittances	Remittances	All	All	Remittances	Remittances
6A R NOR ND UKE	Remittances	Remittances	Remittances	All	All	Remittances	Remittances
6B R NOR ND FE	Remittances	Remittances	Remittances	50%/75%[3]	50%/75%[3]	50%/75%[3]	Remittances
7 NR NOR D	Exempt	Exempt	Exempt	All	All	Remittances	Remittances
8A NR NOR ND UKE	Exempt	Exempt	Exempt	All	All	Exempt	Exempt
8B NR NOR ND FE	Exempt	Exempt	Exempt	50%	50%	Exempt	Exempt

1 Exempt if the taxpayer is abroad for the purpose of the employment for a continuous period exceeding 364 days. There is a special definition of continuous so that short visits to the UK do not break continuity.

2 75 per cent if the taxpayer is abroad for more than 29 qualifying days.

3 75 per cent if resident in 9 of the 10 preceding years of assessment; otherwise 50 per cent.

4 The percentages are the amounts taxable.

5 Complications arising from Irish residence or domicile or duties are ignored.

6 Double taxation agreements normally exempt non-residents who are in the UK for short visits from tax in column 7 on lines 2B, 4B, 6B and 8B.

7 Remittances: only remittances out of income are chargeable. There is in general an exchange control requirement that overseas income of UK residents should be remitted to the sterling area, but remittance to, for example, the Channel Islands does not involve UK tax on this type of income. Remittances to the UK after a source has ceased, or in years of assessment which are not a basis for a year when the taxpayer is resident, escape tax.

that of the United Kingdom. Some overseas administrations use the word more in a sense akin to that of the UK concept of ordinary residence. Because of the strength of the domicile of origin, it is very difficult for the Inland Revenue to show that an individual has acquired a domicile of choice in the United Kingdom, even if he has lived in the country almost all his life, unless he has expressed an intention to stay here. It is because of this that, for purposes of capital transfer tax, there is a concept of *deemed domicile* whereby an individual is treated as if he were domiciled in the United Kingdom if he has been resident for seventeen of the twenty consecutive years ending with the year in which a particular transfer took place. This concept is not applied to income tax.

In Table 21.2 we have summarised the rules as to the extent of the liability of taxpayers with various combinations of the three attributes. In some cases it is

Table 21.3 *Classes of individuals by status as to residence and domicile*

Status[a]	Typical cases
1 R OR D	(a) The normal permanent resident; or (b) Former permanent resident who visits back regularly or has not severed connection with UK.
2 R OR ND	Person of foreign origin who has: (a) been here continuously for a number of years; (b) come here for long-term employment; (c) come here for study or education; (d) been making habitual and substantial visits for more than 4 years; (or (e) an available abode and makes habitual visits).
3 NR OR D	Permanent resident of UK origin spending a complete fiscal year overseas.
4 NR OR ND	(a) Long-term resident of foreign origin spending a complete fiscal year overseas; or (b) Habitual visitor with a blank year.
5 R NOR D	Person of UK origin working or retired abroad making a single return visit of at least 6 months.
6 R NOR ND	Person of foreign origin: (a) making a single visit of at least 6 months; (b) here to work for 2 or 3 years; or (c) here with indefinite intentions and has not yet been here for 3 years.
7 NR NOR D	Person of UK origin who has left: (a) for permanent residence abroad; or (b) for long-term employment abroad (and, if not employed full time, not having a place of abode).
8 NR NOR ND	(a) Foreigner not here or, (b) if here, only for short-term employment or on short visits.

Source: Reproduced from evidence given by the Inland Revenue to the Select Committee on Wealth Tax, Session 1974/75, HC 696, Vol II, HMSO, November 1975.
[a] For key see Table 21.2.

also necessary to distinguish the treatment of non-domiciled taxpayers who are employed by employers not resident in the United Kingdom; and in other non-domiciled cases a distinction is drawn between British subjects and Irish citizens on the one hand and all other taxpayers on the other.

Table 21.3, which is reproduced from evidence given by the Inland Revenue to the Select Committee on Wealth Tax, shows the typical classes of case in which individuals fall within the various combinations of residence, ordinary residence and domicile.

Table 21.4 shows the liability to capital gains tax on UK and foreign property for the same eight categories as those used in the two preceding tables.

We have described the scope of capital transfer tax in Appendix 15.1.

Table 21.4   *Liability to capital gains tax, by status as to residence and domicile*

Status[a]			UK property	Foreign property
1	R	OR	D	All	All
2	R	OR	ND	All	Remittances
3	NR	OR	D	All	All
4	NR	OR	ND	All	Remittances
5	R	NOR	D	All	All
6	R	NOR	ND	All	Remittances
7	NR	NOR	D	Exempt	Exempt
8	NR	NOR	ND	Exempt	Exempt

[a] See Table 21.2 for key.

Appendix 21.2   Investment Subsidy and Double Taxation Relief

We have explained in Chapter 20 (commencing at p. 412) that there are grounds on which it could be argued that it would be overgenerous for an ET country to give relief against its own tax for investment overseas by its residents, and at the same time to give double taxation relief in respect of income tax levied in an IT country on the yield from that investment. In this appendix we examine ways in which such a double allowance might be avoided. We shall illustrate our argument primarily by reference to a UET and an *S*-type corporation tax, but most of what we say is equally applicable, *mutatis mutandis*, to a TTET and an *R*-type corporation tax.

First we consider what happens if both investment subsidy and double taxation relief are given. Our example assumes a UK rate of 100 per cent (tax-exclusive) and a foreign rate of 50 per cent (tax-inclusive), i.e. the same rate in both territories.

	£
A UK taxpayer reduces his consumption by	500
He gets savings relief of	500
He invests abroad	1,000

The investment yields 10%	100
Less Foreign tax 50% (tax-inclusive)	(50)
Yield after foreign tax	50
Less UK tax on the extra consumption 100% (tax-exclusive)	(50)
Double taxation relief	50
Less UK tax after double taxation relief	nil
Spent	50
Yield %	10%

The benefit to the United Kingdom of the overseas investment is the return after foreign tax of £50, and the whole of this is appropriated by the taxpayer, although he provided only half of the investment. In our example the government has had no return on its contribution to the investment; but note that, if the overseas rate of tax had been less than the UK rate, then to that extent it would have had some limited return on its contribution.

If one or other of the two reliefs is denied, the net yield to the taxpayer is as follows:

	Investment subsidy denied £	Double taxation relief denied £
The UK taxpayer reduces his consumption by	1,000	500
He gets savings relief of	nil	500
He invests abroad	1,000	1,000
The investment yields 10%	100	100
Less Foreign tax 50% (tax-inclusive)	(50)	(50)
Yield after foreign tax	50	50
Less UK tax on the extra consumption 100% (tax-exclusive)	(50)	(25)
Double taxation relief	50	nil
Less UK tax after double taxation relief	nil	(25)
Spent	50	25
Yield %	5%	5%

In both cases the UK taxpayer receives a rate of yield on his savings which is equal to the post-foreign-tax rate of return on the physical investment which his savings served to finance. We now examine these two alternative routes in more detail.

THE DENIAL OF INVESTMENT SUBSIDY

A major reason for preferring this route is that the alternative method of denying double taxation relief requires the yield on pre-appointed-day investment to be distinguished from that on post-appointed-day investment if, for the reason given on pp. 416–417, it is assumed that the radical transitional treatment of denying double taxation relief on the yield from pre-appointed-day investment is not acceptable. In some cases (e.g. portfolio investment) it will be easy to make such a distinction; but in others (e.g. industrial plant) it will be impossible to do so except on an arbitrary basis. However, there are several difficulties about this route.

In the absence of investment subsidy the finance needed for overseas investment, even comparatively short term investment, will be greater than that needed for domestic investment. Given that the post-foreign-tax yield on an overseas project was high enough to justify the investment, a UK taxpayer would probably in most cases prefer to receive an investment subsidy and forego double taxation relief rather than to bear himself the whole cost of overseas investment but receive a higher net yield because double taxation relief was allowed.

If the overseas rate of tax equals or exceeds the UK rate, disallowance of investment subsidy on the whole of the overseas investment is justified by the reasoning used above. But to disallow 100 per cent of such investment when the foreign rate of tax was less than the UK rate would be inequitable. To put it in extreme terms, if the overseas territory had no tax on profits, no disallowance would be justified. Only that proportion of investment should be disallowed which is represented by the ratio between the overseas rate of tax and the UK rate of tax. Thus, if the overseas tax were nil, there would be no denial of relief. If it were equal to the UK rate, 100 per cent would be disallowed. If it were greater than the UK rate, there are some who would be content to see more than 100 per cent of the overseas investment disallowed! But there are two difficulties. First, the ratio would have to be established at the time the expenditure was incurred. Perhaps the UK Revenue could establish these ratios for various territories and change them as changes in tax rates took place. Subsequent fluctuations in the rate of overseas tax would vary the way in which the net return was divided between the UK taxpayer and the UK government. (If the rate of foreign tax went up, the UK government would get less and conversely.) Secondly, for individuals there is no such thing as 'a UK rate of tax'.

If overseas investment is not to attract investment subsidy, some way will have to be found of allowing for economic depreciation of fixed assets or capital losses on other investment, since under an expenditure tax regime no specific provision has to be made for economic depreciation or capital losses. (But this problem would not arise under the S-type corporation tax, since under that tax depreciation provisions and profits retained in order to meet capital losses are free of UK tax.)

Under the R corporation tax method, disallowance of investment in stocks sent from the United Kingdom to an overseas branch might be thought to be inequitable, since stocks sent to an overseas subsidiary company would not be disallowed if those stocks were not invoiced to the subsidiary until the moment when they were sold by the subsidiary to third parties (because until that time they would not be an R incoming, since ownership would remain with the parent company).

There would be difficulty in identifying the quantum of overseas investment which should be disallowed. Under the R corporation tax the natural rule would be to say that no $\bar{R}$ outgoing of an investment nature related to overseas branches should be deducted in arriving at taxable profits. Those outgoings would consist of fixed assets and year-end stocks and work in progress. The figure would be computed yearly, and any increase would be disallowed. But if tax relief were denied to foreign investment in this way, foreign disinvestment not exceeding the previous disallowance should not be taxed. This would mean that the proceeds from the running-down of overseas fixed assets, stocks and work in progress would not be taxed unless, for example in the case of a building, there was a surplus over and above indexed cost.

But under a conservative transition (see Chapter 20, pp. 416–417) the proceeds of sale of pre-appointed-day overseas investment should also not be taxed. In those circumstances, it would only be the excess of the proceeds of sale of post-appointed-day investment over disallowed outgoings (as indexed) which would be treated as an R incoming and taxed. In any case there would be apportionment problems when investments or parts of investments involving both pre and post-appointed-day expenditure were sold.

But if the overseas investment were financed by a loan, the interest on which was tax deductible in arriving at profit liable to foreign tax in the overseas territory, then to that extent doubly taxed profits would be reduced and the amount of expenditure disallowed under the R basis ought also to be reduced. Under the S-based corporation tax similar problems would arise, even if interest on any loan were not tax deductible in the overseas territory. Since the S basis is equivalent to $(R - \bar{R} + F - \bar{F})$, it is net rather than gross overseas investment which should be disallowed. But that would raise the problem of matching loans raised and increased creditors with the investment financed thereby.

Under the S-type corporation tax there is also the difficulty of reconciling the fiscal year base of that tax with overseas investment, which would normally be computed on an accounting year basis. This would probably be done either by treating overseas investment in the accounting period as if it were incurred in the fiscal year in which that period ended, or the investment in the accounting year would have to be arbitrarily apportioned between fiscal years. It would no doubt appear incongruous to define the S basis as the net payment by the company to its shareholders plus disallowed foreign investment, but in terms of the equivalence of the S basis to $(R - \bar{R} + F - \bar{F})$ it is explicable.

Denial of investment subsidy, whether under the R or S method, means that the total finance needed to support a given amount of overseas investment (possibly of a short term nature) is greater than that needed for the same amount of domestic investment. Under the R-type tax, that appears as a natural consequence of the disallowance of overseas investment. But under the S method, instead of denying relief on an $\bar{R}$ outgoing, it may appear as if a tax is being levied on $\bar{S}$ outgoings. If the overseas investment is financed out of recently raised share capital, it will be clear enough that, in fact, it is the S-type relief which is being withdrawn rather than a tax which is being imposed. Retained profits used to finance overseas investment have, until so used, been enlarged under the S basis by an investment subsidy, since the capital base from which those profits have stemmed was itself enlarged by the investment subsidy given on the subscription of share capital. What appears as a tax charge on the application of retained profits to overseas investment is thus properly seen as the withdrawal of an investment subsidy.

It remains to consider overseas investment financed by loan. If such investment is treated as an $\bar{S}$ outgoing, in effect an F incoming (the loan) is taxed; no relief is given on the $\bar{R}$ outgoing (the overseas investment), but relief is given on the loan interest (an $\bar{F}$ outgoing). While that treatment is consistent with our analysis of the problem, it would, if satisfactory rules could be evolved for matching loans raised with the expenditure thereby financed, be equally effective if instead of disallowing the $\bar{R}$ outgoing it were the $\bar{F}$ outgoing (the loan interest) which was disallowed. In terms of the strict S basis, that would mean that the relevant loan interest was treated as an $\bar{S}$ outgoing and taxed as such.

THE DENIAL OF DOUBLE TAXATION RELIEF

We have pointed out under the previous heading that denial of double taxation relief on the yield from post-appointed-day investment necessitates differentiating between that yield and the yield on pre-appointed-day investment. In some cases (e.g. portfolio investment or investment in a totally new project) this is easy to do, and when it can be done it is probably to be preferred to the alternative of disallowing the investment subsidy. The government would contribute towards the financing of overseas investment in the same way as with domestic investment, although investment through overseas subsidiary companies under the R method would not receive any investment subsidy unless those subsidiary companies were resident in the United Kingdom for UK tax purposes.[1]

It is a matter for consideration whether rules could be formulated whereby the post-appointed-day yield on overseas investment was arbitrarily divided between that eligible for double taxation relief and that ineligible, e.g. by reference to pre and post-appointed-day investment respectively. It might be sufficient if pre-appointed-day investment were taken as the sum of:

1　Stocks and work in progress at the appointed day.
2　Expenditure on fixed assets in, say, the ten years before the appointed day, indexed to the value at that day. It could be argued that this should be taken less depreciation; but to ignore depreciation could be regarded as compensating for the omission of expenditure more than ten years previously, and perhaps as introducing a deliberate bias in favour of the taxpayer as well as simplifying the computation.

The figure thus arrived at, and post-appointed-day expenditure on fixed assets, would need to be indexed each year. Post-appointed-day expenditure would also include any increase in stocks and work in progress over the indexed appointed-day value or be reduced by any decrease.

Having made this apportionment, it might be reasonable to say that for some years after the appointed day the part eligible for double taxation relief should not be less than the indexed average of the pre-appointed-day profit from the same source in, say, the five years before that day (provided the profits reached that figure).

In the case of the S-based corporation tax, it can be argued that this apportionment should be on the basis of net rather than of gross overseas investment; but because of the problem of matching loans raised and increased creditors with the corresponding outgoings it might be more satisfactory to use gross investment even in this case.

Although double taxation relief might be denied on the yield from investment, it would have to be continued for earned income. In closely owned businesses there is often no easy method of dividing the income between remuneration for work done and the return on investment, so that there would be a temptation to have overseas profits treated as earned income whenever possible.

For portfolio investment by individuals a possible solution would be on these lines:

1　No double taxation relief should be given on such investment after the appointed day except as below. But normal savings relief would be given.
2　Investors holding foreign securities at the appointed day would continue to get double taxation relief on the income from those securities, and would be permitted to reinvest an amount not exceeding the proceeds of sale of such securities in further securities on which double taxation relief would be given.

Most dividends on foreign securities are paid through collecting bankers or paying agents in the United Kingdom, who are authorised to limit the deduction for UK tax in such a way as to give relief for direct foreign tax. (At present portfolio invest-ment by individuals, in most cases, attracts relief only for direct foreign tax on dividends and not for underlying foreign tax on the profits of companies paying the dividends; we assume that limitation would continue.) We do not think it would be possible for paying agents to distinguish those dividends on which, under these proposals, relief would still be due. This would mean that those entitled to relief would have to apply for a repayment at the year-end as part of a self-assessment procedure. This would not present any computation difficulties as, in most cases, the whole of any foreign direct tax on pre-appointed-day acquisitions would be repayable. The problem would be to monitor the sale of pre-appointed-day securities and the subsequent reinvestment. Relief would probably have to be disallowed if reinvest-ment did not take place within a limited period of time.

Similar matching problems would arise when other forms of overseas investment were sold and the proceeds reinvested overseas, perhaps in a different territory.

If relationships between an overseas subsidiary company and its UK parent were on an arm's length basis, it might be sufficient to give double taxation relief on the yield from shares issued before the appointed day and to deny it on shares issued after that day. But, if interest-free advances were made to the subsidiary company after the appointed day, this method would break down. There are other devices which could be used artificially to enhance the yield on shares issued before the appointed day.

INEFFECTIVE RELIEFS

So far our discussion has proceeded on the basis that, whichever of the two reliefs (investment subsidy or double taxation relief) is given, that relief is fully effective at the time when it first arises. This would require, for example, that a newly formed company operating under an S-based corporation tax would get S-type relief on its share capital by way of cash repayment rather than by way of set-off against future dividends. In Chapter 10 (p. 212) and Chapter 12 (pp. 238–239) we have made it clear that if unutilised tax losses are not repaid at once in cash in this way they should be carried forward with interest. There are a number of cases in which this will give less immediate, but nevertheless effective, relief. If the government is not prepared to make a cash payment of S relief to newly formed companies, the question arises whether S relief on new share capital applied to overseas investment is effective if carried forward, even with the addition of interest.

We assume, by way of example, (i) that a newly formed company's only income is from an overseas source, which we shall assume to be liable to a foreign rate of tax equal to that of the United Kingdom; (ii) that it wishes to promote an overseas project involving an investment of £1,000; and (iii) that it is operating under an S-type corporation tax with no double taxation relief. Since the company is paying no dividends – and we also assume that the S relief is not paid in cash – it has to find the whole of the £1,000 itself, which we postulate that it does by issuing share capital. If we assume that the pre-tax yield on domestic investment is 10 per cent, the com-pany is likely to make such an overseas investment only if the post-foreign-tax yield is 10 per cent or more. With a foreign tax rate of 50 per cent this implies a yield of £200 and foreign tax of £100, leaving a yield after foreign tax of £100. The company has unused S relief of £1,000, which we assume to earn interest at 10 per cent a year, so that a dividend of £100 can be paid without any UK tax liability. This is a yield of 10 per cent on the share capital, which is the same rate of yield on share capital as would be obtained from the same overseas investment if an immediate cash investment subsidy had been given, so that only £500 of share capital had to be raised. So long as the post-foreign-tax yield does not exceed the rate of interest earned on the unused *S* relief, this state of affairs will continue. The only disadvantage which the company has had to suffer is that it has had to raise twice the amount of capital that would have been required had the investment subsidy been paid in cash.

We now need to consider what happens if, in our newly formed company, the yield is high enough to use up the initial *S* relief and interest thereon. For ease of exposition, we make the rather odd assumption that in the first year the yield is high enough to absorb the whole of the initial *S* relief. We also assume that interest on the unused *S* relief is given at 10 per cent. The first column in Table 21.5 shows the overseas yield which would have been obtained had a cash subsidy been paid when the initial share capital was subscribed; the second column shows the yield which would be obtained on the investment in the United Kingdom at 10 per cent of the £500 which is not required overseas in the first column because of the investment subsidy; and the third column shows the overseas yield obtained without an initial cash subsidy.

Table 21.5   *Overseas investment (in £s)*

	With immediate cash subsidy		No immediate cash subsidy
	Invested overseas	Invested in the UK	Invested overseas
Share capital subscribed	500	500	1,000
Investment subsidy	500	500	nil
Invested overseas	1,000	—	1,000
Invested in the UK	—	1,000	—
Yield in 1st year (for ease of exposition)	2,200	100	2,200
Less Foreign tax	(1,100)	—	(1,100)
Yield net of foreign tax	1,100	100	1,100
Less UK CT on dividend	(550)	(50)	nil[a]
Dividend	600		1,100

[a] Nil because of *S* relief on initial share capital plus one year's interest thereon.

The excess dividend of £500 in the third column can be regarded by the shareholders as reducing their investment to £500. Thereafter, whatever the physical yield on the overseas investment, the shareholders would get on that £500 the same yield as they would have received had a cash subsidy been given when the initial capital was subscribed. They can now invest the excess £500 to produce the same yield as in the second column.

We should explain the treatment of depreciation provisions. Assume that fixed assets have a ten-year life and that a depreciation provision of £100 a year is allowed for overseas tax. Under the *S* base all retained profit is free of UK tax, so that at the end of ten-years £1,000 will be available for replacement purposes.[2] Under the *R* basis the annual depreciation provision of £100 would be liable to UK tax (unless year by year it were spent on other fixed assets), so that at the end of ten years there would be only £500 available. But expenditure at that time of £1,000 would attract investment subsidy of £500, which might or might not be immediately effective. In this respect the *R* basis is less satisfactory than the *S* basis; but in other ways the position is very much the same.

In the above examples the relief carried forward with interest was effective. But there are other circumstances where relief may be ineffective unless special arrangements are made. Assume that a UK taxpayer under a UET regime has no UK income but draws substantial remuneration from an overseas partnership, and that he wishes to increase his investment in that partnership. If the overseas rate of tax equals or exceeds the UK rate of tax, there will, whatever the level of savings, be no UK expenditure tax payable because it will be fully offset by double taxation relief. In other words, there is no subsidy from the UK government towards the overseas investment. If, as we assume, double taxation relief were not given on the yield from overseas investment, savings of £1,000 yielding £100 of pre-foreign-tax income would only support expenditure of £25 after foreign tax of £50 and UK tax of £25. One way to overcome this problem would be to permit the taxpayer to carry forward to a subsequent year or years such amount of savings as he wished. If the overseas rate equals or exceeds the UK rate of tax, then the whole of the savings can be carried forward, with interest, to be deducted in a future year or years; in this case the situation becomes similar to that of the unused *S* relief just discussed.

However, if the overseas rate is less than the UK rate of tax, the position is not so straightforward, particularly under a progressive tax such as UET. For that reason, we illustrate with an *S*-type corporation tax example and assume (i) that a company is in receipt of income of £1,000 from a pre-appointed-day overseas investment on which it bears overseas tax of £400, which is eligible for double taxation relief, and (ii) that it raises £1,000 of share capital to finance post-appointed-day overseas investment. For the time being there is no yield on the new overseas investment. For exposition reasons we take the UK corporation tax at 108·3 per cent (tax-exclusive) (or 52 per cent tax-inclusive), not the 100 per cent we have generally been using. In the absence of the *S* relief the UK corporation tax payable would be £520 (on a dividend of £480) less double taxation relief £400, i.e. a net £120, which would leave no retained profit. To reduce the £120 to zero there should be set against the £1,000 of *S* relief the gross equivalent of £120 (i.e. £120÷108·3 per cent = £111), leaving £889 to carry forward to later years.

Ineffective reliefs can arise in other circumstances, e.g. when there are losses, and we think that similar arrangements to ensure that reliefs are eventually effective should be devised.

TWO COMPROMISE SOLUTIONS

Since all the methods of dealing with the problem of double relief which we have so far discussed present some difficulty, we now mention two compromise solutions:

1 One solution is to continue to give investment subsidy on all overseas investment but to phase out double taxation relief over a period of, say, ten years by giving it on a diminishing proportion of all post-appointed-day foreign profit. Since pre-appointed-day investment will have been incurred at varying dates and have had varying lives, it is a pretty crude device; but it does recognise that, as time went on, in a good many cases income would be due to new investment.

2 Another compromise method is to continue to give both investment subsidy

and double taxation relief but to reverse the assumptions which would other-wise be made about the matching of outgoings with doubly taxed income and, at the same time, not to permit the carrying forward of unused reliefs. Instead of treating outgoings as being made primarily out of UK income, the com-promise solution would:

(a) In the case of UET, assume that savings were made primarily out of doubly taxed income, so that double taxation relief would only be allowed on the excess of net foreign income over net savings in any one year. There would be no carrying forward to subsequent years of unrelieved foreign tax on foreign income deemed to be applied in acquiring savings.

(b) In the case of S-type corporation tax, assume that dividends were paid primarily out of UK income, with the result that no double taxation relief would be given on retained foreign earnings. There would be no carrying forward of unrelieved foreign tax.

(c) In the case of the R-based corporation tax, treat net investment as coming primarily out of foreign income, so that double taxation relief would only be allowed on the excess of net foreign income over net investment in any one year. Unrelieved foreign tax would not be carried forward.

(d) As at present, permit the taxpayer to elect to forego double taxation relief, in which event the foregoing rules would not apply but foreign tax would be allowed as a deduction in computing foreign income, when relevant.

Because of the denial of carry forward reliefs, all of these methods would in some cases render one or other of the reliefs ineffective and thus to that extent prevent the double relief which is the subject of this appendix. However, there are difficulties about both methods. For example, in the case of UET, dissaving out of the proceeds of sale of an overseas asset might be liable to full expenditure tax, even though the investment, because of the proposed rule, attracted investment subsidy only at a marginal rate of tax, which might have been nil. A similar situation could arise with the method proposed for the R-based tax. On the other hand, in the case of the S-type corporation tax a company could obtain full investment subsidy and full double taxation relief if, for example, it raised share capital with a view to overseas investment at a time when it had only UK income which was fully distributed and later, when the yield on that investment flowed, continued its policy of fully distri-buting its profits so that full double taxation relief was obtained.

NOTES

1 Foreign companies can be resident in the United Kingdom for UK tax purposes if their central management and control are in the United Kingdom.

2 We ignore interest on accumulated depreciation provisions.

Appendix 21.3   Double Taxation Relief

GENERAL PRINCIPLES

Double taxation treaties and the provisions for unilaterial relief[1] distinguish between relief due to:

1   UK resident companies entitled to claim relief for underlying foreign tax charged

on the profits of a foreign company from which the UK company has received a dividend (usually when the UK company controls, directly or indirectly, or is a subsidiary of a company which so controls, not less than one-tenth of the voting power of the dividend paying company); and

2   UK resident companies in other circumstances and resident individuals (when only direct foreign tax on dividends or other income is taken into account; underlying foreign tax, charged on profits from which dividends are paid, is ignored).

Up to April 1965, UK resident companies and individuals were permitted to bring underlying tax on ordinary dividends into account for double taxation relief purposes. The administrative problems of so doing were considerable; and for most (but not all) taxpayers the additional relief thus obtained was out of line with the administrative and compliance costs involved. We think it unlikely that the pre-1965 methods would be reinstated.

The computational methods used are influenced by administrative considerations, but the general effect is that the relief is the lowest of:

1   The overseas tax;
2   The UK tax payable at the taxpayer's highest rate on the UK measure of income from the foreign source; and
3   The UK tax borne by the taxpayer after deducting tax he is entitled to charge to other persons.

In practice, for individuals the method where there is only *one* foreign source is to take the UK tax on the foreign income on a top-slicing basis as being the difference between: (a) UK tax on total income, including the foreign income, without any deduction of overseas tax; and (b) UK tax on total income, excluding the foreign income. Relief is the lesser of: (i) the amount thus computed, and (ii) the foreign tax.

If there is a *second* source, the calculation is repeated, but (a) of the previous computation becomes (b) of the second calculation and the new (a) is UK tax on total income including both foreign sources; and so on if there are further foreign sources. The taxpayer can choose the order in which foreign sources are taken into the calculations; and in a progressive system it will usually be advantageous to use first the foreign source with the lowest rate of foreign tax and to use last the source with the highest rate. If it is obvious that the UK marginal rate of tax exceeds the overseas tax, then there is no need to do these calculations; credit is simply given for the overseas tax.

However, in the examples given later in this appendix, we compute the UK tax on foreign income at the taxpayer's average UK rate of tax rather than at his marginal rate. We do this partly for ease of exposition and partly because we think that average rate methods may be more suitable for self-assessment procedures. The marginal rate method is, of course, more favourable to the taxpayer, but we do not regard this as an issue of high principle since the comparison is with average foreign rates.

The practice of permitting the taxpayer to choose the most favourable method is also observed for corporation tax, where it is a question of: (i) allocating deductions from profits (e.g. interest paid) first against chargeable gains, then against UK income, and thirdly against overseas income with a low rather than a high rate of overseas tax; and (ii) setting advance corporation tax against the corporation tax on the various sources in the same order, but restricting the amount set against any one source to basic rate on that source. The effect of these rules is brought out in the next few paragraphs.

At present a company which derives £100 of income from a UK source can pay a dividend plus tax credit of £71·6 or retain profits of £48, thus:

Example 1

	Maximum dividend (£)	(£)	No dividend (£)
Profit from a UK source		100	100
Less CT	(52)		(52)
Plus ACT	23·6		
CT net of ACT		28·4	
		71·6	48
Less Dividend (£100 − £52)	(48)		—
Less ACT i.e. tax credit (£48 × 33 ÷ 67)	(23·6)		
Cost of dividend		71·6	—
Retained		0	48

If, instead, its profit consists solely of a dividend from a foreign company in which it has more than 10 per cent of the votes and whose foreign tax rate is also 52 per cent, the dividend plus tax credit which it can pay is £48, as is the profit which it can retain, thus:

Example 2

	Maximum dividend (£)	(£)	No dividend (£)	(£)
Foreign dividend before foreign tax		100		100
Less Foreign tax		(52)		(52)
		48		48
Less UK CT	(52)		(52)	
Plus Double taxation relief	36·2		52	
Plus ACT	15·8		—	
UK CT net of double taxation relief and ACT		(0)		(0)
Less Dividend	(32·2)		—	
Less ACT i.e. tax credit (£32·2 × 33 ÷ 67)	(15·8)		—	
Cost of dividend		48		—
Retained		0		48
Unrelieved foreign tax		15·8		0

Thus it can be seen that, in these circumstances, out of a given amount of pre-tax foreign profits the amount which can be paid by way of dividend to shareholders is substantially less than can be paid out of domestic profits. But if the foreign rate of tax is less than the UK rate of corporation tax, the rate of dividend which can be paid to shareholders improves. When the foreign rate is less than 28·4 per cent, the rate of dividend which can be paid from foreign profits is the same as that from UK profits. Companies with mixed foreign and domestic profit can pay a larger dividend than could be paid by two separate companies, one receiving the foreign income, the other receiving the domestic income. In the following example profits of £200 support a dividend of £86·4, whereas the dividends in our two previous examples aggregate £80·2 (= £48+£32·2):

Example 3

	Total		Foreign profit		Domestic profit	
	(£)	(£)	(£)	(£)	(£)	(£)
Profit before tax		200		100		100
Less Foreign tax		(52)		(52)		—
		148		48		100
Less UK CT	(104)		(52)		(52)	
Plus Double taxation relief	42·4		42·4		—	
Plus ACT	42·6		9·6		33[a]	
UK CT net of double taxation relief and ACT		(19)		(0)		(19)
		129		48		81
Less Dividend	(86·4)					
Less ACT, i.e. tax credit (£86·4 × 33 ÷ 67)	(42·6)					
Cost of dividend		129				
Retained		0				
Unrelieved foreign tax		9·6				

[a] This figure not to be more than 33 per cent of the first line.

Considerations of this kind have led companies with mainly overseas profits to seek to increase their profits from UK sources, particularly as double taxation relief is fully effective against UK tax on retained profit (see the second example above).

In our second example the dividend received by the shareholder of £32·2 is less than the shareholder would have received had the dividend been paid direct to him by the foreign company. The rate of withholding tax levied on dividends paid by overseas companies to UK companies which hold 10 per cent of the votes of the overseas company is typically 5 per cent. The net dividend of £48 is therefore a gross amount in the foreign country of £50·5 (underlying tax being 49·5 per cent). An individual UK taxpayer liable at 33 per cent receiving a foreign dividend of £50·5 would pay UK and foreign tax of £16·7, to leave a net of £33·8 compared with £32·2 if paid through a UK company (as in our second example) or £38·4 in our third example where there are mixed profits (£86·4 minus the £48 which could have been paid out of UK profits of £100).

These anomalies are in part caused or aggravated by the imputation system; they would not arise, or would be less acute, under the classical system of a corporation tax coupled with a withholding tax. An alternative procedure to the method used in the second example is:

Example 4

		£
Foreign dividend before foreign tax		100
Less Foreign tax		(52)
		48
Less UK CT	(52)	
plus Double taxation relief	52	(0)
		48
Less Dividend		(48)
Retained		0

The problem now is whether the dividend should carry an imputed tax credit of £23·6 as in the first example. Under the pre-1965 system it would carry such a credit, but it could only be used against tax payable; shareholders not liable to tax (e.g. because of personal allowances or because, as charities or pension funds, they were exempt) would not get repayment. If the pre-1965 precedent were followed, when the foreign rate was less than the UK rate, so that a reduced rate of UK corporation tax was payable, the non-liable shareholder would be entitled to repayment of tax credit at that reduced rate. Thus pre-1965 dividend counterfoils had to state the rate at which repayment was allowed. The administrative burden of these arrangements was considerable, and we doubt if they would be reintroduced.

In some circumstances, UK residents pay income tax on only 75 per cent of foreign earned income (see Appendix 21.1). They can, however, set 100 per cent of the foreign tax against the UK tax on that 75 per cent, provided that the foreign tax does not exceed the UK tax. The effect is that frequently the 25 per cent is free of both UK and foreign tax. The 25 per cent deduction is intended to allow for extra expenses falling on the taxpayer because the income is earned abroad.

We now discuss the application of double taxation relief to the taxes described earlier in this report.

CIT

The rationale of CIT suggests a return to something like the methods in use in the United Kingdom up to 1965. As just explained, we think that, for administrative reasons, it is doubtful whether those methods would be reintroduced.

However, in relation to dividends paid by UK companies which have received double taxation relief, there are two methods which might be acceptable although they are somewhat arbitrary in their effects.

In both the company's liability would be dealt with on the lines indicated in Example 4 above. Under one method the full rate of corporation tax would be imputed to the dividend (i.e. in our example the tax credit would be £52), but non-liable shareholders would get repayment at a lower rate. That lower rate would be the same for all companies, and the difference between the two rates would be fixed yearly by the Revenue at such a level that the aggregate difference was approximately equal to the double taxation relief given to all companies. The result would be that the whole tax credit could be used against higher rate tax (which would be based on the correct gross figure), but that an exempt or low rate shareholder would get repayment of the UK tax element of the tax credit at an average rate instead of at the rate actually paid by the particular company or companies in which he held shares. From the point of view of the Revenue authorities the system would be satisfactory; but an exempt shareholder in a company with only domestic profits would get less repayment than he would receive under the pre-1965 methods, and an exempt shareholder in a company with only foreign profits would get more.

Another alternative would be to give imputation for the full corporation tax rate (taken as 52 per cent in the example) and for the Revenue to make repayment to exempt or low rate shareholders on that basis. There would be some loss of revenue in so far as there were exempt or low rate shareholders who would get more repayment than they would under pre-1965 methods. That loss would be reduced if the corporation tax rate were, say, 33 per cent instead of 52 per cent, although we have argued (p. 432) that it should be the higher figure.

UET

We have pointed out in Chapter 20 and in Appendix 21.2 that there may be circumstances where it would be inappropriate to give double taxation relief. But it is clear that it would have to be continued for earned income and also possibly, for transitional reasons, on the yield from pre-appointed-day investment.

Because a UET gives relief for savings and its tax rates may be tax-exclusive while those of overseas countries are likely to be tax-inclusive, we give a few examples of a way in which double taxation relief might be worked under a UET. The method used here has been chosen partly for ease of exposition and is not necessarily the most suitable for use in practice. In particular, the use of UK marginal instead of average rates ought to be considered. It should also be remembered that, in terms of numbers, most double taxation relief claims made by individuals relate to portfolio investment where relief is likely to exclude underlying tax on the profits from which overseas dividends are paid. Rates of direct overseas tax are frequently demonstrably less than either UK average or marginal rates, and to that extent the computational problems are less acute than may appear from these examples. (It should be remembered that UET presupposes self-assessment.)

Our computations proceed as follows:

(a) Compute expenditure by the methods of Table 8.1 (p. 151), treating foreign tax paid as a deductible 'non-consumption outgoing'.
(b) Deduct the personal allowance from (a).
(c) Compute UK tax on (b).
(d) Express (c) as a percentage of (a+c), to arrive at an average tax-inclusive rate of UK tax applied to expenditure before deducting the personal allowance.[2]
(e) Ascertain gross foreign income before any personal allowance.
(f) Ascertain foreign tax.
(g) Express (f) as a percentage of (e).
(h) Take the lower of (d) or (g).
(i) Take the lower of (a+c) or (e).
(j) Apply (h) to (i): this is the amount to be credited against (c) to arrive at
(k) UK tax payable.

The effect is that savings are deemed to come first out of UK income but that no double tax relief is given on the excess of pre-tax foreign income over expenditure plus UK tax thereon. That excess may be due to foreign tax rates exceeding UK rates or to savings out of foreign income.

In the following example the foreign rate of tax is less than the UK rate. Foreign tax is fully credited and the taxpayer has the same spendable income as he would have if his income were wholly UK income.

UET example 1

		£
UK income		2,000
Purchase of registered asset		1,500
Foreign income before any personal allowance	(e)	10,000
Less Foreign tax	(f)	(3,000)
Less UK tax		(500)
Expenditure	(a)	7,000
Less Personal allowance		(1,500)
Taxable expenditure	(b)	5,500
UK tax thereon	(c)	3,500
(c) as a percentage of (a+c)	(d)	$33\frac{1}{3}\%$
(f) as a percentage of (e)	(g)	30%
The lower of (d) and (g)	(h)	30%
The lower of (a+c) and (e)	(i)	10,000
Double tax relief (30% of £10,000)	(j)	3,000
UK tax payable (£3,500−£3,000)	(k)	500

The foreign rate in the following second example is higher than the UK rate; as a result there is unrelieved foreign tax of £533 ($=£3,200−£2,667$), which is $6\frac{2}{3}$ per cent ($= 40$ per cent$−33\frac{1}{3}$ per cent) of £8,000.

UET example 2

		£
UK income		3,000
Sale of registered asset		33
Foreign income before any personal allowance	(e)	8,000
Less Foreign tax	(f)	(3,200)
Less UK tax		(833)
Expenditure	(a)	7,000
Less Personal allowance		(1,500)
Taxable expenditure	(b)	5,500
UK tax thereon	(c)	3,500
(c) as a percentage of (a+c)	(d)	$33\frac{1}{3}\%$
(f) as a percentage of (e)	(g)	40%
The lower of (d) and (g)	(h)	$33\frac{1}{3}\%$
The lower of (a+c) and (e)	(i)	8,000
Double tax relief ($33\frac{1}{3}\%$ of £8,000)	(j)	2,667
UK tax payable (£3,500−£2,667)	(k)	833
Unrelieved foreign tax (£3,200−£2,667)		533

If savings take place out of foreign income, the taxpayer can only save that income less the unrelieved foreign tax, as shown in the third example.

UET example 3

		£
UK income		3,000
Less Purchase of registered asset		(8,000)
Foreign income before personal allowance	(e)	20,000
Less Foreign tax	(f)	(8,000)
Less UK tax		0
Expenditure	(a)	7,000
Less Personal allowance		(1,500)
Taxable expenditure	(b)	5,500
UK tax thereon	(c)	3,500
(c) as a percentage of (a+c)	(d)	$33\frac{1}{3}\%$
(f) as a percentage of (e)	(g)	40%
The lower of (d) and (g)	(h)	$33\frac{1}{3}\%$
The lower of (a+c) and (e)	(i)	10,500
Double tax relief ($33\frac{1}{3}\%$ of £10,500)	(j)	3,500
UK tax payable (£3,500−£3,500)	(k)	0
Unrelieved foreign tax (£8,000−£3,500)		4,500

The unrelieved foreign tax of £4,500 is made up of unrelieved foreign income used for savings – i.e. £9,500 (= £20,000−£10,500) at 40 per cent = £3,800 – plus the excess of foreign over UK rate on foreign income which is spent – i.e. $6\frac{2}{3}$ per cent $(40-33\frac{1}{3}$ per cent) of £10,500 = £700. The savings of £8,000 come from UK income of £3,000 plus foreign income of £9,500 less unrelieved foreign tax of £4,500.

The third example raises the question of whether foreign tax unrelieved because of savings (£3,800 in the example) should be capable of being carried forward to a year when dissaving takes place. We think that there is a strong case for this, which we have discussed under the heading 'Ineffective reliefs' in Appendix 21.2. An alternative method, which raises this question in an even more acute form, is to regard savings as coming first from foreign income net of foreign tax and to give double tax relief only on the excess of such net income over savings (Appendix 21.2, pp. 463–464). In the third example, this would mean that double tax relief would be given only on £4,000 at $33\frac{1}{3}$ per cent, since on this view, of the net foreign income of £12,000, savings would absorb £8,000.

TTET: TAX ON VALUE ADDED (ORIGIN TYPE) WITH EXPENDITURE TAX SURCHARGE

We have explained in Chapter 20 that under this regime there is no case for giving double taxation relief against tax on value added, whether the foreign income in question is investment income or earned income. Thus the troublesome problem of needing to give double taxation relief against foreign earnings or against the yield on pre-appointed-day overseas investment simply does not arise except in relation to expenditure tax surcharge. In principle the method of giving double taxation relief against surcharge could be the same as that suggested for UET above, but in practice the administrative burden would be much less because of fewer numbers.

TTET: TAX ON VALUE ADDED (DESTINATION TYPE) WITH EXPENDITURE TAX
SURCHARGE

As indicated in Chapter 20, the destination-type tax on value added raises the question
of how double taxation relief would be given against that tax. If tax on value added
has replaced income tax, the cost of living will be relatively high, but UK incomes
will be paid free of income tax. UK residents with foreign earned income or with
income from pre-appointed-day overseas investment that has borne overseas tax
would suffer. It is difficult to see on what basis double taxation relief could be given,
except to make the very arbitrary assumption that net foreign income has borne UK
tax on value added.

TTET: INCOME TAX WITH 100 PER CENT CAPITAL ALLOWANCES WITH
EXPENDITURE TAX SURCHARGE

Whatever view is taken of the double allowance problem (discussed in Chapter 20
and Appendix 21.2), it would be appropriate to give double taxation relief against
UK income tax on the income from overseas portfolio investment, since the purchase of those investments would not attract any investment subsidy against income
tax. In most cases this would present no problems, since foreign direct taxes on
dividends would probably be less than the UK income tax rate. On that basis there
would be no unrelieved foreign tax to be credited against surcharge, so that savings
relief against surcharge would, in any case, be appropriate on the acquisition of
overseas portfolio investments.

But in some cases foreign tax rates will exceed the UK rate of income tax (e.g. on
earned income). With a proportional income tax it would almost certainly be easier
to deal with double tax relief against that tax at the basic income tax rate (if the
foreign rate were higher), rather than by the average rate method suggested for UET.
It should be noted that, in the second example given on page 473, there is no relief
against UK income tax for the unrelieved foreign tax; i.e. it is not deducted as an
expense. Using algebraic methods it would be possible to provide for such relief, but
the amounts at stake would not justify the complexity.

CORPORATION TAX

The questions of double reliefs and of ineffective reliefs (discussed in Appendix 21.2)
are of great importance for companies, and the way in which those issues were
resolved would have a big influence on the method of computing double taxation
relief. That apart, the computational problems of the R or S-type corporation tax
do not appear to be great.[3]

Under the S-type corporation tax, for the reason given in footnote 2 on p. 474,
the UK tax-exclusive rate of corporation tax would be converted to a tax-inclusive
rate by use of the formula $t/(1+t)$. The method would then be to give relief on the
lesser of (a) the gross equivalent of the dividend or (b) the foreign profits; at the
lesser of (i) the UK tax-inclusive rate or (ii) the foreign rate.

The example on page 474 uses a UK tax-exclusive rate of 100 per cent (tax-inclusive
equivalent is 50 per cent). In the first two columns profits are fully distributed; in
the third column there is underdistribution.

		TTET first example £	TTET second example £
ET surcharge before double taxation relief			
UK income		5,500	—
Sale of registered asset		—	3,981
Less Purchase of registered asset		(200)	—
Foreign income before any personal allowance	(e)	8,000	8,000
Less Foreign tax (45%)	(f)	(3,600)	(3,600)
Less UK IT		(1,200)	0
Less UK surcharge		(400)	(281)
Expenditure	(a)	8,100	8,100
Less Threshold		(4,000)	(4,000)
Chargeable	(b)	4,100	4,100
Surcharge payable thereon before double taxation relief	(c)	1,600	1,600
IT payable			
UK income		5,500	0
Foreign income		8,000	8,000
Total income		13,500	8,000
Less Personal allowance		(1,500)	(1,500)
Taxable income		12,000	6,500
IT thereon at 30%		3,600	1,950
Less Double tax relief at 30% on lesser of foreign income or taxable income		(2,400)	(1,950)
IT payable		1,200	0
ET surcharge net of double taxation relief			
Foreign tax not relieved against IT (£3,600−£2,400) and (£3,600−£1,950)	(f2)	1,200	1,650[a]
(c) as a percentage of (a+c)	(d)	16·49%	16·49%
(f2) as a percentage of (e)	(g)	15·0%	20·63%
The lower of (d) and (g)	(h)	15·0%	16·49%
The lower of (a+c) and (e)	(i)	8,000	8,000
Double taxation relief (h ×i)	(j)	1,200	1,319
Surcharge payable (c−j)	(k)	400	281
Unrelieved foreign tax		0	331

[a] It could be argued that this figure should be only £1,200, with consequent effect on the remainder of the calculation.

	At foreign tax rate (tax-inclusive):		
	60% £	50% £	40% £
Overseas profits	100	100	100
Less Overseas tax	(60)	(50)	(40)
Profit net of overseas tax	40	50	60
Dividend	40	50	40
Less UK CT thereon (100%)	(40)	(50)	(40)
Gross equivalent of dividend	80	100	80
Double taxation relief base	80	100	80
Double taxation relief rate	50%	50%	40%
Double taxation relief amount	40	50	32
UK tax payable	0	0	8
Unrelieved foreign tax	20	0	8

In the first column the unrelieved foreign tax is due to the excess of the foreign over the UK rate; in the third column it relates to the retained profit of £12. In our view the unrelieved tax in the third, but not that in the first column, should be carried forward, so that it can be used against the tax on later dividends.

The R-type corporation tax is not compatible with imputation, so that the problem discussed on p. 468 could not arise. It would, however, be present under an S-type imputation system of the kind described in Chapter 12 (pp. 250–251), and also under the imputation system which would be needed for a TTET if it were operated with an income tax with 100 per cent capital allowances.

OTHER TAXES

The Select Committee on Wealth Tax do not appear to have dealt with the question of double taxation relief in their draft reports, but it would not appear to raise any very difficult issues. The PAWAT and LAWAT (discussed in Chapter 15) are very different matters, since they partake partly of the nature of a transfer tax and partly that of equivalence to an annual wealth tax.

NOTES

1 For reasons of brevity we do not refer separately to unilateral double taxation relief, since in general it is treaty relief which is more important. So far as UK residents are concerned, its effect is frequently similar to that of double taxation treaties.

2 We convert the UK tax-exclusive rate to a tax-inclusive rate rather than converting the foreign rate to a tax-exclusive rate, since under the latter method it is easy to overlook the fact that, when UK rates exceed foreign rates, some foreign income may be applied to paying UK tax; double taxation relief on the foreign income thus applied is easily overlooked.

3 A P-based corporation tax with true economic depreciation does not raise any fresh issues. If there is imputation, the problem discussed on p. 468 will arise; but not so if the classical system of a corporation tax coupled with a withholding tax is used.

22 Administration

In this chapter we consider how some of the proposals discussed elsewhere in this Report could be administered in practice. Further investigation is clearly needed, and therefore the conclusions in this chapter are somewhat tentative. We have drawn to a large extent on the report and proceedings of the Select Committee on Tax Credit,[1] which considered a number of problems which are equally applicable here. We shall consider first the changes in the general structure which we propose, such as the taxation of social security benefits, personal allowances and the tax unit; next the problems of an expenditure tax; and finally the possibility of self-assessment. There is no doubt that a system which allows for frequent year-end adjustment, which is a feature of self-assessment, provides a far more flexible framework for a tax system, being able to deal readily with a smooth progression of rate scales – unlike the existing system, which depends upon having a lengthy band at a fixed basic rate. The changes will initially be considered in the light of the rate structure continuing to exist in this form.

CHANGES IN THE GENERAL STRUCTURE

The following statistics give some idea of the numbers involved, this being the main source of difficulty in administration. There were 26 million PAYE (pay-as-you-earn) records kept in 1975/76 (of which 1·29 million were subsidiary employments), there were 4·4 million Schedule D assessments, 478,000 corporation tax assessments and 276,000 capital gains tax assessments. The PAYE system is in some respects an extremely flexible method of collecting tax and results in roughly six out of seven cases not being altered at the end of the year. It can cope with the large number of personal allowances, which include separate allowances for single and married persons, married women's earnings, children, children of single parent families, housekeepers, dependent relatives, daughter's services, blind persons and life assurance. Deductions can also be given for mortgage interest. In addition, untaxed income (e.g. bank interest, $3\frac{1}{2}$ per cent War Loan interest and the national insurance pension) can be taxed by reducing the allowances to be set against the employment income. The system is a cumulative one under which each week (or month) a proportion of the allowances for the year is deducted from the aggregate pay for the year to date and the tax calculated according to tables. This is compared with the figure for tax calculated at the previous week (or month), and the difference is the tax deductible. It can therefore cater for variations in the level of pay and variations in the allowances during the year, e.g. those caused by the taxpayer having another child, taking out another life insurance policy, or moving house and

---

[1] Select Committee on Tax Credit, HMSO, 1973.

changing the amount of his mortgage payments. When an employee changes his job he takes a certificate showing the cumulative position to date, and the new employer carries on using the same figures; in this way the system caters for 10 million job changes in a year, which is 40 per cent of all PAYE records. The flexibility of the PAYE system means that the Revenue need ask a taxpayer whose circumstances are fairly simple to complete a tax return only once every five years in 60 per cent of cases.

The sophistication of the PAYE system also has its disadvantages. When the national insurance scheme started it was found that it was not practicable to include short-term national insurance benefits (e.g. sickness and un-employment) as had been originally intended, and since 1949 these have been untaxed solely for reasons of administrative expediency. It can readily be seen how onerous it would be for the paying department to operate a cumulative PAYE system as if the change to unemployment were a change of job. The Committee shares the general view that all such social security payments should be taxed. Not to do so gives an advantage to an unemployed person, since he can set his personal allowances against his income while working and since, given the same total income, the person who is unemployed for part of the year pays less tax than someone who works throughout the year (see p. 79). The only way in which national insurance benefits could easily be brought within the tax system would be to change the PAYE system to a non-cumulative one, so that payments each week could be dealt with on their own and not be affected by cumulative earnings. By a non-cumulative system is meant a non-cumulative method of collection, and it is assumed that the calculation of the final amount of tax would still be made on an annual basis. It might be thought that to change to a non-cumulative system would in any case simplify administration. While this would be broadly true for employers, it would not be true for the Inland Revenue, who would, unless other amendments to the system were made, have far more year-end adjustments than the present one out of seven cases. Since the tax credit scheme depended upon having a non-cumulative PAYE system, the practicability of these proposals was studied fairly fully by the Select Committee.

Dealing first with personal allowances, we have proposed in Chapters 13 and 18 a single personal allowance for each family coupled with an allowance for working wives. The social security payments would remove the need for many of the allowances, since, for example, a dependent relative would be receiving a benefit and there would be no need for a tax allowance to be given to another person. Removal of this allowance, for which there are 1·25 million claims, would considerably simplify the administration, since the allowance would be variable according both to the amount of support given to the dependent relative and to the income of the dependent relative. The Select Committee on Tax Credit did not see any difficulty in withdrawing all the secondary personal allowances, although the blind allowance could only be withdrawn if it were replaced by a cash benefit.

Some of the items which have hitherto been dealt with as personal allow-ances or as adjustments in the PAYE coding are in process of being altered in such a way that they will no longer need to be dealt with in this manner.

Child benefits are to be paid in cash, and from 1979 when the transitional period is over no coding will be necessary for child allowances. We have proposed in Chapter 13 that child benefits should not be taxable; but even if they were, no coding would be necessary so long as they were paid net of tax. Similarly, the relief for life assurance premiums, which has hitherto been dealt with by coding, will from 1979 be given by deducting tax on payment of the premiums. The main two items left are the relief for mortgage interest and the taxation of interest received gross. Mortgage interest relief can easily be given in much the same way as is proposed for life assurance premiums, by deduction of tax at the basic rate from the interest. Indeed, this system was in force until 1969 except in relation to building societies. The Select Committee on Tax Credit proposed that building societies' annuity mortgages, under which constant monthly payments are made consisting of a varying amount of interest and capital, could be made by calculating the payments using a net rate of interest, on the lines of extending the option mortgage system to everyone. For example, at $10\frac{1}{2}$ per cent a twenty-five-year loan of £1,000 would require a monthly payment of £9·54; instead the rate of interest would be a net 7·035 per cent, and the monthly payment £7·17. Deduction of tax from bank deposit interest was also considered by the Select Committee on Tax Credit and thought to be practicable so long as suitable arrangements were made to exempt non-residents.

The arrangements for carrying forward cumulative totals on changes of job would not be required under a non-cumulative system. Instead an employee would be given a certificate of his gross pay and of the tax deducted for each employer for whom he had worked during the year, and these would be sent to the Revenue or, under self-assessment, attached to his tax return. So long as the employee's income from earnings or social security payments kept him above the threshold and within the basic rate band, the ending of the present arrangements would not give rise to year-end adjustments.

There could also be a standard deduction for expenses for employees, as was also proposed by the Select Committee on Tax Credit which would again remove a number of cases where coding has to be done individually.

These proposals for excluding items which are at present dealt with by coding were also found by the Layfield Committee[2] to be necessary if a local income tax were to be introduced.

The adoption of these proposals removing the necessity for such items to be dealt with in the PAYE coding would mean that a PAYE system could be operated on a non-cumulative basis without the necessity for year-end adjustments in cases where a person was either working or in receipt of social security benefits throughout the year.

We have yet to consider how married women's earnings should be dealt with and the adjustments to be made for higher rate taxpayers. A non-cumulative PAYE system works somewhat badly when earnings fluctuate above and below the amount of the personal allowance, and also when earnings do not continue throughout the year. In such cases any unused part

---

[2] Local Government Finance, Report of the Committee of Enquiry, Cmd 6453, May 1976.

of the personal allowance which is brought forward cannot be set against the current week's earnings and therefore has to be the subject of a tax reclaim at the end of the year. Taxing social security payments removes part of the problem, and the remainder is particularly likely to occur in the case of married women who work part time. The solution to this problem adopted by the Select Committee on Tax Credit was that married women who worked full time should be on a non-cumulative system in the same way as men, but there would be a residual cumulative PAYE system to deal with earnings of those married women who worked intermittently. This scheme does have the disadvantage that two systems, one cumulative and the other not, would have to be operated side by side by employers; but it seems the best solution nevertheless.

Higher rate taxpayers would inevitably be subject to year-end adjustments with a non-cumulative PAYE system, but this is probably the case even with a cumulative one. The number of higher rate taxpayers and those paying the investment income surcharge has increased dramatically in recent years, from 392,000 in 1973/74 to an estimated 2·2 million in 1976/77, although the extension of the basic rate band for 1977/78 will reduce the figure considerably. Arrangements would have to be made so that payment of bonuses did not put a taxpayer into the higher rates for one week, but the Select Committee on Tax Credit felt that a solution to this problem could be found.

Moving to a non-cumulative PAYE system would make it easy to adopt a tax credit system if that were desired for dealing with social security payments (see Chapter 13) such as the two-tier social dividend. Most of the foregoing applies equally to a system of tax credits, except that they would be less suitable for married women's earnings, as they would give a bonus to women with low earnings compared to a tax allowance, which would merely remain unused. If it were accepted that there would need to be a cumulative PAYE system for married women with low or intermittent earnings, a system of personal allowances could be retained for them. Since we do not favour an allowance which can be transferred in part to the husband, we think that retaining a personal allowance would be a better solution than that proposed by the Select Committee on Tax Credit, which involved having a tax credit half of which was transferable to the husband. For higher rate taxpayers the personal allowance could be continued, or the higher rates could merely start at an increased level.

EXPENDITURE TAX

We turn now to the particular problems posed by an expenditure tax on the basis that the simplifications suggested above were adopted. The essence of administering an expenditure tax is to adjust for savings and tax dissavings. This means either that there must be a year-end adjustment or that there must be some method of giving the relief and collecting the tax as income is received and spent.

If the liabilities of taxpayers with relatively simple affairs are to be satisfied without a requirement for action by them to ensure appropriate year-end adjustment, it is necessary that relief should be given simultaneously with saving and that tax should be paid at the same time as dissaving occurs. Life assurance premiums and mortgage payments would present no difficulty; there would be deduction of tax at the basic rate on the full amount of the premium or the mortgage payment, rather than, as proposed above, half the basic rate for premiums and against the interest element only for mortgages. This would simplify the arrangements for annuity mortgages, because tax would be deducted from the whole of the payment.

In other cases the same effect could be achieved for those taxpayers by 'dealing net' with financial institutions, so that payments made to the institutions were grossed up by the basic rate of tax while withdrawals were subjected to withholding of basic rate tax (as happens at present in respect of many interest payments). It might be possible for certain deposit-taking institutions authorised to operate registered accounts to be required to deal on this basis. We shall suppose, for illustration, that the basic rate of expenditure tax is 50 per cent (tax-exclusive) and that the interest rate on deposit accounts is 10 per cent. An individual opens a registered account with a financial institution, such as a building society. In order to do so he is required to provide a tax reference number to indicate that he is an individual entitled to 'grossing up', so as to exclude the use of this system by non-residents, companies and those outside the personal tax net. The transitional problem of identifying which existing accounts were entitled to this treatment in relation to future transactions would be considerable. He then deposits £100 in the new registered account. This is then 'grossed up' by the counter staff of the building society, so that he is credited with a deposit of £150. If he then withdraws any money, the building society also debits him with tax at 50 per cent on the amount withdrawn. If he maintains the deposit for a year, he will earn interest of £15 (10 per cent of £150). If the interest were then sent to the depositor, the building society would withhold $33\frac{1}{3}$ per cent of it (i.e. 50 per cent of the net amount), so that he would receive a net payment of £10. If the interest were instead credited to the account, then the full £15 would be added, giving him total credit of £165. If he wished to withdraw the whole amount, $33\frac{1}{3}$ per cent tax would be retained by the building society, so that on closing the account he would obtain a net £110. At the end of the year the building society would send to the taxpayer and the Revenue a statement of the net and gross additions to the registered account during the year and of the interest credited. The building society would have regular settlements with the Revenue, in which it accounted for the difference between amounts added to deposits and deducted from withdrawals.

If the basic rate of tax changed, then so would the rate of withholding and the factor to be applied on grossing up. It is because of this that it would not be possible merely to credit interest on the account on the grossed-up amount.

There would, however, be taxpayers with marginal rates of tax different from 50 per cent. These would consist of poor taxpayers whose expenditure fell below the tax threshold, and higher rate taxpayers. We suggest that no adjustment should be made for the former group; i.e. it would not be possible for depositors in registered accounts to claim a refund of amounts withheld from withdrawals or interest payments (or to be deprived of the benefits of grossing up). So long as the basic rate of tax was constant, such individuals would be no better (or worse) off in such a registered account than they would be if no grossing up occurred, although they might prefer un-registered accounts since they would pay no tax on the interest received from it.

Higher rate taxpayers would, however, be required to make a return at the end of the year, and an adjustment to their liabilities would then be made. They would be entitled to a remission of the amount by which the grossing up fell short of the relief on savings to which they were due and would have to pay an equivalent amount on withdrawals.

The appropriate treatment of transactions in securities is more uncertain. Many taxpayers who buy and sell shares would normally be completing tax returns in any event, so that retrospective adjustments to their liabilities would pose no major administrative problem. Advantages of net dealings are that it is possible to make purchases without having to wait until the year-end to receive the associated refunds of basic rate tax and the increased effectiveness of the mechanisms for collection. However, it may be felt that to extend the range of those entitled to deal net to include all stockbrokers is to extend it too widely. The case for extending net dealing to unit trusts is stronger, since these are more often used by basic rate taxpayers.

Whatever decision is taken on this, there are bound to be transactions in which an individual withdraws money from an institution which deals net in order to make a purchase of a registered asset to which net dealing does not apply. One instance is the withdrawal of funds from a building society in order to provide some of the money required for house purchase. A possible device which we have considered for dealing with problems of this kind is to permit institutions dealing net to issue cheques for the gross amount of a withdrawal, whose validity is restricted to their endorsement to another authorised dealer. Thus it could be that a 'pink cheque' of this kind could be paid only into another registered account, or into the client account of a solicitor (and perhaps stockbroker), subject to the agent concerned stating and identifying the registered asset purchased with the proceeds.

On the whole we feel that net dealing, although feasible in some cases, would not be easy for ordinary investors to understand, particularly as it would not operate for all savings media. This points to the conclusion that a universal expenditure tax would only be possible under self-assessment.

A two-tier expenditure tax, on the other hand, might be possible to ad-minister under the existing system, because the number of higher rate tax-payers would be relatively small.

IMPUTED RENT

We have explored in Chapter 11 the possibility that an occupier of a house should be taxed on the excess of the annual imputed value of the house over the rent which he pays. To do this under a PAYE system would be a great administrative burden, since it would require individual calculation and coding for each taxpayer based upon the value of his house for this purpose and the rent which he pays. A possible method of administration would be (i) that all rent should be paid net of tax (as was the case with rent under long leases before 1963), and (ii) that the income tax on the imputed rental value should be collected by local authorities. This would not present any great difficulty if the present system of rates were to continue, particularly as it is now proposed that they are to be based upon the capital value of the house. The imputed rent would be this capital value multiplied by a rate of interest and the basic rate of tax, so that the calculation of it would present no difficulty to local authorities, who would be sending annual assessments for rates to taxpayers in any case. A tenant who had been taxed on the annual value ought not to bear the tax to the extent that he had paid for the beneficial occupation by paying rent; he should, therefore, retain the tax deducted from the rent. The computation of the rent payable by tenants whose rent is inclusive of rates and tax on imputed income would involve several stages and would not be well understood.

The other alternative considered in Chapter 11 involves only higher rate taxpayers, and this would be administered by year-end adjustments.

SOCIAL SECURITY BENEFITS

In Chapter 13 we have concluded that all social security benefits other than child benefits should be taxable. Under the proposed new Beveridge scheme the personal allowance would be equal to the supplementary benefit level, so that the tax threshold would be raised to that level. Accordingly no question of taxing the basic retirement or similar benefit would arise, as it would be wholly below the tax threshold. The home responsibility payment would, however, bring the recipient over the tax threshold whenever he was receiving the standard benefit or, unless he was earning less than the personal allowance, whenever he is working. The easiest way to tax the home responsibility benefit is to pay it after deduction of tax at the basic rate, which will avoid any problem of collecting the tax. It would be simplest not to refund this tax in the unusual situation of the person not being liable for it, treating the payment in the same way as building society interest, which is grossed up for tax at the higher rates although no refund of tax can be claimed. There would be no necessity for people to know that the payment was a net one; it could merely be stated that its grossed-up equivalent was liable for higher rate tax, with credit for tax at the basic rate. Unfortunately, PAYE coding does not work well for taxing payments at the higher rates only, and year-end adjustments would be needed as now for most higher rate taxpayers. Sickness benefit would be troublesome, since in most cases it would be paid to people with no other income (and so would be matched by the personal allowance) and in other cases would be paid to people in employment (so that the benefit should be taxed).

THE TAX UNIT

In Chapter 18 we have considered three possible modifications of the present system:

1   The abolition of the married person's allowance, which obviously presents no administrative problems and would indeed be a simplification.
2   Partial income splitting under which investment income under income tax (plus the expenditure tax adjustment under expenditure tax) is split equally between the parties and the personal allowance is not available against investment income. This does not present any particular administrative problems. The PAYE system would operate on an individual basis, and the only effect of splitting investment income would be in calculating higher rate tax, which would be done by year-end adjustment. The restriction on setting personal allowances against investment income would prevent there being repayment claims by wives with no earned income.
3   What in Chapter 18 we have called the partial quotient system, which in its separate treatment of earned income and joint treatment of investment income would only affect higher rate taxpayers and could be administered by year-end adjustment. However, the option to aggregate earned incomes would be administratively complicated because it would be impossible to operate correctly under a PAYE system, in cases where the parties opted for aggregation because the tax payable by one of them depended on the earnings of the other.

CAPITAL TAXES

The administrative problems of an annual wealth tax have been considered in Chapter 16 and by the Select Committee on Wealth Tax,[3] and there is no need to repeat them here. At first sight the administration of a PAWAT (described in Chapter 15) seems extremely complicated, but we believe that with computerisation it would not be too formidable. The records would keep two totals: the PAWAT total, and the amount of equivalent annual wealth tax. At each year-end these would be automatically indexed, which would mean applying the same multiple to all figures in the memory. Late returns would need to be discouraged by a penalty because they would mean going back to the previous year's totals. The calculations necessary on making or receiving a gift are suitable for computer operations, and to facilitate checking by the taxpayer or his advisers we suggest that the assessment should be accompanied by a printout showing the stages in the calculation in a similar way to that set out in Appendix 15.3. It would then only be necessary to see that the correct value of the gift and annuity multiplier had been used.

[3] Select Committee on Wealth Tax, HMSO, 1975.

SELF-ASSESSMENT

A detailed study of the possibility of introducing self-assessment in the United Kingdom has been carried out for the Institute for Fiscal Studies and the Institute of Chartered Accountants in England and Wales by Dr N. A. Barr, Mr S. R. James and Professor A. R. Prest.[4] For this reason the Committee has not duplicated this work. The Committee supports the conclusions in the study that self-assessment in the United Kingdom is both possible and desirable. Indeed, without self-assessment we concluded that a universal expenditure tax would not be possible. The following is not intended to be a summary of that study, to which the reader is referred, but it is intended to draw attention to some of the aspects which are relevant to this Report.

By self-assessment we mean something on the lines of the system in operation in the United States, under which a taxpayer calculates the tax due as part of the process of filling in his return form and remits the tax with the form. To some extent most of this already exists in the United Kingdom, except for the payment of the tax with the return, e.g. when an accountant submits a set of accounts together with the adjustments necessary to convert the accounts profits into taxable profits. But this does not apply to the average taxpayer. The extent to which a system of self-assessment could be operated in the United Kingdom depends largely upon the starting point. If the existing system of allowances were continued, it would certainly not work. This was illustrated by an Inland Revenue experiment described in the study mentioned above, which showed that two-thirds of a sample of 465 taxpayers failed to code themselves correctly. We therefore start with the assumption that the simplifications to the existing system outlined earlier in this chapter have been adopted, that coding is necessary in many fewer cases (because there would be only one personal allowance and few adjustments to be made to it), and that there is a non-cumulative PAYE system or a tax credit system in operation. The new factors which could potentially be accommodated by self-assessment are: (i) a different system for the tax unit, such as partial income splitting; (ii) the adjustments necessary to convert an income tax into an expenditure tax; and, if self-assessment were universal, (iii) the substitution of a smooth progression of marginal rates of tax for the broad basic rate band. In addition, a genuine local income tax would become possible both on investment income and earned income. The Layfield Committee found that for investment income this could not be done under the present system, and that under their proposals even the tax on earned income would be allocated among local authorities by indirect statistical methods.

The theory of the UK system is to add all sources of income together, although using different basis years for certain sources of income, deducting allowable outgoings (e.g. mortgage interest and the personal allowances) and then applying the rate schedule to the balance. The reason why it is not presented in this logical way to the taxpayer is connected with

4 N. A. Barr, S. R. James and A. R. Prest, *Self-Assessment for Income Tax* (London: Heinemann Educational Books, 1977).

the dates for payment of tax. Much tax has to be collected on 1 January during the year of assessment: the first instalment of tax on business income, tax on rents and interest not taxed at source, and casual profits. In order to achieve this the personal allowances have to be allocated to a source of income, as do the higher rates of tax, often on the basis of estimates, and this is carried through at the end of the year when the final figures are known.

Under self-assessment, if the US pattern were followed, it would be the responsibility of the taxpayer to ensure that a minimum proportion of the tax was paid at regular intervals during the course of the year, either by deduction from remuneration or by making payments on account. Any balance of tax shown to be due to the Revenue when the taxpayer compiled his return would have to be paid forthwith to the Revenue; but it is probable that the system would be structured as in the United States, so that most taxpayers would be entitled to a repayment when the return was prepared. This would automatically occur under a non-cumulative PAYE system.

The preceding year basis is necessary at present only because tax is collected before the current year's profit is known; and if the change to self-assessment took place, the preceding year basis could be dropped, as it has already been for companies. Taxpayers could still be allowed to draw up accounts of unincorporated businesses to a date other than the year-end and to use the accounts drawn up to a date in the year of assessment, rather than the preceding one, as the basis for the assessment, although this would mean apportioning the profits if the rate of tax changed.

If these changes were made, there would be no particular difficulty in operating a system of self-assessment for higher rate taxpayers, and this could conveniently be coupled with a two-tier expenditure tax. We set out in Appendix 22.2 an outline return form for two-tier expenditure tax; this is based on the one used in the United States (Form 1040), which has attached, in duplicate, other forms for listing interest and dividends, for calculating capital gains and for calculating the business profits of a sole trader. To avoid confusing the issue this is based on the present system of aggregating the incomes of husband and wife, but it would not be difficult to alter the form to deal with partial income splitting. The introduction of universal self-assessment raises a political question: whether departure from the system where PAYE does not require year-end adjustment in six cases out of seven is possible, particularly since non-cumulative PAYE tends to result in too much tax being collected during the year. It is often said in the United States that people like this form of enforced saving; but it is not clear whether this would be equally true in the United Kingdom, where people are not used to paying additional tax or obtaining refunds at the end of the year. There is also the serious administrative question of the extent to which the Inland Revenue could cope with the increased number of returns and year-end adjustments which would occur in virtually all cases (97 per cent of all cases in the United States). If 60 per cent of taxpayers at present make returns only once every five years, this means that only just over 50 per cent of the population make returns in any year. With self-assessment it would be necessary to obtain returns every year from everyone. There would be incidental advantages of doing this, such as helping to prevent evasion in years in which the taxpayer has some casual earnings but is not sent a return form; it might also help the general under-standing of the tax system through increased familiarity. There would be savings to the Inland Revenue in not having to send coding notices, but the additional volume of paper would still be heavy. It could in practice only be administered by extensive use of computers and by having a sample, but thorough, check of returns. In the United States about 2 or 4 per cent of individual taxpayers are selected by statistical techniques for checking, although all returns can be subject to a complete computer check for mathe-matical accuracy. The United Kingdom is already moving away from the scrutiny of all returns; and in a recent speech the Chairman of the Board of Inland Revenue said that in future business accounts would be selected for investigation depending on the District Inspector's judgment, and those not selected for investigation, which would be the great majority, would usually be admitted by the Inspector as a basis for the tax assessment.

The cost of collecting income tax in the United States in 1974 was 0·55 per cent of the tax collected, compared with 1·75 per cent in the United Kingdom for 1974/75, which has risen to 1·95 per cent in 1975/76.[5] It is difficult to deter-mine the exact cause of this difference, but a lot must depend on the use of highly sophisticated computers and on the sampling methods used in the United States. A major reduction of administrative costs in the United King-dom would depend on the adoption of similar techniques. And it should not be overlooked that taxpayers' compliance costs would be greatly increased. It has been estimated that about half the returns in the United States are pre-pared by someone other than the taxpayer, compared with around 10 per cent in the United Kingdom. A note on compliance costs is included in Appendix 22.1.

The question of detecting evasion is a separate issue from self-assessment; but it is likely to be the case that a sample check which was generally known to be a thorough one, coupled with annual returns from everyone, would help to deter evasion. On the other hand, the fact that only a sample of returns are scrutinised means that there are bound to be innocent errors. It needs a clear policy directive that a harsh view should not be taken of such cases. It would be essential that the transition to self-assessment should be taken on its own and not coupled with other major tax changes. But once this had been done it could deal, for example, with partial income splitting for married couples. In the same way the expenditure tax adjustment could later be accommodated in the return form, this being illustrated in the sample form in Appendix 22.2 in relation to higher rate taxpayers. The introduction of a universal expenditure tax would face people with a tax collection problem which does not exist under the present system. People who dissaved would find themselves faced with a higher tax bill in the same year, perhaps at a time when they were least able to afford it because by definition their ex-penditure would have been higher during the year than their income.

---

[5] US population, 210 million (UK 56 million); US revenue employees, 82,226 in 1975 (UK 80,285 in 1975/76).

Further study of the administrative costs of self-assessment is necessary, and we recommend that these should be carried out.

CONCLUSIONS

Some tentative conclusions are drawn about the feasibility in practice of administering the taxes considered in this part of the Report. A universal expenditure tax would involve self-assessment, which has advantages in its own right. We recommend that further studies of the cost, both public and private, of self-assessment should be carried out.

So long as the present long basic rate band were retained, the personal allowances and the use of PAYE coding could be simplified, which would enable PAYE system to be operated on a non-cumulative basis. This would simplify the taxation of social security benefits, other than child benefits, which we have recommended elsewhere. Both the modifications of the present system for the tax unit discussed in Chapter 18, and partial income splitting, could be accommodated. A method of collecting tax at the basic rate on imputed rent by local authorities has also been put forward.

Appendix 22.1   A Note on the Compliance Costs of Taxation[1]

WHAT ARE COMPLIANCE COSTS?

Compliance costs can be defined as those costs incurred by a taxpayer or by third parties in complying with the requirements of the tax system. They are costs resulting from taxation over and above tax payments to the Revenue (and in addition to any costs arising from price distortion). The term '*administrative costs*' is often used to cover both the costs incurred by the tax authorities and the costs incurred outside the Revenue; but it would seem to be more convenient to distinguish between them, perhaps by using as the comprehensive term *tax-operating costs*, which can be sub-divided into the two categories of compliance costs and administrative costs.

Figure 22.1 sets out the main kinds of compliance costs and the ways in which they may arise.

An important distinction must be made between 'discretionary' and 'non-discretionary' costs. *Discretionary costs* are avoidable costs – expenses incurred by taxpayers in attempt to reduce the total size of their tax bill (e.g. fees for 'tax-planning' advice). *Non-discretionary costs* are costs necessarily incurred in meeting the requirements of the tax system (e.g. time taken in completing tax returns or fees paid to accountants for drawing up tax statements). It can well be argued that the term 'compliance costs' should properly be confined to the latter. Much must depend on our purpose; if we are examining the overall resource costs arising from the existence of a tax system, we cannot ignore the real costs incurred by taxpayers' endeavours to reduce their tax bills.

A second distinction is between 'temporary' and 'permanent' compliance costs. *Permanent costs* are the continuing costs associated with the operation of a tax. *Temporary costs* are costs incurred as the result of the introduction of a new tax or a change in an existing tax. Temporary costs, in fact, can usefully be further sub-divided. The introduction of a new tax gives rise to some immediate once-and-for-all, expenditures, which may be called '*commencement costs*' (e.g. the cost of new accounting equipment or of attending a conference to learn the legal requirements of the new tax). In addition there are temporary costs, which may last some time, before the taxpayer has become fully used to the operation of a new tax; these costs diminish until they reach a fairly stable level as taxpayers develop what they regard as the most suitable methods for complying with it.

THE MEASUREMENT OF COMPLIANCE COSTS

These distinctions illustrate some of the problems associated with measuring compliance costs. There is difficulty in separating out discretionary and non-discretionary costs. For example, an accountant advising a personal taxpayer will assist in completing the tax returns required and suggest ways of minimising the tax bill; the charge he levies will not distinguish between the two. Similarly, there may be difficulty in determining which costs are permanent and which are temporary, because the temporary element in the costs of a new tax or a tax change may continue for some considerable time after the change has taken place.

Another problem, which arises with closely-owned businesses, is determining how far an accountant's fees should be regarded as accounting and auditing work and how far they should be regarded as compliance costs. Were it not for the requirements of the tax system, an individually-owned business would not need the formal

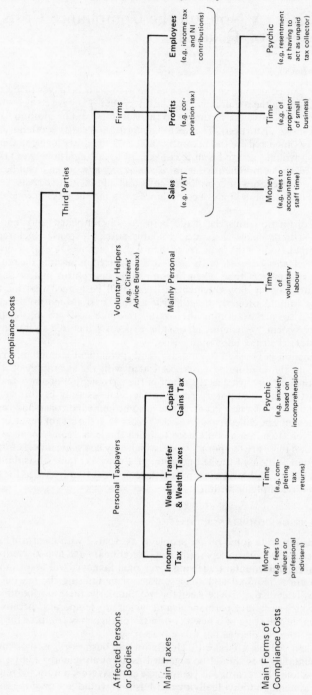

Fig 22.1   Main forms of compliance costs and affected parties

accounts required by the tax authorities. There is therefore a sense in which the whole of the accounting costs of such a business could be regarded as tax-generated. Further, drawing up the accounts and dealing with the tax affairs of a business may be so interconnected that it is difficult to distinguish between them; and, in practice accountants frequently do not present separate bills to a business for tax work and for auditing and accounting. Complying with a tax on a product, like VAT, may require the firm to adopt a more elaborate system of accounts than would otherwise be necessary. The whole of the cost of this system could be attributable to the tax. On the other hand, such accounts, prepared for profits tax or VAT, may be a useful management tool and thus provide a spill-over benefit to the firm.

Two other particular problems of measuring personal compliance costs arise. *Psychic costs* – the worry and anxiety which tax affairs do cause people – are almost impossible to value although they may be very real, especially for the retired, for persons with marital problems (e.g. separated and divorced persons) and for widows whose husbands have always filled in the tax returns. Further, one of the most important costs to many personal taxpayers and to the private proprietors of small firms whose products are taxed, are *time costs*. Their valuation raises all the familiar difficulties which have cropped up in trying to assign an appropriate valuation to leisure time in cost–benefit transport studies.

Very little work has been done in the United Kingdom on compliance costs, and few attempts have been made to measure them. Rather more has been done elsewhere, especially in the United States, but even here the surveys tend to be small scale and suffer from various other methodological deficiencies.

Reference can be made to two studies in the United Kingdom: one on personal compliance costs, one on compliance costs of VAT. Because of their acknowledged limitations, the results must be regarded as indicative rather than definitive, but they strongly suggest that compliance costs are too important to be ignored.

From a series of interrelated surveys carried out in 1970/71[2] it was concluded that upwards of $8\frac{1}{2}$ per cent of personal taxpayers employed paid tax advisers and a further $3\frac{1}{2}$ per cent used unpaid advisers. The total operating costs (administrative plus measurable compliance costs) of personal direct taxes in England and Wales seem likely to have amounted to between 3·8 per cent and 5·8 per cent of tax revenue plus up to 4 per cent more for tax work not billed as such. Measurable compliance costs (which consisted of fees to tax advisers, an estimated value of the time costs of the taxpayer and unpaid advisers, miscellaneous expenses like postage and travel, and the cost to firms of operating the PAYE system) were at least 180 per cent of total administrative costs and, allowing for all tax-generated work not billed as such, might have been more than six times as large. It was not found possible to estimate discretionary and non-discretionary costs separately, so these figures include both.

A recent study of the compliance costs of VAT,[3] which took the form of a series of interviews with each respondent from a sample of twenty-nine small retailers in five types of business (grocers, ironmongers, chemists, clothing retailers and news-agents) during 1973/74, concluded that compliance costs were 78 per cent of tax liability; if chemists (all of whom were receiving credits) were excluded, the ratio of cost to liability was reduced to 31 per cent. Even if this figure were discounted for an element of overstatement by the respondents, a very disturbing figure would still remain. It should be added, however, that this reflects not only the absolute level of compliance costs but also the comparatively low yield (from a low basic rate and a wide range of zero-rated products); that, under VAT with its multistage collection, each registered trader only remits a proportion of total tax liability; and that the compliance costs were probably higher for small retailers than for any other regis-tered trader under VAT.

THE INEQUITY OF COMPLIANCE COSTS

No less important than the size of compliance costs are their characteristics. Despite the paucity of evidence, it does seem to be well-founded that compliance costs generate horizontal inequity and have a marked tendency to regressiveness. This applies both to personal and to third-party compliance costs.

Personal compliance costs tend to fall with disproportionate weight on certain categories of the tax-paying population, in particular the self-employed. The 1970/71 survey showed a bimodal distribution of incomes among high compliance cost taxpayers, with peaks both at £900–1,100 and at £2,000–2,500. Half those with high compliance costs had incomes of under £1,500; this compares with an average income among the tax-paying population of £1,352 in 1969/70. High compliance costs are thus very far from being a prerogative of the rich. Typical low income, high compliance cost taxpayers were small farmers, self-employed tradesmen and retailers and retired persons. The definition of high compliance cost taxpayers, for the purposes of the survey, was people who employed paid advisers or/and spent at least eight hours a year on tax affairs.

The uneven and regressive characteristics of compliance costs emerged from answers by tax advisers to questions about the fees which they would charge in various situations. Because the fee was generally related to the time taken and the complexity of the work, tax advisers' fees for two cases, similar in all respects save for liability, were usually the same for the large liability as for the small; hence as a proportion of liability, compliance costs tended to be larger for the smaller liability.

Capital gains tax particularly illustrated the unevenness of compliance costs. Two capital gains tax cases with the same liability might incur very different compliance costs because in one case the problems of discovering the acquisition price, or an especially complicated share history or valuation, would put up compliance costs, whereas in the other case the same liability would be established with very little difficulty, as in a straightforward disposal of shares in a public company.

Regression in compliance costs also arises from the existence of a threshold. Take, for example, the Green Paper proposals for a wealth tax with a threshold of £100,000 and the provision that persons whose wealth represented X per cent of £100,000 would also be required to file returns. A person with wealth of £90,000 would have to file a return and incur compliance costs in order to establish a nil liability. Someone with wealth of £110,000 would have to value their possessions and submit a return to establish a very small liability. Someone with wealth of, say, £200,000 would have to incur very little more trouble or expense than either of the others, although his liability would be substantially greater. In these cases compliance costs as a proportion of wealth would be higher the less the wealth.

There is also another aspect of regressiveness, relating to benefit received. Where complex negotiations may be involved, as in issues like share valuations for wealth tax or capital transfer tax, the rich, who can afford to employ the best negotiators, are able to get the best terms. Even though the fees of the most skilled advisers will be higher, they may not be higher, proportionately to wealth or income, than those paid by the relatively less well off. In addition the rich will reap the benefit of lower tax bills.

The evidence about compliance costs to firms, partly from the UK surveys, but mainly from foreign studies, strongly points to the conclusion that the costs of collecting taxes from employees, the compliance costs of profits taxes and of sales taxes, all are relatively larger for the small firm than the large. To quote, for example, the conclusions of a study on Canadian corporate taxpayers, which covered both corporation tax and the tax collected from employees: 'The job of acting as a collecting agent for Government bears more heavily on smaller companies.'[4] Or from a study on the costs to retailers of sales taxes in Ohio: 'Sales tax collection costs as a percentage of tax liability are generally higher for smaller stores, lower for larger stores.'[5] The examples could be multiplied;[6] the general conclusion is the same: there are substantial economies of scale in firms' tax-remitting work.

THE IMPORTANCE OF COMPLIANCE COSTS

To some extent administrative costs and compliance costs are interchangeable; different methods of administration may be adopted where the weight falls relatively more on one or other of these two forms of operating cost. If the take-up of real resources were the only consideration, then automatically the method which minimised total resource costs would be chosen. But the position is more complicated than this; other things equal, the balance should be tipped towards administrative costs and away from compliance costs, for at least three reasons.

(1) Administrative costs are met from taxation. They are thus spread among the tax-paying population in a way determined by policy. Given a satisfactory tax system, it can be assumed that the distributional consequences of administrative costs are acceptable and that considerations of horizontal and vertical equity are taken into account. Compliance costs, on the other hand (as has been shown), are uneven with a marked tendency to regressiveness. On distributional grounds, therefore, if the choice is between higher administrative costs and lower compliance costs or vice versa, within the same total operating costs, there are strong reasons for preferring the system with the higher administrative costs.

(2) Compliance costs are likely to be more resented by taxpayers than administrative costs, especially if, as in the United Kingdom, compliance costs are not generally tax deductible. The taxpayer feels that it is bad enough to have to pay taxes; to have to incur further bills in order to have the privilege of paying taxes is adding insult to injury. There is thus a psychic cost, real even though not measurable, which attaches to compliance costs but not to administrative costs. Particular situations occur in which there are special reasons for resentment arising from compliance costs, e.g. with capital gains tax or the wealth tax proposals, where substantial compliance costs may need to be incurred simply to demonstrate that no tax at all is payable. Again, there is the rather special case, brought out by the VAT study of retailers, where most resentment to compliance costs was shown not by those whose compliance costs were highest but by those retailers for whom the ratio of costs to revenue handed over to the Customs and Excise was very high. They resented the fact that all their work as unpaid tax collectors didn't even bring any worthwhile benefit to the community.

(3) Administrative costs are visible in a way that compliance costs are not. A government is always likely to be conscious of that part of tax-operating costs which it incurs directly itself. It is much more likely to overlook the hidden costs of compliance. The larger the proportion of operating costs in the form of administrative costs, the more readily can the costs of tax operation be calculated.

THE EFFECTIVE INCIDENCE OF COMPLIANCE COSTS

Although little work has been done on the measurement and characteristics of compliance costs, even less is known about their effective incidence. There must be a presumption that personal compliance costs, which are not associated with market transactions, are unlikely to be shifted. The presumption is probably the other way with the compliance costs of firms, in so far as there is a basic level of compliance costs which raises costs for them all; however, it is unlikely that the differential in compliance costs between the small and the large firm can be passed forward into price in a competitive market. Thus tax compliance costs tend to reduce the profitability of small firms.

NOTES

1 Most of this note appeared as part of an article, by one of the Committee members, in *British Tax Review*, No. 4, 1976. The Committee thank the editors of the *BTR* for kind permission to reproduce it.

2 C. T. Sandford, *Hidden Costs of Taxation* (London: Institute for Fiscal Studies, 1973).

3 M. R. Godwin, 'Compliance costs of value-added tax to the independent local retailer', unpublished thesis 1975, obtainable from the University of Bath Library.

4 M. H. Bryden, 'The cost of tax compliance', *Canadian Foundation Papers*, no. 25 (July 1961).

5 J. C. Yocum, *Retailers' Costs of Sales Tax Collection in Ohio* (Ohio State University, 1961).

6 Sandford, op. cit., pp. 148–9.

Appendix 22.2   Self-assessment

Table 22.1   *TTET self-assessment form*

	Schedules to form	Tax deducted or tax credit	Income or outgoing before tax (both husband and wife)
Income			
1 Earnings[a] shown on forms P60 (including fees, bonuses, commission, tips, etc.)		XX	XX
2 Other earnings			XX
3 Benefit in kind, taxable expense allowances		XX	XX
4 Retirement pensions		XX	XX
5 Social security benefits (grossed up)[b]		XX	XX
6 Dividends[c]	A	XX	XX
7 Interest[d]	A	XX	XX
8 Business income[e]	B	XX	XX
9 Disposals of registered assets[f]	C		XX
10 Total of lines 1 to 9		XX	XX
11 Total outgoings from line 21 (right hand column)			XX
12 Deduct line 11 from line 10 to leave amount on which tax is payable			XX

Outgoings

13	Expenses in employment			XX
14	Interest on main residence	D	XX	XX
15	Interest on let property	D	XX	XX
16	Interest on other registered loans	D	XX	XX
17	Alimony or maintenance		XX	XX
18	Acquisitions of registered assets	C		XX
19	Personal allowance			XX
20	Tax paid in the year as line 29			XX
21	Total of lines 13 to 20		XX	XX

Tax paid in the year

22	Tax deducted from income during the year as line 10 (left hand column)		XX	
23	Tax deducted from outgoings during the year as line 21 (left hand column)			XX
24	Direct payments of tax during the year in respect of this year	E	XX	
25	Total of lines 22 to 24		XX	XX
26	Total of right hand column from line 25		XX	
27	Deduct line 26 from line 25 to leave		XX	
28	Direct payments of tax during the year in respect of other years	E	XX	
29	Total of line 27 plus line 28		XX	

Tax due for the year

30	Tax on line 12		XX
31	Tax paid in respect of this year as line 27		XX
32	If line 30 is larger than line 31 check here ☐ and enter amount due to Inland Revenue and enclose your remittance for this amount		XX
33	If line 31 is larger than line 30 check here ☐ and enter amount due from Inland Revenue		XX

ᵃ If, as proposed, earnings for work done abroad are given a 25 per cent deduction on a proportionate basis (assuming thirty days' continuous service abroad) this would have to be calculated by the employer and only the 75 per cent of such earnings included.

ᵇ Alternatively, the gross amounts of cash and the tax notionally deducted could be listed.

ᶜ There would be no need to show foreign tax separately.

ᵈ This would include building society interest grossed up in accordance with the table (or supplied by the building society).

ᵉ Corresponding to Schedule C in the US return and including capital allowances. It would be possible to use accounts made up to a date during the tax year. Rents would be included here.

ᶠ It is assumed that CGT is abolished.

PART FOUR   A CONSIDERATION OF ALTERNATIVE POLICIES

In Part Three we examined a number of radical restructurings of the system of direct taxes. We turn in this Part to a consideration of the alternative lines of policy which are suggested as a result of that examination. In doing so we summarise the ultimate reforms of the tax structure which in our opinion might reasonably be chosen as the long-run aims of policy; and we discuss the processes of change in the present tax structure which might serve to move the system towards those final goals.

23 Summary and Conclusions

In Chapters 4 and 5 of our Report we have described two sectors of the economy in which, in our opinion, the present UK tax arrangements are causing confusion: namely, in the muddled choice between income and consumption as the base for direct taxation (Chapter 4), and in the interplay between the tax system and the social security system resulting in the poverty trap with its excessively high marginal rates of implied tax (Chapter 5). We believe that the changes which are desirable to remove the tax anomalies in the choice between income and consumption as the tax base are rather extensive but would not on balance involve any great loss of revenue. On the other hand, the changes which are necessary to remove the anomalies in social security and in the taxation of those with low incomes are inevitably costly if standards of living are to be maintained for all at acceptable levels.

If these anomalies are to be removed, some rather radical rearrangements of the present UK tax system will be necessary. But in Chapter 1 we have expressed our awareness of the clash between the need for such radical reforms and the desirability of avoiding disturbing upheavals of existing arrangements. We seek in this concluding Part of our Report to reduce this conflict of objectives to a minimum (although it is impossible to remove it entirely) by suggesting lines of policy which will enable existing arrangements to be shifted gradually in the direction of certain ultimate radical restructurings, which we have discussed in their ideal final form in Part Three.

The larger part of our Report has been devoted to issues which cover the choice between income and consumption as the main base for direct taxation. But we first give an account of our conclusions on the change needed to prevent poverty and to set an acceptable floor to the standard of living, since these conclusions remain the same independently of the choice between income and expenditure for the main tax base.

A NEW BEVERIDGE SCHEME

In Chapter 13 we have considered two alternative ways of dealing with the problems of social security and the maintenance of low incomes: (i) by means of what we have called a *two-tier social dividend scheme*, and (ii) by means of a further implementation of the principles of the Beveridge Report of 1942, which we have called a *new Beveridge scheme*. Of these two we are of the opinion that the new Beveridge scheme is to be preferred. A major reason for this choice is that the new Beveridge scheme can be approached by a process of gradual change and reform of the existing arrangements, but at the same time does not rule out the possibility of its ultimate further development into a form of two-tier social dividend.

THE BASIC FEATURES OF A NEW BEVERIDGE SCHEME

We shall not repeat in this summary the detailed changes needed for the implementation of a new Beveridge scheme; but it may be useful at this point to enumerate a few of the basic needs:

1   Much of the present trouble is due to the fact that the threshold at which income tax starts has not kept up with what may be regarded as the acceptable minimum standard of living, as measured by the scale of supplementary benefit. As a result of this families may be at a standard below this acceptable minimum and yet at the same time subject to deduction of income tax. A major need is to raise tax thresholds in line with the minimum acceptable standard of living.
2   Similarly, national insurance benefits (e.g. unemployment and sickness benefits) need to be raised to be brought in line with the minimum acceptable standard of living.
3   Personal allowances which determine the threshold for the start of liability to income tax are only of full value to those whose income is as great as the tax allowance. To replace tax allowances with a social benefit confers a benefit on those with inadequate earnings as well as those with adequate earnings. The replacement of child tax allowances with cash payments of child benefits, which is now in the process of introduction in the United Kingdom, is a major feature of the new Beveridge scheme, which rests on the principle that earnings should in any case be sufficient to maintain a man and wife but that there should be social benefits for the support of children.

These three changes are all expensive. They should not, however, be regarded as extravagances invented by the Committee. The child benefits under (3) have already been set in motion by the present government; and any government must inevitably be concerned with the notorious discrepancy which is developing between the supplementary benefit scale and the tax threshold.

There are certain changes which can help to relieve these great costs.

(1)   We believe that all social benefits other than child benefits should be subject to tax. It is a principle of the new Beveridge scheme that benefits should be paid to the sick, the unemployed and the old without special means tests; but in that case the benefits should properly, like all other elements of income, be included in the recipient's tax base. If the main personal allowances under the income tax were brought into line with the scale of social benefits, then anyone receiving such a social benefit would receive it free of tax; but the social benefit would absorb the personal tax allowance and all income over and above the social benefit would thus become liable to tax.

(2)   With the replacement of child tax allowances by child benefits the only remaining personal tax allowances involving large amounts of revenue will be those for single adults and for married couples. Revenue could be saved by the removal of the anomaly whereby a married couple, both members of which are earning, can receive a tax allowance which is approximately two and a half times the tax allowance of a single person. This

anomaly should be removed by disallowing a couple to receive simultaneously both a single person's allowance against the wife's earnings and a
married man's allowance (which is about one and a half times a single
person's allowance) against the rest of the family income.

A more radical modification of personal tax allowances would be to give
personal allowances only against earnings. A single person with only investment income would enjoy no allowance; but social benefits would be treated
as earned incomes and thus with an adequate personal allowance would be
untaxed. In addition, taxpayers over a certain age would be permitted to set
their personal allowances against investment income as well as against
earned income. In the case of married couples of working age, these arrangements would mean that, if only one member of a married couple were working, there would be only one single person's tax allowance and not the present
married man's allowance against the couple's income. A radical reform of
this kind would, however, need to be accompanied by a taxable cash benefit
(which we have called a *home responsibility payment*) payable to those who
had in their charge children or other dependants needing home care and were
therefore either debarred from working or obliged to make alternative costly
arrangements to meet their home responsibilities. Whether, and if so by how
much, the restriction of personal allowances to be set only against earnings
would increase tax revenue thus depends upon the scale and conditions of
receipt of a home responsibility payment. We have discussed possible schemes
in detail in Chapter 13.

THE COST OF A NEW BEVERIDGE SCHEME

Clearly the full cost of a complete new Beveridge scheme will vary considerably according to the arrangements made for the treatment of the personal tax allowances and for the scale and conditions of payment of any home
responsibility payment. We have already given estimates in Chapter 13
ranging from £2,000 million to £3,600 million. To finance these extra expenditures it would be necessary to raise the basic rate of income tax on the
present tax system from 33 per cent to 37 or 40 per cent respectively.

The scheme can, however, be implemented by the piecemeal introduction
of new features and by gradual changes in scales of payments and of tax
allowances.

But whatever is said and done, a new Beveridge scheme will be costly; and
either new sources of revenue must be found, or rates of tax on existing sources
must be kept at higher levels than would otherwise be necessary.

INCOME OR EXPENDITURE AS THE PRINCIPAL TAX BASE?

This fact is of relevance to the choice of tax changes designed to remove
anomalies and confusions in the taxation of savings and investment. As
argued in Chapter 4, much of the trouble in this case lies in the fact that the
UK system of direct taxation is an unsystematic mixture of elements of tax

on income and elements of tax on consumption expenditure. To clear up the confusion it seems necessary to move either in the direction of an income-based tax (we have discussed in Chapter 7 the features of a completely comprehensive income tax) or in the direction of an expenditure-based tax (we have discussed in Chapters 8, 9 and 10 the features of a fully fledged expenditure tax). One of the attractions of moving in the income tax direction is (as shown below) that it could be done in such a way as to widen the tax base and thus to allow a lower average rate of tax to finance any given level of public expenditure.

INCOME-BASED TAXES

A COMPREHENSIVE INCOME TAX

Our examination of the problem in Chapter 7 has convinced us that it would be extremely difficult, if not impossible, to introduce all the features of a comprehensive income tax. In particular, we think that many of the measures which would theoretically be necessary to index the system for proper capital–income adjustments against inflation would not be practicable. Unless it is held that substantial price inflation itself will shortly come to an end, or else that the continuation of inflation as an important but wholly unreliable and arbitrary fiscal instrument for the raising of revenue is not intolerable, the choice of an income-based system of direct taxes should be avoided. However, within these limitations a movement in the direction of an income base is a possibility and would in fact open up new sources of revenue. If, for whatever reason, an expenditure tax regime were ruled out, the following set of changes would make a coherent package of reforms in this alternative direction.

SOME APPROACHES TO AN INCOME-BASED TAX

(1)   Capital gains tax could be levied on government securities, and the charge on assets changing hands at death could be reimposed.

(2)   The investment income of pension funds could be made subject to the basic rate of tax, and their capital gains could also be made taxable.

(3)   Premiums paid for life insurance policies could cease to qualify for any income tax deduction. An exception would be necessary in the case of policies taken out to provide pensions for self-employed persons, provided that, as at present, there was some limit on the contributions which so qualified for relief.

(4)   The special rate of $37\frac{1}{2}$ per cent on income (other than franked income) and capital gains allocated to insurance company life funds could be abolished, in which case the operative rate would be the full rate of corporation tax. Franked income would continue to be taxed at the basic rate of income tax.

(5)   National savings relief could be limited to the basic rate of income

tax. Higher rate taxpayers would then become liable to tax on the income on National Savings Certificates, SAYE investments, etc. The tax would be collected on maturity.

(6)   As far as business incomes were concerned as a basis either for income tax or for corporation tax, the aim could be to go back as far as possible to a system of depreciation allowances which (unlike the present 100 per cent capital allowances) were restricted to the true economic depreciation of the various assets concerned. Such allowances would in fact have to be based on rather arbitrary rates for straight-line or for diminishing-balance depreciation, the rates varying according to the nature of the asset.

If such a return towards true economic depreciation were contemplated, it would probably be necessary to make some allowance for inflation by, for example, indexing historic cost depreciation allowances to the index of gross domestic product at factor cost and, as far as stocks were concerned, to take some measures to enable stock appreciation but not investment in stocks to be tax deductible. We have, however, explained in Chapter 6 how partial indexation against inflation for capital–income adjustment itself causes inconsistencies and anomalies; and some such anomalies would be bound to appear if these elements of business transactions in real assets were indexed, while other transactions were not indexed. In particular, anomalous situations would arise where there was no indexation of fixed money debts incurred for the finance of investment in real assets whose appreciation was taxed on an indexed basis.

(7)   In principle (as argued in Chapter 11), all occupiers of houses should be liable to tax on the excess of the annual value of their house over any rent which they have paid for it. This should be the case both under an income tax and under an expenditure tax, since the excess of the annual value of a house over the rent paid for it is in fact a part of the real income of the occupier, which the occupier is himself consuming in the form of dwelling space. Such a tax on owner-occupiers and on the beneficial element enjoyed by tenants who are paying less than market rents could thus be a proper element in the move towards a true income-based tax. In Chapter 11 we have discussed two possible reasons for modifying this view: (i) that some persons may regard local rates as a tax on dwellings which should not be duplicated by national taxation; and (ii) that the market for houses is so distorted by rent controls and housing subsidies that no tax changes are worth contemplating until the whole structure of the market for houses has been reformed. In case (ii) there would be no change in revenue. To meet case (i) it would be necessary to confine the tax on the excess of annual value over rent paid to the higher rates of tax with exemption from the basic rate of tax and to give a tax credit at the basic rate of tax to private tenants on the rent which they have actually paid; the net effect on revenue would thus be small.

The items in the above list could clearly be implemented piecemeal, and in many cases the individual items could be introduced gradually; thus, for example, the rates of tax on the imputed annual values of houses could be raised gradually from zero up to the full rates. Moreover, some of the items would have to be introduced gradually with transitional reliefs; thus, for example, it would probably be necessary to allow some continuation of tax relief for premiums payable on existing life assurance policies.

REVENUE IMPLICATIONS

In Appendix 23.1 we give an account of estimates of the additional revenue which might be raised by these changes. If all of the changes were fully implemented (including the full taxation of all occupiers on the excess of the annual value of their house over any rent paid, and the extension to government securities and assets changing hands at death of unindexed capital gains tax), an additional revenue of some £3,750 million might be gained. But the contributions of the various items are extremely uneven. If no change were made under item 7 in the present tax treatment of housing, the above total would be reduced by £1,500 million to £2,250 million. If, in addition, it were considered impossible or undesirable under item 6 to reintroduce true economic depreciation into the calculation of business profits, a further reduction by £800 million to about £1,250 million would result.

AN EXPENDITURE TAX

A basic argument for a move in the direction of an income tax is that it would enlarge the tax base – an outcome which (as we have shown) depends largely upon the implementation of items 6 and 7 in the above list. Apart from this possibility, it may be claimed that the balance of considerations points in the opposite direction, namely a move towards some form of expenditure tax. With an expenditure base for the tax no indexation for capital–income adjustment is needed to offset the effects of inflation; and provided that there is adequate bracket indexation of the kind discussed in Chapter 6, this means that the rate of inflation can no longer play the role of an arbitrary fiscal instrument.

But even if there were no inflationary problem, there would be powerful reasons for preferring an expenditure base. A progressive expenditure tax gives the maximum opportunity for business enterprise and development (since all resources devoted to such development are free of tax); but at the same time it imposes a heavy tax on heavy spending by the wealthy, including expenditure out of capital resources. Moreover, even if the rates of tax under an expenditure tax regime have to be somewhat higher than under the alternative feasible arrangements, this does not necessarily imply a more adverse effect on incentives to earn. As argued in Chapter 3 (p. 43), against the fact that the marginal rate of tax on earnings spent on immediate consumption will be greater must be set the fact that the marginal rate of tax on present earnings used to finance consumption in later life will be reduced.

For these reasons, all of us with the exception of one member of the Committee have a decided preference for moves in the direction of an expenditure tax, provided that the problems of transition can be met.

FORMS OF EXPENDITURE TAX

The first step in operating a progressive expenditure tax is to take as the base the taxpayer's total expenditure on consumption; and (as explained in Chapter 8) this total can be calculated only by taking the taxpayer's realised income and adjusting it by the addition of all his other receipts and the subtraction of his outpayments for purposes other than consumption, thereby indirectly obtaining a figure for his expenditure on consumption. This method we have called the *expenditure tax adjustment* of the income base. But a proportionate expenditure tax can be operated by the quite different method of a proportionate tax on value added, which we have called the *value-added method*; and a similar, though less apparent, result can be obtained by a proportionate income tax with allowances against taxable income of 100 per cent of all expenditures on capital goods, which we have called the 100 *per cent capital allowance method*.

This distinction leads to the consideration of two types of fully fledged expenditure tax. In Chapter 9 we have considered a *universal expenditure tax*, which relies wholly on the expenditure tax adjustment method. In this case the schedule of progressive rates of tax can take any shape desired. But if a tax schedule which relies upon a first long band of expenditure liable to a single proportionate rate of tax (comparable to the long band of incomes liable to the present basic rate of income tax) is acceptable then an alternative expenditure tax can be devised which relies upon the value-added method or the 100 per cent capital allowances method for the long band of basic rate and employs the expenditure tax adjustment method only for the imposition of a progressive surcharge on the limited number of taxpayers whose total expenditure exceeds the band which is subject only to basic rate. An expenditure tax of this form we have called a *two-tier expenditure tax*. We have described it in some detail in Chapter 10.

A TWO-TIER EXPENDITURE TAX

A two-tier expenditure tax can be introduced by a more gradual process of change than can a universal expenditure tax. For the upper tier of the tax it would be necessary to treat the higher rates of tax as a separate surcharge; and it would then be possible to change the base of this surcharge from an income base to an expenditure base by the addition or subtraction of the expenditure tax adjustment. This change of base might itself be phased in by the addition or subtraction of an increasing fraction of the expenditure tax adjustment over a period of years, in the way described on p. 207 of Chapter 10. If this process were adopted, it should be possible to make the change for the upper tier of the tax without further transitional arrangements.

If the tax system started to move in the direction of a fully fledged expenditure tax by the gradual change of the higher rates of income tax into a progressive surcharge on expenditure, it would be necessary to consider what to do at the same time or subsequently about the remaining basic rate of income tax.

This decision would have to be influenced very much by a choice between two different long-term goals. If a long band for the basic rate of tax were acceptable as a permanent feature of the tax structure, then this long band of basic rate tax could be moved from an income base to an expenditure base by a shift either to a basic rate of tax on value added or to a general application of 100 per cent capital allowances against income tax. In this case the final objective would be a two-tier expenditure tax of the kind described in Chapter 10. On the other hand, if the phased-in replacement of the higher rates of income tax with a progressive surcharge on expenditure were regarded merely as a first step towards a universal expenditure tax, this would have to be completed by a subsequent application of the expenditure tax adjustment to the basic rate of tax as well as to the higher rates of tax. This would result in a tax structure of the kind discussed in Chapter 9.

THE CHOICE BETWEEN TAXATION OF VALUE ADDED AND INCOME TAX WITH 100 PER CENT CAPITAL ALLOWANCES

If the former of these two final objectives[1] were adopted, an important decision would remain: namely whether to adapt the basic rate of tax by shifting from the income base to a value-added base, or to do so by extending 100 per cent capital allowances to cover all forms of real investment. The generalisation of 100 per cent capital allowances could be a gradual process of extending the application of existing rules and would not require any great upheaval in present tax structures. But against this must be set the facts that it is a less certain form of expenditure tax (since its full effects may be marred by imperfections in the capital market), and also that it would not be perceived and understood by the public as being in effect a tax on consumption expenditure; and we place great weight on the desirability of devising a tax structure whose purpose and real meaning can be clearly and simply understood.

THE TAXATION OF VALUE ADDED

The shift from an income tax base to a value-added base for the basic rate of tax thus has great merit, but it would involve a more extensive restructuring of the tax structure. It could, however, be carried out by a gradual process of change. One possible future scenario is the following. Suppose that it were decided on the lines discussed in Chapter 17 and Appendix 17.1 to consolidate the employer's national insurance contributions and part of the investment income surcharge into a 10 per cent tax on value added. The taxpayer could be required to account for this levy on an annual basis to the Inland Revenue together with his liability to income tax, the charge being an embryo ITVAT of the kind described in Appendix 8.3. Once this machinery was in working

---

[1] The choice of final objective would be much influenced by the weight placed on the merits and demerits (discussed in Chapter 14) of a tax system with a constant marginal, but rising average, rate of tax.

order it would be possible by gradual stages to reduce the basic rate of income tax and to raise the rate of tax on value added.

Such a procedure would, however, raise three very important issues.

(1)   One could not expect nominal money wage rates to be reduced *pari passu* with the replacement of the tax on income by the tax on value added. This implies that there would be a corresponding rise in money costs and prices. The wage and salary earners would take home larger money pay packets as the rate of income tax was reduced, but the money price of products would have to be raised to cover the extra cost of the tax on value added. Clearly the process would have implications for incomes policies and for the control of runaway inflation.

(2)   The reduction in the basic rate of income tax would make personal tax allowances less and less important, but the tax on value added would raise prices relatively to money wage rates for all taxpayers, rich and poor. The shift from income tax to a tax on value added would therefore have to be accompanied by a shift from personal tax allowances either (i) to tax credits or unconditional social dividends of the kind discussed in Chapter 13, or else (ii) to some form of tax subsidy on the first slice of earnings of the kind described in Appendix 8.3.

(3)   The question would arise whether the new tax on value added should, like the existing VAT, be charged on imports and remitted on exports (the *destination principle*). If that were the case, the rise in prices and costs described in (1) above need have no effect on foreign trade since it would not apply to exports from the United Kingdom and since the price of imports for domestic consumers would be raised in just the same manner as the price of home-produced goods. If, however, the new tax were not remitted on exports and not charged on imports (*the origin principle*), its effects on foreign trade would need to be offset by some fall in the exchange rate, which would serve to offset the rise in the sterling price of UK products. In spite of this there would be a strong case for applying the new tax on value added on this origin principle. In the first place, this would avoid a somewhat confusing differentiation between the new tax on value added and the tax on income which it was replacing, since the latter is not remitted on exports nor charged on imports. But more importantly (as explained in Chapter 20), the application of a tax on value added on an origin basis would avoid one of the most awkward problems raised by many other forms of expenditure tax, namely an incentive for persons who have earned their incomes and made their savings under an expenditure tax regime to emigrate in their retirement in order to spend those savings abroad under an income tax regime.

A UNIVERSAL EXPENDITURE TAX

The shift from income tax to tax on value added could thus be carried out in stages, but it would clearly raise tiresome transitional problems of great importance. It would obviously be pointless to go through the agony of these changes if the ultimate objective were, not a more-or-less permanent two-tier expenditure tax with a long band of basic rate tax, but a universal expenditure tax with much more flexibility in the choice of rate structures for those at present subject only to the single basic rate of tax.

Even if the ultimate goal is a universal expenditure tax of this kind, it may well be useful to make a start, as with the upper tier of a two-tier expenditure tax, by replacing the higher rates of income tax with an expenditure tax surcharge. This would give experience with a limited and more manageable number of taxpayers. Moreover, as a progressive expenditure tax almost certainly requires a large measure of year-end adjustment of actual tax payments to tax liabilities, it will be easier to start with those who already pay higher rates of tax, since such taxpayers will already for the most part be subject to year-end adjustment.

We are of the opinion that a universal expenditure tax which permitted a flexibility of tax rates through the whole range of taxpayers (thus making a gradual tapering of rates possible over the present range of those paying tax at the single basic rate) would be feasible only on the basis of a system of *self-assessment* for the payment of tax. The introduction of a system of self-assessment would itself be a major operation, the completion of which would take some years; and we contemplate that the introduction of a full universal expenditure tax would be possible only after this preliminary process had been undertaken. To initiate the introduction of a full universal expenditure tax by turning the higher rates of income tax into an expenditure tax surcharge might be the occasion for gaining experience, not only with the problems associated with the expenditure tax adjustment itself, but also with those associated with self-assessment, for it would be possible to make the first experiments in self-assessment by using it as the means for collecting the expenditure tax surcharge.

Bringing the basic rate of tax into the framework of a universal expenditure tax based on the expenditure tax adjustment method could be done by a once-for-all dramatic change on D-day. We have discussed the problems associated with such a change on pp. 189–192 of Chapter 9. We shall not repeat them here except to say that in our opinion as many types of asset as possible should be treated as registered assets at the time of the change and subject, therefore, to expenditure tax if they were subsequently realised, but that the hardships thereby caused would have to be at least partially offset by allowing some scale of subsequent expenditures out of such assets to be free of tax.

Alternatively, it might be desired to attempt a phasing-in process for the universal expenditure tax over the range of incomes covered by the existing long band of basic rate of income tax. This would mean reducing by gradual steps the level of income at which the expenditure surcharge started, with appropriate increases in the schedule of tax rates for the expenditure tax surcharge and decreases in the basic rate of tax. For the reasons given on pp. 214–215 of Chapter 10 we believe that such a process could work only if there were a previous splitting up of the single basic rate of tax into a number of tapered rates, rising from a low reduced rate on the first slice of taxable income through a number of increasing steps up to the rate at which the expenditure tax surcharge started to operate. In this case the expenditure tax surcharge could be extended downwards in gradual stages, taking in at each stage the whole of the slice of income liable to the highest remaining rate of income tax and with a rise in the rate of expenditure tax surcharge sufficient to make up for the disappearance of that particular step in the rates of income tax.

One possible strategy for long term policy would thus be:

1   To introduce the expenditure tax surcharge in place of the existing higher rates of income tax, the surcharge being collected by a process of self-assessment;
2   To extend the process of self-assessment to cover the basic rate of income tax for all taxpayers as well as the expenditure tax surcharge;
3   To use the process of self-assessment as a means of splitting the single basic rate of tax into a number of progressively rising rates; and
4   To replace the income tax with the expenditure tax surcharge (operated by means of the expenditure tax adjustment method), step by step down the different rate bands of the remaining income tax.

THE BORDERLINE BETWEEN A TTET AND A UET

We have discussed these movements in the direction of an expenditure tax as if there were a clear-cut choice between a two-tier expenditure tax (which necessitates a long band at a single basic rate of tax) and a universal expenditure tax (which allows a progressive rise in rates over the whole range of expenditure levels). This is perhaps to make too sharp a distinction. There may be a strong case for splitting the existing basic rate band into, say, two bands – a first band at a reduced rate, and a second band at a higher 'basic' rate – or perhaps the division should be into more than two such bands. But however many bands there are there will always be a lowest band; and this lowest band could always be covered by some form of tax on value added while all the higher bands were covered by a tax based on the expenditure tax adjustment method. Taxpayers in the lowest band would merely need to confirm that their total expenditure level was below the starting point for the application of the expenditure tax adjustment method. Whether or not it is worthwhile transforming the machinery of the present basic rate of income tax into a machinery for a general tax on value added depends upon the question at what point in the scale of expenditure should the *second* step in the tax scale begin. If those whom it is wished to keep below the tax threshold (whose position can be met by the payment of an unconditional social dividend or tax credit) plus those whom it is wished to tax only at the *first* step in the tax scale make up a substantial proportion of the population, it may be sensible to operate what is in form a two-tier expenditure tax system. Whether or not it is worthwhile to plan to operate a two-tier system thus depends essentially upon how large a proportion of the population is likely ultimately to be found in the first band of the tax schedule.

REVENUE IMPLICATIONS OF AN EXPENDITURE TAX

A shift from the present tax system to an expenditure tax base would not in itself be very costly in terms of revenue, for (as shown in Chapter 4) there are already large elements in the UK personal tax system which are effectively on an expenditure tax base and there are some important elements (e.g. arrangements for pensions and for the taxation of houses) which give even more generous treatment to savings than is implied by straightforward expenditure tax treatment. It is difficult to make any precise estimates; but on the basis of the figures given in Appendix 9.3 it would appear that if all occupiers of houses were taxed fully on any excess of the annual value of their houses over the rent which they paid, the effect on the revenue of the shift to an expenditure tax would be minimal. However, at the other extreme, if no change were made in the taxation of houses, the needed rise in the basic rate of tax might be some 4 percentage points (i.e. from 33 to 37 per cent).

Once again the fiscal importance of the treatment of housing is apparent. As argued in Chapter 11, we believe that the case for a gradual introduction of the full tax on the occupation of houses would be incontestable if local rates could be replaced by a fully effective local income tax or local expenditure tax. This would appear to us to be administratively feasible if a system of self-assessment for the collection of the national income tax or expenditure tax were already introduced; but we hesitate to express a firm opinion on such a major change, many of the implications of which have not fallen within the scope of our study.

The shift to a fully fledged expenditure tax would thus not be very costly in revenue. But there are two further changes which must be taken into account:

1 Allowance must be made for the cost of the new Beveridge scheme, which we have estimated (p. 499 above) would account for 4 to 7 points on the basic rate of tax.

2 If the charges for national insurance contributions and for the investment income surcharge were consolidated into the basic tax structure on the lines discussed in Appendix 17.1, there would be another 7 points to be added to the basic rate. This change represents no change in effective tax burdens on the average[2] or in the effective tax rate; it merely underlines the true cost of the existing levels of public expenditure.

Thus, choosing the least expensive form of the new Beveridge scheme, assuming the full taxation of housing, forgetting about the consolidation of national insurance contributions and investment income surcharge, but allowing for the full shift to an expenditure tax base, the extra cost might involve a rise in a basic rate of tax of some 4·5 points from 33 to 37·5 per cent. If, on the other hand, the more expensive form of the new Beveridge scheme is chosen, no change is made in the taxation of housing, and the consolidation of national insurance contributions and investment income surcharge is

---

[2] To the extent that the national insurance contribution is payable on earnings below the income tax threshold, consolidation would raise the progressivity of the whole system.

allowed for, the basic rate might have to rise to no less than 51 per cent. These figures are, however, all based upon the implementation of the new Beveridge scheme in the conditions of 1976. We may expect economic growth in real output per head in the future which will lead to a rise in the real value of the tax base. If other forms of public expenditure are restrained, revenue available to finance a new Beveridge scheme will grow without any rise in tax rates; the future of tax cannot be judged in isolation from the future prospects for economic growth and plans for public expenditure policies.

SOME SIMPLIFICATIONS OF THE TAX SYSTEM

As shown in Chapters 9 and 10, the change to an expenditure tax base would also bring with it a number of important simplifications in the administration of the tax system. The replacement of the higher rate of income tax with an expenditure tax surcharge would in itself remove the need for much close company legislation, since higher rates of tax would in any case only be levied on what individuals took out of businesses and would be irrelevant for any resources left in the business. The extension of the expenditure tax regime to the whole range of taxpayers (whether by means of a tax on value added or by means of the universal application of the expenditure tax adjustment method) would make the special tax provisions relating to pensions irrelevant and would greatly simplify the tax treatment of trusts (since it would only be what pensioners or the beneficiaries of trusts received and spent which would be liable to tax). It would make capital gains tax in general otiose (since tax would be levied on what persons spent out of the income or capital of assets and not on what they received for income or capital gain),[3] although, in our view, some form of tax on capital gains should properly be retained on the appreciation of value of valuable chattels (such as pictures) which were not treated as registered assets for expenditure tax purposes (see Chapter 9, p. 180, and Chapter 10, p. 211).

A FLOW-OF-FUNDS CORPORATION TAX

We are of the opinion that, if the personal direct taxes are to be shifted from their present base towards an expenditure base, it would be appropriate to shift the existing corporation tax yet further than it is at present in the direction of a flow-of-funds base. We have given our reasons for this view at length in Chapter 12. The existing corporation tax is no longer based simply on the true profit or income of the company; the existence of 100 per cent

---

[3] In general the capital gains tax is needed only to impose on capital gains a rate of tax equivalent to the rate of tax on other forms of income. In the processes of transition which we have outlined, the relevant rates of income tax could be reduced both (i) by those ranges at the top end which become subject to the expenditure tax adjustment, and (ii) by the part of the basic rate which is replaced by a tax on value added. It would be a matter for political decision at what point in this process it would no longer be worthwhile to maintain the existing capital gains tax to offset only the remaining basic rate of income tax.

capital allowances over the most important range of real assets has already moved the base of the tax to a large degree in the direction of a flow-of-funds base. A main feature of the expenditure base for personal taxation is that the rate of return on savings is not taxed unless the proceeds are spent on consumption. Similarly, a flow-of-funds corporation tax (as explained in Chapter 12) means that the rate of return on a company's new capital development is not taxed unless the proceeds are distributed and not reinvested in the corporate sector of the economy; and for this reason a flow-of-funds corporation tax is a suitable bed-fellow for a personal expenditure tax.

AN R-BASED CORPORATION TAX

There is, however, an important choice to be made in the selection of the funds whose flows would be the subject of tax. One possibility (which we have called the R base for the tax) is to tax the excess of the inflow over the outflow of funds in respect of the sale and purchase of all 'real' goods and services, whether these be for current or capital purposes. This base would be achieved by a modification of the present corporation tax through (i) the extension of the principle of 100 per cent capital allowances to all purchases of capital goods and raw materials by the company, and (ii) discontinuing both the deduction of interest payments from the tax base and also the addition of interest receipts to the tax base.

This procedure would have the disadvantage that it would not be appropriate for the taxation of financial institutions which make their living, not through the purchase of 'real' resources and the sale of 'real' goods, but through '*financial*' transactions – through some excess of financial inflows over financial outflows. It would also incidentally cause some transitional problems for highly geared companies which had large net payments of interest which would no longer be deductible for tax purposes.

AN $(R+F)$-BASED CORPORATION TAX

An alternative flow-of-funds tax base would be the excess of inflows over outflows of funds in respect both of 'real' and 'financial' transactions, whether these be on current account or capital account – what we have called an $(R+F)$ base for the tax. The modifications of the existing base which would be necessary in this case would be (i), as before, the extension of 100 per cent capital allowances to cover all 'real' assets, and (ii) the bringing into the tax base all new debts incurred by the company and permitting as deductions from the tax base all repayments by the company of its existing debts. This base would avoid two of the disadvantages of the R base. It would be an appropriate base for financial institutions as well as for companies producing 'real' products and for companies which indulged in a mixture of these two types of activity; and the changes in the tax base due to the addition of the net increase in financial liabilities would probably cause less transitional disturbance than disallowing interest deductibility.

AN *S*-BASED CORPORATION TAX

There is one further great attraction of the $(R+F)$ base. As explained in Chapter 12, to tax the excess of all inflows over all outflows in respect of 'real' and 'financial' transactions is equivalent to taxing the excess of all outflows over inflows in share transactions. Thus to tax a company on the excess of its dividend payments plus purchases of company shares over its issue of new shares and sale of any company shares which it holds (which we have called the *S* base) is to effect an $(R+F)$-based tax by an alternative means. This alternative means has the great attraction of administrative simplicity, in that the tax on net share transactions could be operated on a fiscal year basis rather than – as would be necessary for an *R* or an $(R+F)$ base – on the basis of the company's accounting year, with the added advantage that the avoidance of the tax through intercompany transactions would be more difficult if all companies were taxed on the basis of the same fiscal year.

We think that the *S* base should be borne in mind as an ultimate goal. But to scrap the present corporation tax and to institute in its place a tax on net share transactions would cause an upheaval from a familiar tax to an unfamiliar, and on the face of it unrelated, tax. The present tax base could, however, be gradually transformed into an $(R+F)$-based tax by the piecemeal extension of 100 per cent capital allowances and by the gradual phasing into the tax base of the excess of capital inflows over capital outflows in respect of 'financial' transactions. At the end of such a process the transformation into an *S*-based tax on the same fiscal year would cause a much smaller upheaval.

There is one further argument in favour of this indirect approach to the *S*-based tax. We have given reasons in Chapter 20 for the view that with a flow-of-funds base it is in principle inappropriate to give to new foreign investment both 100 per cent capital allowances against UK tax on the investment and double taxation relief against UK tax on the yield on the foreign investment; and we have discussed in Appendix 21.2 a number of alternative ways of dealing with this problem. The choice lies between restriction of tax relief on the making of new foreign investments and restriction of double taxation relief on the yield from such investment. The choice of method needs further consideration. But with an $(R+F)$ base it would be feasible to adopt either approach. With an *S* base there would be no special obstacle in the way of restricting double taxation relief, but it would be less natural with the *S* base to adopt the method of restricting tax relief on the occasion of the making of a foreign investment. The $(R+F)$ base thus has the advantage over the *S* base that it allows more flexibility in the choice of methods for dealing with the problems of double taxation relief which arise from the application of a flow-of-funds corporation tax.

REVENUE IMPLICATIONS

It appears from Appendix 12.2 that a flow-of-funds base for corporation tax would raise no less and probably more revenue than the existing system. The change could well offset any contraction of the tax base for personal taxation resulting from a shift to an expenditure base.

For the reasons given above we would favour a gradual transformation of the present base for the corporation tax to an $(R+F)$ base, with the possible ultimate objective of applying a straightforward S base if a satisfactory solution can be found for the treatment of foreign investment and double taxation relief.

CAPITAL TAXES

If personal direct taxes were shifted on to an expenditure base, certain changes in the taxation of capital and of income from capital would be appropriate.

As explained in Chapter 17, there are four types of reason why the tax system should properly discriminate in some way against the enjoyment and use of capital wealth.

SOME REASONS FOR THE TAXATION OF CAPITAL

1   Income from property may be more permanent than income from work. Under an income tax regime this may be held to justify some form of surcharge on investment income or of relief on earned income. Under an expenditure tax, however, this argument for discrimination disappears (see Chapter 3, pp. 39–40).

2   The use and enjoyment of inherited wealth may be considered a fit object for special taxation, since the luck of inheritance differs from the fruits of a man's own skill, enterprise and effort. These considerations justify the imposition of taxes on the transfer of wealth by gift or bequest to another owner.

3   The mere ownership of wealth – and particularly of large amounts of wealth – may itself, quite apart from any income which the wealth may yield, confer security, independence, influence and power on the owner. This argument justifies a tax on the holding of wealth (an *annual wealth tax*) or a surcharge on investment income as a rough and ready proxy for an *annual wealth tax*.

4   It may be desired to tax wealth in such a way as to redistribute ownership so as to avoid great inequalities and the high concentration of large fortunes. Capital taxes on the transfer of wealth and/or on the holding of wealth, employed for reasons 2 and 3 above, may be designed and applied for the promotion of such a redistribution of ownership.

INTEGRATION OF THE TAXATION OF CAPITAL TRANSFERS INTO THE INCOME TAX OR THE EXPENDITURE TAX

One way of taxing transfers of capital is to incorporate such transfers into the income tax or the expenditure tax itself. Thus with a comprehensive income tax gifts received could be taxed as part of the recipient's income (as explained in Chapter 7), and with an expenditure tax gifts made could be taxed as part of the donor's expenditure (as explained in Chapter 9). Such an arrangement would cause the rate of tax to be adjusted progressively to the recipient's income level in the case of a comprehensive income tax and to the donor's expenditure level in the case of an expenditure tax. The arrangement would have the great advantage of enabling the whole of the apparatus of a separate transfer tax to be dismantled, although there would have to be some averaging arrangements to avoid the unfair effects of progressive tax rates on large lump-sum receipts (under a comprehensive income tax) or large lump-sum outgoings (under an expenditure tax). To include gifts received in the tax base for a comprehensive income tax is to design a tax geared to the whole of the lifetime resources which a taxpayer receives to dispose of as he pleases; and to include gifts made in the tax base for an expenditure tax is to design a tax geared to the whole lifetime disposal of resources by the taxpayer.

THE TAXATION OF INHERITED WEALTH

It is, however, arguable that there are other objectives which it is the proper purpose of transfer taxes to achieve. In particular, the view may be held that such taxes should be expressly designed to encourage a wide dispersal of inherited wealth and to reduce very large concentrations of such wealth. In this case and *accessions tax*, which acts progressively on the cumulative amount of wealth which the recipient has received by way of gift or inheritance, is preferable to a tax which acts progressively either on the current income of the recipient or on the current standard of consumption of the donor. Moreover, it may be considered desirable to adjust the impact of a transfer tax so that it falls more heavily on those who have enjoyed the inherited wealth for many years than on those who have enjoyed it only for a short period – a distinction which (as argued in Chapter 15) can be made by taking into account the ages of the donor and donee. For reasons of this kind the majority of the Committee would prefer a separate form of transfer tax, rather than incorporating gifts received into the base of an income tax or gifts made into the base of an expenditure tax.

The PAWAT (described at length in Chapter 15) is such a transfer tax, which takes into account both the cumulative amount of inherited wealth received by the donee and the period of years over which he has the possibility of enjoying that wealth. We are much attracted by this tax. But like all taxes, PAWAT has its problems.

(1) The tax involves a refund when inherited wealth is passed on, the refund being the greater (i) the higher the rate of tax paid on the initial receipt of the inheritance, and (ii) the shorter the period for which the inheritance has been held. But in order to allow for possible changes in the tax schedule between the date of initial receipt and the date of the handing on of an inheritance, the averaging procedure described in Appendix 15.3 would probably be necessary. This procedure not only introduces a tiresome administrative complication, but also, for the reasons given on p. 326 of

Chapter 15, dilutes the incentive for persons who have inherited much to pass the inheritance on quickly to those who have inherited little.

(2)   It is difficult to devise any satisfactory way of operating a transfer tax which distinguishes between the ages of donor and donee without subjecting gifts between husband and wife to the tax. In the case of PAWAT, which involves a refund of tax to the donor, this fact opens a troublesome possibility of avoidance. We must assume that it would be impossible to treat a change in the sharing of household expenses between the spouses as a gift from one spouse to another. Given this fact, a husband who had inherited much might make a substantial gift to a wife who had inherited little and thus receive a net refund of tax from the Inland Revenue; and the wife might then over the next years in effect repay the money to the husband without any payment of tax by taking over the whole of their joint housekeeping expenses. If PAWAT were applied, there would probably have to be some troublesome anti-avoidance measures to meet such cases.

(3)   PAWAT, unless it is modified, gives a tax incentive for owners of wealth which they have accumulated out of their own savings to postpone the handing on of such wealth as long as possible.

The transfer tax which we have called LAWAT (see pp. 330–333 of Chapter 15) is a version of PAWAT without the progression of the tax depending upon the total amount of wealth received by the donee. It is a tax on transfers of wealth, with the rate of tax depending upon the ages of donor and donee. The older the donor and the younger the donee, the longer is the average period for which the wealth will be enjoyed by a single owner and the higher therefore the appropriate rate of tax. This tax need not suffer from the same disabilities as PAWAT. It can be applied at whatever rate schedule is in operation at the time of the transfer. It could be operated on the basis that a tax is paid if (as must be the usual case since human beings are not immortal) the donor is older than the donee, but that no tax is payable and no refund is received if the donee is older than the donor. In this case there can be no net refund of tax through interspousal transactions; and it would be possible, if so desired, to ignore interspousal gifts, as is the case with the existing capital transfer tax. Finally (as explained on pp. 332–333 of Chapter 15), LAWAT does not give any incentive to hold on as long as possible to wealth, whether it be inherited wealth or wealth accumulated out of the owner's own savings.

THE CASE FOR AN ANNUAL WEALTH TAX

The absence from LAWAT of any degree of progression of tax according to the total wealth received by the donee would in our view be a fatal objection unless this tax were accompanied by a progressive annual wealth tax. As explained in Chapter 16, such a tax has a number of important merits.

(1)   It is the most effective form of tax for encouraging the prompt handing on of large properties in a dispersed manner to recipients who do not own large properties; for whether the wealth be inherited or accumulated out of his own savings by the existing owner, it will incur a high tax liability each

year so long as it is held in a concentrated form, a tax burden which will be reduced as soon as the wealth is dispersed.

(2) Changes in the rates of tax, which will almost certainly take place from time to time with changes in economic and political conditions, are less arbitrary in their incidence in the case of an annual wealth tax than in the case of a tax on transfers of wealth. In the former case changes of tax rates affect, so long as they last, all owners of wealth equally; in the latter case they fall with exceptional weight or exceptional levity on those owners who chance (by reason of death or otherwise) to make their transfers at dates when tax rates happen to be exceptionally high or exceptionally low.

SOME PROBLEMS OF AN ANNUAL WEALTH TAX

But an annual wealth tax has its own drawbacks.

(1) There are many practical difficulties, which have been exhaustively examined recently both in the reports of the Select Committee on a Wealth Tax and in the book by Sandford, Willis and Ironside.[4] We have briefly reviewed these difficulties in Chapter 16 of our Report. In particular we are impressed by the difficulties of valuation and by the problems of finding an appropriate treatment of pension rights. To include such rights in the tax-payer's wealth presents great difficulty; but to treat the taxpayer who has no appreciable pension rights as being no less wealthy than the man whose pension expectations may be worth over £100,000 seems to us a grave injustice.

(2) There is clearly some clash of objectives in a tax structure which combines an expenditure tax with an annual wealth tax. A main purpose of an expenditure tax is to allow all savings and capital development to go tax free and to levy tax progressively on what is spent on consumption. But the existence of an annual wealth tax will mean that as soon as wealth has been accumulated or inherited on a scale sufficient to exceed the threshold for the annual wealth tax, any additional savings will in fact be subject to this annual tax just so long as they are not either given away or dissipated in riotous living. It is impossible to avoid some such clash if it is desired to encourage savings and to discourage dissavings, and at the same time to tax the advantages of holding wealth and to encourage its dispersal. The only question which can arise relates to the balance between the two objectives and the two taxes. Clearly the combination of an expenditure tax and an annual wealth tax is preferable from this point of view to the combination of an income tax and an annual wealth tax. With the former combination a given tax on holding wealth and a given incentive to disperse wealth can be provided through the wealth tax with a much smaller disincentive to saving and capital development than with the latter combination. Moreover, if the threshold for the wealth tax is reasonably high, an unadulterated incentive and opportunity for business development can be given up to the point at which the business concerned has grown sufficiently in size to increase appreciably its

[4] C. T. Sandford, J. R. M. Willis and D. J. Ironside, *An Annual Wealth Tax* (London: Heinemann Educational Books, 1975).

ability to raise outside capital; and it is not unreasonable to design the tax on the principle that it is only fairly large concentrations of wealth that bring with them great power and influence and which the tax system should be designed to disperse.

TWO ALTERNATIVE TREATMENTS OF CAPITAL TAXES

As a result of these considerations we are attracted by two possibilities: (i) a combination of a progressive expenditure tax plus a PAWAT with a rather severe rate structure designed to tax heavily large concentrations of inherited wealth, but without an annual wealth tax; and (ii) a progressive expenditure tax plus a LAWAT to give a general discrimination against inherited wealth, plus an annual wealth tax with a high threshold to effect the main incentive for the dispersal of the ownership of property.

The former of these combinations would avoid the many very real difficulties and disadvantages of an annual wealth tax; but it would mean that there was no tax on the holding of wealth accumulated out of the owner's own savings, and it would involve some troublesome (but in our view not insuperable) problems in the administration of PAWAT.

The latter combination would be less favourable than the former to saving, enterprise and capital development beyond the threshold for the annual wealth tax, and it would involve the very real difficulties both of administration and of equity in the operation of the annual wealth tax. But it would operate as a more prompt and a more direct tax incentive for the dispersal of large fortunes; and since tax rates are likely to be changed from time to time, it would provide a form of capital tax which was less arbitrary than PAWAT in its incidence.

CONCLUSIONS

Our report has been mainly concerned with three issues:

1 How to remedy the evils (e.g. the poverty trap) which have resulted from the largely unco-ordinated interplay between the tax system and the social security system.
2 Whether to shift the base of the main direct taxes in the direction of an income base or in the direction of an expenditure base.
3 What structure of capital taxes to combine with any reforms of the rest of the structure of direct taxation.

1 TAX AND SOCIAL SECURITY

We favour arrangements (see Chapter 13) based broadly on the principles of the Beveridge Report of 1942, which can be summarised as follows:

1 *Taxable* social benefits to cover unemployment, sickness, old age and other causes of need at an acceptable minimum standard of living.

2 *Untaxed* child benefits on a scale sufficient to provide an acceptable minimum standard of living.
3 A correspondingly adequate single person's tax allowance.
4 The introduction of a home responsibility payment.
5 To help finance the reforms, the elimination of the married man's tax allowance and the restriction of the single person's allowance to earned income (both with appropriate transitional arrangements).

To finance the most ambitious scheme in full would require an addition of at least four percentage points on the basic rate of income tax; but it could be introduced piecemeal, as circumstances allowed.

2 INCOME OR EXPENDITURE BASE

(1) We do not consider it feasible to introduce a fully comprehensive income base (see Chapter 7). However, a number of measures (pp. 500–501 above) would be feasible to move in the direction of an income base. Widening the tax base in this way would permit some reduction in rates of tax, but without correction of the distortions due to inflation.

If all the possibilities enumerated were accepted, some £3,750 million additional revenue might be raised at current tax rates, but well over half would arise from two items: the taxation of housing occupation, and the discontinuance of 100 per cent capital allowances on business investment.

However, all but one member of the Committee would prefer a shift in the direction of an expenditure base, which makes it possible to cope with inflation and, more importantly, gives opportunity and incentive for economic enterprise while at the same time taxing the rich heavily on *consumption* expenditure.

(2) We consider that a shift to a fully comprehensive expenditure tax (the universal expenditure tax of Chapter 9) would be feasible, but that the change would depend upon the prior introduction of a system of self-assessment.

There would be serious transitional problems and problems of international migration (for which possible treatments have been suggested in Chapters 9 and 21 respectively).

On the other hand, the change would simplify the tax system in many important directions (e.g. the tax treatment of pensions, trusts, close companies and capital gains).

A universal expenditure tax would allow a more smoothly progressive rate schedule as compared with the maintenance of a wide expenditure band taxed at a single basic rate.

(3) If, however, the preservation of a long basic rate band were acceptable, a full expenditure tax regime could be achieved by combining an expenditure tax surcharge with a basic rate of income tax with 100 per cent capital allowances or with a proportionate rate of tax on value added (the two-tier expenditure tax of Chapter 10).

This would raise less serious transitional and international problems. It could be introduced more gradually than a full universal expenditure tax; and it would be treated as a first stage towards such a tax.

If the base for personal taxation were shifted in the direction of an income base, it would be appropriate to shift the base of corporation tax back in the direction of a true profits base by discontinuing the grant of 100 per cent capital allowances. If, on the other hand, the base for personal taxation were shifted in the expenditure tax direction, the corporation tax base would appropriately be shifted more completely than at present in the direction of a flow-of-funds base. In this case we would favour the $(R+F)$ base with the S base as a possible ultimate objective (see Chapter 12).

The combined shift of personal tax on to an expenditure base and of corporation tax on to a flow-of-funds base could be achieved in such a way as to involve little, if any, loss of tax revenue.

3   CAPITAL TAXES

We favour some form of tax on wealth which discriminates against inherited wealth, and we suggest ways of designing such taxes so as to encourage dispersion in the ownership of wealth.

1   If it is acceptable to exempt from such tax all wealth accumulated out of the owner's own savings, we see a strong case for relying wholly on a form of accessions tax which levies on the receipt of gifts or inheritances a charge representing the prepayment of a progressive annual wealth tax on the holding of inherited wealth (the PAWAT of Chapter 15).

2   If, however, it is desired to levy tax on the holding of wealth accumulated out of the owner's own savings as well as on inherited wealth, we recommend a progressive annual wealth tax with a fairly high threshold (the annual wealth tax of Chapter 16), combined with a moderate accessions tax levied on all gifts and inheritances received (subject only to minor exemption) and designed so as to represent the prepayment of a moderate proportionate rate of annual wealth tax on the holding of inherited wealth (the LAWAT of Chapter 15).

ULTIMATE OBJECTIVES

We believe that the combination of a new Beveridge scheme (to set an acceptable floor to the standard of living of all citizens), of a progressive expenditure tax regime (to combine encouragement to enterprise with the taxation of high levels of personal consumption), and of a system of progressive taxation on wealth with some discrimination against inherited wealth, presents a set of final objectives for the structure of direct taxation in the United Kingdom that might command a wide consensus of political approval and which could be approached by a series of piecemeal tax changes over the coming decade.

Appendix 23.1 Revenue Implications of Various Possible Tax Changes on Income Tax Framework

The numbers of the sections of this appendix refer to the list on pp. 500–501 of Chapter 23.

1 Extensions of capital gains tax to government securities and assets changing hands at death:
   (a) If capital gains tax were levied only on real (indexed gains) and if losses were deductible in full, the tax would have had a negative yield in recent years.
   (b) The tax yielded £464 million in 1974. The extensions proposed would increase this by less than 50 per cent, say (at 1976 prices) £300 million.
2 Implications of basic rate income tax and full capital gains tax on the interest, dividends and capital gains of pension funds. The rent dividends and interest receipts of life assurance and pension funds together was just over £2,000 million in 1974. Income tax and capital gains tax on pension funds might have raised about £400 million or (at 1976 prices) £600 million.
3 and 4 Withdrawal of life insurance relief and special rate of tax on life funds. Estimates derived from the Page Committee[1] and the Public Expenditure Committee show £400 million.
5 Restriction of national savings relief to the basic rate of income tax. Given the restriction on holdings and the small numbers concerned, this item cannot be very large. Updating Page Committee figures we put it at (June 1976) £75 million.
6 Replacement of 100 per cent capital allowances on plant and machinery by conventional depreciation applied to indexed historic cost. This should remove tax relief on net investment.
   Net capital formation in plant and machinery in 1974 was £1.8 billion, of which two-thirds or £1·2 billion was private. At 50 per cent this would have raised £600 million, say £800 million in 1976.
7 (a) Reimpose Schedule A on owner-occupiers and other beneficial occupiers. The *Blue Book* gives the imputed rent of owner-occupied dwellings in 1974 as £2·5 billion. This is concentrated towards higher rate taxpayers and ignores other beneficial occupants; thus a figure of £1·25 billion revenue in 1974 seems reasonable, say £1·5 billion in 1976.
   (b) As (a) but with a credit at the basic rate for imputed or actual rent paid. Net effect assumed negligible.

REFERENCE

1 Report of the Committee to Review National Savings, Cmd. 5273, HMSO, 1973.

INDEX